Engraved by H. B. Forrest from a Daguerreotype taken by J. H. Clark.

C. M. Clay.

Harper & Brothers New York 1848.

\THE

WRITINGS

OF

CASSIUS MARCELLUS CLAY·

INCLUDING

SPEECHES AND ADDRESSES.

EDITED,

WITH A PREFACE AND MEMOIR,

BY

HORACE GREELEY.

NEGRO UNIVERSITIES PRESS
NEW YORK

Originally published in 1848
by Harper & Brothers, New York

Reprinted 1969 by
Negro Universities Press
A Division of Greenwood Publishing Corp.
New York

SBN 8371-1993-6

PRINTED IN UNITED STATES OF AMERICA

DEDICATION.

HORACE GREELEY—

I ENTRUST to you the writings of which it is proposed to make this work, both because you have displayed in your words and acts a living aspiration for the civilization and happiness of mankind, and because you have been from the beginning my most trusting friend and ablest vindicator.

If I have advanced nothing very new, I flatter myself that I have placed old truths in a striking light, and in a few words. Whilst I am not unambitious of fame, I believe that I am actuated in this by a desire to do good.

In touching the serious subjects of Religion, Morals, and Government, I have looked consequences full in the face. I come not to destroy, but to save. I believe that the Christian morality is the basis of all progress and civilization; the embryo of all amelioration of earth's ills; expansive enough for all forms of governments and social relations, at the same time, the time-serving and gross corruptions of "THE CHURCH" call for unsparing scrutiny from all true lovers of vital religion and pure morals. The tone of many of these articles I would gladly soften, but then I should lose in truth and freshness what I should gain by more gentle phraseology. Those who have taken part in this struggle for the liberties of men, have voluntarily chosen this position; it remains for impartial history to award the deserts of each.

C. M. CLAY.

New York, April 1, 1848.

EDITOR'S PREFACE.

THE Liberty of the Press is the palladium of all true liberty ; with it despotism is impossible ; without it, inevitable. Wherever all subjects may be freely discussed, all wrongs and abuses fearlessly exposed, it is morally certain that the Right must soon prevail. Evil seeks a fancied good for a part, at the expense of the residue ; it triumphs, or seems to triumph, because the few are rendered powerful by intelligence, concert, and the command of material resources, while the many are paralyzed by ignorance, disunion, and poverty. That a majority should persist in perpetuating injustice, after full and free discussion, is scarcely tolerable as a hypothesis, and wholly unjustified by facts. With a Free Press for twenty years in Russia and South Carolina, the former would establish a Republic, and the latter abolish her Slavery. Unawed discussion would gradually make plain to the general understanding that servility corrupts the few while it debases the many, and that the enduring welfare of each demands security and justice for all.

And whenever, in the clear daylight of intelligence, any claim, usage, or institution, repels public scrutiny, shrinks from the ordeal of the general reason, and to argument and criticism opposes the torch and the axe, be sure the knell of that institution has sounded. In proclaiming its own inability to bear the light, it has truly foretold its destruction by the ever-advancing day. Whenever we are told that such or such an arrangement will not bear discussion—that it is too delicate, too critical, too inflammable—that argumentative opposition to it must be suppressed, or blood will flow—then we may understand that such arrangement, however natural or necessary in the past, bears no healthful relation to the present, and is doomed. If it be a matter of form and ceremony, of speculative or unessential import, we may wisely stand aside, and let it decently compose itself to die ; but if it be a serious and practical evil—a denial of primary rights, or an infliction of flagrant wrongs—then we must prepare for the convulsions attending its death-pangs, and endeavor to bury it out of sight and scent as speedily as possible.

It is now some years since public attention, especially that of philanthropists, was attracted to the spectacle of a young man, alone among five millions, raising his voice against the iniquities of human slavery on the soil where they are perpetrated. Known to not many, though bearing an honored name, there was something in his position and course which arrested and fixed regard. Enjoying wealth, and social distinction, and political consideration, he could not be suspected of sinister motives, since he inevitably sacrificed, for a season, if not for ever, the friendship of the loved, and the favor of the powerful, including the voting masses, while he could only hope to secure in return the gratitude of an abject and servile caste, too ignorant even to learn who was daring and sacrificing in their behalf, while their few champions among the governing class were hardly more potent, were regarded with scarcely less contempt, and certainly more aversion. These were all residents of distant communities and states, so that, when CASSIUS M. CLAY first spoke out in condemnation of slavery, not one audible voice was raised approvingly, in the entire slaveholding region, while thousands were loud in fiery condemnation.

Yet it was difficult to discover plausible grounds whereon to assail him. He could not be charged with seeking wealth, for he had enough; nor of seeking to profit by the spoliation of others, for he too was a slaveholder, and only ceased to be so by emancipation some time after. He had public honors, which he knew must be forfeited, and valued friendships, which he felt must be shaken by the course he had resolved on. Yet he took his stand on the side of Universal Freedom—at first defensively, against the aggressive efforts to repeal the law of Kentucky which forbids the importation of slaves from other states for sale in that one, and against the incipient maneuvers looking to the annexation of Texas to this country— but soon he was borne by the irresistible might of principles, and the current of events, out upon the broad sea of opposition to bondage, under all circumstances, and everywhere, but especially in his own Kentucky.

Hence he established and sustained at Lexington THE TRUE AMERICAN— the first * paper which ever bearded the monster in his den, and dared him

---

* The issue, for a brief season, of Lundy and Garrison's "Genius of Emancipation," at Baltimore, in 1829, is an apparent exception, but an exception in appearance only. Slavery was then too strong to manifest alarm, or even indignation, at such an ineffectual invasion of its dark realm, and not one slaveholder in a hundred knew that such a paper existed, until it had been quietly suppressed. If its establishment were intended as a challenge to slavedom, the defiance certainly did not reach the ears of the challenged; and no one will contend that the power of the slaveholders over the Freedom of Speech and the Press, was at all shaken by this noble enterprise and its result.

to a most unequal encounter. Its establishment was a public and widely resounding challenge to the slaveholding oligarchy, to come forward and defend their cause by argument, to surrender it as no longer justifiable, and see their cherished structure crumble and dissolve beneath their feet, or to crush their antagonist by mob violence and brutal force. They chose, most fittingly, the last alternative ; organized a mob through the instrumentality of a mass meeting, broke into the American office while the editor lay dangerously sick at his dwelling, took down his press, types, etc., packed them up, and sent them out of the State. This, it was supposed, put a quietus on the paper, and on anti-slavery discussion within the Slave States.

They miscalculated, for C. M. Clay still lived. He recovered from his illness, and promptly made arrangements for resuming his regular issues. They were henceforth printed at Cincinnati, but published at Lexington (where the editor still resided), and continued for months to expose and combat the evils of slavery, without bating one jot of heart or hope, of plainness or pungency. The paper was finally discontinued, during and in consequence of the editor's long absence in Mexico. He had intended to issue it regularly till its successor was established, but in the absence of any tidings from him, his agent decided to stop it. But its place was speedily taken by "THE EXAMINER," published at Louisville, Kentucky, and edited with great ability and tact by JOHN C. VAUGHAN, a prized associate of Mr. Clay in conducting the "True American." Since then, "THE NATIONAL ERA," another distinctively anti-slavery paper, edited with much power by DR. G. BAILEY, has been established at Washington City, whence it is largely and widely disseminated. And finally, the award by a Kentucky Court, of two thousand five hundred dollars damages to C. M. Clay, in an action brought by him against the leaders in the dismantling of his printing office, may be said to have settled the question of civil right and legal immunity, so that there is no longer a panoply for mob violence, either in the courts or in public opinion, and the Freedom of the Press stands fully vindicated and established. Of the struggle, which has resulted thus auspiciously, the hero is Cassius M. Clay.

The volume herewith presented is mainly important as a virtual history of this struggle. After a single preliminary essay, setting forth the basis of the author's conviction, that man, and thought, and utterance, should be truly and thoroughly free, his speeches and the residue of his writings are given very nearly in chronological order, so as to mark the gradual awakening of an ingenuous mind to a profound conviction of the unmixed and intense evils of slaveholding, and the utter flimsiness of all excuses for perpetuating that evil. Of course, the opinions expressed at one stage are not always consistent with those avowed at another ; and no attempt has been made to render them so. Nor has the editor deemed it within his province to suppress any sentiment of the author, because it differed from his own convictions ; and though he has in one or two places given his own differing view in a foot-note, he has more commonly refrained even from this. It will of course be understood, without being expressly stated, that the editor's notions of war, of warriors, and of the obligation to support the country in injustice and rapacity, are not expressed in Mr. Clay's writings. With regard to the selection of a President, and on some other topics of a temporary interest, his views also differ widely from those of the author, as those who care for the opinions of either already well know; and the fact is noted here to forestall dishonest and tricky perversions. On the great, abiding principle, that freedom and opportunity for all are essential to the assured well-being of each, and that freedom of speech and of the press are conditions without which life would be hardly tolerable, genuine liberty wholly impossible, there is the most entire sympathy between them, and this sympathy has impelled the editor to his very subordinate part in the production of this work.

Yet I think the public will discern in the following pages something to esteem beyond noble sentiments and a self-sacrificing devotion to Right. Unless personal partiality has blinded me, there are passages and pages in Mr. Clay's writings which have rarely been excelled in vigor, in forecast, or in true eloquence. Of this, however, the public will impartially judge. That the whole will tend to awaken generous impulses in many hearts, and to ripen into action those already existing in others, is my earnest and confident hope. That it will prove to some the trumpet-call to the wide battle-field in which the liberties of mankind are now to be struggled for, is my cheering conviction.

New-York, May 1, 1848.

Error—page 20, first line of foot-note: For *offered* read *opposed.*

INDEX.

MEMOIR.

GREEN CLAY,* was born in Powhattan County, Virginia, on the 14th of August, 1755. He was the son of Charles Clay, a descendant of John Clay, a British Grenadier, who came to Virginia during Bacon's Rebellion, and chose to settle there rather than return with the King's troops to England. He was understood to be of Welsh origin. The Clay family maintained a good standing in Virginia, and several brothers of Green were chosen to stations of responsibility. Matthew, who was remarkable for his personal attractions, was long a member of Congress from Virginia. Thomas was one of the framers of the first Constitution of Kentucky, in 1792. Green Clay, having been punished for some trivial offence, by his father, in a way which wounded his pride, left the paternal home, a minor, and determined to push his fortune in the West. He attended school but nine months in his life; yet during that time he learned to read, write, cypher, and acquired some notion of surveying. He was among the first white settlers of Kentucky. He found employment in the office of James Thompson, a licensed surveyor, was soon made a deputy, and became one of the first practical surveyors in the West. By entering lands on the shares, he laid the foundation of a very large fortune. He was successively chosen to fill several important stations, civil and military. He was a representative of the Kentucky district in the Virginia Legislature, and was a member of the Virginia Convention that ratified the present Federal Constitution, himself supporting and voting for the ratification. He was also a member of the Convention which, in 1799, framed the present Constitution of Kentucky, and subsequently represented Madison County at different times in either branch of the State Legislature. He bore an active and influential part in the politics and legislation of his time, and was widely esteemed for his ability, integrity and patriotism. Clay county was named in his honor by the Kentucky Legislature.

On the breaking out of the last war with Great Britain, Green Clay was among the large number of Kentuckians who rallied around their country's standard, and in May, 1813, he advanced at the head of 3,000 volunteers to the relief of Gen. Harrison, then besieged in Fort Meigs. Cutting his way, through the enemy's lines, the British and Indians were forced to retire after this accession of strength. Gen. Harrison reposed the utmost confidence in General Clay, and left him in command of Fort Meigs. In the autumn of that year, the fort was again invested by 1,500 British troops, under Proctor, and 5,000 Indians, led by Tecumseh, but they made no impression, and were soon obliged to raise the siege and decamp. For the gallantry and good conduct of this defence, Gen. Harrison rendered, by special order, thanks to Gen. Clay. Gen. C., admonished by his advancing years and increasing cares, declined public life after the close of the war, and died on the 31st of October, 1826, in the 72d year of his age.

CASSIUS MARCELLUS CLAY, the youngest of seven children of Green Clay

---

* See Collins's Kentucky, 1847, Art. Clay County.

(B. J. Clay being the only other son now living,) was born on the 9th of October, 1810. His mother's maiden name was Sally Lewis, granddaughter of Edward Payne, of Virginia, who struck Gen. Washington for an insult, for which that great man promptly and magnanimously apologized, and Payne was ever after one of his most devoted admirers and friends. Mrs. Clay still lives, is an exemplary member of the Baptist Church, and is distinguished for her industry, energy of will, and love of truth, with which she early and ardently imbued the minds of her children.

The father, feeling keenly the deficiencies of his own education, freely lavished his ample means in procuring the best attainable instruction for his children. Cassius was early committed to the charge of the late Joshua Fry, Esq., of Garrard Co., Ky., a wealthy gentleman, who taught a small number of pupils in his own house, more to indulge his love of teaching than with a view to pecuniary recompense, as he took but few pupils in addition to his own grandchildren, one of whom is the present Maj. Carey Fry, honorably distinguished at Buena Vista. Thoroughness was the grand aim of this school. Hence young Clay passed to Transylvania University, at Lexington, where he pursued the usual routine of study to the middle of the Senior year, when, in consequence of President Wood's leaving to take charge of the University of Alabama, he transferred himself to Yale College, where he entered the Junior Class, and graduated in 1832. While a Senior, he was unanimously chosen by his class to deliver an Address on the Centennial Anniversary of Washington's birth day, which he did. That Address is the earliest of his productions reprinted in this volume.

Returning to Kentucky, Mr. Clay was married the ensuing spring to Mary Jane Warfield, of Lexington, Ky., daughter of E. Warfield, Esq., who emigrated thither from Maryland. Miss W. was one of the most accomplished and most admired women of Kentucky. It is not within the province of this sketch to reveal the priceless treasures of conjugal affection, but it can hardly be improper to state, what is already widely known, that through all the varied fortunes and imminent perils of his subsequent career, Mr. Clay has enjoyed the appreciation and sustaining sympathy of one who has approved and gloried in his every act—has discerned a straightforward rectitude and a self-forgetting philanthropy, where others proclaimed inconsistency, and empty craving for notoriety,—and who, whether he were arming for the defence of his own property and dearest rights at home, or to join the invaders of Mexico in a war he had early, uniformly and unsparingly stigmatized as unjust and abhorrent, has still recognised in him, through all, a generous, self-devoting champion of eternal justice and universal freedom.

The public career of Mr. Clay has been so closely interwoven with and is so fully illustrated by the speeches, letters, &c., contained in the following pages, that little remains to be added. He was first chosen to the Legislature of Kentucky, as soon as eligible, from his native county of Madison, in 1835, (See his speech at the ensuing session,) but was defeated in a canvass for re-election by the influence of a local question respecting Internal Improvement. The next year (1837) he was triumphantly returned. Removing soon after to Fayette county, he was in 1840 elected from that county. Meantime he was chosen a delegate from a district in which he did not reside to the Whig National convention which met at Harrisburg in December 1839, and nominated Gen. Harrison for President. Mr. Clay advocated and voted for Henry Clay throughout that excited struggle. He was for the last time a candidate for the Legislature in 1841, when, having rendered himself intensely obnoxious to the slave power by his course with regard to slavery, he was thrown out by illegal votes, by violence and fraud, a slave-trader being chosen in his stead. He has not since been a candidate for any public station.

While a member of the Legislature, Mr. Clay was an ardent supporter of a common school system, of internal improvements, and of an improved jury system, all of which measures were ultimately carried during his public service.

Having early and earnestly exposed and denounced the project of annexing Texas to our Union, as a plot for the extension of slavery and the slave power in the United States, (see Speeches and Letters), Mr. Clay in 1844 traversed the free states, urging and entreating the opponents of slavery to vote for the whig candidate for President, so as to defeat that flagitious measure. He was partially but not sufficiently heeded. Sixty thousand voters saw fit to give their suffrages to James G. Birney, thus permitting the election of Polk, and insuring the annexation of Texas, with the long catalogue of consequent crimes and calamities. For none of this can Mr. Clay be held responsible.

On June 3d, 1845, he commenced at Lexington, Ky., the weekly issue of THE TRUE AMERICAN, expressly devoted to a discussion of the character and influences of Human Slavery, as it exists in this country, and to the dissemination of truth and concentration of opinion with a view to its overthrow. As the publication of that paper marked an era in the history of the time, and as the concerted, systematic violence which destroyed its office and temporarily suspended its issues was justified by its authors by impeaching not the general bearing and aim but the manner and temper of its strictures. the editorials, without an exception of any consequence, and including all those which especially provoked or were made the pretext for the riot, are in this volume collected and presented in due order. The public will therefore judge whether the personal criticism and the brief passages which, wrenched from their context, were made to threaten the upholders of slavery with the horrors of a servile insurrection, were in truth the causes of the outrage, or whether they were not rather seized upon as pretexts for crushing an adversary whom it was painful to hear, difficult to avoid hearing, and impossible otherwise to silence or to answer.

It were easy to say that a prudent, discreet man, just commencing an anti-slavery journal in the midst of a slave-holding community, would have studiously avoided all severity of language, all personal inculpation, every form of expression calculated to excite angry feeling or provoke hostile demonstrations. A model of prudence would doubtless have cut the matter short and avoided all danger by not attempting such a paper at all. No sensible person supposes that a wrong so inveterate and so interwoven with all its upholders' ideas of comfort and consequence as slavery, is to be pelted out of existence with rose-leaves, or that the wielders of such weapons will ever achieve its overthrow by any means. When Mr. Clay became convinced that his duty to an oppressed and degraded race required of him not merely the emancipation of those held in bondage by himself, but a public and persistent endeavor to awaken in others the convictions which impelled his own course, it was hardly to be expected that those convictions would be uniformly expressed in language inoffensive to the large class who had long ago determined not to be convinced, nor even patiently to listen. From the day that his Prospectus was published, the ultimate suppression of his paper by violence was generally anticipated, and if any one excuse had not been afforded, another would almost certainly have been made to serve. Have we not just seen the office of the National Era at Washington—a paper uniformly temperate and courteous in language—assailed quite as formidably and determinedly as that of the True American, and only saved from destruction because the Police of Washington was more powerful or more faithful than that of Lexington?

The excitement which the bare annunciation of an anti-slavery journal in Kentucky had created, was steadily, daily increased, after its appearance by the bold, fearless, pungent character of its editorials. At length, after the appearance of the strictures on Gov. Metcalf's letter, a leading article by a Southerner and a slave-holder, and the swiftly succeeding article in which reference is made to "the smooth-skinned woman on the ottoman," as sitting there in peace and safety, ever under the protecting shield of law, which it would therefore be most unwise in the slaveholders to overbear or disregard, a secret caucus, and then a public meeting, were called in Lexington, largely attended and most vehemently addressed, at which it was formally resolved that the True American should be stopped—if not by intimidation, then by violence. A committee was appointed to see to the execution of this edict, first by corresponding or conferring with Mr. Clay, and, remonstrance failing, by a resort to overwhelming force, and bloodshed if necessary. Personal hostility very naturally mingled with the more obvious impulse in this business. The chief orator of the lawless gathering was T. F. Marshall, a notoriously bitter adversary of Mr. Clay, and all whom he had offended during the ardent political contests wherein he had been engaged were ready enough to seize so fair and safe an opportunity for revenge. The excitement fanned itself into a fierce and fiercer fury; those who did not share in it were awed into silence, and the spectacle presented was that of a whole community banded and ready to go all lengths for the immolation or destruction of one solitary man.

That man did not shrink from the encounter. To the formal demand that the True American should be stopped, he returned a peremptory and scornful negative. At a day appointed, therefore, on the 18th of August, the mob re-assembled, with the active countenance and under the almost entire direction of men of high social standing and seeming consequence, and, compliance with their wishes being still refused, proceeded to the office, overawed the civil power, the mayor of the city and posse, to whom Mr. Clay had surrendered the keys, by order of injunction from Judge Trotter, tore down the press, packed up the type, &c., all of which was, in such order as may be best imagined, sent off to Cincinnati, and there landed, subject to the owner's order. To this procedure no active opposition was made. Mr. Clay lay severely ill in his dwelling, unable even to witness the outrage, and, as none beside would take the hazard of standing forth against an infuriated multitude, the press was silenced.

Not finally, however. On the partial restoration of his health, Mr. Clay promptly made arrangements for the re-issue of his paper. It was thereafter printed at Cincinnati, but still dated at Lexington, where its editor continued to reside and conduct it, with no abatement in the vigor or plainness of his reprobation of Human Bondage. Thus the paper went on, increasing in patronage and in influence, up to the time (June 7th, 1846,) that Mr. Clay left it in temporary charge of his friend, John C. Vaughan, previously Assistant Editor, to engage in the war in Mexico, for which, according to a long standing pledge, he had volunteered.

Although a war with Mexico had been confidently predicted by Mr. Clay in his various public addresses, in 1844, as certain to follow the Annexation of Texas, and though he had repeatedly declared that, on the breaking out of such war, he should, in obedience to his pledges, and to his view of the duties of a citizen in a Republic, volunteer to aid in its prosecution, it will not be denied that the fact of his so doing surprised and pained the great body of his Northern friends and subscribers, very many of whom were hardly more adverse to Slavery and Annexation than to War, and especially offensive War. To these, his volunteering appeared a complete abandonment of the high moral position and philanthropic aims by which he had been so honorably distinguished. Mr. Clay's own opposite view is so fully set forth in the body of this volume, (See Letters to the Christian Reflector, and to the Tribune, from Camargo), that I shall merely refer the reader to those letters for his defence, simply adding that if his Mexican service shall enable him to exert a more decided influence in Kentucky in favor of the great cause of Emancipation, to which he is still devoted, the most·determined contemner of the Mexican War will surely rejoice that this good has been educed from the reprehended evil.

Mr. Clay left his home on the 7th of June, 1846, as Captain of "the Old Infantry," the oldest company west of the mountains, acting as Dragoons, and having been conveyed by steamboat to Memphis, Mississippi, the regiment took up its line of march south-westwardly, through Arkansas and Texas, more than a thousand miles, to the Rio Grande, near Camargo, Mexico, and thence to Monterey and Saltillo.

On the night of the 23d of January, 1847, a party of seventy-one cavalry, led by Maj. Gaines, and including Capt. Clay, was surrounded and surprised at the hacienda of Encarnacion, 110 miles in advance of Saltillo, where they had too securely and incautiously taken post, by a body of 3,000 Mexican horse, led by Gen. Minon. The surprise was complete, every avenue of escape trebly guarded, and the handful of our countrymen, slenderly provided with ammunition, and without food or water, had no choice but to submit to a capitulation, or to a useless and aimless butchery. They exacted and received honorable terms, and were made prisoners of war. (See Letter to N. O. Picayune, and C.'s reception speech at Richmond.) They marched successively to San Luis Potosi, to the city of Mexico, and to Toluca, where they remained until the conquest of the capital by Gen. Scott. By the magnanimity of Origuibel, Governor of the State of Mexico, they were sent to the city of Mexico on parole, when they were exchanged, and (the fighting being substantially at an end), they returned by way of Vera Cruz and New Orleans to their homes. Mr. Clay reached Lexington in December, 1847, and was received in that city (where he had so recently been mobbed and threatened with death), with public and general rejoicings, —a procession, address, salute of artillery, &c. In the county of his birth, to which he has returned to live, he was also greeted with a hearty Kentucky welcome and public reception; and in Estill county, also, he was tendered a public reception and dinner; and everywhere received with enthusiasm. So much for the past life and services of Cassius M. Clay; the future must speak for itself.

NEW-YORK, MAY 1ST, 1848.

ESSAYS, SPEECHES, &c

BY C. M. CLAY.

HINTS ON RELIGIOUS AND CIVIL LIBERTY.

PART I. RELIGIOUS LIBERTY.

I. BELIEF.—FAITH.

MAN, the earth, the sun, are things. They are said to *be*. The mind of man is a thing; it exists. It is something else than the earth, the sun. It sees differences between the thing earth, and the thing sun; and distinguishes those differences by names, by language, written or spoken. Language is used to convey ideas of things, from one mind to another; or to treasure up those ideas for its own use by assisting the memory. Truth is a representation of things as they are; the things themselves are also, in consequence of the imperfections of language, called truths. Falsehood is the representation of things as they are not. If I say that the earth and the sun have the same properties, the same color, solidity, and form, I tell a falsehood; I state things that do not exist; I represent them as they are not. The object, then, of all inquiry is truth. Living in a world of things, upon the knowledge of whose existence and laws not only our happiness but our very existence depend; it is always useful to know those things, those laws—to know "the truth, the whole truth." For if we know all things that are, we know all things that are not. If we know all truth, we know, as a sequence, all falsehood. When we see, feel, or taste an apple, we have a sensation of something, external to and distinct from ourselves. When those impressions of other things are made upon any or all of our senses, in such manner that the orange is determined by

the mind to be some other thing than the apple, we are said to
know those things. There are three sources of knowledge—
the Senses; Consciousness; and Reason. We see the sun.
We are conscious of our own being, of our identity—that we
are the same persons, who were in sickness, and again restored
to health. By the Senses and Consciousness, is developed a
third power, Reason. I have seen the sun, day after day, rise
and set; I remember this; I am conscious of it; reason tells
me it will rise and set again to-morrow; or, to speak of past
time, I know that it has risen many degrees East of me, for
hours before I see it. Here, then, are three truths, all ascertained through distinct or separate sources of knowledge. There
are no other primary sources of knowledge than these three.
Testimony, written, or oral, or pantomimic, is a secondary *mode*
of knowledge; it depends upon the original sources of knowledge, and can never outweigh them. If one is to be questioned, it must be Testimony; for Testimony can only be received
by the mind so far as it is in accordance with the Senses,
Consciousness, and Reason; and no farther. A tells B that C
has red hair. Now if B has had experience, that A is in a
habit of telling the truth, and his reason does not induce him
to think that A lies for some selfish end; or that red hair is not
so unusual in the nature of things—does not run counter to
known laws of matter—B *believes* him—has faith in A—thinks
that A tells the truth. But if A tells B that C has spike-nails
growing on his head instead of red hair; here B's consciousness
and reason, higher powers of knowledge than A's testimony,
come in, and he does not believe A. It is evident, then, that
belief is founded upon the knowledge derived from the Senses,
the Memory or Consciousness, the Reason, and the evidence of
others Testimony. This last is the weakest of the four, because
it is based upon them; and not they, in the least iota, based
upon it.

 Belief, then, in all cases, will depend upon the Senses, Consciousness, Reason, and Testimony. They mutually aid and
assist each other in ascertaining *truth*. If a juggler puts a
marble in his eye and takes it out of his mouth, though I see it,
or seem to see it, I will not believe it. Why? Because all
the other sources of evidence are against it. Here the senses
are distrusted. Again; A is engaged with B in a fight; under
great excitement, he strikes B and kills him. A had a knife

and a whip : he *thinks,* he is conscious, he remembers, that he used the whip ; but the skull of B is cut with a *"clean cut,"* such as a whip never makes; and his own father and best friends all testify that he cut B with the knife. In spite of consciousness, he *believes* that B was killed with a knife. Here Testimony and Reason outweigh Consciousness. Once more : B tells A that C has turned into an oak tree. A does not believe it. Reason, and Consciousness, are here against Testimony. *Belief* in all these cases then depends upon the weight of *evidence.*

And as the evidence preponderates one way or the other, a thing alleged to be true will be *believed* or *not.* Belief, then, is involuntary. It does not depend upon the will. The will forms not an iota of evidence, upon which only, belief is based. And as a consequence, it is not a thing of praise, nor of blame— of reward, nor of punishment. It cannot be said to be a virtue, nor a vice : a holy thing, nor a sin. I see the sun, that it is red : I believe it. B tells me it is green, I disbelieve it. I am not to be praised nor blamed, rewarded nor punished,* for believing the one, nor for disbelieving the other. There can be no knowledge of truth among men, if this is not *truth.*

II. Toleration.

If belief, or faith, is involuntary, which we have proven, then is *Toleration* a necessary consequence. To punish a man for his belief, is as absurd as to punish him for the color of his hair. Religious belief does not differ in character from any other belief. Whether the mind contemplates *God,* or the *things* that belong to God, it is subject to the same laws. Religious faith, then, is also involuntary. Hence the attempt

---

* I think unbelief may be culpable, or at least the evidence of culpability, in that it implies and proves an unjustifiable inattention to some important subject, or to testimony which establishes some important truth. For instance, A has fitted out a privateer in time of war, and sailed in her, resolved to lie in wait for, and capture a tempting prize, and he is so intent on that prize, that he discredits all reports of Peace that reach his ears. He makes the coveted capture, and returning to port, finds that Peace was ratified a month before. Can we say he was not culpable in obstinately discrediting the first news of Peace ?—Editor.

to *force conformity* of opinion in Religion, Morals, Science, Politics, or any other department of knowledge, is not only absurd, but criminal. For if truth be the legitimate object of human inquiry, and its laws, which are the laws of nature, are to be obeyed in order to our happiness, then any attempt to influence belief or faith by *pain* is in violation of all the laws of nature. For belief, depending on sense, consciousness, reason, and testimony, and not at all upon pleasure or pain, the use of pain to cause it, as it is absurd, so is it criminal; for it *violates every law of nature* applicable to the case, which is *the sum of all crime.* Any person, therefore, who attempts to influence another's belief by any other than the means stated, is a criminal and a madman. "Religious tests"—Taxation for support of Priests—Punishments for violation of the Sabbath—Disturbance of Religious worship—in a word, all attempts to make Religion anything else than a relation between a man's conscience and his God, are *persecution.*

III. Miracles.

I do not say that Miracles are *impossible.* But that, when based upon *testimony,* only one of the four kinds of evidence, and that one the weakest, and in opposition to all the rest—they fail to carry conviction of their truth to my mind. And for this conviction I am· neither to be praised nor blamed. Miracles may induce belief in one to whom they come; but they cease to be conclusive* at second hand, or as soon as they pass from *primary* to *secondary evidence.*

---

* I do not assent to the proposition that Miracles are offered to our Consciousness and Reason. It will be time enough to assume even that a Miracle is a violation of the laws of nature, when we perfectly understand those laws, and can decide off-hand that a particular phenomenon exists by their flagrant violation. To the ephemera warmed into life by the morning's sun, night is a miracle—contrary to all experience—a violation of nature's laws. So is an earthquake or volcano to the man who never before heard of one. But suppose it conceded that a miracle transcends natural laws, we have still to consider the great fact that GOD IS, and that He framed Nature and her laws, and can overrule either at his mere good pleasure. To assert dogmatically that He can never wish to suspend the laws He has established, is to assume a familiarity with His plans and purposes which seems to me unwarranted by the existing

IV. GOD.—REVELATION.

God *is*. I think that the argument in favor of the existence of God, drawn from *design* in the universe, is the strongest of all. To my mind it is conclusive. The wonderful construction of the human mind and body, and the universe, brings conviction of an intelligent cause—of God. The attributes of God are to be drawn in like manner, from the evidences of nature : by the fruit shall the tree be known. Paley's argument upon the benevolence of God seems to me to be especially conclusive. Other attributes also given Him by the most enlightened nations, are likewise known from his works. "Revelation" seems not to be higher evidence of God and His attributes than these, because it is in reality founded only upon "internal evidence" and *testimony*. Revelation is subject to the same laws of belief

---

state of our knowledge. Laws are but means to ends, and when these ends may be better subserved by a suspension of the laws, why not suspend them? To assume that God can never have occasion to overrule the laws of nature, seems to me to border on a confusion of laws with the Lawgiver, and to imply that the laws once established, the Lawgiver is fettered if not superseded by them. And besides, I feel a moral need of the assurance that God is, and that He is not a blind, inexorable Destiny, but a paternal Providence. Yet how am I to know and feel this, except by some clear manifestation of His being and power? Yet every such manifestation is termed a miracle—therefore deemed incredible, except possibly on the direct testimony of the senses. Must God, then, manifest Himself especially to every human being, or leave them to grope in the darkness of heathenism? I think not.

Now, as to the force of Testimony: although a man may lie, it seems to me possible so to combine and interlace testimony that it shall absolutely *command* belief. For instance, that Adams and Jefferson, the two chief authors of our National Independence, should live just half a century to a day after that Independence was declared, and die on the fiftieth anniversary of its declaration, and that the messengers conveying from their distant residences the tidings of their respective deaths, should meet exactly in Philadelphia, where that Independence was matured and proclaimed—I hardly know anything recorded more astonishing than this, nor more suggestive of direct Providential interposition. Yet I know that such were the facts; and any man who lives hereafter may satisfy himself that they were so by carefully examining and comparing the journals and other publications of 1826. The testimony of many concurring witnesses to an occurrence, when collusion between them was manifestly impossible, may establish it more strongly than direct sight or hearing could do. I therefore esteem perfectly rational and logical my belief in Divine Revelation as a verity, and in Miracles, so called, as the strongest possible attestations that Christ, the Savior, came to earth commissioned and empowered by God.— EDITOR.

as Miracles. Revelation is conclusive only to whom it comes in personal identity. When it goes a step farther, it becomes *testimony*—subject to all its laws, as other events : and may or may not produce belief. Its "internal evidence" always being the strongest item in influencing belief, cannot rise, the spring, higher than the fountain-head. "Internal evidence" means conformity to the known laws of things ; which knowledge is based at last upon the Senses, Consciousness, and Reason.

V. The Jewish Bible, or Old Testament.

"The Bible" is the history of the laws, country, customs, and men of the Jewish nation. Its truth must be judged of by the same laws of evidence as the truth of other ancient books. As a code of laws it is no more binding upon me, than the history of the Greeks, and the Romans, and the Chinese.

The will of God, so far as I learn it from the history of the Jews, I, must obey, or suffer the penalty. So, also, I say of the history of the Romans, the Greeks, and all other nations. If, after maturely reading it, studying its internal evidence, and the collateral testimony of others, I conclude that it is Divine— *well ; if not, well.*

VI. The New Testament.—Christ.

The New Testament, the history of Christ, is true. I know no higher code of morals among men. His doctrine is in accordance with all the known laws of nature. The spirit of God is displayed in his whole life. He speaks of God as the father of all men ; and of all men as brothers. As the father loves the children, and as the children love the father and each other, so also is it with God and His creatures. Christ teaches man's whole duty, "Love the Lord thy God with all thy heart, and thy neighbor as thyself ; on these hang all the law and the prophets." *This is the embryo principle of all morality.* Away with the blood of animals, and vain ceremonies, and long prayers, and ascetic debasements ! Here is religion promoting

the great ends of all creation—the happiness of all God's creatures! Eternal and glorious spirit of the Father of all! in
Jesus Christ of Nazareth we know the truest manifestation of
Thyself; inspire our souls with a kindred flame, that "Thy kingdom come, and Thy *will* be done, on earth as it is in Heaven."

VII. Sin.—Evil.—The Devil.

When we put our hand in the fire it pains us. Who created
the pain, God or the Devil? The pain is evidently an incident
of the flesh, one of its laws, one of its attributes. If God made
the man, he made the pain. What! God make pain—make
"evil?" Yes. For benevolent purposes. For if the pain did
not give the man warning that his person was burning, it would
be destroyed; then would human life end, and all this "beautiful world" would to him cease. I say then with Paley, that pain
is not the object of life, but a mere law for the preservation of
man's physical being. "Partial evil is universal good." But is
not death an evil? I would, taking the whole universe of God
in view, say, no. Because, from all the observation which we
can make, it seems, that God created the world for the greatest
happiness of the greatest possible number of his creatures—men,
and other animals. We are bound to believe that he made
them as happy as *possibly* consistent with his own ends. The
law of nature, or of God, seems to be, that there should exist on
the earth the greatest *possible quantity of life* and happiness.
And paradoxical as it may seem, death is conducive to this end.
Take a single instance. In a pond of an acre in size, were
there no eating of each other, or no death, I cannot readily
imagine how a perch of six pounds weight could live. Where
would he get food enough for his subsistence? But he eats the
one pound fish; the one pound fish eats the minnow; the
minnow eats the worm: and the worm eats the decayed
vegetable matter that washes into the pond from the rains, or
that lines its circumference. Here, then, are myriads of lives
in consequence of death; whereas, without death, we cannot
conceive of the subsistence at all of thousands of beings now
existent. Besides, suppose men immortal in the flesh; all young
if you please; what becomes of the parental love, the beauty of

childhood, the promise of early youth, of filial affection, and reverence for age? For if the old die not, the young cannot be born—there is no room for them. I conclude, then, that evil in the long run is swallowed up in good, and mysteriously subserves it. Physical evil brings pain—moral evil brings *remorse*. When the body violates physical laws, pain gives warning. When the laws of mind are violated, remorse gives warning. Both say, stop—turn and live—and be happy. The violation of physical laws is evil—physical evil. The violation of moral laws is moral evil—sin. They are both equally the will of God. They are the similar attributes of distinct things, mind and body. If the first be of God, then is also the second. The Devil, then, has no work left. He is a figure of speech—an allegory. He is not a distinct Being.

VIII. The Immortality of the Soul.

The existence of the mind, or the soul, is as certain as any other known thing. That the body and the soul are not one, or the same, is as demonstrable a truth, as that fire and water are not identical; or that the sun and the earth are not the same thing. The body moves from place to place, grows by eating matter, is subject to certain forms, color, heat, and pain. The mind or soul thinks of the future; remembers the past; collects facts; forms theories; has neither color, heat, nor form. In a word, mind and body, of all known things, have fewest properties in common. If, then, there be in all nature two distinct entities, they are soul and matter. But gross unthinking matter is composed of elements which are imperishable—in other words, matter is everlasting;—how much more then is the ethereal thinking soul immortal!

Since the mind then is immortal, we are induced to believe that its character is unchanged in a future state; the good, is good still, and the bad, bad. Future rewards and punishments then seem necessary sequences of the immortality of the soul; the truth of which has been demonstrated. The "resurrection of the body"—of the identical body—seems to be inconsistent with the known laws of physics—impossible in the nature of things.

In giving my views upon such serious subjects, I have looked only to the establishment of Truth, and human happiness. I come not to destroy, but to save. If I have erred, I shall be happy to be set right. My religion is, that truth is always useful—is God's law; that intolerance, so far from being a virtue, is the greatest of crimes; that liberty of thought is the gift of Deity—the right of every responsible being.

PART II.—CIVIL LIBERTY.

I. State of Nature.

Man, like most animals, is gregarious. Both by sympathy, or instinct and reason, which teaches him utility, he associates in multitudes. The attempt to ridicule what is called the "state of nature," has generally come from *monopolists!* I take it that there is now, and always has been, a "state of nature" in some portion of the world. The reasoning founded on such a state then, is reasoning founded upon *fact,* which is the *legitimate* basis of all *disquisition.* But even if we were confined to reasoning: having no people in a "state of nature:" such a state can be logically, in our eye, deduced. For if man be progressive, as all admit—unlike other animals, accumulating the experience of preceding generations—he must have advanced from an indefinite point. Not, indeed, an *infinite* degree below present civilization, but an *undefined* degree. To go as low as other animal nature is sufficient for our purpose. Say then, that man was once governed by such influences as herd horses or deer; then was he in a "state of nature" sufficient for our purpose; and that he has been in that state is beyond question. In such a state there was no *compulsion* for *association* used by one over another, for such is the law of the beasts. In such a state all did as they pleased; no one attempted to influence another by opinion, or by physical force. That the stronger robbed the weaker, if he pleased, is equally clear. We mean, then, only to say, that each did as nearly as he pleased as he was able. In such a state, then, all were *equal in law*, for each man's own will was the *only law*.

II. Force.

It may be said truly that there was a law other than each man's will, namely, physical force. The stronger killed the weaker, and robbed him, or subjected him to slavery, and by the terror of superior might fed upon the bread of unpaid labor. That law did exist, does now exist. But the *sword* is its *only sanction*.

"They who live by the sword shall perish by the sword." When the strong man slept, the weaker one was then the stronger, and became master. When the strong was sick, the weaker was then the stronger, and grasping the sword he slew the slayer. Such was the case; such is the case. And against the right of the sword there is no other argument but the sword. We do not write a book for men who regard force as a rule of right. Reason, truth, justice, are to them unmeaning terms; their understanding lies in the flesh and the blood vessels; it can be reached only by leaden bullets and cold steel!

III. Mutual Interest—"the Greatest Happiness."

Rising one degree higher in the progress of mankind—higher than that period when individual will and force were the only laws—we come to *mutual interest*. The strong man finding that there were times when he might be weak, was pained by apprehension of future danger, and sought out some other basis of safety than his individual might. Two or more weak men banded together to intimidate the stronger, or actually set upon him and slew him. Here was an *agreement* on all sides, no matter whether expressed or implied, to forego the natural right of killing each other, for the higher good of being safe from the assaults of others; or, to use Bentham's language, there was "more happiness" in *society* and *safety*, than in individual will and *liability to murder.* The same reasonings began to secure first, life, then property, and then character, and such happiness as results from their undisturbed enjoyment—as the American declaration of rights has it, "the pursuit of happiness."

IV. GOVERNMENT.

So soon as force began to give way to reason, or mutual interest, government began. Its foundation then, in all its breadth, and depth, and length, is in the "consent of the governed," and in nothing else. That government uses force is true, but it is force with the addition of an omnipotent *ought.* It is force to *save,* not to *destroy.* Right and wrong, good and bad, injurious and useful, now begin to appear among men. Paley very aptly says a tooth was made to *chew* with, not for the purpose of *aching.* The *object* of the government is to secure happiness to *all* its members ; *not to oppress any.* A, B, and C, and D, are the society ; A *ought* to be, or has as much right to be, protected in the eating of the fish he catches; and B has a right to be protected in the eating of the venison he kills ; so of C and D. Now, if A comes upon B to rob him, he becomes not a useful member of society ; he does wrong, he does not consult the "greatest happiness" of himself, in the long run, nor of the other members of society. B, C, and D, use force against him ; reason has failed to influence him ; the sword must. These men, then, are equal in their *rights.* I say, then, all men are, politically—in respect to all that government can legitimately do, ought to do, can possibly do, *in virtue of being a government—equal.* Because A is six feet high, "born," or "created,"—I care not for terms—and B is only four feet high—in that respect plainly *unequal*—does it follow that C or D, or any other person, shall come upon them and take away their fish or their venison ? Surely not. Again, A, B, C, and D, the society having agreed to protect each one in his accumulations of labor, his property, and having *agreed* that it was most useful, right, conducive to the greatest happiness, for A to transmit his property at his death, to his son, E, and B his property to his two sons, K and M, now, if it turn out that

M is born with *less* property than E, does 'his *inequality* entitle C or D, or any one else, to plunder both, under the contemptible plea that they are not born *equal* in property?

The declaration of American rights is true then in the whole large and broad sense in which it was spoken—Jeremy Bentham and other cavillers to the contrary notwithstanding! "All men are created equal."

V. Monarchy.—Aristocracy.—Republicanism.

From what I have said it is plain that government is founded by "the consent of the governed," either tacit or expressed. It is *possible* to attain all its legitimate objects by any *form.* If a people consent, or without any intimidation of mind, or apprehension of force, submit to a despotism, that is a legitimate government. The despot may perform all his duties, may imprison the thief and hang the murderer, and do anything that best secures the happiness of his people. A, B, and C would commit treason in attempting to dethrone him, and set up a republicanism, so long as a *majority* of the people preferred a despotism. But if the despot kill A to enjoy his wife or his property—let him have a care!—*all allegiance due him is gone!* For he was allowed to be despot to do good, not to do evil; to hold power under the implied understanding that he would be just; would do right; secure the happiness of his people. If he would avoid this awfully precarious position, let him become a constitutional monarch—let him form an aristocracy—a republic, and by sharing his power lessen his danger. For all three of these governments may do wrong, and deserve punishment when they transgress—fail to secure the happiness of the people, as much as the despot, were it possible to inflict it. A *constitutional* monarchy is a government which can exist by the *consent* of the governed, and is better than a despotism; for it is plain that a despotism—its existence depending upon a single wilful crime of the despot, must be in *perpetual revolution,* in consequence of the infirmities of men, or become *illegitimate*—that is, based upon *force* and not the *consent* of the people. A monarchy, on the contrary, by the punishing of ministers, or by co-ordinate branches of power, as the parliament of England, may do wrong and receive punishment, and not cease to exist. So of an aristocracy.

No doubt the legitimate ends of government may be attained under all the *forms* named. We can only say that despotism is least likely to attain the ends of society ; or is, in other words, the worst form of government. For to be secure is one thing ; to have assurance of future security, is another thing. I imagine an aristocracy is the next worst. A constitutional monarchy, like England, is the best of the three ; but a republic is the best of all. All of them may do wrong ; may not subserve the ends of government—security of property, life, and character, and the "pursuit of happiness." All we can say is, that the chances of doing wrong in a republic are less than under other forms of government, and herein Mr. Pope errs—

> " About forms of governments let fools contest,
> That, which is best administered, is best."

We are not satisfied with not being robbed of our property, defamed in character, and killed in person, but the apprehension of such results is an evil to be avoided. It is true, it matters not to me, when the act is done, whether the majority of the people, a mob of " respectable gentlemen," or the Emperor of China, murder me. Still, there is more hope that *laws* in republics will restrain mobs and secure rights, than that despots would do the same, of their own will. That republics will always regard the legitimate ends of government, the security of the rights of all, is not to be hoped ; for man is by nature imperfect, as we have seen in the first part of this essay.

But take an extreme case—that all governments will do wrong, and that continually—still is a republic best ; for a majority of the people, if plunder be a blessing, will enjoy it. The " greatest happiness" will be diffused over the greatest number, and millions preying upon the minority will enjoy, what in a despotism, at the same, or rather a greater expenditure of human misery, will be enjoyed by a single man. But such a case is hardly possible, as *ten* men systematically oppressing the minority, *nine ;* for, when it does assume a permanent form of tyranny, it will soon cease to exist. By nature's law crime works out its own destruction at last—" a lie cannot live for ever." The majority will finally disagree, and bring the former minority into the ascendency, in the same form; or else the minority will join one of the disaffected parts of the former majority, and make some other form of government, more likely to give security to life, property, and character.

VI. Liberty.

Liberty, then, is security from aggression in the possession of life, property, and character, and the happiness accruing from their undisturbed enjoyment, with reasonable guaranties of its perpetuity.

Absolute liberty is attainable only by God. Man in "a state of nature" has some liberty, as I have shown, if my definition be good. A might fish, and hunt, and sleep in caves, and in the thick woods, and be tolerably secure from the death blows, robbery, or defamation of B. Still he would be very much trammeled in his enjoyment of these blessings. He might obtain a hard and precarious livelihood, and the coarser animal enjoyments. But when he planted corn, or fruit trees, B would come upon him and eat; and when he built a shelter against the inclemency of the elements, B would take possession. No government then is so bad, or has so little liberty *permanently* as a "state of nature;" otherwise men would flee to the hills, and groves, and caves, for safety, and society be dissolved. That governments sometimes become so oppressive to a portion of the people, that they possess less liberty than in "a state of nature," is true. Such is the case with slavery in the United States, the West Indies, and South America. To the African *slave*, government brings no boon. It has stripped him of all his natural rights under the *pretence* of protection. It secures him neither life, nor property, nor character; but systematically strips him of all. The wild man of the woods is more fortunate than he; there is no *concert* among his hunters. But here numbers band together, not to protect, but to plunder; not to save, but to destroy! And when intolerable oppression dries up the affections of the heart, destroys all the sensibilities of enjoyment, and degrades men below the beasts of the field, or else plants a field of *unsatisfied desires* in the soul, and the slave flies instinctively to the woods—with overpowering numbers and inevitable bloodhounds, he is hunted back to his earthly hell ! This is an extreme case ; I use extreme language ; but language fails me here !

Here, then, are governments which do not even pretend to the liberty enjoyed in the despotisms of Europe, and Asia, and Africa, and the Isles of the Seas. In our own land, in hot haste to oppress a portion of society, they have struck down their own liberties ! Some of these states have already attained that point when majorities systematically oppress minorities for their own selfish enjoyment; and even when minorities eat the bread of forced majorities, though nature and nature's God have sworn by the eternity of things, a wrong shall not be permament—a lie shall not live for ever ! This wrong cannot be confined to color. Already, as might have been anticipated, the national sense of justice—of right and wrong, languishes ; the majority begins to act upon the principle, that "to the victors belong the spoils," and grow strong in the determination to live upon the forced labor of the minority. There is no hope, for a man who has made up his mind to do wrong systematically, until he abandons his system, and has determined to attempt the right. So also with governments. They have Moses and the Prophets ; they will not hear one though he arise from the dead ! If all time, all moralists, all jurists—if Jesus Christ and his followers have spoken in vain, then most surely must I be silent. Where there is *slavery*, there is not, and never can be, *liberty*. The thing is axiomatic. Human reason and human language stop here.

VII. Guaranties of Liberty.—Suffrage.

If society is formed for the protection of *all* its members, it is plain that *all* have an equal right to choose the mode of government, and if rulers are elective, to vote. That a man, or a set of men have a right to disfranchise themselves, is plain; but then it must as plainly appear that they have willingly done so. The people have at times denied themselves the right of choosing judges, and other high officers, trusting to the judgment of more intelligent electors.

Minors, and idiots, and insane persons, being incapable of

taking care of themselves in "a state of nature," and in society, are in both cases, at the mercy of society. Society is bound to secure their rights also; that is, such rights as they are capable of using without detriment to others; among which *voting* is not one. That idiots and insane persons have no right to marry, seems also plain; for it would be a great injury to humanity, by perpetuating disease and folly, without an equivalent good to the individual authors of them.

Some politicians and moralists have affected to deny to individuals any rights more than the already existing government allows. *Minors* and *women* say they are forbid the right of suffrage; and *therefore* A, B, and C are rightly forbid to vote. The *reason*, why minors are forbidden to vote, is the *presumption* that they are incapable of taking care of themselves. If the reason fails, then the rule fails. And should it appear that men generally at eighteen are capable of wisely governing themselves, then no government ought to restrain their majority till they are twenty-one years of age. But the rule of exclusion does not extend to A, B, and C, men of good mind and mature years, and of course they cannot justly be debarred from the equal right of *voting*. Of course the argument is only a sophism of men who are determined to cover up a wrong with the smoke of logic. Neither is the argument of any weight against universal suffrage, that women are not, or ought not to be, allowed to vote. For should it turn out that there are no guaranties for their security without voting; or should it appear that they are capable of voting judiciously, without a loss of a *greater* good, *then they have a right to vote.*

I believe, and they believe, that the sympathy of the sexes is sufficient for their protection in the enjoyment of life, property, and character; and that voting would not increase, at all events, that security. That the retiring virtues and modesty of women are more powerful than the ballot; and that they would lose power by mingling in the angry and indecent contests of the polls. I conclude, then, that it is best for women not to exercise the right. The argument, then, founded upon the non-voting of women, also falls to the ground.

The saying that "they who own the country should govern the country," though more specious, is equally false. If property were the only right which society proposes to secure, the argument would be conclusive. But as life (in which we include all its minor postulates, preservation of limbs, freedom from blows, imprisonment, and slavery, &c.), and character (in which we also reckon the liberty to attain by legitimate means posts of honor and profit, &c.), are also rights which society ought to protect; and as they are of equal or rather greater moment than property, government has performed only a third part of its objects, when it has protected property. The argument that "when property holders protect themselves, they of course protect others," is not only in logic, a *petitio principii*, but false in fact, and unworthy of refutation.

That there might in legislative bodies be two houses, one in some sort representing property, and the other representing more immediately personal right, seems reasonable. But after all, the best security that property has, in all governments, against the plunder of the indolent and indigent, is in its distribution among a large majority of the people. For a man will stand by his *little*, with as stout a good will and courage, as the millionnaire will by his *millions*.

It becomes all nations, then, to guard, as much as possible, consistently with the undisturbed accumulations of industry, against monopolies and overgrown estates, which arise not unfrequently from fraud or governmental aid. More especially does it become every nation having wild lands, to shape their laws so as to divide them as much as may be among the great mass of her people.

For I confess that I have but little hope of the permanence of any government, when the property of the nation is in the hands of a considerable minority of its people.

It is hardly necessary to state here that the same rules which regulate the formation and sustainment of a government apply to its change and dissolution.

VIII. GUARANTIES OF LIBERTY, CONTINUED.—TRIAL BY JURY.

The next thing after making the laws, is, the insuring their sensible and impartial administration.

The same reasoning which applies relatively to Despotism and Republicanism, may be extended to trial by a single judge, and by a jury. The judge would no doubt be generally the more *intelligent* tribunal; but then he would know more men personally, have more ambitious ends to attain, and be more liable to corruption. A jury of six or twelve men, selected beforehand, from sober and respectable citizens, seems to have more qualifications for *impartiality* than a judge. And after all, we consider impartiality the highest attribute of judgment; for few are so low in the scale of intelligence, as not to be competent for the trial and decision of causes, after full and able discussion by counsel. Absolute justice in human affairs is unattainable; we believe that "Trial by Jury" is one of its surest guaranties.

That in criminal trials the accused should be confronted face to face with his accusers,—and that *oral* testimony should in all cases, where it is practicable, be given, is reasonable. But that depositions should be taken in many instances, as evidence in criminal cases, seems equally plain. Many men being in a transitory state, and living at a distance, conceal their knowledge of criminal offences; because they fear detention in person. This could be obviated by depositions properly guarded. There are obviously other instances in which justice is evaded by this absurd rule.

The law allowing a man to refuse to "criminate himself,"—and to plead not guilty as a matter of course—or to stand mute when questioned—is *utterly absurd.* Mr. Bentham very well observes that the hardship of criminating one's-self "is not harder than being *punished* for crime." If one don't want to criminate himself, let him cease to commit crime. We consider that this is not one of the guaranties of liberty, but one of the abetments of crime.

I agree also with Mr. Bentham that the legal fiction of man and wife's *oneness* should be abolished, for the same reasons. "A man's house is his castle," "habeas corpus," and some other safeguards of liberty, may be ranked under the head of *guaranties,* but hardly rise to the dignity of separate discussion.

IX. The Guaranties of Liberty, continued.—Peaceable Assemblages of the People.—Right of Petition.

One of the chief devices of tyranny for the protection of its *assumed* power, is to raise the cry of mad-dog *sedition*, against inquiry into the abuses and usurpations of rulers. And thus they array, without investigation, the prejudices and passions of all *law-abiding* citizens, against any man, of however lofty and disinterested virtue, who dares to canvass the corruptions of state. *Peaceable* assemblages of the people for the discussion of public affairs are only terrible to tyrants. But on the other hand, when these assemblages, instead of discussion for the *enlightenment* of the constituted authorities, assume the attitude of *threatening* and *intimidation*, they are then traitors and tyrants themselves. For neither the King, nor Parliament, nor the Representatives, nor the *people*, are higher than the *laws*. The *law*, until constitutionally changed, is *the highest power in a nation*.

The assemblage of the citizens of Kentucky on the 18th of August, 1845, at Lexington, Kentucky, who violated the constitution and laws of the state, and of the American Union, were traitors, and merited the death of felons. Crime cannot be modified in its character by numbers; it may by numbers go unwhipped of justice; but it remains, in the eyes of God, and the wise and good of all time, still *crime!*

So the monster meetings of Daniel O'Connell, in Ireland, for which and whom I have the highest respect, through *noble motives*, did undertake to *intimidate* the British crown; and assumed a character of *force*, which was *illegal*. I trust I speak with no personal prejudice, but with the freedom of a moralist, who writes for all countries and all time.

The right of petitioning rulers in a respectful manner, for the redress of grievances, or for special acts of any kind, comes under the same category; and is subject to the same laws of reasoning. Both are, in fact, but *modes of freedom of speech and the press*, and cannot be lost without losing all true liberty.

I regard the act of J. Q. Adams in finally vindicating "the right of petition," as one of the most noble and glorious achievements in all history; which places him eminently above all the men of his country. For in maintaining the liberty of his country, in a *great principle*, he has become the victor, not of a single revolution, nor the benefactor of a single people, but the defender of the freedom of all countries, and of all coming time.

X. Guaranties of Liberty, continued.—Liberty of Speech and of the Press.

I come at last to the chief guaranty of all liberty, civil and religious. As I cannot imagine a despotism to exist with freedom of speech and the press, so I cannot conceive for a moment of a free government existing without liberty of speech and of the press. This is a proposition not only sealed with the blood of the most noble martyrs—but what is more in a logical point of view—established by the unanimous vote of the most brilliant intellects, and the truest spirits of all ages. If all that has been said on this subject were collected in one volume, there is hardly a book in existence that would be filled with more cogent logic, and fervid eloquence, and immutable truth. I shall not, therefore, attempt to reason upon the main proposition. I shall only add that this, like all truth, is *universal*. That the liberty of speech and the press must extend to *all subjects whatever*, or else *there is no liberty at all!* The moment you bind it with the least possible cord—it dies! The Pope says: discuss freely all subjects, but don't touch with profane hands, holy things—don't canvass religion! There is no liberty, then, in Popedom. The Czar of Russia says: discuss all things else, but don't meddle with my tenure of power! There is no liberty in the Russias! The king and parliament of England say: speak freely of science, and religion,—of all things; but don't decry the Constitution of England; don't speak of Republicanism here! There is no liberty in England! The United States say: abuse, if you please, the Pope; denounce the Czar; don't spare the iniquities of British aristocracy and oppression; but don't interfere with *slavery*—that's a *delicate relation*—a *"peculiar institution"*—let that alone, or we'll Lynch you! There is, then, no *liberty in America.* So long as there is one thing in a nation which cannot be discussed— there is no freedom of speech or the press in that nation.

What are called "the abuses" of the liberty of the press and of speech, are utterly distinct from "freedom of speech and of the press." A man may be punished for *slander*, which is a crime, and the "liberty of speech" remain intact. The crime here is not simply in speaking, but in speaking *a lie.* To set about the destruction of the freedom of speech because men sometimes lie, would be about as contemptibly absurd, as to destroy all government for the same reason!

The liberty of the press is not terrible in its lies, but in its *truth :* and *truth is terrible only to criminals !*

The same class of men who advocate despotism—who hold force as a rule of right—who cling to the faith that it is not always meet that the truth be spoken—are the same fellows who are terribly afraid of the "abuses of the liberty of the press." They are afraid of being slandered—are they? not at all; they are afraid *the truth will be told upon them !* To them, indeed, "the greater the truth, the greater the slander!" The propagators of the most criminal errors become suddenly, when some one is about to expose their villany, afraid that unbridled opinion may upset *truth* and *religion !* The most bloody tyrants, when their corruptions are about to be exposed, all at once are awfully shocked, lest some madman may, with reckless innovation, destroy "*the peace and security of the people !*"

Perpetrators of systematic crime of all sorts, are always afraid of "*fanaticism !*" which, interpreted, means *truth with the sword of long delayed vengeance !* The liberty of the press and of speech, is to them as Jesus to the devils of old ! Well may they cry out in wild despair : "*what have we to do with thee, thou son of God !*"

ADDRESS

BEFORE THE

SENIOR CLASS OF YALE,

FEBRUARY 22d, 1832,

THE CENTENNIAL BIRTH-DAY OF WASHINGTON

Gentlemen of Yale College:

WERE a stranger to visit this land, in this time of peace and plenty, this mildness and tranquillity of nature, and hear, at a distance, the loud peals of cannon, and the murmurs of assembled multitudes, behold crowds of both sexes, and every age, moving in anxiety to the churches and places of public convocation, in amazement he would exclaim, "What means this hurried array! this mighty tumult! What threatened invasion; what great political commotion; what impending convulsion of nature, draws together thirteen millions of human beings?"

Illustrious, departed shade! whom we this day call to memory, this could not be. For from what land shall he come who knows not thy great and virtuous deeds? What language shall he speak, who has not heard the name of Washington?

We are assembled to-day, a great and intelligent nation, to offer up our thanks to the Author of our being for the many and signal favors bestowed upon us as a people. To give to departed worth our highest approbation, the voluntary tribute of grateful remembrance. To manifest to mankind, and our posterity, the regard which we entertain for the blessings of religious and political freedom, which our gallant ancestors have bequeathed us. To make ourselves better men, and better citizens. It is enough for one man, that thirteen millions of intelligent beings have assembled in his name. Any efforts which I might make to color his fame by indulging in panegyric, would be trifling with the feelings of this assembly; for, from the throbbing bosom and brightening eye, I perceive that you have outstripped the slow pace of language, and already given way to the grateful emotions of the soul. I shall therefore briefly touch upon a few incidents of his life, and proceed to some other considerations, which may be not inappropriate to the occasion. It was the good fortune of Washington to unite in one personage the far distant and almost incompatible talents of the politician and soldier. It would not, I presume, be considered disrespectful to say, that this circumstance is the only one which made a material distinction between him and some others of his noble compatriots. Other men may have conceived as high designs, and entertained as exalted patriotism; but it was for Washington to conceive, and to execute; and what he declared with the pen in the cabinet, to conclude with the sword in the field. Other men would have been proud of the honor of pre-eminence in either department; but Washington drank deep of the glory of each, and was not intoxicated with the draught: for he was subject to temptation, on a most signal occasion, yet his virtue and patriotism failed not in the hour of trial.

Success had crowned his efforts against a foreign foe. His followers, stung with the ingratitude of a preserved country, who refused the poor tribute of soldier's wages, were united to him by the strongest ties—the sense of common suffering and injustice. Inflammatory letters were industriously circulated throughout the army, by an insidious enemy. The republic, in its very infancy, was about to pass the way of all democracies, and on the eve of yielding up her dearly bought liberties to her chieftain. Then do we see the grey headed patriot, coming forward in deep and sorrowful mood, and hear his faltering voice, entreating them, to spare themselves—to spare him—what? An ignominious death? No! to spare him the titles, the honors, the arbitrary power, for which others have deemed the risk of life not too dear a sacrifice. Raising the intercepted letters to his face, while the gathering tear suffused his sight, he uttered those memorable words, "My eyes have grown dim in the service of my country." Where, in the long annals of the reputed sayings of departed sages, shall we find the equal of this more than eloquence—this pouring forth of the soul? It was then that tyranny was rebuked; and liberty drew immortal inspiration. For selfishness and power were disrobed of their tinsel ornaments, ambition loosed his deadly grasp, and liberty and virtue, in union, winged their heavenly flight!

I pass over his virtues, and his public acts. His virtues are known, and more appropriately mentioned by our fire-sides, and in the private circle. 'Tis there we love to dwell upon the scenes of his infancy, and the virtuous impressions made upon his tender mind, in the day when the destiny of empires is in the hands of a woman. Well for mankind, that he was in the hands of a mother, a woman, who, in those days, filled the high rank allotted her by nature, to be the instructress, as well as the plaything companion of man. His public acts—they are inwoven with our Constitution and laws. They are known and appreciated by the politician and the jurist; and are more immediately objects for the contemplation of those concerned in the administration of the government.

What then remains for this occasion? Washington is gone, and his virtues and his exploits are reserved for mention, at other times. The effects, my countrymen, the effects! "The man dies, but his memory lives." How many like the great Emmet have died, and left only a name to attract our admiration for their virtues, and our regret for their untimely fall, to excite to deeds which they would, but could not effect! But what has Washington left behind, save the glory of a name? The independent mind, the conscious pride, the ennobling principle of the soul—a nation of freemen. What did he leave? He left us to ourselves. This is the sum of our liberties, the first principle of government, the power of public opinion—public opinion, the only permanent power on earth. When did a people flourish like Americans? Yet where, in a time of peace, has more use been made with the pen, or less with the sword of power? When did a religion flourish like the Christian, since they have done away with intolerance? Since men have come to believe and know, that physical force cannot affect the immortal part, and that religion is between the conscience and the Creator only. He of 622, who with the sword propagated his doctrines throughout Arabia, and the greater part of the barbarian world; against the power of whose tenets the physical force of all Christendom was opposed in vain; under the effective operations of freedom of opinion, is fast passing the way of all error.

Napoleon, the contemporary of our Washington, is fast dying away from the lips of men. He, who shook the whole civilized earth—who, in an age of knowledge and concert among nations, held the world at bay—at whose exploits the imagination becomes bewildered—who, in the *eve* of his glory, was honored with the pathetic appellation of "the last, lone, captive of millions in war,"—even *he*, is now known only in history. The vast empire was fast tumbling to ruins, whilst he yet held the sword. He passed away, and left "no successor" there! The unhallowed light which obscured *is gone ;* but brightly beams, *yet*, the name of *Washington !*

This freedom of opinion, which has done so much for the political and religious liberty of America, has not been confined to this continent. People of other countries begin to inquire, to examine, and to reason for themselves. Error has fled before it, and the most inveterate prejudices are dissolved and gone. Such unlimited remedy has in some cases indeed apparently proved injurious, but the evil is to be attributed to the peculiarity of the attendant circumstances, or the ill-timed application. Let us not force our tenets upon foreigners. For if we subject opinion to coercion, who shall be our inquisitors? No; let us do as we have done, as we are now doing, and then call upon the nations to examine, to scrutinize, and to condemn! No! they cannot look upon America, to-day, and pity—for the gladdened heart disclaims all woe. They cannot look upon her, and deride; for genius, and literature, and science, are soaring above the high places of birth and pageantry. They cannot look upon us, and defy; for the hearts of thirteen millions are warm in virtuous emulation; their arms steeled in the cause of their country. Her productions are wafted to every shore; her flag is seen waving in every sea. She has wrested the glorious motto from the once queen of the seas, and high on our banner, by the stars and stripes, is seen:

> "Columbia needs no bulwark,
> No towers along the steep,
> Her march is o'er the mountain wave,
> Her home is on the deep."

But on this day of freemen's rejoicings, and all this mutual congratulation, "this feast of the soul, this pure banquet of the heart," does no painful reflection rush across the unquiet conscience? no blush of insincerity suffuse the countenance, where joy and gratitude should hold undivided sway? When we come this day, as one great family, to lay our poor offering on the altar, to that God who holds the destinies of nations in his hand,

are there none afar off, cast down and sorrowful, who dare not
approach the common altar; who cannot put their hands to
their hearts, and say; "Oh, Washington, what art thou to us?
Are we not also freemen?"

Then what a mockery is here! Foolish man, lay down thy
offering, go thy way, become reconciled to thy brother, and then
come and offer thy offering.

In the language of Thomas Jefferson: "Can the liberties of
a nation be sure when we remove their only firm basis, a conviction in the minds of the people, that these liberties are the
gift of God? that they are not to be violated but with his
wrath? Indeed, I tremble for my country, when I reflect that
God is just; that his justice cannot sleep for ever; that a revolution of the wheel of fortune, a change of situation, is among
possible events; that it may become probable by supernatural
interference! The Almighty has no attribute which can take
side with us in that event." And shall these things be? 'Tis
fit that he should chide who bears the shame! How long, my
own, my native land, shall thy exiled sons dare to raise their
voice only in a land of strangers, in behalf of thy best interests—the cause of reason, religion, and humanity?

But ye philanthropists, if so ye term yourselves—whether
real or feigned, I care not—leave us to ourselves. Give opinion
full scope; examine, scrutinize, condemn, but let us alone.
Know ye not yet the human heart? It has its affections, but it
has its jealousies and its revenge, too! But, if you attempt to
snatch justice from our arms—our destined bride, lovely maid
of every perfection—we will plunge the assassin's dagger to her
heart—to be mourned by her followers as well as by her destroyers!

"Leave us to ourselves," should be the motto of our republic,
the first principle of national legislation. Not license to lawless-
ness and crime; not that liberty which is so often shouted forth
without meaning—defiance of wholesome laws and their severe
and rigid execution. But let us alone—let us exercise reason
and public opinion as regards our temporal interests as well as
our immortal welfare.

If we come to honor Washington to-day, to sanction his principles, which have been approved in times past, I cannot forbear
pressing upon the minds of my audience, from various parts of
the Union, the necessity to concede something to public opinion

in the construction of our federal league; to be indulgent to one another. If you do not, my countrymen, I very much fear that this, the first centennial celebration of the birth of Washington, will be the last, on which a mighty nation will have met.

It is a principle generally admitted, among politicians, that the most despotic government in peace, is the most efficient in war, and the reverse. This principle applied to us admits of much limitation. If we war with foreigners, and all united, I venture to say, we are the most powerful nation on earth, comparing our physical resources; for we war not for a change of *masters*, but for *ourselves*—for freedom. But, if we war with each other, which God forbid, we are the weakest nation in existence; because we are the farthest removed from executive influence; more subject to individual will. Our strength is in public opinion, in *unanimity*. We revolt on the most favorable circumstances. No ignominious death of traitors awaits us; defeat, at worst, is but an unwilling marriage with a haughty, but yet loving lord. *States* come to the contest, armed, provided, unanimous; fighting ostensibly under the banner of the constitution, if not in supposable cases, in the real spirit of our federal league.

I would not speak lightly of the constitution of America; long may it exist to the honor of its framers, and the greater glory of those who support it well; but I should not deem it safe to appeal to the LETTER of any copy, in defiance of the great original, written in the breast of every American.

It needs not the eye of divination to see that differences of interest will naturally arise in this vast extent of territory. Washington saw it; we see it. Let us not flatter ourselves that these differences will be merged by the revolution of time, or the increase of space. While I now speak, a voice is heard imploring concession, founded upon claims, warmly and conscientiously supported—no matter whether they be real or imaginary.

In the political arena the glove is already thrown down; the great northern and southern champions* stand in sullen defiance; bristling crests are seen extending to the extreme verge of the lists; the mystery of intense feeling pervades the hosts; "non tumultus, non quies: quale magni metus, et magnæ iræ silentium est."

---

* Webster and Hayne.

My countrymen, this must not be; the issues are too great to depend upon the fall of one man. 'Tis yours—you, the people of the United States—to look well to it!

The warning voice of Cassandra is abroad! May not a blinded people rest secure in disbelief and derision, till the birthright left us by our Washington is lost! till we shall be aroused by the rushing ruins of a once "glorious Union!"

SPEECH,

In the House of Representatives of Kentucky, upon the bill " to take the sense of the people of this Commonwealth, as to the propriety of calling a Convention." 1835-6.

MR. SPEAKER,—In discussing a subject of such interest to society, as a change, or it may be, the destruction of the charter of their liberties, I shall not urge those arguments calculated to excite our sympathies and obscure our judgment. I pass over, then, the difficulties into which we would plunge those who now hold offices under our government, by withdrawing from them the public trusts, in the faithful discharge of which they have grown old, and who are now perhaps too far advanced in life to obtain a livelihood for themselves and families by other pursuits. I pass over the probability that our system of internal improvements so lately, yet so auspiciously, commenced—when Kentucky seems to be just shaking off the lethargy which has so long prostrated her—would be retarded, perhaps stayed for ever. I omit to mention the bitterness of party strife which the passage of this bill must bring home to every fire-side, when the elements of society are dissolved, and political theories are mingled with personal vituperation and insult. Such considerations as these should be lost sight of, when a grave assembly are about to pass judgment upon the constitution of their country.

I, sir, when I weigh the arguments of gentlemen upon this floor, and elsewhere among the community at large, can see but two leading designs in calling a convention. They are the emancipation of our slaves, and the destruction of the independence of the judiciary department of this government. For I cannot believe that the movers of this project are of so humble and contemptible an ambition, as to disturb the very elements of society for the purpose of ridding themselves of an odious magistrate, or venting their spleen upon a peculating constable. I think I do not flatter the gentlemen over the way, when I say for them that they would scorn such an imputation.

First, then, the slave question—and I address myself to the

advocates of emancipation. Is this a time—when the arm of the law is averted, and deeds of violence go unredressed throughout the land, when a horde of fanatical incendiaries are springing up in the North, threatening to spread fire and blood through our once secure *and happy homes?—I ask, is this a time to deliberately dispose of a question which involves the political rights of master and slave—the liberties—it may be the lives of one or both parties? I am bound to confess that there was a time when I favored gradual emancipation. Having had some experience of the state of society in slaveholding and non-slaveholding communities, to say nothing of the moral and social condition, in a political point of view, I am candid in saying that the free states have largely the advantage. I cannot as a statesman, shut my eyes to the industry, ingenuity, numbers, and wealth which are displaying themselves in adjoining states; nor can I look with indifference to that time when argument fails and arms decide the fate of nations. Such considerations, sir, belong to the past, not to the present. When I see a spirit of dictation and interference rising in the North— where we looked for amity and aid; when I hear the genius of discord speaking in threatening accents in the federal legislature, to whose halls I looked for concession, co-operation, and effectual assistance; when I behold the lame and feeble effort of the Colonization Society striking off one hydra's head, whilst a thousand spring up in its stead, I almost cease to hope —I almost give way to the belief that slavery must continue to exist till, like some uneradicable disease, it disappears with the body that gave it being.

What, Mr. Speaker, is the other great end which the advocates of this bill propose? It is to disturb the sources of justice, and batter down the walls of *constitutional* responsibility. This is no novel project—the seeds of anarchy, deception, and misrule, which were buried some twelve years since, which were trodden under foot and forgot, have been germinating, and are now assuming a new and luxuriating growth, and if unchecked, will be as fruitful of discord and evil as the most ambitious and restless spirits could desire. The advocates of this bill go for electing all the officers of the government—the legislature, the judiciary, and the executive departments are to be brought all under the control of the popular will. The senatorial term of office is to be shortened, the judges, clerks, sheriffs, constables, jailors, hangmen, and grave-diggers are to be elected annually, biennially, or for a longer term of years. All the officers of the government, from the highest to the lowest, are to be chosen at the polls; the country must be harassed from day to day, and from year to year, with the intrigue, strife, electioneering, and disgusting struggle of this horde of office-seekers: hungering like Egyptian locusts, even for the stunted leaf that vegetates upon the treasury walls. These, sir, are minor evils which fade away from the vision, when we look at the insecurity, confusion and injustice which must result from such a system. Property, life, reputation and liberty are all at the mercy of an excited multitude. The dominating party pervades the halls of legislation, the courts, and the fireside; before the excited mind can cool, some cruel act of injustice has been done which time may reveal, but can never remedy. Experience is perfect and full upon this subject. The ancient republics, England, all Europe, are full of the deplorable injustice done by the popular will, unchecked by wholesome laws and constitutional restraint. There is one instance within the memory of many now in this house, more horrible than all in times past. Look at France, that people who fought under the same flag with Washington, who caught the spirit of liberty on the American shore, bore it across the Atlantic, and planted her image upon the throne of her antiquated kings. What did France, republican, democratic France? She made her judges immediately dependent on the popular will—she "afraid to trust the people?" No, sir, the blood of her best citizens which flooded her streets—the cries of murdered women and children—the pale and mute language of despair stamped upon the innocent faces of the young and beautiful—the mutual distrust, accusation and death—bear witness that she did not " fear to trust the people."

The Hon. Gentleman (from Hardin) answers this argument by rejoicing that he is in Kentucky, not in France—among freemen, not slaves—not a Frenchman, but a Kentuckian. I, too, rejoice that I am a freeman, a Kentuckian: and as I am a freeman and a Kentuckian, the heir of a controlled and constitutional liberty, and not a slave, or a Frenchman, I therefore abhor the policy of France, and call upon my countrymen to reject and put their seal of eternal disapprobation upon doctrines which lead to despotism, slavery, and death.

I have said, that I did fear to trust the people to *choose their judges*, and I am warned that I stand upon dangerous ground. The heroes of our revolution, the sages of our federal constitution—Washington, Adams, Hamilton, Jefferson, and a host of the advocates of equality, of universal suffrage, and republican liberty—believed that the judges should not be elected by the people, and that the Senate should not be broken down, and all the strength of the government subject to popular impulse. The experience of more than half a century, the liberties we now enjoy, and the privilege by which I now stand here to defend their doctrines and enforce what they and I believe to be republican principles, prove that they were worthy of the trust which the destiny of nations deposited in their hands.

I am warned, sir, against the advocacy of measures upon this floor, which gentlemen conceive are too unpopular elsewhere; and I am told that Webster and Calhoun are now prostrate on account of speculative opinions, against which this people have decided.

I do not conceive that I am called upon to say how far the Hon. Gentleman, holding the position which he does, is justifiable in alluding to such names in such a manner: nor do I conceive myself necessitated to defend such names. But I do say, sir, that if, by the advocacy of truth, and what I believe to be the best interests of a free people, I am cut off from the popular approbation, and commit political suicide, I thank the gentleman for the honorable interment to which he has assigned me. For I had rather be remembered with Webster and Calhoun, than to be associated with the most *successful demagogue*, feeding upon the breath of applause caught from a deluded and self-destroying people.

The gentleman last up, (from Morgan) has undertaken to construe to this house what he believes to be the tenor of my argument, and asserts that I "distrust the capability of the people for self-government." No, sir, I answer that assertion now, and I hope for ever. It is such persons as we have heard upon this floor, who appeal to the worst passions, who excite the "poor" against the "rich," the "mountains" against the "valleys," who are for ever flattering the people for their own aggrandizement, and watching the tide of human misfortunes, distress, and confusion, for the purpose of running into power. These, sir, are demagogues I do distrust. I believe that the *people* are the proper depositaries of *all power*—but I believe also that there should be constitutional restraints for its wholesome exercise.

I do not fall short of gentlemen in my confidence in republican governments. I go farther—that I shall be the last to give up my confidence in the capacity of the people for self-government. But I do most solemnly avow to this house, that if ever this people cease to be free, and are compelled to throw themselves into the hands of a self-constituted chief or military despot—no man will have contributed more to produce so lamentable a result than he who continues to stimulate the passions of the multitude, till they shall have thrown off all constitutional restraints, and amalgamated all the elements of government into one uncontrollable will.

I may be thought, sir, to have taken too excited a view of this subject; it may be so. I feel that this question should be met in the outset; ground once lost can never be recovered. ' Your vote here to-day may decide the question, whether our constitution shall be sustained or lost. And I beg gentlemen that if they shall have a shadow of doubt concerning the propriety of calling a convention, to vote against the bill : return to your constituents, convince them, if possible, of the impropriety of the measure, and, should you at last fail to convince, leave it to more willing hands to strike a blow at the constitution of your country, which neither your consciences nor judgments can approve. For myself I shall go against it, and should such a course shut me off from the confidence of my constituents, and should I never again be allowed to taste the sweets of popular applause, I shall carry into retirement and obscurity, the proud and imperishable consciousness of having used my every effort for the preservation of human—" *republican* "—liberty.

SPEECH

On the bill conferring Banking Privileges upon the Charleston, Cincinnati, and Louisville Railroad Company, before the Committee of the whole, in the House of Representatives of Kentucky, 1837–38.

Mr. C. spoke in opposition to the bill, as follows:

Mr. CHAIRMAN,—The American people have been from the beginning jealous of incorporated institutions. Kentucky, of all the states in this union, has had most fatal experience of the evil influence of bank corporations. While I now speak, there is one voice coming up from all classes and all parties of our sagacious countrymen, attributing the prostration of our trade and business, the wide-spread bankruptcy of our citizens, and the derangement of the currency, to an over-issue of bank paper —to a redundancy of bank capital. Our banks, in common with others, have suspended specie payments. The anxieties of our whole people; the threatened suits, executions, and demands for specie; the wide-spread panic and fearful apprehension of other and unforeseen evils—all, call for whatever of firmness and judgment and patriotism the council of our state may possess, to sustain our own banks, and to restore a currency convertible into specie at the will of the holder. At this crisis, we are gravely asked to lend our aid in bringing into existence a bank with twelve million dollars of capital, capable of throwing into circulation twenty-four million dollars of paper, which it can refuse to redeem without *forfeiting*, or even *impairing* its corporate powers.

The bill asks, that four million dollars of bank paper be admitted into our own state—our *bank injured* state!

I for one, I am not prepared to grant it. Before I disappoint the just expectations of the people, hazard the healthful existence of our state institutions, bestow upon an alien and irresponsible directory the control of our finances, I ask myself what remuneration my state is to receive in turn? Shall I be told, grant the bank charter, and the railroad will be made from Charleston to Lexington, Kentucky? I deny the proposition. The bill provides, that when the company shall have subscribed three million dollars, the bank shall go into existence; that when the road shall have been built to the southern border of Kentucky, the bank capital may be increased to nine million dollars, and have corporate powers for thirty-one years. Thus we may have a bank issuing eighteen million dollars of notes, dealing in exchange and discount to an unlimited extent; holding real estate to the amount of twenty-seven million dollars, dividing annually (if it makes no more even than our banks, eight per cent. per annum), seven hundred and twenty thousand dollars—nearly a million of dollars; capable of raising and depressing at will the prices of our property; under the control of a directory at Charleston, South Carolina, whose interest it is to lower the price of live stock, having the entire power of removing the directors in this state, and of withdrawing the capital at will, without being compelled to expend one dollar, or make one foot of road, in Kentucky.

Our state has begun a system of internal improvements, the progress and completion of which depend upon the sale of state scrip or bonds; the sale of those bonds depends upon the punctuality with which the interest is paid; to meet the payment of that interest the state has formed a sinking fund, the means of which consist mostly in the dividends of the stock she holds in our banks. That part of the stock which the state holds in the banks was paid in bonds, bearing interest of five per cent. per annum : but the banks are bound to pay the state, dividends as the other stockholders, being about eight per cent. per annum; thus leaving the commonwealth a clear gain of three per cent. per annum, making during the last fiscal year about sixty thousand dollars. Now, admit this railroad bank into competition with our banks, reduce their dividends to five per cent. per annum, and you lose the three per cent. excess; you lose the sixty thousand dollars, destroy the sinking fund, injure our credit abroad, violate the faith of the state, hazard the whole system of internal improvement, merely to enrich a foreign corporation !

Shall I be told, that our stock drivers require some medium which will relieve them from the excessive rate of exchange now demanded by the banks of Kentucky and South Carolina? Let us see if the evils I have enumerated are counterbalanced by any saving in exchange. The notes issued at the Charleston bank are not redeemable at the branch in Kentucky, and the notes of the Kentucky branch not made payable at Charleston; thus the railroad bank has it as much in its power to demand a premium for exchange upon its own notes, as the present banks of Kentucky and South Carolina have to ask a premium upon their notes.

But for argument sake, I will go so far as to grant that the railroad bank charges nothing, and that our banks charge five per cent. premium upon bills of exchange on Charleston. What then shall we gain or lose in dollars and cents? The amount of stock which passed the Cumberland ford during the year 1835, which may be taken as an average year, was six thousand six hundred and sixty-seven horses and mules, two thousand four hundred and eighty-five beeves, sixty-nine thousand one hundred and eighty-seven hogs, two thousand eight hundred and eighty-seven shoats, and one thousand three hundred and twenty sheep. Now, the custom of this country is to pay for stock on the return from market with the proceeds of the sales, and of course bills of exchange are wanted merely to procure expense money : suppose each horse and mule and beef to cost twelve dollars per head, each hog four dollars per head, and each shoat and sheep two dollars per head, to carry them to market, and we have nineteen thousand seven hundred and forty-nine dollars and thirty cents, the premium at the rate of five per cent. upon three hundred and ninety-four thousand nine hundred and eighty-six dollars, the total amount borrowed. Suppose one-third of the stock to come from Ohio, Illinois, Indiana, and Missouri, and you leave for Kentucky thirteen thousand one hundred and sixty-six dollars twenty cents; but grant that half of the drovers use borrowed capital for expense money, and we have only the contemptible sum of six thousand five hundred and eighty-three dollars ten cents paid by all Kentucky for exchange. But to cover all quibbles, double the sum, and there is only thirteen thousand one hundred and sixty-six dollars twenty cents paid in exchange to our own banks—to our own citizens. To relieve the good citizens of this commonwealth of this evil—this burden, the friends of this bill propose to introduce two million dollars of foreign capital, dividing, and carrying out of this state for ever, eight per cent., one hundred and sixty thousand dollars per annum. Subtract the thirteen thousand one hundred and sixty-six dollars twenty cents, and you leave a total loss to the state of Kentucky of one hundred and forty-three thousand eight hundred and thirty-three dollars eighty cents per annum. Save me from such economy! I cannot, to use the language of a certain British orator, boast of bringing a miserable pepper-corn into the treasury at the loss of a whole continent!

I object to the bill because it wars against a national bank. You enlist all in these four states, who may hold stock in this bank, through direct and personal interest, against a national bank.

And who can limit the power of this large moneyed corporation over the political will of all the south and southwestern states? I shall not give my sanction to this silent and gradual influence, which strips the general government of one of its most salutary powers, that of regulating the commerce of these twenty-six states, by an equal and uniform currency—a uniform *paper* currency; for such is necessary to the high-wrought commercial and social intercourse of the civilized nations. Let me not be told that by a national bank I would increase the evils of foreign influence and a redundant paper medium. Give us a bank, in which the states may hold stock proportionate to their representation in congress, with directories controlled in part by the states; with a capital sufficient to effect foreign and domestic exchanges—all under the supervision of our national representatives—and you reduce the rates of exchange, free us from a mean dependence upon irresponsible state corporations, drive in the spurious issues from local institutions, and restore us to a convertible paper currency. Gentlemen tell us that it is too late to talk of a national bank. Others may doubt, and falter, and make terms with the enemy; but for my single self I shall hold out for the best interests and most ardent wishes of this people. I shall ever struggle, till the union be strengthened by the restoration of one of its most legitimate and appropriate powers—till our country, by its financial skill, shall be reinstated in the admiration of all nations.

I oppose this bill because it is anti-national in its conception and in its consequences. I will not, Mr. Chairman, cast any reflections upon the motives of any man or set of men in or out of this house; but when it is proposed to give to a foreign directory the control of the finances and the politics of my own state, I will not shut my eyes to the past, nor turn away my face from the signs of the future; I shall speak with the freedom of *history*—from her only do I fear rebuke. There is a class of politicians who have solemnly declared themselves at war with the system of American manufacture, sustained by Kentucky, at some sacrifice, for the good of this whole nation. There are men who have avowed themselves inimical to a system of national internal improvements; casting from them those ever-during bonds which compress us by intercourse, by association, and by diminished space, into one consolidated people. There are men who have deliberately set at defiance the decreed laws of these states, and declared eternal war against their enforcement. There are men who have succeeded in prostrating the best bank circulation known among any people; and who now refuse the aid of the general government to sustain, by the deposit of specie, our state banks—our last resource! There are men who declare in convention that they will throw off a "servile dependence" upon the eastern cities of this union, and call upon the southern citizens of these states to import, at a sacrifice, from foreign and alien merchants, kingly subjects, rather than sustain the freemen of our common country. They propose to import goods for the south and southwestern states— to transplant New York to Charleston—whilst they are now compelled to buy of that same New York, the daily clothing for the sons and daughters of their ocean city. There are men whose names in national history will not be the most illustrious —whose prospects of promotion to national honor are not the most flattering. These are the men who are now asking from the state of Kentucky, the grant and uncontrollable exercise of all those powers which they consider "monstrous" and "dangerous" in the hands of our representatives in congress assembled!

They are now agitating the slave question; that question which of all others is most terrible to the hopes of this union. Give them this "monstrous moneyed power," and do you not tempt, do you not precipitate that crisis, to which all these things in long and unbroken succession fatally lead—when the "north" and "south" shall be far severed, like the names they bear, never again to unite? I admire the south; I love her feelings of independence; I commend her spirit of enterprise and self-elevation; but I must stop here; my courtly complacency will carry me no farther; I cannot join in enslaving my own state! in prostrating the general government! in the dissolution of the union! While the union lasts—amid these fertile verdant fields, these ever-flowing rivers, these stately groves, this genial healthful clime—this old Kentucky land; hallowed by the blood of our sires; endeared by the beauty of her daughters; illustrious by the valor and eloquence of her sons; the centre of a most glorious empire; guarded by a cordon of States garrisoned by freemen; girt round by the rising and setting seas; we are the most blessed of all people. Let the union be dissolved—let that line be drawn, where be drawn it must—and we are a border state: in time of peace with no outlet to the ocean, the highway of nations, a miserable dependency. In time of war, the battle-ground of more than Indian warfare, of civil strife and indiscriminate slaughter! When, worse than Spanish provinces, we shall contend not for glory and renown: but like the aborigines of old, for a contemptible life and miserable subsistence! Let me not see it! Among those proud courts and lordly coteries of Europe's pride, where fifty years ago we were regarded as petty provinces, unknown to ears polite, let me go forth great in the name of an American citizen. Let me point them to our statesmen, and the laws and governments of their creation, the rapid advance of political science, the monuments of their fame, now the study of all Europe. Let them look at our rapidly increasing and happy population; see our canals, and turnpikes, and railroads, stretching over more space than combined Britain and Europe have reached by the same means. Let them send their philanthropists to learn of our penitentiary systems, our schools, and our civil institutions. Let them behold our skill in machinery, in steamboat and ship building—hail the most gallant ship that breasts the mountain wave, and she shall wave from her flag-staff the stars and stripes. These are the images which I cherish; this the nation which I honor; and never will I throw one pebble in her track to jostle the footsteps of her glorious march!

I oppose the bill because we have denied to the United States Bank of Pennsylvania, what we now propose to confer upon a Charleston bank. When I had the honor, two winters ago, to hold a seat in this House, there came from the citizens of Louisville, the emporium of our own commerce, the pride of our own state, a petition signed by many and distinguished names, praying that a branch of the United States Bank of Pennsylvania be admitted into our borders. A committee of thirteen, one from each congressional district, was appointed to consider it. That committee decided unanimously against the admission, and the House unanimously sustained their decision. The advocates of this bill were then found voting with me. No new light has been shed upon my mind. The considerations which influenced me to vote against that, impel me now to vote against this bill. If it was not necessary, in order to regulate exchanges with the east, that place where *three-fourths* of our commerce is carried on, then to admit a foreign bank into our border, it is not necessary now, for the same purpose, to admit a bank from that place to which only *one-fourth* of our commerce is extended.

If it was bad policy to admit foreign influence then from that quarter, it is worse policy to admit it now from this quarter. If I dislike Hartford Conventionism* much, I hate Nullification more. I am willing to yield to both parties the best of motives; I will put myself under the influence of *neither*. If my own state was contaminated by the *imported* dicta of '98, the " Kentucky resolutions," I would lustrate her by the legislation of '38, by guarding against a like result! I will join roads and hold friendly intercourse with both; I will enter into entangling alliances with neither.

I was for the road in the session of '35–'36, when the present† advocates of this charter were against it. I am still for it. We are told by the report of the Board of Directors that each state is expected to make its own road within its own border; we are told now by the letter of the President of the Board of Directors, lying on your table, that we must grant the bank charter and make our own road also. I thank him for his candor: it relieves the advocates of this bill of many a long argument to prove the contrary, and the people of this commonwealth of many of their delusive hopes! The admission is not only candid, but fair. When Kentucky is prepared to vote a tax of three or five millions of dollars to make this railroad to the southern border of the state, from Lexington or elsewhere, I am prepared to aid, as becomes a good and faithful citizen, to

---

* Mr. Wickliffe, of Fayette, alluded to the partiality of Mr. C. for the east, the seat of Hartford Conventionism; and deprecated Mr. C.'s allusions to the Nullification of the south, inasmuch as Kentucky, by the resolutions of '98, was amenable to the same censure.

† The Fayette delegation.

the extent of my means in purse and mind. I wait to hear her voice. Till then I vote against this charter: because the bank does not aid the making of the road in our own state: because it increases the already too great irredeemable paper currency: because it is controlled by a directory at Charleston, capable of depressing the prices of our property, and influencing our political will by withdrawing the capital at pleasure: because it carries out of our state for ever, annually, thousands of dollars: because it injures the dividends of our own stockholders, for the benefit of aliens: because it decreases the dividend of the state stock, lowers the sinking fund, and thereby jeopardizes the whole internal improvement system of the state: because it would be granting to one portion of the union privileges which we have unanimously refused to another part of the same union: because it wars against a National Bank: because it is anti-union in its tendency and effects—giving the states powers which properly belong to congress only—and creating sectional in opposition to national interests. And lastly, because my constituents have given me no intimation that I should do this thing. I hope the house will vote with me against the bill.

SPEECH,

In the House of Representatives of Kentucky, January, 1841, upon the law of 1833, " To prohibit the importation of slaves into this State." The House being in Committee of the Whole, Mr. C., of Fayette, having the floor, said:

MR. CHAIRMAN :—The result of your deliberations upon this bill must affect the destiny of this state, and perhaps that of the Union itself. Pamphlets and speeches have gone forth among the whole people, and all the leading journals of the state have taken ground upon one side or the other. If I were pleading my own cause only, however much I might hazard in the result, I should ask your attention with diffidence. But I stand up here in behalf of a whole people. Your state, yourselves, your posterity, are so nearly concerned as to demand a patient hearing and an impartial determination.

The gentleman from Breckenridge,* and the gentleman from Louisville, have done me the honor to allude to me personally, and to the late canvass in my county. And, although they have done so in a manner most complimentary to myself, yet to me it is a source of regret, because my opponents are not here to answer what I have to say. I shall therefore speak of them in terms of scrupulous respect. The influences which were arrayed against me were indeed great. A young man, in intellect at least, my equal, with all the advantages of great wealth and thorough education; in the country of his nativity, and among the associates of his childhood and youth; the son of an old politician, who had done some service in the commonwealth, and whose legal attainments at all events had no small consideration in the public estimation, was my opponent. I, on the contrary, was a new comer. If I bore with me any reputation for ability it must have been, of necessity, but little; whilst if I had any social qualities, my limited associations barred their influence. It was, then, the policy and the justice of the cause I advocated, which, in a county of ten thousand slaves, sustained me triumphantly. The discussion of this subject is deprecated

---

* Mr. Calhoun, the ablest advocate of the repeal.

here ; and so it was deprecated *there.* And by whom, in both instances ? By those who will not rest while this law stands ; who would claim a judgment against us by default ; who by bitter denunciation would drive us from our integrity. They beg the question, and ask us to be silent. They have demanded the repeal of this law for three years ; at every period the law has gained friends ; and yet they dare tell us *" the people "* require its repeal.

Epithets strike no terror into my spirit ; denunciation shall not silence me. It has been said that money is power, that knowledge is power ; but more powerful than both these combined is *truth.* She is the high priestess of republican liberty. Let me ever worship at her shrine ; let my voice be lifted up for ever in her cause.

Shall the slaves of our State be increased ? If slavery be a " blessing," by all means repeal this law. But, if it be an evil, as I hold—as Jefferson held, as held Madison, and Washington, and Henry, and all the illustrious statesmen of the world, since seventeen hundred and seventy-six to the present time—then you dare not touch that law, which stands like a wall of adamant, shielding our homes, and all that makes that name most sacred, from more than all the calamities that ever barbarian invaders inflicted upon a conquered people.

The gentleman from Breckenridge avows slavery to be " a blessing," and undertakes, by scripture, to hallow it with the sanction of Deity. This is strange doctrine to be heard in any country ; but to urge it here among Kentuckians, is not only strange but monstrous. I utterly dissent from the argument ; I oppose it on every principle of truth and expediency, now and for ever. It saps the foundation of all liberty. If you sanction it now, when and to what shall you appeal when the *purple* and the *sword* are arrayed against you ? No: let not gentlemen, in their blind zeal to make slavery *perpetual,* cleave down the banner under which our forefathers fought and triumphed ; the barrier against the oppressor of all lands, that *" all men are created free and equal."* The *Divine* right of kings has fallen before the advance of civilization ; the most loyal sticklers for royalty or despotism, speak now only of the *historical* right of princes to rule. Can it be that this doctrine shall have fallen only to give place to its more monstrous counterpart, the *divine right of slavery ?* I understand our religion to leave the form of government, and the municipal institutions of nations untouched. Nay, sir, the Savior of men disclaimed the design to interfere with them. "Give unto Cæsar the things that are Cæsar's," was his doctrine. It is also my doctrine. I am no reformer of governments. I leave slavery where I found it. It is not a matter of conscience with me; I press it not upon the consciences of others; "let him who formed the heart judge of it alone." I admit, with the gentleman, the antiquity of slavery that it has existed from time immemorial to the present day; yet, sir, in all that time I find nothing to commend it as a source of wealth, of glory, or of humanity. Its first mention is in Genesis, where Isaac subjects Esau to Jacob. Esau rose up to slay his brother, and Jacob was forced to flee from his country. Evil in the beginning, as it is now. The Jews were enslaved by Pharaoh in Egypt; what, again, were the consequences? In the metaphorical language of the historian, unheard of "*plagues*" came upon the Egyptians, which were terminated only by the entire destruction of Pharaoh's host in the Red Sea. Slave-holding Jerusalem was destroyed; and the Jews led captive by Nebuchadnezzar and held in bondage in the Assyrian empire. What to her, in turn, was the result? Glory, and dominion, and safety? No, sir; these slaves were the cause of the destruction of Babylon, and the utter ruin of the empire. The inspired writers imputed it to a judgment for their oppression of God's people. The profane agree in the same result; whilst it would require no great sagacity to discover, that slavery, by the universal and immutable laws of nature, was a cause adequate to the result. It is true, that Cyrus and Darius turned aside the Euphrates, and entered through the dry channel beneath the walls into the city; but it was by treachery only that they could pass the massive gates that blocked the streets that led from the river to the palace. The hand writing upon the wall was *Hebrew:* Daniel, the *Hebrew,* only could interpret it to the doomed Belshazzar! Effeminacy, and luxury, had caused a *slave* to rule over that once powerful and proud people. They were betrayed in the hour of revelry and self-confidence; they were destroyed in a night; and Daniel, the Jew and the *slave,* was made vice-regent, under Cyrus, over all the shattered provinces of a once glorious empire. Thus passed away, without a struggle, most impotently and for ever, leaving no vestige behind, the most splendid city the world has seen. I am gravely told, that

in those countries of antiquity, where slavery existed, the human
intellect reached its highest development. Yet did slavery exist
in all countries at that time. How came it that a cause so
general produced effects so limited? No: the Roman and
Grecian states were great in spite of slavery. The ancient historians say but little upon the subject of slavery; perhaps they
thought as some do now, that nothing should be said upon the
subject of so "great a blessing."

Yet, whenever we do hear of it, it is mentioned only in connexion with the evils of its sufferance—the desolation that for
ever marks its progress. Plutarch and Thucydides tell us that
during the reign of Archidamus, an earthquake threw Mount
Taygetus upon Sparta and destroyed it; their slaves, the He-
lots—those natural enemies of their masters—immediately rose
up and set upon the Lacedæmonians, and this proud and war-
like people were forced to call in their rivals, the Athenians, to
protect them from "domestic violence." We may judge of the
prolonged and aggravated desolation of the war, when we learn
that Ithome was besieged for ten years before it was taken.

The effects of slavery upon the moral sensibilities of that people may be learned from the bloody "Kryptia," under which
law two thousand slaves were massacred in a single night. Of
course, the perpetrators of the deed escaped all inquiry or punishment, the whole community winking at the crime. The
servile wars in the Roman empire are too well known to be
dwelt upon at length. The Roman eagle, which never quailed
before a foreign foe, was struck down by the slaves of Italy; and
whole consular armies were driven back in dismay and defeat.
Slavery, then, certainly, formed no element of strength or greatness. If the slaves, who were the principal cultivators of the
soil, had been free yeomanry—a check upon the enervated city
population, and a bulwark against barbarian invasion, Cæsar
might not have been the master of Rome, and the Romans have
yet been *free*. In modern times has slavery been more than of
old the foundation of glory and civilization? Why then have
slave-holding Asia and Africa been subject to non-slave-holding
Europe; and South America, with all her slaves, remained stationary, whilst free America has become the first among civilized nations? Modern slavery, more marked and distinctive in
its character than ancient, is so much the more terrible in its
consequences. Formerly, the color being the same, it was easy

to merge the slave into the freedman, and the freedman into the citizen.   But now the difference of color is an eternal badge of former servitude and lasting infamy—an impassable barrier between the two races.   The massacre of St. Domingo and the insurrection of South Hampton, tell they of blessings, of power, and of peace?   The most overweening self-delusion cannot be deaf to the despairing energy with which all history cries aloud, that Deity has decreed that slavery cannot be the basis of civilization and liberty.*   If the Jewish history seemed to sanction the institution of slavery—and what phasis of human action under the sun does it not sanction ?—there is nothing surely, in the Christian religion, which regards slavery with eyes of peculiar approbation !   Those precepts upon which are said to rest "the law and the prophets," certainly, are not the foundations upon which involuntary servitude can intrench itself. The Virginia statute, of 1753, first making slaves, excepted Moors and Turks in alliance with the British king, and *Christians*, and persons once free in a *Christian* land.   Thus it seems that the founders of slavery in America so far respected the Christian religion, that in whatever land its banner was raised, it should be the shield of the weak and defenceless, the palladium of liberty to the vilest wretch who clothed himself with the panoply of the Christian name.

I have thus been compelled reluctantly to answer some of the arguments in favor of the *Divine right of slavery*.   Reluctantly ; because I would have avoided the necessity of treating this subject in its bearing upon conscience ; whilst, at the same time, I cannot silently acquiesce in this wresting the religion, of all others among men most favoring freedom and equality, to the unnatural sanction of the most despotic of all known governments—that of master and slave.

Christianity, then, was the beginning of the anti-slavery movement.   Then came the American Revolution.   One of the grounds of rebellion was the importation of slaves against the consent of the colonies.   In 1778, Virginia imposed the penalty of one thousand pounds, and the forfeiture of the slave, upon the importer of any slave into that commonwealth.   The act of 1785 makes some amendments to that of 1778.   The act of 1794 modifies the above acts, and introduces a clause of *emanci-*

---

* See Gov. McDuffie's Inaugural Address : and R. Wickliffe's Speech, 1840.

pation. The act of 1798 again modifies, and carries out the prohibitory clause of the Constitution against foreign importation. The act of 1815 imposes the penalty of six hundred dollars upon the importation, and the *oath.* The law of 1833 does but *the same.*

Thus, from 1778 to the present time, has a law similar to this, with the same oath in all, been upon the statute books of our country. Such has been the policy of the slave states, from the Revolution to the present day. All the original states were slave states. Through the silent and safe operation of laws similar to this, has slavery gone south of Mason and Dixon's line. The importation of slaves is forbidden by the Constitution of Mississippi. Georgia makes the domestic slave trade felony—a penitentiary offence. The United States have made the foreign slave trade, since 1808, piracy: so, also, have Great Britain, Holland, and France. Although the African be a slave in Africa, yet is the trade in such slaves punished with death. Well may gentlemen become the advocates of the foreign slave trade, who go for the repeal of this law.

Having thus attempted to repel the Divine right of slavery; and to prove that this law, so far from being an innovation, and contrary to precedent, is in accordance with the settled policy of all our eminent men, from Washington down to the present time; that it is in unison with the Christian religion, and the advance of civilization, and the moral sentiment of mankind; I shall now vindicate its constitutionality. I might, indeed, pass on with the remark, that if the law be constitutional, I need not prove it; but if it be unconstitutional, then the courts will declare it so, and it will be null and void. But since the honorable chairman of Courts of Justice has dwelt upon it with some semblance of triumph, the house will pardon me, if I travel over the same ground. The argument, so far as the state constitution is concerned, is so fully treated of in the pamphlets of myself, and the late member from Woodford, T. F. Marshall, in reply to R. Wickliffe's speech, now lying upon your tables, that I shall briefly recapitulate it.

We live under two constitutions, the Federal, and the State. In the Federal Constitution no powers are vested in the legislature but those *specifically* named; and such subordinate powers as are necessary to carry those named into effect. But in the State Constitution, all powers are in the legislature which are not expressly *denied* by the constitution, or given up specifically to the general government.　In other words, the state legislature has all the power which the people in convention would have, save the restrictions imposed by the written constitutions.　Now look, *first*, into the State Constitution and say, where is the restrictive clause; where is the mandate not to close the door to the importation of slaves?　Nowhere, save as to *emigrants*. About citizens nothing is said, and of course, nothing is excepted. The legislature can do as it pleases, so far as citizens are concerned: but how as to "emigrants" (immigrants)?　"They shall have no power to prevent emigrants to this state from bringing with them such persons as are deemed slaves by the laws of any one of the United States, so long as any person of the same age or description shall be continued in slavery by the laws of this state." Art. 7, Sec. 1.　Now had the constitution stopped here, a doubt might well have arisen, whether we could have prevented emigrants from carrying on the slave trade under this clause.　But the constitution comes to the rescue and declares that: "They shall have full power to prevent slaves being brought into this state as merchandize:" and puts this vexed question to rest for ever.　Let no man who has the least regard for his legal reputation dare again disturb it, unless he would become the laughing stock of the very school boys who frequent our moot courts; for even they deem it not debateable ground.　The other minute arguments urged against the constitutionality of this law, under the State Constitution, such as "the oath," "the jury of the vicinage," and such like special pleading, I leave to those illustrious dialecticians who have whilome filled the worthy county courts, with a most profound estimation of their legal acquirements, by making "confusion worse confounded,"—or to that more acute class of logicians, skilled

> "To divide
> A hair 'tween North and Northeast side,"

whom the good natured Butler has made no less distinguished.

Next : does the Constitution of the United States give any power to congress to permit, or to forbid the importation of slaves from one state to another?　The argument under Art. 4, Sec. 2, Clause 1 : "The citizens of each state shall be entitled to all privileges and immunities of citizens in the several states," has been abandoned by common consent: since by this law the citizens of the several states have not been denied any privilege allowed the citizens of Kentucky. I come, then, to the Art. 1, Sec. 8, Clause 3: "The congress shall have power to regulate commerce with foreign nations, and among the several states, and among the Indian tribes;" so strongly urged by the honorable chairman. I warn gentlemen of the dangerous ground upon which they entrench themselves. In their over-heated zeal to flood our state with the refuse slaves of all the south, they are advocating and strengthening the only principles on which the Abolitionists rest all their hopes of destroying the tenure of slaves. Wherein do the Abolitionists differ from the great mass of the citizens of the non-slaveholding states: nay, from the whole civilized world? The Abolitionists believe slavery to be an evil: so do all other men of free states. The Abolitionists do not believe slavery to be the foundation of civil liberty: all men of free states believe the same; and despise the paradox. The Abolitionists contend that they have the right, under the Constitution, to abolish slavery in the District of Columbia, to abolish the slave trade between the several states, and having the power, they are bound to carry that power into sudden execution. Therein they diverge from the mass of their fellow-citizens of the free states, and begin for the first time to become dangerous to the slave states.

I, too, have been called an Abolitionist. I now challenge the gentlemen to the test. I stand opposed to the power of congress to interfere with the slaves at all: they stand up for congress, and avow her power. The Abolitionists stand up for congress, and avow her power. Nay, if the gentleman's position be tenable, and he gain a triumph over me, he will have proved, not only the power of congress to abolish slavery in the District of Columbia,* and the trade between the several states, but he will have also proved that congress has the power to declare that men cannot be subjects of property; and that the entire slave population of this Union are *free.* For, under the same clause they have declared, whilst *regulating* "commerce with foreign nations," that men are not and cannot be property, by making the foreign slave trade piracy. And the same language is used;

---

* The power to abolish slavery in the District exists, or rather slavery ceases under another clause of the United States Constitution. 1848.

and "among the several states." The conclusion follows in such fearful magnitude, that I need not utter it.*

I pray gentlemen to pause, to reconsider, to retreat, to abandon this untenable position. Standing here in my place, one of the representatives of the independent state of Kentucky, I most solemnly protest against it. I declare war upon it. I am prepared to meet it with argument: I will meet it, if necessary, with the sword.

The gentleman from Breckenridge says, that slaves are *not persons*, but merely "goods and chattels"—tobacco hogsheads and whisky barrels—subject to the same rules as other merchandise! and inasmuch as no state can lay a tax upon *them*, Kentucky, by imposing a tax of six hundred dollars upon each slave imported, assumes the power of congress. He states further, that the northern states contended in convention that slaves should not be considered as *persons;* and that the journal of the convention will so show. It must be a bad cause indeed that can drive sensible, ambitious men to such absurdities as these. Slaves not persons? And the free states so contended? Indeed! And suppose they did so contend, was the south so wanting in common sense as to admit it? No: the contrary was agreed upon: it was determined that slaves *were persons.* That they were not, and should not stand upon the same footing as lard kegs and cider barrels: and because they *were persons*, they became the foundation of representation. What are they called in the Constitution; Art. 1, Sec. 2, Cl. 3: "Three fifths of all other *persons.*" Again, Art. 4, Sec. 3, Cl. 3: "No *person* held to service." Once more; Art. 1, Sec. 9, Cl. 5: "The migration, or importation, of such *persons.*" In these three clauses, the only ones in the whole Constitution in which allusion to slaves is made at all, they are called *persons!* Shame on those hypocritical assertors of human liberty and equal rights who, believing slavery to be "a blessing, and the foundation of freedom," did not dare to put the word slave in that sacred instrument! Slaves, then, are not mere things, but *persons;* the foundation of representation: possessing all the feelings of humanity, and some of the privileges of free white citizens.

---

* It needs no act of congress, nor of the state legislature: the slave, whenever he passes out of the bounds of a state by the consent of his master, is free, under the United States Constitution.

So far as they are *suffered* to be property at all, they stand alone, and sui generis : the objects of jealousy in the formation of the constitution.   Congress, it is true, have entire control over the foreign slave trade, because *all* power over commerce abroad is *denied* to the *states*, and especially granted to congress ; and this power over slaves is acknowledged in Art. 1, Sec. 9, ch. 1 : " The migration or importation of such persons."   But so soon as they pass the line of a state, the power of congress ceases ; you find no grant of power to interfere with the subject.   On the contrary, the whole power of slavery is *passed over* as being in *the states only*.   Slaves, then, are persons, and exclusively the subject of municipal regulation by the states.   I beg to read the decision of the supreme court of the United States in the case of the Mayor, Aldermen, and Commonalty of the city of New York, plaintiffs, vs. George Miller ; Peters' Reports, vol. 2, p. 102.   The corporation of New York imposed certain penalties upon all masters of ships who failed to register the names of passengers, as prescribed by law ; and brought suit against the master of the brig Emily for the penalty incurred by the importation of *persons* from a foreign port.   The defendant contended that under the clause of the constitution giving congress power to regulate commerce, the statute was unconstitutional.   But the supreme court decided otherwise.   I quote some parts of the decision.   " This does not apply to *persons*.   They are not subjects of commerce.   It is not only the right, but the bounden and solemn duty of a state to advance the safety, happiness, and prosperity of its people, and to provide for its general welfare, by any and every act of legislation, which it may deem to be conducive to these ends ; when the powers over the particular subject, or the manner of its exercise, are not surrendered or restrained by the Constitution of the United States."   " All those powers which relate merely to municipal legislation, or which may more properly be termed internal police, are not surrendered or restrained ; and consequently, in relation to these, the authority of a state is complete, unqualified, and exclusive." *Persons* are not the *subjects of commerce ;* and not being imported goods, they do not fall within the reasoning founded upon the construction of a power given to congress to regulate commerce, and the prohibition of the states from imposing a duty upon imported goods."   Now, could a case be more applicable, possibly, to my position : that slaves are *persons*, subjects only of " municipal legislation :" that, there being in the Con-

stitution of the United States no *restraining* power, nor power
surrendered, they of consequence come "exclusively within the
authority of the state:" and that the state is solemnly and in
duty bound to advance the "safety and happiness, and prosperity
of its people?"

Thus, to sustain my ground, I have the implied intentions of
the founders of the constitution; the constitution itself; the
actual precedent of all the states of the union, from the beginning till now. What more will gentlemen ask? what more can I
give? The ablest jurists Kentucky can boast formed this law;
thanks to the simplicity of genius, the humblest of her sons is
able to defend it against all the shafts that baffled ambition can
hurl against it.

Shall the law of 1832–'3 be repealed? Shall I not, says the
advocate of repeal, be allowed to bring in a slave for my own
use? He might also ask, shall I not be allowed to bring in a
slave from Africa, if I want? Yet the laws of the union impose
the penalty of death upon the foreign slave-trader. And the
domestic slave-traders become, in the eyes of some, very *respectable gentlemen!* and native Kentuckians are denounced as
abolitionists, and enemies of the country, because they oppose
the same traffic which the United States denounced with death.
And while the President of the United States is calling on
congress to break up more effectually the trade in African
slaves, they are demanding no less earnestly that this state shall
be impoverished, and desecrated, and brutalized, by an overflow of the slough of slavery from the jails of all the South, to
gratify those lovely specimens of human philanthropy—the professional slave-traders! This indignation at restraint comes
with a bad grace from those whose freedom is to trample with
an iron heel upon the *will of others*. Laws are made for short-
sighted selfishness to bend the wayward impulses of individual
mind into subservience to the general good.

The gentleman from Breckenridge tells us all men are
governed by self-interest; and that, disguise it as we may,
selfishness lies at the bottom of our own actions.—That I,
the representative of a county with ten thousand slaves, favor
this law because it makes them more valuable to the slaveholder; but that the gentleman from Louisville is for the law,
because they there have "*white slaves*," who are *cheaper* than
blacks. I pass over the inconsistency of the argument. I confess I am moved by self-interest. But there are two kinds of

se.   One is a narrow, short-sighted, unstatesman-like
self-   'ch looks only to immediate consequences; it
subse.   .sser passions and appetites; it is the basis of
all men   ..al, and physical debasement; it is the counselor
of crime; and its end is death. But there is another, enlarged,
and far-seeing, and statesman-like self-interest, which looks not
only to immediate, but to secondary and remote consequences;
it yields not to impulse nor to passion, but is subservient to
reason; it is the groundwork of virtue, wisdom, and immortality. In private life, it is the essence of morality; in the public
man it is patriotism.* Fortunately these distinctions are not
necessary to Fayette; both interests impel her with concentrated
force to sustain the law of 1833. For as the owner of ten
thousand and twenty-six slaves, valued at three millions seven
hundred and forty-three thousand one hundred and twenty-
three dollars, there is none so blind as not to see that the free
importation from abroad, by all the laws of trade, reduces the
value of her home slave population, in proportion to the increase
from abroad; while on the other hand, the far-reaching eye
of patriotism will discover, in the increase of the whites over the
blacks, security, wealth, and progressive greatness to the whole
state. Again, if you draw the line between the slaveholder and
the non-slaveholder, you will find that all the interests of both
parties again unite in sustaining the law. For, if by the law
the value of slave labor is increased, so also by the same law is
the value of white labor; for they are the *same* labor in the
same market; and the price of slave labor must influence *pro
tanto* the labor of the free. And as it is admitted that nine-
tenths of the free whites of Kentucky are non-slaveholders
and *working men*, will they ever be so blind and infatuated
as to lower the price of labor, and starve their own families, to
"diffuse the slave population over all the states," that southern
nabobs may sleep in security, whilst their own children cry for
bread and die? It is the interest of all Kentucky, then, to
decrease the number of slaves. Let us see if the law of '33 has
had that effect:

---

* That I was at this time advocating the *immediate* interests of the slaveholder there can be no question, for they have sustained the law but sacrificed
me. The avowal of these elevated sentiments, they well knew, would soon
make me the *acting enemy* of slavery: for *it laughs at all virtue!* At this time I
was *honest;* a sincere love of *truth* has since gradually placed me upon *higher
ground.*—C. '48.

TABLE No. I. *Showing the number of Whites and Blacks in Kentucky.*

CENSUS.	WHITES.	SLAVES AND FREE BLACKS.	RATIO OF BLACKS TO WHITES.
1790, - - - - -	61,133	11.944	1 to 5.11
1800, - - - - -	179,871	41,084	1 " 4.37
1810, - - - - -	324,237	82,274	1 " 3.94
1820, - - - - -	434.644	129,673	1 " 3.35
1830, - - - - -	517,787	170.130	1 " 3.04
1840, - - - - -	587,017	190,342	1 " 3.06
Absolute increase of Whites and Blacks in last ten years, from 1830 to 1840, - - -	69,230	20,212	1 to 3.42

Thus, from the admission of Kentucky into the union down to 1830, the slave population steadily increased upon the whites : but since 1843, and the last decade, in the third year of which the law of 1833 began to act, the whites have increased on the blacks : making the absolute increase in ten years of three and forty hundreths whites to one black.

TABLE No. II. *Showing the rate of increase of the White, and the combined free colored and slave population in Slave States in forty years : Florida and Delaware omitted.*

STATES.	FROM 1790 TO 1830.	BLACKS. INCRE. PR. CT.	WHITES. INCRE. PR. CT.
Maryland,* - - - -	1790	40.3794	39.5204
Virginia, - - - -	"	68.8820	57.0406
North Carolina, - - -	"	151.2094	64.0654
South Carolina, - -	"	196.9117	339.8112
Georgia, - - - -	"	641.7470	461.2185
Kentucky, - - - -	"	1324.3972	746.9844
Tennessee, - - - -	"	3768.6607	1573.5264
Mississippi - - - -	1800	1702.7241	1260.1661
Louisiana, - - - -	1810	198.9656	160.6773
Missouri, - - - -	"	609.2316	566.3669
Alabama, - - - -	1820	147.7971	97.8347
Arkansas, - - - -	"	178.4534	104.0782
District of Columbia, - -	1800	204.7181	173.8228
Total increase pr. ct. in 40 years,		207.4671	200.0080
Total increase in the *U. S.,* pr. ct.		207.4671	232.1512

* Maryland *decreased* her slave population in forty years, by emancipation and exportation, 0.0408 per centum. The consequence is, that of all the slave states she is most prosperous.

By reference to the pamphlet on your desks,* and the table marked number two, in my hand, you will find that in the slave states the increase of the black upon the white population has been slow but *progressive ;* whilst, in .the whole Union, the whites have increased upon the blacks, from 1790 to 1830 ; the whites increasing at the rate of 232.15 per cent., and the blacks increasing at the rate of 187.87 per cent.; which shows that in the free states the whites increase in a greater ratio upon a given basis than they do in the slave states, and that slavery is a drawback upon population. Or else it shows that immigration is greater, or emigration less ; in either case the slave state is the loser. If a free white population *be* itself an element of strength and greatness, or the *increase* of population *indicates* prosperity, as economists all agree, then surely the law of 1833 should stand. As population is not only the basis of strength and wealth, but of representation, in the Union, a contrast between a free and a slave state, cannot fail to strike the most unthinking. Kentucky has the advantage of Ohio in age, in extent of territory, in soil, in climate, and in mineral wealth ; yet, by the census of 1840, it had a total of seven hundred and seventy seven thousand three hundred and fifty-nine inhabitants ; increasing, in ten years, thirty-three per centum ; whilst Ohio had one million five hundred and fourteen thousand six hundred and ninety-five of souls ; having increased, in the same ten years, sixty-two and fifty-one-hundredths per cent. ; having now a greater population than Virginia, the "mother of states." And whilst South Carolina has increased her whole population two per cent., Massachusetts, of about the same age, with less land and natural advantages, has increased twenty-one per cent., in the same time. What statesman, seeing these facts, can vote for the repeal ? Who, that has the soul of a Kentuckian, would not rather that this law had formed a part of the constitution itself ?

The gentleman from Breckenridge has spoken of the lower classes of New England as " slaves—worse than slaves ;" and, because we have alluded to the genius of that people, as developed in literature, and especially in the useful sciences and mechanic arts, we are taunted as being allied in feeling to " *Yankees.*" Since the ever memorable reply of Daniel Webster to

---

* Review of R. Wickliffe's Speech, by C. M. Clay, 1840.

the South Carolinian on Foote's resolutions, I had supposed that
no one would venture to deride the name of "*Yankees.*" They
need no defence at my hands; I shall make none. I am a Kentuckian, of the Virginia descent; I have not been taught to consider praise given to another as so much detracted from myself;
nor have I thought it necessary, in order to establish my claims
to true blood, to abuse all the world besides. It is the part of
friendship to supply defects and to correct errors. Because I am
proud of my state, and love her renown, I call upon her, by all
the triumphs of the past, to seek the true road to permanent
happiness and ultimate glory. [Mr. C. here read from a newspaper, showing that there had been orders from all parts of the
world for American machinery—grist-mills for Holland; steam-
cars for England: ships for Russia: and cotton-gins for India.]

I ask the friends of slave-labor how long shall we wait till
we shall be able to supply Europe and the world with such
things of manufacture? How long before Holland will send to
Kentucky for grist-mills? How long before we shall look upon
such steam-cars, of home make, as Philadelphia has lately
had the honor of shipping for the admiration of other lands?
How long before we shall here see such a steam-ship as lately
floated in the harbor of New York, for the emperor of Russia?
We have waited for more than two hundred years to see these
things, in vain. How many years more shall our hearts fail
with the sickness of "hope deferred" before we shall share the
triumphs of these creations of "Yankee" genius? Like the
doomed Jew we wander on in darkness and sullen expectancy,
clinging with desperate fondness to the cast-off idols of days that
are gone, unconscious of the heavenly light which surrounds
us, and the Deity that moves in our midst!

Have we succeeded better in literary eminence? I might ask
of the South, with the British reviewer of America, "who reads
a southern book?" Where are our Irvings and Coopers; where
our Percivals and Hallecks; our Sillimans and Hares, our Ful-
tons and Franklins? Our very paper, and primers, and presses
are of Yankee make. It is true, that in politics and law—those
ever tense and exciting professions, those hot-beds of human intellect—we have produced some splendid specimens of mental
energy. But they only make us more deeply regret that so
much mind should lie for ever dormant—perishing in embryo,
and sunk in the stagnant pools of luxury and indolence which

slavery spreads afar, like the fabled Stygian lake, an eternal barrier between its doomed spirits and a higher Heaven !

Shall I, then, be taunted with Yankee feeling because I would dispel the lethargy which rests upon our loved state ? I am not insensible to the glory of her triumphs upon every battle field from Lake Erie to the Gulf of Mexico; of her eloquence, which, whether uttered in the rude language of the stump, or in the more polished phrase of the halls of legislation, fears no rivalry. I know her Boones, her Kentons, her Estills, and her Bryants; the hardy stock upon which were engrafted the more polished scions of fairer bloom and more mature fruit. Shall I aggregate her glory and give names to its impersonations ? Shall I speak of her Breckenridges, her Nicholases, her Marshalls, and her Clays?—those names which live with Kentucky; to die only when she dies ; they who formed the constitution of the state, and breathed into that charter the same free spirit which animated their own bosoms ? What said they ? That slavery was a " blessing?" " the foundation of liberty?" that it should be *perpetual ?* No, sir, no. The law of '33 but carries out and fulfils their just expectations and cherished hopes. The same impress of wisdom and patriotism which characterizes that instrument—signed by my father and by your father, (Mr. Calhoon's)—marks this law. And it is with pride and increased confidence that I find the descendants of those same Breckenridges, Marshalls, and Nicholases, all, now standing up the advocates of this much-abused law. It is the cause of our fathers that we vindicate ; we are degenerate sons if it fail.

Gentlemen would import slaves "to clear up the forests of the Green River country:" "the south of the state demands the repeal." Take one day's ride from this capital, and then go and tell them what you have seen. Tell them that you have looked upon the once most lovely and fertile land that nature ever formed : and have seen it in fifty years worn to the rock : tell them of the clay banks and drains and brier fields : tell them of houses untenanted and decaying : tell them of the depopulation of the country and consequent ruin of the towns and villages: tell them that the white Kentuckian has been driven out by slaves, by the unequal competition of unpaid labor : tell them that the mass of our people are uneducated : tell them that you have heard the children of the white Kentuckian crying for bread, whilst the children of the African was clothed, and fed, and laughed! And then ask them if they will have blacks to fell their forests. Tell them yet more: that Green River is acquiring new strength in this house, whilst the representation of the interior counties is fast fading away: tell them that Clark has but one representative here, and that Bourbon, which once voted three thousand, is reduced to sixteen hundred voters. Tell them that Fayette has ten thousand slaves, as many as she has horses. Tell them all this: and, my life for it, they will stand for this law for ever.

It may be doubted whether the worn and waste land seen in the most fertile portions of the state is owing to slave labor. But ignorance and carelessness, which are necessarily combined in the slave, make his the most slovenly and wasteful of all labor. The field is plowed one way: a cross-furrow is run another: the rains fall: the water collects into the common trench: the land is washed to the rock. The slave may be punished: but the evil is not remedied: the soil is lost and the field turned waste. These things will not be seen in the free states. Land, which is here turned waste, or being white oak, is unoccupied, is better than some in New England which contributes to the sustenance and education of respectable families.

The easy life of the slaveholder destroys his vigilance and activity: supersedes the necessity of economy, and the habit of accumulation; and in the long run brings on poverty. Let not, therefore, gentlemen be astonished that the North is radiant with railroads, the channels of her untold commerce: whilst the South hobbles on at an immeasurable distance behind. I shall not dwell upon the fact that most of our *educated* mind is *idle* and *unproductive:* nor press the fact that idleness leads to innumerable crimes—saps the foundations of all morality, whilst it is surely bringing on final destitution and disgrace. Nor shall I consider the effects of slavery upon the temper and affections. Such painful considerations I pass in melancholy silence.

With all these unhappy facts pressing upon my every sense, I am denounced because I will not admit slavery to be a blessing and receive *more* of it. And the gentleman undertakes to threaten me and hold me responsible for every word I may utter upon this floor. Sir, I strike hands with the gentleman. And when he admits that "White labor is cheaper than slave labor," and that "slave labor drives out white labor," and declares that "white laborers are slaves"—in the name of five hundred thousand freemen of Kentucky, I denounce the gentleman, as warring upon their dearest interests, and as pursuing a reckless course of policy, which he knows dries up their sources of subsistence, and outlaws and banishes them from their native land. No! he, and not I, is the defender of aristocrats. Let him tell us again, as we have been told before, that slavery stands in the way of education: let him be consistent: let him bring in a bill, as I am told he threatens to do, to abolish the common school system: let him monopolize the learning as well as the wealth of the country: let the people rest in deep ignorance for ever: let them never learn their rights: then, and then only, can this law be repealed.

This is not the first time I have heard the cry of abolition. It has no terrors to my ear. Bowie-knives, and belted pistols, and the imprecations of maddened mobs, have not driven me from my country's cause. My blood, and the blood of all whom I hold most dear, is ready when she calls for the sacrifice. But I shall be a tame victim neither to *force* nor to *denunciation.* Whilst there is abolitionism in the north, backed by Holland, England, and France, and urged on by a world in arms, there is in these states a party far more dangerous to all that makes life desirable, or liberty glorious. Never, till after the ever memorable and impotent attempt of South Carolina to dissolve this Union, did I hear or read of slavery as the foundation of human liberty! The message of Governor McDuffie, of South Carolina, has the bad eminence of having first set forth this monstrous and absurd doctrine, that filled the civilized world with disgust and dismay. A distinguished gentleman from Fayette, and the honorable member from Breckenridge, are the only avowed converts to this new religion that I have ever seen. I am bound to believe that the honorable gentleman is not initiated into the greater mysteries of this new sect; nay, sir, I will undertake to say that he is not. Yet, with all the weighty responsibilities which rest upon me as a man, and the representative of a gallant state, I declare that there is a party in this country, who, disregarding all the sacred memories of the past, and the yet more glorious anticipations of the future, would *destroy the union of these states.* They are the advocates of *perpetual slavery*—they are the last "state nullifiers," *Southern unionists*—they are the *disunionists.* Conventions must be held, says South Carolina; conventions must be held, say some in

Kentucky; conventions must be held, says the governor of Alabama; the slave population must be diffused over all the slave states; rules must be adopted for mutual safety and permanent security of slave property! Can any man in his senses affect not to understand to what all this leads? I declare, sir, that Kentucky is called upon this day to act; to take her stand now and for ever. I know not what course others may pursue, but, for myself, I have made up my mind: "Sink or swim, survive or perish," I stand by the Union.

Shall we rest in fatal security till this law is repealed; the slave population diffused; conventions held; till we are shorn of our strength by calumny, bound hand and foot, and given over to this Southern union? No; I lift up my voice now; here, in the face of all Kentucky, I most solemnly protest against these *treasonable schemes*. The banner of the United States constitution is my shield and only safety; tear not my state; let not, I beseech you, Kentucky pass from under its hallowed panoply. Let it not be in vain that Adams, and Franklin, and Henry, and Jefferson, and Madison, and Hamilton, have lived; not in vain that Washington, and Greene, and Lincoln, and Lafayette, and heroes innumerable, have bled and died; not in vain that liberty has been proclaimed for all the world! Let not the treasure and blood, which in the last war, the second revolution, added fresh laurels to a nation of brothers, have been spent in vain! Let not the Thames, and Erie, and Champlain, and New Orleans, perish from the memories of men. By the aspirations of the soul for all that is good and glorious, let not our hopes be lost; let not the Union be dissolved! In that day there shall be one Kentuckian shrouded under the stars and stripes; one heart undesecrated with the faith that slavery is the basis of civil liberty; one being who could not exist in a government *denyin g the Right of Petition, the Liberty of Speech, and the Press ;* one man who would not be the outlaw of nations—*the slave of a slave!*

SPEECH

Against the Annexation of Texas, in reply to Col. R. M. Johnson and others, at the White Sulphur Springs, Scott County, Ky., Saturday, Dec. 30, 1843.

The following resolutions were offered by C. M. CLAY, as a substitute for those presented by the majority of the Committee, and supported in a Speech which has been reported as follows:

RESOLUTIONS.

1. *Resolved*, That the annexation of Texas to the American Union, without the consent of Mexico, will be a breach of the Treaty of Amity with that Nation, contrary to the Laws of Nations, and just cause of war, on the part of Mexico, against the United States.

2. *Resolved*, That the annexation of the Slave State of Texas to the United States, is contrary to the Federal Constitution: involuntary slavery, under Act of Congress, being in violation of Art. 5, of the amendments: " That no person shall be deprived of life, liberty or property, without due process of law:"— being also in violation of the principles of the Declaration of American Independence:—and being also at war with the existence of real liberty among our own free-born people.

3. *Resolved*, That Kentucky, above all other States in the Confederacy, it vitally interested in the perpetuity of the American Union.

4. *Resolved*, That the annexation of the Slave State of Texas to the United States, would be just cause for the dissolution of this Union: and would, most probably, array the Northern States, Mexico, and all Christendom, in wars against the Slave States. which could not but result in ruin and slavery to the whites themselves.

5. *Resolved*, That in such a most deplorable event, Kentucky owes it to herself, to posterity, and to mankind, to refuse to expend her treasure and shed her blood, for the extension of Slavery among men:—on the contrary, all her interests, temporal and eternal, demand of her speedily to extinguish slavery within her borders, and to unite her destiny with the Northern States, who, relying upon God, liberty and equality, will be able to stand against the world in arms.

6. *Resolved*, That these Resolutions be sent to our Representatives in Congress, to be laid before the American people.

[These resolutions were rejected.]

SPEECH.

Mr. President, and Fellow Citizens:

In presenting the resolutions which I have offered as a substitute for those reported by a majority of your committee, I do not hope to be more successful here, than I have been in the committee itself. This place of meeting, the presiding officer (Col. R. M. Johnson), and the audience who favor me with a hearing, all forbid any expectation on my part, of carrying the substitute. But I rejoice, humble as I may be in ability, unknown to fame, and of no consideration among men, that association with your name, in this day's deliberations, will give me a factitious importance which will recommend what I shall say to a hearing from the people of the United States. My opinions, of little intrinsic value, may excite the minds of my countrymen to reflection ; and then, after mature consideration, I dare venture the assertion, that the position I have this day taken, will be maintained in practice, and vindicated at last by a recognition of those principles, which it is the province of history to enforce and consecrate in the affections of mankind.

Regarding the questions at issue, as second only to those which have for ever illustrated the year 1776, I shall speak with that freedom which I inherit as my birth-right, and which I so much desire to transmit unimpaired to posterity. Though yet young, I am old enough to know, from sad experience, what history, in such melancholy strains, has uttered in vain to the deaf ears of men : that the best of council is far from being always the most acceptable. When the storm-cast vessel is threatened with wreck, the man who would save her by throwing over-board the boxes of gold or other things of more cherished endearment, is hardly heard, whilst he who maintains that all is safe, is too often trusted, till both life and treasure are irrevocably lost. He, who from good motives gives even bad advice, is entitled at least, to just forbearance ; whilst the man who advances the best of counsel for selfish purposes, deserves no consideration for his services.

Those gentlemen who would annex Texas to the Union, and hurry us blindfold down this precipice of ruin and dishonor, have here, in these slave States, at least, popular prejudice in their favor. On one side are honor, power, wealth, and easy access to fame ; on the other side, denunciation, banishment, poverty, and obscurity threaten. If I, then, speak freely the truth, when you, my countrymen, are to reap all the fruits of the sacrifice, no man can say that I ask too much, when I pray you to hear me with a patience which a subject of such deep interest demands.

First of all, then, I protest against this appeal to our sympathies in behalf of Texas, and these unjust denunciations of
Mexico, as foreign to the true issue, and eminently calculated
to lead us into error. Though truly, and with sorrow be it said,
of Anglo-Saxon blood, bone of our bone, and flesh of our flesh,
in the language of gentlemen, I ask you what claims of sympathy has Texas on the people of the United States? Enjoying all the blessings which the Constitution guarantees to her
people,—with all the offices of honor and profit open to the
humblest citizen—with an unoccupied domain extending to
the distant Pacific—like our first parents, going out from Eden,
with the world before them where to choose, in any clime, a
home—they voluntarily banished themselves from their native
country, disavowed the glorious principles of the American
Declaration of the rights of man, renounced the inestimable
privileges of the Federal Constitution, which was their inheritance, and, forgetful of all the ties of common blood, language,
and home, they became the fellow subjects with a half barbarian
people, of a distant Spanish Prince. Yes, without becoming
the advocate of Santa Anna (whom we have heard denounced
as a tyrant and a traitor, for the purpose of prejudicing the
cause which I vindicate), trusting to indestructible truth and
avenging history, I challenge a comparison between Texas and
Mexico. The Mexican people, inspired by that Declaration of
American Independence which recreant Texas had renounced,
in 1821, vindicated by a glorious revolution, their title to independence of the Spanish monarchy: and illustrated, in act, the
postulate taught by our Revolutionary heroes, that a people cannot of right be governed without their own consent. In 1824,
Mexico, following the example of the United States and Great
Britain, who, in 1820, had declared the slave trade piracy, and
punishable with death, prohibited, in the language of Judge
Story, "this infernal traffic." In 1829, once more, unlike Texas, she made it part of her constitution, that no person born
after the promulgation of the same, in the several provinces,
should be a slave. Again, in 1836, this much abused Mexico
declared that slavery was extinguished in the Republic; and,
elevating the dread standard of "God and Liberty," she called
upon the sons of freedom by arms to vindicate this immortal
decree! And where, now, throughout this vast empire, did this
glad note of liberty fail to receive a willing response? Alas!

for the recreant Saxon, Texas—the descendants of Washington, and Jefferson, and Adams, and Franklin—Texas, who had received from a paternal government a gratuitous fee simple in the finest soil on earth, exempt from taxation for ten years, and without other sacrifice, save allegiance to the government and to the Catholic Religion, which she had most solemnly sworn to yield—Texas was the first to raise the black flag of "slavery and no emancipation"—ay, Texas was the only people who dared to brave the indignation of mankind, by resisting that liberty, which has made the nineteenth century for ever memorable in the annals of the world. And yet Santa Anna is a most horrible despot, and much injured and oppressed Texas is the defender of liberty! Santa Anna, who has civilized the barbarian and revolutionary spirit of his people—who has suppressed the daring bands of robbers who infested the highways, making life unsafe, property insecure, and commerce impracticable—who has encouraged education and the useful arts, who has caused to be recognised the principles of equal rights and representative government—who, in the midst of the embarrassments of the world, and the exhaustion, arising from revolutionary and civil wars, which have especially harassed his own country, has preserved the Mexican faith inviolate—whose many gallant deeds in war and peace, have, by the almost unanimous acclamation of the people, again and again elevated him to the Presidency of the republic—Santa Anna, who has often liberated American citizens under circumstances which induced England to send them into hopeless exile—Santa Anna is an odious tyrant; and Texas, renegades from the land and religion of their fathers—Texas, the ingrates to their adopted and fostering country—Texas, the propagators of slavery—Texas, the repudiators of their debts, the violators of public faith—Texas is so lovely in the eyes of gentlemen, that we must take her to our embrace, although we fall with her into one common grave!

But, in truth, we have nothing to do with the republics of Texas and Mexico; whether they be the same or two independent nations, is to us a matter of no concern. We have no evidence that she seeks our alliance, even if we were disposed to grant it. I am no propagandist—I am satisfied to maintain the principles, the independence, and the honor of my own country. The same impulse which moves me to repel foreign interference and to defend my own rights, constrains me also to keep aloof from, and respect, the peculiar organizations which other nations have deemed most suitable to secure their rights.

I contend, then, in the language of the first resolution, that the annexation of Texas to the United States is contrary to the Laws of Nations, and just cause of war on the part of Mexico. The recognition of the Independence of Texas by the United States may or may not have been a sufficient cause of war. It remained with Mexico to vindicate her injured honor or to pocket the injury or insult, as to her seemed best, relying upon her own capability of maintaining the integrity of her empire. But when the United States, not confining herself to just, or, it may be, unjust sympathy, not restrained to an opinion that Texas is, or ought of right to be, an independent people, makes herself an active and principal party, by taking hold of the province in controversy, thus for ever making it impossible for Mexico to recover the country which, up to that time, was but partially or temporarily, in her view, alienated from her : then I say that Mexico has not only just cause of war, but that she would be disgraced in the eyes of all gallant nations if she did not use her every power for the vindication of her injured honor and violated territory. Learned authority has been quoted here, with the vain expectation of persuading us that Mexico has no cause of grievance in the event supposed. I dare not insult common sense by acquiescence in such mysterious jurisprudential jargon as this. I appeal to the reason, to the instincts, the consciences of men, for the establishment of the law of nature upon which the laws of nations are, or ought to be, for ever based. What, sir, have we a solemn treaty of amity with Mexico, to say nothing at present of natural right; and is it the part of friendship to seize with a rapacious hand, a portion of the territory which she still claims, and appropriate it to ourselves ? Do not these learned jurists know that a breach of treaty is contrary to the laws of nations, as laid down by all the writers upon that most obscure science, and, without reparation, just cause of war ? And what reparation could we make whilst we continued to hold the price of blood and violated faith? What war was more unjust than that carried on by the United States against the Florida Indians ? Suppose, at some time after its commencement, Mexico had agreed with the Indians, that they were, as they declared themselves to be, free and independent; and suppose Mexico had subsequently thereto, thus addressed us: "You have expended forty millions of dollars, you have lost a white man for every Indian slain in battle; you have called to your aid blood-hounds, in vain, to the horror of all Christendom; for eight years you have, with the whole force of the empire, carried on a hopeless war of recovery; it is time hostilities should cease; we will take the Floridas ourselves, peaceably if we can, forcibly if we must." I shall not stop to ask whether we should have deemed this a just cause of war, or to say what would have been our laconic reply. Cases have arisen, and will doubtless again arise, which, when a people are struggling to throw off an unjust and tyrannical rule, have, and will again justify a virtuous nation, even when in alliance with the tyrant, in sympathizing with, and recognising the independence of the oppressed. Here the rectitude of the motive and just cause of the injured, cure and sanctify the breach of the treaty of amity. But when Texas is the wrong-doer, and Mexico the injured party—here, where not even studiously disguised motives, wearing the semblance of virtue, but shameless and openly avowed rapacity, impel us to the breach of faith and the disregard of natural right: she will not only, and ought not only to declare war against us, but she will justly claim the universal sympathy and aid of all nations, to enable her to vindicate her desecrated soil and insulted sovereignty.

The wrongs of Mexico, the wishes of Texas, the armed arbitrament of other nations aside, the case is still far from being stripped of its embarrassments. It matters not so much what other men may think of us, as that we may think well of ourselves—happy, happy indeed, are they who condemn not themselves. If we had our own consent, and also the consent of the north to this annexation, still I deem it questionable whether Texas, as a free state, could constitutionally be admitted into this Union. I do not deny that the necessity of the case, the dread alternative of war, might not, under the treaty-making power, compel us to cede away or to acquire territory. Whether the provinces of Louisiana and Florida were acquired constitutionally or not, I shall not, at this late day, undertake to question. They were admitted, however, by the sovereign proprietor's consent; one of them, lying around the mouth of the Mississippi river, threatened with eternal embarrassment the trade of the whole valley of the west; no breach of violated national faith was insinuated; no disastrous wars threatened; and yet, able jurists and patriotic statesmen denied the constitutionality of the acquisition, and threatened its ratification with resistance and dissolution.

But where is the necessity for the annexation of Texas, even if she desired it; even if Mexico did not denounce war; even if there was no violation of national faith; even if she was not a slave state? where, I ask, is that overwhelming necessity which generates a power not given the constitution, nor anticipated by its authors? It is not territory that we want: our wide unoccupied domain stretches from the Mississippi to the far Pacific: we have already more land than we are able to defend from savage incursion and British usurpation. "We want more slave states to offset the fanatical free states." Let the world hear it: you admit, sir, that we want Texas to extend slavery among men! Unutterable emotions agitate my bosom: I ask the charter of my liberty—of your liberty; I call upon the Declaration of American Independence upon which it is founded; I invoke the spirit of freedom, which, in the day of suffering and threatened despair, inspired its utterance, as solemn protests against this most unholy scheme. Shall we not blush to draw the veil, which has hardly shielded us from the contempt and loathing of mankind, for proclaiming liberty and practicing servitude? shall we no longer gull them by the hypocritical plea of necessity, the sole defence of tyrants? Anew, we incur the guilt of slavery, and are ready to do battle, even unto death, for its extension. Then expunge from your annals the declaration of rights; repeal the law of 1820, which makes the slave-trade piracy; down with the gibbet, and bind the laurel upon the brow of the suspended culprit; withdraw your fleet from the coast of Africa; tell Great Britain, and the world, that you have been enacting a solemn farce, when you talked so loudly of liberty; that tyranny is the best government, and slavery the truest liberty; that now, at last, you begin to be in earnest—fifty years' constraint wearies the impassible muscles of the most wooden face—you give it up—now you hold slavery sacred at home, and, like the Oriental prophet of Medina, you are ready to propagate your faith by fire and sword throughout the world; that henceforth and for ever your watchword shall be " slavery or death." I care not for the precedents of the past, I declare that there is no power in the Federal Constitution by which a slave state can be admitted into this Union. Slavery cannot exist by the law of nature: it cannot exist by act of congress. Slavery did exist by the laws of the sovereign states; in the formation of the Constitution they that far retained their sovereignty, denying it to that extent to the creature of their united will; if they vested in congress the power to make a slave, then they at the same time yielded the power to unmake him. If, then, the congress can make a slave state, she can unmake a slave state; and if she has that power, it is her bounden duty not to add new slave states to the Union, but to purge it immediately of this fatal disease, which threatens death to the liberties of the whole country.*

---

* Since the publication of this speech, some of the presses have affected not to understand, or, what is worse, have wilfully perverted and misrepresented the argument. The avowed object of the Constitution is, "to secure the blessings of liberty;" and another clause says "No person shall be deprived of life, liberty, or property, without due process of law" Art. 5, amendments. I take it for granted that blacks are "persons," for even black slaves are so called in other parts of the Constitution; and that "without due process of law" means without some *offence*, which shall be ascertained by law. Now, if the Federal Government has only special delegated powers, and no others, then here is a special power to prevent slavery, and there is no special power to create slavery. If it has inherent and sovereign power, notwithstanding the clauses here quoted to the contrary, to create slavery, then it must have inherent and sovereign power also to destroy slavery; and the spirit of the whole instrument compels its exercise: and this seems to be an axiom which cannot be elucidated by argument. Whether, then, congress be the organ of a sovereign, or of a limited will—the Constitution—it cannot, in either case, make a slave. If the laws of congress are the supreme laws of the land, all state laws to the contrary notwithstanding, much more then is the Constitution forbidding "persons" to be "deprived of liberty," superior to any *territorial dependent state law!* The original thirteen sovereign states are only excepted, because they created the Constitution itself, and prohibited it by *implication* and *collateral clauses*, in that instrument, from abolishing slavery within their respective borders. I contend, then, that the original thirteen states had, and now have, *exclusive* control over slavery within their borders; that in all places where congress had, or now has, exclusive control, where slavery did not previously exist by the sovereign power of the original thirteen states, there slavery does not and cannot now exist; that in no territory in this wide empire is there now a slave; that the Supreme Court, under a writ of *habeas corpus*, is bound to liberate any person so claimed as a slave; that in the District of Columbia, congress has the right to abolish slavery, by compensating masters; that the slaves therein are not now free, *only* because of the laws of cession emanating from the sovereignties of Virginia and Maryland, guaranteeing the rights of owners to the same, till congress should give compensation and liberation; that Texas, coming into the Union, loses, in the act, her sovereignty, and that slavery falls with it; that there is no power in congress to revive it; and that henceforth, and for ever, an addition of slave states to this Union is impossible.

They who contend, then, for the admission of the slave state of Texas, are handling a two-edged sword: it cuts both ways; the assumption of such a power must therefore be abandoned at once and for ever. The contemptible jargon that slavery already existing in Texas or other territory acquired by conquest purchase or voluntary cession by municipal law, congress may form them into slave states and admit them into the Union, is unworthy of consideration : it involves the absurdity of having the power to do, through an agent, or indirectly, that which they cannot do directly, or of themselves. Nothing but sovereign power can make a slave; the moment a state, once having been independent, unites itself with this Union, at that moment its sovereignty is lost, and with it falls slavery at the same time. If the state about to be admitted was originally a part of the territory of the United States, it never had any sovereignty, and of course never could have made a slave.

I repeat once more, that, independent of Article 5th of the amendments to the Constitution, slavery cannot exist by act of congress ; but, when we there find the express language, "No person shall be deprived of life, liberty, or property, without due process of law," all subterfuge is at an end, and the learned and unlearned must unite in one voice; there is no power under Heaven, whilst the Constitution remains inviolate, by which Texas, as a slave state, can be admitted into this Union. When gentlemen are driven from all their strong-holds, having no ground to stand upon in making out a case of necessity, they at last come out with the old bug-bear, which has been so often paraded up and down, with tin pans beating and cows' horns blowing, whenever any party ends are to be achieved, that it has ceased to attract even the passing boys who are accustomed to shout after such unfamiliar shows—yes, England is the monster they would get at, and they are surprised, when this old enemy is in the field, that a military man, like myself, should be the last to come to the rescue.

Although, in the eyes of some, it be treason to say a kind or just thing about this haughty power, the brave cannot, at last, but honor the brave. I scorn to compliment myself indirectly, when I say, that the greatest warriors are, in the main, the stanchest friends of peace. The man who intends to run away, cares not how soon the battle may come on ; but he who has determined to die or conquer, will be slow in seeking the fight. Soult and Wellington are said to resist the war-like spirit of their people; and the correspondence of Scott and the Governor-General of New Brunswick, during the difficulties on the Maine border, is an honor to them and to their respective nations. In a bad cause, a woman may put me to flight; but plant me upon the right, and I am proud to say, that the man does not live whom I dare not look in the face. If we conquered in the war of Independence, it was not because of our physical strength; with Lord Chatham, I say that England, in a good cause, could have crushed America to atoms. It was the consciousness of justice which nerved our people in the hour of trial. Yes, it was the right, in which we conquered; it was the right, that called the gallant of all lands to our standard: it was the right, which made the veteran British Lion, who had traversed the world unscathed, at last crouch, in dishonor, before the unfledged bird of Jove. It was the glorious principles of life, liberty, and the pursuit of happiness, inscribed on our banners, which, like the letters of fire on the Babylonian walls, struck terror into the enemies of our country. But in this war which you are madly projecting, this inspiring banner will not be borne, alas! by us, but by them. Go, tell the six hundred thousand free laborers of my state, before they leave home, wife, children and friends— before they shoulder their musket and march afar, to shed, on the plains of Texas, their blood, for the extension of slavery, to ask themselves what they are to gain! When they lie bleeding and dying on the burning sands of a foreign country, or writhing in the deadly grasp of the terrible epidemics of the swamps of Florida and Louisiana, what maddening reflections will then await them—the blood of our sires has been shed in vain, the Constitution has been violated, the Union has been dissolved, our homes have been desolated, our wives and children have become outcasts and beggars; our country is lost; all nature fades from our dim, reluctant eyes; we sink, unwept, into dishonored graves, accursed of God and man:—if our cause triumphs, the sighs and tears of millions enslaved will mar the fruits of victory: but if it fail, as seemingly it must, then have the chains which we have forged for others become the heritage of our posterity for ever!

No, Mr. President, it cannot be. If the worst comes to the worst, and the Union shall be dissolved, I, for one, will join my destiny with the North. Here, in Kentucky, my mother earth, I shall stand unawed by danger, unmoved by denunciation, a living sacrifice to her best prosperity. I shall not fear death itself if she may but live. But if mad counsels shall press her on to ruin, and she shall prefer destruction to the relinquishment of her idols, then, and not till then, taking up my household gods, an unwilling exile, I shall, in other lands, seek that liberty which was hopeless in my native home. I would to God that my voice could this day reach every log cabin in this wide and lovely land; then, indeed, would I feel assured that this dread alternative could never happen; but my words are feebly echoed from these walls, and the press is sealed like the Apocalyptic books, which human power cannot open, and darkness broods over the land once more, till God himself shall say " Let there be light!"

Gentlemen, I know, flatter themselves that there will be no dissolution of the Union. In 1803, and in 1820, we are told, there was the same loud talk that there is now, about separation; that it will wear away once more, as it did then. "It is natural for man to indulge in the illusions of hope; we are apt to shut our eyes against the painful truth, and to listen to the voice of that syren, till she has transformed us into beasts," alas! that these lines of other days, made familiar by school-boy declamation, should rush back upon the memory with their primitive, awful energy. I know the North, at last they are in earnest. Twenty of her leading minds, her ablest, most patriotic citizens, have most solemnly declared in the face of men, that in the event of the annexation of Texas to this country, the Union shall be no more. Yes, sir, they have said it; depend upon it they will do what they say they will do. Since the time when, in the vindication of the law of 1833, I found it necessary, in order to prevent the flood of Southern blacks from desolating our state, to appeal to the first great principles of natural and American law, to sustain my policy against blind and maddened avarice; I have received from all parts of the Union letters and papers upon the vital subject of slavery: and I think I know as much about the true feelings of northern men as any other man in Kentucky.

They are divided into three parties upon the subject of slavery. First, there is a small band of abolitionists, who are for violence, if necessary, in the extermination of slavery. They are few indeed, and deserve, as they receive, the execration of

good men in both the north and the south.   Then come the
liberty party, embracing a large portion of the virtue, intelligence, and legal knowledge, the Christianity, and patriotism of
the north.   Taking the ground first occupied by Washington
himself, that slavery was the creature of the law, and should be
abolished by law, they appeal to the ballot-box, not to the bayonet; like the great Irish reformer, having faith in the power of
reason, truth, and virtue, they expect to achieve a bloodless revolution, more glorious than any yet arising from force and
arms.   This party, a few years ago, numbered but seven thousand voters; now, in 1843, they poll sixty-five thousand men at
the ballot box; having doubled themselves every year from the
time of their organization.   At such a continued rate of increase
I leave it to the reflecting to determine how long it will be before they absorb the whole political power of the North.   Lastly, there is the great mass of northern men, who are opposed to
slavery in principle, but who forbear to take any active part for
its removal; not because they do not feel many of its evils, but
because they fear the consequences of entering upon untried
scenes, preferring, in the language of the oft-repeated maxim, to
bear the ills they have, rather than fly to others they know not
of.   Then, there remains a fragment of men, who are shameless advocates of slavery, with a perverse nature, such as in-
spires the unworthy bosoms of convicts; they pride themselves
upon pre-eminence in guilt, and challenge the abhorrence of
mankind to elevate them to that notoriety which they have
despaired of obtaining by virtuous deeds.   In estimating northern feelings, I shall pass them over entirely, as in speaking of
the morals of Kentuckians I would not enter the penitentiary
for illustration, so, in speaking of the north, I mention not these
men, regarding them rather as those reprobates, whom God in
his vengeance has inflicted upon all nations, and who are peculiar to none.

Then, sir, these twenty men, at whose head stands the immortal name of ADAMS, of whom I have before spoken, are the
true exponents of the sentiments of the great mass of northern
freemen, and of course, also to that extent, of the two fragmen-
tary parties which I have enumerated.   You know the opinions
of those men—they have avowed them in congress—they are
before the world.   They say that slavery, not content with the
immunities allowed it in the original compact, has transcended

its assigned limits, and recklessly trenches upon the liberties of the north, through a violated constitution.

They complain that the right of petition is denied—that the freedom of speech and of the press is suppressed—that members of congress are censured for opinion's sake—that the post-office is wrested by violence from the purposes of its creation. They are outraged, that their colored citizens, cooks, sailors, and others, contrary to the express language of the Constitution, instead of being allowed the privileges of citizenship, are thrown into prison and deprived of their rights without just cause. They are indignant that her free white citizens are horribly murdered in the south for opinion's sake, without having violated any state or national law, or without having been tried by a jury of their peers, which is their inalienable right. They are disaffected, that the most solemn treaties of the United States should be nullified by the extension of the laws of Georgia over the Cherokee nation, by which, the Missionaries, free citizens of the North, were thrown into prison, and there kept contrary to law, and in disregard of the Supreme Court of the Union. They are aggrieved at the cause and progress of the Florida war, by which forty millions of dollars have been taken from the hard earnings of the people,—by which many thousand valuable lives have been sacrificed by disease and the Indian rifle—by which our national honor was tarnished in the employment of blood hounds, to drive the unoffending savages from the homes of their fathers, which were their rightful inheritance—all of which they attribute to the sole cause of saving runaway slaves from fleeing into those impassable swamps. They are solemnly of opinion, that of right, no new slave state could have been admitted into this Union. They believe that there is no good reason why slaves held as property should be represented in congress, to the exclusion of all other property, and that justice, as well as their own interest, calls for a change in the Constitution, so as to destroy this inequality. They are opposed to the continuance of slavery in the District of Columbia, and in the territories, and to the impunity of the coasting and the domestic slave trade. "Annex Texas," say they, "and slavery will acquire such strength as to destroy the remnant of liberty that yet lingers in the North and in the South." All these grievances they have reluctantly borne for the peace, harmony, and permanency of the Union, bought by the common blood of our ancestors. Should the south, now anew, violate the Constitution for the sole purpose of extending slavery, they are not true descendants of the men of Lexington and Bunker's Hill, if they do not part from slavery and its ruinous consequences at once and for ever. And because I will not shut my eyes to the danger which threatens us with immediate dissolution—because I dare to speak fearlessly the truth : holding with Jefferson, that there is no error so dangerous that it may not be successfully combated with reason and argument—because I will not, for popular favor, prove a renegade from the faith of my ancestors—because I will not, for the sake of office and political promotion, prostitute myself to the basest and most dishonorable purposes, by denying in public, what, in private, every one who is not a madman, daily acknowledges to be utterly false, that "slavery is a blessing,"—because I am willing to allow that the six hundred thousand free white citizens of this commonwealth have some rights as well as we slave-holders, I am to be run down as an abolitionist, and the ban of the empire is to be denounced against me. I cannot write an answer to a complimentary letter from Mr. GIDDINGS, of Ohio, but I am published throughout the land as an enemy to my country. And when, in the New York Tribune, I set forth my true position, and in the defence of which I challenge both North and South to shake me, my letter is denied publication in the presses of both political parties; and yet still goes on the eternal prating about the *freedom of the press;* sycophantic speeches are daily poured into the ears of the *dear people, whilst that same people are barred by despotic intolerance from receiving any light by which they can know their rights, and free themselves from the competition of slave labor, which brings ignorance and beggary to their doors.* I appeal to mankind against such fiendish injustice. If public opinion be indeed omnipotent, then let its thunders strike terror into the faithless sentinels on the watch-tower of liberty—the false prophets who have basely usurped the tripods of the press.* To say that I am an aboli-

---

* NOTE.—Rotteck, the profound historian of the world says :

"It is far more difficult to *maintain* liberty than to acquire it. It may be gained by a momentary elevation, by the power of transient enthusiasm ; but it can be maintained only by constant exertion and virtue, harmony, vigilance, and the *hard victory over selfishness.*" Speaking of the first *censure of the press,*

tionist, in the sense in which the enemies of all moral progress would have you believe, that I would sanction insurrection and massacre: my wife, children, mother, brothers and sisters, and relations and friends are all hostages for my sincerity, when restraining myself to the use of courteous terms, I repel the unjust and dishonoring imputation. That I am an abolitionist in the sense, that I would take away, without just compensation, the rights of property in slaves, which the laws secure to me and to some thirty or forty thousand citizens of Kentucky, my letter to the Tribune which is before the world disproves.

Still, sir, I am an abolitionist. Such an abolitionist as I have been from my boyhood—such an abolitionist as I was in 1835, when I declared in my place in the House of Representatives to which I was just then eligible, that if the Constitution did not give us power to protect ourselves against the infernal slave trade, that I renounced it, and would appeal to a Convention for a new one. Such an abolitionist as I was again in 1840, when I declared in the same House of Representatives, that I wished to place the State of Kentucky in such a position, by sustaining the law of 1833, that she could move at any time she thought it conducive to her highest interest, to free herself from slavery. Such an abolitionist as I have ever avowed myself in public speeches and writings to the people of this district, that if Kentucky was wise enough to free herself from the counsels of pro-slavery men, that slavery would perish of itself by the voluntary action of masters and the irresistible force of circumstances which would convince the people to the use of free, instead of slave labor, as every way most advantageous. Such an abolitionist as were the band of immortal men who formed the Federal Constitution, who would not have the word "slave" in that sacred instrument, am I. Such an abolitionist as was Washington, who, so far from lending countenance to the propagation of slavery, as you are now doing, declared that

---

he cannot subdue his indignation to the usual historical denunciation, but he thus breaks forth: "Pope Alexander VI., the most detestable of all tyrants, first established it. Curse on his memory! The press is to words what the tongue is to thoughts. Who will constrain the tongue to ask permission for the word it shall speak, or forbid the soul to generate thoughts? *What should be free and sacred if not the press?*"

The New York Tribune has gained an enviable fame, by maintaining the true freedom of the press in America.

on all proper occasions, his influence and his vote should be cast for the extinguishment of slavery among men, am I also. Such an abolitionist as was Jefferson, the great father of democracy, whom you all profess to follow, who foretold what has since partially come to pass, that slavery, if not destroyed, would jeopardize and finally extinguish the liberties of the whites themselves: who foresaw, with an unerring glance, that the slavery of the black race, if not remedied by the whites, would at last remedy itself, such an abolitionist am I also. And being such, I take issue with the opinion, which has been here to-day, as it has been often elsewhere, most dogmatically advanced, that the question is, "whether the whites shall rule the blacks, or the blacks shall rule the whites." Such an assumption is false in theory, false in practice, and so proven to be false by all experience. It is derogatory to human nature and blasphemy against God himself.

All America, except Brazil and the United States, have freed their slaves; and are the whites slaves in consequence? At the Revolution, on the day of the Declaration of Independence, all the states held slaves, not excepting Massachusetts. Now, there are thirteen non-slaveholding states; are those ten millions of Northerners slaves? Great Britain, in conjunction with all Europe, except the miserable anarchies of Spain and Portugal, has long since emancipated many slaves, and now, in the year 1843, to her honor be it spoken, having liberated thirty millions of her East India serfs, in all her wide domains which touch on every sea, and embrace every clime under the whole Heavens, there is not, nor indeed can be, a single slave: and is she enslaved? No, she has sense enough to know, and heart enough to feel that it is justice, honor, and glory, which secure the liberties of a people, and make them invincible and immortal.

Do gentlemen take the absurd position, that one hundred and eighty thousand freed men could enslave Kentucky? West India emancipation proves that the great majority of freed men could be employed economically in the same offices at small wages, which they now fill, with, perhaps, more ease and safety than now exist. But should they prove turbulent, for which there would be no cause, and which no man in his senses believes would happen, and were I disposed to indulge in that vaunting spirit, which, to-day, has so powerfully infected us:

with five thousand such troops as those I have the honor to command, to whom gentlemen have been pleased to allude in a manner so complimentary, at my expense, I would undertake to drive from the state the assembled one hundred and eighty thousand in arms. They further tell us, with most reverential gravity, that "God has designed some men for slaves, and man need not attempt to reverse the decree: it is better that the blacks should be slaves, than the whites." This proposition, which I denounce as utterly false, passes away before the glance of reason, as the dew before a summer's sun.

I shall admit, merely for the sake of argument, that some men always have, and possibly will perform menial offices for the more fortunate. Let the law of nature or of God, have its undisturbed action—let the performance of those offices be voluntary on the part of servants, and that beautiful harmony by which the highest intellect is united, by successive inferior links to the lowest mind, will never be disturbed. The sensitive and highly organized, the intellectual, will gradually rise from servitude to command: the stolid, the profligate, the insensible, and coarsely organized will sink into their places: the law of God and enlightened freedom will still be preserved, and the greatest good to the greatest number be secured for ever. But when, by municipal law, and not by the law of fitness, which is the law of nature, not regarding the distinctions of morals, mind, or body, whole classes are doomed to servitude: when the intellectual, the sensitive, the foolish, the rude, the good, the bad, the refined, the degraded, are all depressed to one level, never more to rise forever ; then comes evil, nothing but evil, like as from dammed up waters, or pent up steam, floods and explosions come slowly, but come at last—so nature mocks with temporary desolation, at the obstacles man would oppose to her progress, and at length, moves on once more in all the untrammeled vigor and unfading loveliness which, from eternity, was decreed. That the black is inferior to the white, I readily allow ; but that vice may depress the one, and virtue, by successive generations, elevate the other, till the two races meet on one common level, I am also firmly convinced. Modern science, in the breeding and culture of other animals than man, has most fully proved this fact, which the ablest observers of man himself, all allow, that mental, and moral, and physical development transmit their several properties to the descendants—corroborating by experience, the divine decree, that the virtues and the vices of the father shall be visited on the children, to the third and fourth generation. In the capitals of Europe, blacks have attained to the highest places of social and literary eminence. That they are capable of a high degree of civilization, Hayti daily illustrates. There we have lately seen a revolution, conducted in a manner that would do honor to the first people on earth : one of the avowed grounds of which was, that President Boyer neglected to secure general education to the people, a consideration that should make some of the states blush in comparison. After the expulsion of the tyrant they set about forming a more republican Constitution, admitting the whites who had participated in their dangers and success, into all the rights of citizenship. If history be true, we owe to the Egyptians, said to be the modern Moorish race, the arts and sciences, and our early seeds of civilization. How many centuries did it take to bring them to perfection? When we reflect how little time the negro race has been under the influences of other civilized nations, and the rapid progress they have made in an upward direction, we have no reason to treat them with that absurd contempt, which, in both the eye of reason and religion, stands equally condemned. Why then, I am taunted by both pro-slavery and anti-slavery men, do I hold slaves? Uninfluenced by the opinions of the world, I intend in my own good time to act or not to act, as to me seems best in view of all the premises. Yet, I thus far pledge myself, that whenever Kentucky will join me in freeing ourselves from this curse, which weighs us down even unto death, the slaves I own, she shall dispose of as to her seems best. I shall ask nothing in return, but the enhanced value of my land which must ensue gradually from the day that we become indeed a free and independent state. I will go yet further, give me *free labor*, and I will not only give up my slaves, but I will agree to be taxed to buy the remainder from those who are unwilling or unable consistently, with a regard to pecuniary interest, to present them to the state, and then I shall deem myself and my posterity richer in dollars and cents even, than we were before.

But I return from this digression. We are told that England almost surrounds us, and that if we do not break away from her fatal grasp, our days are numbered ; and to excite our patriotic indignation we hear the taunt, that by our last treaty, territory was lost, and the country betrayed! Indeed! and where then

were the swords which to-day are so restless in their scabbards ?
where were your indignation meetings, your chivalric defiance,
your patriotic ardor ?   If we must meet England, let's meet her
in defence of our western border : there let us vindicate our sul-
lied honor : there, battling in the name of liberty and the right,
let us not doubt for a moment on whose standard victory will
perch.   But no ! you don't want to fight England.   In Oregon
are no titles in lands to be confirmed, no bonds to be redeemed,
no plunder to be indulged, no slavery to be perpetuated.   When
miserable Mexico, exhausted by revolutionary and civil wars,
was inundated by armed troops from the United States, marching
from our very cities in open day, with colors flying, led on by
land-mongers and bond-speculators, to violate the neutrality of
a country at peace with us—whilst she protested and implored
us by the ties of republican sisterhood to spare her—we answered her entreaties and just complaints by sending Gen.
Gaines into (if necessary) her very borders, under pretence of
guarding our own country, but in fact to aid in the rescue of
Texas from the invading foe.   But when the Canadians, inspired by sentiments of true liberty, invoked the God of battles
and the sympathies of nations to her rescue from the British crown
—that Britain, who we are now told, is about to seal us up herme-
tically—that Britain, with whom we had two exasperating wars
—that Britain, whom the gentlemen so much denounce,—dared
to come into the borders of the United States, and to cut out an
American vessel lying in our own town—and to destroy the
lives of American citizens, resting under the folds of the broad
banner of the stars and stripes.   And when McLeod, one of the
perpetrators of the deed, was taken in our border, where he had
tauntingly intruded himself, and held to answer for the murder,
this same haughty Britain, defyingly assumed the responsibility, demanded his unconditional release, and denounced war as
the consequence of refusal.

Where, then—where, I ask once more, was that military fervor which to-day would hurry us to battle ?   You heard not,
then, the blood of our brother, crying to us, from the ground, for
vengeance !   Silent as the still waters which had for ever closed
over our murdered countryman, you opened not your mouth !
Aye, more yet—your Major-General was sent in hot haste to the
northern border, not like Gaines, to enter into the enemy's country,
but to keep the peace at home, lest England might not bear with

your pitiable humility.   Your Attorney-General was hurried off
to New York, to guard, with all the inviolability of a great national officer, McLeod from harm.   Your Secretary continued to
write frequent and explanatory letters to the British Minister,
anxiously protesting that the laws of New York would no doubt
release the prisoner after trial, which the General Government,
if they had the power, would immediately do.   All this we had
to bear, not because we were not indignant, not because we regarded ourselves as in the wrong, not because whether right or
wrong, at other times, we would not have hung McLeod as high
as Haman.   No—it was because we were unprepared, utterly
unprepared for war ; that although England stood single-handed
against us, we pocketed the insult and the injury, and at last
released the prisoner.   And now, when these ten millions of
northerners—they who cast our cannons, build and man our
navy—who make our swords and munitions of war—who are
capable of inventing more infernal machines than ever the de-
mon of war has yet dreamed of, and who have the iron nerve to use
them—now, when they are not only not for us, but against us—
now, when we are opposed, not to England single-handed, but to all
Christendom, united with Mexico—now, when we are in a worse
state of defence than before—now, in a manifestly bad cause,
where we are losers, whether we stand or fall—now we are to
be hurried into the miserable policy, only worthy of madmen,
of seizing on Texas, and waging a general war !   For one, I
dare not, I will not do it.   I pray you to consider this matter
yet a little while longer : sleep on it a few nights, if sleep you
can—scrutinize the admonitions of an unerring conscience—see
if it be a cause that you can pray for—a cause upon the justice
of which you dare invoke the dread arbitrament of the God of
battles.   If it be not, desert it now and for ever—renew your
vows upon the desecrated altars of an injured country—spurn-
ing all party trammels, trample into dust the black flag of war,
slavery, and dissolution, and, from every house-top throughout
this boundless empire, let there be thrown out, once more, the
soul-cheering banner—"Liberty and Union, one and insepara
ble, now and for ever."

SPEECH,

Against the Annexation of Texas to the United States, delivered in Lexington, Kentucky, on the 13th day of May, 1844, in reply to THOMAS F. MARSHALL.

[THOMAS F. MARSHALL having addressed for three hours a large and attentive audience, in an impassioned and eloquent manner, in favor of the immediate annexation of Texas to the United States, C. M. CLAY replied substantially as follows :]

I am not insensible, men of Fayette, of the hard task which I have voluntarily imposed upon myself. I have often witnessed, as you have done, the powerful influence which the honorable gentleman who has just addressed you never fails to exercise over a popular audience ; and I frankly admit, that I should have much preferred that some one more able than myself should have undertaken the vindication of the cause which I now advocate ; but since no one has thought fit to enter the lists, I could not consent to sit still when measures of such a ruinous character were urged, without raising my feeble voice in solemn protest against a scheme which I cannot regard otherwise than revolutionary, mad, and fatal to my country.

The gentleman has not anticipated me as he supposes, and I regret that he has thought it necessary to refer to my anti-slavery opinions, which may indeed prejudice me in the consideration of this audience, but which are not at all necessary to a triumphant vindication of the integrity of "the Union as it is." Nor do I come as the advocate of Henry Clay, or the whig party, with whom I and the gentleman have so long acted. No ! I stand here as a citizen of Kentucky, and of the United States, a southerner in birth, association and feeling, and united irrevocably in the destiny which awaits us all in common ; yet I trust that if I know myself, I shall this night rise superior to the trammels of party, and feel and speak only as an American, not knowing the faint lines of separation between Whig and Democrat, or the more miserable distinction between the North and the South. I shall not say that the gentleman is influenced by motives less elevated than these; yet I cannot but regret that he has till this late hour withheld his light from the people, and now, when both the great party leaders have denounced this project, that he should, upon the eve of an exciting national election, press it upon the consideration of the country, when the public mind is so little prepared for issues of such overwhelming interest. And allow me here to return my thanks to Martin Van Buren for the high stand he has taken in behalf of our national honor, and to commend that greatness of soul which, for the first time nascent in this well-drilled partizan, has enabled him to break away from the dishonoring shackles which some of his party seemed over-ready to impose upon him.

The gentleman has with a most vivid imagination portrayed the beauties and fertility of Texas; he has spread out the map of the world before us,* and holding up the plunder and conquests of other nations, he hopes to lull our consciences, whilst he stimulates in us a taste for rapine. I profess not to be learned in geography, or history, yet, as I glance my eye over this scene of the world's history, I am forced to confess, that I see nothing in the eventful changes of past times to encourage, but much to deter us from the extension of boundary; more especially, when that extension is founded upon rapine and injustice. I have read in my school-boy days of objects yet more lovely than Texas, painted, as she has been, with all the artist's skill, which the gentleman possesses in so eminent a degree. Here lies, in the Mediterranean sea, the petty peninsula of Laconia, a mere spot on the wide waste of waters; there, in the midst of Asia Minor, the most fertile and once the most wealthy portion of the world, the prolific mother of nations, was the site of the world-renowned Troy, embracing I know not how much of territory, men, and military strength. Her proud and God-defying prince, yielding to those unlawful passions of stimulated desire which the gentleman would foster to-day, seized on the lovely bride of Sparta's monarch, and bore her in secure triumph, as he vainly supposed, into the brazen walls of his time-honored city. The contemptible hill-bound city of Sparta at once grew strong in the pressure of her wrongs: in the name of outraged humanity, violated hospitality, and omnipotent justice, she summoned to her standard the gallant spirits of other lands, and

---

* Mr. M. spoke with the Map of the World before him.

invoking the avenging Gods, and inexorable destiny, she carried fire and the sword to the very citadel of this vaunted den of robbers. The rude home of Menelaus yet blooms amid its waste of woods and hills, eternal in the memory of men; the antiquarian searches in vain for any traces of the golden palaces and silken bed-chambers of the dishonoring and dishonored Paris. Here on this other neighboring peninsula stood Athens; by brilliant talents, and lofty public virtue, she rose to an eminence which vast territories and unjust conquest could not confer upon the proudest nations of the world. Already the first naval power in the world, and standing in prowess at the head of confederated Greece—having part of the continent and many isles of the sea tributary to her—she was not yet satisfied; in the Isle of Sicily, the granary of the Mediterranean, she saw another Texas, necessary, as her demagogues would have her believe, to her lasting glory and secure existence; unhappily, she forgot to ask herself, not what she wanted, but to what she had a right! Under the walls of Syracuse the best blood of Athens was shed, her fleet was destroyed, and with it passed away the glory and independence of the Athenians.

The Turk now keeps watch in the Acropolis of Athens: the tread of slaves is heard along the Piræus: and the plains of Marathon and the names of Salamis are forgotten. Here lies Macedon, a first-rate empire when all her energies were constrained within her natural boundaries, but when she poured her troops in fiery floods of conquest over the greater portion of Europe, Asia, and Africa, her blood sank down into barren sands, and she that lived by the sword also perished for ever.

Shall I speak of the Persian, the Roman, the Mongolian, the Goth, the Celt, the Frank, the Hun, all wasting themselves in vain and empty conquests—meeting in quick and dread succession the same doom by them imposed upon others? It were a useless repetition of the same oft-told tale, that the *unjust* thing, lingering out a forced existence for years, till men of limited vision took courage and denied the existence of God himself, and impartial retribution, shall utterly perish and pass away at last. Come to this, boasted Spain, herself—reaching from sea to sea, the mistress of Europe and the monopolizer of continents—here, within these narrow bounds, not so large as Texas even, she grew to be the first power in Europe; but the date of her conquests was the beginning of her downfall; not all the gold of

Mexico and Peru could satisfy her crimes, nor the chivalric valor and romantic glory of a Cortes and a Pizzaro shield her from the retributive sword and the vengeance and the contempt of nations. In these lawless conquests, though sanctioned by the desecrated majesty of Israel's God, in the impious decrees of the Pope, the seeds of anarchy, misrule, and contempt for all those obligations, which from the days of chaos and night to the nineteenth century of the Christian era, have ever been recognized by the wise among men, were broadly sown ; go now among her revolutionary hordes and remorseless bandits and see the mature fruit.

I am not so sure that England—England, the gentleman's everlasting raw head and bloody bones, his dread object of hatred, envy, and fear, his epilectic fit, that maddens him with convulsions, and turns the kindly currents of humanity and brotherhood into floods of passion, vengeance, and blood—I am by no means sure that England is not upon the eve of some great catastrophe in consequence of her very great extension, not unlike those which history has so often in trumpet tones uttered in vain. I dare venture the assertion that a nation may grow too great for the government of a single intellect; and such is the nature of mind that when a certain degree of talent is called for in the history of a nation and cannot be found, then also will a combination of secondary talent strive in vain to master the destinies of a people. I implore you, then, my countrymen, be not deceived by these fatal allurements which are held out to move us from our integrity ; for while you have followed me in this hasty review of the decline and fall of empires, you cannot fail to perceive, if you have given ear to the dread revelations of history, that the beginning of decay comes from a vain-glorious spirit, resulting in injustice and rapine ; ever forgetful that they who sow the wind shall reap the whirlwind ! It seems to me that the nature of human society is overlooked entirely by gentlemen ; the object of all association is mutual protection, and when a nation has grown strong enough to protect herself, comparing her strength and numbers and territory with the other nations, what more can be done ? Have we reached that point ? Having stood against England in two wars, with less than twelve millions of people, and possessing territory, with a population less dense than that of England and France, capable of maintaining more than one hundred millions of people, possessing all the minerals, soils, and vegetables, and climes of the globe, I say we are large enough; we have all the elements of greatness, security, and independence; it is avarice, madness, and crime to seek more. Here, sir, in the midst of the changes and desolations of nations, for ages, is the little, gallant, and independent Switzerland—contented with her poverty, her freedom, and her mountain home, she has turned no lascivious eye upon the rich lowlands which woo her descent on every side; seeking no conquests, she has successfully resisted all aggression—she has ventured to be just, and the world stands awed in her presence. Clinging to the highest attribute of Deity, she feels sure of His omnipotence, standing eternal as the basis of her hills. Let us, too, listen to that voice which, whether by sage, in caves and forests wild, and on ocean's waves and earth's secret places, wrested from unwilling nature, or coming in paternal tones of security and love through divine revelation, speaks alike to individuals and nations, and bids us "be just and fear not!"

The gentleman holds us up the map and presents us the hideous and deformed step of Texas obtruding herself into the harmonious valley of the Mississippi, and marring the beauty and arrondissement of the empire, claiming the waters of the Mississippi and all its tributaries as ours. Here also lie the British possessions south of the St. Lawrence, marring the beauty of the map, thus: dare he extend his rule there also? Oh no, the British lion slumbers upon the banks of the St. John's, and the gentleman, with all his boasted gallantry, is not the man to "lay him by the beard."

Whilst we look on this picture, let us not forget that it is but the body of the nation: the nobler, better part, beams out in its glorious deeds and its undoubted good name. From the hour of our existence to the present time, we hold no land by conquest or rapine. Justice and good faith have marked our intercourse with all nations; I shall not be the first to sully the purity of my country's escutcheon.

We are told of the long line of border which exposes us to savage warfare and foreign incursion on the West: and Texas must be seized to shorten this border, and diminish the necessity of defensive outposts. Now, sir, I utterly deny the proposition. It is the established doctrine of European policy, that the safest border, next to an impassable waste, for one nation, is the inter-

position of a weak nation. If this be true, and who will doubt
it? for Mexico and Britain could not strike us till they had thrust
Texas through the side, what better barrier could we have than
Texas on the south; and especially as a shield from savage incursion?   For Texas would fear our power when unexerted,
and be at peace by treaty and interest; but the savage, who
knows no law but force, actually pressing upon his existence,
would only be kept at bay by continual war. I say, then, that
Texas, at her own expense, as an independent government, or
as a Mexican province, guards us from the mouth of the Sabine
to its source, and thence to the Red River: then come the
wastes of the volcanic soil of Western Arkansas, the best frontier a nation could have. But take in Texas, and so far from
diminishing our frontier, you give us twelve degrees of latitude
to guard, running from the Rio del Norte, in twenty-six, to latitude thirty-eight, north, being about one thousand miles on a
parallel of longitude, and near fifteen hundred following the Rio
del Norte—along the whole space of which we should have to
keep up defences, to us now uncalled for, against the untold
thousands of savage warriors, who have already held our nation
at bay in Florida, and be exposed to the attacks of Mexico from
the thousand streams which flow east through a fertile country
to the Rio del Norte; the worst possible, instead of the best border for a nation. So that, as a question of border and defence,
I strip the gentleman of every foot of ground upon which he has
entrenched himself.

I declare to you, my countrymen, that throughout the long
and impassioned speech which we have heard, there has been
but one argument of any force urged, to which all the others
indeed have been merely subsidiary, and that is this, "If we
don't take Texas, Britain will." I will not call this the robber
argument, as this has been protested against, but I will say that
it is this much: Sir stranger! you are traveling in a dangerous
wood, you are among thieves, if I don't take your purse, some
one else will, so stand and deliver, or else I will knock you on
the head and help myself. For two long hours this haughty
power has been held up to our distrustful gaze: and neither
geography, history, nor eloquence, spared in portraying the net
which she is spreading for us.

We are told of her eternal policy of conquest by arms and
diplomacy—her world-wide power is drawn in giant outline

before us—she, not satisfied with the greater portion of the old
world, already holds more land than any other nation on this
continent—she runs along our whole northern border, in Oregon and on the little island of Vancouver—she has traveled
around Cape Horn, traversing two seas to take a point of attack
on our western border, and then getting hold on the soil of
Texas, she will extend her sway through Mexico to the Carri-
bean sea—she will cut off the outlet between Cuba and South
America, and seizing on Cuba, block the Florida stream, and
shut us up in the Gulf of Mexico—and passing through Texas
to Oregon, meeting her forces on Vancouver's isle, she will "rein
us in" on the west, and like an old spider with a fly in her web,
she will devour us at her leisure.

With all due respect for the gentleman's facts and logic, I
must say, that this splendid array of English policy is based
upon his own vivid imagination, and on that only. She borders
on the north, 'tis true, yet it cannot be supposed that she can
long hold supremacy there over her own colonies; and some of
her ablest statesmen have debated in Parliament the propriety
of not waiting for a revolution, but of giving up peaceably a
colony which destiny decrees to be free. It is not necessary for
England to pass through Texas and round through Mexico and
Columbia, to command the pass between Cuba and South
America. Does not the gentleman know that England already
owns several of the small islands lying in the straits of which
he speaks; and so far as it is possible for her in any event to
shut us in by her navy she already does so now?

As to Cuba, we have already declared that she shall not hold
it, except we are first prostrated by arms. This voice, efficiently
coming from us, when we were several millions weaker than we
are now, does any man here suppose that England would dare
now to take Cuba, when we are still more strengthened for the
strife? The geographer just read with so much interest has
told us that the whole coast of Texas is not gifted with a single
harbor capable of affording anchorage, fit for vessels of war.
But she is bordered from the Sabine to the Rio del Norte with
shallow lagoons, which will hardly ever hold a first-rate war
steamer, and this, the gentleman himself well knows. And
were it otherwise, where would be the propriety of passing by
land three hundred miles through an unprovisioned country
from Texas to the Mississippi, when she could any day by a

ruse burn New-Orleans ? Such a track of attack, giving us time to pour our troops, from the Aroostook to the lakes, as well as from the whole valley of the Mississippi, upon her as soon as she touched the Mississippi, is unheard of in the history of war and utterly idle and absurd. The idea of passing through Texas two thousand miles to the Columbia, and then three thousand miles over the Rocky Mountains, one thousand of which is incapable of subsisting an army, being almost barren, covered with prickly pear, and deserted by the beasts of the forest even, is the most Quixotic anticipation that these prolific lands have yet bred to startle the credulity of a wonder-loving people. I say then, that the whole fabric of the gentleman's argument tumbles to the ground.

The remarks of Lord Brougham in the House of Lords have no weight with me as to the policy of England. We all know the embarrassment which the opposition in this country, as well as in England, throws in the way of the government ; but here I have Lord Aberdeen's declaration, made to Mr. Everett, which is conclusive as to the policy of England with regard to Texas.

[Mr. Clay here read from Lord Aberdeen's statements to Mr. Everett.]

Now then, England has gone further than she need to have gone, and to strip us of all excuse for seizing Texas, she has declared to the world her intention, " to *continue* to treat Texas as an independent power." Not only so, but if this be not enough, I stand by the gentleman in saying to England and the world, let Texas alone. This is a quarrel between Mexico and Texas, the United States will not permit other nations to interfere. And if, as the gentleman supposes, there is a fixed destiny that these two great nations, England and America, brothers, and joint depositors of constitutional liberty among men, are running a course of rivalry, which leads at last to collision, and the ultimate ruin of the one or the other—a proposition which every idea I have, of God and nature, utterly repudiates—I say I should not make haste to seize on Texas, a vacant club which will be used to bruise our heads, but I should not only let her seize the club, but strike the first damning blow, which, like that of Cain, would eternally ostracise her from the fellowship of humanity. Ay, sir, I would have her, if we must fight her, palpably in the wrong—as much in the wrong as we would be, were we now to seize on Texas, on any such miserable pretence of dread necessity as this! I would have inscribed on our banner once more that sentiment which rallied us in 1776, and was the strength of our arms, "right against might." This robber argument was not the argument of the revolution : the man who grew immortal in that contest, who had more at stake in our continued independence and glory than all here present, gave no such miserable advice as this. Looking at those universal and immortal principles which have governed the world from the beginning, he solemnly warned us to do right, that we might suffer no wrong.

As I stand here this night—as I love my country, and would leave her a safe depository of all that I would not have perish with me, I would say to you, do no wrong, that your spirits may be calm in the hour of trial, and your nerves strong in the day of battle. I cannot but admire the ingenuity of the gentleman, in mixing up Oregon with this Texas annexation. He has gilded the pill that we may swallow it—disturbed the water that he may catch his prey ; for while I am ready for Oregon, if it *be ours*, as I believe it is, to fight to the death, so I am free to avow that nothing short of the alternatives of slaveholding or personal dishonor could induce me to make an aggressive war for Texas, which is *not ours*.

The most important objection to this annexation, the breach of treaty existing with Mexico, has been overlooked, and as there seems to be (judging from the public press), a very slight appreciation of treaty obligation among our people, I shall read a few clauses from celebrated writers upon this subject. First, a word upon the glory of a nation. Vattel says : "True glory is the favorable opinion of men of wisdom and discernment : it is acquired by virtue, or the qualities of the mind and the affections, and by the great actions that are the fruits of these virtues." "It is then of great advantage to a nation to establish its glory and reputation." And this is done "by virtue," not by unjust extension of border. Again. "It is shown by the law of nature, that he who has made a promise to any one, has conferred upon him a true right to require the thing promised ; and that consequently, not to keep a perfect promise, is to violate the right of another : and is as manifest an injustice, as that of depriving a person of his property. All the tranquillity, the happiness and security of the human race rests on justice ; on the obligation of paying a regard to the rights of others." "Nations and their conductors ought then to keep their promises and their treaties inviolable. This great truth, though too often neglected in practice, is generally acknowledged by all nations ; the reproach of perfidy is esteemed by sovereigns a most atrocious injury ; now he who does not observe his treaty, is certainly perfidious, since he violates his faith.' Not satisfied with his treatment of the subject once, in another place he returns to it again, " Who can doubt that treaties are in the number of those things that are held sacred among nations ? They determine the most important affairs; they give rules to the pretensions of sovereigns ; they ought to make known the rights of nations, and to secure their most precious interests." "The faith of treaties, that firm and sincere resolution, that invaluable constancy in fulfilling engagements, of which declaration is made in a treaty, is then holy and sacred between the nations, whose safety and repose it secures : and if people would not be wanting to themselves, infamy would ever be the share of him who violates his faith." Chancellor Kent, the greatest jurist of modern times, says in his Commentaries : " The violation of a treaty of peace, or other national compact, is a violation of the law of nations, for it is a breach of public faith." "No nation can violate public law, without being subjected to the penal consequences of reproach and disgrace, and without incurring the hazard of punishment to be inflicted in open solemn war by the injured party." And this, Mexico has in the most public and formal manner declared she will do in case we annex Texas, which she claims as part of her territory, and which we have acknowledged so to be, by a solemn treaty on our part, containing promises of perpetual amity and good offices, besides an acknowledgment of boundary.

Let us beware then, how we incur the imputation of bad faith, lest like the Carthaginians, we become a bye-word among nations ; as slaveholders and repudiators of debts, we are already well nigh infamous in Christendom, let no new title of bad eminence be branded upon us. Nor let us, because Mexico is weak, rest secure in our strength, for no man knows what allies she may bring into the field. And even if not a single sword is thrust into the sides of my countrymen, our commerce may be cut up by privateers of all nations, sailing under Mexican colors, who are hungry from the long peace of the world for slaughter and

plunder. But even if no physical injury should await our perfidy, should not a generous magnanimity and a becoming shame
restrain us from seizing on Texas, under a pretence of protection
from England, whilst we gave up to Lord Ashburton a military
pass-way from the colonies South of the St. Lawrence to the
Canadas, when the very object avowed was warlike security,
and when the land yielded, was voted by a unanimous Senate
to be ours—indisputably ours.

That a corrupt press should use the argument that because
Texas was once ours (which is, however, by no means certain)*
it should be now taken again by us, in spite of treaty obligation,
I was not surprised ; but for one who aspires, here in the city
of Lexington, and in the county of Fayette, to lead and give
tone to public sentiment, to adduce this consideration to influence
us, I must say with all respect to the gentleman, is unworthy
of him ; [here Mr. Marshall interposed and remarked, that he
had no pretensions to be a leader] ; very rightly, for although no
man is more ready to acknowledge than I am the great interest
which the gentleman, with a gorgeous imagery and most captivating declamation, throws around any subject he discusses, yet,
indeed, it sometimes seems to be to him a matter of no importance which side he takes : and justice to the great interests now
at issue constrain me to say, that there is no man in Kentucky,
whose lead, in my estimation, it would be more difficult, as well
as more unsafe, to follow.   What is the substance of the argument ?   I sell you my watch for a fair equivalent ; to-morrow I
meet you on the street and say to you, this watch was once
mine, it suits me to regain it—peaceably if you will—forcibly
if I must ! Upon the same principle Spain may reclaim Florida ;
France, Louisiana ; England, the United Colonies ; and we
should be surprised on waking up some morning, to find ourselves pushed into the ocean, with not a foot of land to stand
upon ; and yet barred the glorious Anglo-American privilege of
even complaining ; for the gentleman's argument and precedent
would close our mouths in eternal silence.   It is equally vain to
tell us, that Texas having been acknowledged independent by
several nations, including the United States, we are thereby
relieved from all treaty obligations, and may lawfully acquire

---

* See a very able pamphlet styled " Thoughts on Texas :" New York. Supposed to be from the pen of T. Sedgwick.

her. It is and has been our habit to acknowledge the govern-ment *de facto ;* and the acknowledgment of the independence of Texas was therefore no breach of treaty, nor did Mexico so treat it; for I am not apprised that she made a single remon-strance through her ministers, who were at all the courts who admitted Texan independence. But she now declares that the seizure of Texas is a very different affair, depriving her of a province, which she deems herself (and which the world also knows she is) capable, if let alone, of recovering. And is Texas really independent? I say she is not. In the very treaty of armistice entered into lately, she admits herself by express lan-guage "the Department of Texas." General Washington, though a mere agent of the revolted colonies, and not a direct representative of the sovereignty of the states, refused to receive a letter from the enemy, unless it had the superscription giving him his title, as conferred by the congress : such is the caution, with which a power really independent guards, even in word, her independence and sovereign dignity. But even the misera-ble traitor and madman, now accidentally marring the honor and prosperity of these United States, as reckless as he is, has virtually acknowledged the supremacy of Mexico, by sending a minister there to buy Texas, giving blank millions of dollars as an equivalent. So that all things preclude the idea of Texan independence, and what we now do, we must do with the fullest light : and if we sin, then we sin without a shadow of excuse.

It is in vain for the gentleman to press the fact, that Mr. Clay wished to purchase Texas of Mexico, whilst Spain had not yet acknowledged her independence, for it is well known that Spain was utterly incapable of recovering her revolted colonies; and up to this time she is struggling for existence herself, in the midst of the wildest anarchy and the most frequent revolutions. The gentleman must remember that Mr. Clay's opinions were never carried into effect, and cannot therefore at all become a precedent ; for what a nation may actually do, and what some individual acting in a diplomatic station may wish her to do, are entirely different things ; and I cannot but regard the gen-tleman's supposititous precedent as a virtual abandonment of the whole ground which he once assumed, and it would be ungene-rous to attempt further to force him from this harmless retreat.

Having now considered this subject in its connexion with other nations and our foreign policy, a more important view remains to be taken of its influence upon ourselves as members of the American Union. And with regard to the annexation of Texas, if it did not violate public faith and bring on a ruinous war, it would be eminently injurious to the prosperity of the present states by carrying off our population and our capital. That England should seek to throw off from her over-filled hive her starving population, is both humane and economical. But it is our policy to encourage population, not to thin it out, for it is a plain proposition, that so long as we have more food than we can use, there is room for more mechanics, manufacturers, and artists ; and the greater the division of labor, the more perfection in art ; and the more of all the luxuries that civilization affords, the more comfort there will be among all classes, if there is an equitable division of the proceeds of labor. Let us simplify this idea. If a farmer be thrown upon a deserted isle, he might raise corn plentifully, and to spare, yet need clothing and shelter ; if a manufacturer of cloth and maker of clothes should come, he could give him grain for his clothing, and both would be gainers: having yet corn to spare, if a house carpenter should come, he could give another portion for a house, and be still a gainer. So one after another could all operatives advantageously be received till the isle refused to bring a surplus of corn : and this would be the limit, and the only limit, that would be placed on the farmer's enjoyments, as well as upon the necessaries and luxuries of all the occupants of the isle. Suppose under the system of culture the farmer had adopted, he had supplied himself with all the ordinary comforts of life ; but he yet lacked musicians, painters, and litterateurs, and other luxuries ; by a judicious invention of farming tools, and the application of suitable earths and manures, he might largely increase his corn crop, till he would be able to supply these new comers, and at last no luxury known to men would be wanting. Thus, I say, that the only limit to the wealth of a nation is the point at which the earth ceases to afford food for the consumption of its people : up to that point, every accession of population, with corresponding industry and division of trades is an absolute advantage to the whole community. America has not reached that point : she has not reached it by two centuries, and yet it is proposed in this treaty of the accidental President to pay ten millions of dollars as a premium to cause our own hearths to be desolated for the sake of building up Texas. It might well become us to pay our own debts before we undertake to assume the debts of the other states, who, by repudiation, have brought dishonor on our household. But what shall I say to those men who, denying the general government any power to rescue one of our own daughters from ruin, would levy a tax upon the hard earnings and exhausted resources of our people, to rescue this profligate child of a strange house from her self-willed abasement.

And it is not ten millions only, my countrymen, we are compelled to pay, but whatever Texas owes. For, I contend that no agreement between us and Texas, can in the least effect the just indebtedness of Texas; if we take her, we, like man and wife, become identified, and we must take her with all her incumbrances; and if her debt amounts to fifty millions we are bound it to pay. No principle of national law is better settled. For although the rule of Napoleon was revolutionary, and the subsequent dynasty so declared it null and void, yet France could not quit herself of the debts and responsibilities incurred during his reign, and under the threat of war from Andrew Jackson, the French indemnity was promptly paid. If, then, the subsequent government was bound for the debts of a dynasty which she repudiated, much more will America be bound for the debts of Texas, which is the same party that made the debt, still perpetuating its identity. I call upon every farmer and mechanic, and laborer, and professional man, here present, are you willing to be taxed for the benefit of the monopolizers of the lands of Texas, from which you receive so many injuries and losses, and from whose fields not a single orange or lemon, or pound of sugar will pass your lips without an ample equivalent? It is in vain to tell us that the public lands of Texas are pledged to the liquidation of the debt; for when you remember the extravagant grants of land held by individuals in Texas, embracing all the better portions of the country, and the millions of acres now in market in the United States, at low rates, is any one so mad as to believe that the whole burden of this debt will not fall immediately on us?

I have said this annexation was revolutionary. The powers of our government have been widely misconstrued; the state constitutions are vested with all power not reserved expressly to the people; but far different is the character of the national government. It is an instrument of limited powers, and all powers not expressly granted, are reserved to the people; it is a power of attorney, which they hold from the United States severally; when it acts it must show specific words for action, else its action is null and void. They who contend, then, for Texas, must either show that there is a specific power to annex it, or they must show that its annexation is "necessary and proper" for carrying into effect some other power specially granted. I defy the gentleman, with all his known ingenuity, to make out any such a case. What then becomes of the splendid eulogies upon constitutional liberty, which he has so often in times past poured pathetically into our ears? Nor can he find refuge in that clause of the constitution which allows the admission of new states into the Union, for Texas is not proposed to be admitted as a new state into the Union, but as a territory ; and it is by Congress, composed of a Senate and House of Representatives, that a new state is to be admitted, and not by the Senate and the President, as this treaty proposes. But even if Congress should undertake to admit it, there would be an equal assumption of power, for all the debates upon this subject, as reported by Mr. Madison, show that "new states" are meant to be the then territory of the United States, and not designed to include foreign nations. In the construction of instruments of limited powers, no rule is better ascertained by jurists, political and civil, than that the meaning of the words are not to be enlarged, but confined to the will of the grantors ; and when a latitudinarian construction is admissible by the words, and a close construction also, that construction is to be given which comports with the general design of the instrument. There is not a man in this house or in this country who believes that the founders of the Constitution anticipated any addition of foreign nations to this Union. I admit that the acquisition of territory may be had by treaty, for it is necessary to exercise sovereignty in the disputes to be settled between nations, and as no state has power to act in this capacity, it is manifestly a power belonging to the general government, arising from the clause giving "necessary powers."

When a controversy arises between nations about territory, they must either appeal to arms or to compromise; and it does often happen that it is more "proper" to buy or cede territory, than to appeal to arms. Thus the United States lately acquired and ceded territory in the Maine treaty. But these great state necessities must come up of themselves, the Senate has no right to make difficulties, in order to settle them.   And before Texas can be taken under the treaty-making power, it devolves upon its advocates to make out a plain and palpable case of necessity. This they have not, and indeed, men of Fayette, cannot do. The case of Louisiana was not parallel to this; yet he who made the treaty even denied its constitutionality.   I acquiesce in the past action of the nation; let Florida, and Louisiana, and Mississippi and Arkansas, and Missouri, receive all the security and blessings of our common constitution; but, at the same time I protest most solemnly against the precedent.   Here was the mouth of the Mississippi, our highway to the great ocean, blocked up by a people actually threatening by arms our egress and ingress.   No principle of national law is better settled than that a nation has a right of passage to the ocean, the highway of the world.   This was a real and urgent state necessity; its amicable settlement was only to be made by a final and entire occupancy.   Here the mighty Mississippi, bearing on its bosom the products of the larger portion of the empire, watering the most extensive and productive lands of any river under the wide Heavens, was barricaded at its mouth.   If we sailed securely through French batteries there, we met England in one of the straits of the Gulf, and Spain in the other, and were effectually blockaded once more.   I cannot, therefore, but rejoice, that Louisiana and Florida are ours.   In Pensacola and St. Augustine, we have two of the best ports on the southern portion of the continent; and in the quick descent of our armies from the St. John's to the Lake of the Woods, through the Mississippi, we may defy the world to the invasion of our southern coast, so long as we remain an united nation.   The precedent, then, fails—utterly fails!

A war now exists between Texas and Mexico.   The day that this treaty is consummated, we are at war also.   If the Senate and President can declare war, what a farce is your parchment of pompous restrictions and dialectical distinctions? In vain shall the power of the Senate and the House be separated, and the House only invested with the power of declaring war, if the Senate may, under the pretence of making a treaty, knowingly plunge us into war—*bellum flagrans.*   If you sit silently by, and suffer all this, men of Fayette, in vain was the war of '76.   If we have not secured constitutional liberty, then have we obtained no liberty at all.   If we have gained nothing by the representative system, by employing agents to carry out our wills in a prescribed manner, then have we gained nothing over the fallen republics of antiquity—if we are at the mercy of the caprice of a single President and fifty-two Senators, then are we slaves indeed, and may no longer boast of, but weep over our Colonial separation !   If the Senate may unite a nation to us to-day, she may unite us to a nation to-morrow, and merge our very nationality into the first despotism which shall be able to insinuate gold enough into their pockets to outweigh the patriotism in their bosoms.   Yes, be assured that this is indeed a revolutionary movement, despotic in its character, and fatal in its results ; we are unmindful of the illustrious dead, suicidal to ourselves, and damned in the estimation of posterity, if we slavishly bow our necks to the yoke !

The gentleman has not acted with his wonted magnanimity in alluding to slavery ; he has already too many personal advantages over me, to avail himself of any supposed unpopularity which may attach to me on account of my opinions upon this subject.   I flatter myself that I am able to maintain my position, irrespective of any aid arising from this source : but if the time and occasion were suitable, I should not fear to meet the gentleman upon this broad ground.   He has not allowed me to forget that we once stood upon the same principles ; the letters of that gentleman to the Commonwealth in denunciation of slavery, have given him more reputation than all the other acts of his life summed up together.   If we are now found moving in divergent paths, let the world say who has deserted the high way of right and enlightened patriotism.

I trust that I shall never shrink from the stern and unwilling duties which an elevated love of country shall impose upon me. I shall not at one time indulge in honeyed tones of an exalted philanthropy and a self-sacrificing patriotism, to please the ear of mankind, but when the day of action comes, by my weight and influence deny the sincerity of my purpose.   I shall not undertake to denounce the gentleman, but I cannot forget the graphic description of the lamentable evils which he attributed to the introduction of slavery into the South, and his concluding "curse on the tyrant hand that planted this dark plague spot upon her virgin bosom."   Let him render not to me, but to that God whose curse he has to-day denounced in an opposite direction, an account, for his instrumentality in now attempting to plant this same "*damning curse*" on the unborn millions of Texas. If slavery was denounced by God on Ham and his descendants, then the blacks are not the legitimate inheritors of the curse, for, from the beginning of the world to the year 1442, Europe, at least, was free from negro slavery. Not till 1503 were blacks seen in America. If the curse of God in this respect rests upon any portion of mankind, then, till within the last three centuries, it rested only upon the whites ; for up to that period the larger portion of the slaves of the world were whites. But I scorn to repel such an argument, better worthy of some cunning priest of the dark ages, than creditable to a statesman of the nineteenth century. I have formed no such degrading idea of God as this. My reason and observation teach me another lesson.

I look abroad over all harmonious and lovely nature, and conclude that God has willed the enjoyment of all animated beings, and that he has provided room enough for even the black to enjoy "liberty and the pursuit of happiness."

There is no portion of history that fills me with such feelings of solemn and despairing interest, as when the Athenians, indulging a most fatal indolence and self-delusion appropriated those revenues which sustained her navy and made her illustrious in Greece, to theatrical amusements and idle shows, and denounced death upon any man who should dare to propose a law to restore them to the cause of the country, and the re-establishment of the glory of her name. Though Philip surrounded her with armed battalions, and traitors infested her inmost sanctuaries, and gave the sanction of the betrayed Gods to the ruin of their country—the patriots of Athens looked on the impenetrable phalanx that was about to crush them to powder, and could not open their mouths to arouse their countrymen from their fatal security and apply the remedy that wooed them to touch and to live.

I cannot, I will not, I dare not, submit to this morbid sensibility upon the subject of slavery, which strips us of our strength, and delivers us up naked and defenceless into the hands of our enemies.

As a southern man, and in behalf of the south, I call upon the gentleman to know who has authorized him to place our safety upon any such self-destroying ground as he has assumed?

What, because the North will not lend herself to this crusade against other nations—this fiendish propagandism—this forcible extension of slavery among a people, now declared by Mexico to be free and equal—shall we be told that the south will separate, and with Texas, form a southern union? Has the southern paradise, wrought out by Mr. McDuffie, in his late senatorial speech, so won upon the imagination and affections of the gentleman, that he is willing to take the Lethean draught, which will sink all identity with the illustrious dead and living of a once glorious Union, and to appear in this elysium beyond the dark and damning Styx which eternally surrounds it? Washington! the just, the immortal, speaks to you to-night in his farewell address—he warns you against the terms north and south—he bids you brand those as traitors to all true liberty, who would produce disaffection between these states, and boldly bids you ever to remember that the palladium of your happiness and independence rests in the eternal union of the states. Who shall dare to counsel us to its dissolution? Have you counted the cost? Have you looked consequences in the face? Have you numbered the whites and the blacks of a southern republic? Have you seen the indignant countenances of all Christendom turned towards you? Have you heard their voice? These American repudiators of their just debts—violators of treaties—these men who have disturbed the world with the cry of liberty, and caused blood in the name of equality to flow in every field in Europe, and redden every sea that surrounds her—they are now the propagandists of slavery—and the red and black flag of war is raised in its perpetuation and extension!

What do you ask of the north? Have you the souls of men, and can you ask them to play the supple tools in any such mad schemes as this? I shall not say what they have borne from slavery. I would have them love us as brethren, not hate us as the most dangerous of enemies. I would calm their rising spirits, not goad them on to madness and revenge. No, I will not say what the north have suffered from slavery. Yet I thank God that the spirit of freemen is not yet extinguished in their bosoms : nor Plymouth, nor Lexington, nor Bunker Hill, nor Trenton, nor Plattsburg, nor Erie, forgotten. Had they said less than they have said, they had not been fit compatriots for Kentuckians. Here is the letter of that world-known jurist, Chancellor Kent, and the speech of Albert Gallatin, the associate of Jefferson, at the New York meeting, men of other days, speaking as it were from the dead, they warn us to forbear—to stand by "the Union as it is." Where is Webster, and Everett, and Adams, and Van Buren, and Seward, and Greeley, and Wright, and Birney, and Morris, and Corwin, and Pierpont, and Longfellow, and the other leading minds in politics and literature? They tell us to stand by "the Union as it is." They say to us, "we have forborne till forbearance has ceased to be a virtue—we must stop here, our courtly complacency will carry us no further—we cannot join in misfortune and disgrace." The question is no longer whether we have anything to do with slavery in the states now existent, but whether we shall anew, become participes criminis; it is not, with Texas and a slaveholding Senate, whether we assent to slavery, but whether we ourselves shall be slaves! The cry of other days comes back upon our slumbering memories, "Americans, liberty or slavery." This shall yet swallow up the murmurings of party—no more the name of Democrat and Whig shall be heard among us—Federalists, Jeffersonians, Abolitionists, Nullifiers, and all other designations, shall be merged into a single designation: on one side "Slavery, Texas, and disunion"—on the other, "Liberty and Union, now and for ever, one and inseparable." That day has not yet come; but in the language of Adams, if come it must, I say, "let it come." Yes, I take up the language of the gentleman, (Mr. Marshall) and repeat, "let it come—let it come."

I do not fear to trust the gallant sons of the wild and untrammeled forest to choose my banner: and if my country calls me to the fight, it must be where virtue shall wreath the crown of triumph for the living, and glory consecrate the memory of the dead.

LETTERS

TO THE

LEXINGTON INTELLIGENCER:

WRITTEN DURING THE PENDENCY, BEFORE THE SENATE OF KENTUCKY,
OF A BILL FROM THE HOUSE OF REPRESENTATIVES,

REPEALING THE LAWS OF 1833, 1840, AND 1794,

PROHIBITING THE SLAVE TRADE.
1843.

I have told,
O Britons! O my brethren! I have told,
Most bitter truth, but without bitterness;
Nor deem my zeal, or factious, or mistimed,
For never can true courage dwell with them,
Who playing tricks with conscience, dare not look,
At their own vices.   COLERIDGE.

—

Yet let us ponder boldly—'Tis a base
Abandonment of reason to resign
Our right of thought—our last and only place
Of refuge; this at least shall still be mine.
                CHILDE HAROLD.

—

"Congress shall pass no law," &c., "abridging the FREEDOM OF SPEECH or of the PRESS," &c.—*Constitution of U. States—Art. I. Sec. I.—A.*

"That the general, great and essential principles of liberty and free government may be recognised and established: *we declare* . . . . that the printing press shall be free to every person who undertakes to examine the proceedings of the legislature, or any branch of government: and no law shall ever be made to restrain the right thereof. The free communication of thoughts and opinions is one of the inalienable rights of man, and every citizen *may freely speak, write, or print on any subject*, being responsible for the abuse of that liberty.—*Constitution of Kentucky—Art. X. Sec. VII.*

LETTERS

PEOPLE OF KENTUCKY.

No. I.

THE six great Christian nations, England, France, Austria, Prussia, Russia and the United States of America, are making most extraordinary efforts, by specific and elaborate treaties, for the suppression of the slave trade. Our own United States, have just concluded the treaty of Washington, by which we are bound to keep a squadron on the coast of Africa, carrying some eighty guns, expending millions of money, and endangering thousands of the lives of our gallant seamen, to prevent this traffic, which the united suffrage of Christendom has declared piracy, and justly punishable with death. Proud and noble spirited Kentucky, after years of bitter and elaborate discussion, by continued and increased majorities, has solemnly declared to the world, that she would permit no more slaves to be brought within her borders; thereby giving the strongest assurances, that she looks upon *slavery* as an *evil*, and that she would have no more of it; only permitting slavery to exist through necessity, in obedience to our *Constitution* and laws, and allowing the transportation of slaves out of the state, under the stern rule of self-defence, and social and political security. Now in the face of all these facts, the present House of Representatives—without any evidence of a change of public sentiment—when the whole people had every right to suppose that this embarrassing question was settled for ever—when no mention of slavery was made during the last August election—suddenly and insidiously pass a law, opening deep wounds, not yet cicatrized, and again subjecting our beloved state to the influx of foreign degraded slaves, the refuse of cotton and tobacco plantations, the scourings of jails, and the escape-gallowses of yet more debased populations than ours—house-breakers, poisoners, rogues, perpetrators of rapes* and midnight murders.

The tide of black population, which under the law of 1833, and the more stringent amendments of 1840, was turned away from our land is to sweep with more than Etnæan desolation among us. The blacks are to hurry on to that fast approaching crisis, when they shall out-number the whites. The Elysian prospect of South Carolina civilization, wooes us in the distance. Each city, and town, and village, and cross-road, shall boast its magazine of arms, not to repel a foreign invader, but to crush domestic insurrections. The night owl shall arouse the timid female and the restless husband from their turbid dreams —the one to grasp in bitter mockery that Bible, in whose infinite promises of mercy and support, no vestige of hope or alliance can now be found—the other to seize those arms upon which he nightly slumbers, not with the vain expectation of successful defence, but with the desponding purpose of selling life as dearly as possible.

To make way for this most glorious consummation, our free white laborers are to be driven out; our manufactories, already too inconsiderable, are to be destroyed; our cities are to crumble down; our rich fields are to grow sterile; our frequented places to be deserted. Our morals are to be still more corrupted; more universal debauchery to exist among our male whites; more mulattoes to stand as eternal curses, before the lovely eyes of our wives, our daughters, our mothers—most damning monuments of our self-abasement and crime, diluting the boasted purity of our Saxon blood, with those who, in our holy regard for the dignity of mankind, we will not allow to aspire to the common name of men. The flush of anger and petty tyranny is for ever to disfigure the bright faces of our little ones. Education must perish among the people; idleness and unbridled

---

* During the discussion of the slave bill in 1839, Judge F. Ballinger told the following tragedy : " A respectable woman and infant child, were sleeping in the absence of the husband and father, with the window raised, in the summer season; a slave entered through the window and committed a rape upon the woman, killing the child in the struggle." Here were two offences punishable with death. The miserable offender confessed under the gallows, that he had been " *run off* " from *Carolina* for the *identical offence of rape*, and supposed that his fate would only be a new transfer to the far south. And these are the men who are to inhabit this most lovely land, to the exclusion of the Saxon blood.

passions must characterize the rich ; poverty and contempt for
labor degrade the poor. Our state must dwindle away yet
more in political importance, till we shall become the contempt
of mankind, with the only consolation that we most richly
deserve it—blindly rushing into a secondary oriental civilization,
to fall by the Yankee arm, as the multitudes of haughty
Chinese, were mowed down by British power. And all this for
what purpose? That a class of men whom the general government has just pledged millions of men and money to bring
to the gallows,* may grow rich by feeding on the very life-
blood of our devoted state ! Is not this monstrous? Are we
already so infatuated? Has retribution so soon overtaken us?
Have the Gods already maddened us for destruction? Is this
indeed the deliberate voice of Kentucky ? Has she made up
her mind that her representatives should do this deed? Is she
not shamed by the gaze of Christendom ? Is she utterly
blinded to self-interest ? Does she defy the stern mandates of
religion? Does she spurn all the experience of wise men, coming down to us from all ages, trampling under foot all that is
redeeming in philosophical morality or Heathen Mythology ?
Is the boundless universe spread out before her, and does no
voice come up from its mighty depths in terrible energy, striking
through the triple steeled bosom to an awakened conscience—
there is a God ? Has she said with the fool in the fable, He is
not God ? Has she with rebellious infidel France, dethroned
Him ? Does she acknowledge with Jefferson, that He has no
attribute by which He can side with her—and tremble ? Or
does she defy the Omnipotent God to arms ?

No ! Kentucky has not done this. These men have slandered her fair fame ; they have dishonored her past history.
Twenty years ago, here, in this state, in tears and sorrow be it

---

* No moralist can or will discriminate between the foreign and domestic
slave-trade. In Africa the slaves are already made so by native masters. The
true African is far lower in intelligence and consequent sensibility than the
American negro. The balance is against the home trade, so far as humanity is
concerned ; as a matter of economy and safety the *foreign* is infinitely preferable to the home slave-trade. The society of Friends, in an address at Philadelphia, 1839 says, "neither can we discern any material difference between
the foreign and domestic slave-trade. Scarcely an evil is seen in the former
that has not its parallel in the latter." It will be seen from the extract appended to the third No. of these papers, that the bill from the House of Representatives, *repealed the law of* 1794, *against the slave-trade.*

spoken, was struck the first blow at self-government; here chains were first forged for the "toiling millions" (alas for the prostituted epithet); here the standard of liberty was first struck down. How? The despotisms of Europe, said man was not capable of self-government. We said he was. Why not? All history proves it, said they; democracies all end in the disregard of property, and consequently all social rights; for without property is secured to the producer of it, there is no possibility of social or governmental existence. Even savages, with their meagre effects, must have despotic chiefs for mutual protection, submitted to without appeal by the necessity of self-preservation. We admit, said Americans, that without security to property, there is no liberty, nor even existence. We also admit, that all previous republics, or rather democracies, ran to anarchy and suicidal destruction: but we have discovered a new principle of written constitutions, submitted to in times of peace and unexcited mind, by which, in times of excitement and popular rage, the weak will be protected, and the multitudinous majority restrained within the bounds of right. The ignorant shall not meet to govern in mass as in Athens or Rome; but we will choose representatives, intelligent, honest men, who will act for the great mass, and justice shall prevail among all. The multitude will be corrupt, said Europe. The representatives will be assimilated to the lower mass, and cater to its prejudices and dishonest appetites, and ruin will come in the end. Yes, my country, this did come to pass. They, who cried out, "the people—the people."—"Democracy"—the "toiling millions," did that which we so much feared would come upon us. They trampled the written constitution under foot—for what? To take from the industrious, to give to the idle; from the honest, to give to the profligate; from the sober, to satiate the drunken; from those who accumulated by the sweat of the brow, to give to those who *sang* in the summer months, and when the winter came, still wished to turn out the labor-worn, to *dance* by his winter fire. Yes, Kentuckians, we had relief measures, stay laws, and constitution breaking, then. America looked on in tears, and despair; Europe hissed and curled the lip; and hugged more closely the chains of despotism; and brightened yet more the bayonet: saying the masses were only fit food for gunpowder. You rose up like a startled giant from your delusive slumber, and hurled these false gods from the temples of

Liberty. Kentucky, yesterday, so fallen, to day, stood against the world; and all men said, "the honesty of the people is proven; liberty is vindicated; let the Republic live for ever." Who then supposed, that, in twenty years, before another generation succeeded, while the white heads of these patriots were yet lingering among us, in that same legislative hall, this ill-boding voice of "the *people*," "the *democracy*," "the *toiling millions*," would again be heard, that our sacred Constitution would be again trampled in the dust? Yes, the Philistines are again upon us. Go, mechanics; cheat sleep of her hours of welcome nature sustaining repose; practise self-denial; know no luxury; let untimely age succeed a youth devoid of pleasure; be confident; let him who rides in chariots, and wantons with the summer flies, knowing no toil, keep your hard earnings. Fear not, you shall never have your own again, unless the lordling's carriage brings "*two-thirds of its appraised value.*" That time *may never come.* But what of that? Are not these lawgivers the *people's friends, the true democracy.* Go farmer, and laborer, and ploughman, till the land; rest not long under the summer's shade; for the landlord offers large prices; look with hope to the cheerful winter's fire, and well clad wife, and laughing children, and the plentiful board. Fear not, the landlord says, "go sell my land at *two-thirds* of its value and take pay for your corn"—*that* it may *never* bring. What, though the matron shiver in the cheerless cot, and the little ones cry for bread; the *democracy* are for the "*toiling millions.*" They are "the people's friends." It is true, this is all contrary to old-fashioned ideas of honesty—true, it is against the precepts of the Bible—true, it is not in accordance with heathen morality—true, the Indian of the dark forest and the predatory Arab of the desert, would spit upon any one, who, with a grave face, would contend that this was right—true, it *violates* the *Constitution*, and sinks for ever the best hopes of self-government and true liberty—true, one sows and another reaps—true, one gathers and another scatters abroad—true, this subverts the foundation of all government, and in the end brings on *despotism, bloodshed,* and *depopulation;* but—"we are the PEOPLE'S FRIENDS; we are for the TOILING MILLIONS; we are for LIBERTY and EQUALITY."

Now, if you were to see such a set of men, with such words of peace and good will upon their lips, and most consummate robbery and debased injustice in their actions—is not this the very set of men that you would foresee would *repeal the law prohibiting the* SLAVE TRADE? Suppose that you were to hear men admit, that education "was the cheap defence of nations," that "learning was power," that intelligence was the only security for free governments, that the people were the foundation of all power, and without education, that power would become suicidal, and freedom sink into anarchy and then into despotism. And suppose they were to profess to be the people's friends, and yet, when common schools were established to educate that people, these same men should cry out that *common schools cannot exist in a slave state*, and yet vote for the admission of more slaves, and do all in their power to make slavery perpetual. Are not these the very set of men that you could foretell would trample under foot the constitution of their state, and with the cry *liberty* and *equality* on their lips, would consummate their dishonor by *repealing* the laws prohibiting the *slave trade*, which the despots of Europe punish with death and lasting infamy?

No. II.

IT is vain to tell us that slavery and the slave trade existed before the authentic history of men—that all people have been infected with slavery—each enslaving its color and nation. That all this has measurably passed away, is an indication of human improvement; that slavery yet remains among us in its worst form, is more eminently a reproach to us. The Egyptians allowed the Hebrews separate lands, houses and flocks; only a part of the nation were under "task masters;" and that part was mostly males. Though among the Hebrews themselves, the father might sell himself or his children; though free men were degraded to slavery, by being made captives for debts or for crime; yet the time of Hebrew servitude was limited to six, and that of all other people made slaves, to fifty years—the day of universal emancipation returning every fifty years. At the time of emancipation liberal allowances were made to freed men, so that at last it resembled more the English apprentice system, than American slavery. They were more lenient in the recovery of slaves, when runaway, than we. The Egyptian might escape to the temple of Hercules, and claim a discharge; the Hebrew's house was an asylum to his neighbor's runaway; and he could not be delivered up without the slave's own consent. The Hebrew servant partook of the religious festivals with his master, and they were so numerous as to employ, including the Sabbath, nearly half the year. Among the oriental nations of Asia, surrounding the Jews, slaves were entitled to many of the posts of honor in households; and in many states were capable of holding public office; slaves not unfrequently became—the women, the honored wives of potentates and masters—the males, captains and vice-regents. The nations of Asia Minor, from the time of Troy and before, all those holding the Grecian mythological religion, allowed their slaves many privileges. That they were treated with great humanity may be inferred from the custom, during the feast of Mercury, of masters taking the places of the servants; and thus being made sensible of the *golden rule* afterwards matured by the Christian religion. The people of Athens considered their slaves as occupying a more exalted position than free barbarians; but this might arise from the same causes by which many are now moved to compare our own slaves to British laborers. At all events, the temple of the Gods was an asylum to the fugitive slave; and the right of holding property and self-purchase, existed among them. It is certain that learning was common among them, and many of the most distinguished Grecians were freed men.

The state of servitude among the Spartans was worse than that at Athens, as the Spartans were a more rude people than the Athenians. But even here they enjoyed a liberty unknown to Americans, for they could not be sold out of Laconia; and their power, from the excess of wealth and personal liberty, excited too often the jealousy of their masters, and gave rise, no doubt, to the cryptia—those cruel and sweeping murders which so much disgraced that republic.

With Roman slavery we are more familiar—embracing all nations, not excepting their own people, as well as the doomed Africans; which last, however, constituted a very small portion of the entire class. They had, it is true, the power of life and death over their slaves; but they had the same power over their own children. They were allowed the use of money, and accumulation of property, by custom and education. Self purchase and emancipation were not uncommon. But the great numbers of slaves in Italy and the Roman province of Sicily, were the cause of unnumbered woes to the empire.

England, Scotland, Ireland, Russia, France, the German kingdoms, all Europe, have held slaves and fostered the slave trade; but the foundation of slavery has dissolved beneath the Christian religion and advancing civilization; and the base trafic no longer disgraces these rigid governments, save, perhaps, Portugal and Spain.

The Africans, also have, from time immemorial, held each other in slavery; but even here, to our shame be it said, it wears a milder form than in Christian America. Z. Macaulay, formerly governor of Sierra Leone, before the British House of Commons, said, "I never was able to discriminate between the son and the domestic slave of any chief. Field labor is performed by free people and by the domestic slaves jointly and indiscriminately."

The American Indians, also, in common with the barbarous people of all countries, made slaves of their captives in war for short periods, when they were at length burnt at the stake, to appease, according to their superstition, the spirits of their own friends slain in war, or else were set free and adopted into the tribe; no longer performing the degrading offices which were exclusively performed by the women. The wild stoic of the woods could not steel his own untutored and savage spirit to submit to or inflict *perpetual slavery.*

The Christian religion, has, at times, stood forth in its mighty purity, and stayed for a season the dictates of confirmed selfishness and inhumanity. Pope Alexander III., even many centuries ago, said, "Nature having made no slaves, all were alike entitled to liberty"—the germ of the immortal declaration of American independence. Yet even Christianity itself is shamed, in practice at least, by the imperfect precept of Mahommedan theology; for the Turk will not hold in bondage a captive of the Prophet's faith. The odious distinction of having first initiated England into the African slave trade, is awarded to Sir John Hawkins. This took place in 1562.* In 1620 a Dutch ship first landed African slaves upon the banks of James River, in the colony of Virginia. Here, then, we can pause a moment, and draw the

---

*Bancroft's History of the United States, vol. I., p. 173.

melancholy conclusion, after we have traversed all time, and all people, of all religions, and all grades of civilization, that here, in these United States of America, professing to be the only people on earth free, *slavery stands pre-eminent in degradation.* 'Tis true that our laws make the slaying of a slave murder, and punishable with death; but I will venture to say that although numerous murders of slaves have taken place, never has a single white man been capitally punished for this offence in any of the slave states. The writer of this article has reason to believe that he knows of three slaves who were slain by masters, neither of whom were ever punished. It is also true, that the laws insure, by word, that cruelty shall not be inflicted, else the slave shall be sold to another; yet never have we heard of a sale for such a cause.

The contrast between American and Roman slavery, is fairly given by the Society of Friends; "Philadelphia, 1839;" that sect of pure and practical Christians, who gave the first impulse to emancipation in America, who composed the society of which Benjamin Franklin was President, whose last official act was to petition congress for the suppression of the *slave trade.* They say:—"1st. Negro slavery, as it exists in the United States," is aggravated by the difference of color. "2d. The slave is held as a personal chattel, and in most of the slave states is liable, at all times, to be sold, removed, mortgaged, or leased, at the will of the master, or his executors, or at the suit of creditors. 3d. The master may determine the kind, quantity, and time of the slave's labor. 4th. The master may supply the slave with such food and clothing only, both as to quality and quantity, as he may think proper, or find convenient. 5th. The master may, at his discretion, inflict any punishment upon the person of the slave, save power over life and limb, which exclusion is nugatory, as slave evidence is never taken against the master. 6th. Slaves have no legal rights of property, in things real or personal. 7th. A slave cannot be a party before a judicial tribunal, in any species of action against his master. 8th. Slaves cannot redeem themselves; and in several of the states emancipation, without removal, is prohibited. 9th. If injured by third persons, their owners only may bring suits, and recover damages. 10th. Slaves can make no contract, nor be party to a civil suit, nor be witnesses against a white person. 11th. The benefits of education are mostly withheld from the slave, and in some of the southern states, to teach him is punishable as a crime. The means of moral or religious instruction are seldom or but sparingly granted him—(American Quarterly Review). 12th. No effectual provision is made to restrain the slaves from the grossest licentiousness, by laws to encourage marriage, or other means. 13th. Slaves escaping from their masters can be recovered within any part of the United States, by an act of congress called the fugitive law."

Of the Roman slaves, on the other hand, it may be said— "1st. No particular color or origin marked him out for proscription. 2d. He was often allowed, by the master, to accumulate property, called the slave's peculium, on which he traded for his own benefit. 3d. In the time of Augustus, the slave was heard, and *his testimony admitted against his master*. 4th. Their heathen temples afforded them safety. It was deemed an act of sacrilege to drag them thence. 5th. Many of them were carefully instructed, and under the Christian Emperors, their *spiritual welfare* was not neglected. 6th. No laws existed against their being emancipated or instructed. 7th. A large share of human happiness or misery arises from comparison. The severe Spartan discipline imposed upon the free, made the sufferings of the slave to be less felt."

Is this contrast so flattering to Kentuckians, that they shall honor the memory of the House of Representatives, when they shall have compelled us, by increase of numbers, to restrain the little liberty with which we may now indulge our miserable dependents? Do they look with evil eye upon that clause in our constitution, where emancipation is guarantied to all those who, not blinded by gross idolatry of "perpetual slavery," believe that a freeman is safer than a slave? Are our towns and cities to be yet more infested by lawless bands of robbers and ruffians, who—under the specious garb of police assistants—shamelessly assuming a name for doing that which impartial history proclaims that the wild savage of the woods would utterly abhor—in violation of the constitution and laws—*spare from violence neither age nor sex, bond or free*, so that they be guilty of a partially colored skin—under the desecrated pretence of *reforming the morals of the town?* Shall the very foundations, I will not say of society, but of imperative self-defence, be broken up, and Lynch law go unrebuked among us, under the infamous pretence that the laws are not sufficient protection for the citizens of Kentucky, a state that has, in days past, vaunted herself amidst this glorious Union, for chivalry and honor?

If these are the legitimate results of slavery, are they so flattering to those, who should imbibe inspiration from the glorious name and unspotted honor of our own native state, that their pride and self complacency are gratified? Are they so precious in the eyes of a statesman, that he would have *more of it?* But yet, if slavery be "the foundation of liberty," then most surely is the corollary, that Lynch law is the foundation of good order and pure morals, most admirable logic, and the "Black Indians" most honorable men.*

The bells from seven churches weekly toll in my ears till I am deaf with the sound, calling up the people to the worship of the Ever Living and Omnipotent God. No rakish Jupiter, nor drunken Bacchus, nor prostituted Venus, nor obscene and hideous Pan, rule the consciences of the illuminated people of this city and state—yet these scenes, which would have added fresh infamy to Babylon, and wrested the palm of reckless cruelty from Nero's bon-fire Rome, have been enacted "not in a corner," and the sentinels of Him whose "*arm is not shortened,*" from the watch-towers of Israel, have not ceased to cry out, "all is well." If the illustrious Emmet could "look death and danger in the face," for a far off petty sterile isle, because it was his *home,* and *he would have it free,*—shall no one—for a far more glorious home, spreading from North to South, from far distant sea to sea, filled with every association that can move the heart,—attracting the eyes of all mankind—to whose trust is committed the fondest, and proudest, and dearest hopes of the whole human family—speak out also for his country. Though no Athenian

---

* It may not be uninteresting to the prople of Kentucky to know, that the "Black Indians" are about seventy-five in number. On the day of the election of the City Council for Lexington, 1843, a card from this band was laid upon the tables at the places of voting, calling a meeting, and signed "Capt. Split Log"—for what purpose? Because some of the *blacks* "*had not paid city taxes.*" O, tempora! O, mores! and this during the free exercise of the right of suffrage!

Following the example of this slave-begotten moral code, a few days since in an adjoining county, a lawless band, with blackened faces and hearts, took Doctor W. from his home, in the night, aud lynched him nearly to death. For what? To gratify private and cowardly revenge, under the pretence of punishing him for whipping his wife, *seven years ago,* which whipping the wife utterly denies.

trumpeter may hurry through the assembled and terrified people, in bitter anguish, crying aloud, " will no man speak for his country ?" yet from mute, and unresisting, and down trodden innocence, there comes up a language, no less powerful, to awaken whatever of sympathy and manly indignation may be treasured up in bosoms, nurtured on Kentucky soil—rich in associations every way calculated to foster all that is *just, honest, and true, without which chivalry is a crime, and honor but an empty sound!* For them, once more, then, I denounce those who would, by legislation or otherwise, fix the bonds of " *perpetual slavery* " and the *slave trade* upon my native State. In the name of those, who, in all ages, have been entitled to the first care and ultimate protection of men, I denounce it. In the name of those, who, in '76, like they who sent back from Thermopylæ the sublime message, " go tell it at Lacedemon that we died here in obedience to her laws,"—illustrated by their blood the glorious doctrines which they taught, I denounce it. In the name of Christianity, against whose ever lovely and spirit-stirring sentiments it for ever wars, I denounce it. In the name of advancing civilization, which, for more than a century, has, with steady pace, moved on, leaving *Cimmerian regions of slavery* and the *slave trade* far in the *irrevocable* and *melancholy past*, I denounce it. In the name of that first great law, which, at creation's birth, was infused into man, *self-defence*, unchangeable and immortal as the image in which he was fashioned, and in *His name*, Whose likeness man was deemed not unworthy to wear, *I denounce slavery and the slave trade for ever !*

No. III.

THE most lamentable evil of slavery is the practical loss of the liberty of speech and of the press. The timid are overawed by the threatening array of physical force; the conscientious, who are naturally lovers of peace and good will, sink under bitter hate, and unceasing persecution; the ambitious and spirited are overwhelmed by the insupportable anticipation of sudden proscription, certain obscurity, and eternal oblivion. Thus truth ceases to be a virtue, and hypocrisy a crime; most severe retribution of the violation of nature's laws; the limbs of the apparent slave are fettered with iron, but the living and immortal spirit of the master wears heavier and more insufferable chains !

Under this, the only intolerable servitude, how many noble and sensitive spirits have perished in inactive and despondent repose ! They knew too well that truth and justice were the foundations of glory, and like those who go out to battle in a bad cause, their hearts failed them and they perished. Was there one whose eye and soul were quick and sensitive to the sublime and beautiful in nature ? History said to him "liberty and poetry have ever been allied." Was there one who was moved by the grandeur of empires, the luxuries of wealth, the social refinements of civilization, the power of earthly rule—one who would have his nation great ? In slavery, he saw no elements of strength ; a house divided against itself, sparse in numbers, indolent in production, wasteful in economy, dull in mechanic arts, debauched in morals, weak in purpose ; possessing *many* elements of gradual decay, and *none* of regeneration and renovation ; despair chilled the glow of patriotism, and the embryo statesman perished ! Where could the divine, the jurist, the historian, find refuge from this all-pervading curse, that with a triplicate force sapped the foundations of religion, marred the beauty and harmony of the sense of justice, and wrested from experience all the strength of its moral ? For such the land of slavery was no abiding place. Year after year they have passed off from the home of their birth, in mighty silence, among strangers, suppressing the agony of a lost home—an exiled country ; to which conscience allows no words of commendation : pride no language of rebuke !

Modern prudence would have pointed out to me, in the melancholy future, a similar fate, and have said to me, be wise —be silent ! But constitutional organization, and a large and living faith in the omnipotence of truth, and in the gradual improvement and perfectability of the human race, have led me to give utterance to the emanations of my own mind. Look there at the declaration of our illustrious sires : it is my birthright : while life lasts no man dare, no man can rob me of it ! I now hold, as I have ever held, that here, in the slave states, is the legitimate and proper place for *the consideration, the discussion, the perpetual retention or the final eradication of slavery. I have ever resisted, as I ever shall resist, foreign interference ;*

*they who bear none of the consequences of action, shall never,
by my consent, act at all.* But I must live or perish with my
country. All my interests, my life, liberty, and pursuit of happiness, and the interests of my nearest and dearest relations, of
my friends whom I love, and of all the rest of my countrymen,
between whom and myself for ever exists the right of mutual
protection—all are bound up in the common word COUNTRY.
She has claims on me for my *vote,* for my *opinions ;* and though
the humblest of her sons, when she calls for my help, whatever
of physical, moral, or intellectual power I may possess, shall be
freely exhausted in her cause ; and no human power shall, in
the most minute manner whatever, influence me to say or act
otherwise than my conscience, however false or unenlightened
it may be, shall sternly dictate. The two previous numbers of
this series of publications, were put forth in accordance with
these principles of action. The repeal of the laws of 1833, and
the amendments of 1840, in the House of Representatives, was
one of those crises in which *I dared not be silent.* Its consequences, in my limited view, were so utterly horrid and suicidal
to my country, that I should in being silent have been for ever
recreant to all that is sacred in my own estimation. And even
upon the subject of slavery, lying at the foundation of all our
social and political institutions, I was bound by all considerations, human and divine, not only to speak, but to speak with a
thoroughness, and candor, and boldness commensurate with the
occasion ; to probe the wound to the very seat of vitality ; to
save by all hazards ; for failure was death, certain as it was
horrible. Here was not the doubtful and debatable point of
political ethics, whether it was a matter of conscience for us
having slaves, no matter whether willingly or unwillingly, to
retain them still ? Or whether, having them by purchase or
inheritance, we could be forced by the Christian religion, or
philosophical morality, to give up that which the original compact, the *Constitution, guarantied* to us and our descendants ?
No, this was not the question. No ; the question was *the
original proposition,* whether we, having full power and *free
will,* with all the chances of good or evil clearly seen and illustrated by history and experience, should *anew* determine, in the
face of all mankind, to give sanction, in the most solemn manner, to African slavery. The question was, whether we Kentuckians, in the face of the action and denunciation of Christian

Europe and our own United States, should, in the most formal manner, legalize the slave trade. The question was, whether we, after due deliberation and repeated warning, had made up our minds, *not for ourselves only*, but for *our posterity* also, that Kentucky should remain a slave state for ever! Upon this subject, instinct, which sometimes grovels in the dark, flashes like lightning upon the dark paths of reason, and the crooked ways of blinded self-interest; and its echoes rush back in tones of thunder—*go not for perpetual slavery!* Upon this subject, though I were bound to life by ten thousand more sweet and endearing ties than were they whom the wise warriors of Israel sent back from battle in the trying hour of mortal conflict, lest their hearts should fail them, I would, with joyous enthusiasm, lay it down, and my parting spirit should be exhaled, in words which should be immortal among men, "*go not for perpetual slavery.*" Can it be that I wander, as a sick man in a fever? And are these images which seem to stand before me like rocks of adamant, the airy phantoms of an excited and diseased imagination? As the sick reach forth and touch a dear friend, to be reassured that it is indeed the one so much loved, I lay my hand upon my political bible—the immortal Declaration of Independence. I read its life-sustaining and soul-cheering precepts—"*go not for perpetual slavery.*" Here, too, on my table, lies all that remains of one of the most remarkable men the world has seen; a man born in the eighteenth century, concentrating in his own person all the mighty developments of brilliant genius, with all the virtues which had before been falsely considered to belong only to mediocrity of intellect. A great warrior, a great statesman, great in the successful defence of his country against the most powerful nation in the world, but greater still as the founder of the civil institutions of liberty among men; believing in a pure and all-wise Providence; practising all the Christian morals; yet of philosophic tolerance, and utterly devoid of fanaticism. A man eminent among his contemporaries, who were themselves illustrious, for calm judgment and profound wisdom—GEORGE WASHINGTON. His voice, in paternal tones of warning and undying tenderness, implores me, "*go not for perpetual slavery.*" Again, I turn to him who was the author of a new political religion; a man eminent for his knowledge of men; sceptical in his opinions; a calculator of chances; a nice balancer of motives; so given to incredulity as to question even the Christian religion; yet a believer in one all-wise and omnipotent God; a man in all senses of the expression, "worldly wise"—THOMAS JEFFERSON. I hear his voice of powerful denunciation, "*go not for perpetual slavery.*" At last, I consult him, the greatest philosopher as well as statesman of modern times; a man of whom it has been most proudly and justly said, "He wrested the lightning from the heavens— the sceptre from kings;" a man of the coolest and clearest head, with a most dogged and stoical control over his imagination, his appetites, and his passions—BENJAMIN FRANKLIN. By the most close, laconic, and convincing logic, he binds my intellect and senses in a net which human power cannot rend, impelling my action, "*go not for perpetual slavery.*" Yes, here lie upon my table, the parting voices of *Washington, Jefferson,* and *Franklin*—the greatest warrior, the acutest statesman, and the most profound philosopher, that modern times have seen—all saying to me in the most imploring, and convincing, and affectionate language, "*My son, go not for perpetual slavery and the slave trade.*"

Kentuckians! do you love these men? But yesterday, the Revolutionary Sword of WASHINGTON, and the Walking Staff of the venerable FRANKLIN,—a present to his friend, the father of his country,—were presented to congress. Party strife perishes, the soul of a great Nation is stirred within her; the hearts of the assembled representatives are melted down; tears are stealing along alike the cheeks of age, manhood, and youth; the names of her illustrious benefactors are swelling up oceans of gratitude and manly resolve, and patriotic determinations in the bosoms of America's sons. Kentuckians! you felt this scene; you honor, you reverence, you love these men: *they have said on the subject of slavery all I have said, and more.* I interpose their sacred persons between me and your uplifted arm, and dare you to strike.

The same paper that bore to you my last number, bore also the good news of a conservative spirit in the Senate of Kentucky, and that *the repeal bill was defeated!* My task is ended! I retire to that privacy, where the public ban has placed me, for baring too boldly my breast to the shafts, which, piercing me, a common soldier, perhaps yet saved my country. There I shall remain till the same causes again call me forth; when I shall deem it my greatest honor again to stand for the defence of the vital interests of Kentucky, though I perish in the conflict. My enemies declare me a *factious* and dangerous man. And though I shall, with an undaunted, and proud, and uncomplaining spirit, bear all the full consequences of the calumny —I appeal from their decision to posterity, if my name survive me. I say that my action as a citizen has been, with one exception, which I deeply regret,* eminently *conservative*. Holding the same opinions which I now hold, and have always, on proper occasions, avowed, and which at no very remote period were held, and are now held by a great majority of the people of Kentucky, and which it was not then deemed treason to avow, so soon as I was eligible, I took my seat in the House of Representatives of Kentucky. There then arose, during the pendency of the Convention question, an effort to repeal this law *prohibiting the slave trade*. My honorable friend, the present speaker of the House of Representatives, for whom, as a man, I entertain sentiments of personal friendship, which I trust are reciprocal, although I have as little tolerance for some of his political opinions, as he has perhaps for some of mine— will bear me witness, that I then denounced the slave trade as boldly and, as some would say, as fiercely as I do now. I then declared, that if we had not the power, under the Kentucky Constitution, to sustain the law of '33, that I would go with him heart and soul to hold a Convention for its change ; yet I went against the Convention in all its stages. Was not this conservative ? For four years more I was in and out of office, and I challenge all Kentucky to say that I uttered, by word, speech, conversation, letter, or print, one word upon the subject of slavery that was not approved of, in all respects, by all who knew me. Did this look like a factious spirit ? In 1840 (the citizens of Fayette, I believe, at this period at least, are prepared to do me justice to believe, when I say, once more), I had no share whatever in bringing the subject of slavery before the people, yet when it was up, with my opinions fixed beyond the shadow of a doubt on the justice and expediency of the policy which I advocated, I spoke with the freedom of a man, who, in the largest slave-holding county in the state, had made up his mind to bear political ostracism, rather than swerve from the path of duty and truth.

---

* The duel with Wickliffe.

The people of Fayette generously sustained me by their suffrages; and in the Legislature, in spite of the pretended instructions which were sent me by a threatening minority, I sustained, to the best of my ability, the instructions which I had received at the only legitimate place of power—the polls. In '41 the slave question was again brought up—not by me. I was first attacked through the press, and I replied through the same channel, in a manner equally free and undisguised as I now do. I was beaten in effect, although I most solemnly reiterate that I believe that I received a majority of the legal votes of Fayette county; but a man is a partial judge in his own case—let that pass. With all the aggravating circumstances of that election surrounding me—with a burning sense of injustice from slander and misconstruction, and from other sources, unusual and before unheard of, as they were unexpected and overwhelming, had I been a *factious* man, of selfish ambition, seeing then and now little prospect of political regeneration, would I not have continued to trouble the waters which had submerged me, and have, if possible, Sampson-like, thrown down the pillars of the temple of social and political safety, burying my enemies in the common ruin with myself? For two years more I have held my peace; and not till the repeal of this same law, was for the first time, I believe, in the last ten years, actually accomplished in the House of Representatives, to the sudden astonishment of all Kentucky, did I again come forth. Have I not stood against the bankrupt law, because I thought it not a conservative law. And, although I have sympathized in common with all humane men, with the sudden, unexpected, and cruel bankruptcies which have swept over our land like a summer cloud—has not my voice on all proper occasions been against it? And yet I am a *factious* and a *dangerous* man. The Judiciary is a *conservative* power in our government. I have met *popular defeat* to sustain the judges, by placing them, by adequate compensation, beyond the reach of bribery and intimidation. Was this the act of a factious man? Relief laws have been agitated, which struck at the roots of that Constitution, which is the sole protector of slavery. I stood by the Constitution! Was that factious? I voted for the law providing for the payment of the interest of the state debt; and warred to the last against the restriction to two years; and now, as I foresaw, our state is threatened with *practical repudiation,* in consequence of a want of a *conservative* spirit in the government. Yet I am denounced through the press, and threatened with violence, as being *factious !* Two men were hung in our state without, and contrary to the law and the Constitution ; that, too, I did and do now, denounce ! Yet, I am a *factious* and a dangerous man ! Seventy-five *lawless* men are now banded together, for unconstitutional and illegal purposes—through the press avowing their design to go on and through with it, as long as it suits their royal will and pleasure—in a state of open rebellion and anarchy, having already torn asunder the *Constitution,* the *sole tenure* by which the right to your slaves is secured, as a filthy rag and trampled it under foot with most consummate, cool, and provoking impudence. I denounced them in language that falls infinitely short of the deep and damning consequences of their action ! and I am blown through the city and county as a soiled feather upon the breath of an infuriated people. Yes, I am a *factious* and *dangerous* man ! The press is threatened with a mob ; my crime is so great that the innocent and patriotic editor is to be ruined in person and fortune, to atone for a *constructive* participation in the guilt of a dangerous and factious correspondent !

Let no man impute to me a vain-glorious spirit, when I say, that the writer of these papers has too much soul, to sacrifice, for his own ambition, far less, for his self-preservation, the humblest or the highest of those who may, in the most remote manner, have allied their fortunes with his. I only, myself am answerable for myself ! Yes, even to those, who, of all men living have the least right to know my name, I give it.

Kentuckians ! I subscribe myself one of the humblest of those who would be the last to wound the proud and gallant state, to which he owes his *being,* his *honor,* and his *first* and *last* allegiance.

Cassius M. Clay.

ANNEXATION AND SLAVERY

For the New York Tribune.

LEXINGTON, KY., April, 1844.

To THE AUTHOR OF "TEXAS:"

SIR—In addressing you through the press, I hope I shall not be thought wanting in courtesy. It does not beeome me to draw aside the anonymous veil which any good citizen may rightly assume in conferring with his countrymen, so long as he confines himself to principles and refrains from personalities; yet at the same time, in replying to the arguments and reflections set forth in a pamphlet headed "Texas," it would be the most absurd affectation to seem to be ignorant that the author is yourself. It was my fortune to have been a member of the Kentucky House of Representatives in 1836 with you, when the Convention was proposed to be holden. This project we both opposed, because, unless I very much misunderstood you, the public mind was not prepared for the only necessary reform— the Emancipation of Slaves. When no favors are to follow, no flattery will be imputed: allow me, then, to say that your course as a Legislator excited my admiration: already eminent as a Jurist, you seemed also to possess the necessary characteristics of a statesman—that boldness and self-elation which trampled under foot all the arts of the demagogue, and evinced a spirit which based its eminence upon the lasting ground-work of the public good. It has been, therefore, with great interest that I, in common with the American public, have read all the emanations from your pen. Like you, a private citizen, I profess to be operated upon by the same motives assumed by yourself—the formation of a just public sentiment, and the establishment of the honor, prosperity, and permanent security of our whole country.

In venturing to dissent from one whose opinions are entitled to so much consideration, I shall not be regarded as presumptuous, for this cannot be a contest for supremacy, and whether you or I be the "better soldier," our object is equally attained, and our common standard, "Truth and our Country," shall still

be borne aloft unsullied and intact. I know it is common in
the nineteenth century to solve all great political problems
upon economical principles. If man were a beast only to be
fed, then to this course there could lie no solid objection. But
when we regard our moral and intellectual nature, as well as
our mere physical well-being, then I contend that there are far
weightier considerations than mere economics in determining
any great national and social interest. When Agesilaus, the
Spartan king, and generalissimo of the Grecian forces, held a
public conference with the luxurious Satrap of Persia's wealthy
monarch, arriving first at the place appointed he sat down
upon the turf under the shade of a tree. When Pharnabazus
arrived, his people spread skins upon the ground, of exceeding
softness from the length of their hair, with rich carpets of
various colors, and magnificent cushions. But when he saw
Agesilaus, the mighty king and warrior, sitting merely upon
the ground without any preparation, he was ashamed of his
effeminacy, and sat down also upon the grass. Far distant be
the day when Americans shall be less sensible to virtue, noble
poverty, and true greatness of soul, than the minion of an
Eastern despot!

Passing by, however, these appeals, though unhappily of late
too impalpable to the common apprehension, or too sublimated
for the stern reason of modern statesmen, I shall follow the method which you have laid down. I agree with you, then, that
the annexation of Texas would injure the present United States
by subtracting her labor and capital ; which it is admitted on all
hands to be wise, especially in a new country like ours, to increase
rather than diminish   More especially would it injure the cotton and sugar planter, by inviting more capital into the culture
of those articles, which are already too plentiful in the market
for the planter's interest. It would add to the burthens of government, by extending its laws and protection over very nearly
the same labor and capital, spread over a greatly expanded surface of country. For if Texas be admitted as a slave state,
and no other result is now anticipated, experience fully proves
that there would be little immigration except from the slave
states of America. For the same reason there would be no
new consumers of northern manufactures, whilst dispersion
would, according to well ascertained laws, weaken their capability of purchase. The *alleged* fertility of Texan lands,

would be no equivalent for all these *ascertained* losses. I agree with you also on the other hand, that from Texas, allowed to exist as an independent state, we have nothing to fear. Because, in the event of her becoming a free state, white labor could not compete with us in the planting business, and because as a slave state she must ever be almost impotent in all respects. Having nothing to fear from her in an economical point of view, either as a planting or as a manufacturing state; either as an independent free or slave state ; neither can we fear her arms in war: this, surely, needs no debate. Nor can Texas be feared as a fulcrum of aggression for a more powerful hostile nation, as General Jackson would have us suppose : the absurdity of whose views you have so fully shown, that his opinions, where he is so evidently jaundiced, cannot have the least weight even with the men the least skilled in military defence. The scare-crow of England occupying Texas as a colony, or forming any alliance seriously injurious to us, you have fully exposed ; and we have her declaration, both in parliament and through her plenipotentiary here, that she disclaims any unjust interference in the affairs of Texas; and besides, we have the guaranty of our own potent, armed intervention, against any illegitimate consummation injurious to us, whether diplomatic or forcible. The assumption of Texas for the sole purpose of extending the bounds of the national dominion, with all the fatal lights of history beaming full upon us, is too absurd for refutation, and can only be used for effect by the most reckless demagogues, which class of men it was not your, nor is it now my, purpose to address. As a measure of economy, as a means of defence, and as a mere extension of boundary, we both agree that Texas cannot be admitted. All those high moral and constitutional considerations which I have declined using for the present, are most certainly against its annexation. Every one would conclude, then, that we both would come to the same Q. E. D. Texas, therefore, is not to be admitted. But no ! Setting out with the same data, granting the same postulates, following the same method of demonstration, we còme to utterly different conclusions—I, that Texas *ought* not, *will* not, and, so far as I form an integral portion of the national power, *shall* not be annexed—you, that she *ought* not, perhaps, yet *will*, and so far as you are concerned, *shall* be allied to us ! If I am right, you are wrong—if you are right, then is the American people stultified and dishonored by your own showing. For, if pecuniary interests, good policy, and good faith lead them to abstain from Texas, then no "insatiable craving for good land" excuses their rapacity, nor any "determination rightfully or wrongfully to have it," evidences their wisdom or conceals their dishonor. What terrible power is this, then, which, overriding all considerations of moral and material interest, determines us to seize on a foreign nation, and, in spite of the faith of treaties, the feelings and wishes of a majority of the nation, in violation of the national constitution, and at the hazard of the dissolution of the Union, "wrongfully" to appropriate it to ourselves? You are constrained to make the humiliating confession—it is *slavery*, which makes the "south desire the annexation, though contrary to *her* interests, and the north to refuse the alliance though contrary to *her* interests." But here you seem to contradict your previous showing, that the admission of Texas would be injurious to the north. And it may be farther safely said that no monopoly of trade in Texas secured to the north by alliance can compensate her for her losses by the perpetuation of slavery, which Texas, at least for some centuries would probably insure. For we are consumers, not mostly because we have slaves, but because we are planters; and every slave made free is so much the greater consumer of northern manufactures, as an intelligent, educated freeman, produces more to give in exchange than an uneducated slave. Add to this, that by emancipation the whole class of masters is added to the producing class, instead of being merely the agents of the consumption of the fruits of others' labor.

Am I right, then, when I plant myself upon physical wellbeing, and say Texas cannot be admitted? Am I right, when I stand upon the faith of treaties, and declare, she ought not to come in? Am I right, even if Mexico assent to the union, when I interpose the bulwarks of the Constitution, and proclaim that, till these shall be leveled to the ground, she cannot be ours? Am I right, when I gather about me all the glorious principles and hallowed associations which illustrate the American name, and confess, that all these must perish, before Texas can become one (or more) of these United States? Then no more of this inexorable necessity—this ill-omened "must!" It is the command of a superior to an inferior—the language of a king to his subjects—the voice of the master to the slave. We are yet free—the day on which Texas must be wedded to us—the day on which, as you seem to anticipate, she shall be thrust upon us—we are free no more! In Kentucky, the gross population may be set down at 800,000; 31,495 only, the Auditor's books show to be slaveholders; not one in four or five, as estimated by you to be the ratio in the five states of Maryland, Virginia, Kentucky, Tennessee, and Missouri, but *one in twenty-five* only, is a slaveholder; and this is probably the ratio in all the five states named, the number of slaveholders decreasing as you go farther South.* To this insignificant minority we have sacrificed common schools—we cannot sustain them; the supremacy of the laws—it has not been vindicated; the national and state constitutions—they have been trampled under foot; liberty of speech and of the press—there is not a despotism in Europe that has less than we; a navy—it cannot be ours; manufactures—they are impossible with slave labor; all the arts and sciences, the useful and ornamental—they perish here; the Christian morality,—"the salt has lost its savor"—high intellectual development, such only as can exist where the spirit is free in its flights and untrammeled in its utterance—slavery, like the fabled Stygian lake, paralyzes the wings of genius—dread, gloomy and remorseless, she suffers none—none to escape—each victim but adds more and more to that noxious atmosphere which infects her inhospitable shores, making her very weakness, exhaustion, and decay, her impregnable defence. Have the less than one in twenty-five, to say nothing of the entire ten millions of the North, imposed upon us all these sacrifices, and do they now come on once more with that everlasting word "*must?*" Surely, this is unworthy of us! or else are we most unworthy of our patriot sires. If slavery has already grown so great that you are forced to cry out, "It is time for every statesman, wherever located, to look it full in the face;" is it not, then, also become too large for compromise? Nay, is not the institution in itself incapable of compromise? When, out of the original thirteen states a new government was formed to "establish liberty," the compromise was to reduce slavery gradually to extinction—read the Madison Papers and

* The London Non-Conformist, of April 3d, gives the number of slaveholders, and those *interested* in them, at 32,700, in a population of 600,000, in South Carolina.

deny it! Search the Constitution for the word "slavery" in vain, and deny it! When Kentucky, and Tennessee, and Alabama, and Mississippi, were successively taken into the Union, it might seem that slavery should have rested satisfied for ever—the wide bounds of constitutional empire, were they verge enough for slavery? No! then comes Louisiana, and hard upon her footsteps, Florida hastens to the sacrifice. Louisiana, and Arkansas, and Missouri, acknowledge the devouring appetite of slavery—and is she yet content?—does she abate anywhat in her demands? No. She knows too well that liberty and slavery cannot exist under the same government; and with an unerring instinct she hastens us on to enlarge her dominion, growing more openly rapacious and shameless as she feels that she has less to fear from the slumbering and perishing friends of liberty and equal rights. Texas spreads out her "banks and braes" in the distance, and the "insatiable craving" of slavery hurries us once more, at "the price of blood," if necessary, to its acquisition. And yet, in view of all these facts, you would give her "the eastern part of Texas, another single slave state," for a compromise! Suppose her safely enthroned in Eastern Texas, and she scents once more the orange groves of *Western* Texas, exciting again her "insatiable craving"—I ask you, with all the fearful energy of self-defence, what new guaranty for the preservation of the compromise do you offer us? Can you suppose that the few half-starved negroes who should find their way to this new colonization Elysium would oppose their westward progress? Can you bring any new constitutional or moral barriers more strong than those which already oppose the dreadful "*must*" in vain? Will the addition of three or five slave states, by giving slavery preponderance in the Senate, strengthen the defences of constitutional liberty, and oppose more effectual barriers to the expansion of the limits of servitude, than a senatorial equality can now do? Have not the mad projectors of this fatal scheme already proclaimed from the high sanctuary, the inner temple, of the world-wide republicanism, the American Senate, that this whole continent is, or should be, ours? Aside from this, could a free black colony exist alongside of slaveholding Texas?— would not the slaves flee to it from oppression?—and would the colonists return their black brethren once again into bondage?—and would not a Texan invasion be the sure consequence? Can all the power of the Union now shield the harborer of the runaway slave from vengeance?—did it protect the Cherokees of Georgia or save the tribes of Florida from extermination?—would a miserable black colony fare better, in a word, than native, free-born, white American citizens have done? The idea, then, of a free black colony alongside of slaveholding Texas, with due deference to your more mature reflections, I pronounce absolutely absurd and impossible. Louisiana, Arkansas, and Missouri, I am willing to recognise as states possessing equality with the rest; I submit to the past decision of the nation; at the same time I most solemnly protest against the precedent, and deny the constitutional possibility of the annexation of new slave states to this Union. Let slavery subside into its constitutional limits—I stand by the Constitution. If, in the dread necessities of coming time, Americans shall, like the Spartans, in a night thin out Americans, as you intimate, let not this blood be upon our garments—not for all the cotton and sugar which, since creation's dawn, has grown on the green earth beneath the dewy heavens, would I have posterity of mine look upon this "sorry sight." Let the aspirations of Kentuckians ascend in gratitude to the Father of Destiny, that our own loved native state is subject to no such miserable slave growing cotton and sugar necessity as this! Maryland, Virginia, Kentucky, Tennessee, and Missouri must then, as you say, soon become non-slaveholding states. J. Q. Adams thinks that the slave trade cannot be suppressed till Africa is Christianized, and the supply of slaves cut off. I, with great deference, contend that the *market* must be destroyed before the trade can be suppressed. Do you stop the vent for slaves from these five states by taking in Texas? No. Then never let these states take in Texas. No, we must stop here—now; the time grows stringent, fearfully pressing. Americans, liberty or slavery?

"Under which king, Bezonian? speak, or die!"

I am firmly of the opinion that you are mistaken in the supposed necessity of colonization; all additional expense and complicated arrangement for the disposal of emancipated blacks, I regard as so many obstacles to doing any thing; it but adds new links to a "lengthening chain." Free blacks are not a tax on the north, as "we have been taught to believe"—they would be a better class here, because of the climate. Whenever Kentucky moves in earnest on this subject, as move she will—the great mass of slaves will be removed and sold elsewhere. There will not be more left than we will be glad to employ in such menial offices as they now fill; where they will not be at all in the way of that increase of intelligence and provident labor which adds so much to the substance and glory of a people. The time has passed when we are to console ourselves with vain reflections upon northern abolitionists; the time has come when we are to regard not names but things; not inquire what one may be called, but whether he be *right*. Is not all injustice retributive? And while we join in feeding the false and morbid appetite of pro-slavery men, by denouncing abolitionists, do we not place the very obstacles in the way of progress of which you so bitterly complain? If a wayfarer say to me, "You *rascal!* get out of the way, that steam-car will crush you!" shall I shut my eyes and in blind obstinacy, be crushed? Or shall I not rather first save myself, and then nurture my gratitude or vengeance for a fit opportunity of manifestation? If the former course be folly in a single individual, how much more should a great state be ashamed to practise such absurdities! And the statesman who dare not meet and expose them is more a coward than he who shows his back to his country's invaders. I conclude, then, that the bounds of American slavery should not be enlarged—that the five middle slave states, as you say, will not *allow* the dissolution of this Union; we are a nation, and nothing but revolution can sever us; there should be no new slave state added to this Union; slavery will be abolished in the district of Columbia; the north will by the ballot box drive slavery into its constitutional limits, the present thirteen slave states, and there leave it to ourselves, to our consciences, and to destiny; all the non-cotton-growing states will, by peaceable means, free themselves from slavery. Kentucky will be among the first to take the lead; this will be done by first gaining supremacy in the legislature, then by calling a convention, and at last, by legal emancipation, which will be easy and light, as many slaveholders, with their slaves, will have been removed from the state. When seven southern states shall become free, slave representation will be abolished; and this, in conjunction with all the rewards of political promotion and the spirit of the age operating upon the ambitious and the virtuous, will induce the sacrifice of slavery even in the cotton-growing states, or else the extinction of one or the other of the races in all that region; and, at last, our land will be redeemed, and liberty and union shall reign supreme among us. If there be, indeed, as you say, a majority of slaveholders with us in our belief that slavery ought to and must fall, I solemnly commend my plan and yours to their calm consideration, and most cheerfully exclaim, "God save the right!" Thus far only I must for ever dissent: I cannot but regard the annexation of Texas to this nation as treason against the republic, the virtual revolutionary overthrow of the American government; and so esteeming it, should arms be opposed to arms, as Gen. Hamilton vauntingly threatens, on the part of the land of "all the chivalry," I shall not hesitate to strike for the constitution transmitted me as my birthright, from a gallant ancestry. Here, in this Texan Thermopylæ, we must take our ground; here some of our countrymen must stand—ay, and if the worst comes to the worst, must fall, too—or else no Marathon shall ever bring glory, safety, and liberty, to our homes.

A
REVIEW
OF THE
"PHILOSOPHY OF SLAVERY,
AS IDENTIFIED WITH THE
PHILOSOPHY OF HUMAN HAPPINESS.
AN ADDRESS BY PRESIDENT SHANNON,
TO THE FRANKLIN SOCIETY OF BACON COLLEGE, KY.,
27th JUNE, 1844.*"

I.

NATURE has not designed, nor are we so unreasonable as to
expect, every man to be a martyr. We do not blame even a
professed follower of the self-sacrificing and uncompromising
Author of our faith, for not making open war upon *slavery*,
when his bread may be stopped and his character and person
exposed to continual attacks. There may be deep and silent
longings for the true and the right, a well of undying charity
and love in the heart's core, and yet the importunate cravings
of the flesh may bend the crushed spirit to its unholy ministry.
There is in negative characters, who fail to reap the pleasures
of lofty virtue, something which requires us to withhold the
pains of censure. Even in crime there is much to commiserate,
and a sense of our own frailty should ever make us an indulgent
judge. Give us a bold, daring villain, a shameless cut-throat,
a stern scorner of the right, a follower of all-conquering passion,
a man owning allegiance to neither men nor gods, we shall
wonder if we cannot defend, look on the chaotic elements of a
possibly great character, and mingle some sentiments of admiration with unpitying horror and inexorable vengeance.

But a cold, calculating hypocrite, a puling, canting defender

---

* This address is published in the Christian Journal, Harrodsburgh, Ky.,
and largely circulated in extras for political effect. It has been ably re-
viewed by some one of the same sect, and I believe is by no means approved
of by most of that large and respectable class of Christians—the Reformers.

of the wrong, a moral assassin, an emasculate who without passion steals upon unsuspecting virtue, and prostitutes her to other men's uses; one who pursues evil for its own sake without hope of reward, or sense of remorse; not entirely a beast, because knowing sin, yet not man, for lack of soul enough to damn the body—what shall be said of a thing like that? I put it to the calm response of every honest man, if there be aught in nature that moves our indignation, and so cries aloud to all mankind, by all the quickened virtues of nature's great first law—beware! Let no man misunderstand me: I come to denounce not men, but measures; not individuals, but classes. The President of this College is, so far as I know, an amiable gentleman. I shall not say that he is not a Christian, in its ordinary acceptation among men; but he has volunteered against the best interests of mankind, is warring against all that is vital in religion, or valuable in morals, committing treason against republicanism, shutting off the light of peace, justice, and mercy, from the earth, and filling the future with impenetrable gloom and utter despair. He shall go down with the curses of millions to the grave, and his name shall be a by-word of contempt and infamy, or rot for ever from the memory of men! The great and good, even among the heathen, taught that *Liberty* was the greatest boon of the Gods to men; and the youth of all countries went up to this temple of glorious faith, and learned to become heroes among nations. The man who in this republic undertakes to teach the young to be slaves, can hardly hope to stand against the just resentment of those who believe, that the American Declaration of 1776 is not a lie, and the Christian religion not a cunningly devised fable, full of promise to the lips, but filling the soul with poisoned drugs of bitterness and woe!

This address is delivered before the "Franklin Society." The true "Philosopher" should have been spared this cruel irony, and covert insult. Franklin was the friend of *liberty*; he believed a Christian defender of slavery worse than a Turk, and has given utterance to some most withering sarcasms upon the "Philosophy of Slavery," which I commend to the sapient President and his pupils. I know nothing so mal-apropos as the association of this address with the name of Franklin, unless it be Featherstonhaugh's slave-trader, who wore a huge fold of black crape upon a great white hat, in memory of Lafayette, the martyr of freedom!

The first four columns are taken up with an elaborate argumentation to prove the very recondite truth, that every one desires to be happy, and that the way to be happy is not to violate any of those laws of our being which produce happiness! Having come to this broad and deep foundation, through much delving into the dark and hidden recesses of unwilling nature, who only reveals herself to the enlightened few, the ingenious President, I know not by what strange and unheard-of association of ideas, builds up the great superstructure, "The Philosophy of Slavery as identified with the Philosophy of Human Happiness." It would, perhaps, be enough to proclaim to all the world, that the President, so far as we are informed, has not submitted himself, his wife and children, to unconditional servitude ; but it may serve a purpose, by displaying the utter inanity of this Sophomorean address, to make falsehood and crime ridiculous as well as hateful to men.

"All the misery on earth originated in self-will, prompting the violation of law ; " the President has before stated, that no man "wills" his own misery ; there is, therefore, an absurdity truly exquisite in saying, that all his misery arises from his *will* (self-will). The foundation of this theory is not only absurd, but false. We have every reason to believe, that man is now essentially what he was from the beginning ; and every man's observation teaches him, that the great mass of misery is entirely independent of his will altogether. Hunger and thirst, cold and heat, and disease and death, (to say nothing of the pains of the mind, which might require some reasoning to produce conviction, such as two men's loving the same woman) are surely not the creatures of the will, or, if the learned gentleman prefer, of "self-will." Nor will the President mend the matter by running back to Adam ; it is "with philosophy, not with theology," that we have to do—for all animals, without exception, are subject to necessary evil ; had they too their Adams ? If self-will be the cause of all misery, in the sense in which it is here used, then take away self-will, and man is inevitably happy. Yet men are so short-sighted as to object to solitary confinement for life, as not only undesirable, but as absolutely insufferable— perhaps the strongest case possible when a man is most completely deprived of self-will in practical life, save in the Elysian state of slavery ! The President's logic is only surpassed by his gallantry. Now it is unfair to bring lovely woman to his help ;

by all that is sacred in common-place, let Eve rest, for if she is brought into the field I am undone; here is a case where self-will does lead men into perpetual slavery. Again, "there is no created being on earth to which *man* could be made subject." Then is slavery *impossible*, as well as foully *wrong;* and here is an end of the argument! If "children were placed in bondage to their parents, to arrest the ruinous tendency of ignorance and self-will," by what "philosophical" deduction from Adam's fall is a kitten put in bondage to its parents, who gather it by the nape of the neck, and bear it where they list? and pray, what ruinous tendency is arrested in the little blind creature?

Is not this worse than contemptible; shall such stuff flow from the head of a learned institution under the huge name of "philosophy," without a horse laugh as loud as the Katskill thunder which aroused Rip Van Winkle from his sixty years' sleep of universal stupidity? I pass over the three or four columns vindicating slavery from the Bible : my province, I repeat, is with philosophy, not with "Theology." I may be allowed to remark, however, that the Old Testament may prove any crime under the sun to be right, by a similar process of specious reasoning from isolated examples. We are not Jews, but Christians, and I say, without fear of contradiction, that there is not, and never has been a code of ethics so full of liberty and equality as the Christian. Let the professed become the real followers of Christ, and slavery falls in an hour.

II.

The President has ventured into the same shallow water, where so many minds of small tonnage have before stranded. Because Christ did not by special command in all cases denounce slavery, therefore it is right. The instance given by Thomas Clarkson, of the gladiatorial shows (which none will now defend, and which were not by name forbidden, though existing at the time; yet the spirit of the gospel reached them and they perished before the spread of its precepts) is one of many cases which it is useless to cite. The truth is, if all the actions of men were to be specially commanded or denounced, so far as moral good or evil is involved, the whole of Bacon College would not contain the volumes of the Christian law; and a man in a long life time would not be able to read the one thousandth part of them! See the untold books of temporal institutes and precedents, and yet the profession can hardly find in a life time of practice an actually occurring case in exact point with the written law. No, the great *principles* of the Christian morality are laid down, and reason and conscience must apply them to individual cases.

When the deists of the American revolution proclaim slavery a curse—when all civilization denounces it—when a cold philosophic statesman, Lord Palmerston, speaks of it as evolving more sin and misery than all other *crimes* from the beginning of the world—when the same language is echoed by the principal statesmen of all nations—when our own country gives us so terrible an example of its influence upon morals, intelligence, and economical interests—your argument is vain—your cause must be lost. Yes, if by any forced interpretation of the Scriptures the belief shall prevail that Christianity sustains slavery, then shall its once glorious and sacred temples be hurled into the dust! Let the priesthood beware, it is a critical posture for the church to be behind the morals of the world. If France was desolated, as is contended, by "self-will," and crimes perpetrated, in the name of Liberty, and Infidelity, it was because the insufferable and infernal corruptions of the professors of religion, and the prostitution of its sanctity to the defence of the most palpable abuses of civil government, had rooted out all reverence from the minds of men—happy indeed if President Shannon shall read the French revolution aright, and take timely warning of the untold miseries which similar infatuation cannot fail to bring upon our own loved land. The author of this address then proceeds to vindicate governments upon the principle that the restraint of self-will is the true happiness. Now, so far, from the government which most subjects my will to that of another, as in the case of slavery, being the best, political writers of all ages and countries have agreed in the very reverse proposition. Does not this man, living in a republic, see that he is vindicating the despotism of the Turk, as the best rule on earth? In a true republic I may do as I please—follow every bent of my own will, except that I must not trench on the rights of others—the largest liberty and *happiness* consisting in a mutual determination that each is to steer clear of his neighbor's path ; and if this rule *was to be* fully enforced by law, so as to ensure its *entire practice*, each man would be as free as if he stood alone in the world—the point at which government ceases to be necessary at all!

But if I am in a despotism, I may be so circumscribed by the will of my sovereign—at one time sent to the field of unjust war, at another subject to unrepelled insult—now forced into prison, and then compelled to hard labor unrequited—till life itself shall become insufferable, and all this without any self-will on my part—the least moral delinquency.

With a most leaden stupidity, he fails to see, that if it be dangerous for a man's will to be without a master, that it is doubly dangerous in the master, to have not only the control of his own will, but that of another also. All this miserable nonsense even so far as the slave is concerned, arises from his overlooking the fact that the will may be, and alas ! too often, is constrained to *evil* as well as to good. Though the master may prevent the slave from being idle, and getting drunk, he may deprive her (if a female) of her chastity, and him (if a male) of his virility.* If slaves were but men, and masters angels or gods, then would slavery be a blessing ; but not till then. "Communities of men therefore have a *jus divinum*, a divine right to organize it in such manner as may be necessary to secure their permanent safety and happiness." What precious stuff is this ? In the "divine right" of tyrants there was some sense, if no truth, and men were taught to submit to what they could not without infidelity change ; but here is neither sense nor truth. If slavery be of God, then man can't change it ; if it be of man, then how comes it to be divine ? What is the community ? all the individuals, or a part ? If a part, which part ? the black or the white ? If you say a majority, suppose that a majority are black, as in South Carolina, shall the blacks rule ? Long ears and a silent tongue, says nature ; violate no more her laws ! The *truth* every ass, it seems to me, might see ; *all* the individuals have a right to equal action and

---

* I know there are many good and virtuous slaveholders : but the misfortune is, that bad men have unlimited power—law nor public sentiment cannot control them, for all indignation is lulled in the consciousness of a common guilt. The crime of castration has been perpetrated with impunity in South Carolina : the master has the life of the slave in his power—the greater includes the less.

security, or else none have, either from God or their own wills. Then, by his own showing, once more, slavery falls.

The President thus sums up his whole argument:

"1st. Happiness is the end and aim of our being." Well, so is death the end; tautology can not save us.

"2d. This happiness can be secured only by acting in harmony with all the laws of our nature," and not then.

"3d. Self-will and insubordination to law is the cause of all our unhappiness, individual and social." False in grammar as well as in fact. What becomes of the millions of ills that are utterly independent of moral action. Even within the scope of the *will*, virtue does not always lead to happiness; as in the physical world, so in the moral, accident, or fate, is a disturbing influence daily displayed. Probably all that can be said upon this subject, at last, is that by an ever active and wise regard to the laws of his being, man may cause good to preponderate over evil. The life of Franklin is in point.

"4th. Freedom, or liberty to act as we please, is a blessing only so far as we please to act right. Beyond these limits bondage is a blessing, and freedom a calamity, highly prejudicial to our interests, even in the present life." If the master be wise as well as good, true—if not, not. A sensible slave might belong to a fool master; then the proposition is at least doubtful. He might belong to a fool and knave, then is it glaringly false. In the first instance the fool master might hurry himself and the slave along in the dark, knocking their shins, "against the laws of being" at every step; in the latter case, the master might damn the poor devil to utter misery, out of an excess of *self-will*. If this magniloquent dogma is a mere show of wisdom, having no reference to slavery, then say, instead, the moon is or is not, as some suppose, a green cheese; that is shorter and more easily assented to.

"5th. The destruction of self-will and the cultivation of a law-abiding spirit—a spirit to do right in every thing at all hazards, is identified with our highest happiness, both in time and eternity." Amen, say all good men; the moral law tells you to let the oppressed go free, will you do it?

"6th. For the attainment of these benevolent ends, God, at various times instituted, by positive enactment, bondage of different grades—including domestic slavery." I appeal to nature, to reason and to every man's conscience, if this be not false!

"7th. Human government is a divine ordinance or appointment for the accomplishment of the same benevolent object; and absolutely indispensable to its accomplishment, at least in the present life. When we say that human government is a divine ordinance, we refer to its authority, and not to its peculiar form or mode of organization," &c. The same thing may be said of a threshing machine, or a tailor's goose; human government is just as divine as they, and no more! When we say that a tailor's goose "is a divine ordinance, we refer to its authority, and not to its peculiar form or mode of organization." Surely this must be the brother of the Mexican diplomatist.

"8th. As bondage in all its forms is a curse on man for the indulgence of self-will and of a lawless spirit, it is obvious that it should exist in no government in no *greater degree* than might be necessary to secure the general good." "Bondage is a curse," ah! then there's an end of it—then is slavery no blessing. "*No greater degree*," of course let slavery enter the kitchen, but stop at the steps of the mansion! Yet if this "curse" be a "blessing," I say let it walk into the President's house. I am not so impious as to wish a "blessing" to be excluded from the parlor of the man of God.

"9th. As among the lawless and self-willed, bondage is a blessing (a curse?) alike indispensable to the existence of society and of individual happiness, even in this world, it is obvious that God wills its existence in every government to such a degree, be it more or less, as, may be necessary to the attainment of these ends," &c. Massachusetts, then, is much more virtuous than Kentucky, as she prospers, having no need of bondage. God help us to a speedy purification of spirit—a sudden deliverance from this "blessing," for which we miserable sinners most frankly confess we have no feelings of gratitude—no hearts of thankfulness.

III.

The eloquent divine, after denouncing the French revolution, as most tyrants do, who affect not to see that this kingdom is infinitely better off now, in consequence of that change, than she ever was in any former period of her history, thus gives utterance : "Had I a voice of thunder, that could penetrate to earth's remotest bounds, I would say to the misguided though amiable enthusiast everywhere, who is toiling for the universal extension of freedom, regardless of the foregoing principles— beware ! "

"O qui rex hominumque Deo-rumque ! "

Misserere Domine—keep cool, Mr. Shannon.   You may have a voice somewhat louder than Amos' baby-wakers—you may get Joe Smith's brass plates and make a quasi thunder, which may frighten some of the good people of Campbelldom, and cause them to fall down on their bellies like beasts, and feed on the garbage that slimes the track of South Carolina nullification and pro-slavery despotism—but the " amiable enthusiasts " who dwell on this side " of earth's remotest bounds," having a spark of that Promethean fire in their souls which assimilates them to Deity—something of the ken of immortal vision, distinguishing good from evil—will perhaps find out, that you are at last but the locum tenens, and not the veritable Jupiter Tonans ; yes, some daring clown, irreverent of majesty, shall pluck up spirit to whisper in the ground, till the very reeds shall cry out, " *Midas has ass' ears.*"

Ye " amiable enthusiasts," who of old with the sun, moon, and stars held companionship, and with a lover's heart communed with the infinite in time and space ; ye who gazed on the " beautiful visible world," with fondest eyes intent, o'er hill and dale, by lake and stream, old ocean's waves, in forests wild and earth's dark secret caves—and seeing all—

"A torrent sweeping by,
And an eagle rushing to the sky,
And a host to its battle plain,"

did think, of the ideas caught from all created nature, *Liberty* was the most lovely ideal of the soul's imaginings, and inspired, so sung of her in moving strains of sweetest harmony, till men listened, loved and died in her willing worship : Homer, Virgil, Dante, Milton, Byron, go to, with your rusty harps, Shannon says, " beware," you sung in vain !

Ye " amiable enthusiasts," orators, statesmen, and philosophers, who ventured to search that deep, unfathomable thing, the human heart—the hopes, the fears, the loves, the passions, the hatreds, conscience, instinct, reason—this "harp of a thousand strings," and marked out at last the all-ennobling sentiment *Liberty*, as the thing divine, in itself at once the most glorious motive, and the highest end of mortal deeds: Plato, Socrates, Demosthenes, Cato, Cicero, Chatham, Franklin, Jefferson, Henry—babblers "beware," when had you "regard," to Shannon's "principles" of philosophy?

Oh Epaminondas, and Miltiades, and Cincinnatus, and Bruce, and Tell, and Washington—"amiable enthusiasts," your laurels shall wither, and the "night-shade of death-distilling fruit" shall henceforth encompass your brows for ever! Your heaven-born aspirations were all in vain—Shannon's "philosophy of slavery" was unknown to you! Marathon, and Leuctra, and Bannockburn, and Waterloo, and Bunker Hill, and Yorktown, in vain was the best blood of long ages shed on your plains—"freedom" is an unattainable thing! No more shall your sacred soil drink of the tears of the "amiable enthusiasts" who in times past have gone up to thy altars, to rekindle the fires of Liberty in heroic hearts—the President of *Bacon* College has spoken in a "voice of thunder, penetrating to earth's remotest bounds;" avenged be the blood of tyrants—henceforth you shall grow only cabbages, and the yearning bowels of the youths of America shall be filled with grass!

You are no enthusiast, Mr. President—not given to the ideal—oh, no, too much stern stuff for that—believe in the universal extension of freedom? not you: you only believe in the universal extension of the Christian religion, and the coming of the glorious millennium! When the lion and lamb shall lie down together; when the wild beasts of the field shall be disarmed of their ferocity; shall the master at last continue to appeal to the fears of his slave? or shall every bond be broken and the oppressed go free? Which, now, Mr. President, will you give up, your "philosophy," or your religion?

> "Hypocrisy, in mercy spare it,
> That holy robe, O din-na tear it,
> Spare it for their sakes who wear it
>   The lads in *black!*
> *   *   *   *   *   *   *
> "Think, wicked sinner wha ye're skaithing,
> It's just the *blue-gown* badge an' claithing
> O' saunts; take that, ye lea'e them naething
>   To ken them by,
> Frae ony unregenerate heathen
>   Like you or I."

I put it to you, then, not as a Christian, but as a philosopher, when before in the history of the world did mankind enjoy more liberty and happiness than now? Have you not heard how many nations have not only become free themselves, but how they have been just enough to remember that all men were made of one flesh—the children of the same father? If since the American Revolution such progress has been made towards "universal freedom," how do you know that the final goal may not be at last reached? that it may not be at least spread over this nominal republic?

If it be true, as you quote from Dr. Wayland, that government must either be formed upon *morals*, or upon *fear*—are you not ashamed, being a religionist, to give up the Bible for the sword? Is there not in all this something worse than most lame and impotent reasoning? is it not contemptible cant and rampant hypocrisy?

The remarks upon mob-law would be well enough in a treatise upon liberty, but are utterly out of place in a studied defence of slavery. When he puts up the bayonet in the place of moral appeal—when he arms me with a pistol over the every will of the slave—is it not absurd to say, that one man may do in good conscience what, when done by ten or more, becomes a crime of the darkest dye? I make the bold assertion, that slavery is lynch-law—mob-law—the law of force, unmeasured by any check but the unbridled will of an irresponsible master: *the day "mob-law" ceases, slavery dies!* What alliance, then, can slavery have with Christianity? The conclusion of this address touches my sensibilities as the most absurd mockery, and the foulest blasphemy against God and virtue; it will be read by the enlightened portion of mankind with the same horror with which Judge O'Neal's sentence of death upon Brown filled all Christendom.

I repeat, I have not dealt personally with President Shannon further than his principles demanded unqualified denunciation. When the interests of seventeen millions of free laborers are trodden under foot, by the same inexorable laws which consign three millions of "native American" blacks to hopeless slavery; when *Republicanism* is stabbed in its vitals, and *Liberty*, under any form of government, sought to be extinguished; when the inner temple of virtue is desecrated to base uses, and the sanctity of the living God invoked in a most unholy cause; when all that is just, and great, and lovely, and sacred—all that makes life desirable, or death supportable, is attempted to be struck down at one insidious blow ; in the desperate energy of self-defence, I shall not stop to ask, whether a frothy, lying dema-gogue, or a canting, sniveling priest shall be the foe.

He may be unconscious of his guilt, but I freely declare my most solemn conviction that there is no crime known among men greater than the one committed by this man. A single murder may extinguish the hopes and fears, the joys and sorrows of one poor mortal—the horridly repulsive features of a special individual crime will check the contagion of the example —but this sanctimonious advocacy of lynch-law, slavery, and wholesale assassination, is infinitely more disastrous in its ultimate results.

When I see the innocent eyes of these young and true hearts raised to their respected teacher, asking some noble, virtuous and sin-defying principle—some glorious and vital sheet-anchor of faith, hope, and safety in a world of temptation and sorrow— when I see slavery instilled into the deep recesses of the soul, drying up the sweet sympathies of the heart, stifling the noblest aspirations of the spirit, substituting crime for virtue, leading down to death and despair—I find no language to give vent to the emotions of pain and indignation which crowd upon me !

Had this man lived in the days of Socrates, the Athenians might have been saved their greatest reproach : as a corruptor of youth, he would have been justly compelled to drink the hemlock. Had he dwelt in Judea of old, our Lord might have been betrayed, and the twelve pieces of silver have been saved.

I shall not insult the slave trader of Louisiana, or the man-pirate of the seas by a comparison with the Christian defender of slavery—for here is one who, without gold, prostitutes his soul to the greatest of crimes, is proud of his abandonment, and glories in his shame !

LETTER.

Col. J. J. Speed, of Ithaca.

Lexington, Ky., July 10, 1844.

Dear Sir—I have received your letter of the 2d instant, inviting me to your state this summer. I am sensible of the high compliment which you pay me ; and would gladly comply with your wishes, if public and private duties did not call me elsewhere. In the meantime I am not idle, and my correspondence with both whigs and liberty men is extensive. I confess that my interest in the cause of the whigs is founded on the supposition that they will act up in good faith to their profession. If whiggery means anything it means opposition to tyranny— all tyranny. If it is dear to me at all, it is because it promotes the great principles of equality and individual prosperity which can only result from real republicanism. I regard no aristocracy in Europe so coercive and anti-republican as Southern slaveholding. The North is equally implicated in this tyranny over *master* as well as slaves. The whigs must come up to this high ground or fall, and their fall will not be regretted by coming generations. If you cannot have my services, you can have those of a greater. SEWARD is a name that New York may well be proud of; call him into the field. Such a man leading, the whigs must triumph. To succeed when such a man is not a fit leader brings no success at which a lover of the principles of '76 can rejoice. Let the whigs of the North put the battle on its true basis and fight it bravely—on one side, *Polk, Slavery, and Texas*—on the other, *Clay, Union, and Liberty*. If we cannot beat on such issues then let us fall: and in our fall we will be remembered by the good for ever. Can it be possible that, while Mr. Clay shall lose some three or four slave states, which were sure to him before, by opposing Texas, that there is not sufficient spirit of freedom, honor, and good faith in the North to carry those large states where his success was before doubtful? Mr. Clay, and his friends, have taken high and holy ground. We must raise the war-cry, soul-stirring as the great questions at issue are expansive, and lasting in their consequences for good or evil. With Polk's election Texas comes in; with Texas the North and South are inevitably split, and away goes the fruits to us here, at least, of the American Revolution.

It is in vain to put off the evil day; it is at hand now. Slavery or liberty is to be determined in some sort this coming election—not the liberty of the black only, but of the white also. I do not mean to say that Mr. Clay is an emancipationist; but I believe his feelings are with the cause. I know that those most immediately within his influence approximate to myself in sentiment upon the subject of slavery. The great mass of whigs are, or ought to be, anti-slavery. If so, then you have no need of me; but if principles give strength, then strengthen yourselves, for I claim nothing above the humblest of my whig friends in ability. If ardent and sincere zeal in the cause of my country's highest and best interests, have given me any consideration, go you and do likewise, and your success will be equal.

The great question of the age in all countries is slavery or liberty. The American Declaration of Rights has leavened the world—the waves first started in the old hall in Philadelphia in '76 have encompassed the earth, and are now returning with accumulated power to the centre where they started. Slavery must fall. Whether we will give it up or go down with it remains with ourselves. "The fault is not in our stars, but in ourselves that we are underlings." It begins to be an *effort* in Europe to treat Americans with civility. Let us take care to retire from Christendom, or vindicate our title to respect. Ten years I have labored silently and cautiously in this cause—forsaken by the whigs, I have stood by them in good and in evil report. I cling to them yet. I implore them to come up to the standard made by Washington and his noble compeers. Save us from disgrace and ruin—elevate us among nations to that post of honor which we once held, and from which slavery and repudiation—twin-brothers—have dragged us down. Let God and liberty be once more our battle-cry—and at last freedom, union, and equality may be ours for ever.

Yours, in the cause of the union and liberty,

CASSIUS M. CLAY.

SPEECH

At the Tremont Temple on the evening of the nineteenth instant, after the adjournment of the great convention on BOSTON COMMON. Sept. 1844.

IT would be ungrateful in me to affect to be insensible to the respect and enthusiasm with which I have been received here, as elsewhere, in the whole North, yet my gratification is diminished by the reflection that I cannot point to any achievement of my own—any great public service which deserves so much distinction as you are pleased to bestow upon me. Still, if fixedness of purpose, an ardent love of country, and a fearless advocacy of *truth* are worthy of consideration, I trust I may prove not altogether undeserving your generous confidence. I stand here under very peculiar circumstances. Having been ever true to the whig cause, from my earliest manhood down to the present hour, I find myself denounced by leading whigs as ultra in my opinions. I owe the whigs nothing—once having possessed their confidence and support, because I would not submit my conscience and my reason to their will I—have been by them, or at least by a portion of them, joined by the democratic party, proscribed for ever. It is unnecessary to say that from the democratic party, I meet with no favor. I myself, am then, only responsible for myself. I know too well that I am denounced at the South as an enemy of my country; I know also who they are, that pursue me with inexorable malice, which neither time, nor distance, nor any thing short of utter ruin of my name and person, can ever satiate. To the pro-slavery party of the South I owe nothing; no—not my life. Once more now, as heretofore, I scorn their wrath and defy their power. I appeal from the thirty-one thousand four hundred and ninety-five slave-holders to the five hundred thousand *free white laborers* of my own loved state. Yes, to Kentucky, place of my nativity, home of my boyhood, the early and fond associations of childhood, and more mature age, I owe my first and lasting allegiance—there I shall ever live and there I shall repose in death. To my country, to posterity, to God, I look for slow coming justice and ultimate judgment.

Shall I repeat that the present crisis is the most eventful in the annals of our history. It is the same great struggle, which from time immemorial down to the present hour, has never ceased between liberty and slavery. In the language of Mr. Choate, the question is not how we shall be governed only, but who shall govern ? It is the same issue which the colonies of America, in seventeen hundred and seventy-six, made with the tyrannical parliament of Britain, except that now we are called upon not only to vindicate the right that taxation and representation should be equal and inseparable, but to stand by, or for ever lose, many of those great safeguards of liberty which we enjoyed under the British rule. Mr. Webster has asked to-day " where, out of America, save in England, exist trial by jury, a free press, public assemblies, the right of free discussion and the habeas corpus act ?" I ask you, where but in England do they exist ? do they exist here ? No, you know too well that they do not. These great bulwarks of human liberty founded on the blood and unspeakable woe of the great and good, who have for long ages fallen a sacrifice to the vindication of the eternal principles of right and truth, are now trampled under foot by the despotic pro-slavery party of this republic.

Yes, it is to slavery and to the temporizing policy of our fathers, owing that the war of '76 was incomplete, and that we are now called upon in 1844 once more to fight the battle of liberty. I will not reproach our illustrious sires, or detract from their glorious fame; they did more, by the American revolution and the constitution of the United States, to establish the cause of human freedom, than any other men whose deeds illustrate the annals of the world. Still, sad experience has too well proved to us, that they left much undone, and the permission of slavery in the United States government has well nigh left us nothing of our original franchises. Let us look the evil boldly in the face; and if it be not already too late, retrace our steps, and be yet saved from ruin. It cannot be denied that the whole people of the Union were *participes criminis* in the establishment of slavery; when they allowed the importation of slaves up to 1808; when the North agreed to return slaves to the South; and allowed three votes for every five slaves in the federal representation. Yes, if they did not use the word *slave* they *meant* it—they meant what they said—if they did not say *all* they meant. On the other hand I deny, now and for ever, that there was any sacred and inviolable compromise between slavery and liberty.   Adams, and Sherman, and Morris, and others of the North; and Madison, and Jefferson, and the immortal Washington, and others of the South—yes all, with few exceptions, of the illustrious founders of the Constitution, were opposed to slavery.   And all—all, every one that voted for the Constitution, agreed that all alliance with slavery, so far as expressed in the three clauses named, the only ones in the Constitution on that subject, should *cease* whenever three-fourths of the states should *will* its fall.   The only compromise in the Constitution is that every state, small as well as large, shall for ever have *two senators;* all other clauses of the Constitution but this may be changed in accordance with the express permission of the instrument itself.   And since the object of the Union, in its preamble, was to establish justice and perpetuate liberty, then, it is not only the right but the inexorable duty of this great republic to purge the Constitution of these clauses, which blot its fair escutcheon, and make its great fabric indeed the temple of the free.   The national government has no power over slavery in the slave states, because none was given it by these then independent sovereignties.   Let each state act on its own responsibility—looking to its own interests, to conscience, and to God.   *I stand by the Constitution—yes, with my life I will defend it.*   But as the general government has no power to abolish slavery, so it has no power to make slavery: and the admission of slave states into this Union I declare to be unconstitutional: and the *permission* of *slavery* is its *establishment.*   Within the district of Columbia and in the territories of the Union, slavery does not constitutionally exist. For the fifth article of the amendments says expressly that " no person shall be deprived of life, liberty, or property without due process of law "—which means without some crime committed, and ascertained, and punished by law.   Then if Congress cannot make a slave, she cannot allow a new state to do it— she cannot transfer to others more power than she has herself —the agent cannot do more than the principal—then she cannot permit slavery in states or territories, or any other place where she has sovereign and uncontrolled power.   Nor can the miserable pretence be set up, that blacks are not "*persons,*" for slaves are called " persons " in *every clause* where they are alluded to in the constitution.   And if A, B, and C, calling themselves states, or Congress itself, can make, or allow to be made, a black man a slave, then I and the best man in Massachusetts may be reduced to slavery, and there is no power in the Constitution to restore us to liberty. The states of Louisiana, and Missouri, and Arkansas, which have been unconstitutionally admitted slave states, have now been by us, the Union, admitted to be SOVEREIGN, and entitled to all the privileges of the other states. I would not, *if I could,* now interfere with slavery there. Experience teaches us that stability in the affairs of men is much ; and it is often better to bear some ills than lose all good by an attempt too late to remedy   But I say, that in the District of Columbia and in the Floridas, as we have, contrary to the Constitution, allowed slavery, we should now pay the masters, and let the slaves go free. Yes, I would tax myself doubly to liquidate the penalty of the bond—give them two prices, if necessary, that in the capital of this great republic, and throughout its vast jurisdiction, the American eagle should spread its sheltering wings for ever over all, of whatever tongue, clime, or color. Here, then, on this broad ground, I take my stand, and I defy the combined talent of all the lawyers and statesmen of the republic to move me.

Thus far, the pro-slavery power, by the concentrated interest of having $1,200,000,000 of so called property represented, has triumphed over the power of liberty and free labor. Our offices of honor and profit have been monopolized almost by slaveholders; our foreign policy has been subsidary to the fostering of *slave labor,* at the expense of *free labor.* The system of internal improvements, as carried on by the general government, the land bill, a national currency, and above all, the tariff, have all been prostrated at the feet of the slave power. And now, when the people of the North seem to be opening their eyes to the real sacrifices which they have made in the desecrated name of democracy, to the rule of slavery, by the ruinous results of the reduction of the tariff from 1832 to '42, John C. Calhoun and his southern clique, seek once more an accession of slave territory to strengthen their power and assist them in over-ruling the tariff of protection, and to reduce us once more to free trade and perpetual slavery. They are determined to rule or ruin; to wield the whole power of the Union, or else dissolve the Union, and establish a slave despotism in the South. Hence the democratic party in 1844, although they went up to Balti-

more instructed to vote for Mr. Van Buren, threw him overboard.
So they rejected Cass, and Buchanan, and Stewart, and took
the unheard-of name of James K. Polk, of Tennessee, Mr. Calhoun's, and Andrew Jackson's most supple tool, imposed upon
them by the same nullification power which had prostrated all
the interests of free labor at the feet of the free trade and perpetual slavery party of the South. And Mr. Polk was suited to
their purposes, not only because he was for Texas and free
trade, but because he was, from his position in a slave state, necessarily identified with the great scheme of ultimate disunion.
Do I state untruth? What say the convention? They are
for immediate annexation! What says Mr. Calhoun? He is
for Texas, to prevent the ultimate overthrow of slavery. What
says R. M. Johnson? We want Texas to form new slave
states, to balance the coming in of the free states of Wisconsin
and Iowa. What say Messrs. Holmes and Rhett? They will
have Texas with the Union, or, if necessary, without the Union.
What says the ex-nullification governor, James Hamilton? He
will resort to *arms* for Texas and dissolution! And last, not
least, what says T. H. Benton, the leader of the democratic party for the last quarter of a century, up to May, 1844—a man of
more sense than all the nullification party consolidated into one?
He tells us in his Booneville speech, that "*dissolution of the
Union*" is the end proposed by these Texas annexationists.
Jackson tells us, Texas is *the* question; the Richmond Enquirer, the leader of the southern democratic wing, says that
"free trade and Texas are the questions." If then these be the
issues, and I am compelled to choose between Polk and free
trade, and Texas, on the one hand, and Henry Clay, home labor, and the Union, on the other, then, by all that is sacred
among men, I go for Clay and the whig party, and against Polk
and the democratic party. Free trade with other nations is impossible—they do not, and will not allow it—and they ought
not if they would. I lay down the broad ground, that has been
practised on for centuries by intelligent nations, repeated once
more by Thomas Jefferson, and engrafted into our system, by
the first law ever made by our government, the end of which
was to perfect its execution, that "the farmer and mechanic
should be set down alongside of each other."

If I raise a bushel of wheat, and carry it to England, and
there exchange it for a hat, I have to pay the entire cost of

transportation, or, if it is divided between me and the hatter equally, I lose half the cost of the carriage. If I sell my bushel of wheat to the hatter living alongside of me, I lose nothing in carriage, neither I nor the hatter. Again, if I carry my bushel of wheat to England, or send it, and sell it, I get one hundred and ten cents a bushel, but it costs me sixty cents to get it there, leaving me but fifty cents at last a bushel for my wheat; but if I can by volition, or by legislation, move the hatter from England, and place him by me, he gives me one hundred and ten cents for my wheat, and I more than double the product of my farm. I say that the whole navy of the world, not engaged in fishing, and similar pursuits, but in carrying on exchanges between countries, which might each for itself make the same things within themselves, is *a dead loss to the world.* The ships must be built and manned, and the men fed at the common expense of the grain grower, and the manufacturer, and they produce nothing in return. England was wise enough long ago to find out this thing; and by her tariff of protection, whereby the farmer found a market at home, and the manufacturer a market in the agriculturist, she has elevated herself to the first position among nations. Nor can her starving millions be urged as an argument against her protective policy. If human life be a blessing, and it be the will of Deity that the earth should support the greatest amount of animal nature possible, in comfort and luxury, then has England done as much or more than any other European nation, in the fulfilment of her true destiny. Suppose that the lower strata of society embraces five millions of people, subject to famine, disease, and death; then you have the remaining twenty millions out of the twenty-five millions comfortable, and enjoying, some of them, many luxuries; reduce the high living of the court, clergy, and aristocracy, and you bring comfort to many millions more. Poverty, disease, and the sword, are, by the stern laws of nature, the checks upon population; destroy England's tariff and machinery, and reduce her population ten millions, still there would stand these same inexorable laws, destroying human life, and limiting population. All animal and vegetable nature are prolific in seed, but perish for want of sustenance; a thousand fish are spawned, where ten live to maturity; so with man, he is limited by the pressure of misery on the under strata. Take the thin, sparse tribes of American savages, there is no class enjoying comfort and security; but the chief and commoner, the squaw and papoose, are all subject to fear, the sword, cold, hunger, and death. Then let not the tariff system be sacrificed to the dictation of the slave power—but let here in our own republic many centuries intervene, before we shall be subject to the stern laws which press upon the laboring poor of Europe. And cursed be the statesman for ever, who would degrade the laborers of this happy country to the level of foreign labor, and precipitate them into premature and unnecessary decay, and untimely and utter ruin.

In order to accomplish the overthrow of the free labor of the country, north and south, then Texas must be taken into the confederacy. It was for this, that the naked project is now presented to this people; whether they will now, in the nineteenth century, in the face of Christendom, without any outward pressure—such as in times past was urged, that England forced slaves upon us, without the salvo to an awakening conscience, so often potently applied—"what are we to do with the slaves when free?" in direct violation of the Constitution, through breach of treaty, and by war—cruel, unprovoked, unhallowed war—vote to extend slavery over three hundred thousand square miles of territory, now declared by Mexico to be free and equal in all its population, in order to perpetuate the bonds of three million slaves and seventeen million whites! For one, if I stand alone, I am against it now; I am against it for ever! Let us examine, for a moment, some of the miserable pretences for this acquisition, which are thrown out to deceive the honest portion of the democracy, and delude them to their own ruin. For, what kind of democracy is that which, contrary to the principles upon which were based the American revolution, allows the most infamous man, who by the slave trade, or piracy, acquires possession of one hundred slaves—his fellow men—in Texas, to stand, by admission into the Union, against you, sir, (Abbot Lawrence) and any other sixty of the wealthiest and most intelligent freemen, whether whig, democrat, or abolitionist, in the North? We want Texas, they tell us, to prevent smuggling into the United States! That is, the men who have sworn to dissolve the Union, or break down the domestic industry of the country, want Texas for fear England will do the same thing, which they are rushing to war, even, to accomplish! Into such absurdities do men fall

when they leave the straight road of justice and truth! Here
lies England along our whole northern coast. We are accessi-
ble through the whole of the eastern and southern border, and
yet we are to be told that Great Britain will sail around the
dangerous seas about Florida, and into the shallow lagoons of
all southern Texas, and pass through the swamps of the Mississippi lying between these and the Sabine, to smuggle goods
into America! The same reasons which forbid its being used
as a place of smuggling, apply with greater force against the
idea of Andrew Jackson, that Texas would, in the hands of
England, become a point of attack. If it were not from the
source whence this argument came, it would deserve to be passed in contemptuous silence. What? when we are unable to
guard the line from the mouth of the Sabine to the southern
border of Arkansas, a few hundred miles, extend the line from
the mouth of the Rio Grande, eighteen hundred miles including
Santa Fe, to its source—embracing one hundred thousand
square miles more than the kingdom of France—and then we
can defend it? But if names are thus to weigh down common
sense, I put Napoleon against Jackson, and he tells us that a
desert is the best barrier against foreign incursions. And should
England be fool enough to land in the shallow bays of Texas,
unfit for the first class of war steamers, and hazard her army
through the *unproductive* swamps between the Sabine and the
Great River, we would have time enough to rally a half million of freemen, from the lakes to the Gulf, to give her ball and
steel as soon as she showed herself from the canebrakes of
the Mississippi. The idea that England seeks to surround us
is equally absurd. If she did, she would only weaken her
force, and enable us more easily to break through her serried
ranks, wherever drawn up in battle array. But England seeks
not to possess Texas; she has again and again, in the most
formal manner, disclaimed any improper interference, of any
character whatever; and if she should attempt it, then let us,
by arms, if necessary, stand for Texan independence.

I would always treat an opponent with respect, but I must
confess that I lose my patience when I see such men as Mr.
Bancroft urging the annexation of Texas, under the damnable
pretence that it would ultimately lead off slavery from our soil.
Manufacturers, do you lower the price of your goods by acquiring additional markets? Farmers, do you diminish the price

of your produce by having two manufacturing towns to sell to, instead of one? Then tell me no more that you will destroy slavery in the states by finding in Texas new markets for slaves, and thus enhancing the profits of slave breeding in all the grain-growing slave states in the Union. What presumption is it, for men here to set up such opinions against the combined experience of all who live in the slave states, both, those who are in favor of emancipation, and those who advocate eternal slavery, agreeing in this only, that the admission of Texas will tend to make slavery secure in the United States for centuries to come! Nor do we want Texas for the purposes of emigration and expansion of our population. Every principle of political economy teaches us, that up to the time when the earth ceases to afford sustenance for its inhabitants, it is desirable not to diminish population, but to increase it: because all the burthens of civil government, moral and intellectual improvement, are lessened to each individual by the accumulation of numbers, to say nothing of the perfection of all the arts which accrue from the division of labor and the laws of intelligent observation and heightened competition. We are capable, on our present soil, of sustaining more than two hundred millions of men. Far distant, then, is the day, when it will be the interest of our people to leave us. No, we do not want Texas to prevent smuggling—we do not want it to prevent England from getting it as a point of attack—we do not want it for purposes of emigrating—we do not want it to destroy slavery. Oh, no! I ask every democrat here to-night, to tell if there be under heaven, any reason why this project then is urged upon us, in all this hot haste, but for the avowed, the single, the damnable purpose of extending slavery over the unborn millions of Texas, and perpetuating the slave rule over us and our posterity! Once more, I repeat, I am against it, now and for ever. The Romans made their prisoners of war pass under a yoke, to remind them of their servitude: here is a yoke labelled *war and perpetual slavery*; shall the future historian write it, that the descendants of the patriots of '76 went forward to the polls in 1844, and voluntarily submitted their necks to bondage, gladly prostrating themselves before the heel of the tyrant?

But if you take Texas you must pay her debts, twenty-five million dollars, says Mr. Benton, who also tells what we all believe to be true, that not a single foot of unappropriated land remains in Texas proper to come into our possession and liquidate the debt we pay for her. How dare the men who will not give us our own land money, to pay our debts and relieve our own states from repudiation and dishonor, to thrust their fingers into the pockets of the freemen of America, to pay twenty-five millions of money for a foreign nation, incurred in propagating slavery among men? We trample upon the most solemn treaty between Mexico and the United States, and rush over the Constitution, to war in this fiendish propagandism; and in such a war, according to the laws of nations, it is not only the right, but the bounden duty of all Christendom, to come in to the help of Mexico, and reduce us to a sense of common justice. And in such a war, when the banner of 1776, "right against might," once borne by us, is now borne by them—when I shall be called upon to rally to the standard of my country, inscribed with "eternal slavery"—I am bold in the avowal, that, though I profess to be as brave as most men, I have no heart for such a contest, I am a coward in such a cause! On our own soil, in defence of our own rights, I defy the world in arms; but in such a cause as this, if the Bible be true, we cannot succeed; if history be not a fable, we cannot hold permanent conquest; "they who live by the sword shall perish by the sword;" and at all times, dominion based upon unjust conquest, has fallen to sudden ruin and ultimate retributive desolation! This republic must stand upon *justice*, a *high moral sentiment*, or else it cannot *stand at all;* there must be either a regard for right, or a resort to the sword; either a pure ballot-box, or the pestilential cartridge-box! The day that the nation deliberately violates right, the Constitution of our country crumbles into dust, and is gone for ever, and upon its ruins rises force and utter despotism. And now we are called upon, in the very outset, to perpetrate this outrage against the laws of nations and nature, by trampling the Constitution under foot in two several instances; once, as I have shown before, by violating the 5th article of the amendments, by admitting Texas as a *slave state;* and again, by admitting her at all. The Constitution is an instrument of delegated powers; all powers not given are reserved to the states, or to the people. Where, I ask every democrat here, is the clause, giving the federal government authority to add a foreign nation to us, or us to a foreign nation? Nowhere! You cannot show it; it does not exist. I admit, with Chancellor Kent that Louisiana was constitutionally admitted as territory, saving the allowance of slavery; although every Jeffersonian democrat would be forbid the use of the precedent; for Mr. Jefferson agreed there was no power in the Constitution to accomplish it. But there lay Spain at the mouth of the Mississippi, threatening by arms to resist our entrance into the Gulf of Mexico, the great highway of nations, to which we had a right to pass, by the laws of God and man. Kentucky could not treat with her; she was forbid to do so by the federal Constitution; war was likely to ensue: there was necessarily some soverign power to come forward, and anticipate a ruinous war by a timely treaty; it *necessarily* accrued, then, to the *Senate of the United States* to acquire, or cede territory, in order to determine this eternal cause of enmity and war. I say then that Louisiana was rightly acquired of France; and the same thing was rightly done at the treaty of Washington, when land was acquired and lost in Maine. But far different is the case with Texas; we have no cause of quarrel, no point of contact; there is no *necessity* for the interference of the Senate, and its power only belongs to it.

When you vote for Polk, then, you vote for Texas; for Mr. Webster has very well to-day remarked, that it is " Polk *and* Texas, or neither Polk nor Texas.   If, then, you elect Polk, you vote a tax of twenty-five millions of dollars—you vote a war—you vote the violation of treaties—you vote a double violation of the Constitution, by annexing foreign states, and also *slave* states, to the Union. And if the president and fifty-two senators may to-night annex Texas to us, they may to-morrow unite us once more to the British crown, or to the Russian despotism. If they may enslave the blacks to-day, they may enslave me and you the day after; and there is no power under heaven which can give us liberty, if this Constitution does not. Men of Boston, what say you? Will you give up the Constitution, or will you stand by it for ever? What shall we do, then, to avoid these accumulated evils that threaten us on all sides? Who can save us from this gulf of ruin? Can Mr. Garrison do it? He will not if he has the power! Can Mr. Birney do it? He cannot, if he would. Mr. Polk will be sure not to save us, but to sacrifice us. What other man, then, in all this wide land, except Mr. Clay, can, from his talents, his patriotism, and his fortunate position, stay the wild waves of anarchy, violence, and dishonor? No other—none. Then must I vote for Mr. Clay. He has told us in three several letters that he is against Texas. So long as it costs more than a fair rate, he is against it. It was thought, by the Jackson cabinet, to be worth four millions of money only. Now, when there is not a foot of land to be sold to refund the money, we have no reason to believe that Mr. Clay would be willing to give twenty-five millions of dollars. So long as it costs us dishonor, by breach of treaty, Mr. Clay is against it. So long, then, as Mexico shall choose the treaty to remain, so long is Mr. Clay against annexation. So long as it costs us a war, Mr. Clay is opposed to Texas. War now exists: and Santa Anna, her president, tells General Hamilton that as long as a drop of Mexican blood flows in the veins of her patriots, they will resist the desecration of their soil, and the dismemberment of the Empire. And although bribes have been offered, and ministers have been sent to negotiate, and every thing tried, it is all in vain to move the Mexicans to acknowledge the independence of Texas. And they know full well that the loss of Texas is the downfall of Mexico. Already has Mr. C. J. Ingersoll said this whole continent is, or should be, ours; and so soon as Texas falls, then falls California, then Mexico proper, and so on, till our own government, as well as theirs, shall be for ever wrecked.

So long, then, as Mexicans shall love their homes, the graves of their sires, the illustrious dead, who achieved her independence, so long will she resist Texan independence, and so long is Mr. Clay bound to oppose annexation. So long as Texas cannot come in by the common consent of the Union, so long is Mr. Clay pledged against it. He will not look to the Democratic, the Whig, or Liberty party in the states, but to the *states themselves*. He regards them as forming in the Union individuals, parties to a common compact. No new partner can come in, without vitiating the whole agreement; and if this view be his, as we are warranted in saying, then, so long as a single state opposes it, Texas cannot be ours. Five states have almost unanimously, in their state capacity, protested against the unholy project. So long, then, as they—as one of the smallest states is against it—she cannot, by Mr. Clay's consent, come in. So long, then, as you are true to the great principles of 1776—so long as you remain worthy descendants of the pilgrim sires—so long as the vestal flame of liberty shall burn in your bosoms, eternal and inextinguishable—*so long* is Mr. Clay, three several times in the most solemn manner, before the nation and all mankind, irrevocably bound to oppose the annexation of Texas to these United States. Then, my countrymen! be persuaded to trample under foot prejudice and party rule, and quietly and conscientiously review the whole ground; then look to your country and to God, and do your duty now in November 1844, before it is for ever too late !

Be not deluded by the enemies of all liberty, who, under the honeyed name of *democracy*, would reduce you to perpetual servitude. Do not suppose that you are doing anything for the cause of human freedom by opposing Mr. Clay. Of all men now present, I have the greatest cause to take care that I am not deceived in this matter. I can go—I say it before God and man—with a good conscience for him, because I believe it will save my country from ruin if we shall secure his election. The blood of all those, who in all ages have gone up to the scaffold and the cannon's mouth, in defence of the true and the right, calls on us to-night. Remember the mighty agony, the voiceless woe, of the generous and brave hearts who have perished in the cause of human liberty. Oh, be faithful to this last hope of freedom among men : let our battle cry be liberty and union —*God and the right*. If we triumph, mankind will rejoice in our success; if we fall, then all that is worthy to stand, the noblest aspirations of the soul, the desire of glory and immortality, shall fall with us.

ADDRESS

PEOPLE OF KENTUCKY.

WHILST I was battling in the North, in a triangular fight, with Whigs, Abolitionists, and Democrats, for the postulate that " what the law makes property, is property," and that all good citizens should abide by the law, till they can, in a legal and constitutional manner, conform it to their conscientious standard of morality ; the Southern press was denouncing me as wishing to employ the army and navy of the United States in the liberation of the slaves. The many calumnious insinuations against my fidelity to the laws and state allegiance, I shall not condescend to repel. I say to those who are so insidiously attempting to prejudice me in the confidence of the whig party, that I shall nothing palliate nor deny ; conscious of my own duty to the American people, I have fearlessly discharged it ; and as I never played the *sycophant* to *men* for the sake of office, though *sacrificing some personal pride* in the cause of the political *principles* of that party, to some portion of which I owe nothing, so, in defeat, I have nothing to deplore but the common calamities of the country.

To the *people* of Kentucky I would humbly suggest, that I am the son of one of the first pioneers of the West—a man who, in an obscure way, rendered some service to his country, both in the council and in the field ; he was one of the founders of the state Constitution, and his services were not unappreciated by those who have perpetuated his memory, by giving his name to one of the counties of the commonwealth. I speak not of these things in a vain spirit, or from overweening filial affection, but to remind those men of yesterday, that they are presuming too much upon popular credulity, and their own significance, when they set themselves up as the exclusive guardians of the honor and welfare of the state, and undertake to denounce and ostracise me as an enemy of the country. Having some small interest in the soil, as well as in the good name of the commonwealth, with all of my humility and love of equality, I cannot but give utterance to some touches of contempt and indignation towards those feeders upon the crumbs which fall from other men's tables, who affect so much sensibility about the *property* of the country. If there is in our state something improper or dangerous to be talked or written about, I put it to every true and manly Kentuckian, if that thing is not improper and dangerous in its existence among us? And if so, is he who undertakes to remove the evil the enemy of his country? Or rather, is not that man, who, seeing the wrong, for the sake of popularity, and a narrow self-interest, in opposition to the welfare of the great mass of the people, dares not attempt its extinction, a traitor and a coward, and truly deserving the execration of his countrymen? I am not ashamed to admit, that I am the uncompromising foe of tyranny, wherever displayed; and I proudly avow myself the eternal enemy of slavery. At the same time, experience-taught charity warns me to lose none of my sympathy for the slaveholder, because of his misfortune or his fault: and whilst I would be just to the black, I am free to confess, that every feeling of association, and instinctive sentiment of self-elevation, lead me to seek the highest welfare of the white, whatever may be the consequences of liberation to the African.

Bred among slaves, I regarded them with indifference, seeing no departure from morals or economical progress in the tenure. The Emancipation movement about 1830, affected me as it did most persons at the time; and I felt some new and pleasing emotions springing up in my bosom, when I had resolved, in common with my lamented brother, to liberate my slaves. I authorized him to put my name to the Emancipation Society, formed about that time in Mercer county. In the same year I went on to Yale College, in a *free* state. I was not blind, and I therefore saw a people living *there* luxuriously on a soil which *here* would have been deemed the high road to famine and the alms-house. A city of ten or fifteen thousand inhabitants rose up in the morning, passed through all the busy strife of the day, and laid down at night, in quiet and security, and not a single police officer was anywhere to be seen. Here were more than five hundred young men congregated from all climes, of various habits and temperaments, in the quick blood of youth, and all-conquering passion, and there was not found in all the city, so far as the public were aware, a single woman so fallen as to demand a less price for her love than honorable marriage. A grey-haired judge of seventy years and more, in a life-time of service, had pronounced sentence of death upon but five criminals in a whole state; and three of these went down to ruin by intemperance. I had been taught to regard Connecticut as a land of wooden nutmegs and leather pumpkin seed—yet there was a land of sterility without paupers, and a people where no man was to be found who could not write his name, and read his laws and his Bible. These were strange things; but far more strange, passing strange will it be, Kentuckians, if you shall not come to the same conclusion to which I was compelled, that *liberty, religion, and education,* were the cause of all these things, and the true foundation of individual happiness and national glory. In 1835, I introduced a common school bill into the house of representatives of Kentucky; it was lost. In 1838, I had the pleasure of voting for the present common school law, in common with a great majority of my compeers. Before 1840 I was firmly convinced, that universal education in a slave state was impossible! Whilst I now write, the eight hundred thousand dollars set aside, from the proceeds of the sales of the public lands, for common schools, surreptitiously appropriated to internal improvements, confirm my conclusion. There is not a single cent, in the great commonwealth of Kentucky, appropriated to the education of her people! C. A. Wickliffe, in a convention of teachers in 1840, at Frankfort, said; "If slavery and common schools be incompatible, I say, let slavery perish." The sentiment was met with tremendous applause. Men of Kentucky, what say you? Time has proved that they are incompatible: not a single slave state has succeeded from the beginning, in the general education of her citizens. Governor Hammond, of South Carolina, says, in his message to the legislature; "the free school system is a failure;" "its failure is owing to the fact, that it does not suit our people or our government." Experience and reason have long since proclaimed the same unwelcome fact.

Whilst Mr. Wickliffe was speculating I was acting. By aid of the law of 1833, I hoped ultimately to emancipate the state from ignorance, poverty, and crime. Kentucky called upon all her sons, by all the glorious memories of the past, by all the fond hopes of the future, to resist those who, by the repeal of that law, and a retrograde movement, would sink her into the ever during night and "lower deep" of perpetual slavery. The time had at last come when I was to play the selfish time-server for office and temporary elevation, or, planting myself on the eternal principles of truth, justice, and reason, looking to conscience, to posterity, and to God, to fall proudly in their cause. What though I be a "fanatic or an enthusiast" in holding that slavery is contrary to the declaration of American independence; the Constitution of the United States; the common law of our English inheritance; and in violation of the laws of nature and of God—the effects of it are beyond all controversy—the monumental hand of time has written them in characters of horrible distinctness, turning the dewy heavens into brass, and scathing the green earth with sterility and decay. The whole South cries out with anguish against this and that measure of national injury; implores and denounces in alternate puerility; makes and unmakes presidents; enacts and repeals laws with a petulance and recklessness, more worthy of manly indignation, than the pitiable forbearance of the North. Yet no relief comes to the sinking patient; her hypochondriacal illusions are not dispelled; she cannot, she will not see that slavery, nothing but slavery is the cause of her ruin. Her fields relapse into primitive sterility; her population wastes away; manufactures recede from the infected border; trade languishes; decay trenches upon her meagre accumulations of taste or utility; gaunt famine stalks into the shattered portals of the homestead; the hearth-stone is invaded by a more relentless intruder than the officer of the law; and the castle that may stand before the sword, falls by this slow, secret, and resistless enemy; the blood of the body politic is frozen at the core; atrophy paralyses all its limbs; sullen despair begins to display itself in the care-worn faces of men; the heavens and the earth cry aloud, the eternal laws of happiness and existence have been trampled under foot; and yet, with a most pitiable infatuation, the South still clings to slavery. The competition of unrequited service, slave labor, dooms the laboring white millions of these states to poverty; poverty gives them over to ignorance; and ignorance and poverty are the fast high roads to crime and suffering.* Among the more fortunate property holders, religion and morality are staggering and dying. Idleness, extravagance, unthriftiness, and want of energy, precipitate slaveholders into frequent and unheard of bankruptcies, such as are unknown in free states and well-ordered monarchies. The spirit of uncontrolled command vitiates our temperaments, and destroys that evenness of temper, and equanimity of soul, which are the sheet anchors of happiness and safety in a world of unattainable desire and inexorable evil. Population is sparse, and without numbers there is neither competition nor division of labor, and, of necessity, all mechanic arts languish among us.† Agriculture drags along its slow pace with slovenly, ignorant, reckless labor. Science, literature, and art, are strangers here; poets, historians, artists, and machinists; the lovers of the ideal, the great, the beautiful, the true, and the useful; the untiring searches into the hidden treasures of unwilling nature, making the winds, the waters, the palpable and the impalpable essences of things, tributary to man; creating gratification for the body, and giving new susceptibility and expansion to the soul; they flourish where thought and action are untrammeled; ever daring must be the spirit of genius; its omnipotence belongs only to the *free*. A loose and inadequate respect for the rights of property, of necessity follows in the wake of slavery. Duelling, bloodshed, and Lynch law leave but little security to person. A general demoralization has corrupted the first minds in the nation; its hot contagion has spread among the whole people; licentiousness, crime, and bitter hate infest us at home; repudiation, and the forcible propagandism of slavery, is arraying against us the world in arms. I appeal to history, to reason, to nature, and to conscience, which neither time nor space, nor fear, nor hate, nor hope of reward, nor crime, nor pride, nor selfishness, can utterly silence—are not these things true? A minute comparison of the free and slave states, so often and ably made, I forbear. I leave this unwilling and bitter proof to each man's

---

* In 1843 there were in Kentucky but 31,495 slave-holders; the ratio of the slave-holders to the whole population of the South, is about 1 to 25.

† It is estimated that in 1833, the mechanical power of machinery in England performed the labor of 400,000,000 of men. What else than poverty can we expect when slavery and free trade expose us to this awfully unequal competition.

observation and reflection. There is, however, one consideration which I would urge upon all, because it excludes all
"fanaticism and enthusiasm." Kentucky will be richer in dollars and cents by emancipation, and *slaveholders will be the
wealthier by the change.*

I assert, from my own knowledge, that lands of the same
quality in the free, are from a hundred to a hundred and fifty
per cent. higher in value than in the slave states: in some cases,
probably, six hundred per cent. higher! Lands six miles from
Cincinnati, in Ohio, I am credibly informed, are worth sixty
dollars per acre, whilst in Kentucky, the same distance from
that city, and of the same quality, they are worth only ten
dollars per acre! Now the slaveholders of the state are, with
rare exceptions, the landholders of the state; they, therefore,
absolutely increase their fortune by liberating their slaves, even
without compensation. Thus if I own a thousand acres of
land in Fayette, it is worth fifty thousand dollars; say I own
twelve slaves worth five thousand dollars, the probable ratio
between land and slaves; if my land rise to the value of the
free state standard, which it must do, my estate becomes worth
(losing the value of the slaves, five thousand dollars), ninety-five
thousand dollars.* If it rises to a hundred and fifty dollars per
acre, three times its present value, as I most sincerely believe it
would do in twenty years after emancipation, the man owning
a thousand acres of land, now worth fifty dollars per acre, would
be worth, under the free system, a hundred and forty-five
thousand dollars. Now this assertion is fully proven by facts
open to all. Kentucky was settled by wealthy emigrants;
Ohio by mere laborers mostly. Kentucky has forty-two thousand square miles in area; Ohio but forty thousand. Kentucky
is the senior of Ohio by nearly one half of the existence of the
latter. Kentucky is the superior of Ohio in soil, climate,
minerals, and timber, to say nothing of the beauty of her
surface—and yet Ohio's taxes, for 1843, amounted to two
million three hundred and sixty-one thousand four hundred
and eighty-two dollars, and eighty-one cents, whilst Kentucky's

---

* The recent visit of the Quakers to the West Indies confirms this view.
They say in many places the land is now worth as much as both land and
slaves were during slavery.—See "Visit to the West Indies, 1840–41," published
1844, Philadelphia.

tax is only three hundred and forty-three thousand six hundred and seventeen dollars, seventy-six cents.   Thus showing Ohio's superior productive energy over Kentucky.   Ohio has twenty-three electoral votes to our twelve, and outstrips us in about the same ratio in all things else.   A comparison of the older free and slave states will show a much more favorable balance sheet to the free labor states; whilst the slave states have greatly the advantage in climate and soil, to say nothing of the vastly greater extent of the territory of the slave states.*

Massachusetts produces more in gross manufactures yearly, than all the cotton in the Union sells for !† Let Louisville look to Cincinnati, and ask herself how many millions of dollars slavery costs her?   All our towns dwindle, and our farmers lose, in consequence, all home markets.   Every farmer bought out by the slave system, sends off one of the consumers of the manufactures of the town : when the consumers are gone, the mechanic must go also.   A has acquired another thousand acres of land, but B has gone to Ohio with the fifty thousand dollars paid for it, and the state is that much the poorer in the aggregate.   A has increased in his apparent means, but his market has flown to lands governed by wiser heads than the land of slavery can boast.   Beef from Fayette sold this spring in the city of New York for six dollars per hundred ; but the expense of carriage was three dollars per hundred ; thus, for want of a home market, which cannot exist in a slave state, the beef raiser *loses one half of the yearly proceeds of his farm.* Slavery costs every man in the community about the same price—one half and more of the proceeds of his labor, as the price of lands have shown !

Political difficulties thicken round us ; war for the perpetuation of this curse, threatens us in the distance ; dark clouds of bloodshed, dissolution, and utter ruin, lower on the horizon : the great national heart lies bleeding in the dust, under the relentless heel of the slave power !   It requires no very quick eye to see that the political power of Kentucky is gone for ever, unless she takes a new tack, and revives under the free labor system.   Having, in truth, no common interest with the slave-

---

* There are, in the free states, leaving out Michigan, 291,435 square miles : and the slave states, leaving out Arkansas, 482,780 square miles.

† See the address of James Tallmadge before the American Institute, 1844.

holding policy of the South, we bear all the evils of the alliance, without any of the supposed compensating benefits which slavery confers·upon the cultivators of rice, sugar, and cotton.* The South is beginning to be supplied with produce from states nearer them in distance and facilities of transportation than ours, whilst she is already too poor to buy from us; we look for markets almost exclusively to Cincinnati, and New York, and New Orleans, which last is but the outlet to the other nations. Until Kentucky is prepared to go all lengths for slavery, she is powerless; not pro-slavery enough for "the chivalry," nor free enough for the *free*, between two stools she flounders on the ground.

Christians, moralists, politicians, and merely let-live laborers feel these bitter truths. Kentucky never will unite herself to the slave empire, born of Southern disunion: then let her at once lead on the van of freedom. Is the cry of liberty less powerful than slavery to move the hearts of men? Let us, then, be just and fear not. Let us liberate our slaves, and make friends instead of enemies for the evil day; for all the signs of the times proclaim that the elements of revolution are among us; when the crisis comes, if we are free, all will be safe; if not, no man can see the end.† British emancipation has gone before us, proving all things safe. The price of land in the colonies is admitted on all hands to have risen in value, in spite of all the enemies of freedom; these are the eternal and undisputable proofs of successful reform.‡ The day you strike off the bonds of slavery, experience and statistics prove the prophecy of Thomas Jefferson, that the ratio of the increase of the blacks upon a given basis, diminishes, compared with the increase in slavery; whilst the influx of white immigration swallows up the great mass of the African race, in the progress

---

* The only argument left to the pro-slavery party is, *hemp* cannot be raised without slave labor! If ridicule be more potent than argument, then is slavery perpetrating suicide most effectually. Quattlebum can't save it.

† See the appeal to the people of Massachusetts on the annexation of Texas.

‡ Some thick headed "anti-fanatical" politicians affect to consider British emancipation a failure, because the imports and exports are less since emancipation than before. Every one knows that in planting with slave labor, simplicity is always aimed at, hence great exports of sugar, &c.; but under the free system, many articles of subsistence are cultivated instead of sugar. The price of land is, therefore, the only true test of prosperity.—See "Visit to the West Indies."

and civilization of the more energetic white. Amalgamation of the two races, so affectedly dreaded by some pro-slavery men, is far less in the free than in the slave states; this all men know from observation; what a little reflection would have enabled them, *a priori*, to have determined. Many of the more faithful and industrious slaves may be employed by their quandam masters, whilst the idle and vicious must suffer the consequences of their folly. Stealing will not increase, as some argue, but be diminished; for vigilance will be more active, and punishment more certain and severe. *Let candidates be started in all the counties in favor of a convention, and run again and again, till victory shall perch on the standard of the free. Whether emancipation be remote or immediate, regard must be had to the rights of owners, the habits of the old, and the general good feeling of the people.* To those who cry out for ever, What shall be done with the freed slaves? it will occur that upon this plan, no more will be left among us than we shall absolutely need, for we have every reason to suppose that many of the opponents of the movement will leave us before its consummation, taking their slaves with them: and the state ought not to, if she could, at once deprive herself of the slave laborers now here.

Then let us, having no regard to the clamors of the ultras of the North or the South, move on unshaken in our purpose, to the glorious end. Shall sensible men be for ever deluded by the silly cry of "abolitionist?" is this not becoming not only ridiculous, but contemptible? Can you not see that many base demagogues have been crying out wolf, whilst they were playing the traitors to their party and the country for personal elevation? Is it not time that some sense of returning justice should revive in your bosoms, and that you should cease to denounce those who in defeat do not forget their integrity, and who, though fallen, do not despair of the republic?

Washington, Jefferson, and Madison, and the great founders of the republic, are my standard bearers—Liberty and Union is my motto. Never yet has a Kentuckian deserted his country's standard, and fled the field. Shall I be the first to prove recreant to the sentiment which should ever be uppermost in the bosoms of the gallant and the free, when danger, no matter whether of the sword, or more damning despotism threatens his native land?

—" Think through *whom*
Thy life-blood tracks its parent lake,
And then strike home !"

I have given my slaves freedom for the public good. Is more needed? Tax me to the verge of sustenance and life, and make my country *free!* I call upon all Kentucky to speak out upon this subject; let each man come to the press in his own name: let us hear others—hear all. *Trust not those who in private whisper approval in your ear, but denounce the open advocates of the same admissions.* I do not profess to be infallible; if I am wrong, show me the right; no man will do more, suffer more for conciliation. I listen to advice, I implore counsel; but neither denunciation, nor proscription, nor persecution, shall silence me; and so far as the voice of one individual makes up the omnipotence of public will, I say, Kentucky shall be free. Let no man be startled; a few years ago most men looked upon slavery as a matter of course; a thing of necessity, which was to live for centuries. Now, few are so hardy as to deny that some twenty or thirty years will witness its extinction.

The time is, in my judgment, yet nearer at hand. A space of three counties deep, lying along the Ohio river, contains a decided majority of the people of the state, as well as the greater part of the soil. How long before slaves there will be, from obvious causes, utterly useless? Soon, very soon, will they find themselves bearing all the evils of slavery, without any, the least remuneration. Does any man believe that they will tamely submit to this intolerable grievance? If slavery does not tumble down of itself, they will vote it down, for they will have the *power*, and it will be their *interest* to do so. The rich interior counties of the state have the least need of slave labor of any portion of the globe. The mountains are ruined by the decreasing population of the lowlands, and the inability to consume their products, where slaves abound. The Green River country should remember that if Pandora's box was opened again upon mankind, two greater curses and forerunners of poverty and ruin, than slaves and tobacco, could not be found! Kentuckians, be worthy of your past fame—be heroes once more. God has not designed this most favored land to be occupied by an inferior race. Italian skies mantle over us, and more than Sicilian luxuriance is spread beneath our feet. Give us *free labor*, and we shall indeed become "*the garden of the world.*" But what if not? Man was not created only for the eating of Indian meal; the mind—the soul must be fed, as well as the body. The same spirit which led us on to the battle field, gloriously to illustrate the national name, yet lives in the hearts of our people; they feel their false position; their impotency of future accomplishment. This weight must be removed. *Kentucky must be free.*

CASSIUS M. CLAY.

Lexington, Ky., January, 1845.

From the New York Tribune.

LETTER TO MR. CLAY.

NEW-YORK, 9th Jan., 1846.

CASSIUS M. CLAY, Esq.:

DEAR SIR—Having heard with pleasure, of your arrival in New-York, we venture to express the hope that, before your departure, you may be induced to address a public assembly on the subject with which your name and character have been of late so prominently identified. Believing it to be alike due to you and to the cause of human freedom, that you should have an opportunity, untrammeled by any party associations, to lay before the people of New-York the views of slavery, which, as a southern man, you are known to entertain, we take the liberty of asking you if it will suit your inclination and convenience to address a public meeting on some evening during your stay amongst us.

We should, for ourselves, be pleased to hear you, and we doubt not that there are other of our citizens who have a similar desire, and would cheerfully attend a meeting for that purpose.

We are, dear sir, with great respect.

Your fellow-citizens,

EDWARD CURTIS,	ORVILLE DEWEY,
E. C. BENEDICT,	HIRAM KETCHUM,
R. M. BLATCHFORD,	JAMES HARPER.
JOHN INMAN,	HORACE GREELEY,
EDWARD DAYTON,	DAVID B. OGDEN,
HENRY W. BELLOWS,	JOHN JAY,

ISAAC T. HOPPER.

Mr. Clay's Reply.

ASTOR HOUSE, Jan. 9, 1846.

GENTLEMEN:

I had the honor of receiving to-day your very kind and flattering letter, inviting me to address the citizens of New York, " in the cause of human freedom."

Believing, as I do, that the cause in which I am engaged—*Constitutional, Equal Liberty*—is not bounded by the imaginary lines of states or nations, I accept your invitation; hoping to excite in the minds of New Yorkers, a train of reflection that will result in some good to our unhappy republic.

Standing, as I do, to some extent, isolated from party rule and the power of numbers, with no other support and alliance than truth, and the unerring instincts of an honest heart, my only guide, I shall ever gratefully appreciate that true nobility of soul which has moved you—men, whose elevated standing and acknowledged judgment will not be questioned, in a time-serving age—to come up and give me a helping hand, at this critical time in my humble life.

I will address you at any time and place you may name, between now and Wednesday next.

I have the honor to be, your ob't. serv't.,

CASSIUS M. CLAY.

To Messrs. Edward Curtis, Orville Dewey, E. C. Benedict, Hiram Ketchum, R. M. Blatchford, James Harper, John Inman, Horace Greeley, Edward Dayton, David B. Ogden, Henry W. Bellows, John Jay, Isaac T. Hopper.

THE MEETING AND THE SPEECH.

The largest and most respectable concourse ever assembled under one roof in the city of New York, convened at the Broadway Tabernacle last evening, to testify their admiration of, and sympathy for Cassius M. Clay of Kentucky, in his intrepid struggles and generous sacrifices for the cause of universal freedom, and to hear him speak in behalf of the policy, economy, necessity, and eternal justice of emancipating all who are held in bondage, except for their own crimes. The spacious Tabernacle was crowded before the hour (seven o'clock) fixed for the

opening of the meeting, though it will accommodate some three
thousand persons, and soon every nook and aisle was densely
packed with eager, enthusiastic freemen. No such audience
was ever before crowded into the Tabernacle, and thousands
went away unable to obtain standing room within the walls of
the edifice.

Precisely at seven o'clock, Mr. Clay was introduced to the
audience by H. Greeley, with a few words of allusion to his
past history and present attitude, and was received on rising
with rapturous acclamations. Mr. Clay took the· stand, and
enchained the auditors for fully two hours, laboring under some
embarrassment at first, from the immensity of the audience,
the enthusiasm of his reception, and the difficulty of making
himself heard by all, but warming as he proceeded with the
fervor of patriotism and love of humanity, stimulated by the
cheers of the sympathizing thousands, and gradually rising to
higher and still higher flights of the noblest eloquence. The
following is a condensed report of his speech:

He commenced with a few preliminary remarks, in which he
stated that if we looked back through past history, and noticed
the development of the human mind and its results, we were
always enabled to trace something upon the tablet of time, by
which to guide us in carrying on the progress of mind to a still
higher state of human development. He added that, therefore,
he claimed for himself no merit for originality in his efforts; he
had merely attempted to take up that which he had learned by
rote, and to add his mite to that which was already before the
intelligence of the world.

We, of the United States, claim to be the first people who
laid down the true basis of the government of men. It is this:
that government consists of one omnipotent principle—that men
associated together in a civilized state shall obtain a greater
amount of liberty than they can whilst living in the natural
state. That it should give to all associated under it, the same
rights and equal liberty; and if a government does not show
that it does this—if it shall in any way trench on the rights of
any portion of the governed, then I say that that government
ought to perish, whether it be a republic or a monarchy. [Here
there was considerable applause, and a few faint hisses.]
And that government which cuts off a portion from any of
their rights, and leaves them even worse than they were in the

natural state, ought not to, and cannot by any possibility, be a permanent government. [Applause.]

Whilst I am not insensible to the injuries inflicted on the African race—the almost countless miseries and tortures which many of them have endured for centuries; whilst I admit fully that God has given rights which are marked clearly on the most dusky face of that injured race, still I must insist, that I am mainly actuated by a still higher motive—the greater motive of achieving the complete independence and liberty of my own, the white Anglo-Saxon race of America! [Much applause.] And God has so ordered it that you cannot trench upon any— the humblest, meanest link in the great chain of humanity—but the injury will reach to the highest link, and draw all down with it to destruction. [Applause.] I advocate, then, not only the interests and liberties of the African, but also those of the eighteen million of whites who should have been freemen on this soil of the United States. [Loud applause.]

Men, we are told by some, are influenced in the long run by their interest; others there are who say, that most men are mainly influenced by the nobler and truest principles of the human heart. But I wish you to bear in mind this higher truth; which is, that justice and interest go together. [Much applause.] When will men learn it?

I do not assume any peculiar sagacity, or any peculiar merit, for advocating emancipation in all the slave states of the Union. I had only to lift up my eyes and see what was going on around me daily, and the conviction forced itself upon me. [Applause.] Was I ambitious of power, of wealth, of numbers? The conviction forced itself on me that these were much more abundant in the free states of the Union. Was I fond of the fine arts— of painting, of sculpture, of music, of poetry, of all that constitutes the embodiment of the beautiful and true? I saw that all these existed in a much higher degree of excellence in the free than in the slave states. Did I look at the subject of education? I saw that the mind developed itself to a far greater degree in the free than in the slave states, with the added conviction, that it always had so done, and would continue so to do through all time. [Applause.] So that, if in the course I am pursuing, I am a madman, if I am a fanatic, I do not desire to destroy those glorious developments of art and science—those luxuries of refinement and high civilization, of which those who affect to cast such an imputation on me, claim to be the executive conservators. [Applause.]

If I had seen this thing only once developed, if I had seen the struggle only once tried, I might have doubted. But thirteen times has the battle been fought on the question, whether man most usefully belongs to himself, or to another; and thirteen times has it been decided in favor of liberty! [Applause.] Was not this enough?

Until since the period when it has been customary to take the census of all the products and manufactures of the United States, if you talked to a man about freedom as compared with slavery, he'd say, "look to the cotton crop." And he'd tell you it was the great staple—the only source of wealth we produced, to take to Europe, in order to get back thence what we wanted for our use in this country. But Gen. Tallmadge told us in his recent address before the American Institute of this city, that the little state of Massachusetts produced more in manufactures (in the gross, it is true) than the value of the whole cotton crop of the United States. [Loud applause.] But the slaveholders argue that this manufacturing wealth is produced from a part of the cotton crop itself. How is this? Let us see. You see the $60,000,000 of cotton that goes from the ports of Charleston, Savannah, Mobile, and New Orleans, annually: but you do not see the $60,000,000 which comes North, to buy mules, and clothing, and implements of agriculture, and other matters for the negro. So that after all, the assertion is true to the letter, that the little state of Massachusetts *does* produce more wealth than the value of the whole cotton crop of the United States. [Applause.] Will you look to that?

You hear of an intended railroad that is to be constructed from Memphis through the wilds of the far West. Why, you'll find that there is not capital enough in the whole South to build it. [Laughter and applause.] But, you'll find, by and by, when there are a sufficient number of people who desire to travel in that direction, some shrewd and enterprising Yankee will start up, and find the capital, while other ingenious Yankees will go out and build it. [Increased laughter and applause.]

Look to the Mechanic Arts. If you inquire at the Patent Office at Washington, relative to those results of the extraordinary skill, ingenuity, and inventive faculties of our countrymen, you will find that ninety-nine out of a hundred are from the

Northern states. [Applause.] Have you thought of that, men of the South? for I know that I am speaking to many Southern men, besides many from my own state of Kentucky. This is enough to prove that position, though in relation to matters of mechanical skill, I might go on *ad infinitum*, to show the superiority of the free over the slave states. [Applause.]

How about agriculture? The actual territory—I mean that which is strictly tillable and profitable territory or susceptible of profit is in the South perhaps *four* times greater than that of the North, and yet look at the products. Have you ever reflected on this? And with regard to all those great public works of improvement, there is hardly any thing in the South that can begin to compare with those of the North. And if there is no political change there, we shall remain so for ever! Remain so? No, we shall recede farther and farther from being able to hold any comparison with the North. [Applause.]

I know that there are shrewd men and intelligent, as they are accounted, who contend that it is better to keep these 3,000,000 of human beings in slavery, because we get the proceeds or profits of their labors. But if this be true—which it is not,—if this were true—frightful as it would be thus to obtain wealth only by human suffering and blood—by trampling into the dust all human rights and blessings,—how much more horrible it must be to find, that with all this outrage such is not the case;—that gold being the God they worshipped—when by violation of all laws human and divine they expected to grasp it—they found nothing but an ashen apple remained—to their utter destruction. [Much applause mingled with a few hisses.]

The truth is, that free intelligent labor will effect twice as much as labor driven with the whip or by compulsion. Have you thought of that? In the South there are 3,000,000 of blacks, and 5,000,000 of whites. Now, throw out of consideration, if you please, the 3,000,000 of blacks, and take the 5,000,000 of whites, who, not so accustomed to toil, we are satisfied, perform at least not more than one-third the labor of those at the North; say one-half. Admit that the laborer at the North produced $25 a month, that at the South would be $12 50. The white laborer at the South would then produce $150 a year, and the Northerner $300. Multiply this by 5,000,000, it gives you $1,500,000,000 annually; which would be produced by the whites at the South, if they worked as those do at the North. But with only half of this labor, it gives a result of $750,000,000, which might easily be produced annually, by free white labor at the South. [Applause.] Turn round and put this $750,000,000 against the $60,000,000 cotton crop [applause], and they would have by this means $690,000,000 more to exchange for the products of the North, than they now have by means of slavery and the cotton crop. [Applause.] I know it is said that the whites would be in the habit of more nearly living up to their income; but no man who has been an observer of the commercial concerns of the country, can fail to observe that all classes, under such a system, would have largely more to expend, even if they did live more extravagantly, than when they had a total of only $60,000,000. [Applause.] So that justice and truth are the true policy. It is the best expediency. Honesty, as in the old proverb, is the best policy after all. [Applause.] And you have only to have the heart to wish, and the energy to carry it out, and blessed as it will be by God, it must succeed. [Applause.] The history of all past time, and the very nature of things, prove incontestibly that this must be so. [Loud and continued applause.]

Let us inquire as to mental development between the two sections. A young man [a school-mate of mine at Yale College] went from New-Haven to Virginia; and, in order, I suppose, to make his book sell, he gave the private history of several of the F. F. V.'s. He came to Kentucky, and I said to him. "Well, you've come from the land of wooden nutmegs and leather-pumpkin-seeds [laughter], and you've been to the Old Dominion, the land of the F. F. V.'s, and what have you found there?" "Why," said the young man, "I've found nothing; there are not three *literary* men in the state." [Laughter.] And it is so, out of politics and law. The remnants of the nobility and the cavaliers have gone down to oblivion, leaving nothing bright or permanent behind them. And yet, in that small state of Connecticut, not less than fifty-nine men have made for themselves a national reputation that will live with the land's language, beside their great and varied achievements in the mechanic arts, science, and philosophy. [Applause.]

Who are your historians? There is but one response. Turn

to Griswold's book of the Poets of America, and how many do you find there that come south of Mason & Dixon's line? Go to the courts and high places of Europe; look at those who have distinguished themselves honorably abroad, in numerous ways ; and whom do you find? · Northern men, who have risen from the body of the people by the power of their intellect ! [Applause.] 'But yet sirs,' say the Southern men, 'we have hitherto always governed you !' It is too true ! 'We have our feet on your neck.' It is too true. [Applause and a few hisses.] Almost now, certainly in a short time, and you'll not find a man or woman in the Northern states who cannot read or write. [Applause.] And yet what numbers you may find in the South, who can do neither !

I love the South ! [Applause.] It is my birth-place. I am not a Southern man with Northern principles ! [Applause and laughter.] I love my country, and I would make her great and glorious. [Much applause.] And it is because I *would* make her great and glorious, that I thus tell her of her faults. [Very general applause.]

Shall I speak of the morals of the South ? That other portion of the human being, forming the great unity ? They tell us in the South, that slavery is the great shield of morality, in the whites. If that were true, which it is not—if that were even true, yet who could say that God is a God of justice and of mercy, and yet admit it as an argument? As well might you point to the state of society in Great Britain, and argue in relation to the classes there, that there was less crime among the aristocracy of England, than among the great mass ? Would that be a fair comparison ? No. You must take the mass of men and women as you find them ; and thus, in your statistics of morals, you would have there to dot down three million of abandoned men and women, the slaves, to begin with, and that at once shuts out all comparison. Have you looked at the records of blood and murder ? at the fatal rencontres ? at the street fights ? at the duels ?—where, not by man's code, though in the eye of God, the deliberate killing of a man in an arranged fight, is as much murder as stabbing him in the dark· Where are your divorces most numerous ? where but in the South, with several hundreds annually ; and yet we are told that chastity in the South far exceeds what exists in the North. [Applause.]

It is an inevitable result of the laws of God and man, that

where a man habitually violates one great law, he will—but with here and there an exception—sooner or later, violate all the rest. This very principle of slavery is the subversion of the greatest law of nature, self-defence. It is the law of force ; and when that law of force—when Lynch law is abolished—then slavery dies. [Much applause and considerable hissing.] And yet there are many who smooth back their hair and look grave, and roll up their eyes, and say that they wish that man, Clay, well, but that he's too violent; he's too harsh; he uses arms in his own defence. [Laughter.] But suppose a man were to be stopped on the highway, or fall into a band of robbers (I use the terms here in no offensive sense), and he had a sword by his side, which ought he to use, his tongue or his sword ?

[A gentleman (sitting right in front of Mr. Clay, with a lady by his side), "His sword, to be sure." [Much laughter.]

Mr. Clay, Why, certainly ; for if he did n't, he might be call-ed a pretty good fellow, but he'd be sure to have his pocket thoroughly picked. [Increased laughter.] So, therefore, I say to you, churchmen, who sit in the high places of the sanctuary, and enter into the inner places of the temple, that so far as we know any thing of the Divine nature, slavery subverts it com-pletely; and where slavery exists, there true morality cannot exist. There are men amongst those institutions that I love and re-verence ; and, therefore, I tell them they stand on a sandy foundation—one that cannot stand the test of Divine law, and, therefore, I would have them leave, and leave suddenly. [Ap-plause.] It is true, that in some quarters the conscience may be touched, but there remains still, the seminal evil. [Applause.]

I told them long before the mob of the eighteenth of August, that though there was a love of morality and order amongst them, yet that the few bad spirits would concentrate and over-turn their good purposes. And so it will ever be. And be-cause I fully acknowledge that the Church has in all ages sown the seeds of truth, virtue, morality, therefore, I invoke all its leaders to see if slavery be sin or no. They will see that it will not stand the test. Thus, I ask, that they warn their fellow-men, that those who hold their fellow men in bondage cannot belong to the church of Him who said, "Do unto others as ye would others should do unto you." [Much applause, with con-siderable hissing.]

Slavery has powerfully affected us politically. Our forefathers felt this when they were about to inquire what was just and true. They started then with this fact, that all men were born equal—equally entitled to life, liberty, and the pursuit of happiness. Nor was this a mere rhetorical flourish, as has been so frequently, so impudently asserted. [Applause.] It is true that some pretend to combat this, and say that all men are not born equal. In one sense, this may be argued to a very limited extent; but I am prepared to prove, that the Declaration of Independence is true in theory, and true in fact. [Applause.] Some men are born with much wisdom, and some are born fools; are they equal? No. Some are born with much personal beauty, and some deformed; are they equal? No. So with the one born wealthy, and the other poor. But what was the sense in which our fathers meant that all men are born equal? In a political sense—in his being governed by man, and as between God and his fellow-man, he is, to all intents and purposes, equal. [Applause and hisses, and a cry of "A nigger is not a white man's equal.] And though I be born poor, and dirty, and ragged, and crooked, yet I am entitled to equal protection from the laws, and to equal political rights. [Much applause.] And, if anywhere within the range of this government, as now administered, it shall be found that man is not considered as entitled to equal political rights, that portion of it must fall, and every good man will say, "Amen." [Loud applause, and considerable hissing.]

The great principle of government is, that it is bound to procure man more liberty in the social state than he can procure in the natural state; and the government which says to a man, "You shall not possess your own wife, you shall not have your own child, you shall not select and enjoy your own home, you shall not take medicine from the doctor of your own selection," &c., &c., that government subverts every principle for which it was formed; and if God is just it will be dissolved. [Much applause and hisses.]

At the formation of the Constitution, in 1789, we had then fought a long and doubtful war; and our fathers were induced to form a certain alliance with the South; and thus that clause was introduced which has been subversive of all those principles for which they began the war. They agreed that slavery should exist in the South until the South should choose to throw it off in its own good time and pleasure. This fact, it is true, has been denied by some, who in their zeal for freedom have gone too far. But I regret that any man should go beyond the true principle for which he ought to contend, because such a course is calculated to bring the whole cause into disrepute. [Applause.] There was, then, an agreement that slavery should exist in the Southern states. And there was a farther agreement—more's the pity—that if a slave escaped to a free state the latter should return him into slavery; and also, that none should be introduced from Africa, subsequent to 1808. [Applause.] So, therefore, the North joined hands with the South in this matter, and departed from the great principle for which they had fought the bloody battles of the revolution. [Applause.] So, therefore, if slavery still exists in the South, you of the North are equally guilty of its existence. But if there be an extension of slavery over other territory of the Union, you men of the North, are far more guilty than others, because *you do evil with far less temptation!* [Much applause.]

Let us see how this operated in actual practice. The framers of the Constitution (with the exception of the slave states), of 1789, formed a free Constitution, so far as they had the power to do so, and pledged themselves to the world to work for human rights and liberty; and that this should be a government of freedom so far as it should be extended in all time. Nor should we forget the blood they had shed for this purpose! [Applause.] They said that none should be deprived of life and liberty without law! What crime, then, have the black people of Virginia, Maryland, the Carolinas, Georgia, Florida, Alabama, Louisiana, Arkansas, Mississippi, Missouri, Tennessee, and Kentucky committed, that, so far as they are concerned, this Constitution lies slumbering with the dead usages of past ages? Our fathers meant that this Constitution should be carried out and fully vindicated. For this they freely shed their blood and treasure. And if we are but true to ourselves (so far as our blood and treasure are concerned), *it shall be vindicated.* And God save the right. [Great applause and hissing.]

You will find that Washington, and Lee, and Henry, and Madison, and most of the Southern men (except those of Georgia and South Carolina), the entire delegation from the South to the Convention, looked to the time as not far distant when there would be no slavery at the South. And all their actions clearly showed that they wished it so thoroughly abolished that both the name and the memory of it should soon pass away from the minds of men. [Applause.] In Madison's speech you find he says that "Man can have no property in man." And still more strikingly is this feeling shown in the private correspondence of these men. Washington, writing to a friend in Pennsylvania, tells him to come to Virginia, for that when slavery should be extinct, and that soon, the land, now more valuable and cheaper than in Pennsylvania, would then be three times more valuable. [Applause.] But what has been the result? Could Washington have contemplated it? In Pennsylvania, the land is now worth from one hundred dollars to three hundred dollars per acre, whilst that Virginia land is unoccupied by man, and traversed only by the wild beasts of the forest. And many of those beautiful farms that were cultivated to such great advantage by Washington, are now deserted, and the houses unoccupied. [Great sensation.]

Many intelligent gentlemen have declared that these glorious designs of those great men would have been carried out, if it had not been for the invention of the cotton gin, and the rise in value of that staple. But as it was, our fathers took the back track, and declared, as far as they were concerned, that Liberty should be extinguished. Shall it be done?

SEVERAL VOICES. No.

MR. CLAY. Now let us see how the South progressed in their plan to perpetuate slavery. They set about to monopolize all the important offices in the country. And they got them. [Laughter and applause.] They then set about to pass laws by which free labor should be less valued than slave labor; and they accomplished that. They then devised ways and means by which slave labor should be especially looked after and protected; and they accomplished that. And all the laws which they passed were to elevate the labor of the slave, and depress that of the free white man. And they accomplished all this. [Laughter and applause.] And, notwithstanding all this, they were determined to have a large extension of slave territory; and they accomplished all this too. [Increased laughter and applause.]

First, they took Louisiana (three states.) Let us say that Louisiana is the great entrepot for the commerce of the southwest—admit all its peculiar advantages; we should have bought it, but have let it be free. But they confounded the two interests together, and made a slave empire of it. They then turned their attention to Florida, for another small slave empire to check the march of freedom; and they accomplished that. And not only did they get all this extent of slave region, but they farther willed to take a territory, Texas, making *forty states as large as Massachusetts;* and they accomplished that also. [Much applause and laughter, and loud hisses.]

Mr. Clay. You hiss, because you have guilt upon you. You fight with a mask, but I mean to tear it off. [Applause.] You call yourselves Democrats. [Roars of laughter, applause and hisses.] What did the Democrats fight for in 1776? I should be very much pleased if any one of you would tell me.

A Voice. That freemen should vote, not niggers.

Another. Liberty!

Mr. Clay. Liberty! Have you given it to the unborn millions of Texas? [Laughter and applause.]

A Voice. Yes.

Mr. Clay. You say 'Yes.' And our friends may judge of the value to be put upon the balance of your arguments, by this very answer. [Shouts of laughter and applause.]

The Voice. Let's go out, Joe.

Why, the leading principle for which our fathers fought, was, no taxation without representation. [Loud and continued cheering.] That they should go together. [Cheers.] And yet here comes up a man from Texas owning 100 slaves; he takes his seat in the House of Representatives, and thus has as much power as he who represents sixty-one of the best freemen of New York, John Jacob Astor, or any one else included. Is that equal representation?

A Voice. Yes. [Laughter.]

Another. No. [Laughter.]

Mr. Clay. You send your members to Washington— 10,000 votes (about), to one representative; and a man comes from Texas, who-has only 1250 votes; for there are only about 4500 there in all. [Laughter.] And yet you call it equal representation. [Applause.] Suppose a stranger was to come among you; he'd say it was a queer state of things. Your 10,000,000 of the northern freemen allow 5,000,000 of slaveholders to get the upper hand of you. And by whose money, and by whose blood is the country sustained? By that of northern men; and there would be no money, if Northern men did not furnish it.

[Hisses.] The money to buy Louisiana came from Northern men; and in Florida the blood of Northern men was .shed in order that Northern men might make themselves and their children slaves. [Applause and hisses.]

MR. CLAY. You hiss again! Is it not true? If we desire to differ from former republics, and regret that they lived so short a time, let us ask, why was it that their life, so glorious and so brilliant, was so short? Because they had not a Constitution for which they had any reverence. They had the same despotism that we suffer under to-night—the despotism of numbers. And if I had a choice to-night, so help me Heaven, I had rather live under the despotism of the Emperor of Russia, or the Sultan of Turkey, than under the despotism of numbers. For there, if you keep yourself humble and insignificant, you may slink away into peaceful obscurity; but here, no matter how humble yourself or dwelling—on the loneliest creek or bayou, the tax-gatherer is sure to find you out; for, as they say, there are two things from which no man can escape—Death and the tax-gatherer. [Laughter and applause.] The man who basely submits to one act of tyranny, will submit to all, and is a slave. And if I know anything of slavery, it is a miserable dependence on the will of another. Our fathers framed the Constitution that it should not be subjected to the despotism of numbers, particularly against the acquisition of territory by numbers. [Applause.] And yet what have we lately seen?

MR. CLAY then compared the conduct of the South on the Texas question, with that on the Oregon affair. He said that Oregon was ours by discovery, exploration, and beneficial and successful occupancy. He deprecated the last resort—the *ultima ratio regum.* But if it was necessary to take a slave state by force, he would take this free state by force, and leave it to sensible men, on whom the guilt of the blood spilt should rest. Our title is perfect. England cannot, and dare not, go to war for it; and if hot-headed men on both sides will keep still, we shall have Oregon without a war.

MR. CLAY jocosely proposed to buy out England's partial right to Oregon with Texas and South Carolina money, since the North was so liberal as to buy Florida and Louisiana for the slaveholders.

He contended that, as all history proved, we must all either be slaves or freemen. What would we do? Declare we will

all be free.   How was this to be accomplished?   By standing
only on the Constitution and laws.   Give the South the pound
of flesh, but no blood.   If they violate a single right of the free,
they violate the entire franchise of the North, and the peril of
the strife be on their head.

The course he desired, was not to vary the ninth part of a
hair from the Constitution.   If you wish to be generous, be so;
if you wish to be conciliatory, be so; but stand close up to the
Constitution.   Wherever slavery can be constitutionally reached,
there reach it [applause], and with the extension of territory,
extend only freedom.   [Much applause.]

Mr. CLAY then went on to speak of slavery in the District of
Columbia; and to show that ten million of free Northern men
have something to do with slavery there, seeing that the
national government has entire jurisdiction over the ten miles
square, and that these ten million constitute a majority of the
constituents of the government.   [Applause.]

There was another way which slavery could be constitutionally reached.   It could be banished from the seas, so far as they
were under the jurisdiction of the United States government.
The domestic traffic in slaves now carried on between the
states could be driven from the ocean under that clause of the
Constitution, which empowers Congress to regulate commerce.

If the question were again asked, What had the North to do
with slavery? he would answer, that they could destroy the
monopoly of office and patronage so long enjoyed by the slave
power, and place the administration of the government in the
hands of those who would wield it in conformity to the great
principles of liberty.   On this point he spoke with much
emphasis, but we cannot follow him farther.

There was another point of still greater delicacy as pertaining
to the peculiar duties of the North.   He alluded to the restriction which the free states might put upon the right of suffrage.
On this subject, he called upon the audience and the reporters
for the press to mark his language when he said that on no
subject was the South more sensitive than upon this.   If the
North would reach slavery effectually, let her be just to her own
free black population, by giving them their political rights.   If
she would aid in freeing the South, she must herself be free
from all taint of oppression.   He would not enter upon the
question of the natural equality of the black with the white

race. When he considered the progress which the latter had made, from a state of rude barbarism to their present comparatively high intellectual condition; when he considered what England was in the time of Elizabeth, and what she is now, he would not undertake to say what might yet be done to elevate the blacks. It had been affirmed by those wiser in such matters than himself, that the arts and sciences were received by the Romans from ancient Egyptians, who were negroes; and he could not tell whether in the progress of events, the blacks might not be elevated to the highest point of civilization and refinement. On that point, he would neither affirm nor deny anything, but leave it to be settled by the developments of time, and the action of Divine Providence. That the blacks, in their present condition, were vastly behind the whites, he admitted; and he did not stand there to plead for amalgamation, or for entire social equality. Here was an important distinction which he begged his audience to note—that between equality of social condition and equality of political rights. Suppose he were to meet in the street a live Yankee, a sucker from Indiana, a corn-cracker from Kentucky, or even a poor miserable drunken vagabond. He might not prefer such men for associates, but would he therefore knock them down and rob them? Would he deprive them of all political rights, because he did not choose them for his companions? No—if he did not want to associate with them, he would let them pass by in peace; but he would say to them, "You shall be permitted to have a voice in making and administering the laws by which you are to be governed." [Great applause.] He had enjoyed the privilege of taking Webster, and Adams, and Everett by the hand, and he did not feel that those men were degraded because they came from a state where the colored man was allowed the right of suffrage. O no! And if, unfortunately, the Union were to be severed into fragments by the struggle between slavery and freedom, to what quarter could he turn for safety, and where would the principles of liberty be longest preserved, but in the land of Bunker Hill and Lexington, where justice is not outraged by a denial to the blacks of their political rights.

He was willing to let by-gones be by-gones, and wherever he saw any man laboring according to his best light in the cause of freedom, whether he were a Garrisonian, a liberty man, a whig, or a so-called democrat, he could not find it in his heart to throw cold water upon his plans.   No, let him go on his own way, and God prosper the right.   But as he had besought the liberty party, in the late presidential campaign, not to cast their votes in such a way as to promote the election of Polk, and ensure the annexation of Texas, so he would now beseech them not to throw their votes and influence in such a way as to defeat the effort to extend to the blacks of New York the right of suffrage.   The two great parties were taking their ground on this question, the one in favor, and the other against this measure of justice; let the liberty men not sacrifice this object by a too rigid adherence to their abstract theories.   He had told them beforehand what would be the effect of the election of Polk upon the annexation of Texas, but they were sceptical, and disregarded his admonitions.   They had seen all his predictions on that subject verified, and he would now warn them not to sacrifice, in the same manner, this great question of suffrage.

Mr. CLAY concluded his speech as follows:

As for myself, though the cause has apparently gone against me, and the liberty of speech and of the press, and the right of habeas corpus have been struck down in my person, I am resolved not to give up!   I may indeed be an enthusiast. Webster, Clay, Calhoun may better comprehend the destiny of this republic than I; but I cannot but give utterance to the conceptions of my own mind.

When I look upon the special developments of European civilization—when I contemplate the growing freedom of the cities, and the middle class which had sprung up between the pretenders to Divine rule on the one hand, and the abject serf on the other—when I consider the Reformation and the invention of the press—and see on the southern shore of the continent, an humble individual, amidst untold difficulties and repeated defeats, pursuing the mysterious suggestions which the mighty deep poured unceasingly upon his troubled spirit, till at last with great and irrepressible energy of soul, he discovered that there lay in the far Western Ocean a continent open for the infusion of those elementary principles of liberty which were dwarfed in European soil, I have conceived that the hand of destiny was there!

When I saw the immigration of the Pilgrims from the chalky shores of England—in the night fleeing from their native home—so dramatically and ably pictured by Mr. Webster in his celebrated oration—when father, mother, brother, sister, lover, were all lost, by those melancholy wanderers, "stifling," in the language of one who is immortal in the conception, "the mighty hunger of the heart," and landing amidst cold, and poverty, and death, upon the rude Rock of Plymouth—I have ventured to think that the will of Deity was there !

When I have remembered the revolution of '76—the seven years' war—three millions of men standing in arms against the most powerful nation of history, and vindicating their Independence—I have thought that their sufferings and death were not in vain ! When I have gone and seen the forsaken hearth-stone—looked in upon the battle-field, upon the dying and the dead—heard the agonizing cry, " Water, for the sake of God ! water"—seen the dissolution of this being—pale lips pressing in death the yet loved images of wife, sister, and lover —I will not deem all these in vain ! I cannot regard this great continent, reaching from the Atlantic to the far Pacific, and from the St. John's to the Rio del Norte, a slave empire, a barbarian people of third-rate civilization.

Like the Roman who looked back upon the glory of his ancestors, in great woe exclaiming,

> " Great Scipio's ghost complains that we are slow,
> And Pompey's shade walks unavenged among us"—

the great dead hover around me. LAWRENCE, " Don't give up the ship"—HENRY, " Give me liberty or give me death"—ADAMS, "Survive or perish, I am for the Declaration"—ALLEN, "In the name of the Living God, I come !"

Come, then, thou ETERNAL ! who dwellest not in temples made with hands, but who, in the city's crowd, or by the far forest stream, revealest Thyself to the earnest seeker after the true and the right; inspire my heart—give me undying courage to pursue the promptings of my spirit ; and whether I shall be called, in the shade of life, to look upon sweet, and kind, and lovely faces as now—or, shut in by sorrow and night, horrid visages shall gloom upon me in my dying hour—OH ! MY COUNTRY ! MAYEST THOU YET BE FREE !

Mr. CLAY having concluded his remarks amid deafening and prolonged acclamations, three resolutions, handed up to the desk, were read by H. Greeley, and submitted to the meeting.

[They were instantly spirited away by some of our contemporaries, but their purport was as follows]:

Resolved, That we regard the destruction of the True American Press by a mob, at Lexington, Ky., as a direct attack on the Rights of Free Speech and the Rights of Man, and that the authors of that outrage are deserving of the severest reprehension.

Resolved, That we tender to CASSIUS M. CLAY our fervent gratitude for his struggles and sacrifices in the great cause of Universal Freedom, and we trust his devotion will yet be crowned with the amplest and most gratifying triumph.

Resolved, That we are deeply indebted to Mr. CLAY for his Address this evening, in favor of the great principles of Justice and Liberty, and we assure him that our ardent sympathy will attend him in all his future efforts in behalf of Universal Emancipation.

Which resolutions were unanimously adopted, with six unanimous cheers for CASSIUS M. CLAY and the Freedom of the Press.

The meeting then [half-past nine o'clock] adjourned.

SLAVERY: THE EVIL—THE REMEDY

To the Editor of the Tribune:

" And can the liberties of a nation be thought secure, when we have removed their only firm basis, a conviction in the minds of the people that these liberties are the gift of God ? * * * Indeed, I tremble for my country, when I reflect that God is just : that his justice cannot sleep for ever : that, considering numbers, nature, and natural means only, a revolution of the wheel of fortune, an exchange of situation, is among possible events : that it may become probable by supernatural inter-ference ! The Almighty has no attribute which can take sides with us in such a contest."—*Jefferson's Notes on Virginia.*

Thomas Jefferson never thought of the absurdity of debating the question, whether slavery be an evil, nor was he indulgent to the delusive idea that it would be perpetual He reduced the subject to its certain elements : the master must liberate the slave, or the slave will exterminate the master. This conclusion is not weakened by the history of the past. The same color in the ancient republics enabled the state to use emancipation as a safety valve ; yet notwithstanding the thorough amalgamation of the freed man with the free born, servile wars nearly extin-guished by violence the noblest nations of antiquity : while no man dare say that slavery was not the secret cause of their ultimate ruin. But if " His justice" should "sleep for ever," and the tragedy so awfully predicted should never occur, still must we regard slavery as the greatest evil that ever cursed a nation.

Slavery is an evil to the slave, by depriving nearly three mil-lions of men of the best gift of God to man—liberty. I stop here ; this is enough of itself to give us a full anticipation of the long catalogue of human woe, and physical and intellectual and moral abasement, which follows in the wake of slavery.

Slavery is an evil to the master. It is utterly subversive of the Christian religion. It violates the great law upon which that religion is based, and on account of which it vaunts its pre-eminence.

It corrupts our offspring by necessary association with an abandoned and degraded race, ingrafting in the young mind and heart all the vices and none of the virtues.

It is the source of indolence, and destructive of all industry, which in times past among the wise has ever been regarded as the first friend of religion, morality, and happiness. The poor despise labor, because slavery makes it degrading. The mass of slaveholders are idlers.

It is the mother of ignorance. The system of common schools has not succeeded in a single slave state. Slavery and education are natural enemies. In the free states one in fifty-three, over twenty-one years, is unable to read and write; in the slave states one in thirteen and three tenths is unable to write and read !

It is opposed to literature, even in the educated classes. Noble aspirations and true glory depend upon virtue and good to man. The conscious injustice of slavery hangs as a mill-stone about the necks of the sons of genius, and will not let them up !

It is destructive of all mechanical excellence. The free states build ships and steam cars for the nations of the world ; the slave states import the handles for their axes—these primitive tools of the architect. The educated population will not work at all ; the uneducated must work without science, and of course without skill. If there be a given amount of mechanical genius among a people, it is of necessity developed in proportion as a whole or part of the population are educated. In the slave states the small portion educated is inert.

It is antagonistic to the fine arts. Creations of beauty and sublimity are the embodiments of the soul's imaginings : the fountain must surely be pure and placid whence these glorious and immortal and lovely images are reflected. Liberty has ever been the mother of the arts.

It retards population and wealth. Compare New York and Virginia, Tennessee and Ohio—states of equal natural advantages, and equal ages. The wealth of the free states is in a much greater ratio even superior to that of the slave states, than the population of the free is greater than that of the slave states.

The manufactures of the slave as compared to those of the free states, are as one to four nearly, as is shown by statistics. I consider the accumulation of wealth in a less ratio.

It impoverishes the soil and defaces the loveliest features of nature. Washington advises a friend to remove from Pennsylvania to Virginia, saying, that cheap lands in Virginia were as good as the dear lands in Pennsylvania, and, anticipating the abolition of slavery, would be more productive. His anticipations have perished ; slavery still exists; the wild brier and the red fox are now there the field-growth and the inhabitants !

It induces national poverty. Slaves consume more and produce less than freemen. Hence illusive wealth, prodigality, and bankruptcy, without the capability of bearing adversity, or recovering from its influence: then comes despair, dishonor, and crime.

It is an evil to the free laborer, by forcing him by the laws of competition, supply, and demand, to work for the wages of the slave—food and shelter. The poor, in the slave states, are the most destitute native population in the United States.

It sustains the public sentiment in favor of the deadly affray and the duel—those relics of a barbarous age.

It is the mother and the nurse of *Lynch law*, which I regard as the most horrid of all crimes, not even excepting parricide, which ancient legislators thought too impossible to be ever supposed in the legal code. If all the blood thus shed in the South could be gathered together, the horrid image which Emmett drew of the cruelty of his judges would grow pale in view of this greater terror.

Where all these evils exist, how can liberty, constitutional liberty, live? No indeed, it cannot and has not existed in conjunction with slavery. We are but nominal freemen, for though born to all the privileges known to the Constitution and the laws, written and prescriptive, we have seen struck down with the leaden hand of slavery, the most glorious banner that freedom ever bore in the face of men ; " Trial by Jury, Liberty of Speech and of the Press." The North may be liable to censure in congress for freedom of speech; may lose the privileges of the post office, and the right of petition, and perhaps yet be free; but we of the land of slavery, are ourselves slaves ! Alas for the hypocritical cry of liberty and equality, which demagogues sound for ever in our ears ! The Declaration of Independence comes back from all nations, not in notes of triumph and self-elation, but thundering in our ears the everlasting *lie*—making us infidels in the great world of freedom—raising up to ourselves idols of wood and stone, inscribed with the name of Deity, where the one invisible and true God can never dwell. The blood of the heroes of 1776 has been shed in vain. The just expectations of Hamilton and Franklin, and Sherman, and Morris, and Adams, of the North, are betrayed by the continuance of slavery. The fond anticipations of Washington, and Jefferson, and Madison, and Mason, of the South, have not been realized. The great experiment of republican government has not been fairly tested. If the Union should not be perpetual, nor the American name be synonymous with that of liberty in all coming time, slavery is at once the cause, the crime, and the avenger!

Are we indeed of that vaunted Saxon blood which no dangers can appal, no obstacles obstruct, and shall we sit with shivering limbs and dewy feet by the running stream, with inane features and stolid gaze, expecting this flood of evils to flow past, leaving the channel dry? We, who can conquer all things else, shall we be here only subdued, ingloriously whispering with white lips, there is no remedy? Are the fowls free in the wide heavens, the fishes secure in the depths of the ocean, the beasts untrammeled in the forest wild, and shall man only, man formed in the image of Deity, the heir of immortality, be doomed to hopeless servitude? Yes, there is a remedy.

There is one of four consequences to which slavery inevitably leads: A continuance of the present relative position of the master and the slave, both as to numbers, intelligence and physical power; or an extermination of the blacks; or an extermination of the whites; or emancipation and removal, or emancipation, and a community of interests between the races.

The present relative position between the blacks and whites (even if undisturbed by external influences, which we cannot hope), cannot long continue. Statistics of numbers show that in the whole slave states the black increase on the white population. The dullest eye can also see that the African, by association with the white race, has improved in intellect, and by being transferred to a temperate climate, and forced to labor, and to throw off the indolence of his native land, he is increasing in physical power; while the whites, by the same reversed laws, is retrograding in the same respect. Slavery then cannot remain for ever as it is. That the black race will be exterminated seems hardly probable from the above reflections, and because the great mass of human passions will be in favor of the increase of the slaves, *ad interim.* Pride, love of power, blind avarice, and many other passions are for it, against it only fear in the opposite scale. We are forced, therefore, to the conclusion that the slave population must increase, till there is no retreat but in the extermination of the whites. Athens, Sparta, and Rome nearly, Hayti in modern times, did fall by servile wars. I have shown elsewhere that the slavery of the blacks in the modern, is more dangerous than the slavery of the whites in the ancient system; then the intelligent slave was incorporated into the high castes of quondam masters, an eternal safety-valve, which yet did not save from explosions eminently disastrous.

The negative of the second proposition, then, establishes the third, unless we avail ourselves of the last—*emancipation.* If my reasoning and facts be correct, there is not a sane mind in all the South who would not agree with me, that if we can be saved from the first named evils, by all means emancipate. *Emancipation is entirely safe.* Sparta and Athens turned the slaves by thousands into freedom with safety, who fought bravely for their common country.

During the revolution many emancipated slaves did good service in the cause of liberty. We learn from Mr. Gurney, and other sources to be relied upon, that British West India emancipation has been entirely successful, and productive of none of those evils which were so pertinaciously foretold by interested pro-slavery men. The British have regiments of black men, who make fine soldiers—protectors, not enemies of the empire. But above all, I rely not upon sound *a priori* reasoning only, but rather upon actual experience. There are in the United States, by the last census, 386,265 free blacks; 170,758 of whom are in the free, the remainder in the slave states. There are also 2,485,145 slaves—so that, in fact, about one-sixth of the whole black race in America are already free ! No danger or evil consequence has ensued from the residence of these 386,265 freedmen among us. Who then will be so absurd as to contend that the liberation of the other five-sixths will endanger the safety or happiness of the whites? *I repeat, then, that eman cipation is entirely safe.*

Emancipation must either be by the voluntary consent of the masters, or by force of law. I regard voluntary emancipation as the most probable, the most desirable, and the most practicable. For the slaveholding landholder would not be less rich in consequence ; the enhancement of the value of land would compensate for the loss of slaves. A comparison of the price of lands of equal quality in the free and slave states will prove this conclusively. If, however, by force of law—the law having once sanctioned slaves as property, the great principle which is recognised by all civilized governments, that private property cannot be taken for public use, without just compensation—dictates that slaves should not be liberated without the consent of the masters, or without paying an equivalent to the owners. Under the sanction of law, one man invests the proceeds of his labor in slaves, another in land : in the course of time it becomes necessary to the common weal to buy up the lands for redistribution or culture in common—how should the tax be laid? Of course upon lands, slaves, and personal property—in a word, upon the whole property of a whole people. If, on the other hand, it should nearly concern the safety and happiness of society, both the slaveholder and the non-slaveholder, that slaves should be taken and emancipated, then, by the same legitimate course of reasoning, the whole property of the State should be taxed for the purpose. If emancipation shall take place by force of law, shall it be by the laws of the states, or by the law of congress? Let congress abolish slavery wherever she has jurisdiction—in the military places, in the territories, and on the high seas, and in the District of Columbia, if the contracts of cession with Virginia and Maryland allow. I lay down the broad rule that congress should do no more for the perpetuation of slavery, than she is *specially* bound to do. The debates in the federal convention prove that the free states did not intend to assume the responsibilities of slavery. In the language of Roger Sherman, and others, they could not acknowledge the right of " property in men." There is then no moral obligation in the Union to sustain the rights of the South in slaves, except only they are morally bound to regard the contract with the South, and in the construction of that compact, the presumption in all cases of doubt is in favor of Liberty. On the contrary, the United States are morally bound by all means consistent with the Constitution to extinguish slavery. The word slave is not used in the Constitution, because the promises of all the southern members of the convention led to final emancipation, and a noble shame on all hands induced the expulsion of the word from the charter of human liberty. I cannot agree that there is any law superior to that of the federal Constitution. It is the part of Christians to model human laws after the divine code, but the law in the present state of light from on High, must be paramount to the Bible itself. If any other practice should prevail, the confusion of religious interpretations of the Divine will would be endless and insufferable. In a country where Jews, Christians, and Infidels, and Deists, and Catholics, and Protestants, and Fourierists, and Mormonites, and Millerites, and Shakers, all are concentrated into one nation, it would be subversive of all governmental action, that each sect should set up a Divine code as each "understands it," superior to the Constitution itself. If a case ever arises where conscience dictates a different doctrine—that the penalty of the law is rather to be borne than its prescriptions obeyed—then also there arises at the same time a case where the sufferer must look to God only for approbation and sustainment—he has passed from all appeal to mankind.

I dissent, then, from the ultra anti-slavery and the ultra pro-slavery men. I cannot join the North in the violation of the Constitution. I cannot stand by the South in asking the moral sanction of the North ; nor do I regard it as a breach of the constitutional compact that she should seek a higher grade of civilization by using all legal means for the entire expulsion of slavery in the United States. Congress, having no power over slavery in the states, the states, each one for itself, where its Constitution does not forbid, certainly has, and should exercise the power of purchase and emancipation. In Kentucky the Constitution forbids the legislature to act upon the subject.* We must therefore look to a convention, or that which I most hope, to voluntary emancipation. Enlightened self-interest, humanity and religion, are moving on with slow, yet irresistible force to that final result. Let the whole North in mass, in conjunction with the patriotic of the South, withdraw the moral sanction and legal power of the Union from the sustainment of slavery, then our existence as a people with undivided interests may yet be consummated. May the Ruler of all nations, the

---

* Without payment—which is impossible in practice.

common Father of all men, who is no respecter of persons, and whose laws are not violated with impunity by individuals nor by states, move us to be just, happy, and free. May that spirit which has eternally consecrated in the admiration of men Salamis and Marathon, Bunker's Hill and Yorktown, inspire our hearts, till the glorious principles of '76 shall be fully vindicated, and throughout the land shall be established "Liberty and Union, one and inseparable, now and for ever."

CASSIUS M. CLAY.

Lexington, Ky., Nov. 1843.

PROSPECTUS

FOR

THE TRUE AMERICAN.

A NUMBER of native Kentuckians, slaveholders and others, propose to publish in the CITY OF LEXINGTON, a paper devoted to gradual and constitutional emancipation, so as at some definite time to place our state upon the firm, safe, and just basis of liberty. The time has come when a large and respectable party, if not a majority of the people, are prepared to take this subject up, and act so as to secure the end proposed, without injustice to any, but with eminent benefit to all. A press is only necessary to give concentrated effort and final success, by free conference of opinion, and untrammeled discussion.

We propose to act as a *State Party*, not to unite with any party, state or national; expecting aid and encouragement from the lovers of liberty of all parties. we shall treat them with studied courtesy and forbearance, so far as it may be consistent with the integrity of the principles which govern us.

It is not proposed that our members should cut loose from their old party associations. The press under our control will appeal *temperately* but *firmly* to the interests and the reason, not to the passions, of our people; we shall take care rigidly to respect the legal rights of others, because we intend to *maintain our own*. We shall attempt to sustain in good faith the "*freedom of the press.*" Whilst our organ will conscientiously vindicate and uphold the Christian morality in ethics, and constitutional republicanism in politics, its columns shall be open to all sects in all things concerning human action; believing, with Jefferson that there is no error so dangerous but that it may be left safely to the combat of reason; we utterly repudiate that false philosophy and time-serving expediency which caters to the tyranny of opinion, by excluding from the press whatever does not suit the fastidious tastes of "patrons." Our readers shall not be our masters; if they love not truth they may go elsewhere. The times call for language plain, bold, and true ; our cause is good ; our press shall be *independent* or cease to exist ; designed to accomplish great purposes, to vindicate principles of interest to all mankind, it shall subserve the elevation of no man, disdain personal denunciation, and share the glory of its triumphs among all its supporters. A native born Kentuckian has engaged to edit " *The True American*," and as his opinions and feelings are expressed in the above outline of party action, he will be untrammeled in his independence, so long as he is faithful to the principles of his adoption.

"The True American" will be published weekly, in the city of Lexington, Kentucky ; and it is proposed to make it embrace all the matter common in newspapers ; especially will it regard the high place which labor holds in the economy of nature, and insist upon its enjoyment of a fair distribution of the products' of capital. The size and appearance of the paper shall be as studiedly becoming and tasteful as its means will allow.

THE TRUE AMERICAN.

"GOD AND LIBERTY!"

LEXINGTON, TUESDAY, JUNE 3.

EDITORIAL DEPARTMENT.

Some of the ablest statesmen and scholars of this state, have agreed to assist in editing this paper, and as my pursuits will not always allow me to revise and comment upon their editorials, some diversity of opinion, upon the great questions at issue, will necessarily occur.

CASSIUS M. CLAY.

SINCE the proposition to publish this paper was made, events have transpired which sink our original design, important as we deemed it, into utter insignificance, compared with the great principles which are now at issue.

The question is now no longer, whether six hundred thousand Kentuckians shall postpone their true prosperity to the real, or supposed interests of some thirty-one thousand slaveholders : but whether they are prepared to yield up, absolutely, all their liberties, and submit themselves willing slaves to a despotic and irresponsible minority. The slave party have undertaken to say, not—that they claim the Constitution as the title-deed to their slaves, which no man can cancel until the very foundations of the government be forcibly overthrown, or peaceably changed by *legal* means, through the omnipotent will of the majority—but that they themselves, trampling under foot all the vital principles of that Constitution, will set at defiance its special injunctions, by an anarchical and revolutionary power —violating natural right, Divine revelation, and the conscience of the civilized world.

The representatives of this faction, " *Junius*," in the Observer and Reporter, and " *A Whig*," and *Robert Wickliffe*, in the Kentucky Gazette, whose letters we publish to-day, have more or less taken the ground, that the subject of slavery shall not be discussed, and that violence shall suppress our press.

Here, upon this issue, then, we take our stand, and are ready to " try conclusions" with these gentlemen, before a gallant people, in the face of the world. We most frankly admit, that we are not so Quixotic as to seek to fight with a mob ; we know that we can be overpowered by numbers ; yet, from the defence of our known rights, we are not to be deterred by vague threats or real dangers, coming from any man or set of men. As we should deem ourselves a base citizen of a commonwealth, if we were not prepared at all times, if necessary, to fall in the defence of our country against a foreign foe : so, we shall ever fearlessly meet the treasonable and revolutionary enemies of constitutional liberty at home. Though under the ban of popular proscription —baited by the wide-spread tongue of slander, and the relentless denunciations of men in power—set on by bands of hireling assassins—still, undismayed, planting ourselves upon the firm basis of our birthright, constitutional liberty, and the world-wide principles of truth and justice, we hurl back indignant defiance against these cowardly outlaws. We can die, but cannot be enslaved.

The Constitution of the United States, Article IX., A, says : " Congress shall make no law　*　*　* abridging the freedom of speech, or of the press." Article X., Section VII., of the Kentucky Constitution, declares, that " The free communion of thoughts and opinions is one of the invaluable rights of man, and every citizen may freely speak, write, or print on any subject, being responsible for the abuse of that liberty." Now every tyro in the lowest attorney's office knows that this responsibility is, for *libel*, or treasonable matter, (if, after the definition of treason in the Constitution of the United States, anything less than " levying war," &c. could be considered punishable) and to a "*jury of our peers*," as James Kent has nowhere denied, and not to a " *mob*," as Junius would have it. For, if this man, grossly ignorant as he is of the great principles of common law and natural right, had looked at the very next Section VIII., of the Kentucky Constitution, he might have saved himself from the ridicule and contempt, if not from the indignation of men.

If, then, Junius shall, single-handed, fall upon us when alone, and take our life, and suppress our publications, he will be guilty of murder. If he shall come with numbers to back him, he will most probably find us too, sustained by some Kentuckians who yet dare to be free. The contest, in that event, may aspire to the dignity of a civil war, in which we shall be found fighting in the cause of the Constitution and Liberty, and they in the cause of slavery—in rebellion against both. In such a contest, I shall not fear the result :

> " That point
> In misery, which makes the oppressed man
> Regardless of his own life; makes him, too,
> Lord of his oppressor's."

Still we are not men of blood ; and to show the pacific that we are economical in that precious fluid, if nothing but a fight will satisfy this rampant *knight of the scalpel*, we propose that he supersede this projected civil war by the less heroic, but more harmless mode of the duel. If he slay us, the press shall stop; if we slay him, then never shall doctor's lancet draw blood more. Here, I must confess, I make but little show of courage, for I fall in with the opinion which generally prevails among my own gallant countrymen, that *mob-leaders* are inevitable *cowards*. Genuine bravery and magnanimity ever go together ; and a man of large chivalric soul scorns to take odds against a single foe. " *Ne sutor ultra crepidam.*" Let *Junius* stick to his bolus ; there is more death in his mortar than in his sword ; none but *unresisting* victims mark his prowess. A man outlawed from the social circle by his infamy, may well aspire to become a cut-throat, if numbers should ensure him his wonted impunity in the perpetration of crime.

I should rather judge "*A Whig*," from his hesitating tone, to be a tame and harmless villain, and we can hardly waste indignation enough to repeat,

> " Thou cream-faced loon,
> Where gottest thou that goose look ? "

Of all men living, *Robert Wickliffe* should be the last to speak of popular vengeance. He stands a living, but ungrateful monument of the forbearing mercy of the people. The victims of incendiary publications have not yet imbrued their hands in the blood of this man, who for years.has not scrupled to aggrandize his political power by the most dangerous insinuations against the lives and property of the community. The armies of men, women, and children, whom he has robbed by the dishonest *juggery* of the *law*—men, who have seen the beds stripped from the sick and helpless women—bread from the mouths of crying infancy—the plough-share run sacrilegiously over the buried ashes of their fathers, mothers, brothers, sisters, and children, by this inexorable fiend of the *law*—have not come up in mass, in their great and remediless woe, and thrown his torn limbs to the dogs : and yet he stands, at the age of seventy, advocating violence. Let this old man beware ! Does he want another family picture spread out upon those walls, built up by the tears and blood of the poor and oppressed, whose cries for redress and vengeance, he confesses, shake him in his guilty home ?

Here, midst the settled gloom which rests upon a house for ever dishonored, may be seen BRECKENRIDGE, returning after a long exile of patient wrong and unresisting persecution, and with one fell blow, crushing into the lowest depths of infamy, the man whom the sincerest follower of the long-suffering Martyr of Judea, could no longer look upon, and live unavenged.

Here is HENRY CLAY, of Ashland, his friend in the days of his deepest woe, who saved the only one of his race worthy of such a champion from a felon's death—the blood flows from a thousand wounds inflicted by the tooth of cruel and remorseless slander—foremost among the bloodhounds who thrust their insatiate muzzles into his very life's blood, is Robert Wickliffe.

Here is a great and gallant and confiding party, who have stood by him in good and evil report, through a long life, conferring upon him its repeated, though undeserved honors : at last, in 1844, in the day of its greatest trial, he basely deserts, and goes off, he and his, to the enemy ; and yet he, with a face of more than metal, dares insult a virtuous community by talking of double-dealing in politicians !

Here is a young and lovely girl, raped by a ruffian negro. When her imploring and streaming eyes were upturned to him, as one of the propounders of the law, asking vengeance for the violated purity of a virgin soul, he dared to strike a yet more deadly blow, by insinuating that this humble daughter of the people was a common prostitute. How can he talk of a mob, at this late day, without trembling at the remembrance of the popular indignation, which had then well nigh executed on him the vengeance which his crimes so richly deserve?

When a citizen of Fayette was poisoned by that degraded population which he would make perpetual among us, who covertly and insidiously procured her pardon of the Executive of the state? And yet he ventures to impute to others the encouragement of rape and poison! Old man, remember poor Benning; remember Trotter, the avenger; remember Russell's cave; and, if you still thirst for bloodshed and violence, the same blade that repelled the assaults of assassin sons, once more in self-defence, is ready to drink of the blood of the hireling horde of sycophants and outlaws of the assassin-sire of assassins.

We pass from these men, whose frontless baseness has turned us from our purpose of avoiding, if possible, all personal controversies, to the great mass of slaveholders, whom they, I know, do not fairly represent. I beg them to remember, that the Constitution is the sole basis of slave tenure, as well as of landed estate; they who have every thing to lose, and nothing to gain by revolution, in my humble judgment, should be the last to avow the doctrine, " *Sauve qui peut,*" and cut loose from all Constitutional moorings. We are not anarchists or agrarians; we claim to be conservatives of the highest order; and for this reason, and no other reason, than because we are such, we intend, if our humble life is spared, to look into the very bottom of this thing of slavery, and see whether it be a safe foundation of prosperity to us and our children, or not. We come not to bring war, but peace; to save, not to destroy. We have no interests separate from those of the great mass of our fellow citizens. We intend to share their dangers, or rejoice in their rescue; but in good and evil report, we are enforced to abide the same destiny. We feel deeply the responsibility of our post; it strips us of all personal ambition and private ends; we ask, therefore, the just and patient forbearance of our countrymen. Far be it from us to wound unnecessarily, their sensibilities, or to run wantonly counter to their rooted prejudices; but we are constrained to speak boldly and honestly, looking neither to the right nor to the left, in our search after truth; advocating our cause as if, not Kentucky only, but all mankind were our judge, and posterity the jury of our award.

If we fail in our purposes, our friends shall not blush for us, nor our enemies lightly triumph. When our mission on earth shall have ended, it shall be said of us, if we attained not the high mark of our fondly cherished aspirations, we dared much, in our humble way, for the vindication of the liberties of men; if we, by the stern and inexorable decree of fate, fell short of the establishment of the right, we never, knowingly, defended the wrong.

Lynch Law.

The following extract from J. H. Green's account of a visit to the New York Auburn State Prison, we commend to "Junius" and his comrades:

" I looked at the murderer and could scarcely believe my own eyes; yet he stood before me a living marvel. I have pledged secrecy as to his real name until after his execution. I interrogated him on his first steps in vice, and how he became so hardened. He told me to remember the treatment he had received fron the lynchers' lash at Vicksburg. I did, but my eyes could scarce credit reality. I had known him in 1832, '3, '4, and the early part of '35, as a barkeeper in Vicksburg.

" He was never a shrewd card-player, but at that time was considered an inoffensive youth. The coffee-house he kept was owned by North, who, with four others, were executed on the 5th of July, 1835, by Lynch law. Wyatt, and three others, were taken on the morning of the 7th, stripped, and one thousand lashes given to the four, tarred and feathered, and put into a canoe and set adrift on the Mississippi river. It makes my blood curdle and my flesh quiver to think of the suffering condition of these unfortunate men, set adrift on the morning of the 7th of July, with the broiling sun upon their mangled bodies. Two died in about two hours after they were set afloat. Wyatt and another remained with their hands and feet bound forty hours, suffering more than tongue can tell, or pen describe, when they were picked up by some slave negroes, who started with the two survivors to their quarters. His companion died before they arrived. Wyatt survives to tell the horrors of the lynchers' lash. He told me seven murders had been occasioned by their unmerciful treatment of him, and one innocent man hung. I know his statements to be true, for I had known him before 1835, and his truth in other particulars cannot be

doubted. He murdered his seventh man, for which crime he will be executed. I have another communication for your paper, concerning the murderer, and his prospects in the world to come. Yours, truly, J. H. GREEN."
" *Auburn, April* 10, 1845."

The lynching of the gamblers in Vicksburg has ever been regarded by reflecting men, as murder. It is vain for the perpetrators of that notorious crime, to tell us that these gamblers were outlaws and cut throats ; there were also there judges, jurors, police officers, and a populous country. These men, however abandoned, had thrown themselves upon the majesty of the law for defence, and by that law they should have fallen, or have stood for ever intact. If a single citizen had stolen in the night and stabbed the gamblers to the heart, when wrapt in slumber, the crime would have stood out in its real colors. A number of citizens, going in mass, in open day, in *overpowering odds*, only in degree reduced the crime in the ratio of the number and armament of the attacked. Crime is ever shortsighted ; in fact, that conduct which the wise of all ages have marked as destructive of man's best interests—*that* is crime The ends of this mob have never been attained ; they thought to secure peace and security by violence, what was the result ? Some of the best blood in Vicksburg was shed in that contest : the gamblers were ousted ; but the blood of the murdered men still cries aloud from the ground for vengeance. It is said that this fraternity have sworn eternal enmity against Vicksburg. It has been burnt again and again, by these armed men, who have sprung up as from the sown dragon's teeth : and no man can foretell the end of these woes that hang over the doomed city. This convict confesses *seven murders* in consequence of this outrage—what else can men expect ? They who sow the wind shall reap the whirlwind !
Monstrous cruelty and wrong never deter from crime ; but on the contrary, by disturbing the elements of virtuous intent and religious faith, as well as the basis of wholesome public opinion, which, with weak minds is often the only rule of action, they quicken into life the worst passions and the foulest deeds. The theory of society is taken to be this : every man yields up to government *his right of offence* for any injury, and *his right of defence*, in all cases where it is possible for the strong arm

of the law to come to the rescue. And the great law of self-defence does not exist, except in extreme cases, when it is incumbent on the defendant to show that to have awaited the slow progress of the civil power would have been utter ruin, for which society could have made no amends. Now I take it, that if these postulates be true, then in all cases whatever, Lynch law is a *crime* of the darkest dye in organized society, and in no case justifiable. Or we may state the case thus: If any offence is punished by Lynch law, before it can be justified, the lynchers must show that it is better that all society be dissolved, than that the offence should go unpunished. By this rule, the slayers of Utterback (I believe this is the name of the man lynched by the Kentuckians, near Cincinnati), were murderers. Because it is better that this murderer should have gone unwhipt of justice, than that all law should have been trampled under foot; or that the tacit covenant which every man has made with all the members of society, to yield up the right of offence or vengeance, should have been perfidiously and sacrilegiously broken. And when the murderers of Utterback say to us, what! should this man, who has cut the throat of his fellow man, for the sake of gold, and left him for dead, go unwhipt of justice, because the law had not anticipated just such a case? We say yes: and you yourselves have done in very *fact* what he in *design* merely attempted; and yet you are still yourselves unpunished—the very thing you complain of in others. Give us back our savage life, the scalping knife, the poisoned arrow, the war club, the cave, the brushwood, the prairie grass, the sharpened sense of aggression, vengeance, and defence: or spread over us the sacred panoply of inexorable and eternal law. The great master of the human mind and heart surely never conceived that there could be a conservative principle in Lynch law:

> *Shylock.* What judgment shall I dread doing no wrong?
> You have among you many a purchased slave,
> Which, like your asses, and your dogs, and mules,
> You use in abject and in slavish parts,
> Because you bought them:—Shall I say to you,
> Let them be free, and marry them to your wives?
> Why sweat they under burdens? let their beds
> Be made as soft as yours, and let their palates
> Be seasoned with such viands? You will answer,
> The slaves are ours. So do I answer you:

The pound of flesh, which I demand of him,
Is dearly bought, is mine, and I will have it;
If you deny me, *fie upon your law!*
There is no force in the decrees of Venice:
I stand for judgment; answer, shall I have it?

And again:

Shylock. If you deny it, let the danger light
Upon your charter and your city's freedom.

Here this "damned inexorable dog," (to use the words of Gratiano) plotting the murder, in cold blood, of the worthiest man in Venice, shielded by the inviolate sanctity of the law, defies the omnipotent council of the haughty republic:

Bassanio. And I beseech you
Wrest once the law to your authority.
To do a great right, do a little wrong;
And curb this cruel devil of his will.

A "Junius" he, except he had a soul. But such was not the wisdom of the immortal poet. In the ever-memorable words of Portia, Lynch law finds its grave—no Junius, nor banded outlaws can ever resurrect it from its sleep of death:

Portia. It must not be: *there is no power in Venice*
Can alter a decree established.
'Twill be recorded for a precedent:
And many an error, by the same example,
Will rush into the state. *It cannot be.*

LEXINGTON, TUESDAY, JUNE 10.

PROGRESS.

Revelation, as well as natural philosophy, teach us that creation itself has been progressive; organism, both vegetable and animal, has slowly reached its present perfection; history confirms the combined evidence of the anterior theory, till speculation has subsided into fact. It is foreign to our purpose to moot the vexed question, whether man is the immediate work of the hands of God, or whether his existence is the necessary result of original elements, combined by antecedent laws of omnipotent will. We imagine that there are few at the present time, who will contend that he was from the beginning, and that he is at the head of all intelligences, *known* and *unknown*. Atheism has perished from the convictions of mankind. Passing on, however, to known truths, we lay down the broad proposition, that from the earliest time man has been improving in his social condition, or advancing in those complicated developments and relations which are understood by the term civilization. We dare say that our race is better guarded against natural evils than ever before; better housed, better clothed, better fed, and better provided with medicines against disease and casualties. Particular nations have at times excelled in particular arts, but what was once peculiar to a single people is now world-wide in its diffusion. The Grecian temple now illustrates many a "barbarian" hill; and provincial peasants, since the cultivation of cotton, and the preparation of chemicals, rival, in lovely raiment, the Tyrian purple of princes. The intellect has not fallen behind the physical part in its progress. Men no longer bow down to stocks and stones, and shed each other's blood in submissive sacrifice to wooden gods; the eclipses of the sun and moon fill them no more with vague terror; comets move on serenely through the Heavens, and pestilence and war are flung no more from their fiery hair. The angry voice of an avenging Deity is no more heard in the midst of the storm; and the red lightning comes not with the flash of death, but passing harmlessly into its great reservoir, the earth, silently aids in the evolution of vegetable and animal life. Wars are less frequent and less disastrous than of yore; first, men, when captured were put to the sword, then enslaved, but now exchanged with scrupulous fidelity. Formerly every tribe, or embryo nation, was a predatory horde; and all strangers were regarded as enemies, and legitimate spoil. The most refined nations, before the Christian era, were but robbers on a large scale. The Greeks regarded all others than Greeks, as barbarians, and lawful prey to their victorious arms. The motto of the Romans was, that the God, Terminus, should never retreat, but that the bounds of the empire should enlarge for ever. In primitive societies feeble children and aged parents were alike exposed to death; and blood was avenged by blood, without any nice discrimination between the innocent and the guilty. Religion itself has its epochs of progress; and many degrees lie between the time of sacrifice of human beings to avenging Gods, and that when Christ taught the ever-glorious doctrine of universal love to God and man. The political rights of men have in the mean time, by no means, remained undeveloped. The divine right of kings to rule, and their sanctity of person and irresponsibility to man, are long since exploded : and every monarchy bases itself upon the common good, and the tacit assent of the governed.

The reformation was as much a political as a religious renovation. The independence of the English Church and the emigration of the Puritans, were but the results of a progression of the democratic principle. The declaration of American independence was not so much the work of the profound reflections of particular men, as the exponent of the spirit of the age, and the sum of the freedom of the world. The enunciation of the political equality of man was in politics, what the great law of love was in religion ; both the eternal rocks of man's best happiness and highest glory—imperishable elements in progressive civilization. The sacrilegious hand of political tyranny and priestly superstition have in vain essayed their demolition.

For the first time in the history of nations was the conservative principle of *mutual interest, equality*—absolute equality, so far as God by the inequality of organization would allow—distinctly avowed. There was force in it, tremendous, irresistible force, the force of truth and justice. All human obstacles fell before it like the bent reed before the whirlwind. The most venerable monarchies, with their prestige of antiquity and Divine right, crumbled into dust : the dark veil of political Jesuitism was rent for ever; the priesthood, who wielded the thunders of usurped Divinity for long centuries, crushing the body and soul, were spit upon in their sanctuaries. The bent oak, grown to maturity, shivered with its rebound the mad hands who thought to trail it in the dust. No ! Americans ; the spirit of liberty, though seemingly retarded and turned back, is *onward*. Like as on the fabled wandering Jew, the hand of destiny is on the nations of the world ; they shall *not rest ;* the great, the wealthy, the refined, cut off from all physical pressure, are touched with drowsy lids ; they would sleep, and be at peace, but labor, and famine, and woe, and contempt, are crushing the hearts, extinguishing the immortal aspirations of God's creatures ; a voice which walls of chiselled marble cannot shut

out, bids them awake—"*March! march!*" till justice be no
more "compromised," and man's political redemption shall
come.

———

Men do not differ as to what are the elements of National
prosperity and glory ; wealth, numbers in new countries, literature, industry, the mechanic arts, scientific agriculture, &c.,
these are indisputable elements of prosperity. Now, if New
York had excelled Virginia in a bare majority of these elements
of strength, we might have concluded that the cause was in
some superior advantages that New York had in position, in
climate, in soil, in extent of territory, in minerals ; but no ; Virginia has the advantage in all these ; slavery then would seem
to be the cause of Virginia's inferiority. But what will men
think when told that there is not an element of strength and
glory in which New York does not excel Virginia in spite of
all her natural odds ? Slavery must then be set down as the
sole cause. If a single State only illustrated this contrast, then
there might still be room for argument. But here are twenty-
six States covering a continent, embracing all climates and
soils, and most unequal spaces in favor of slavery : and yet
thirteen times has this struggle of ascendency between liberty
and slavery taken place in these United States, and thirteen
times has liberty borne off the palm ; not in one of the elements of national strength and glory, only, but every one, yes,
every one, without a single exception. The cause is as shallow
and transparent as the result. Here in the South are three
millions of slaves, doing only about one-half of the effective
work of the same number of whites in the North : because they
are not so skilful, so energetic, and above all, have not the stimu-
lus of self-interest, as the whites ; next they waste as much
again through carelessness and design. The twelve hundred
millions of capital invested in slaves is a dead loss to the South ;
the North getting the same number of laborers, doing double
the work, for the interest on the money ; and sometimes by
partnerships, or joint operations, or when men work on their
own account, without any interest being expended for labor.
Will any mathematician undertake to tell us the astounding
consequences which would result from this, in half a century ?
Next, then, three millions are of necessity, with rare exceptions,

cultivators of the soil; of course mechanic arts, and all other arts than those of agriculture, cannot exist. Then all the necessaries and luxuries which are used in the South must be got by a double exchange, and of course double freights are to be paid by her. We have undertaken to show elsewhere that this exchange costs us in many cases one absolute half of all of one year's production. Having lost then all chance of availing ourselves of the physical discoveries of the last half century, how do we stand in other respects? The three millions of slaves make all those kinds of labor in which they are engaged especially, and all other labor, indirectly, dishonorable; there is a mental debasement in compulsory service, which attaches to the thing done; and men may moralize and homilize as much as they please, and they never can, as they never have put labor on a respectable footing in slave states. *To make it honorable, you must make it free.* Well, the five millions of whites in the slave states do as little work as possible: idleness being one of the seeming regalia of wealth and refinement. Whatever of mechanical talent or intellect, capable of illustrating a nation, there is in the three millions of slaves, is lost for ever for want of education : whatever mind capable of achieving anything in the laborious departments of human knowledge and mechanism, there is in the free five millions, is almost entirely lost : because indolence is the fixed habit of the people, industry the exception. How as to morals? is there anything in favor of slavery in this respect? There is more crime in slave states than in any other form of society under the sun. In the eye of God there is no respect of persons : so with the moralist. Here, then, to begin with, are three millions of slaves, almost without exception, practising adultery, fornication, and theft, whilst in other respects they commit as many, if not more crimes, than the same numbers in any portion of the civilized world. One need but read the newspapers to see that crime is in proportion to the numbers, about five times as great in the slave states, as in the free. How else can it be, when the sense of public justice is poisoned by slave tenure, and indolence and pride and self-indulgence pervade the masses of the people? The less we say about religion the better : the Romans had a niche in their temples dedicated to the "Unknown God;" if some of the remarks of certain Divines of the far South are correctly reported, the worshippers of the "Unknown God" have not perished with the seven hilled city. Education in slave states has been proved impossible. It is impossible, because the interest of the slaveholding is an antagonistic one to that of the free laborer : the ignorance of the free is the security to the holders of the enslaved : and if a better spirit prevails in spite of interest, over the slaveholder, the extent of the farms in slave states absolutely excludes the poor from coming within reach of a teacher. Where is their school fund, won by the common blood of the people, and as justly theirs, as the coats on their backs ? Where is it ? we ask. Where is it ? is heard from the children of the poor, perishing for mental light and moral instruction ! let the slaveholders answer ! The press—they are unfaithful sentinels !—the churches, they have not cried aloud and spared not ! " Great statesmen !"—they have built upon a sandy foundation !—economists, they have been walling against the stormy ocean with pebbles. Americans, the British nation is become the defender of liberty. Webster, Clay, Calhoun, you who have the ear and confidence of our people—help ! or we shall sink down into Oriental barbarism—our place among nations will be for ever lost.

TO ALL THE OPPONENTS OF SLAVERY.

Friends, have you counted the cost ? If you are not for slavery you are against it : be assured there is no middle ground ; between liberty and slavery there is not, there cannot be, any compromise. We have been told often, with an air of triumph, that R. S., Esq., lost his nomination because he took the " True American " for six months, whilst humble men are continually informing us, that they are *proscribed* for opinion's sake. You will be assaulted and shut in on all sides ; traduced in your character ; injured in your persons, in your business, and in your families. Never fear, brave hearts : oat meal can be had at twenty cents per bushel ; they can't starve us yet : " every dog has his day." Only let us, like our revolutionary sires, be true to ourselves, and to the liberty of our inheritance, and triumph awaits us : as sure as God regards the right, *Kentucky shall be free.*

Lawyers, merchants, mechanics, laborers, who are your consumers; Robert Wickliffe's two hundred slaves? How many
clients do you find, how many goods do you sell, how many
hats, coats, saddles, and trunks, do you make for these two hundred slaves? Does Mr. Wickliffe lay out as much for himself
and his two hundred slaves, as two hundred freemen do? "I
am a maker of saddles; formerly I had two hundred farmers
purchasing saddles; A, B, and C, slaveholders, bought them out;
they took all the money they got, from circulation, and went to
Illinois. I have now only A, B, and C, three customers, they are
not sufficient, I am starving: I, too, must pack up, and leave
my native home: a slave takes my place." We stand for the
whites: Mr. Wickliffe for the slaves. If any fighting is to be
done, will you stand by us, who would put bread in the mouths
of your children, or by Mr. W., who hates and fears you because
he knows he injures you? Some of our mechanics are building
homes here on their own account: this will do very well if it
is to become a *free* state; if not, I advise them to desist, for as
sure as life or death, they must lose: a town cannot outlive its
consumers. The roads into this city have swallowed up some
of the small towns around, by taking their customers; but if
the farmers continue, as they have done, enlarging their farms,
and increasing the slave population, your consumers will, as
they have, become daily, fewer. You may linger out your lives
with trade continually decreasing, but your children will be left
absolutely without employment; they must emigrate or die.
But under the free system the towns would grow and furnish a
home market to the farmers, which in turn would employ more
labor; which would consume the manufactures of the towns;
and we could then find our business continually increasing, so
that our children might settle down among us and make industrious, honest citizens.

Fallacy of the saying among Laborers, that the "Decay of Work is the Strength of Trade."

There are five men: A is a farmer, B a tailor, C a manufacturer of cloth, D a hatter, and E a house builder. Now, A,
having labored ten days, has made five bushels of meal, which

he exchanges, with B, C, D, and E, for such things as they make; but in order to get the selling of another bushel of meal, he has sold it hot, so that one half of it spoils before it is eaten. B, C, D, and E, also acting upon the same principle, sell A the coat, the cloth, the hat, and the house, all intentionally damaged, in order that the decay of work may cause A to return sooner. What have they all gained? Nothing; on the contrary, they have each one lost five days' hard work in ten, trying to cheat each other. A has had to work enough to pay for two hats, &c., when one good one at half the money would have lasted him just as long as two under the cheating system. B, instead of getting a bushel of meal that would last him a week, has been compelled to make two hats instead of one in exchange for meal to keep him going. Now, let each one do his best in improving himself in the making of their several articles; then each one may live as well on half the labor, and have half his time for recreation, improvement in mind and morals. Surely "decay in work is not the strength of trade," but "*honesty is the best policy.*"

President Bascom's Review and Slavery.

We have read this review carefully and painfully. As a chronicler of the times, we would be doing him injustice to pass with seeming indifference this work, lying right across our path, so deeply mixed up with the engrossing political movements of this and all countries. Yet we must let this cup pass from us: we venture to call Mr. Bascom our personal friend; we regard him as a man of large soul, but the *victim of a false position :* if we are right, no reproaches are needed; if wrong, all would be in vain. We confess that we have, in spite of our attempt at neutrality, ever felt a certain softness about the heart when we are thrown in company with the Methodists. When we have seen, in some of our mountain excursions, one of these self-denying men, on a salary of one hundred dollars a year, facing the rain and chill blasts of coming winter, alone among the bleak hills, with his Bible, searching out the remote occupant of some rude hovel on a deep ravine, or the mountain side, carrying with a confiding and sympathizing spirit, the hopes and the consolations of the Gospel to the humble and the afflicted, without hope of earthly reward, we have said to ourself, this is indeed a son of God : with him we will share our hearth and board, to the last faggot and crust of bread. Whilst the millionnaire feeder on the flocks of cities has never failed to excite our instinctive sense of, beware! these Methodists are strong and true-hearted men, said we, and if any man shall open up a way whereby slavery shall be attacked, even unto death, without conflict with the civil power, which it is not the part of Christians to resist, except by the saving influences of the Gospel, these will be his friends, and strengthen his hands in the unequal contest. This may have been a gleam of boyish enthusiasm—a passing reverie—yet we have cherished it long and fondly ; if it be a delusion, time will dispel it soon enough.

LEXINGTON, TUESDAY, JUNE 17.

THE LETTER OF EX-GOVERNOR M., UPON THE "MISSOURI RESTRICTION, ABOLITION, SLAVERY, EMANCIPATION;" *Published in the Frankfort Commonwealth, Feb.* 14, 1845.

This letter we re-publish to-day in order that our readers may see it for themselves, and that we may always give our opponents a fair hearing. It purports to have been written in reply to charges made against the ex-Governor, before the Presidential election in '44 ; and when we consider its temper, we are somewhat at a loss to know why the gentleman remained so long quiescent under imputations which now excite in him so much indignation. We think the public will agree with us, in our inference, that Mr. M. has taken up some flying reports, as a mere pretext for striking a deadly blow at the cause of real liberty and pure republicanism, through the odious persons of other states, whom it has ever been the policy of the slave party, both in the South and the North, to calumniate ; with a view to strike down the friends of safe and rational emancipation at home, by transferring, at a word, the accumulated vengeance of long years upon any one whom these patriots, par excellence, may stigmatize as "*mad dogs.*" This shallow game, whilst all the presses were on one side, was easy enough. But now, since there are two avowed emancipation presses in the State, and many more whom an enlightened self-interest leads to favor the cause of truth, this wily politician will find it can be no longer played, except at a ruinous loss, not only of logic, but of character.   Now, we tell the people of Kentucky, that we are not responsible for the opinions of the abolitionists of the North; yet, after all this bugaboo of long years, what will the community think when we assure them that there are just as good, and religious, and moral, and peaceable men among the "abolitionists," as T. M. himself.   Take William Lloyd Garrison, upon whose devoted head a price has been set by the state of Georgia, who has been shamelessly hunted like a wild beast through the land; yet Garrison is a man who is opposed to bloodshed, in all cases, a *non-resistant*, an enemy to war and to the gallows!   It is true, that latterly, the Garrisonian party have come out for the dissolution of the Union; "no union with slaveholders" being their motto.   This, we by no means wish to palliate; but between the *disunionists* and *perpetual slavery* men, the world will not hesitate to say, that the disunionists are the *truest men*.   Take the "liberty party;" they stand by the Constitution in its whole letter and spirit, and are for *legal* and equitable reform only.   There are some evil, and malignant, and fanatical spirits among the abolitionists, it is true; but it is as unjust to denounce them as a class, as it would be to call all slaveholders murderers, because some dastards among them, plot against the lives of the friends of liberty in the South.

Were it not for the Governor's violent protestations against any suspicion of aspiration for office, one would imagine that he has given way to a temper exasperated by the loss of "the spoils," when one so "*sweet*" towards the abolitionists before November, should now esteem those, loathsome "*vermin*" in February '45, who even suspected him of having fraternity of feeling with that contemned party.   Surely he is a much injured man, for the public have regarded him for years as a standing candidate for any good sinecure that might fall uppermost.   And if his songs and his hunting shirt, have not proved as useful to him or the community of late years, as his stone hammer did in early life, he ought to submit with a becoming grace to the progress of the times and the shrewd good sense of the people, who might very well honor the honest mechanic, whilst they contemned the shallow tricks of the political mountebank. The Governor attaches some importance to himself for having voted with Mr. Clay, for the admission of Missouri into the Union ; now, if this is the basis of his fame with posterity, his ambition is low enough to meet with ample satiety ; and the stone walls which he has built as a mason will much outlive the fame of his acts as a statesman. We never approved of this vote of Mr. Clay's; and whilst we regard his action on that occasion as evidence of his intellectual eminence, and superior control over his contemporaries, we at the same time, esteem it the unfortunate beginning of a course of policy, which has well nigh lost us our liberties, and driven our republic upon the very verge of ruin. As well as the loss of that moral power on his part, which has shut him out from the presidency of the United States, and from that culminating ray of glory which for all time would have illuminated his name, if this people had found him in '44, as they did in 1799, the fearless advocate of the universal liberty of men. He should have said to Missouri, " The Constitution which I love, and have sworn before God and the world to support, has no clause providing that any human being, either red, white, or black, or mixed, shall be enslaved ; but on the contrary, it says in its preamble, that it was formed to 'establish justice' and to secure the blessings of liberty to us and our posterity, and we know not where you get the authority to enslave the African more than the Indian, or the Asiatic, or the European, or the Anglo-Saxon American. Moreover, this same Constitution says, art. V. of A, ' No person shall be deprived of life, liberty, or property, without due process of law,' that is, unless for some offence ascertained by law, and punishable by the verdict of a jury. Now an African is as much a ' person' as a Saxon, or a Frenchman ; and, since no one has asked that the courts should put in force the habeas corpus, another constitutional right to cause these holders of the blacks in durance, to show by what authority these 'persons' were held, in opposition to the Constitution and laws of the Union, the only sovereign, to which the people of Missouri, being in the territorial bounds of the same, owed entire allegiance—in consideration of all these positive laws and natural right, we declare before all men, that you shall never be admitted into fellowship with us, a republican and free people, whose every fundamental principle of equal liberty your Constitution tramples in the dust." Such, Mr. M., should have been the declaration of the sons of Washington; and if this had dissolved the Union and drenched the land in blood, then, by the God of battles, every lover of the human family should have cried out, let it perish from the place of nations, and from the memory of mankind. But such was not the dread alternative; there is not, and never has been, and God forbid that there ever should be, a time in the history of this nation, when the South shall dare to dissolve this Union, with the diabolical design of maintaining African slavery; and if that day ever does come, then will the crime and its atonement be but one deed!

We follow this champion of the slave party in the order of his letter. He "differs radically in opinion with those of our countrymen, who maintain that Kentucky is at no distant day to become a non-slaveholding state." Thus far an unimportant opinion only, for he speaks for the slave party: but when he undertakes to speak for us, the free white non-slaveholders of the state, we say, softly, governor, we are the best judges of our highest interest, and a friend of perpetual slavery is not a safe keeper of our conscience. We say, then, that T. M., holding interest not only different from, but antagonistic to ours, has no right to speak for us. "It is a great error to suppose that those of our countrymen who own no slaves, will ever go for emancipation, and the retention of the emancipated within our borders." Here is the great battle ground, M. knows it, we feel it; we enter upon it cautiously, but without trembling. We say, look to reason and your own conscience, and then speak boldly to your countrymen, as men of sound heads and true hearts, and leave the result to God. I. Then, we are opposed to banishing the liberated blacks from the state, because we deem it, in many respects, *inexpedient*. II. Because it is *unjust*. We believe it to be inexpedient, because, to be plain with our readers, at home and abroad, the great obstacle to emancipation is the *loss of the money*, vested in the slave. To colonize, you increase the loss, to the amount of the land purchased for the colony, the necessary outfit of clothing, provisions, implements of agriculture, and trade, and the cost of transfer. If slaveholders dread the loss of slaves by emancipation, will they love it the more when, by colonization, you propose an increased expenditure? Shrewd slaveholders see this difficulty, and with that jesuitical cunning, which characterizes the friends of perpetual thraldom, they attempt to make us the slaves of our own prejudices, by exciting us against the black, till we are unwilling to live with him, when free, whilst they believe themselves secure against emancipation and removal, by the difficulties of its achievement. Thus, you hear them with alternate words of honeyed tone and bitter denunciation, saying: "I am as much in favor of liberty as you, if you will send the blacks to the moon; but unless you send them to the moon, I'll see you damned before I assent to their liberation among us." Is not that the argument, governor? Worse yet, just read his jesuitical letter. "Heavens, the monster talks of banishing the poor negro to the moon!" "So," to cut the matter short, "we go for perpetual slavery." No, M., we will not advocate the "banishment" of the black, because all nations have thought expulsion from one's native home sufficient punishment for the greatest crimes; we will not, therefore, go for banishment. If we fall in this cause, we will fall on solid ground, that our body may be a rampart to the gallant spirits who shall succeed us in an undying cause. We will not be driven by our foes into bottomless quicksands to be swallowed up, "like dumb dogs,"* to be forgotten for ever. Yet this is merely one individual opinion, we do not presume to dictate to the *emancipation party* in Kentucky. All we say is, we are opposed to emancipation with banishment; yet sooner than see slavery made perpetual, we are willing, if there be no other alternative, to yield up our own wishes to the majority of our countrymen. Leaving this part of the question here now, intending to give it an ample discussion hereafter, we pass on.

We think every honest, self-respecting laborer in Kentucky, will repel, with just indignation, the Governor's shallow sycophancy, in calling them "nature's noblemen," for doing the very *thing* which he dares in a few subsequent sentences to characterize as an act of "*intolerable inhumanity.*" If such is the Governor's code of morals, we doubt whether any are so poor as to envy that "eminence" which he boasts over his former compeers. Which by no means for the first time in the history of men, has hardened the heart, vitiated the soul, obscured the

---

* This is the elegant language of some of our pro-slavery friends—that in struggling against the stream of public opinion, we will go down like "dumb dogs." The Governor, in his letter, reiterates the same idea. We may go down as "dogs," but the Governor, as well as some others, shall long have cause to remember that we are not "*dumb.*"

reason, and caused the unbalanced sons of blind fortune to look down with contempt upon the humble companions of earlier days. We should despise ourself if for any unworthy purpose, we should excite unjust prejudices in the minds of one portion of the community against the other. And if we tell our fellow-laborers the real sentiments of such slaveholders as M., it is because he has attempted to corrupt their minds by unjust and ignoble appeals to the lowest of human passions. They impoverish you by the tremendous and overpowering competition of slave labor, and then cry out in extenuation of their conduct towards the blacks, "they are better off than the poor whites." They first take away your bread, your schools, and all social advantages, and then add insult to injury, by placing you, in the category of economical progress, a degree below the slave. You all understand very well, my countrymen, how penitentiary labor ruins your business, and the mechanics have petitioned the legislature to prevent them from manufacturing in the penitentiary such articles as they themselves were engaged in making. Now slave labor is penitentiary labor, the master standing in the same relation to the slave, that C. does to the convicts : each getting their labor done for the mere outlay of victuals, clothes, and shelter, without either giving wages. Thus every laborer in Kentucky is injured by the one hundred and eighty thousand slaves, as if the same number of Irishmen, Dutchmen, or Englishmen, should come in here and agree to work as the convicts or the slaves do, without wages. Free the blacks, and they either would not work at all, or they would require wages; which would prevent you from being underbid as you now are. We know that many of our mechanics and laboring men have accumulated estates, and live in as refined and luxurious a manner as many slaveholders. But these are exceptions, arising from superior intelligence, energy, and long hours of steady toil, which surmount all the counteracting weight of slave competition. It is a great fallacy to talk of the wages of laborers in the slave states, being higher than the wages of laborers in the free states, for our articles of purchase here are higher than in the free states ; and a man getting one hundred dollars in the free, can live as well as one getting two hundred dollars in the slave states. Let no laboring man allow himself to be insulted by this vulgar aristocracy of slave tenure, by the continual cry of "association" with the blacks. Every

man and woman in this country can choose their own companions; and, so far as my knowledge goes, the wealthy have
been more frequently in dishonorable intercourse with the
blacks than the laboring poor. We say, fearless of contradiction, that there is more amalgamation of the two races in the
slave states, according to numbers, than in the free states. The
injustice of the free states towards the blacks, is not a matter at
issue. One wrong is no justification of another wrong: and we
are pleased to see that the free states are beginning to place the
blacks upon a better footing than of yore; so that the Governor
will soon find himself, without the apology of companionship
in evil, the last miserable refuge of little souls.

So far as the "slow progress of colonization" is concerned,
we throw no obstacles in the way of this benevolent scheme
of Christianizing and civilizing Africa. For those purposes
we wish it well, and have become a life member of the Colonization Society, but, regarding it as no remedy for slavery, we
throw it out of all estimate of the elements of emancipation at
home; unless some great change upon this subject takes place
in the minds of the people of the free states, which we do by
no means anticipate. There can be no doubt but that, preceding the calling of a convention, many slaves will be sent out
of the state, notwithstanding its "inhumanity." And we merely allude to it to show that the Governor's foresight is as shallow
as his compliments, or as *real* as his *affected sympathies :* for
he knows that there is a yearly trade of thousands of human
souls, carried on between Kentucky and the South, and this, his
*humane system of life-long legislation has never attempted
to stop !*

The Governor attempts to grow facetious, and ranks the
friends of gradual emancipation with the "Millerites," and
"Live-for-evers." "I thank thee, Jew, for teaching me that
word." The lovers of justice, those who, through many perils
and much contempt, battled on for the right, who gave up their
whole intellect to the defence of the liberties of mankind, though
humble and obscure, with large souls and untameable spirits,
trusting on to the last, shall not pass from the memory of men.
From generation to generation, lighting up congenial sentiments
in the hearts of the brave and the true, they shall not perish,
but "*live for ever.*" The charge against the abolitionists, of
failing to throw the balance of power, which they held in their

hands, in favor of the Whigs, and thus exclude slaveholding Texas from coming into the Union, is true. God knows we labored in this cause with a devotion and sleepless energy, worthy of better success than awaited our party, or than the cold recognition of the services rendered by our humble self, which awaited us on our return to our native state. Yet, to say that the abolitionists were operated upon by less lofty, or sincere and pure motives than T. M., or ourselves, has never had the slightest proof to sustain it. And we do not scruple to characterize such insinuations as unworthy of any man of right principles and honorable bearing. Whether the Indian or the African are to be "ever held as inferior to the whites," remains with God only to determine. But to exercise perpetual despotism over them "because the whites have the power," is a sentiment only worthy of the source whence it emanated, and cannot fail to excite disgust and indignation throughout all Christendom. If despotism is to be perpetuated, give us a splendid monarchy over our equals, where the magnitude of the game will stir the spirit, and exercise the intellect. If the finer feelings are to be crushed, and all the sympathies of the heart dried up in one stern and inexorable passion for supremacy and glorious achievement, well; but for vulgar, imbecile, negro slavery aristocracy—for this, no—not for this, will "I file my mind." The Governor says, in connexion with Texas and slavery, that he "had no compunctions whatever, on the score of extending the slave boundary," and proceeds to exhort his countrymen to be ever ready, like him, to shed their blood in the defence of Texan slavery. Well, we don't complain of this, we know not what cause such blood would better grace; but we protest in the name of the immortal patriots, who declared that all men were entitled to life, liberty, and the pursuit of happiness," against shedding the blood of the Americans in such ignoble cause. With Texas and her slavery we have nothing to do, farther than that we are ready to guaranty her independence against the unjust interference of any European government. But we tell the ex-Governor, that if Texas comes into this Union as a territory, and she can come in in no other way, *that her slaves are free.* And if she comes in as a state, contrary to the Constitution and laws of this confederacy, as soon as we have the power we will *put her out again.* And transmitted down from generation to generation, shall go the watchword, "*no more slave territory added to the Union: and the constitutional extinction of slavery in the present states.*"

If T. M. had discussed the subject of slavery and emancipation without going out of the way to take an impotent blow at England, he would have at least preserved some show of originality; and not have followed a track made disgusting to all enlarged minds by reiterating the spiteful remarks of ignorant and shallow demagogues. No doubt England might spare much from her splendid and munificent church and state establishments to her laboring classes. Yet, notwithstanding all this, England supports more numbers in comfortable circumstances than any other same number of square miles under the sun. And if the sustaining of human life in its fullest numbers in comfort, be the design of God, then has England best accomplished her mission on earth. It is true, that the lower strata of society are bitterly oppressed by want in England, but this is a necessary result of human existence. Want, disease, and the sword, cut off the human species in all old countries, which, like all created vegetable and animal existences, has many more embryo lives than there are places for, or nourishment on earth to nurture into maturity. We deny that there are "slaves in England." The lowest laborer in the mines of Cornwall or the factories of Manchester may become the Premier of Great Britain, a power greater than the throne; and from the lowest haunts of famine may and will again arise as there have already arisen, many of the first jurists, statesmen, and men of letters, in the British empire. How many from the three millions of slaves here may aspire to similar eminence? Here statute law sets at defiance the law of nature and of God; there nature as she should be, is the only arbiter of the destinies of men. We envy England her freedom and her glory: she has become the defender of the liberty of mankind; and America, once glorious and proud America, has become the propagandist of slavery among men. If the slaveholders expect to maintain the war against Liberty and Republicanism, they must get some more Herculean champion than the man with the hunting shirt: and let the ex-Governor return once more to his proper sphere of hammering stone: or singing the really good old song of "*Wife, Children, and Friends.*"

DEATH OF ANDREW JACKSON.

ANDREW JACKSON died at the Hermitage, on the 8th instant. Whatever difference of opinion may prevail about his measures as a statesman, every true-hearted American cannot but be be proud of his military fame. That Jackson was a great man, no one who regards the remarkable impress which he made upon the millions of his day, can deny. His strength was that of the will and the passions, rather than the force of eminent intellect. Like Sylla he never spared an enemy or forgot a friend : he must of course then go down to posterity with a divided fame. The man who, like WASHINGTON, would live in the affections of a whole people or of the world, must, like him, be just : for justice is the only basis of universal admiration and sure immortality.

DIVORCE.—BEAUTY IN WOMEN.—PHYSICAL LAWS.— SLAVERY.

The number of divorces in the slave states is startling to the statesman as well as the moralist. As the marriage state is one sanctioned by the Christian code, as well as by the judgment of the wise of all times and nations, we shall at the risk of injuring the delicacy and refined sensibilities of women, inquire into the causes which load the tables of our halls of legislation with thousands of applications for divorces. These petitions come mostly from women, praying to be divorced from their husbands ; generally on the ground of infidelity to the marriage vow. Many persons have supposed that climate is the cause ; giving way to the common opinion, that warm climates favor the rage of lawless passion. Not so. It is true that warm climates are inclining, but not immediate and necessary causes of animal or ideal passion. Warmth of temperature produces lassitude, and consequently idleness, and the old saw, from time immemorial, is, that "an idle brain is the devil's workshop ; " thus far, then, only, is a warm climate favorable to passion. In cold climates on the contrary, the pulse beats much quicker than in southern latitudes. And persons who are wealthy and self-indulged, under the same pressure of moral restraint, we undertake to say, are equally, if not more passionate in the North than in the

South. Modern science and modern statistics are overturning many hoary errors; and the world was astonished to find, that Sweden and Russia have turned out to be as frequent in sexual crime as Italy and France. As this difference, then, between the North and the South is not owing to climate, nor to religion, nor to government, for these two last are the same in both countries, how comes it that the applications for divorce are monstrously greater in the South than in the North, although there are twice the numbers in the Northern that there are in the Southern States? We believe that we may, without fear of refutation, ascribe this difference to *slavery*. The moral influence of slavery upon the marriage vow cannot but be, by unhinging all the instinctive ideas of right and wrong, disastrous. But the physical and moral laws are inseparably connected; and we shall here confine ourselves solely to the consideration of slavery as being antagonistic to the physical laws of our nature; and in consequence subversive, in respect to divorce, of the moral law, and man's true happiness.

The many guards which nature has taken against the loss of any known species, vegetable and animal, as all naturalists know, are of tremendous power. In the human species, *beauty in women* is especially designed, as the eccentric and witty Burton would have it, to cause that "a man be not too much absorbed in his books, seeing that there are other things that must need be attended to." A sense of gratitude and duty, habit, propriety, common interests, and convenience, in the *absence of religion*, may keep man and wife together well enough, without "physical beauty" and its consequence, sexual love. But when in that case a really lovely object meets the unaccustomed eye of a man of quick sensibility to the beautiful, it takes a higher degree of virtue than falls to the lot of most men, if there is not some weakening of the foundations of connubial devotion. The Southern women in the United States are admitted by foreigners, as well as claimed by our gallant countrymen, to be among the most beautiful in the world: but at the same time they are the most fragile of all beauties. They begin to fade in a few years after marriage; and maternity, in a great many cases, leaves but a wreck of what was once most lovely. From infancy our girls, who have slaves, begin to be waited upon, till locomotion becomes a most painful thing. The young women grow up with a fair skin, and from generous feeding, are apparently full in development, but there is no muscle, nothing but fat, which the first trials of the physical frame dissipate, and the whole system is collapsed. For the want of exercise in the house, and in the open air, added to the infamous and disgusting pressure of the waist and all the vital organs, the secretions are faulty; the skin, instead of being of a firm velvet feeling texture, becomes pale and sallow; then come low spirits, peevishness, ennui, disgust, and then *divorce.* Put away your slaves : nature never made provision for a slave, having decreed that work, health, and happiness should be inseparably and inexorably united. If you want to drink, go to the pump or to the spring and get it; if to bathe, prepare your own bath, or plunge into the running stream ; make your own beds, sweep your own rooms, and wash your own clothes; throw away corsets, and nature herself will form your bustles. Then you will have full chests, glossy hair, rosy complexions, smooth velvet skins, muscular, rounded limbs, graceful tournures, elasticity of person, eyes of alternate fire and most melting languor ; generous hearts, sweet tempers, good husbands, long lives of honeymoons, and—*no divorces.* When we read of the free clothing, the gymnastic exercises, the household duties of the Greeks, we are not surprised at the exquisite loveliness of the marble copies of those most perfect exemplars of Burke's line of beauty. But, when, under the Southern system of dress and no exercise, we see great profusion of clothes piled up in most rigid opposition to nature's known lines of gradual swell, and imperceptible declension, and attenuation of limb, we do not fail to remember, that the owl, of all birds, having the greatest bulk of feathers, has also the most ragged person. And "flaccid skins," and "forked radishes," "come o'er the spirit of our dream—what business had they there at such a time?"

"GIVE THE DEVIL HIS DUE."

In our first article, in allusion to Robert Wickliffe, we followed common rumor in imputing to him mercenary motives in the defence of the slave Moses. We are credibly informed that Bill, who was also hung, being the guilty culprit, Mr. Wickliffe showed a noble boldness in attempting, in opposition to great popular excitement, to save Moses, who, from accounts, was entirely innocent. Now we are always ready to admit, that the "Old Duke" has some good traits, among which we do not number the unrelenting steadiness of denunciation with which he pursues a *good-natured* fellow like ourself.

LEXINGTON, TUESDAY, JUNE 24.

THE CONSTITUTIONAL QUESTION.

We publish to-day the two numbers signed " *Madison,*" first published in the Observer and Reporter, and afterwards republished in the Frankfort Commonwealth of February 25th, 1845. The pertinacity with which the author forces these essays upon our notice, either proves that he courts the honor of a reply, or that he vainly imagines that his arguments are conclusive against the positions of the speech which he reviews. " Madison," it will be seen, though apparently courteous, (as a lawyer can never brook that sandaled feet should enter upon ground hallowed by the priestess of the green bag, " the perfection of human reason," which was and is from everlasting to everlasting, " from the time whereof the memory of man runneth not to the contrary—*that is, from the time of Richard the First* ") gently chastises our presumption in entering upon a subject of so " much delicacy" "which the wisest and ablest statesmen the nation can boast," and " Madison " even, " approach with *timidity*." Well, to tell the truth, that is the very reason why we have approached it : we enter upon the constitutional question of slavery, because it is full of hoary error and sanctified fraud. We enter the sanctuary of American Liberty, sword in hand, determined to expel, if possible, the wearers of the blood-stained ermine, who have prostituted its holy places to the sustaining and perpetuating slavery among men.

We shall, without following " Madison" through his long evolution of *trite facts* and distorted construction, restate our ideas of the power of the national government over slavery, and sustain them by such arguments as history, the Constitution, and *common sense*, may present us.

I. I contend, then, that the original thirteen states had, and now have exclusive control over slavery within their borders. II. That in all places where Congress *had*, or now has exclusive control, where slavery did not previously exist by the sovereign power of the thirteen states, there slavery does not and cannot exist. III. That in *no territory* in this wide empire is there now a slave; that the supreme court, under a writ of *habeas corpus*, is bound to liberate any person so claimed as a slave. Here then, are our three propositions, word for word, as quoted by "Madison;" upon these we will stand or fall.

The proposition in clause I, is not a matter of controversy between us and the slaveholders, whom "Madison" represents; in that we all agree. The thirteen original states were, at one time, dependent on the British crown, and on that only, having a separate and distinct organization with regard to each other. When, by the successful maintenance of the Declaration of 1776, and by the assent of the British nation, they became independent, they stood, by the laws of nations, equal sovereigns with the other nations of the globe. African slavery existed in all the states at the time of the formation of the Constitution, except a few who had abolished slavery since the declaration of American independence. No nation on earth had any right to interfere with the internal laws of these sovereigns, for Vattell says, "nations" are "free and independent of each other, in the same manner as men are naturally free and independent. From this liberty and independence it follows, that every nation is to judge of what its conscience demands." "In all cases then, where a nation has the liberty of judging what its duty requires, *another cannot oblige it to act in such or such a manner.*" "*For the attempting this would be doing an injury to the liberty of nations.*"—Vattell, Pref., p. iii: London edition, 1773. Here, then, before the formation of the Union, without controversy, no state had a right to interfere with any other state. Whether slavery be in accordance with natural law, or revealed Divine law, it matters not, the ultra-abolitionist of the North is forbid to interfere: just as the United States denying the natural and divine right of man to more than *one wife*, is forbid by the law of nations from interfering with the Turk, who claims, by the internal laws of his own Ottoman Empire, the right to *two or more wives.* When the Union was formed, the states lost none of their power over slavery, except what was yielded up ; and as none was yielded up, none was lost. For the national Union is a government of special, delegated powers, and it declares that " the powers not delegated to the United States by the Constitution, nor prohibited by it to the states, are reserved to the states respectively, or to the people.—Art. X., A. The first proposition is tenable then, beyond the power of cavil.

II. " That in all places where Congress had, or now has exclusive control, where slavery did not previously exist by the sovereign power of the thirteen states, there slavery does not and cannot exist." Remark, now, that we are arguing this question as jurists, not as statesmen. With jurists the question is, not what is expedient or best, or what will be the consequences, but *what is the law* ? Now, as a statesman, with regard to the district of Columbia, a place where Congress *has* exclusive jurisdiction, we would vote as a member of Congress to liberate the slave, and *pay the master a fair equivalent*, because the whole nation has sanctioned the error, and the whole nation should bear the loss. Such was the opinion of the British nation with regard to West India slavery ; although, no doubt, every slave in the British dominions under habeas corpus, might have been liberated by the same considerations in respect to the Constitution, which declares all men in England free. But sitting as a judge of the United States, being restricted to the bare question, what is the law, we should declare every slave in the District of Columbia *free*. If Madison had put the word "government" in the place of "legislature," in the following sentence, it would have been *true ;* as it is, it is *false :* " The rights of property and the rights of persons, included within their boundaries, are under the *absolute dominion* of one national legislature." We can scarcely restrain expressions of infinite contempt for such a declaration. In the simplicity of our heart, we had supposed that this was a " Constitutional " government, and that the Legislature was not " ABSOLUTE." " The rights of persons" then living, in places of the "exclusive control " of Congress, are to be ascertained, not by the will of an " absolute Legislature," but by the *Constitution ;* to that then let us look. Now, the preamble of that instrument has it, that the government was formed to " establish justice, and to secure the blessings of liberty to ourselves and our posterity." By this clause, then, without a more latitudinarian construction than that which in England and in Massachusetts liberated the African, there cannot be a slave in the district of Columbia. Paley declares that "Natural rights, are a man's right to his life, limbs, and liberty; his right to the produce of his personal labor, to the use, in common with others, of air, light, water." *Paley's Works*, chap. X., p. 42. Philadelphia edition: 1831.

"Natural liberty consists properly in a power of acting as one thinks just, without any restraint or control; unless by the law of nature; being a right inherent in us by *birth*, and one of the gifts of God to man at his creation, when he endowed him with the faculty of free will." *Chitty's Blackstone*, p. 89. New York edition: 1842.

The Declaration of American independence says: " We hold these truths to be self-evident: that all men are created equal, that they are endowed by their creator with certain inalienable rights, that among these are life, liberty, and the pursuit of happiness." Now these various high authorities all agree, that it is right and " just" that no man shall be enslaved without crime —and of course, if the preamble of the United States' Constitution be enforced, slavery in the district falls. But it seems that our fathers did not intend to rest our liberties on such vague foundations : they bring the slaveholder up to the bar of the LETTER as well as the *spirit* of the instrument. " *No person* shall be deprived of life, liberty, or property, without due process of law."—Art. V, A. Here is the omnipotent law of the District, from which there is no appeal. If James K. Polk holds us in slavery in the district, we ask for a writ of habeas corpus, which brings us before Judge Taney—we plead that we are a person guilty of no crime, not that we are *white* or *black* or of Yankee or Virginia descent. Mr. Polk. " The defendant is a slave by the laws of Maryland and Virginia." Mr. Taney. " They became extinct by the deed of cession—this instrumentality is the supreme law of the land here, it asks you only what crime this man has done." Mr. Polk. " None." Mr. Taney. " The defendant is free." Mr. Polk. " The deed of cession guarantied slavery by the assent of the legal organs of the Union—good faith requires that you restore me my slave." Mr. Taney. " An act done by a single individual, or by the combined authority of the whole Union, contrary to the Constitution is *void ;* let the defendent go." Mr. Polk. " Well, I acknowledge the justice of your decision, but this

defendant does not come under the law : he is a "*thing*" not a
"*person*," he is my "*slave*," and that you know makes one a
thing—by the slave code, everywhere." Mr. Taney, looking
intently at the defendant, and then turning over to Art. V., A. sec.
II. and III. " He has every semblance of a man, but perhaps
is only a beast, yet here I find the only *slaves* known to
this Constitution, called "*persons*." The *thing* then being a
" person," no matter whether white, red, or black, " for all of
those colors in the South are *slaves*, and as Upham has it, and
common sense agrees, " words are not to be used without meaning"—the language can mean nothing else—and " we are not
to use the same word in the same discourse with different mean-
ings"—[*Up. Phi., p.* 194, *Portland edition*, 1828] the " slave,"
the " thing," the "*person*," must go "*free*." If this be not
good law and right reason, we are a slave, and " Madison" may
come in any place of exclusive national jurisdiction, and take
possession of us and ours, and there is no power in the American
Constitution, or the Union of these states to save us ! The
word "HAD" in this second clause, we admit had reference to
the new states, formed out of what was *once* territory, *never
having been a part of the land over which the original thirteen had extended slavery.* Up to the time, then, when the
independence of those states was acknowledged, by the formal
act of admission into the Union, *whilst* the power of the
national government was over them as *territories*, notwithstanding the treaties of cession from Spain and France, *every
slave therein* was FREE. That these "*persons*" having been
at one definite period free, could not be barred the right of
habeas corpus, and *restoration to liberty*, on the ground that
the territory had become a " sovereign state," the case lately
decided by Judge McLean fully sustains. A slave was carried
by his master to Illinois ; but the master finding that this act
made him free removed to Missouri ; subsequently the slave
escaped to Illinois ; a certain citizen assisted the slave to elude
the pursuit of the master, who had come upon him in Illinois.
The master brought an action against the citizen of Illinois.
Judge McLean decided that the slave was free, by the act of the
master carrying the slave to Illinois—once free, always free—
and that an action for damages could not be sustained. We
leave it to jurists to say if we have not sustained our second
proposition. Yet, as we said at the Tremont Temple, in Boston,

we are willing for one, as a mere citizen, that the new states having become "sovereign," by admission into the Union, should be left to the entire and undisturbed responsibility of holding slaves in their *own limits*.   Whether these "persons" held as slaves will be returned into slavery again under the Constitutional requisition, after having escaped from the place of municipal jurisdiction, is a question which we imagine, as it cannot endanger the peace or safety of those states, will be decided after the same manner as Judge McLean's late judgment.   So much with regard to the present slave States—as to Texas, we, in common with a great portion of the American people, give them warning in time, that if she comes in as a territory, her slaves are FREE, if she comes in as a sovereign, it is contrary to the United States' Constitution—there is no law in the Union requiring her slaves escaping from "service" to be returned into bondage—*and we will put her out whenever we have the power.*

Proposition III. is but another specification of proposition II. and is maintained by the same reasoning, which need not be repeated, for it is hardly worth while to contend among men capable of appreciating a legal argument, that if Congress cannot make slaves in the District by *immediate legislation*, she cannot make them *indirectly*, by allowing her agent a territorial legislature, or a convention of her subjects, in remote places, to make them.   As has been justly and forcibly said, Congress can no more make a *slave* than she can a *king*.   It will be perceived by the reader that the whole of "Madison's" second number, is based upon a misconception of our argument: we have never, anywhere, contended that the 5th article of A. had a force penetrating beyond the *exclusive jurisdiction* of the Union to the rescue of citizens or persons of the states *legally* held in durance; and if the slaves were free in the states formed by the addition of foreign territory, it was because of the action of the Constitution, before the *sovereignty* of the states by admission into the Union was acknowledged.   And *once a freeman, always a freeman*, is an admitted principle of law; and in accordance with natural justice and the spirit of the age.   I will only strengthen my position by one quotation from Alexander Hamilton, and leave the matter to the serious consideration of those clothed with the judicial power of this republic.   "For why declare that things shall not be done, which there is no power to do ? The truth is, after all the declamation we have heard, that the Constitution is itself, in every rational sense, and to every useful purpose, A BILL OF RIGHTS."—*Fed., p.* 402–3. Such was the language of Hamilton before the 5th Art. of A. was made ; but our fathers, to put the thing beyond the power of cavil, afterwards spread it out in broad and eternal characters. Cursed be the sacrilegious hand that would destroy or pervert this the sole palladium of the liberty of the whole American people and the friendless wanderers of the world.

Whilst we are upon this subject, we will give our opinion upon the remaining bearings of the Constitution upon slavery, which are not brought by "Madison" into the field of discussion. There are only three clauses bearing upon slavery: the one allowing, after 1808, the prohibition of the slave trade: the second touching slave representation ; and the third concerning the return of fugitive slaves. Now, we have heard a great deal of silly talk about "compromise" as if slavery was sacred ; whilst the truth is, there are but two *inexorable* "*compromises*" or binding *agreements* in the whole Constitution.

The one is, that each state shall *for ever* have equal representation in the senate: the other is, that the Constitution shall not be changed, except in the manner prescribed in the instrument itself. Every clause in that Constitution was a subject of "compromise," in one sense, and one sense *only*. That is, each member of the convention did not get all he wanted ; and had to submit to some things that he did not want. Such was the subject of Franklin's speech in convention. But with the two exceptions abovenamed, every clause in the Constitution stands upon equal ground, subject to the judgment and deliberate will of subsequent generations. So far from slavery being intended to be held *more sacred* than any other *rights*, we have by us *voluminous testimony, of the most prominent men of the North and South, looking forward to the day of universal emancipation*. When as the word slave was not mentioned in that immortal instrument, so in this wide-spread nation there should not be a single soul who could not claim the Declaration of American Independence as his—and the American Union as the palladium of freedom and equal rights. Our fathers saw that liberty and slavery could not co-exist—they *believed* and *hoped* that slavery would perish—they were mistaken. Slavery now triumphs over even those liberties which we inherited under the British yoke; taxation and representation are yet *unequal*, and the liberty of speech and the press, habeas corpus, and trial by jury *are lost*. The blood of '76 was shed in vain; the Americans are the slaves of slavery.

"Turning Loose."

"What," says the slaveholder, "shall the blacks be turned loose among us?" Permit me to ask, in the most childlike simplicity, if they are not loose already? Men talk as if all the slaves were chained to a block, and some mad hand was about to sever the links, and let them go, like wild bears to ravage the land! Now, all this bugaboo is founded upon the false idea that the aggregate power of the community is less than that of an individual slaveholder, which is absurd. By liberation we do not withdraw the force of *legal restraint, but enlarge it;* because we bring a high moral power to sustain the civil arm in the execution of justice. The whole population of Kentucky, we take to be now, 840,000: blacks, 180,000; for since the last census of '40, the whites must have increased, whilst the blacks, perhaps, have remained about stationary, owing to the Southern trade: that is 660,000 whites, to 180,000 blacks; an excess of whites over blacks, which would insure the whites absolute power of control, for ever, over the blacks, in case of liberation: more especially, as statistics of the North and South show that, upon the same basis, the black increases faster in slavery than in a state of freedom, *among whites, when all the stimulants of acquiring position in society, and rising to eminence, are withdrawn.* To say then, that turning them loose, would endanger the peace of society, is absolutely contrary to all experience, as proven in the West Indies, and in the Northern states; and contrary to every law of the human mind; for it involves the gross absurdity, that a man would revenge a favor, or love his enemies, not as well as, but better than his friends! We are not for turning any man *loose, black* or *white;* but in case of liberation, we repeat, we would not only have the same civil power over the blacks, which we now have, but the *superadded power* of the combined moral power of the master and the slave ! The master strengthened in his position by a sense of being based upon justice, and the freedman constrained to quiet subjection to the laws, by every grateful affection of the heart. But if we do not turn them "*loose*," they will go on increasing, till they get in a majority ; when, at last, they will turn themselves loose, for *every law of nature*, in time, vindicates itself. Man never has, and never will hold his fellow man in perpetual slavery. South Carolina, has gone on with the "let alone" system, and will it "right itself" policy, till she is on the very eve of utter ruin. A single citizen, from the state of Massachusetts, where Bunker Hill lifts its eternal granite brow to the eyes of equal freeman, throws the whole state into a consternation, greater than if an hundred thousand mail-clad men, with fire and sword, had landed on the shores of a *just* people. In spite of all the silly vaporing of this unhappy state, we are full of pity when we look upon such a "sorry sight." They are now set about giving the slaves "moral and religious culture," most tame and impotent conclusion: the only remedy is to slay them—remove them—or make them *free*. Kentuckians, you know the right, you feel the wrong : in South Carolina you see *the end*.

A SMALL BUSINESS.

G. D. and Robert Wickliffe seem to be contending which is the most ready to yield up the right of petition, one of the *necessary* rights of a *free* people, and which is solemnly guarantied to us by the Constitution, won by the blood of revolutionary sires. It is enough to make the heart sick to see the once proud bird of Jove, the American Eagle, cowering in the very dust, beneath the cold, dark, and slimy folds of slavery ; this serpent, which now rears its defiant head over eighteen millions of men ! Mr. D. is said to be a proud and honorable man—if so, the gods have punished us awfully for our crimes—when, whatever is noble, generous, and brave, must prostitute itself to base uses, utterly abhorrent to all that is demanded by the eternal laws of God and nature.

E. Needham.

The pro-slavery clique of Louisville, seems wonderfully in-dignant at the remarks of Mr. E. Needham, in the Cincinnati Liberty Convention. They seem more sensitive to words than to acts. The only question to be asked in this case, is, did Needham tell the TRUTH? If the crimes of which he spoke be true, every voter in the state of Kentucky is responsible for their perpetration. It is time that this solemn farce should cease. The truth is, no language can *misrepresent slavery.* "*Mob*" Needham, indeed! that is a *double* game. The slaveholders and their *sycophants*, will find that the *free white laborers of this land, composing four-fifths of the population, at the lowest estimates, are not slaves.* Slavery is doomed—it must die!—*the first act of violence in its cause, will hasten its fate!*

The Fourth of July.

Some of the Southern people seem to wonder that this once glorious day has begun to be neglected by our people—in many places "not celebrated at all." Why should it be otherwise; are we not, in the face of men, a living lie?—shall we be so silly, as yearly to proclaim our own abandonment? We cannot lift up our hearts to God, in holy aspirations of gratitude and ex-pectancy, because we have been *partial* in the appropriation of his mercies. We cannot come together, and exchange joyous congratulations, because selfishness is solitary in its manifesta-tions. The Fourth of July, 1776, saw us proclaiming liberty to all mankind—the Fourth of July, 1845, will look down upon the American people, as the *sole propagandists of slavery among men.* Henceforth, till the rights of men be vindicated, let the fife be mute—the drum be muffled—the American eagle wear mourning—let Christians pray that our holy religion be restored to its life-giving purity—our statesmen re-baptize them-selves in the exalted spirit of the patriotism of Washington, Adams, and Jefferson—let the people mourn their apostacy— let the Fourth of July be a day of fasting and prayer, that the nation be lustrated of its great and self-destroying sin.

WE PUBLISH below the note of Mr. R. S. we repeat that we were taunted with the remark that R. S. lost his nomination for the legislature, (we had no reference to the fact of his being or not being upon " the convention") because he took the *True American.* His letter proves that he deserves his fate. We return Mr. S. his one dollar and twenty-five cents : the cause of human rights asks nothing but the free gift of true hearts. Our readers will, in reading this singular note, remember the story of the wolf, the lamb, and the running stream—or the more marked history of a certain adjunct reformer of ancient times, who dipt his hand into the same dish with his Lord in prosperous times—but who, in the day of trial, *swore* that *he knew him not.* Mr. S. is certainly in a "*wrong position.*" We told him in our prospectus, that we were no beggars, and therefore intended to speak the " *truth ;*" that those who had no sympathy with that, must go *elsewhere.* If Mr. S. had unobtrusively withdrawn his name, like some five other subscribers, he would have spared us the mortification of saying that he imputes to us doctrines which *he knows* we do not advocate.

LEXINGTON, TUESDAY, JULY 1.

HEALY AND HART.

There are now in our city two artists, who would do honor to any country, and to any age. Healy, the painter, is in the meridian of his fame, patronized by the first monarch of Europe, in the very inner temple of the fine arts : Hart, the sculptor, a scholar of nature, in the wild woods of the great West, following the unerring instinct of Genius, has proved himself, in our humble judgment, equal to his more favored rival. We do not hesitate in saying, that Mr. Healy has taken far the best portrait bust of CLAY, that we have yet seen : indeed, it seems to us, perfect of its kind. Mr. Clay is represented in a plain black dress coat, buff colored vest, dark blue stock, plain shirt bosom, with a full face, and sitting in an arm-chair : the back ground, like as in the picture of Jackson, of simple dusk color. Mr. Healy has not attempted an ambitious picture, as did Neagle ;

but he has succeeded better in his design. He represents Mr. Clay in a calm, easy, conversational face, and has succeeded to the life; he has Mr. Clay's peculiarly penetrating eye, his color, and above all, his mouth, in that suspended state of the passions, when the great original, having spoken, awaits a reply, or is in the act of taking a pinch of snuff! We conceive Mr. Healy to be very happy in the eye, giving it the luminous transparency of the real convex humors of the natural eye: the shaded side of the full face shines through inimitably. It has been, again and again, remarked by connoisseurs, that there have been more caricatures made of Mr. Clay than of any man living. This is true; and it is because of the great mobility of Mr. Clay's features; especially, are the muscles of the mouth, and chin, and cheek, very variant under different emotions. The consequence is, that none but an artist of the first rank can take him at all. One who sets about mapping his face, is sure to make a caricature; because the face cannot preserve life-like harmony, if a part of the features express one emotion, and the others another emotion. And, just here, is the reason, why we contend that no ideal picture has ever equalled one taken from *nature:* no man's genius is equal to the combination of beauties, taken from various models, into one harmonious whole. You may produce a seemingly faultless figure; but at last, the *soul, which reaches the soul, is wanting.* Mr. Neagle attempted to give Mr. Clay, in a "heroic" mood, in an animated speaking mould: he did not, exactly, succeed; the mouth is faulty: the upper lip looks as if the foreteeth were too long, and the lip stretched over them; producing both an ungraceful, as well as an unintellectual expression. Now, Mr. Hart, in his bust, has succeeded in effecting that, in which Mr. Neagle failed to some extent. He has made a *heroic bust* of Clay, and yet a *good likeness,* which is the very essence of genius. He has attempted Mr. Clay, in a tumultuous mood of excited feelings; the head is thrown up, aside, and slightly back, the eye full, the nostril expanded, the mouth widened and compressed, the brow elated, the cheek and chin in a tumultuous play—to be compared to nothing better than Hell-gate, in the Sound near New York, when wave seems to meet wave, and upper and under currents come together, in most inimitable confusion. If we were Mr. Clay, with his bold, impetuous, defiant eloquence, we should deem ourselves happy in going down to posterity in Hart's marble; for fully are we convinced, that no one has, or ever will again succeed in taking him, at once heroic as a statue of Jupiter, and as true to life as is possible in the nature of things. The Kentucky Monumental Society, instead of building some huge, uncouth, Indian mound of stone, should send HART to Europe, to take CLAY's full statue in marble, which would be favoring the fine arts of the world, adding to our own reputation, and rewarding a true son of genius.

EDGAR NEEDHAM.

We publish to-day the letter of this true man tó his persecutors. He talks like one who had a soul in him to be saved, and after a manner that must win the admiration of all good men. Mr. Needham might well say to the newspaper press of Louisville, as the Satyr of the fable said to the man, "Get you gone, for you blow hot and cold with the same breath."

What are the circumstances? Mr. Needham is a democrat, and believes in the political equality of man, and seeing that slavery not only deprived the blacks of Kentucky of this; but that the system subjected the great mass of his fellow citizens to a *necessary political* and *social inequality*, he sets about, like an honest and sensible man, to reduce his faith to practice.

All over the Union, yes, in our own state, the democrats have been abused for *professing* liberty and republicanism, but practising servitude and despotism; and yet, when a strong-hearted man undertakes to put himself in the true position which an enlightened conscience and this Pharasaical press have taught him; these same men come down upon him with all the terrors of unmeasured denunciation. Mr. Needham, seeing that the statesmen and moralists of the state are callous and indifferent to all the accumulated curses and crimes of slavery, goes up to a convention of his fellow-citizens, of the same great republic, to devise the ways and means to free his country from her greatest evil; and for this, too, he is bitterly denounced; although no one is so shameless as to deny his legitimate right so to act. But last year there was called a convention in "*all the slave states,*" not only *avowedly treasonable,* in some places, but from the very face of the proposition itself, revolutionary and antipatriotic; and men went up to it from "Old Kentucky," too:

yet these same fastidious gentlemen were as mute as any sucking doves!

Mr. Needham says that the Kentuckians are as humane as any set of slaveholders in the world (*and in this he no doubt told nothing but the simple truth*), but the *system* of *slavery* is utterly *wrong ;* because even here, within his own knowledge, two horrid cases of barbarity, which he instances as having occurred in his own city, have taken place; and urges this as a cogent reason why the institution should be overturned.   Will any man of common sense or common honesty deny the blameless legitimacy of such a course?   Yet some of the sycophants of power pour forth the most scathing abuse, as if he were the author of the crimes alleged.   Let justice be done, though the heavens fall.   We say that Mr. Needham not only showed himself a man of soul, but a moralist, *with a remnant of common sense ;* which seems to have departed utterly out of the heads of some professing to be the followers of God.   They have found out some poor foreigner, untouched with the true genius of republicanism, who did this deed.   Pray, Messieurs, who armed this man with the power to do it with impunity?   *Every voter in the state of Kentucky, these Pharasaical journalists among the rest !*   Who put it in the power of any foreigner, or home villain, in the land, to do the same deed, or worse, over again, whenever it suits them?   These same journalists !   Who legalize a domestic slave trade, which is worse than burying a dead child without a shroud?   These same journalists !   Who enable the heartless to separate husband and wife, father and child, sister and brother, lover and lover, with impunity, which is worse than burying a child without a shroud?   These same journalists !   Who take the care of the intellectual and moral discipline of the child, generally to the utter neglect of both, out of the control of parents, a thing worse than burying a babe without a shroud?   These same journalists !   Who allow the master to deny the slave the selection of his own physician, and enable some horrid quack to pour down unmeasured quantities of calomel into the throats of unresisting victims?   These same journalists !

Who take the Bible, if it be the only means of the salvation of the souls of men, from the hands of a great portion of the blacks—destroying not the body, but the soul—a thing worse than burying a child without a shroud?   These same journalists! Who encourage habitual prostitution of both sexes by denying to slaves legal marriage—a thing worse than burying a child without a shroud? These same journalists! Who by the unlimited control of the master over the slave, by the thousand enforcements short of legal criminality, has the virtue of every female in his power, in the eye of common sense and of God—has given the lustful the power of rape upon every female slave—a thing worse than burying a child without a shroud? These same journalists! Who disarms the black, and gives the master the power, by excluding negro testimony, of life and death over his fellow man—a thing worse than burying a child without a shroud? These same journalists! Who has given the lie to the immortal declaration of independence, that all men are "born free and equal, and entitled to life, liberty, and the pursuit of happiness"—a thing infinitely worse than burying a child without a shroud? These same journalists! What say you, gentlemen; guilty, or not? Are you not ashamed of yourselves, then, to come up in full pack, with thundering tones, and blood-thirsty tongues, after one poor little mechanic and democrat, who mustered up soul enough to say, this slave system is a horrid affair, when it puts it in the power of *one villain*, in the midst of Kentuckians, to bury a miserable, unclad child without shroud or coffin? Do you understand us? We say that Needham spoke the truth, and spoke it like a man, and, if *Kentuckians are men, he shall be upheld, triumphantly, honorably upheld!* If he falls, truth falls with him! If he is dishonored, then are Washington, and Adams, and Franklin, and Jefferson, and Madison, and Sherman, and Morris, and a host of names, which the world deemed illustrious, damned for ever! If he is wrong, the Declaration of '76 cannot be right! If he is crushed, the pillars of the Constitution go down with him! If he has sinned, then is Christianity a miserable fable! If he dies, justice dies with him! If he is lost, let him perish, with the bitter yet neutralizing reflection, that he leaves a home, unworthy of his soul's expansive aspirations—that he quits a world not worth living for! It cannot be! We regard these as but the spasmodic grimaces of the wounded monster. *Slavery cannot be defended: it must be abandoned; it is doomed!* IT MUST DIE!

Six hundred thousand Free White Laborers of Kentucky—Men, Women, and Children.

If slavery deprives us of political and social equality; if it impoverishes us by the ruinous competition of unpaid wages; if it fails to educate our children, and places large farms between us, so that we can't get our own schools; if it degrades labor, so that slaveholders rank us below slaves—some of whom play idlers in the houses of the rich—if, above all, after suffering all these curses, we and ours are to be involved in the common ruin, which as sure as fate awaits the catastrophe which follows the violation of the laws of God and nature—shall we any longer support it, by our countenance, or our votes? No! Let us say, with one loud and unanimous voice, *slavery shall die!* and the Heavens and the earth shall respond, *amen!*

Liberty?—or Slavery?

The Governor of South Carolina, in his correspondence with the venerable Thomas Clarkson, the pioneer of British emancipation, takes McDuffie's ground, that slavery is the corner-stone of liberty! How? by excluding "*poor white folks*" from power in the government! This head of the "*democracy*," also *denies and ridicules the declaration of American independence!* Democrats, all over the Union, do you hear? Whigs, North and South, do you hear? Americans, awake! the time has come; take your ground. Liberty? or Slavery? "*Under which king, Bezonian? speak or die!*"

Non-resistance.—Our first number.—The Northern Press.

Whilst we have the greatest respect for non-resistants, we beg leave to think and act for ourselves. If Washington and his compatriots had relied upon "*moral power*" only, the paw of the huge lion of Britannia would be now quietly resting upon the necks of the American people. If non-resistance be right, then is self-defence in individuals and societies *wrong;* and the walls of every penitentiary in the Union ought to be knocked down, and the inmates turned loose to ravage the land with impunity. We say, that when *society fails to protect us,* we are authorized by the laws of God and nature to defend ourselves; based upon *the right,* "the pistol and Bowie knife" are to us as sacred as the gown and the pulpit; and the Omnipotent God of battles is our hope and trust for victorious vindication. "Moral power" is much; with great, good, true-souled men, it is stronger than the bayonet! but with the cowardly and the debased it is an "unknown God." Experience teaches us, common sense teaches us, virtue teaches us, justice teaches us, the right teaches us, instinct teaches us, *religion* teaches us, that it loses none of its force by being backed with "cold steel and the flashing blade," "the pistol and the Bowie knife." Without these, "moral power" has been and will be again, ridden on a rail; it will be graced with a plumigerous coat of less enviable colors than that of Joseph of old, and not so easily torn off! Moral power stands by and sees men slain in Vicksburg; Catholic churches plundered in Massachusetts; good citizens murdered in the defence of the laws in Philadelphia; public meetings broken up in New York; the envoys of Massachusetts mobbed in the South; United States citizens imprisoned in Charleston and New Orleans; men hung to the limbs of trees in the Southern states for exercising the "liberty of speech;" Lovejoy murdered in Illinois; Joe Smith assassinated in the sanctuary of the law. She stood by in Paris, during the French revolution, and saw the peasant and the prince, male and female, "the young, the beautiful, the brave," brought to the block. She looked coldly on when Christ himself was crucified in Judea! We say, then, she is powerless of herself. Meet mobs with "moral power!" not so thought the "little corporal" of Corsica; they are to be met (when will the American people learn it?) with "round and grape—to be answered by Shrapnel and Congreve; to be discussed in hollow squares, and refuted by battalions four deep." Yes, they must be met with "cold steel" and ball, the "pistol, and Bowie knife," and subterranean batteries, for they will never come to their senses while the ground is firm beneath their feet! Let us hear no more of this sickly cant, and mawkish sensibility. People at home and abroad greatly underrate *Kentuckians* if they suppose them capable of lawless outbreaks; the *few assassins*, who infest the best of communities, we thoroughly understand; and we must be allowed to deal with *them* as they deserve, *and after our own manner.*[*]

FOSTER'S POWER PRESS.

We invite our *pro-slavery* friends—for we are the enemies of *slavery*, not of *slaveholders*—to come and see this beautiful piece of mechanism, the product of *free labor*. If any man is proud of mental achievement let him look on this and reflect that slavery deprives us of such as these. If any one is covetous of wealth, let him see this, and reflect that slavery has sent millions of our money to *free states, to purchase machinery*, that ought to have been made at home. If any body is fond of the "*toiling millions*," let him show his faith by his works, and see to it that our own money shall be spent among our own "people." Let those men who have spent the people's school fund in building locks, and dams, and turnpike roads, over which there is nothing to be carried, remember that there are thousands of Fosters in Kentucky, who for the want of proper education and encouragement, are lost to the world. First *make* your articles of commerce, and then the means of *conveyance*. Those who take pride in large cities, ask yourselves why we have been compelled to send sixteen hundred dollars from Lexington, the older, to Cincinnati, the younger city, for a press and printing materials. Those farmers who want home markets and high prices, can know why their beef and pork and other things, have to be carried to distant and uncertain markets. Where the manufacturing mouths are, there is the farmer's market also.

If pious parents are grieved that their sons or daughters are spendthrifts and profligates, how can they blame any one but themselves. Make *labor free* and you make it *honorable*. How many men are starving at the desk, at the bar, at the counter, who, like Foster, might have been useful to themselves, and an honor to their country, if slavery had not made manual labor "*unfashionable*."

---

[*] I believe now, as ever, that had I not fallen sick, I never would have been mobbed. C. 1848.

If any man deems us a fanatic, let him look upon this press, the result of *free labor :* the source of light, liberty, civilization, and religion, and then ask his own secret emotions, if he should be regarded as an enemy to his country, who would wish that Lexington, too, might make these.

Above all, if there is any father of ten sons, so unfortunate as to have *one* poor, miserable, sun-burnt, foxy-headed negro, let him come and see our press, and go with us, and make Kentucky *free.*

LEXINGTON, TUESDAY, JULY 8.

THE RIGHT OF SEARCH—THE SLAVE TRADE.

In saying that the American people have become the sole propagandists of slavery among men, we wish, if possible, to arouse the public to the fact, in order, if we are not dead to our peculiar glory of being the " defenders of liberty," that we may retrace our steps, before it is for ever too late. We do not propose, in this article, to notice the supremacy which the slave power has acquired since the formation of the Constitution, contrary to the expectations and wishes of its illustrious founders, in the home administration—how it has monopolized all the offices of honor and profit—in the civil administration—in the army, and in the navy ; this would require more space than a newspaper article would allow. We shall therefore confine ourselves, mainly now, to our foreign policy. Up to the year 1845, says the Foreign Quarterly Review, April No., 1845, the right of belligerents to search neutral vessels " was not questioned." Lord Stowell sums up ·the whole international law upon the subject, by these propositions :

I. " That the right of visiting and searching merchant ships upon the high seas, and not merely their papers, but their cargoes, whatever be the ship, its cargo, or its destiny, is an incontestible right of the lawfully commissioned cruisers of every belligerent nation.

II. " That the sovereign of the neutral country cannot, *consistently with the law of nations, oppose this right of search.*

III. " That the penalty of opposing this right of search, is the confiscation of property so withheld from visitation." The Quarterly goes on to say, that, this doctrine is sustained by Bynkershoek, Vattel, Voet, Zuarias, Soccaenius, and Abreu, and is also set forth in " Il consolato del Mare." Bynkershoek says, " Non ex fallaci forte aplustri, sed ex ipsis instrumentis in navi repertis constare oportet navem amicam esse. Si id constet dimittam : si hostilem esse constiteret occupabo. Quod si liceat, ut omni jure licet et perpetuo observatur, licebit quoque instrumenta quæ ad merces pertinet excutere et inde discere si quæ hostium bona in navi lateant."*

Vattel admits (Que. Pub. Jur : Vattel, Droit des Gens, lib. II., ch. 7, p. 114), that without searching neutral ships at sea, the commerce of contraband goods cannot be prevented. He says also : " Si l'on trouve sur un vaisseau neutre des effets appartenants, aux ennemis, on s'en saisit par le droit de la guerre."†

Valin, a French lawyer of European reputation in his " Traité des Prises," justifies the French ordinances, by which both ships and cargo are subject to confiscation, if the smallest part of the lading belonged to the enemy, for, he observes :—Parceque de manière ou d'autre c'est favoriser le commerce de l'ennemi et faciliter le transport de ses denrées et marchandises ; ce qui ne peut s'accorder avec les traités, d'alliance ou de neutralité."‡ Monsieur Hubner, he adds : " entrepend de prouver fort sérieusment que le pavillon neutre couvre toute la cargaison quoiqu'elle appartient à l'ennemi. Mais cet auteur est absolument décidé pour les neutres, et semble n'avoir écrit que pour plaider leur cause. Il pose d'abord ses principes qu' il donne pour constants, puis il en tire les conséquences qui lui convient. Cette méthode est fort commode."§

---

* " Not from the fallacious chance of the Flag, but from the papers found in the ship, it ought to appear that the ship is a friend (a neutral). If this appears, I dismiss it, if it turns out an enemy, I occupy it. If which act is allowed, as it is allowed and always observed, there also follows the right of searching the articles of trade, and thus learn if any of the goods of the enemy (articles of contraband) should lie concealed in the ship."

† " If one finds upon a neutral vessel goods belonging to the enemy, they are seized by the right of war."

‡ " Because it is to some extent favoring the commerce of the enemy and facilitating the transportation of his goods and merchandise ; which is not in accordance with treaties of alliance or neutrality."

§ " Undertakes to prove very seriously, that the neutral flag covers all the cargo, although it belongs to the enemy. But that author is absolutely on the

The learned reviewer then goes on to prove incontestibly that the French courts sustained, under the old régime, most fully the propositions laid down by Lord Stowell; and concludes his argument by a quotation from the Spanish of Abreu, upon the subject of blockade and the rights of neutrals, which we omit. Now, it is plain that "the right of search or visit" was the admitted law of nations up to the time of the declaration of war against England, in 1812. It was not the right of search against which the American people battled. Let us go back a little. In May, 1806, England declared the coast of France and her allies blockaded from Brest to the mouth of the Elbe. The error here was, declaring blockade *without sufficient power of enforcement*. We, as neutrals, were carrying on a profitable trade with the continent, and England, through envy or an arrogant supremacy, determined to break it up. Bonaparte immediately issued his celebrated Berlin decree, declaring the British Isles in blockade; then followed, in 1807, the orders in council of Great Britain, declaring all France in blockade, and requiring all ships to touch at British ports and pay duties before they would be allowed to enter French ports. Napoleon retorts from Milan that the British Isles are in blockade, and that all neutrals trading with them, or allowing her *imposts*, are *"denationalized"* and confiscate : following this up with his tremendous continental system that all British goods even on land are *"contraband."* The United States, thus between two fires was literally crushed. She first tried the embargo—then protestations and diplomacy—and at last appealed to arms. "Millions for defence—not a cent for tribute," was the war-cry : "Free trade and sailors' rights." Not a word denying the right of "visit" was uttered in the whole lengthy correspondence and state papers between the United States, and France, and England, until the usurpations of England drove us and the Emperor to take ground, at last, that the *flag* covered the *goods* —even to the other extreme, that neutral goods under the enemy's flag were confiscate! Amer. State papers, volume 8, 1810–'12. In 1813, after war was declared against England, Mr. Clay, on the New Army Bill, said in the House of Repre-

---

side of neutrals, and seems to have written for no other purpose than to plead their cause. He first lays down his principles, which he takes for granted, then he draws from them whatever deductions suit him. That method is very convenient."

sentatives, " *As to myself, I have no hesitation in saying, that
I have always considered the impressment of American seamen as much the most serious aggression.*" This was said
by the leader of the war party, and *after* the odious *orders in
council* were rescinded. England denied the right of denatu-
ralization—we defended it. England allowed aliens to enlist
in her men-of-war—we, none but citizens. England, after
"two years' enlistment," extended to aliens the protection of her
flag—we did not. England *impressed seamen*—we did not.
England returned deserters from our ships-of-war, as a matter
of grace, because more deserted from her than from us—we refused, on the ground of *criminality*, to return deserters from
British ships, for, by the laws of nations, we are not bound
to return fugitives from justice, except by *treaty*. England refused to return neutrals from our merchantmen—we only
claimed the right to protect our own *citizens*. Now in all these
points of controversy, the right of search does not once come
up. It was because England seized upon naturalized American citizens, under pretence that they were British subjects,
that we fought. It was because England seized on and impressed *native born* Americans, that we took up arms, and proclaimed, "free trade and sailors' rights." It was only when they
violated, under *pretence* of search, the most sacred rights of
nations and individuals, and when it was proposed to give our
citizens *certificates* as a mark of distinction from British men,
that Mr. Clay said, "The colors that float from the mast-head
should be the credentials of our seamen." The battle was
fought—the war ended—peace made—England ceased to *impress*—and we ceased to complain! the law of nations—the
"right of search" remaining just where it was before. Subsequently the slave trade is made between the principal powers of
Europe, including the United States, piracy. Great Britain,
with a consistent philanthropy, moved by the horrors of this
"infernal traffic," establishes a navy at the cost of millions of
money to suppress it : she liberates, at great expense and much
self-sacrifice, her own slaves in her own colonies, and abolishes
slavery as far as it lies in her power, throughout her vast domain.
But the people of Washington, forgetting the faith of our forefathers, array themselves under the slave banner—concentrate
their power at home, in the trade which they denounce abroad.
Maryland, Virginia, Kentucky, New Jersey, and Delaware, and

Tennessee, and Missouri, monopolize the trade which was world-wide when carried on from Congo, Abyssinia, and Guinea, till the whole cotton and rice and sugar country is filled with American slaves. What next? Is she still of the opinion of our ancestors, that it is an " accursed traffic," which, after 1808, was to be abolished? Does she still regard slavery as an *evil*, but a *necessary evil*, inflicted on us by British tyranny? No, slavery has suddenly come to be the "corner-stone of republicanism— the basis of liberty." A systematic attack is made upon the free labor of the country, all the measures of national policy are turned to prostrate the free spirits of the republic, and sustain the slave power. But the North is rapidly growing upon the South—nature's ever victorious laws triumphing over governmental tyranny—something must be done! Well, Louisiana and Florida, foreign territory is added: " the area of freeedom," in opposition to the express language and spirit of the national Union is spread over four new states: *the free, of course being taxed to pay for their own enslavement!* Twenty-five years pass on, and once more free labor comes up in the race and threatens supremacy. The cry goes out, "*we must have more new slaves states to counterbalance the power of the free North.*" The eyes of the slave power are fixed upon Texas, the legal and sacredly admitted possession of a friendly republic. We offer them again and again through agents of the slave party, unknown to the great American public, millions of money. Mexico, seeing no alternative but the integrity of her whole empire, or ultimate subjection by this "tumultuary people," absolutely refuses to sell out. Persons high in the confidence of the President of the U. S., emigrate to Texas—she is peopled by American citizens. Liberty is proclaimed by Mexico to *all* her inhabitants. Forthwith the standard of rebellion is raised; from all parts of the Union organized corps of armed men, with colors flying and music playing, hurry to the rescue; in disgraceful contrast to the Canadian revolt, troops are sent by Andrew Jackson, Houston's godfather, " into " the borders of a power at peace with us, not to prevent war, but with our own U. S. soldiers to achieve conquest. The banner inscribed with "God and Liberty " sinks into the dust, and the black piratical flag of " perpetual slavery " waves triumphant over the land of the *once free!* In the meantime, England, taking the lead in the affairs of nations, after having overthrown Napoleon at

Waterloo, and established the liberties of Europe, forms the treaties of 1831 and 1833, with the first rate powers for the suppression of the slave trade, and the better vindication of the natural rights of men. In 1840, she projects a treaty with Russia, Prussia, Austria and France, with a view to lead the United States into a *cordial sympathy* in the suppression of the slave trade. In 1841, it is signed at London by the five powers. In the mean time, subsequent to the projection, and before the signing of the treaty by the French Minister, M. Thiers meditates the extension of the French power over the Levant and Asia Minor, by creating a revolt in Egypt, and placing her tool, Mohammed Ali, in power, and by conquest overthrowing the Ottoman empire. M. Guizot, the Minister at St. James, is outwitted; Russia, Prussia, Austria, and Great Britain, form in July, '40, the Quadruple Alliance, and before the French had time to concentrate their measures, Lord Palmerston had Bairout bombarded, and the Sultan established in his independence beyond the power of change. The American government, ever watchful of the British nation, as the *enemy of slavery*, was not an uninterested observer of these various events. Mr. Lewis Cass, our Minister at Paris, seeing that the time approached when, out of *many rivals*, choice was to be made for the Presidency very soon, must needs bow down to the slave power at home, and ingratiate himself into their good graces, as the *only* means of riding into power ! Taking advantage of *the soreness of the French nation, from their defeat on the Turkish question*, he ventures upon the bold and unusual plan of appealing from the throne to the people—committing an offence for which citizen Genet was justly, in times past, driven from the United States. In 1841, so soon as the treaty was formally signed by the four powers, he denounced it as a trap set by England to usurp the dominion of the seas. The opposition in the Chambers play the same chord—the deputies are furious—the Ministry is overawed, and the treaty falls. The right of search in the *slaying of men was all right, but in saving men from death and slavery was horribly wrong !*

Thus was the "right of search" lugged in and repudiated to the all possible ruin of two continents, Africa and America. England takes the alarm ; Lord Aberdeen, the Minister of Foreign Affairs, sends Lord Ashburton (the whig ministry, under Melbourne, being overthrown in England) to Washington to settle the old controversy with the United States about the *Maine boundary !* Mr. Webster, with that great ability which ever characterizes his diplomatic intercourse, whilst on the one hand, he gives the Michigan General a lasting rap over the knuckles for his officiousness, cares not to stem the deep current of slaveocratic feeling which had insidiously mixed up the sacred rights of 1812 with the "right of visit," and the slave trade. He *argues, convinces,* and forms the treaty of Washington, by which a double navy is kept on the African shore to touch hats at each other, whilst any slave trader may run up the flag of either nation, and set them both at defiance ! In the mean time Iowa becomes adolescent ; she and her young sisters are about demanding admittance to sovereignty and equal representation in the Senate ; they must be met by the slave power. Florida, although the Indians have been whipt out at the rate of forty million dollars, again paid by the *free* for their own *enslavement,* does not populate fast enough. What must be done ? Van Buren is a "Northern man with Southern principles," but unhappily he has committed himself, not *against* Texas, oh, no ! but against the unjust and *illegal acquisition* of it ! He is the favorite of his party—the *instructed choice* of the American Democracy ; the case is stringent; it admits of no delay ; Texas must come in, *right or wrong ;* Van Buren is thrown overboard ! Mr. Cass makes a most profound bow, "Gentlemen, I broke up the quintuple treaty—*right* or *wrong*, I am your man." A gallant man, this Cass !—strong in the field, and in the council !—but—but—he is too far *North*. "Texas must come in, with or without the Union." In the latter alternative he would not answer ! Mr. Clay is a great and strong man : but he loves the Constitution ; "do you love slavery better ?" "No ! but only less." For the first time in his life he falters. He is lost ! Mr. James K. Polk is for it *right* or *wrong ;* and if the worst comes to the worst, *South* of Mason and Dixon's line—*enough; he is elected !* By a joint resolution of the two houses of Congress, Texas is annexed ; the Constitution is once more trampled in the dust; the "area of freedom is extended over territory forty times as large as Massachusetts ; the balance of power is secured to the slave party ; new markets are opened for the home slave trade, and the American people have become the sole propagandists of slavery among men !

BUSTLES.

A writer in a Boston paper, undertakes to deter the lovely sex from the use of these unseemly enlargements, by the terrors of damnation, as being a trenchant attack upon the *virtue* of *men*. This would-be moralist is very wide of the mark, in his treatment of this epidemic disease. He knows nothing of "horse flesh," or of woman flesh. We tell him, if it be true that huge bustles too warmly move the blood of a man, and the fact should come to the knowledge of the fair devils, our cause is lost! Now, if we know any thing at all, it is all about these same dear creatures; upon whom, Burns swears, nature would not try her "'prentice hand." And we tell them, that if they would "put us as mad as a hare," they must preserve a due proportion between the breadth of the shoulders and the plumigerous developments. Say, for instance, as sixteen is to eighteen, never more, for if they cannot fall within these lines, we pity them, for they must be of the Flanders breed, and are surely wanting in mettle, if not in bottom. Now the truth is, we hold it to be consistent with nature, and the highest morality, for every woman to make herself as lovely as possible in our eyes; we speak now with regard to physical beauty; and at this, every woman of sense and feeling does and ought to aim. When they go into these extravagances of fashion, which are so annoying to men of true taste and exquisite susceptibility, it arises from sheer ignorance of natural laws, and a want of tact in dress.

Some poetaster of the kid glove, white cravat, and poodle genus, in some Magazine story, tells of a heroine with an *infinitely small waist*. Forthwith the silly girl plies herself with silk cord and canvas, till a man would sooner put his arms around a lamp post, than one of these unpliant, mummy-wrapt sticks. The ribs may interlock, the skin lose all its vitality, the limbs all their elasticity and freedom of motion; the yellows, blue-devils, and death, may threaten the disgusting victim, and still the waist is not as small as Miss Sophronisba Waspandbottle's. Well, the power of *contrast* must be invoked to the aid of compression and exhaustion; the dealers in raw-cotton, sail-duck, feathers, and wheat-bran, are patronized, till at last, a church door is too small for our anti-Venus di Medicis. Miss Sophronisba Waspandbottle is thrown entirely into the shade, and our friend in Boston. in horror and despair, denounces eternal damnation against the monster! Now the best cure for all this, is to import into this land—heathen in all things else but this— some of the best models of beautiful sculpture. Let our girls see that SMALL waists are not à-la-mode; au fait; as they say in Arkansas, "*the thing :*" and that a consistent harmony is to be preserved in all the members. This can best be obtained by free exercise and household duties, exercising the arms, the chest, the legs, the whole person, in the freest clothing possible; and if they are at last compelled to resort to dress, to cover over defects, or heighten beauties, they will be wise if they study the natural form, and its imperceptible departure from straight lines. At all events, let them never forget, that *modesty*, in dress and manner, is the divinity, at last, which men adore; so that if there be any luckless lassie destitute of this, which all love most in wife or mistress, let her be at least *apparently* miserly in the display of her most valued treasures; moderate in her stride, and "slow to anger," for the intellectual poet of the age, represents her, whom he would paint in most captivating atti- tude, "saying she would not consent—consented!"

LEXINGTON, TUESDAY, JULY 15.

LET US AGREE TO DIFFER.

Friends of emancipation, we have the power to free ourselves from the accumulated curses of slavery. Interest, pride, self- respect, justice, religion, mercy, call upon us to exercise it. *Let all agree that slavery shall fall!* ABOUT THE DETAILS LET US AGREE TO DIFFER. You have one opinion about the time, the mode, and the reasons of emancipation; we another; and our neighbor a third. What does common sense tell us? Submit our several views to the *will of the majority.* We pray you not to let us quarrel among ourselves—divide, and be crushed! When we meet in convention all our differences of opinion can be settled in an hour. Does one man say that male and female shall be free on a certain day: well and good: if not, vote it down. Does one man say liberate only the females: well and good: if not, vote it down. Does one man say buy all the

females, and thus have the next generation free : well and good :
if not, vote it down.   Does one man say buy, and emancipate
on the soil, for few would be left unsold, and wise policy does
not dictate that one hundred and eighty thousand laborers should
be expelled at once : well and good : if not, vote it down.   Does
one man say buy, liberate, and colonize : well and good : if not,
vote it down.   Is any other *mode* of emancipation, any other
means of freeing us from the worst of all evils known to men,
absolute slavery, proposed, which better suits the friends of
liberty : well and good : let that be adopted, and all the others
be voted down.   *We have now laid down ground broad enough
for every statesman, moralist, and Christian, in the state of
Kentucky,* IN FAVOR OF FREEDOM, *to stand upon : the time
has come : the question is made : liberty, or slavery ?*

FREE LABORERS OF KENTUCKY.

For half a century we have appealed in vain to the magnanimity of the slaveholders to have some little regard for our
welfare ; to remember that we too have bodies to be fed, and
clothed, and sheltered, minds to be educated, and souls to be
saved.

When a journeyman printer *underworks* the usual rates he
is considered an enemy to the balance of the fraternity, and is
called a "*rat.*"   Now the slaveholders have RATTED us with
the one hundred and eighty thousand slaves till forbearance
longer on our part has become-criminal.   They have *ratted* us
till we are unable to supply ourselves with the ordinary comforts
of a laborer's life.   They have *ratted* us out of the social circle.
They have *ratted* us out of the means of making our own
schools.   Twice have common school funds been provided for
our education ; and twice have they *ratted* us out of them !
They have *ratted* us out of churches, by the same means, and
the opportunities of religious worship.   They have *ratted* us
out of the press.   They have *ratted* us out of the legislature.
They have *ratted* us out of *all the offices of honor and profit.*
Judges, sheriffs, clerks, state officers, county court judges—all—
all are slaveholders !   They have *ratted* us into a scale inferior
to the slave : yes, in this state, in South Carolina, and other

slave states, you have seen it in print, how they have added insult to injury, by calling us slaves, and "white negroes." What words can we use, to arouse you to a sense of our deep and damning degradation! Men, we have one remaining, untried, omnipotent, power of *freemen* left—the ballot-box : yes, thank God, we can yet *vote!* Our wives, our sisters, our children, raise their imploring eyes to us; save us from this overwhelming ignominy—this insufferable woe; place us upon that equality for which our fathers bled and died. Come, if we are not worse than brutish beasts, let us but speak the word, and *slavery shall die!*

————

The Alabama Preacher and a Lay Sermon.

An Alabama preacher has been abusing us, and invoking the Kentuckians to mob us. We say nothing now of the impertinent intermeddling with our "peculiar state institutions," which this reverend cut-throat has been denouncing in "Northern Abolitionists," we merely wish to inform him, that he may play the assassin in the Christian land of Alabama, but that we Kentuckians only go in for a "free fight," and are *heathen* enough to disgrace native grown hemp, by stopping the nasal twang of any sniffling hypocrite, who in "Kendall green," or "saintly black," should attempt anything else than "an open ring, and a fair shake." Should this bellicose parson stray off this far from his flock, the chances are more in favor of our making a *scapegoat* of him, than of his making a *slain lamb* of us. Now, let Kentuckians stand aside—take no offence, it is to the Alabamians that we preach our sermon. One man does not see the injustice of slavery; he has not reflected upon *general* principles ; he has from this relation many *immediate* advantages to himself; he has heard that the Bible sanctions slavery—that many men deemed pure patriots, in days past, held slaves; he has hardened his heart, and goes in blindly for perpetual slavery. This man is no hypocrite, yet in the eyes of God he is guilty. Nature avenges her violated laws, a thousand evils of unknown cause come upon him and his, in life, and upon his descendants, perhaps insurrection and death! Another man knows that slavery is wrong—a violation of natural right, and in opposition to the aggregate economical progress of the commonwealth; he sees that it is a libel upon our system of professed republicanism; he feels that it is in opposition to every principle of Christianity; he treats with due contempt the idea of a "mark" of slavery having been put upon the African, seeing that history proves, without controversy, that the great majority of slaves, in all ages, have been whites; he gives you the wink, and tells you frankly that he loves power. This man is no hypocrite, and if God ever looks upon sin with the least degree of allowance, he slips him into some comfortable quarters in the world to come. For this slaveholder is a humane master, a good companion, a true friend, and has many other redeeming virtues. Here is one who feels the wrong—a man of heart and much sensibility, a lover of virtue, in the main a good man; he is a lawyer, a physician, a minister of the gospel, a mechanic, a tenant at will, a dependent laborer; his bread depends upon slaveholders; "the spirit is willing, but the flesh is weak." We have no reproaches for such men; they are on the side of the right at heart; they will be felt in time; they are more sinned against than sinning; the fault and the atonement are *one*. There is another class of men who know that slavery cannot be justified; they feel as full of guilt as a sponge is of water; they are desperately in love with republicanism and equality— are the people's men; their tastes degrade them to seek illicit commerce with the negro; yet they proclaim from the housetops most fastidious horror against *amalgamation*. For the first time in their lives they take up the Bible and affect to find that they are doing God's service in enslaving the "children of Ham." They are the foes of the freedom of the press—the liberty of speech; if they could muster one hundred men to one, they would Lynch you; whenever it suits their purposes they are slave traders, and for a good price have no objection to selling their own children; if you pull their noses, they go home and quarrel with their wives, and whip their slaves for revenge. These are no *hypocrites;* they do not reverence virtue enough to affect it—vice they set up for virtue; these men are simply *villains.* There is a class worse than this—than all the others —having all the vices of each, and the virtues of none. Among these is the Alabama preacher: they are the professed guardians of the morals of men—the representatives on earth of the holy, sin-hating God; they shed crocodile tears over the miseries of men, whilst they waste the body and soul, and gloat on the groans, the crushed affections, the deluded hopes, the despair, and the temporal and eternal damnation of immortal spirits. We speak not in a thoughtless vindictive tone, but as the claims of outraged humanity enforce us. ' They are the robbers of the poor, *would be* seducers of women, betrayers of friends, the overbearing contemners of the humble sons of fortune, the sycophants of power ; " they bend the supple hinges of the knee that thrift may follow fawning ;" nothing but abject and craven fear restrain them from highway robbery and secret murder. Murrel, in comparison, was a Christian and an honorable man. Like the veiled Prophet of Korassan, they wear a silver veiled visage over secret features of disgusting horror and fiendish malice : *these men justify slavery from the Bible, and prostitute to base uses of crime and woe the sanctity of the pure and living God.* Against these the Savior of men, full of patience, and charity, and long sufferance, uncomplaining at all times, though great drops of blood stood upon his sacred and lowly brow, in the mighty instinct of injured humanity, and offended virtue, cried out " Hypocrites—that devour widows' houses, and for show make long prayers : the same shall receive greater damnation."

Plain Talk.

The slave party are in the habit of denouncing us as incendiary. We say in our paper, that the slaves are impotent : their press teems with talk of murder, insurrection, rape, fire, and poison. We tell of the necessary submission of the slave and freedman ; they, of the tumult and insubordination of both. Now we leave it to every candid man to say, whose paper is the most dangerous to fall into the hands of slaves, theirs, or ours ? For long months, the whole city press here, was most violent and denunciatory and *murderous* in its tone against us, aud *no defence allowed us in their columns.* Yet none of their great men spoke out for us ; no public meeting was called to denounce the plotters against the lives of loyal citizens ; but so soon as we took measures for our own defence, and civil war was threatened, the slave party were the first to turn around

and ridicule all idea of mobs! And yet they now have the
hardihood to affect horror at insurrectionary matter being put
in print! Just as false is the insinuation that we are disturbing the old course of events, that we are the aggressors against
the present rights of slaveholders. The law of '33 was passed
with the inherited belief and faith of our people, that slavery
was a curse, which all sensible and honest men were bound, by
patriotism and religion, to throw off whenever it could be done
with safety, and without producing greater evils than actual
slavery. We appeal to all if this was not public opinion, "the
unwritten common law of the South." Then arose up a party
who repudiated the doctrines of Washington and Jefferson, and
began to cry in the wilderness, the new doctrine, that slavery
was of God, and true republicanism. The repeal of the law of
'33 was projected by this sect; its overthrow was a direct assault upon our old faith; it proposed to stay the progress of free
principles, and turn back the tide of safe and gradual emancipation. It avowed its design of amalgamating our interests
with the ultras of the South; that school which had made up
their minds to slavery, or death! A party without God or hope
in the world! Not to go with this party, was treason; no neutrality was allowed: "they who are not for us are against us."
Against this course of policy, we had no other help, than to appeal from the slaveholders, to the people—from our masters to
our own brothers! "Let them alone!" we did let them alone
for half a century; but not satisfied with our tame and base
subserviency, they would impose upon us new chains and make
our bondage eternal! Well, then, war is declared; it depends
upon the slave party, who proclaimed it, to say, whether it is to
be carried on by the ordinary laws of civilized nations, or
whether it shall be savage and heathen—"*war to the knife!*"

THE TIME HAS NOT COME!

Such is the cry of our masters; this was the cry in 1789—it
has poured its syren notes upon confiding and deluded ears, for
half a century—it has not yet come! The Greeks told a story
of a man, who attempted to learn his horse to live without eating; his plan was to subtract each day, one straw from his

accustomed food ; at last when the last straw was fed away, the horse died ! Now my readers suppose, of course, that when the foolish master saw his false system, he was sorry for his poor horse! Not at all; he complained, that so soon as he learned to live without eating, then foolishly he died ! The time for our masters to free us from our impoverishment and death from the straw-subtracting system of slavery has not yet come ! When did men as a body ever in the history of mankind, lay down voluntarily unjust power? Never ! The time has never, with them, come !—it never will ! When the last straw shall fail us, and death come upon us, in bitter mockery they will cry " fools, as soon as they learned to live without eating, then they died." Free laborers of Kentucky, let us not lie down and die like beasts in the hands of those who have for half a century been taking from us straw after straw ! From the garrets and the cellars, and the cheerless alleys of slave-oppressed cities—from the rocky hills and remote neglected valleys—let the cry be borne on every breeze that sweeps over our long down-trodden and slave-ridden state—" *The time has come ! and Kentucky shall be free !*"

THE CONVENTION.

It is a great mistake to suppose, that the defeat of the convention, a few years ago, shows that slavery is firm on its throne of despotic and unrelenting power. Thousands, who went against the convention then, were the emancipationists, among them we were numbered. When a convention is called again, it will be upon the main issue, slavery or liberty! Our power will be fully known, before we go into convention : we will come up to the polls, like regular soldiers, with the spirit of '76, Liberty or Death !

LO ! HERE—LO ! THERE.

The pro-slavery party of the North are mistaken, when they take the press of the South as a criterion of public sentiment : they are the mouth-pieces of the slaveholders, who are the property holders of the country: they hold the bread of the press in their hands: to expect them to speak out like men, is to expect every mother's son of them to be Martin Luthers, Emmets, and Hampdens, which is absurd. Politicians are no better; where is the man among them, who will sacrifice present power, to the contingency of hereafter rising with the swelling tide of freedom? The Church continues to take great pleasure in talking to their self-complacent auditors, "of the beauty of holiness—the exceeding sinfulness of sin." The seeds of an independent party is planted—a party of slow but sure growth, but of certain success and lasting power—traitors and rebels in the eyes of the American slaveocracy—but patriots and immortals in the grateful appreciations of coming generations.

Blowing Hot and Cold with the same Breath.— Sally Muller declared Free.

"Judgment was yesterday rendered in the Supreme Court in favor of the plaintiff in the case of Sally Muller vs. Louis Belmonti and John F. Miller, called in warranty. The decree was read by his honor, Judge Bullard, and is said to be a document characteristic of his high judicial attainments. The counsel for the unfortunate Sally, were, Christian Roselius and Wheelock S. Upton; and we learn that it is in contemplation by those. who have taken an interest in the fate of the plaintiff to pay them some public mark of respect.

"Some twelve months ago when this case was before the district court, we gave a brief sketch of its features. Sally claimed to be born in Germany and of German parents; of having come to this country when an infant with her father and mother, who reached here as "redemptioners," and died shortly after their arrival. John F. Miller alleged that she was born a slave and as his property; as such he brought her up, and as such sold her to Louis Belmonti; and now, after being for a quarter of a century, or thereabouts subjected to all the degradations of domestic bondage and servile labor, she is, by our highest tribunal, declared free!"—*New Orleans Picayune.*

Because Sally happens to be a German, the Picayune affects to be heart-struck! J. F. Miller with a sweet and quiet humanity sells Sally—and he is a villain: Mexico, the supreme power over Texas, declares *all persons of all colors free:* the United States citizens, with blood, fire, and death, violently subvert the decree, and all is glorious! Are the Lynchers dead in New Orleans, that the Picayune dares to sneer at the "blessings of the Patriarchal Institution?" Henry Clay, out of regard for Charles' fidelity, liberated him: the press is full of Pæans at this act of justice and mercy which moves editorial hearts! Another man undertakes to enlarge the bounds of uncompromising justice, to the liberation of the whole human race: immediately thunders of denunciation overwhelm "the fanatic." All at once it is found out that slavery is the greatest of blessings, and liberty the height of cruelty! Out of some 50,000 fugitives from slavery, some one or two cases of voluntary return from a cold and cheerless exile, to home, "wife, children, and friends," are hunted up to stop the mouths of all cavillers! Now, we undertake to say, that out of three millions of slaves, *not one* able-bodied man, woman or child, can be found who will refuse emancipation, on the soil. Is there no drug in the shops—no vegetable leaf, or earth-covered root—by sea and shore, "no mute nor living thing,"—that will cure our people of this Janus-faced morality?

LEXINGTON, TUESDAY, JULY 22.

T. M. Again!

The reply of ex-Governor T. M. to our former article, we lay before our readers to-day. We do not so out of any claim which he has to be heard; but because we wish to show the people of other states, the kind of men we have to deal with; and that we may meet here together, many calumnies, which singly, or coming from another source, are unworthy of notice. If we ever harbored any personal feeling against this silly old man, it would be fully gratified by letting him thus expose himself to the world: but the contrary is the truth. If we denounced him in our former article, it was because of his principles; and because justice to our cause and the claims of humanity, demanded their utter reprobation. It is true, that we made him *ridiculous;* a thing which our comparative ages should have forbid; but when the ex-Governor himself ventured upon ridicule, we could not refrain from a penchant we have for contemning all humbug; and we could not but take a pull at "old stone-hammer's" hunting shirt and songs, at the risk of spoiling much good sport in future.

The Governor begins by terming us the aggressor in a *personal* way. It is true he did not allude to us by *name;* but it seems that he is not only conversant with our personal history, but our political views. Our address to the people of Kentucky was out, and our prospectus for publishing an emancipation paper was published, just before the ex-Governor puts out his denunciation of *all emancipators.* Every one who has read both of our pieces, will see that Mr. M.'s former letter is more "personal and abusive" than our own, although he had the shrewdness to use indirection then, as he does now, in preference to open and manly battle. The Governor will not refute us before the public in "argument;" neither will he "fight" us! What then? Believing that our prowess consists in *words,* he is ambitious of showing us that he can beat us *blackguarding!* We learn that Mr. McDuffie declined meeting him once, because he proposed to fight with ungentlemanly weapons. We, too, for the same reason, refuse his weapons. We shall not, therefore, retort in kind to the Governor's fire; for our moral elevation places us out of the reach of his batteries. We shall notice his long letter in detail, in order that the name of one who has been set at the head of affairs in this commonwealth, shall not hereafter be set down in sustaining against us these calumnious charges, which have not even the merit of novelty to recommend them.

It is true we wear a "dagger;" but we deny ever having been in our life an aggressor upon any man; so that if we be a "daggered assassin," we ask the Governor to produce the proofs! And if we be an assassin, the fact that the Governor "marched into France, and then marched out again," proves that he does not deem us a "dastard assassin." The truth is, that we should much have regretted a personal contest with T. M.; and we feel obliged to him that he has deferred "personal chastisement till Texas shall be put out of the Union;"

because, whether we had lost or won, we should have reaped
no laurels. But if he came up here from Frankfort to attack
us, as we are credibly informed, it comes with a bad grace from
one who has practically concluded "that discretion is the better
part of valor," to reproach us with cowardice! Whilst we protest against expressions made previous to the revelation of his
true character being used in bar of subsequent action, and the
indelicacy of the Observer and Reporter, in detailing a familiar
conversation, we are willing to admit, for argument's sake, that
we are rightly reported, in language of whose accuracy we
cannot now, of course, be sure. And as much as he depreciates
us, we are too mindful of our own self-respect to deny that we
believe T. M. incapable of *deliberately* telling an untruth;
while his first and second letters prove beyond doubt, that in moments of excitement, he makes allegations injurious to others,
which are without any other evidence than the creation of his
own "heat-oppressed brain." In the same spirit, if he or any
of his friends will prove to us that we have in the least "slandered" him, we are ready to retract, and make all the amends
in our power. But until this is done, as there is in our former
article "nothing extenuate or aught set down in malice;" so
now after reading his defence, we still contend that there is
nothing there which we would "palliate or deny." We have
nothing to say in reply to the foreign matter which he lugs in,
about our early education, Yale College, and New Englanders.
The Northern people can fully vindicate themselves; and our
native state knows full well that we censure her for the love we
bear her; and if we blame rather than praise, it is because we
are more careful of her honor than of our own elevation. We
imputed to him his "stone hammer" as an honor, not as a reproach. It is he, not we, who attach disgrace to labor and its
implements. "Vain," as we are willing to admit we are, we
have ever avoided singing our own pæans. We are willing to
leave it to others to sit in judgment upon our humble history.
The ex-Governor was born poor and obscure, and has become
rich and famous: in his prosperity he forgets "the widow and
the orphan," and shows his gratitude to God by using his elevated name to the eternal oppression of the bodies, minds, and
souls of men. We were born in the circle to which he has at
length in spite of many vulgarities which attest his origin, forced
his way; having wealth, position, and high political prospects, we

deemed them naught while the poor were oppressed by our monopoly. If there is anything consoling in the comparison, the Governor is welcome to run it out in full: for really we consider this trifling unworthy of us and the public ear.

We supported Garrison and his friends because we believe that right is ever in the long run expedient—because we love justice more than power, and fear God more than men. This man's letter will, before the American people, prove that slave-holding fanaticism is worse than anti-slavery fanaticism ; and that we spoke but now proven truth when we said that Garrison is a better, infinitely better man than T. M. The Governor, after indulging in insane and impotent rage, and unqualified epithets, undertakes to give our personal history and political life. And again falsely charges us with being a hypocrite and traitor. This people know that what honors we have received, have been won by a fair and honorable reliance upon our merits and measures, and never by hanging upon the skirts of great men ! Whilst we have been a consistent friend of Mr. Clay, we never played the part of *sycophant* as some others have ! When in 1840, in the National Convention, we in common with a great many of Mr. Clay's supporters, were sitting in tears and silence, overcome with the sense of injustice that he was betrayed in the house of his friends—this same M. sprang to his feet, in obedience to his eternal instincts of waiting on the source of power, and passed the most fulsome eulogies upon Harrison, in a manner that was out of place and repugnant to the feelings of every Kentuckian then present, under the peculiar circumstances which surrounded them. We have consistently supported Mr. Clay from our earliest youth to the last: and we are yet a member of the whig party, and hold the same principles which we have ever held. We avowed in the canvass of 1840, in Fayette, our opposition to perpetuating slavery : we did the same in '41. See our Review of 1840 and speech in the Legislature of the same winter, and then let the public say if we have ever in our life, changed a principle, betrayed a party, or deserted a friend.

We were beaten by R. Wickliffe in 1841, by illegal votes, as we have elsewhere, again and again shown by the records of the county.* A man, however, is not always an impartial judge in

---

* We were elected in our native county to the Legislature as soon as we were eligible; the last time we were a candidate there, we were the *foremost*

his own cause; let that pass. It is not true, that we spent thousands of dollars in that contest, nor one thousand! It is true, we suffered much from securityships, then, before, and since. It is true that we bought votes that offered themselves in the market; unhappy country where such things are—and more unhappy still, when an ex-governor imputes to others, faults which he confesses in his own person! The Governor imputes our conduct in establishing a paper, to our personal chagrin at "the cold reception we met on our return from the North." Fortunately, there are letters now in the hands of several eminent citizens of the republic, showing our design of publishing a paper before we left home, which will prove once more the accumulated slanders of this man. The contrast between his policy and ours, is again grateful to our self-respect. We both courted the abolitionists for Mr. Clay, we for principle, he for power. We were the same to them after as before defeat; he became their slanderer, we their defender from his unfounded calumnies! The ex-governor, after having finished our career, as he vainly hopes, then proceeds to speak of his own success in life. This is in harmony with the exquisite taste of his own soubriquets of "the same old coon," and "the hard-faced old stone-hammer," and "*the lump of innocence!*" We have too much self-respect to follow in his lead, else we could fill our sheet, not with what we, but what others say in our praise. He then attempts to prove that we slandered him in saying that "the public regarded him as a standing candidate for any sine-cure which might fall uppermost." We repeat the charge. He was a candidate for the Senate, when we were in the Legislature; he was voted for; he was in Frankfort, and, of course, must have approved it. He was nominated at a public meeting as a candidate for Governor, and he never formally declined, and was generally considered a candidate. When he got to

in the race. The first year we moved to Fayette, in 1840, so soon as we were eligible, we beat R. Wickliffe, the most talented, and wealthy, and prominent young man in the county, if not in the state. In 1841, we were swindled out of our election by the slave party—every judge of the election in all the precincts being against us What then was the "damning infamy" which all at once ruined such seeming prosperous career? We turned "traitor"—worse than "Burr or Arnold"—we turned TRAITOR TO SLAVERY! We did that which a South Carolina divine deemed "worse than slaying his own mother, or losing his own soul in hell." We denounced it then, we denounce it now, and we will denounce it for ever!

Louisville, and found Owsley too much for him he made a virtue of necessity, and then, and not till then, declined! He has
lately been regarded by his friends, in the list of candidates for
Congress, which he admits; he declined the nomination, very
likely, because his *letter* would have assisted in adding another
item to the evidence that the people of Kentucky had long since
lost confidence in him! And, to cap the climax, we find him
in the actual possession of a *sinecure*, for which every one must
admit he is utterly unfit; and yet, in the teeth of all these
proven facts, he ventures to impute to us "slander," and calls
upon us to retract the charge, or admit ourself "a liar and
scoundrel." We have thus, at the hazard of wearying our readers, gone over all his charges, and refuted them, by reference to
witnesses and records, who and which are familiar to our people; whilst every allegation we made, stands eternally against
him. This task was not at first, nor now, an agreeable one.
The disparity in our ages gives him the sympathies of men,
and, for this very reason, no doubt, he was put forward by the
slave party to overawe and brow-beat the friends of emancipation, as he incautiously admits, "*it is much more my (his) true
policy to provoke your (my) ire.*" Slave champions have found,
or will find, that we are not so easily, by passion, thrown off our
guard as is supposed, that in action we are very cool in the use
of our blade; and even the governor may have reason to exclaim, with the hectoring knight of the play:

> "Had I known he were so cunning in fence,
> I'd have seen him damned, ere I had challenged him."

Texas is annexed: believing it to have been unconstitutional
by joint resolution to annex foreign nations to us before the election, we are of the same opinion still. Those who look to the
source of office more than principle, will no doubt quietly submit. But, as we love our Constitution more than slavery, all
impotent as we are, "never will we lay down our arms!" So
we bid the "LUMP OF INNOCENCE," more in sorrow than in anger, farewell! If the slaveholders expect to maintain the war
against liberty and republicanism, they must get some more
Herculean champion than the man with the hunting shirt; and
let the ex-governor return once more to his proper sphere of
hammering stone, or singing the really good old song of "*wife,
children, and friends.*"

We have long expected this servile taunt of being unfriendly to Mr. Clay, because we have not and will not yield up our convictions to him or any other man. We were born as free as Cæsar; we call no man master. We say nothing of intellect; but the moral part of our being is under our own control. In the untrammeled expansion of our own spirit, we have diverged from Henry Clay's lead, upon the vital subject of the liberties of men. Posterity shall justly assign us our relative rank!

That is Property which the Law makes Property.

The Signal of Liberty asks me to answer the argument of the Albany Patriot, against the postulate that "what the law makes property is property." It is the doctrine of republican governments that the majority should rule according to the fundamental law; a man who resists the law is a traitor and outlaw, and is liable to be, and ought to be shot down with impunity. *No government upon earth can stand an hour upon any other principle than that,* " *That which the law makes property is property.*" One man has as much natural right to the land as another: yet if we intrude ourself into our neighbor's field, we are shot down, and the world exclaims, " Well !" Why? because it is the *law !* Mr. C.'s wife is in love with us, we reciprocate her affection, if we attempt to seize upon her, or we voluntarily escape from the husband's house, and he comes upon us and shoots us down, he is guiltless! and all say well! Why? because the law has made it so! My son at twenty is full grown in person and mind, B decoys him from my employ with more advantageous offers: we sue him for damages and recover, and all say well! Why? because the law is so! We are a Turk, and have two wives, the Patriot comes and wins the affections of one, and takes her : we shoot him down, and he has no redress! Why? because it is the law! A thousand similar cases might be adduced, both in accordance with and in opposition to natural law—both in accordance with and against revealed religion—both in accordance with and against the conscientious impressions of men with regard to right and wrong! Upon the same basis, then, does slavery stand: and the same course of reasoning might induce any one to attack any other positive institution of law, that leads him violently, or by physical force or fraud to resist slavery. In reply to the case put: If we were invited to dinner in New York, and seized upon and reduced to slavery, what would we do? We reply, that we would use all the means which we deemed most *expedient* for our liberation for an unjust bondage—a bondage in violation of all natural law. But if such were the law of New York, and the patriot should attempt to resist the authorities by force, and was shot down, however much we might gratefully sympathize with him, we would be constrained to acknowledge the justice of his fate. Because, in resisting, by violence, even a manifestly unjust act, he violated the principles of all government by not submitting to the laws, till changed by constitutional means. Because in resisting an isolated case of oppression, he opened the door to the loss of every man's liberty in the state of New York, for without *law* there is no *liberty*. The resistance of law by violence is rebellion and treason, in all cases, and should be punished with the severest infliction; because it is the greatest of crimes by inducing *all others*. If the laws of New York legalized the betrayal of hospitality to the grossest fraud and oppression, what ought the Patriot to do? *He ought to use neither violence nor fraud.* He ought to call moral power and the laws of nature and of God to his help, to cry aloud and spare not, to *stand to his arms* in the defence of his *constitutional* right of speech and of the press, and implore all good men in all the world, to aid him by their countenance in sweeping the infamous statute from the code of the state. The people of the United States see us in that position! Will they embarrass us with frivolous denunciations about force and childish technicalities? or will they, in the true spirit of reason, religion and humanity, aid us in their cause and ours?

You are either for slavery or against it—if for it, be manly and say so! "and there's an end on 't." If you are against it, you shall not shield yourselves from the guilt of *doing nothing*. If we are too ultra, we stand less chance of carrying our point: if we do not go far enough, go ahead of us. If you carry the blacks to the moon, and everybody is for carrying the blacks to the moon, then go into the movement and into the Convention, vote us down and carry your point, and if to the moon the blacks shall go, we shall say well done! Why do you stand waiting and complaining of others? Are you not willing to submit to the majority? then you are a traitor to our republicanism! Let us hear no more of this silly hesitancy ; be either for or against, either hot or cold, lest the manly of both parties "spew you out of their mouths!"

Moonlight.

For the last few nights we have had the most lovely moonlight. We have heard much of Italian skies and Oriental trees and shrubbery; but if in any portion of the globe the stars look down more numerously bright from deeper and purer heavens, nowhere do their soft and twinkling rays, or the calm melancholy beams of the Queen of Night fall upon more magnificent masses of luxuriant vegetation. When we throw open the lattice and look out upon the glorious harmony and heavenly beauty of the visible world, how painfully do we feel that man's own wild passions are his only foes:

> "We make, ourselves, more pointed still,
> Regret, remorse, and shame!"

The same, unsullied and unchanged, is the face of that moon which shone upon our earliest youth; the same, those old trees which bask in its ethereal light; the catydids, the crickets, and tree-frogs pour their unceasing, melancholy notes upon the ear, the same as when they moved our boyish heart to strange emotions, and filled our heavy lids with unbidden tears! But oh, how changed that scathed and strife-riven spirit of our advancing years! Is not the memory of joys departed, the true remorse? Is not crime but the destruction of the capabilities of the soul for that perfect happiness which is found only in exact obedience to nature's laws? Does any man remember when he first, in silent, oriental idolatry, looked upon the face of some beautiful girl, and poured forth the intoxicating incense of the heart in the language of looks, which words would not and could not express? Do the affections, like some lovely flower bud, gloriously bloom, and then, in fallen and scattered leaves, perish for ever ? Are friendship, filial, and parental, and brotherly, and sisterly, regard, subject to the same laws? and has the time come when we shall in despair learn that they are past ? No; men, and women, look out upon all lovely nature, these moonlight nights ; •the vivid emotions of youth come back again, and all may joyously exclaim, "the soul but sleepeth; it is not dead !"

LEXINGTON, TUESDAY, AUGUST 12.

Our leader to-day is from one of the very first intellects in this nation ; and as he is a large slaveholder, we allow him to speak his sentiments in his own language. We shall give our plan of emancipation in our next.

We are called once more to our hard and responsible task from a bed of long and painful illness. The inquiry has been frequently made, we are told, whether we were living or dead, with hopes for the worst, in the bosoms of some. We are proud to say that the man does not live, whom we would, if we could effect it by the mere exertion of the will, cause one moment's pain, far less compass in desire, his death. "To freemen, the disgrace attending our misconduct is, in my opinion, the most urgent necessity. 'Is Philip dead?' 'No, but in great danger.' How are you concerned in these rumors? Suppose he should meet some fatal stroke: you would soon raise up another Philip, if your interests are thus regarded." It is the weakness and disease in the state that has forced us into our present position ; and if we should perish, the same causes would raise up many more and abler than we to vindicate the same cause.

We had hoped to see on this continent, the great axiom, that man is capable of self-government, amply vindicated. We had no objections to the peaceable and honorable extension of empire over the whole continent, if equal freedom expanded with the bounds of the nation. Gladly would we have seen untold millions of freemen, enjoying liberty of conscience and pursuit, of resting under their own vine and fig tree with none to make them afraid, standing upon a sacred and inviolate constitution at home, and just towards all nations—such was the vision of the immortal Washington, and such was ours. But we are told the enunciation of the great and soul-stirring principles of Revolutionary patriots was a lie; as a dog returns to his vomit we are to go back to the foul and cast off rags of European tyranny to hide our nakedness. Slavery, the most unmitigated, the lowest, basest that the world has seen, is to be substituted for ever for our better, more glorious, holier aspirations; the constitution is torn and trampled under foot; justice and good faith in a nation are derided; brute force is substituted in the place of high moral tone. All the great principles of national liberty which we inherited from our British ancestry are yielded up; and we are left without God or hope in the world. When the great hearted of our land weep, and the man of reflection maddens in the contemplation of our national apostacy; there are men pursuing gain and pleasure, who smile with contempt and indifference at their appeals. But remember, you who dwell in marble palaces, that there are strong arms and fiery hearts and iron pikes in the streets, and panes of glass only between them and the silver plate on the board, and the smooth skinned woman on the ottoman. When you have mocked at virtue, denied the agency of God in the affairs of men, and made rapine your honeyed faith, tremble! for the day of retribution is at hand, and the masses will be avenged.

We are informed that there is a lawyer in this city of very small intellect, and infinitesimal shade of a soul, who has been busying himself about our paper from the beginning, and latterly reporting that we give papers to slaves, both our own paper and papers from our exchange list. Now our publisher has gone so far, although there is nothing in our sheet that a slave might not safely read, as to adopt the rule to require subscribers to write an order when they send by slaves for their papers. We have, out of regard to the opinions and prejudices of slaveholders, avoided printing and circulating tracts gratuitously, which every one sees would greatly forward our cause, by reaching a class of men who rarely take or read newspapers, because they are very liable to fall into the hands of slaves, and thus subject us to censure. Our exchange list is open to the perusal of any white citizen, and no others. We know that there are evils attending the discussion of this subject; but every sensible man is aware that they will never grow less, but will ever increase; they must be met now or never. Slavery does not slough off of itself, as some suppose. In those parts of Maryland where slavery prevails most, and where now her ablest men admit that it has become utterly useless and eminently injurious, the slaves have increased on the whites up to the present hour: and so also in Virginia; and so also in Kentucky. So that we must come up to this subject, cautiously but determinedly. There are some men who suppose that our efforts will be abortive; if so, it is not our fault, but the fault of others. But we are of a far different opinion; from the late political movements in Louisville, we are induced to believe that to-day our friends there are in a majority; when this city takes open anti-slavery ground, the institution cannot long stand. In conclusion, we give this officious lawyer a gentle hint, that if he does not let us alone, we will *brand him* so that his children will not outlive his disgrace.

SPEECH OF G. D. ON TAKING HIS SEAT IN CONGRESS.

Compeers and descendants of Washington, among those great principles of human liberty for which millions of our English ancestors were willing to lay down their lives, was the right of the people to petition their rulers for a redress of grievances. And our forefathers wisely incorporated this essential right of freemen into our organic law, that in all time there should be no cavil or misunderstanding upon this subject. And this Constitution I have solemnly before God and men sworn to support; yet there has arisen in this land a power higher than the Constitution, more exacting than conscience—the slave power. It demands that I should yield up the right of petition, and I have done so. I have thus proven myself loyal to them, and by abandoning one great principle of liberty, I have shown myself a willing servant ready to do their will in all things whatever. All I ask in return, is the prefix of honorable to my name, eight dollars a day, rock fish, and oyster patties!

T. F. Marshall.

We had intended to say something upon this gentleman's handbill. But when we reflect that we have gone to the expense of republishing his letters upon slavery for distribution, as the ablest argument against the "*unmitigated curse*" which we could lay before the public, we feel that it would be trifling with the good sense of the people to set about refuting his poor ragged argument, lately put forth in opposition to his earlier, manlier, and sincerer views, when no miserable purpose was to be subserved at the expense of high and holy principle. He is beaten, and we have no heart to pursue the subject farther.

TRUE AMERICAN—EXTRA

No. I.

LEXINGTON, AUGUST 15, 1845.

To a Just People.

I deem it due to myself, the cause of the people, and the constitutional liberty of my state, that I make a few explanations before the enemies of these proceed to extremity, that they may be left without excuse in the estimation of all just men. I learned a few moments before 3 o'clock, that a public meeting was to be holden at that hour in the Court House, to take measures for the suppression of the publication of the True American. Immediately, unwell as I was, I proceeded to the Court House, to vindicate, as I shall ever be ready to do, the principles and policy maintained in that paper. I found about twenty individuals, including some two or three personal friends who followed me in. I knew them all to be political, and three-fourths of them violent personal, enemies. I saw but one so-called whig, and he has been ever since the publication of the paper, one of its most violent opponents. I will give the names of these men, hereafter to the public. Two speakers proposed to dissolve the meeting : and one Henry Johnson, a cotton planter, declared that although he was ever ready to act boldly upon this subject, he would not then, nor hereafter, take any action in regard to the True American, unless the whig party also came up and incurred the same responsibility. T. F. Marshall said that he had regarded it as a public not a private meeting, and that he conceived that the public dissatisfaction and excitement were based upon the editorial published by me in the last " American," where I spoke of the consequence of the disregard of the principles of justice by the leading men of the nation ; and another person remarked, that the dissatisfaction was also founded upon the opinion set forth in the leader of the last paper. Here several persons contended that it was a private meeting, upon which I started to leave the house, explaining to Mr. Marshall, in passing, that a construction had been put upon my article which it never entered my head to convey, and which any sensible man who will read the piece will see, who knows the circumstances in which I am placed, having regard to common sense, the effectuation of my own purposes, or the safety of myself and relatives, I could never have intended to give it. It will be perceived by the reader of that article, that the whole piece alludes to national policy, and the loss of a high sense of justice in the administration of our national affairs, resulting from the influence of negro slavery upon the national action, even to the habitual violation of the Constitution. And further, I meant to convey the idea, in my elliptical manner, that in a country like ours, where suffrage is universal, and standing armies impossible, that those men who are drawing substance and power from the existence and extension of slavery, at the expense of the interests of the great masses of the legal voters of this Union, who are now and have been sacrificed at the shrine of slavery—that these men, the white millions (having no allusion whatever to the blacks of the South) would, in the course of time, when that poverty pressed upon them which slavery had been the most instrumental in causing, follow the example of their plunderers, and in turn plunder them. Such was the case in France, when the oppressed rose upon the oppressor, and spared neither property, life, nor sex.

As to the blacks, we have ever held in our printed arguments, and in our secret opinion, that the slaves, whilst the Union lasts, are utterly impotent for any very extensive mischief, even in the cotton countries. And I regard the idea of insurrection in Kentucky, where there are about six whites to one black, as ridiculous, 'and only used by the slaveholders as a bugaboo, to maintain the ascendency of their power in the state; and even if an insurrection should take place, I feel myself as much bound, as any citizen in the state, to shoulder my musket to suppress it, and in the discharge of my duty I am not willing to admit that any person is more ready. With regard to the leader of the same paper, I said in the beginning that I intended to allow full freedom of discussion upon the subject of slavery, and I said for several weeks, at the head of my editorial columns, under my own signature, that I intended to allow, under the editorial head also, great latitude of opinion, without comment. Differing as I did in some important points from the writer of this article, who I repeat is a large slaveholder, I intended to give my individual views on the same subject, in my very next number, which when given will put my enemies under the necessity of denouncing, when they denounce me, the immortal Washington, a name sacred to the lovers of liberty of all time and place. I had not expected, in the abundance of my charity, that the most fallen men would have taken advantage of my helpless condition, arising from a long and painful illness, to sacrifice me; when even in health I stood almost one man against a thousand. I tell these men, however, that they much mistake their man, and that if they do succeed in accomplishing their purposes and seal their triumph with my blood, that their banners of victory shall wave over a violated Constitution, the grave of liberty, and the impious defiance of the laws of God, and the moral sense of all mankind. If I stood in defence of my own right only, I might be deterred from the unequal contest; but when I stand for the six hundred thousand free white citizens of my native state, to which, and her interests, concentred by all republican principles, in the majority of her people, I owe eternal allegiance, I cannot lay down my arms. To my children and friends, wherever found, if I know myself, it shall never be said, at least of one citizen of Kentucky, that he preferred life to honor and duty to his country.

Cassius M. Clay.

Thursday, August 14th, 1845.

P.S. Since writing the above handbill, I have received the following letter from the hands of Thomas H. Waters, on my sick bed, at my own house.

Lexington, 14th August, 1845.

CASSIUS M. CLAY, Esq.

SIR :—We, the undersigned, have been appointed as a committee upon the part of a number of the respectable citizens of the city of Lexington to correspond with you, under the following resolution :

Resolved, That a committee of three be appointed to wait upon Cassius M. Clay, Editor of the "True American," and request him to discontinue the publication of the paper called the "True American," as its further continuance, in our judgment, is dangerous to the peace of our community, and to the safety of our homes and families.

In pursuance of the above, we hereby request you to discontinue your paper, and would seek to impress upon you the importance of your acquiescence. Your paper is agitating and exciting our community to an extent of which you can scarcely be aware. We do not approach you in the form of a threat. But we owe it to you to state, that, in our judgment, your own safety, as well as the repose and peace of the community, are involved in your answer. We await your reply, in the hope that your own good sense and regard for the reasonable wishes of a community in which you have many connexions and friends, will induce you promptly to comply with our request. We are instructed to report your answer to a meeting, to-morrow evening, at three o'clock, and will expect it by two o'clock, P. M., of to-morrow.

Respectfully, &c.

B. W. DUDLEY,
THOMAS H. WATERS,
JOHN W. HUNT.

To which I made the following reply, which will be delivered to-day, at the hour appointed :

SIR:—I received through the hands of Mr. Thomas H. Waters, one of your committee, since candle-light, your extraordinary letter. Two of your committee and myself are not upon speaking terms, and when I add to this the fact that you have taken occasion to address me a note of this character, when I am on a bed of sickness of more than a month's standing, from which I have only ventured at intervals to ride out and to write a few paragraphs, which have caused a relapse, I think that the American people will agree with me, that your office is a base and dishonorable one: more particularly when they reflect that you have had more than two months whilst I was in health to accomplish the same purpose. I say in reply to your assertion that you are a committee appointed by a respectable portion of the community, that it cannot be true. Traitors to the laws and Constitution cannot be deemed respectable by any but assassins, pirates, and highway robbers. Your meeting is one unknown to the laws and constitution of my country; it was secret in its proceedings; its purposes, its spirit, and its action, like its mode of existence, are wholly unknown to and in direct violation of every known principle of honor, religion, or government, held sacred by the civilized world. I treat them with the burning contempt of a brave heart and a loyal citizen. I deny their power and defy their action. It may be true that those men are excited as you say, whose interest it is to prey upon the excitement and distresses of the country. What tyrant ever failed to be excited when his unjust power was about to be taken from his hands? But I deny, utterly deny and call for proof, that there is any just ground for this agitation. In every case of violence by the blacks since the publication of my paper, it has been proven and will be again proven by my representatives, if my life should fail to be spared, that there has been special causes for their action independent of, and having no relation whatever to the "True American" or its doctrines. Your advice with regard to my personal safety is worthy of the source whence it emanated, and meets with the same contempt from me which the purposes of your mission excite. Go tell your secret conclave of cowardly assassins that C. M. Clay knows his rights and how to defend them.

C. M. CLAY.

Lexington, August 15, 1845.

KENTUCKIANS:

You see this attempt of these tyrants, worse than the *thirty despots* who lorded it over the once free Athens, now to enslave you. Men who regard law—men who regard all their liberties as not to be sacrificed to a single pecuniary interest, to say the least, of doubtful value—lovers of justice— enemies of blood—laborers of all classes—you for whom I have

sacrificed so much, where will you be found when the battle
between liberty and slavery is to be fought? I cannot, I will
not, I dare not question on which side you will be found. If
you stand by me like men, our country shall yet be free, but if
you falter now, I perish with less regret when I remember that
the people of my native state, of whom I have been so proud,
and whom I have loved so much, are already slaves.

C. M. CLAY.

Lexington, August 15, 1845.

No. II.

TO THE CITIZENS OF FAYETTE COUNTY, AND THE CITY OF LEXINGTON:

As my opponents, notwithstanding my sickness, will not wait
to hear my plan of emancipation, and seem determined to precipitate measures to extremity, without giving me a hearing,
and as they insist upon branding me as an "abolitionist"—a
name full of unknown and strange terrors and crimes to the
mass of our people—I will make a brief statement of my plan
of emancipation. Although I regard slavery as opposed to natural right, *I consider law, and its inviolate observance, in all
cases whatever, as the only safeguards of my own liberty
and the liberty of others.* I therefore, have not given, and
will not give, my sanction to any mode of freeing the slaves,
which does not conform strictly to the Laws and Constitution
of my state. And, as I am satisfied that there is no power under
the present Constitution, by which slavery can be reached efficiently, I go for a Convention. In a Convention—which is politically omnipotent, I would say that every female slave, born
after a certain day and year, should be free at the age of twenty-one. This, in the course of time, would gradually, and at
last, make our state truly free. I would further say, that, after the expiration of thirty years, more or less, the state should
provide a fund, either from her own resources, or from her portion in the public lands, for the purchase of the existing generation of slaves, in order that the white laboring portion of our
community might be as soon as possible freed from the ruinous

competition of slave labor. The funds should be applied after this manner: Commissioners shall be appointed in each county, who shall, on oath, value all slaves that shall be voluntarily presented to them for that purpose. To the owners of these slaves shall be issued, by the proper authorities, scrip, bearing interest at the rate of six per cent., to the amount of the value of their slaves; and to the redemption of said scrip this fund shall be applied, principle and interest. By this plan the present habits of our people would not be suddenly broken in upon, whilst, at the same time, we believe that it would bring slavery to almost utter extinction in our state, within the next thirty years.

With regard to the free blacks, I would not go for forcible expulsion, but I would encourage, by all the pecuniary resources that the state had to spare, a voluntary emigration to such countries and climates as nature seems particularly to have designed for them.

With regard to the political equality of the blacks with the whites, I should oppose in Convention their admission to the right of suffrage. As minors, women, foreigners, denizens, and divers other classes of individuals are, in all well regulated governments, forbidden the elective franchise, so I see no good reason why the blacks, until they become able to exercise the right to vote with proper discretion, should be admitted to the right of suffrage. "Sufficient for the day is the evil thereof." The time might come, with succeeding generations, when there would be no objection on the part of the whites, and none on account of disqualification of the blacks, to their being admitted to the same political platform; but let after generations act for themselves. The idea of amalgamation and social equality resulting from emancipation, is proven by experience to be untrue and absurd. It may be said by some, what right would a Convention have to liberate the unborn? They who ask equity, the lawyers say, themselves must do equity; and whilst the slaveholders have rights, they must remember the blacks also have rights; and surely, in the compromise which we have proposed between the slave and the slaveholder, the slaveholder has the lion's share.

I have thus, in a very rambling, and feeble, unsatisfactory manner, given something of an outline of the plan which I had intended to present.

It may be that my paper has not been conducted in the most pacific manner, but is there not cause for mutual reproach between myself and the public, in which I am placed? And those who now most denounce me, should remember that my paper was denounced, even in advance, in the full avowal of all the incendiary purposes which my enemies now affect to impute to *me*. I am willing to take warning from friends or enemies for the future conduct of my paper, und whilst I am ready to restrict myself in the latitude of discussion of the question, I NEVER WILL, VOLUNTARILY, ABANDON A RIGHT OR YIELD A PRINCIPLE.

CASSIUS M. CLAY.

August 16, 1845.

No. III.

To the Public.

Since writing my last handbill concerning a Convention, I have seen the handbill put out by Henry Johnson, Thomas H. Waters, and Dudley M. Craig, committee, and Beverly A. Hicks, chairman. I thank God, that in his mercy, I am not yet "MAD," although these men, the public will perceive, since they know the state of my health, have done all in their power possible, to destroy not only my reason but my life: for I have had the typhoid fever for thirty-three days, during which time, almost incessantly, my brain has been affected. It will be perceived that they do not characterize their meeting as a private caucus, which all Lexington know it was. And I now thank God that a lifetime's regard for my word will enable me, I feel confident, whilst I am lying on my back unable to hold a pen, and dictating all these handbills which I have put forth, unable to procure authority and testimony to sustain it, to use with the power and truth of evidence, my bare assertion against a thousand calumniators. When I appeal to LABORERS for help, in my handbill, and I say, I meant white laborers and no others, all who know me will believe what I say. And all who do not know me—when they remember that every blood relation I have in the world that I know of, and every connexion, are slaveholders, and that with all these, with few exceptions, I am upon terms of the most harmonious and friendly feeling and association, although we differ about this thing of slavery—they will also know, that I speak the truth. ⸱ Yes, I say it, the publishers of this handbill believe it and know it. If these men have had a six-pounder cannon and some sixty or one hundred balls, as I am credibly informed, ready to batter down my office, before the publication of this editorial of which they complain, it is proven to every honest man that they are now playing upon me the story of the "wolf and the lamb." Whether *they* "*are putting forth a counter manifesto, or advertising for recruits,*" not only from our own city and county, but from adjoining counties, let the public judge. They say that I am "ASSOCIATED" with the abolitionists of the North.* The gentlemen either

---

* From the Ky. Commonwealth.

CASSIUS M. CLAY'S POSITION IN REGARD TO SLAVERY.

We insert the following letter from Mr. C. M. Clay, at his request, in order that his true position, which has been entirely misconceived by many, may be correctly understood by the country. Those who have supposed him an abolitionist, in the sense of the term, as commonly understood in political circles, will see that they have misunderstood him.

T. B. STEVENSON, Esq.:

Sir:—I ask the liberty to make, through your columns, a summary statement of my views upon the subject of slavery. By a portion of the people of this state, I never expect to be fairly represented. To the great mass of the people who have no *interest* in suppressing truth, I would appeal against the calumnies of unscrupulous partizans.

Slavery is a municipal institution. It exists by no other right and tenure, than the Constitution of Kentucky.

I am opposed to depriving slaveholders of their slaves by any other than Constitutional and legal means. Of course, then, I have no sympathy for those who would liberate the slaves of Kentucky in other ways. I have no connexion with any man, or set of men, who would sanction or undertake the illegal liberation of slaves ; and I feel bound, by my allegiance to the state of Kentucky, to resist, by force, if necessary, all such efforts.

Whilst I hold that the United States Constitution has no power to establish slavery in the District of Columbia, or in the Territories, or in any place of its exclusive supremacy ; so I contend, that in the states, once admitted into the Union, and thereby become *sovereign* and *independent,* Congress has no power or right to interfere with or touch slavery, without the legitimate consent of the states.

I believe that the addition of new *slave states,* or *slave territory,* to this Union, is *unconstitutional* and impossible.

I am the avowed and uncompromising enemy of slavery, and shall never cease to use all Constitutional, and honorable, and just means, to cause its ex-mean political association, or nothing; for personal association at this distance is impossible. I utterly deny that I have any political association with them, other than that the opinions of all political parties whatever, meet and mingle upon some common grounds. In my prospectus, which was published for months in this city, I said that I should form alliance with no political party, but act as a "state party," so that then, once more, if I speak truth, these men do not. In the "True American," July 29th, in my letter to the Cincinnati Anti-Slavery Convention, I declined to be present, and in the same letter I used the following language: "I abide the destiny of that party in which I have grown to manhood, until some other, numbering more friends of liberty than we, shall give indication of a more speedy success. I claim to be a WHIG, because I stand upon the same ground of the illustrious declarators of 1776." Now, my countrymen, is not here most triumphant refutation of the assassin calumnies of these men? For if I have said to the abolitionists themselves that I am a whig, whilst they were supporting me as one of *their party*, how could I hope to be estimated by them in any other light than as a base and false political adventurer. That I have many subscribers among them, is true; but to say that I am "SUSTAINED" by them, in the sense here meant, is false. I believe that they do not compose more than one-fourth part of my subscribers in the Northern states; and I would far rather have their support, than that of such men as one of this committee, who comes blubbering like a great fat baby into secret caucus, calling himself my "friend," whilst at the same time, as soon as my back is turned, he stabs me to the vitals. Now, my countrymen! when you remember

---

tinction in Kentucky, and its reduction to its constitutional limits in the United States.

Born a Kentuckian and a slaveholder, I have no prejudices nor enmities to gratify; but, impelled by a sense of self respect, love of justice, and the *highest expediency*, I shall ever maintain that *liberty* is our only safety.

For the freedom of speech and of the press, I never shall cease to battle while life lasts. If there is any Kentuckian so base as to yield these Constitutional and glorious privileges, without which it is the veriest mockery to talk of being a free people, I envy him not. A slave to slaves, let him be sodden in his infamy. With such I hold no fellowship; from such I ask no quarter. All I ask is an open field and a fair fight. Your obedient servant,

CASSIUS M. CLAY.

Frankfort, Ky., Jan. 8, 1845.

that such *far-seeing* and *clear-headed statesmen,* whose names are appended to this handbill, and who have undertaken to become the guardians of the honor and interests of this state, must have seen these written declarations of mine, you must be convinced that they wilfully misrepresent me on this occasion. If "defiance and threats" were my earliest heralds, they came, if report be true, from one of this committee. They were the same heralds of "defiance and threats" which now once more come from them; and if Lexington be true to the glorious name she bears, and if Fayette be true to the glorious name she bears, they will meet with the same fate—a dishonored grave of undisturbed centuries. I am satisfied to trust the explanation of my editorial of the last paper to the people whom I address. But one more suggestion, in addition to those which I have already made, if they torture my meaning from the general context, which none but *clear-headed* men as these will do—not upon mere verbal, and grammatical criticism, and *literal* interpretation—could I have meant the blacks not in the South; for there are five millions of whites to three of blacks—not in Kentucky, for there are six whites to one black. So, then, if a class is to be taken, and choice is to be made between the whites and blacks, even then the whites are the "MASSES." No, these men cannot, they do not, believe what they say. They say that I deny the VALIDITY of the laws in one of the most important "of all its relations." This is absolutely false. Turn to the number of the American in which Thomas Metcalfe's letter was published, and strange to say they will there find an article from my pen, where I maintain with all the power of intellect of which I am capable, against the Albany Patriot—one of those abolitionists with whom these men say I am allied—the proposition in relation to slavery, that "that is property which the law makes property." It is one thing to admit the legality of a thing, and another thing to deny its justice. Oh! Henry, Thomas, Dudley, Beverley, surely ye are "Daniels come to judgment!" To say that "*regard for the public peace*" induces Henry, and Thomas, and Dudley, and Beverley, to shoulder their muskets, and drag one poor editor out of his bed, when they know that he can neither pull a trigger nor wield a pen, and shed his blood—thus violating not only the express language of the Constitution, but every principle of right, religion, and justice—is about as logical as it is magnanimous, or likely to be carried into execution.

But if I am mistaken, and an outrage is to be perpetrated which will stain, with eternal dishonor, Fayette's heretofore proud and fair escutcheon, I pray you, people of Lexington and Fayette, get some men of more truth, of more sense, of more eloquence than these men possess, to give you an excuse to say that you were driven from your propriety to the perpetration of this deed, by the power of genius, which can at times obscure the clearest intellects, and madden the noblest hearts into crime.

CASSIUS M. CLAY.

August 18th, 1845.

No. IV.

LEXINGTON, AUGUST 18, 1845.

THE CHAIRMAN OF THE PUBLIC MEETING ASSEMBLED TO-DAY, WILL PLEASE LAY BEFORE IT THE FOLLOWING COMMUNICATION:

Fellow-citizens of Lexington, and County of Fayette: Being unable from the state of my health, to be present at your meeting, and even unable to hold a pen, having been sick for thirty-five days with the typhoid fever, I dictate to an amanuensis, a few lines for your just consideration. Having been the unwilling cause, in part, of the present excitement in my county, and feeling, as I do, respect for the safety and happiness of others as well as my own, I voluntarily come forward and do all I conscientiously can do for your quiet and satisfaction. I treated the communication from the private caucus with burning contempt, arising not only from their assuming over me a power which would make me a slave, but from a sense of the deep personal indignity with which their unheard-of assumptions were attempted to be carried into execution. But to you—a far differently organized body, and a constitutional assemblage of citizens—I feel that it is just and proper that I should answer at your bar; and as I am not in a state of health to carry on an argument or vindicate properly my own rights, I shall, voluntarily, before any action is taken on your part, make such explanation as I deem just and proper.

During my sickness my paper has been conducted by some friends. The leading article in the last number, which I am told is the great cause of the public disquietude, I have never read; because at the time it was put to press I could not have undergone the fatigue of reading such a paper through. Although it was read over to me at the time, yet I am fully persuaded now, that had I been in health it would not have been admitted into my columns. But I felt the less hesitancy in admitting it, because it has been my avowed policy heretofore to admit free discussion upon the subject of slavery, by slaveholders themselves, and the author of this article is largely interested in that kind of property. You have seen before this time that the course of policy which I commend, myself, to the state, is widely different, in many essential points, from this author's views. The article written by myself, and published in the same paper, was written a few days after the leader was in type, and which has also been the cause of so much dissatisfaction, the justice of which, to some extent, I am willing to acknowledge. I assure you, upon the honor of a man, it was never intended to mean, or to bear the construction which my enemies have given it. I was pursuing the reflections of my own mind, without thinking of the misconstruction that could be put upon my language.

Had I been in the vigor of health, I should have avoided the objectionable expressions, for by sharply guarding against the cavils of my opponents, I would best guard at the same time against anything which could be considered of an incendiary character. I cannot say that the paper from the beginning, has been conducted in the manner I could have wished. The cause of this it is not now necessary for me to mention. Satisfied, however, from past experience, that the free discussion of the subject of slavery is liable to many objections which I did not anticipate, and which I had allowed in an excess of liberality, arising, no doubt, from the fact that I had been denied the columns of the other presses of the country myself, I propose in future very materially to restrict the latitude of discussion. I shall admit into my paper no article upon this subject, for which I am not willing to be held responsible. This, you perceive, will very much narrow the ground; for my plan of emancipation which I put forth a few days ago, is of the most gradual character. My other views put forth there also, are such as I learn are not at all offensive to the great mass of our people. By this course, I expect to achieve two objects, to be enabled to carry on the advocacy of those principles and measures which I deem of vital importance to our state without molestation: and to avoid subjecting the people to the apprehensions and excitement which are now unhappily upon us. You may properly ask, perhaps, why was not this thing done before? I reply, that I did not foresee any such consequences as have resulted from a different course. The denunciations of the public press on both sides, I conceived, and am still of the same opinion, arose from the desire to make for both parties political capital. And you will see also, when the excitement is worn off, that there have been many selfish purposes sought to be accomplished at the expense of your peace and mine, by men who are professing to be actuated by nothing but patriotic motives.

Having said thus much upon the conduct of my paper, I must say also, THAT MY CONSTITUTIONAL RIGHTS I SHALL NEVER ABANDON. I feel as deeply interested in this community as any other man in it. No man is, or has a connexion, more deeply interested, in the prosperity of this state, than myself. You ought not, you cannot, if you are just to me as you are to yourselves, ask me to do that which you would not do. I know not, in reality, what may be the state of public feeling. I am told it is very much inflamed; I, therefore, directed my publisher, after the publication of to-morrow's paper, to exclude all matter upon the subject of slavery, until, if my health is restored, I shall be able myself to take the helm.

My office and dwelling are undefended, except by the laws of my country, to the sacred inviolability of which I confide myself and property; and of these laws you are the sole guardians. You have the power to do as you please.* You will so act, however, I trust, that this day shall not be one ACCURSED to our county and state. Your obedient servant,

CASSIUS M. CLAY.

---

* My enemies have affected to say that in saying they had the " power" I yielded the right. How could I yield the right when I had just said I never would "abandon" it? How could the day be " accursed" if right was done? Of course, physical power only was meant.　　　　　C., 1848.

LEXINGTON, TUESDAY, OCTOBER 7.

Our Appeal.

They, who on the eighteenth day of August, 1845, rose in arms, overpowered the civil authorities, and established an irresponsible despotism upon the Constitutional liberties of this commonwealth, in justification of their conduct "appeal to Kentucky and to the world." So be it. Let Kentucky and the world judge.

When the public peace is disturbed, when the laws are defied, when the Constitution is overthrown, and when, by the avowal of murderous purposes, natural right and Divine justice are impiously violated—not the loss of property, not the individual wrong and suffering, not even the shedding of blood, are to be weighed a moment. But the *great principles of liberty only* are to be borne in mind, whilst individuals, however high or low, are to be forgotten. If it shall turn out that these principles were by me violated or endangered, then was it right that my house should have been rudely entered by personal enemies, threatening me with the dread alternative of death or dishonor. Then was it right that the sick chamber should not awake in the bosoms of the stern vindicators of the law some feeling of pitying sympathy, or magnanimous forbearance. Then was it right that my wife and children should for long days and nights suffer the terrors of impending ruin. Then was it right that I should have my property confiscated. Then was it right that I should be outlawed and exiled from the land of my birth, and the buried ashes of my own loved blood, and ever cherished friends. But if, on the other hand, they, and not I, have done this deed, then let me be restored to the confidence of my countrymen ; to the security of the laws ; to the inviolate sanctity of the home of my native land : and let them be consigned, not to a felon's fate, which is their due by the Constitution and laws of Kentucky, but live out their days with the reflection, that the most they can hope for in the future, is, that their dishonored names will be swallowed up in the magnanimous forgetfulness of coming generations.

In the spring of 1845, I, in connexion with some other Kentuckians made proposals to publish a paper, devoted to *free dis-*

cussion, and gradual emancipation in Kentucky. On the third day of June, of the same year, the True American was issued from the press, having about three hundred subscribers in this state, and about seventeen hundred in the other states. On the twelfth day of August, 1845, the last number of this paper was sent to about seven hundred subscribers in Kentucky, and about twenty-seven hundred in the other states of the Union. These facts are verified by the books of the office, which friend or foe is at liberty to examine. That my readers in Kentucky should have run up, in this short space of about two months, from three to seven hundred, in the face of all the violence and proscription of the enemies of emancipation, voluntarily, without any agencies, and without the distribution of circulars or papers on my part, is a most extraordinary circumstance. And when we reflect that about twenty persons read the paper of each subscriber—making fourteen thousand readers in Kentucky—it proves beyond all controversy, that the principles and tone of my press were taking a powerful hold upon the minds and affections of the people.

The democratic papers were comparatively silent. The whig press was largely in my favor. The Christian Intelligencer soon raised also the standard of emancipation. The people of Louisville had taken the initiatory step for starting a similar paper there. A democratic print of the Green River section—the most pro-slavery part of the state, had copied an article from the True American, showing the ruinous competition of slave labor with that of the whites, and seemed ready to wage a common war. For the first time since the formation of the Constitution of the state was a political party organized for the overthrow of slavery in a legal way; and in the most populous city in the commonwealth a candidate was announced ready to fight the battle upon the stump. A convention of the friends of emancipation was proposed to be held on the fourth day of July, 1846, and met the approval of many able and patriotic citizens. The principal movers in this cause were slaveholders, so also were a majority of the readers of the true American. And the great mass of laborers, who are not habitual readers of newspapers, began to hear, to consider, and to learn their rights, and were preparing to maintain them. So that all things, moving steadily towards the same glorious end, proclaimed, that Kentucky MUST BE FREE !

Previous to the issuing of the ninth number of the True American, I was taken sick with the typhoid fever. A few friends edited the paper till the eleventh number was in press, in which was a leading article written by a slaveholder, and the following editorial written by myself.*

After I had written this, a ride to the office caused a relapse Whilst I lay prostrate with disease, it was told me a few minutes before three o'clock on the fourteenth day of August, that there was to be held at that hour, a meeting of the citizens at the court house, in Lexington, for the purpose of suppressing the True American. I immediately rose and dressed myself, and in opposition to the remonstrances of my family, and at the risk of my life from the exertion, I determined to confront my enemies face to face, and vindicate my cause at all hazards. At the court house I found about thirty individuals, including a few who came in after I left; their names were taken down by a couple of friends and are now in my possession. All these men had grown from political opponents to personal enemies, because of my devotion to the whig cause, except two, "a whig" and "Junius," who were influenced, no doubt, by feelings of revenge on account of the castigation which I had given them in the first number of the True American, for their menace of the murderous infliction of lynch law. After a silence of about half an hour, E. Q. Sayre said he would speak out just the same as if I was not present; he was for suppressing the True American as libellous, by legal means. Henry Johnson, a cotton planter, and the brother of R. M. Johnson, said he understood this meeting was to have been equally composed of whigs and democrats, and for one, he would take no action against this abolition press, unless the whigs came up boldly and shared the responsibility. Thos. F. Marshall, the apostate whig, and late hybrid candidate for congress, said he understood this to be a public meeting,† and was here by an *invitation ;* he held the True American in his hand, and would read what he conceived to be the cause of the public excitement. He then read the article written by me, and took his seat.

Up to this period, no whig had made his appearance. D.

---

* See pamphlet. Lex., 1845.

† In a pamphlet published afterwards under his signature, he says he got up the meeting, and that it was *secret !*

M. Craig now made his entrance; he was a whig: but the supposed author of "a whig," as before stated. He was in a most lachrymose mood—avowed himself my personal friend, but at the same time his determination to use his musket against my life: he said this was a *private* meeting, and in this he was clamorously seconded by the whole mass. During all this time I lay upon a bench, only at intervals being able to sit up. I said I was far from intruding myself upon any set of men—that I had understood this was a public meeting—I threw myself upon their magnanimity—I acknowledged I was in the midst of enemies, yet trusted I would be allowed to explain the article read by Mr. Marshall, which, from his few comments, I found was utterly misconceived, and tortured from its true meaning. I was promptly refused a hearing. Faint, and with lips parched, I turned to T. F. Marshall, as the most chivalric of my enemies—a man whom I had met but a few months before in this same court house, in the presence of an impartial audience of my countrymen, and driven to the wall, upon this same subject of the liberties of men—a man from whom I had extorted an open avowal, "that he had (putting his hand to his heart), *the most profound respect for the gentleman and his opinions and arguments, so new and strong as to demand his more deliberate consideration.*" Who coldly replied: "That he had no more power here than I, being a single individual." I then protested against his construction of my writings, and retired.

Exhausted by this effort, I returned once more to my bed. But feeling the necessity of meeting the vindictive machinations of my enemies, I dictated a handbill to the people, (No. 1) which was taken down by my wife, explaining the offensive editorial, and asking a suspension of public opinion and action, till my health would allow me to be heard.*

I had hardly got through with this when my chamber was entered by Mr. T. H. Waters, my personal enemy, with the following letter:

(See letter.)

---

* In this handbill I briefly narrate the circumstances of the meeting, as here stated. D. M. Craig being the only whig present, I supposed it a party affair, and so stated it. B. W. Dudley, and I. W. Hunt had not then come in, who are whigs, but are said to have been present after I left there.

I now saw that the union of which H. Johnson had spoken, had been consummated, and that a portion of the whig party, sure enough, were about to give me up as a sacrifice, to the malice of foes, made by venturing my life in their cause.* Being determined to die in the defence of my birth-right, the freedom of the press, and the liberty of speech, I appended this short appeal to all true men and friends of law: and sent it to the press:

(See No. I.)

I immediately made preparations for the defence of my office —warned my chosen friends to be ready, to which they manfully assented—wrote my will—and next morning sent my camp bed to the office, as I was unable to sit up. I had thus made every preparation to meet these men of chivalry, who on Monday ventured to hurl defiance at a prostrate foe. They had demanded of me to give them an answer, to discontinue my paper, or that after three o'clock on that day my "personal safety" was lost! Did they come up to their threats? Not they. They found I was still able to drag my feeble body to the place of attack, and rally around me many brave hearts.

With five hundred or more "unanimous" men in the court house, on Friday, at three o'clock, they basely cowered: gave up all hope of a successful attack, and put off the contest for three days, well-knowing that before then, from the report of my physicians, I would be dead, or unable to head my friends. They abandon the *secret* conclave, and appeal to the *public.* On Saturday, the inflammatory piece, "a Kentuckian," made its appearance, and on the same day, they issued a long and lying handbill signed by the committee, to the " People of Lexington, and county of Fayette." Yet they send this with runners and private letters to the *adjoining counties,* calling in the printed bills upon all the enemies of liberty to rally to the " suppression of the True American," but writing on the backs of the same, " to hell with Clay." Seeing that my handbills were relieving the public mind in this county and city, and giv-

---

* The part which the Johnsons took in Wickliffe's and Brown's attempt to assassinate me, a few years ago, is generally believed to have arisen solely from political motives of getting rid of a formidable opponent. The system they imported from Scott county, was to bully opponents in the canvass or at the polls: and this game they were beginning to play quite successfully with the friends of Garret Davis, till the affair at Russell's Cave, taught them that impunity would not await them.

ing way to their fears of being entirely thwarted in their murderous purposes, they issued another handbill, calling for help from the "adjoining counties," from the whole district where Marshall had but just finished a most bitter canvass, and where it was too well supposed that there would be many desperadoes ready for any deed. In their pamphlet, they say this last handbill was authorized by the meeting of Friday, which is *false :* the resolution, as reported by them, confines their call to "the people of Fayette and city of Lexington !"

Finding that the "*secret conclave of cowardly assassins*" had backed out from their purpose of making my "personal safety" "involved in my answer," and had appealed to a public "constitutional" meeting, I told my friends to disarm the office, and leave it to the untrammeled decision of the citizens.

I then wrote my plan of emancipation, addressed to the people :

(See No. II.)

On Sunday I replied to the committee's handbill of Saturday (in No. III.), showing their falsehoods, and denouncing them, and appealing to the justice of the public, at whose bar I intended to appear, if possible. Late on Sunday night, finding myself still more than ever prostrated, and despairing of being able to be present at the meeting on Monday, I dictated this last handbill, read the proof-sheets an hour after midnight, and had it circulated Monday morning, fearing that if it was put off to be read in manuscript, it would be suppressed or unheard :

(See No. IV.)

Here, then, was as conciliatory an offer as any honorable man could ask. I wrote just as I would have spoken, had I been present in a mixed audience, where a few were attempting to hurry on the many to thoughtless deeds of irrevocable infamy. Had I been personally severe in the "True American," on some citizens high in the confidence of the state, I but spoke the real sentiments of my heart when I regretted it. Had I, when worn down with disease, with no friend of similar views to stand by my bedside and give me counsel upon which I could implicitly rely, given utterance incautiously, to language which might by any possibilty be the cause of disaffection among the slaves, I was willing to be more guarded in the future. Had I dangerously given, when incapable of judging, too much liberty to correspondents, who are not always the best qualified to know the effects of their reflections upon a community surrounded by a large slave population, I was willing, for the future to sit in more restrictive judgment upon the freedom and latitude of discussion. All these concessions were freely, frankly, and in good faith, made to save my country's cause and mine. Kentuckians! Americans! was not this enough? Oh no; it was not the manner but the thing; it was not the *words* but *actions* which they feared. They wanted me to say that I would cease the discussion of the subject of slavery; for well did they see from a brief experience, that slavery and a free press could not live together. They wanted me to abandon the exercise of my legal rights. Is any man so base as to say I ought to have yielded? No, my countrymen, remembering what state had given me birth—what I owed my country—what was due my suffering fellow-men—and my obligations to a just God—I replied in words which I supposed to be my last to man, "*my Constitutional rights I shall never abandon.*" But, horrible and fatal necessity! slavery knows not the language of remorse, and cannot indulge the undying instincts of generous magnanimity over a defenceless foe.* She had the decency to listen to my appeal, and I am told that tears stood in the eyes of many— yet the deed must be done, and with melancholy, yet firm despair, she bent herself to the task—and the press fell! and Kentuckians ceased to be free!

On the morning of the 18th of August, George R. Trotter, Judge of the city of Lexington, issued a legal process enjoining the "True American" office and all its appurtenances; and on demand I yielded up the keys to the city marshal. At eleven o'clock on the same day about twelve hundred persons assembled in the court house yard; a chairman and secretary were appointed: a manifesto and resolutions were reported by T. F. Marshall, and adopted. A committee of sixty were appointed † to take down the press and type, and send them to Cincinnati. The committee proceeded to the "True American" office, where

---

* Every one of these handbills was dictated by me to an amanuensis, whilst my hands and head were continually bathed with cold water. to keep the fever down to a point below delirium. Every relative believed I would be murdered on Monday, and all, but my wife and mother, advised me to yield up the liberty of the press: but I preferred rather to die.

† James B. Clay, the son of Henry Clay, was chairman of this committee. C.

the mayor of the city, (who by law has the whole militia of the city at his command) James Logue, warned them that they were doing an illegal act, which he was bound to resist, but that he was overpowered by superior force, and then yielded up possession and the keys. After boxing up the press and type, and all the furniture of the office, and sending them to Cincinnati, they reported again to the meeting at the court house, at three o'clock; and after a speech from Thomas Metcalfe, disavowing all connexion with abolitionism on the part of the Whigs of Kentucky, the meeting adjourned.

Thus, on the 18th day of August, 1845, were the Constitutional liberties of Kentucky overthrown; and an irresponsible despotism of slaveholding aristocracy established on their ruins. They who did the deed call it "dignified," and they supposed that its dignity would shield them from the indignation and curses of men, did they? No, they were not so contemptibly silly as that. They found it necessary in order to cover up the enormity of their crime—(murder, cool and premeditated, and only not consummated because no resistance was offered, according to their own admission, but in reality, because they found hundreds of brave men looking on in sullen silence, ready to die in my defence)—to publish a manifesto to the world, full of darkly studied and damning calumny, in order to shut me off from the sympathies of men and abate the horror of their criminal avowal and dastardly revenge.

They supposed, no doubt, that I would either fall by disease or violence; and, as "dead men tell no tales," it would be easy to blacken my memory, and cover up their own infamy. This last finishing touch was needed to complete the dark portrait of perpetual slavery—that mankind looking upon this picture of slaveholding cruelty, wrong and smooth-faced hypocrisy might be no longer deceived for ever!

In this manifesto, and indictment, and verdict, I am accused:

I. Of being an abolitionist in its southern sense: my northern visit is imputed to me as a crime: and I am declared returning home "the organ and agent of an incendiary sect."

II. I am accused of desiring to put into practical operation the sentiments of the leading article of the "True American" of the 11th number, where I am spoken of as the very author of the same—"The western apostle transcends if possible his mission."

III. It is imputed to me as a crime that I had prepared to defend my property and press against the illegal violence of the people.

IV. I am accused of crime in characterizing American slavery as "the lowest, the basest, the most unmitigated the world had seen;" of being a "daring incendiary, hurling his fire-brands of murder and of lust;" of "responding as a haughty and infuriated fanatic, in terms of outrage, to a committee of gentlemen, who made a wonderfully mild request," and of "denying the right of the citizens to consult together on such a subject;" of being a "madman," and of "preparing himself for a civil war, in which he expected the non-slaveholding laborers, along with the slaves, to flock to his standard;" in calling on the "laborers for whom I have sacrificed so much;" of summoning slaves to my help.

V. I am accused of "attacking the tenure of slave property;" of being "a trespasser" upon slaveholders, and of pushing the community to extremity.

These are cruel charges, and most cruelly have they been avenged. Time was when men were heard, tried, and punished; now, being punished, may I yet be heard?

With regard to the first allegation: I am so far an abolitionist as certain men, named George Washington, and Thomas Jefferson, and some other such "fanatics," who got together in 1776, and enunciated some very "mad and incendiary" doctrines. I followed up the same Washington who, some years after that memorable event, declared that so far as his vote could go towards the abolition of slavery, it should never be wanting. The same Washington, at some time subsequent, liberated all his slaves; I was "fanatic" enough to follow his advice and example, and would have others do likewise, thinking it better to be just than rich. On the other hand, I am opposed to the violation of law in any respect, either for the purpose of liberating a slave, or of murdering by mobs a loyal citizen. I look upon the rebels of the 18th, who bore death and arms in their hands in order to perpetuate slavery, as infinitely lower in crime and infamy than the "incendiary sect," *if such there be*, who would use similar means to liberate the slave. God forbid that I or my countrymen should form an alliance with or submit to the despotism of either. Neither the liberty party, nor the Garrisonians, hold any such murderous doctrines; they are monopolized by the "respectable gentlemen" of the 18th of August. The Garrisonian abolitionists are non-resistants; they hold with O'Connell that no revolution, or change of government, is worth a single drop of human blood. The liberty party holds the doctrine put forth by their convention held at Cincinnati, on the 11th day of June, 1845. They say of slavery, " we believe that its removal can be effected *peaceably, constitutionally*, without real injury to any, with the greatest benefit to all." So that if I was an abolitionist, in its broadest sense, there is no cause or excuse for any number of respectable gentlemen to come upon me and murder me, or trample upon the constitutional liberty of speech, and of the press. The whigs call me a whig: I wrote to the abolitionists on the 11th of June a letter, published in the True American, where I call myself a whig: the abolitionists call me a whig; and the democrats call me a whig: I hold the principles of the whigs of 1776, "eternal resistance to tyrants." And all the renegades, apostates, and traitors in Kentucky shall not shake me from whatever measure I choose to advocate, nor from whatever men I choose to ally myself.

When my visit to the North is imputed to me as a crime, and so voted by prominent whigs of Kentucky, it is time that I should cease to suffer in reputation for their sakes, and speak plainly to them and the nation. Time after time did I receive the most urgent invitations from whigs of the North to come and aid the cause; yet as often did I refuse. I had a great work to perform, and did not wish to place my opponents on the vantage ground. For well did I know that whatever honors I might receive at the North, would be construed by the enemies of emancipation in Kentucky into an alliance with abolitionism.

When at last, however, serious apprehensions began to be entertained that Texas would come into the Union with its unequal representation, slavery, and national dishonor, I felt it my duty to go and give aid to the cause of my country in whatever field of battle she called me. I went by the advice of one of the central committee for the whigs of Kentucky; by special invitation from about fifty whig clubs of the North; by the request, before and after my departure, of four hundred and sixteen committee men, representing clubs, counties, and conventions; by the irresistible persuasion of fifty patriotic whig women of Ohio, and, last of all, by the tacit approval of the leader of the whig party, Henry Clay. The day before I left Lexington, I called upon Mr. Clay, and told him the purpose of my mission ; that it was thought by our friends, that I could have an influence, from my peculiar position, with the anti-slavery, anti-Texas voters of the free states, which no other man could, and that I was willing to go if I could aid the whig cause. Mr. Clay said nothing, but nodded his head with an approving smile ; and after some unimportant conversation he offered me letters of introduction, which I declined as unnecessary. Whether I accomplished any good there or not remains for others to say. It is enough for me to know, if I were vain enough to assume to myself consideration which belongs to the vital interests which were at stake in the canvass, that never did any man of my age in America draw together such large and intensely interested audiences. The greatest intellect of the nation, the greatest orator of any age, said to me, " They had rather hear you than me." The most large-souled, uncompromising man in the Union was pleased to compliment me : " We regard you as one of the pillars of the great temple of American liberty." I mention these things not with the silly vanity of self-elation : I knew them undeserved, and the overflow of hearts touched with sympathy for a man who had suffered proscription in the cause of justice and truth—for a man of proper feeling is less wounded by censure than unmerited compliment, and loves more to deserve praise than to receive it—but because much enmity and denunciation have been poured upon me here, charging me with being the cause of Mr. Clay's defeat, by my visit to the North, and by forcing him into the Gazette letter !

The Speed letter—ay, the Speed letter ! Well, then, if the whole truth must be told, the whigs of New York are solely responsible for the effect of that letter, if any it had ; they published it *without my advice, and in opposition to my consent.* The letter, on its face, shows itself to be confidential, and not intended for the public eye. I have by me, Mr. Speed's letter, apologizing for the action of his friends in publishing it in his absence, and without his consent, because of the eminent service it was thought it would render the cause. As soon as Mr. Clay's letter to the Kentucky Gazette was received by me, I immediately sat down to a table and wrote to him, that I was grieved if I had misunderstood his sentiments, drawn as my opinion was from his whole history, and repeated written declarations ; that if he was not favorable to emancipation I regretted it on my own account, on his account, and on account of our common country. That I was devoting myself unweariedly and honestly to the success of that party whose triumph was to result in his elevation ; but if *he* conceived me doing any injury to the cause, that I would not again open my mouth in the canvass. His answer was that stolen from Horace Greeley, and published without my ever having seen it, by the democracy of New York. During my whole visit to the North, although I was cordially received by the anti-slavery men of all parties, I addressed but two abolition meetings, and then it was to defend the proposition of Henry Clay and the slaveholders, that "That is property which the law makes property." Everywhere among abolitionists I made some enemies by defending this dogma ; which now, by the disregard of all law, avowed on the eighteenth, is of no more effect, but null and void. Everywhere, among abolitionists especially, did I make enemies by defending Henry Clay. How then dare Henry Clay's son, and Kentucky whigs, sit in solemn conclave and vote me to be "the organ and agent of an incendiary sect ?" and under this pretext, to rob me of my property and threaten me with murder ? To my brother whigs throughout the Union, I appeal from this ungrateful and calumnious accusation.

The second charge, holding me responsible for being about to enforce the sentiments of the author of the leader, in the eleventh number of the "True American," who is of their own brotherhood, not *mine*, being a *slaveholder*, when they had my own written opinions before them, utterly different in many essential respects, is as false as it is impudent. Denied myself the use of the press of all parties, on my return from the North, criminally accused in my absence, and not allowed to vindicate myself, it would have been strange indeed if I had refused even a slaveholder a hearing, who uttered his thoughts boldly and honestly. My paper was intended to embody the differing opinions of all Kentuckians; and I said in the beginning that all the editorials would admit of very variant opinions without comment from me. In the same number with this leader, I promised in my very next to give my "individual opinions" upon emancipation. But these they did not want to hear; for well they knew that they would give the lie to all they had been saying about my abolitionism, for months and years. Have our masters grown so fastidious that they cannot bear simple propositions, which are safe and peaceable, stated, without becoming mad with impotent rage? For none of these "respectable gentlemen" have said that the leader was either *unjust* or *untrue*, or that it was incendiary. How then, even if I had endorsed it, could it have been imputed to me as a crime?

In regard to the third allegation : it is indeed a strange state of civil society, when the very basis upon which all associations of men are formed, is imputed to a man as a crime. If self-defence which is so much an axiom : so commanding the instinctive approbation of all men and times as to be known as the "first law of nature," has to be defended, I might as well quit the field in despair. But if it was not a virtue of the highest order, to resist mobs, which are violators of the peace, and in derogation of the dignity and safety of the commonwealth, I need but bring the National and state Constitutions to my defence, which place the right of the citizen "to bear arms in self-defence," beyond the power of legislation, higher and more sacred than the Constitution itself. I was threatened with mobs by all the city papers, before I began to publish the "True American"; then, and not till then, did I prepare for defence. Against partial mobs, emeutes, and black Indians, whether one or a thousand, I was prepared to defend myself; yes, against the "secret conclave of cowardly assassins" I prepared myself, and dared them to the onset; and as I anticipated in the beginning, by them I stood unharmed, only because I was defended. Born free and independent, with my name associated eternally with the commonwealth, whose honor and safety I was bound by the laws of God and nature to support, I did not come secretly sneaking as a traitor with bated breath, *whispering treason and murder;* but glorying in my birthright, I proudly spread my banner, "God and Liberty," to the eyes of men, and vowed my determination to defend it or die. But in that once proud state, for whose best interests I was ever willing to risk my all, I never anticipated a total overthrow of the *civil power;* for upon that, and the justice and magnanimity of the great mass of my countrymen, I relied for security, after I had swept down, if necessary, thousands of traitors and murderers, who were as much their enemies as mine. My office, if a fortified, was not a provisioned fort; so these men, not I, are mad, when they would represent me as warring against the whole community. But let no man misunderstand me. Still, in that case, I would yield only to superior *brute force;* if every man in the district was against me, I do not admit the *right* even of a whole community to do an illegal act. The case of invasion by a foreign power is not a parallel case: that is only not forbidden by law, but these men acted not only *without* the sanction of law, but against it, and in violation of its most sacred purposes; which are, to guard the weak against the strong and many. No, my countrymen, there is no liberty here, if every man in this state should join to enslave the press, whilst the Constitution stands an eternal barrier to, and in stern condemnation of the crime.

In the fourth and principal charge, the editorial already given is urged against me. It is true that I spoke of slavery as I felt and knew it to be. Whilst I admit now, and ever have, the humanity of many masters, and whilst I have *never denounced slaveholders as a class*, still I maintain, that American slavery, its system, its laws, and its possible abuses, make it " the lowest, the basest, and the most unmitigated the world has seen." The Jews had their jubilees; the Romans and Greeks admitted the freedman at once into the class of masters; the Turk makes his slave his wife, and admits her equality in the household; the Asiatic, and the African, and the European slave fall not to the level of ours. For here color, and natural differences of structure and capacity, heighten the deformities of slavery, and increase its difficulties, its cruelties, and its dangers. On this question I spoke as one man to his equal: and who shall be my censors? It can be offensive to none, but the basely guilty. If false, let it be proven! If true, let it be remedied. But as for mere clamor—I contemn it. "Go, show your slaves how choleric you are, and make your bondmen tremble. Must I budge? Must I observe you? Must I stand and crouch under your testy humors? By the Gods, you shall digest the venom of your spleen though it do split you." Impartial men must remember, that this was written by a man just able to wield a pen, after a most dangerous and brain-oppressing fever. It is the dreamy abstract speculation of the invalid purified by suffering, unguarded and unsuspecting, because conscious of a high and elevated motive. It is not an invitation to evil, or a vicious gloating upon suffering foreseen, but the great yearning of a heart full of humanity, to save others from impending ruin.

There are in it, I frankly admit, words which seem to look to a servile insurrection, and to name such an event is, as the author of "A Kentuckian," also, ought to know, to invite it. This I simply regret, not on my own account, but on account of the cause, which is more dear to me than life. My war is upon slavery, not upon slaveholders, I repeat once more. As no man in Kentucky had more to lose, so no man had more reason than I to avoid even the suspicion of insurrection. All human probabilities conspire to sustain me, when I assert before heaven and earth, that such a thought never entered my head. Come, then, ye testy cavillers, I say the proposition is true, in its letter, and in its spirit, and in its broadest meaning! Yes, this much abused article but reiterates *that virtue is the only secure basis for republics.*[*] Such has been the doctrine from Longinus, running down through all writers upon government till the final repetition of it in Washington's Farewell Address to the American people. The consciences of slaveholders bear testimony to its immortal truth, and neither calumny nor murder can eradicate it from the convictions of mankind. Need I maintain an argument to prove that slavery is subversive of virtue, and consequently dangerous to republics, and death to liberty? Go, listen to your Hammonds, and let pulpit hypocrites stultify themselves and you, in discussing and refuting the language, reason, and the irrepressible axioms of the heart. Shall I contend that slavery is at war with the virtue and justice of this nation? Behold our broken constitutions, our violated laws, our tarnished faith, our wounded honor, our rapacious wars, our plundering conquests, our insulted ambassadors, our imprisoned citizens, our robbed presses, our murdered people, and tell me if I be a "fanatic" when I say that slavery threatens all law, and our whole system of republicanism, the ruin of property, and the loss of life. Whether, then, slavery stood by the avarice and selfishness of the farmer of Kentucky, the planter of Louisiana, the manufacturer of Lowell, the cotton merchant of New York, the pork dealer of Cincinnati, or the speculators upon slave labor

---

[*] "Sine summa justitia, rempublicam geri nulla modo posse."—CICERO. "I must fairly tell you, that so far as my principles are concerned, that I have no idea of liberty unconnected with *virtue*. Nor do I believe that any good constitutions of government can find it necessary for their security to doom any part of the people to a permanent slavery." Burke. See Montesquieu's L'Esprit des Lois; Vattell's Laws of Nations; Paley, etc., passim.

-all over the Union; I wished to appeal to the strongest motives of the human heart, the love of money and the adoration of women, to arouse them to its inevitable and disastrous consequences. Will any one of these men tell me the guards which they propose to thrust between the "silver on the board," and the daughters of wealth, with hands unhardened by toil; yes, the "smooth-skinned women on the ottoman," and the plundered poor, the lawless whose existence is pre-supposed by the very necessity of government at all? Come, now, fastidious statesman, you who have had time to reflect, please tell me, that I may in the future avoid your wrath, and my country escape this great woe! Shall it be by law? That you have sacrificed to slavery! Shall it be by a long instilled and sacred reverence for the Constitution? That you have trampled under foot! Shall it be by an appeal to a common interest between the rich and the poor—the only basis of republicanism? You have separated the great mass of the American people from you, by slavery, by studied contempt, and the impassable barriers of ignorance and poverty! You will appeal to a strong government and a king—will you? Look back through history and learn, that no republic has passed into a monarchy without long years of blood and anarchy, in which perish property, men, women, and children; and when are not spared the statues of dead men, nor the temples of the living God! The last clause in the article, which has been basely tortured into the *present now*, every sensible man will see is dependent upon the contingency *when* virtue is lost. It may be now, to-morrow, next year, the next hundred years, and if virtue is *never* rooted out of the minds of the people, *never!*

Has it come to this, that I am to be drawn up, and publicly censured for speaking in plain and manly language to men, who order me to relinquish my birthright, or die. "Go tyrants, I am not yet a slave." Are you *men?* Kentuckians, is not this shameful? Alas! have we so soon "lost the breed of noble bloods?"

It is not true that I "denied the right of the citizens to consult together on such a subject."

On the contrary, I did acknowledge their right, by my repeated appeals to them; not only to consult, but to advise—to warn; but then their office was at an end. They could no more than a single person, go farther than the laws allowed. Had they confined themselves to this, much good would have resulted. There is a moral power in the proceedings and counsel of the assembled people in the public discharge of duty, when within the bounds of law and justice, which no sensible man will disregard, so long as principle be not violated. But when they transcend their power, they sink into the dust, impotent and contemptible as the meanest faction, and all *men* will stand by me when I defy them, as I do now Whether they will best accomplish their purpose by the course pursued, time will develope, and may God defend the right!

For whom "have I sacrificed so much?" *For the six hundred thousand free white laborers of Kentucky!* Against whose every vital interest slavery wages an eternal and implacable war! For them I lost caste with the slaveholding aristocracy of the land! For them I liberated my slaves! For them have I sacrificed all chance of political elevation in my native state! For them have I lived, and for them have I stood ready to die! They who have never eaten of my bread, and stabbed me in the dark; they, who have stood by me again and again, without hope of reward; they, whose children gazing in my face with lovely eyes and reproachful confidence, seemed to say, "what are you, as a legislator, doing for us? Shall we not be enabled to be fed and clothed as the children of slaveholders? Shall we not have school-houses and churches, and be taught to know how to work to advantage? Shall we not be so placed, as to be able to possess a small piece of land, or at all events, if we are manufacturers, to sell our wares, or if we are mechanics, to find continual employment at fair wages? Shall we not change our log cabins daubed with mud, and chilled by the winds of winter, into comfortable little cottages, with some evidences of taste, in yards of flowers and shrubs? Save us, we pray you, from *necessary idleness* and *dishonorable work*—spare yourselves the expense of jails and penitentiaries, and rescue us from the chances of a felon's fate!" Yes, these are the men, the great majority of the people of Kentucky, whose interests, in 1841, I swore I would never betray— for whom I then fell, and now suffer. How long, my countrymen, seeing you have the power of the ballot-box, shall these things be? Will you not at last be removed from prejudice, which poisons you with hatred and injustice to the blacks? Enslaved by passions which our masters cunningly infuse into us from our very cradle—will you never open your eyes and be free? Will you not at last awake, arise, and be men? Then shall I be delivered from this outlawry, this impending ruin, this insufferable exile, this living death!

Not upon the slaves did I call. How could I? Is any man in Kentucky so base as to charge that I have held secret conference with the slaves? No, not one! How then could I call upon the slaves, who could not read, one in a hundred? With all my relations and kindred, slaveholders, many of them ministering in turn at my sick couch, by day and by night—all to be involved in one common ruin—warring one county against a whole state—and I prostrate, and unable to raise my head—to call upon the slaves to rally to the standard of civil war! I refrain from expressing the great indignation which such gross and monstrous calumny cannot but generate in the coldest bosom. Go search my secret and public life, from the cradle up, and tell the world by what steps I have gradually prepared myself for this last round of unmixed depravity! When have I stript the poor? When played the sycophant to the powerful? Where have I lied? What party betrayed? What friend deserted? When have I stolen or robbed? When did I counterfeit? Whom have I secretly injured? In what penitentiaries have I served an apprenticeship to crime? Whom have I secretly poisoned? Whom have I openly murdered? Then, before this charge, in the face of Kentucky and the world, I stand mute! Poor and friendless—broken in spirit and in hope—outlawed and exiled though I be, there is something yet remaining, of what a man, a proud, just, honest man should be, and I shall not stoop to plead not guilty, not here, nor now!

In the fifth and last count of this indictment, I am accused of "attacking the tenure of the property of slaveholders," of being a "trespasser on them," and of "pushing the community to extremity." Now, I deny that I have ever attacked the legal tenure of slave property. The justice of a law is one thing, its validity another. I call for proof. My writings for five years are before them and the world. I challenge them to the proof. They can never produce it. How then can I be a "trespasser upon them?" I have ever vindicated their legal right to *their property:* they have robbed me of *mine!* They have taken more property from me than the average value of the slaves held by masters in Kentucky. If then their accusation were true, and not false, perpetual silence should have sealed their lips : the robber, if I be one, has been doubly robbed !

I did not push the community to extremity. For, in addition to my other concessions, I was willing to suspend the paper till my health was restored. No, by all that is sacred among men, it was not the community, but slavery, which I was pushing to extremity ! Those slaveholders who favored emancipation, cared not what I said of slavery, as my subscription list proves : those who did not and never did intend to favor it, I was not fool enough to attempt to persuade. If slavery never falls till it falls by the consent of slaveholders, it will never fall " in the tide of times." How many of all the monarchs of the world will any man of sense undertake to persuade to lay down the sceptre ? Governor Hammond, in speaking of " moral suasion," addressed to slaveholders, tells but simple truth, when, in writing to the venerable Thomas Clarkson, he says, " *you know it is mere nonsense.*" John Green, of Kentucky, one of the mildest, the best, and most impartial men that ever lived, said in the Luminary, in 1836 : " It is but natural that a stranger, in passing through our state, should take up such impressions, from the liberal tone in which our politicians, and other intelligent men, speak on the subject, so long as they are permitted to deal in generals, and to qualify their remarks by the important word IF. But if you call upon them to propose some plan, and to commence *action*, they will *almost universally* draw back. I think I know something of our public men, and I tell you they are for doing NOTHING." Let me be no more, then, " damned with faint praise " that my motives are good, but that I am rash and denunciatory." No, my countrymen, it is not *words*, but *action*, for which I am now outlawed.

The slaveholders of the other counties have dropt the stale and shallow plea of *incendiarism*, and say that *slavery shall not be discussed*. This is the only and true issue. This manifesto means it, though it was ashamed to say it. Else why speak of its constitutional guaranties ? Now the United States Constitution leaves it fairly within the power of change. The Kentucky Constitution, article II, section 1, thus reads : " The General Assembly shall have no power to pass laws for the emancipation of slaves, without the consent of their owners, or without paying their owners previous to such emancipation, a full equivalent in money for the slaves so emancipated." It is true,

we of the emancipation party have never pressed this power, because we deemed it impracticable in execution. Yet, here is a
clause putting the whole question fairly within the field of discussion, because in the field of *action*—which relieves us of the
necessity of claiming in our defence the constitutional rights
and specific guaranties of the liberty of speech and the press.

I say, then, that this last, and all these allegations against
me are *false and calumnious*, and for my own justification, I
appeal to Kentucky and to the world.

Having said thus much upon this subject, in connexion with
my own name, in order to develop its injustice and studied cruelty and determined wrong, I shall now consider it in its far
more important bearing upon the liberties of the State and the
Nation.

Section II., article VI., Kentucky Constitution, has this definition of treason : "Treason against the commonwealth shall
consist only in levying war against, or in adhering to its enemies, giving them aid and comfort." Now here was a great
party of men who rose up and declared themselves *armed*—
"We are armed and resolved"—they go to the civil authorities,
the Mayor and Marshal of the city of Lexington, officers of the
commonwealth, who warn them that an illegal act is about to
be perpetrated—and with arms and an overpowering force eject
them and take property which was yielded up to the possession
of·the law. Not only do they fail to make restitution, but they
avow their determination to continue their illegal action, and if
necessary, to shed blood—to commit murder upon peaceable
citizens. Now if this is not "levying war against the commonwealth," then is human language utterly incapable of conveying any thing intelligible. It was a *revolution*, bloodless,
only because no physical resistance was made, as they themselves avow. What is the commonwealth? its officers? Against
them they levied war. What is the commonwealth? its constitution? That they avowedly set aside as being incompetent
to meet the case. What is the commonwealth? its laws? They
proclaimed that there was no legal power for their action. They
put it down in writing that there was usurped an original or
revolutionary power. The assembly was called in open day—
its president was a magistrate, a sworn conservator of the peace
at other times—its action was deliberate and "dignified"—its
numbers were large, and its force irresistible—its end the sup-

pression of the press and the Constitution of the State—and lastly, it solemnly appealed to the world in justification of its proceedings. If this be not a revolution, then never has one taken place in the history of men. No matter what may have been the provocation on my part—even though I had been proved an insurrectionist—even though I had been caught applying the torch to dwellings of defenceless women and children —even though I had been taken with hands red with the blood of my fellow-citizens—still the character of this action is unchanged in the least respect. The press had passed from my possession—it was stopped by legal process—whatever danger it threatened, if any, was past—it had become inert matter, incapable of moral or legal wrong—and even if it had not, the commonwealth only was responsible for its influence, whether good or bad upon the safety of the community, which these men effected to believe endangered, but of which, in reality, they themselves were the only enemies.

On the 18th day of August, then, were the constitutional liberties of Kentucky forcibly overthrown, and an irresponsible oligarchy of slaveholders established on their ruins.

They may allow Governor Owsley to retain his seat at the head of the executive department—they may permit the legislature to pass such laws as suit them—they may, in a word, suffer the forms and machinery of a free government to go on —but be assured, men of Kentucky, you are nevertheless *slaves.*

Be assured that you live under an anarchical despotism. The same men who robbed me of my press, have sat as a jury and justified the deed, and declared there was no offence against the laws! What care they, who plot murder, for violated oaths? The respectable slaveholding mob of the 18th, sat in judgment upon the " ungentlemanly" mob of the 19th by arms and force, claiming for themselves only supreme irresponsible power. The " canaille" of the 19th were drawn up before the courts and punished—the " respectable" gentlemen of the 18th beyond all human computation more guilty, went unwhipt of justice. Surely the king can do wrong! Whilst I speak there are now ordered some hundreds of armed men by the Governor into Clay county to preserve what little remnant of civil authority, and the old form of government may yet remain. What will this come to? Where does it all lead? It requires no prophetic eye to see blood flowing knee deep ere this damnable usurpation come to the still grave of unresisted and hopeless despotism! Did they say to Stevenson of Georgetown, print no more upon the subject of slavery? Has the Louisville Journal been silenced? In Lincoln, and Jefferson, and Nelson, will a peaceable citizen be drawn from his bed at midnight and be hung to a limb or shot down like a dog in the day if he venture to read one-half of the newspapers of America? Are not these men mad? Are they not spinning for themselves a web, which, like the shirt of Nessus will, instead of *protecting*, involve them in utter ruin and despair? Who in South Carolina dare now discuss slavery? Can Calhoun—can Hammond plead, if he would, for emancipation? Have they not raised a Devil which the combined intellect of the state cannot lay, though death look them in the face, and the grave open beneath their feet? " Madmen and fanatics," would you place Kentucky in the same category? Will you not allow us to be saved now while it is to-day—and whilst the evil years come not?

By what tenure do you hold your slaves? Is it by natural right, or by the Constitution? If the Constitution be overthrown is not the slave free? Will the other states return him into bondage? Will they interfere to put down domestic violence, when by you all legal security is first destroyed? When you avow yourselves murderers in purpose, will the North be thus cured of dangerous fanaticism? Will not blood answer to blood, and the earth cry out unceasingly for vengeance? Is not the liberty of the press the common concern of the whole American people? Can you plant your iron heel upon the ten million of northern freemen? Are Bunker Hill and Lexington ideal names? and do I dream when I find myself planted upon a soil which was named in solemn dedication and remembrance of that land which was wet by the blood of those who knew not how to be slaves and live? Can any people be free who voluntarily yield to illegal force a single right? Do I not owe allegiance to the National government; may she not call upon me at any hour to lay down my life in her defence? Then does she not in turn owe me protection? Can the sheep be safe when all the watch dogs are slain! Can the nation be free when all the presses are muzzled? Have not the organs of two administrations made relentless war upon me, a private individual? What is there in my person so terrible to the slave power? Is there any thing more terrible to tyrants than

the liberty of the press? Will not emissaries from a slaveholding President do in the free states to-morrow what is done with
impunity here to-day? Do not the cries of the blood hounds of
national patronage, crying for my blood as freely as the despots
of the South, strike terror into the souls of Northern men?

Can it be that the liberty of the press is so small a thing?
Know ye not, Americans, that when the liberty of speech and
of the press is lost, all is lost? Heavens and earth! must I
argue this question with the descendants of Washington and
Adams? Well, then, Euripides said: "This is true liberty,
where free-born men, having to advise the public, may speak
free." Said Chatham: "Sorry I am to hear liberty of speech
in this house imputed as a crime; it is a liberty I mean to exercise; no gentleman ought to be afraid to exercise it." John
Milton: "And although all the winds of doctrine were let loose
to play upon the earth, so truth be in the field, we do injurious-
ly, by licensing and prohibiting to misdoubt her strength. Let
her and falsehood grapple. Who ever knew truth put to the
worse in a free and open encounter?" Daniel Webster, speaking of the freedom of opinion: "It may be silenced by military
power, but cannot be conquered. It is elastic, irrepressible, and
invulnerable to the weapons of ordinary warfare. It is that impassable, inextinguishable enemy of mere violence and arbitrary rule, which, like Milton's angels,

> ' Vital in every part,
> Cannot, but by annihilating, die ' "

Until this be propitiated or satisfied, it is in vain for power
to talk either of triumph or repose. Erskine: "The proposition
I mean to maintain as the basis of the liberty of the press, and
without which it is an empty sound, is this, that every man not
intending to mislead, but seeking to enlighten others, what with
his own reason and conscience, however erroneously, have dictated to him as truth, may address himself to the universal reason of a whole nation, either upon the subject of governments in
general, or upon that of our own particular country; that he
may analyze the principles of its Constitution, *point out its errors and defects, examine and publish its corruptions*, warn
his fellow citizens against their ruinous consequences, and exert his whole faculties in pointing out the most advantageous

changes in establishments which he considers radically defective, or sliding from their object by abuse."

John Milton, again : " For this is not the liberty which we can
hope, that no grievance should ever rise in the commonwealth ;
that let no man in this world expect; but when complaints are
freely heard, deeply considered, and speedily reformed, then is
the utmost bound of civil liberty attained that wise men
look for."

Plutarch nobly says : " Without liberty there is nothing good,
nothing worthy the desires of men."

Rotteck : " Curse on his memory ! The press is to words
what the tongue is to thoughts. Who will constrain the tongue
to ask permission for the word it shall speak, or forbid the soul
to general thoughts ? *What should be free and sacred if not
the press ?*"

Benjamin Franklin : "*Freedom of speech is the principal
pillar of a free government : when this support is taken
away, the Constitution of free government is dissolved, and
tyranny is erected on its ruins.*"

Erskine : " It is because the liberty of the press resolves itself
into this great issue, that it has been in every country the
the last liberty which subjects have been able to wrest from the
hands of power. Other liberties are held *under* government,
but the liberty of opinion keeps *governments themselves* in
due subjection to their duties. *This has produced the mar-
tyrdom of truth in every age, and the world has only been
purged from ignorance with the innocent blood of those who
have enlightened it.*"

James McIntosh : " One asylum of free discussion is still inviolate. There is still one spot in Europe where man can exercise his reason on the most important concerns of society ;
where he can boldly publish his thoughts on the acts of the
proudest and most powerful tyrants.

" The press of England is still free. It is guarded by the
free Constitution of our forefathers ; it is guarded by the hearts
and arms of Englishmen, and I trust that I may venture to
say, that if it be to fall, it will fall only under the ruins of
the British empire."

Curran : " What then remains ? The liberty of the press
only ; that sacred Palladium which no influence, no power, no
minister, no government, which nothing but the depravity or

folly of a jury can ever destroy. As the advocate of society, therefore, of peace, of domestic liberty, and the lasting union of the two countries, I conjure you to guard the liberty of the press—that great sentinel of the state, that grand detector of public imposture—guard it; because, when it sinks, then sinks with it, in one common grave, the liberty of the subject, and the security of the crown."

Such are the opinions of some of the great and good of other times, which seem to burst from agonized souls amid tears and blood.

But our fathers did not leave this basis of all liberty to the uncertain opinions of men. The United States' Constitution, article 1, of A., says: "Congress shall make no law, abridging the freedom of speech, or of the press." The Constitution of Kentucky, section 7, article 10, says: "The presses shall be free to every person who undertakes to examine the proceedings of the legislative, or any branch of government; and no law shall ever be made to restrain the right thereof. The free communication of thought and opinions, is one of the invaluable rights of man, and every citizen may freely write, speak, or print, on any subject, being responsible for the abuse of that liberty." Then I call upon William Owsley, Governor of Kentucky, to protect me in the constitutional re-establishment of the liberty of the press. This is a case of domestic violence. If he has not power enough here in Kentucky, I demand of him, in the name of the spirit of the fourth article of the Constitution, to call upon James K. Polk, President of the United States, to assist, with all the power of the national arm, in vindicating the violated laws, and a broken Constitution. The liberty of the press is my inheritance. It is mine, by the common law of the land. Congress has no power to take it away, but to make it secure. I implore the American people to vindicate their birthright and mine. To the national government I owe allegiance, and in turn I claim of it protection; I demand of the congress of the United States to pass suitable laws, by which the rebels of the 18th, if they attempt to redeem their pledge and renew their violence, may be brought to summary punishment, so that I be protected in the liberty of speech and of the press. Yes, Americans, if you are not slaves, this thing will have to be done. It is your cause and not mine. Justice demands it—the Constitution demands it—

your own safety demands it—virtue and humanity demand it— then, in the name of God and liberty, let it be done.

In the meantime, I stand here on my native land, for which my kindred have bled in every field of honorable achievement —one amidst a thousand—undismayed by the dangers and death, which, like the plague, with mysterious and impassable terrors, by day and by night, hang over me and mine—trusting that my position may arouse in the bosoms of Americans, an honorable shame and a magnanimous remorse—that they may rise up in the omnipotency of the ballot, cast by fifteen millions of freemen, and peaceably overthrow the slave despotism of this nation—and avoid the damning infamy which awaits them for all time, in the judgment of the civilized world, if they leave me here to die !

To the liberty of my country and of mankind, then I dedicate myself and those whom I hold yet more dear—and for the purity of my motives, and the patriotism of my life, the past and the future, I "appeal to Kentucky and to the world."

CASSIUS M. CLAY.

Lexington, Ky., Sept. 25, 1845.

LEXINGTON, TUESDAY, OCTOBER 14.

SLAVERY.

In pursuance of our original plan, we insert in the editorial columns to-day, an able article. We intend to allow our fellow-citizens, whose ability entitle them to the place, to speak there for themselves, without comment from us.

LEXINGTON, TUESDAY, OCTOBER 21.

OUR PRINTING OFFICE,

Was moved one day in our absence, to Cincinnati, by some of our friends. It puts us to some inconvenience, but we are good natured, and used to ill-usage; we *don't* say much about it, *they can't!*

POWDER !

The slaveholders of the 18th admit that there is pressing danger from our slaves—fire—lust—and murder. Yes, slavery is a " powder house," say they, which a madman may blow up ! Say you so, my respectable masters ? Then, by all the instincts of self-preservation, we demand of you to remove this powder-house from among us. What right have you, the 31,000, to keep " powder " in your houses, which may blow up the 600,000 free whites of our unhappy country ? In the name of our wives, our children, our daughters and sons, our friends and relations, our homes and our country, we demand that this " *nuisance*" be removed, as utterly intolerable, and dangerous to our peace and safety.

LEXINGTON, TUESDAY, OCTOBER 28.

THE KENTUCKY PRESS

Is rallying again ; they begin to denounce the mob indirectly. Well, " every dog will have his day," at last.

EUGENE SUE.

We have seen this celebrated and most interesting novelist decried of late, as grossly vicious in his works, by many of our own, and foreign lands : and some have gone so far as to deny him genius and extraordinary power. The latter allegation is too absurd for refutation ; in the language of logicians it would be " proving too much." We are willing to admit, that many of the scenes, and characters, and persons, to us of original and simple manners and unclassic education, are too warmly colored.

But there are extremes among men; and extremes, says the adage, meet: the most refined and the most savage nations, in some respects, stand upon the same platform, when things are called by their right names, and persons seen and described as they are.

The retired countryman supposes that the city belle, with anti-Procrustian dress and manners free, is necessarily impure. And the secluded American and Englishman, with oriental ideas of the sanctity of womankind, look with a suspicious eye upon the French—the modern Greeks of Europe. With the same scale they weigh the gregarious Parisians, in which they balance the staid English or American woman—the fireside—the bed-chamber—the *home*. Now there is equal folly or ignorance displayed by the countryman and the Puritan: and men of the world, of enlarged views, laugh at the conclusions of both.

The people of Paris live mostly in hotels: they have not even a word in their language which signifies *home*. Paris is full of paintings and statues of the first masters and the most free and classic school. She has been the centre of refinement for centuries: not only the higher classes, but the sans culottes and fish-women, of this Babylon of all tongues and climes, are admitted to public exhibitions from their very infancy. They thus see and become familiar with all parts of the human person *before the passions are developed*, and learn to look on with indifference, and speak without shame, because without sense of impropriety or guilt. An American woman looks for the first time upon the Medicean Venus, and blushes of course: but she gazes into the eye of the passing stranger till his very soul is electrified with her mysterious and enchanting influence, and deems herself within the strictest bounds of propriety: for what are the souls of men made for but to be volatilized in her magic crucible? The French woman looks on the Apollo with cold unconsciousness, because she is used to it: but she blushes to gaze into the eager eyes of the stranger, because custom forbids it; and to her it is unchaste. The man, then, who would undertake to judge of these two distinct nations of women by the same indications is little else than a fool. Mr. Sue is a Frenchman; he writes for the French people; he must reach the French heart, or he had better not write at all!

But when he treats of virtue, is she not made more lovely under the golden touches of his pencil? If of vice, does she not gloom into horrid deformity and ugliness under his remorseless pen? If he speaks to the poor, does he not open up to them industry, perseverance, long suffering, hope, and ultimate happiness? If to the rich does he not show them wherein their riches may doubly bless them—the giver and the receiver? Thanks to Eugene Sue that he can discern virtue in rags, and strip vice of its Khorassan veil. Thanks to him that he removes from the humble their envy and malice, and from the rich, their supercilious contempt and haughty indifference towards their humbler brothers of earth. Honor to his sagacity, and wide judgment of intellect, that he sees at a glance, the only basis of safety to society, mutual interest and mutual respect between the humble and the exalted, the rich and the poor, the beautiful and the deformed, the happy and the miserable. A true philosopher he, who, in the glorious and good, sees something earthy and unsanctified—and in the debased and fallen some elements of regeneration and undying hope.

We admit there is something wanting in his universality—something too proscriptive against the Catholic religion, in his Wandering Jew, which we do not sanction or commend : but he says himself that he desires to expose its abuses ; not disturb its faith and truth. He wars against remorseless power where-ever displayed—in religion—in politics--in the social circle ; priestcraft—servitude and exclusiveness—all sit heavily upon the wings of this high soaring son of liberty and equality among men. Neither the power engrossing machinery of the Catholic religion ; American slavery ; nor social oppression find favor with him. Sue is not a mere novelist, nor simply a moralist, but he combines many of the higher qualities of both in the far seeing and man-regenerating statesman. Not in the halls of legislation, live always the rulers of men. The democratic principle grows apace among the nations of the world, and many begin to hear her voice in the wilderness. Priests worthy of her glorious ministration speak once more from her long mute altars of Delphic prescience, and among the highest, holiest, and most loved of these is Eugene Sue.

The Beginning of the End.—Mason, (Ky.,) Meeting.)

We gave, last week, the proceedings of the citizens of Mason county meeting, called after a long and deliberate call, with a hurried notice of the same.   Although we have received rough handling, it is yet our pride to hail these proceedings as the first *victory* of the emancipation party in Kentucky.   The resolutions of Reid, and those of Waller, sustaining the Lexington rebels, were *voted down!*   Thanks, sons of Kentucky, for thus much.

We subscribe to the first resolution with all our heart; it damns for ever the action of the 18th.

We subscribe to the second resolution, with this qualification, that the "irreparable" injury must be *greater* than the one inflicted by the use of revolutionary power.   The claim of Great Britain "to tax the colonies in all cases whatever," was a case of that kind.   Here the injury threatened was wide-spread, eternal, and utterly destructive of all liberty.   But the case of the Vicksburg mob, the Joe Smith mob, the Boston convent mob, and no other mob which has taken place in this Union, justify the second resolution.   Not even a revolution, however necessary and seemingly expedient, can have the sanction of the second resolution, unless that revolution be founded on justice. The mob of the 18th were using urgent means in an unjust cause.   We cannot, if we are about burning a man's house, take his life, even in self-defence, because our unjust action bars all the means of enforcing it, and forfeits original as well as incidental rights.   Far less will mere suspicion that an unjust action will be punished by others, warrant a defensive attack.   Even if servile insurrection were a consequence of the discussion of slavery, which it is not, and slaveholders could prevent insurrection by emancipation as well as by the suppression of the liberty of the press, every principle of religion, reason, and justice, would say, *emancipate* or *stand condemned.*

But so far from free discussion inviting insurrection, it is the sole preventive; for, as sure as fate, if despotism prevents discussion, insurrection follows of course, unless slavery be eternal, *which is impossible!*

About the third resolution there is an honest difference of opinion.   The violence of our opponents drove us from our desired position—no personalities.   It is christian not to resent injuries; but we are, we confess, not thus far imbued with that glorious spirit of "forgive them, Father, for they know not what they do." We were threatened with violence before we published a single number of the True American! Why then, men of Mason, shall we only be censured? Americans, how long shall it be true that those only who are striving earnestly for the right and the true, shall be marked in their minutest errors, whilst the desperately wicked are passed over in silence? We say once more, our crime was not in the manner, but in the thing—not in the tone, but in the action. Kentuckians will yet see this to their sorrow.

Against the fourth resolution we shall ever most bitterly protest whilst we live. The resolution does not state the truth. We never were waited upon "by a committee of the people of Lexington." On the contrary, it was a committee representing, with some few exceptions, thirty as infamous men as ever met in secret conclave to plot treason and murder. Had we replied otherwise, we should have been unworthy of the name of Kentuckian; the poorest slave in Kentucky might well have despised us. The people of Mason dishonor themselves by such a resolution.

The fifth resolution meets our approbation if "abolition" is taken in its worst sense—if not, not! The True American is not an abolition paper. We have no objection to the passage of laws to prevent the circulation of "incendiary" publications.

About the sixth resolution there may be an honest difference of opinion. We are not yet ready for a convention.

We differ about the first part of the seventh resolution. The last proposition to colonize, meets our decided approbation: provided it be done by the voluntary consent of the free blacks.

We give the eighth resolution our hearty approbation as a scheme of Christian benevolence. We do not believe that Colonization is the remedy for slavery! It never has been; and we think for obvious reasons never will be. The true obstacle in the way of emancipation is the real or imaginary pecuniary loss: colonizing adds to that loss.

The ninth resolution is the first victory of liberty over slavery in this State. God defend the right!

With regard to the last resolution, we believe that any agitation is better than the lethargy of the last half century. Under the let-alone-system, the slaves in this Union have increased from a few thousands to three millions; the local "cancer" has become a constitutional disease, which is sure to kill, if let alone. Even a quack doctor is better than none, for he might stumble on some efficient remedy. So far as modern abolitionism meditates unconstitutional action, we go as far as the farthest in condemning it. But we still more condemn the fanaticism and unconstitutional action of the ultraists of the South: the one errs on the side of virtue and humanity, the other in the cause of crime and the destruction of the natural rights of a large portion of the human race.

The denunciation of abolitionists is a herculean club in the hands of the ultraists of the South, with which they propose to knock out the brains of all opponents of slavery. We deny that it is either wise or just to cater to this criminal appetite. For our own part we are simply saying what every sensible citizen knows to be true, that every sincere man does, and ever will sympathize with every other sincere, and honest, and sensible man, engaged in the same cause. We should as soon think of denouncing a Northern tariff man for agreeing with us on that measure, as denouncing a Northern anti-slavery man for agreeing with us in proposing to array the whole constitutional power of the Union against slavery.

That slaveholders should denounce those, who oppose slavery, is to be expected; but to denounce the friends of liberty is not the province of one contending to make his country free. We would have every man in this Union agree with us and act with us on this subject: were it otherwise we were a fool or a knave.

In conclusion, we see no essential difference between our own opinions and those of the people of Mason: and although we may personally suffer at their hands, we are free to avow that Messrs. McClung, Chambers, and Phister, deserve the thanks of every lover of liberty and republicanism, and that they, and all the favorers of these resolutions, will receive the glorious reward of a good conscience and the admiration of the republic.

PRISONS AND MORALS.

We have been favored by the author with "Remarks on Prisons, and Prison Discipline in the United States, by D. L. Dix," a pamphlet of 104 pages, Boston, 1845.

We have no doubt, however much we apprehend serious evils from the result, that the public mind of this, and perhaps of all civilized nations, is fast becoming opposed to capital punishments. The subject of prisons and prison discipline, therefore, is a subject of pressing interest to statesmen and moralists. When we see twenty-six states pouring out yearly, perhaps, above an average of fifty criminals, each from their penitentiaries, making a total of 1300 desperate and degraded men and women, turned loose upon communities possessing but little reverence for "law and order"—who can wonder at the burnt cities, robberies, swindlings, mobs, and murders, which fill the columns of our journals?

It is a startling reflection, that just in proportion as crime seems to increase in frequency and degree, so does the objection to capital punishment gather strength in the public mind. With interest, therefore, have we examined this book, full of good sense—of philanthropy, without any morbid sensibility in favor of *criminals*—and of impartiality in the examination and statement of facts, which rarely attends devoted zeal to any particular theory or pursuit.

Miss Dix seems to think the number of reformed criminals greatly overrated, from the fact, that few comparatively are returned to the same prison. For they would, of course, seek distant places, and a strange society—change their names and vocations, and thus elude detection, and, even when imprisoned again, would rarely be identified. She considers *prevention* far better than *cure;* in fact the *only* sure remedy against wide-spread crime. This can only be done by universal, *mental* and *moral* education in early life. In addition to this, she would have provided, by public or private means, associated effort and expenditure, work and employment for the children who are destitute by orphanage or parental neglect. What crimes then may we not expect in the slave states, where 3,000,000 of the population are barred from all mental cultivation, and are in the most unfavorable condition possible for moral infusion! Then look at our vast number of whites uneducated, and when educated even, cut off from the respectability of labor, and its mere physical advantages, arising from the occupation of land, or the certain sale of manufactured wares! Instead of our prisons being schools of moral reform, and returning self-respect and intellectual culture, they are made slave factories in the domestic traffic.

Miss Dix recommends the "Pennsylvania system," of separate cells day and night for prisoners, in decided preference to the "Auburn system," of a common place of work by day, and the hardly possible maintenance of silence. She regards the objections and prejudices against this plan, as unfounded and unjust. Absolute solitary confinement, where no person is seen or heard by the prisoner, is no doubt intolerable, and would perhaps in many cases bring on madness, disease, and death. But this is not the thing proposed by the cellular system. For there the prisoner may see the warden, the steward, the minister of religion, and occasionally the visiting public, all of whom would exercise a wholesome influence on their minds and hearts. But this is impossible where they are sustained by the company of hardened and guilty companions in obduracy or shamed by the base against penitence and virtue. Partial solitude certainly gives more vigor to the reflective faculties, which are generally deficient in criminals, whilst it deepens the natural affections, which, properly directed, are at last the surest checks upon injurious and criminal actions towards men. At all events, by this system, if the bad are not made good, the good are not made bad; as is always the case nearly, where all are confined in common. The outer world is thus only protected against dangerous combinations, which result from mutual shame and long companionship in common prisons.

Miss Dix regards the reflections of Charles Dickens, and some others, upon solitary confinement, as founded upon misapprehension of the facts, and a poetic and dramatic fancy, which surely is not the kind of mind most to be regarded in things of so great importance.

Prisons, she holds, ought to support themselves, but not be made a source of revenue to the state. The surplus funds should be applied to an enlargement of moral and intellectual facilities for improvement, or held as a reserve fund for the better class of industrious prisoners to commence life with anew. She is in favor of starving and solitary confinement for a breach of prison discipline, in preference to the infliction of stripes, though she thinks they should not be forbidden—but be held in terrorem over the convicts, to be used as a dernier resort. Nothing is more deplorable than the common jail system, where before and after trial, the guilty and the innocent, the old and the young, the pure and the impure, of all sexes, are tumbled together in one common room. Where the expense forbids the cellular system, she recommends some degree of classification of age, sex, and crime.

Miss Dix seems well versed in all the statistics of foreign and home prisons. But we forbear entering upon all the subjects treated in this little volume—expense, cleanliness, air, heat, water, &c., as our object is mainly to call the public attention to the moral influences of the penitentiary system, which so much affects individuals and states.

LEXINGTON, TUESDAY, NOVEMBER 4.

Voice of a Kentucky Freeman.

We proudly give place to the following noble letter of W. S. Campbell, Esq., of Lincoln county, Kentucky. It will be recollected that a few slaveholders got together in Lincoln, and resolved that the True American should not circulate in that once gallant and free old county; one in which such men as Boone, and Estill, and other noble spirits loved to roam the untamed forest. We will now see whether Lincoln is full of freemen, or cowardly slaves; whether they will stand by the Constitution and laws of Kentucky, or quail before the despotism of the slaveholders: and may God defend the right.

Cassius M. Clay, Esq.

Dear Sir :—I have seen a few copies of the True American, as well as heard of its suppression in Lexington, Kentucky, by an unholy mob—the leaders of which were ex-governor M. and the Hon. T. F. Marshall, together with various other distinguished gentlemen. *The Liberty of Speech and the Press are sacred to political vitality in America.* If you will send me one copy of your paper for a year, I will pay you by remittance the first day of April next.

Yours truly,

W. S. CAMPBELL.

Stanford, Lincoln Co., Ky., Oct. 1845.

Thus,—when will the world learn it?—our cause gathers strength from persecution. *Our subscription list in Kentucky is once more making slow but steady progress*, notwithstanding some about Lexington have fled the field!

THE JUDICIAL ACQUITTAL OF THE MOB.

We have too much regard for *common sense*, to attempt to dispute this matter with man or fool. Some things lose clearness by being disturbed: all axioms are such. Are the vague and misty conjectures of Buckeye lawyers to outweigh the letter of the Constitution, and pure reason? It was a one-sided affair, gotten up by the mobites: they presented, tried, and acquitted themselves.

If any man, or set of men, may abate by violence what he conceives to be a nuisance, what, or who, can stand? This reminds us of the quack who with red hot iron converted all his patient's sores into burns—he could cure burns! But some of our good citizens were anxious to gaze upon the length of Minister S.'s ears: at a court nearer home, they may be seen, not only long, but *green*.

The rebels on the 18th said they were acting without law: the long eared jury of acquittal say they acted with law: *which lie?* We suppose we shall now hear no more of bitter and relentless denunciation of Andrew Jackson, for over-riding the laws to save New Orleans. The one was fighting an enemy; the Lexingtonians a friend: Jackson fought one against a thousand; the Lexingtonians a thousand against one! If that one were sick—would not the world be lost in admiration?

Decrease of Blacks in Freedom.

The decrease of the blacks, living with a more energetic race in a state of freedom, like that of the Indians before the whites, (which we have so often maintained against the alarmists,) is most elaborately proven by the statistics of Massachusetts, beginning 1790, as reported in the African Repository for this week. This may be urged by some as an argument against setting the poor blacks free. It is better for us, and *they prefer it.* Injustice towards the free still oppresses them; how then can they flourish? We are, then, for encouraging them to emigrate to a colony, somewhere, of entire blacks.

Plan of Emancipation.

The plan of emancipation which we have proposed is the most gradual possible.

To free all the slaves now living at once; the West India experiment has proven to be both safe and economical. To free all born hereafter, male and female, would seem to be gradual enough. But that slaveholders might have no excuse. we have proposed to emancipate only the *females* born after a certain time, to be agreed upon by a convention.

By this plan there would be no sudden breaking in upon the habits of the present generation. At thirty years time after the young began to be free, by providing a fund in the manner we proposed in the twelfth number of this journal, to buy in all that were offered voluntarily by masters to the state for purchase, slavery could be extinguished in that period. For all those who did not want to sell their slaves into perpetual slavery in the cotton or sugar regions, and who yet did not feel able to liberate them here, would be gratified in seeing them free in their native land, and yet not be ruined by the sacrifice. Those slaveholders who did not want to sell to the South, nor to liberate here, nor to take a fair equivalent from the state, but who would want to hold on to their slaves just for the luxury of having their fellow-men in bondage, would soon be compelled by public sentiment to yield them up; for the difficulties of keeping them, from a combination of causes, would far outweigh any supposed advantage to be derived from their retention.

Suppose, now, after the 4th day of July, in the year 1847, all female slaves were to be free at twenty-one years of age, what would be the effect ?

Rather than be at the expense of rearing and educating them the great mass of masters would move off or sell their slaves into a climate more congenial to the African than this, and thus relieve our people from their imaginary difficulties, of a large free population. And philanthropy would not be the loser. But all those who were allowed to remain would be learned to read, write, and cypher, and taught some trade : and, of course, be better citizens, and safer far than slaves. Thus far then would philanthropy be a nett gainer of all the remaining 180,000 blacks at length changed from slaves to freemen, or the fractional part of the same, more or less.

In thirty years more every one by the state coming in as purchaser, would regard this as virtually a free state, and make accounts accordingly. All men of the age of forty years, who are too old easily to change their habits of life, would have passed off the stage of life ; all men under forty would be able to effect in thirty years a revolution in their previous habits, and the household and plantation economy, so as to adapt them all agreeably, and without pecuniary loss, to a state of freedom. Immediately all discussion of the slave question would cease, and the councils of our state become moulded in unison with the interests and feelings of the great mass of American freemen.

All the slaves sold out of the state would be capital, ready to be invested in manufactures, which would invite as many laborers from the North into this genial climate as we would require. Also in addition to this, there would be poured into our state a great many men of capital, who would come among us to enjoy our pleasant climate, and get clear of the cold and long winters which now oppress so much all the cultivators of the soil north of Mason and Dixon's Line. Thus would the towns begin to grow once more ; mercantile and all city employments " look up ;" home markets be secured for the productions of the soil ; and land rise in value, till it would make many who are now living dogs' lives—the slaves of slaves—independent and easy in their circumstances. The invigorated culture of land would call for more labor, and all our laboring whites find homes and employment—becoming in turn consumers of the produce of the towns. Education would become practicable and universal; labor be scientific, productive, and honorable, because *free*. Then would there be no more fears of insurrection, civil war, and unknown disaster: each one could sit under his own vine and fig-tree, and there would be none to make him afraid.

We call upon slaveholders to look upon this picture, practically. Weigh on one side emancipation, its certain advantages and *its safety :* on the other, slavery, its dangers—its turmoils —its catastrophe : and then say if we are mad when we ask you in all good feeling to carry out our system.

If they are however bent on their melancholy and blind devotion to slavery, they have but to open their eyes and see long lives of tumult, insult, angry strife, insubordination, and running away with slaves, agitation, in strife of mobs suppressing papers, imprisoned citizens, murdered patriots, broken constitutions, lost liberties, then at last civil war, anarchy, despotism, and death. We pray you, my countrymen, not to deceive yourselves; be assured that though you may carry the victory over the True American, and a hundred other such papers, your work is but just begun. The world is your foe, and truth, religion, and justice, its ally. As sure as God rules omnipotent in the heavens, you will fall at last, and bitter indeed will be the end.

The great objection against my plan seems to be that colonization is not annexed to it. Now if colonization is agreeable to the mass of our citizens, and found practicable, we say, amen. We do not object to colonization. We are for emancipation at all events. We are for anything but slavery. Give us liberty and take all things else. We are a life-member of the colonization society: we have paid our twenty dollars: until our defamers show their works let them be dumb! We are for colonization as a means of Christianizing Africa. We do not honestly regard it as a remedy for slavery. We believe the obstacle to liberty, is the pecuniary loss from emancipation : does colonization add to this loss ? Then how can it aid the cause ? We put it thus. Suppose we were to say that we would not go for emancipation unless J. J. Astor should give us a legacy of a million of dollars at his death. The improbability of such an event would readily show the absurdity of our conditions; yet does any one suppose us so silly as to refuse such a legacy? Not at all.

We say then to colonizationists, come on; aid us first to liberate; and we will aid you to emigrate. Let us not differ, but *unite* in the same cause. Let the end of all be the same—the salvation of our country, and the freedom and Christianity of the world.

LEXINGTON, TUESDAY, NOVEMBER 11.

The Annexation of Texas.

Americans, thus far the slaveocracy has trampled the Constitution under foot, and *usurped* a power unknown to its letter or spirit, in annexing this foreign slave nation to us. Shall we tamely sit by and see this damnable deed accomplished? Who is a traitor to his country? He who defends her laws and her rights, or he who tramples upon both? We are proud in the avowal once more, that for one, we never will submit quietly to this horrible consummation. Had we physical power we would as quickly resist it, as we would a foreign nation's invasion of our soil by fire and sword. Shame on the craven spirit that would cower before a seeming or real majority, and give up to hopeless despotism by saying the thing is done, and resistance is useless! Americans! in the name of the oceans of patriot blood poured out in the cause of liberty in all ages; by the immortal soul and its undying aspirations; by the shame, the sorrow, the suffering, and tears, and crushed hopes of the oppressed living and dead, and yet to be born, let not Constitutional Republicanism be now vitally stabbed, and the hopes of mankind perish for ever! Say now, my countrymen, that this thing shall not be done! When we hear one ask how will this affect cotton, another, how will it influence manufactures and trade, and another, how will it affect every party?—when we see so much trimming, so much base subserviency cloaked under the thread-bare rags of self complacent and sagacious expediency; so little faith in justice, in truth, in mercy; so little re-

verence for God or man—we are sick at heart! Can liberty
be bought with gold, or is gold worth the loss of liberty? Or if
it were possible, to secure property, and for the base body to be
clothed and fed in security, in slavery, what have we gained?
The soul—the immortal part—too, must be fed and sheltered;
man does not live by bread alone! Oh, Henry! indeed thou
wert not mad when, in great woe, thou didst cry, "Give me
liberty, or give me death!"

INDIAN SUMMER.

That season of the year which is said to be peculiar to the
Mississippi valley has come. The air is pure, calm, and genial;
the sun seems unusually brilliant; rising in the morning, its
rays are refracted by the slight hazy smoke which pervades
the whole atmosphere, which magnifies its size, and gives it a
warm crimson hue. As it ascends higher in the heavens, and
its beams assume a more perpendicular direction, the smoky
medium is lessened in mass, and it now shines with a white,
and brilliant, and glorious light. For six weeks it hardly ever
rains; not a cloud is seen, and not a breath of air stirs the
leaves, which now begin to fall like Newton's apple, as if impelled by some unknown and mysterious will.

There has been much speculation among travellers and naturalists, about the cause of the haziness of the atmosphere. In
our mind the cause is certain, and known. So soon as the
frost has cut down the leaves, and the dry weather sets in, the
farmers begin to burn logs, brush, and briers; the prairies are
set on fire to burn away the old grass, to give place to the
young and succulent herbage of the spring, or to force game
into the stands of the hunters. The immense mass of mountains and waste lands, lying between the great valley and the
Alleghany mountains, are set on fire from various motives, or
from accident. Sometimes they are burnt by chesnut gather-
ers, to clear the leaves from the fruit, that they may find it
more readily, as the rough exterior hull or burr, prevents the
fruit from being injured by the fire. In passing from Wheel-
ing to Baltimore we remember to have witnessed the most sublime spectacle of miles of woods on fire by night; when,
turning some sharp angle of the mountain, the great sea of

fire was spread before us! The leaves, fallen logs, and dead trees, are all consumed, and sometimes immense tracts of country are swept of briers and shrubs ten feet high, by the devouring flames. As the smoke, when cool, is of a specific gravity greater than the atmosphere, it sinks down into the valleys, and spreads itself over the great west. No winds disturb and dissipate it, and it remains, some times so pungent as to affect the eyes, until the rains of November extinguish the fires and the searching blasts of coming winter sweep it away. In passing from the lowlands to the upper waters of the Kentucky river, on our autumn hunts, this cause is very manifest. In Fayette or Madison counties, and the country round about, the air is merely misty, not at all unpleasant to the eyes; but as you approach the mountains the mist grows more dense, and at times we have been compelled to move our tents in regions more remote, when the woods were on fire in the neighborhood, so intense was the smoke, and so pungent to the eyes.

We suppose every one is more or less affected by the change of the seasons. Some prefer one, some another. The gay and cheerful, and industrious, perhaps, most love the spring. When the grass grows green, and the buds are bursting, and blossoms are opening, and birds are singing, and all nature seems turned out into one universal jubilation, there is a responsive swell in the bosoms of the young, the hopeful, the gay. Behold the beautiful girl, just budding into womanhood; what harmony between soul and body and all surrounding nature—health, purity, beauty, and promise. The inspiration of the blossom-scented gale, seems right incense for such a temple of purity and beauty. The voice is electric with the glad notes of a happy soul, and the pleasure of simple existence, harmonious with the laws of nature—sweeter far than the Æolian breeze, or the song of birds. On her pupils of dilating transparency, as on the heavens, beautiful and many tinctured forms and colors of earth, fall and leave no trace; but the joyous spirit gives back its unstained loveliness, which language cannot convey, nor physical existences delineate; and this, men call *divine*. They too are responsive—the hearts, the hopes, the minds of boys. Ambition now, like exhilarating gas, fills them with glorious anticipations of wealth, conquest, love, admiration, and fame. This is the drunkenness of life; welcome, then, spring to these; heaven put off the hour of soberness! But it comes at last.

Ah me!—the faltering step, the languid, blood-shot eye, the shriveled cheek, the anguished soul! Pain, perfidy, poverty, hate, envy, slander, crime, have come at last, and the drunken are sobered!

Shattered are the leaves of flowers; withered the blades of grass; bare the boughs of trees; hushed the song of birds; nature mourns her departed joys, and to the miserable welcome is the fall! Yet is there not something left? nothing gained by experience, self-possession, strength, wisdom, greatness of soul?

Yes; the flower is gone, but the fruit—if one were at pains to gather it, lies hid in the rough and uninviting hull.

Come, then, ever welcome autumn, to the thoughtful, the contemplative, the serene! Nature, ever kind and true, and forgiving, and providing parent, has something even for the miserable and sobered sons of earth.

Men of leisure, the air, if not exhilarating, is bracing and healthful. The chesnut and hickory nut lie under the trees; there is game in the brakes, quails in the stubble, pheasants in the fern, deer and turkeys in the forest, bass and pike in the streams. Anglers, gunners, netters, ahoy! Men of wealth and show, the earth is firm to the foot'of the blooded steed; up for the gilded coach, for travel, and away! Men of business, on with the bang-up coat, and the long whip; and with mules, and cattle, and horses, and hogs, off to Charleston, and "Porkopolis;" and in leathern purse bring back the guilty god. Let the "cit," with his ironed hat and polished boots, shuffle from home to the shop, and from the shop to the house; the merchant praise his "articles;" the banker count his gold; the doctor kill his patient; the lawyer strip his client; the preacher wool his flock. We are off for a mountain hunt. A club of four is *the number;* all clothed in thick leaf-colored linsey, that will pull up a brier by the roots, or break the snag of a black-jack hickory sooner than tear; moccasins or coarse boots; a leathern shot-pouch, with coon tail flap, and powder-horn; a belt and butcher knife, and tomahawk, and rifle, from sixteen to thirty balls to the pound; with a close fitting leather or fur cap, and the hunter is personally equipped! Then, two tents, one for the servants and one for the hunters; camp stores, bedding, and an axe; ground coffee, crackers, sugar, pepper, salt, baker's bread, and cornmeal, unbaked; cheese, dried herring, and bacon, and a few crocks of butter, and pickles; a camp kettle, aud frying pan, a tin cup, (silver is forbidden !) tin plate, and spoon, each, with knife and fork, a buffalo rug and blanket coat, with a carpet bag of sundries; the four on horses, and away! If you have arranged your business, well; if not, let it go; all the year you may attend to business—hunting time comes but once. If your wife loves you, she is glad to see you enjoy yourself; if she does not, you had better be in the mountains; "fire in the mountains" is more tolerable than fire at home; so, in either case, it is better to be off!

Two days' journey brings us to the upper Kentucky or Cumberland.   Find some level spot, near a mountain rill, and sheltered by rocks from the cold winds, and then pitch tents.   In the first place, halter the horses; then all hands assist in getting up the tent; some spread down all the rugs on leaves gathered up; each man's carpet bag forms his pillow, and the four blankets for covering, all make a most delightful bed. Others get wood.   This is laid across the mouth of the tent, and beyond, a *sheet is hung across a pole, to act as a chimney;* never fail to hang this sheet; it prevents effectually the smoke from entering the tent, which deters many good fellows from hunting at all.   As you approach the camp ground you must provide turnips, potatoes, and corn for the horses.

As soon as all things are made ready and comfortable, then you may either make a hunt, or rest yourself after the fatigues of travel.   The next morning, each one takes a separate route, and the hunt commences.   The country is either mountainous or table land, or both; with deep ravines, rocks and benches, covered with chesnut, white oak, and beach, hazel bushes, black-jack, and green briers, mostly.   You steal gently along, and shoot such game as you like, or can find—deer, bears, turkeys, pheasants, quails, and squirrels.   When a deer is shot down, load again, the first thing, and then approach, and if he is approachable, bleed him, bend a sapling, hang him, take out his entrails, strip the skin from the haunches, cut them off, and tie the legs together with the skin, swing them like a shot pouch, and off to camp.   If you wish to pursue the hunt, run up the sapling top with a fork, cut by your tomahawk, so that he may be out of the reach of the wolves, and leave him till you return from camp, and get a horse and pack him in. If ravens are about, it is well to tie a handkerchief to the deer, to scare them away.

The hunt for the morning being over, now for cooking and eating. If turkeys or pheasants are killed, roast them on spits ; if a deer, put on the camp kettle, well-filled with pure water, cut the ribs, back bone, and neck into small pieces, and after well washing them, put them into the kettle ; then peel the turnips and potatoes, and put them in, then salt, and a few pods of red pepper, and a few grated crackers, and boil it all well together : the longer the better : dish it, and with buttered bread—corn cake baked on a clean chip cut from a tree—kings might envy you ! For if they ever had as good a dish, of which we are not certain, they never had as good an appetite, of which we are certain ! Then wind up with a roasted potatoe and butter, or a cup of good coffee. Perhaps we might just as well tell our better-selves here how to make good coffee. First get good coffee, and "a heap of it ;" roast it *very slowly*, and to a dark cinnamon color, *no more ;* only grind it when used, or if ground, keep it in a close vessel ; let the water be boiling all sorts of ways before you put the coffee in, and *put it all in— all that you have got, and all that your neighbors have got ;* let it boil just as long as you would have a half-boiled egg, and *no longer.* You then have the *aromatic flavor* of the coffee. If you roast it black, *forget* to put any coffee in the vessel, or boil it two days and nights, or boil the same grounds over again for a few months ; then, by all means, give us stump water, greasy milk, rue, or rhubarb, but don't give us coffee, madam ! All this cooking, if you have not a well-taught servant, must be done by *yourself ;* that is, let him do the mechanical part, you show him how it must be done. A clean split log makes an excellent table, and needs no cloth. The hunt being over, then before the cheerful fire, stretched on the rugs, you forget the rascally world—tell anecdotes—the adventures of the day— praise camp fires—rig the *green horns,* if any—if you ever " liquor," now's the time—never drink of a morning—if you drink at all, drink at night, or what is better, not at all—or if you will not be persuaded, then drink—water ! If you are in the reach of civilization. have a venison supper : clear off the planks : get a fiddle or so, and gather the " gals " together, and then for a real, unsophisticated, heart and soul frolic. But be sure you never tell your wife about it : if you do, the next time you start, your horse will be crippled, and your tent made into carpet rags.

We have seen as many as twenty deer hung around camp at once. If they are to be brought in, they should not have the hide taken off. When you have hunted ten days, or two weeks, and have game enough, and begin to want to see the children—yes, and the children's mamma, too! sling tents, pack the game, and be off. Roast the saddles of the venison: stew the ribs: spit the pheasants and quails: invite your friends: eat, drink, and be merry. Single men cannot resist the mysterious influence which besets them, from the lovely lassies, whose lips receive a more inviting polish from stripping a deer's rib. There's more blood in the cheek, more fire in the eye, and more love in the breast, and more soul in one real woman at a hunter's table, that would make ten of your pickle eating, coal chewing, famished beauties. As for the hunter's wife, she loves him as if she had never been married to him, unless by ill-luck he speaks of the " frolic," when she downs upon him like a summer cloud! Who shall say there is not poetry in woman and the Indian summer?

LEXINGTON, TUESDAY, NOVEMBER 18.

Why Mechanic Arts cannot Flourish in Slave States.

In slave states, the tendency of things is for land to accumulate in the hands of a few. The former occupants of the soil emigrate to new countries. Now, B. is a saddler; he supplies twenty farmers with saddles; well, if no depopulation takes place, he may live on very well; but what are his children to do? Make saddles too? There is no one to buy: the father supplies the demand. Sell saddles in the great marts of commerce? That is impossible; because slave states do not afford roads and canals, and such facilities of transportation as the free states. And even if the roads were made, there is not division of labor and energy enough to enable the maker of saddles in slave states to sell as cheaply as saddlers in the free states. B.'s children are then left without employment; for all other trades are full as well as that of saddle making. Hence, in the great mass of slave states, free white laborers are necessarily impoverished! But suppose half of B.'s customers buy out the other half; B.'s means are reduced one half: he becomes poorer. Suppose one buys out the other nineteen of the twenty farmers, filling the twenty farms with slaves; then B is ruined: he can't sell but one saddle: he is out of bread, and must move, or die! Thus the tendency of slavery is to destroy every free white laborer, or reduce him to the physical necessities and mental subserviency of the black slave! The state loses all her middle class; effeminate aristocracy ensues on one hand, and abject slavery on the other. *This is barbarism!*

WHAT DOES THE SLAVEHOLDER GAIN BY SLAVERY?

We say now nothing of its influence upon the temper, the mind, the body; we say nothing of its indolence, prodigality, injustice, and crime; we say nothing of "lust, fire, poison, and insurrection," which its advocates affect to dread whenever the cry of wolf suits them. Can slaveholders stand against the physical power of neighboring states? They cannot! Money is the sinew of war; the fighting of the world is done not in the battle-field only; in the coal mines, the iron foundries, the cotton factories, the structure of rail-roads, steam cars, and steamboats, in the workshop, and in the scientific culture of the soil—there is the battle of conquest and dominion fought in the nineteenth century. It is proved in the above article, that in all these freedom rules it in triumph over slavery! How then can slave-holders stand? They must fall! As soon as the national Union is knocked from under them, they fall an easy prey to the first invader! If nations of equal power are at war, which conquers? The one that can first concentrate its force upon a given point, other things being equal. There is no plainer problem than this in the art of war. Now if the free states, by superior internal improvements, and larger capabilities of endurance in the field, by accumulated capital, to say nothing of strength of limb and spirit, can sooner concentrate their forces than the South, and longer keep them there, when met, is not victory already theirs? Come now, ye testy and valiant champions of the 18th of August, answer us! Are you not far-seeing and able statesmen to lay us all powerless at the feet of those "damned fanatics of the North?" We tell you the time is coming when high-sounding words will not avail you! When hard knocks in some coming time shall fall fast and heavy upon the heads of you or your children—remember the 18th of August! and write down in a book, *if you have any*, who was the *True* American! and who, the "traitor, fanatic, and madman!"

Spirit of the People.

In giving on our first page the "spirit of the press and of the people," we have omitted the hundreds of abolition meetings of sympathy for us, and denunciation of the mob, because their opinions would have no weight with the people of the slave states just now. We are neither afraid nor ashamed to acknowledge our gratitude. If we had thought proper to have *slandered* the hundred thousand abolitionists of the North, some say we never would have been mobbed! Had we been as base as those who make the suggestion, we would now be lolling in some fat office, and "hurrah for Cash. Clay," uttered by some foxy-headed negro children, would never have caused "respectable" men to make fools of themselves! Whilst we say thus much, we must tell the liberty party and abolitionists, that to reproach us for not deserting our party is, to say the least, in exceeding bad taste. Do they suppose that a man can change his principles as he can his coat? Or would they have us degraded enough to desert what we conceived to be the highest interest of our country, through personal pique, the ingratitude of friends, or disappointed ambition? There are selfish and base apostates enough in this Union. Heaven give us spirit to bear all things for our country, and the liberty of men!

Elevation of Labor—Fourierism—Factory Strikes— The World's Convention.

Having in reality the same sympathy with laborers as with capitalists and no more, because both are men and have equal claims upon us as such, we consider ourselves in a very fair position to give an impartial word upon these several projects of "the elevation of labor" which stands at the head of our columns as one of the purposes of this journal. First, then, we have no faith in society's ever having a very decidedly different organization from what it now has, and which it has had from the earliest historical times. We believe that there are essential differences in the organization of men—in the mind—in the body—in the senses, and in the sensibilities. That God designs some for honorable places, or the first places, descending down to positions of neutrality or public indifference : as in a single man, there is the head—the body—the legs—the feet—so in society there are men filling correspondent places. Or again : suppose society—its privileges—its possessions—its enjoyments—to be likened to the sea, men of different capabilities mental and physical, as bodies of different density or specific gravity, rise or fall to their proper sphere, provided there be no obstructing force.

So far then as we understand Fourierism, we regard it as opposing, to some extent, natural laws. You cannot make *all* labor agreeable ; because some labor to persons of certain degrees of refinement is essentially disagreeable, which to others is neutral or indifferent, because of a coarser structure. You cannot place a higher motive in the breast of any man than an enlightened self-interest ; a man who will not labor for himself, will not labor for another ! If one man by himself is incapable of taking care of himself and family, when allied to another of the same sort he will hardly better his condition. We know that there is some gain in the economical laws by association ; such as several families eating at the same table ; using a common fire ; a common garden ; pump, and all that ; but these gains already exist in society as at present organized, whilst individuality of person and property are still preserved just so far as each one likes. We have known several persons to keep house together, very harmoniously and more economically than if living separately. But then they were of peculiar temperaments, and similar tastes. We do not undertake to say that Fourier association will not prosper ; on the contrary, some of them no doubt will turn out well. We mean to say that they will never supersede the present order of society. We wish they may do much good ; and at all events evolve some new truth which may be usefully engrafted upon the old stocks—the present organization of states.

Upon the subject of trades unions and factory strikes, we believe that no laws ought to be made to prevent them; at the same time we are convinced that they rarely, if ever, do the working classes any good, whilst they often do infinite evil. So far as persons "striking" undertake to hinder others from laboring in the same trade by force, we regard it as the most infamous despotism—another name for lynch or mob law, which is at war with all order and human society. Suppose the capitalist or head manufacturer is making more than a fair interest, and the laborer is worked harder than is right, and does not receive a just proportion of the common product; what is the remedy? Let the laborers combine and start a factory themselves; or if they have not the means, let them intelligently show how a large profit may be made, and as sure as death some new capitalist will come in and employ them at such rates as can be afforded. The truth is, capital is generally quick sighted. If A and B are making too large profits, C comes in and takes away a portion of the laborers of A and B, by giving them higher wages; competition here, as elsewhere, always in the long run producing an equilibrium. If A, B, and C still give too little wages, D comes in. If A, B, and C give too much wages, C breaks. and his hands are thrown out of employment! Suppose A, B, C, and D are making a living profit, and their hands receiving living wages and some reverse in trade takes place for the worse, they must stop or run at sacrifice, or the wages must be reduced. If they stop, the hands must seek some other employment, or starve. If they run at a sacrifice they must do so only to keep the laborers up till better times—they go through—break—or stop. In this case the laborer ought to work at the lowest possible price at which he can live; for it is his interest as well as his duty; unless some other employment of better pay offers itself. Thus we have gone through all the stages of prosperity and adversity in manufacturing, and assure our countrymen and countrywomen, that a strike is not the remedy in our judgment, *in any case whatever*.

We have no objection to a county convention or a national convention—or if it please them more—even to a "World's Convention" upon any subject whatever. "The free communication of thoughts is one of the invaluable rights of man." But the late World's Convention was the richest thing of the day. We never shall be able to cancel the deep obligation of gratitude

which we owe that convention. We believe we should have
died of the mob, had it not been for the report of their proceedings in The New-York Tribune. There is one man of eminent
genius in Gotham, and he is the *reporter* of The Tribune!
Reader, in whatever portion of the globe you are, eat, drink—
and read that—and you *shall be merry!* If you are sick, you
shall laugh : and if laughing will make and keep you well—
you shall never be sick any more! When ever before was Philanthropy put to such exquisite torture? Some one no doubt
put a bat's wing into our shoe? No. Caused a hare to run
across our road; put pealed alders into our well; or in some
other mode "*tricked*" us? No! They have no doubt called
us *philanthropist!* It's a wonder the people had not killed
us!

If neither Fourierism, nor strikes, nor the "World's Convention," are to be looked to for the elevation of labor, how shall
we proceed? *Repeal all laws which obstruct man in the use
of all the powers which God has given him : and then render
those powers as perfect as possible!*

Under this broad rule slavery dies! Under this broad rule it
becomes the bounden duty of every nation under the sun to
give all her citizens, as far as practicable, an intellectual and
moral, and physical education, so as to give full scope to the
body, the mind, and the affections. Let every man have a fair
start in life, and "the Devil take the hindmost!" If a man
beats us fairly in the race, we say, well done—God speed you
—we shall not repine! But if you clog us, if you trip us, if
you maim us, by laws of injustice destroying the power God
and nature have given us—then by the eternal instincts of the
undying spirit and unconquerable will—let the Heavens fall,
and the earth crumble into dust, but we shall be righted! And
gods and men respond, Amen!

What then, are those legal clogs which obstruct us in life's
race? That law of the South which subjects three millions
of men to the absolute will of others, and near five millions
more to the desolating influences of slave labor, is one. All
laws of privilege, as in our state, when the county courts are a
self-perpetuating body, is one. All monopolies such as banks
where citizens are forbid to bank, and roads of toll, where persons are forbid others, when they become more profitable to
individuals than to the public, are such! A bank, so long as

it confines itself to affording a safe and portable currency, and facilities of exchange, &c., and a fair rate of interest to stockholders, though in one sense a monopoly,—yet is a monopoly for the public good—it is the state's machine. But when it becomes a shaving shop in the hands of its friends and owners, stripping the labor of the country by usurious profit, then it is an unfair clog upon industry—foul play in the race of life—and should die.

We have given these briefly as examples of what we mean, believing that the rule we have laid down is a good one, and broad enough to embrace all the ends of the " World's Convention !" and certainly as practicable as some of their schemes of amelioration of society's ills !"

In conclusion, we recommend less haughtiness and indifference on the part of the rich towards the poor, and less invidiousness toward the rich on the part of the poor. In a word, let true Christianity prevail, and earth will become the foreshadowing of Heaven.

LEXINGTON, TUESDAY, NOVEMBER 25.

THE UNCONSTITUTIONALITY OF SLAVERY, BY LYSANDER SPOONER, BOSTON, 1845.

This pamphlet, of 156 pages, we have read through very carefully; and although it is full of elaborate research, and able and plausible argument, yet it fails to convince us of its truth. We are satisfied that slavery exists in all the old thirteen States, where it now exists, *constitutionally.* We have a phrase in the West that is very coarse, but to the point: so far as the Constitution sanctions slavery, it is best frankly "to acknowledge the corn." Every argument which is merely specious, but really, in the honest convictions of sensible men, *untrue,* weakens the cause, however good. Surely the cause of liberty and political equality of rights needs no meretricious aids! Words are intended to convey meaning: we know not how it may affect others, but for ourself, when we read the Constitution of the United States, we feel as surely as we read, that slavery is there alluded to, and allowed to the States then in being, and parties to the contract. The North reluctantly yet certainly became a joint actor in this crime against man. Let them now, while it is to-day, rise up in their power and wash their hands of this thing! Saying in a manly and constitutional mode, we will no longer give the lie to the Declaration of 1776!

RELIGION AND SLAVERY.

We have before us " A condensed anti-slavery Bible argument, by a citizen of Virginia," a pamphlet of 90 pages: New York, 1845. We are ever pained when we see or hear religion and slavery mentioned in connexion. Here, we confess, we lose all that charity which we can at times feel towards the greatest criminals, and the worst of crimes. We imagine that no one looks upon the lion and the snake with the same feelings, although death may be threatened by both. Go to the field of battle, and see the brains scattered from the crushed skull, or the great gush of the hearts blood! and the greatest work of God has been marred! This sight is horrid enough. But go to the gloomy chamber of the victim of secret poison! See the wasted form—the anguished eye—the dread of friend and foe— the horrible war of the necessary craving for food—and the instinctive keen sense of fatal poison—now, when all that God has intended for support in the trying hour, are turned into the bitterest curse—look there, misery and madness struggling for supremacy—and cold, certain, inevitable death, the sole arbiter and giver of rest! Tell us now the untaught impulse of the heart of man, is not this worse than death in the battle field? Go see the "cat o' nine," buried in the flesh of the unprotected slave—see his ashy shriveled form—his rags—his foul and comfortless hut—tear him from his home—blot out from his eye the loved images of wife, children, and friends—and who are the men who do this thing? Every citizen who, by his vote, allows the vilest wretch to do the deed with impunity! But the citizen was born to it: love of wealth, pleasure; and pride, have usurped the place of unbought conscience. Many palliatives come to his help: and if conseience awakes, heaven help us!

there is a great, and merciful, and omnipotent God, who can purify the most deep stained soul, and upon repentance, make the tortured spirit happy once more.

But when and how shall we class that man who knocks from under our tottering and weary feet, this last scaffolding of hope, and makes God himself the worst of tyrants—the falsest of friends —the most unjust of fancied existences? The man who attempts to justify slavery from the Bible, is that man! If he wins us to his opinions, he makes us an infidel—we lose our belief in the existence of a God—our idea of the immortality of the soul—all distinction between right and wrong—we sink from the man into the beast—we would not scruple to murder our mother for a meal of victuals—or scatter the desecrated remains of a dead sister, or father, or wife, to manure our cucumber vines! We thank God that instinct is stronger than reasoning, and conscience more powerful than argument. We do most sincerely believe, and we deliberately weigh what we say, that all the books and papers which have been written to prove slavery a divine institution, have never convinced a single man or woman that it was *right—no not one!* We have not read the argument above referred to: life is too short for a man to read a long discourse to prove that a man may not murder his father, or sell his country for gold, or enslave his fellow man! If then we will not and cannot read the argument of our able friend, "A Virginian," in defence of the right, what shall we say of the God defying defender of the wrong? We promised to give the "Alabama Preacher," and his class, a round, when we got *cool:* we now postpone it for ever, for until this miserable and dying being of ours becomes yet most deserving of all the ills that flesh is heir to, we never can associate in our mind religion and slavery, without the most unqualified loathing, and hot indignation!

LEXINGTON, TUESDAY, DECEMBER 2.

COUNTY COURTS.

The county court system of Kentucky has long been regarded by the people of Kentucky as a "nuisance," and has grown so corrupt as to be intolerable. It is notorious that one of these conservators of the peace was president of the mob, and another one the avowed originator of it. Is there no statute in the commonwealth to punish perjury? They would no doubt plead like the other rebels—necessity! For, in truth, there is no doubt, if a convention shall be called, that these perjured "respectable gentlemen," and all their associates, will be quickly trounced from their places, which they have dishonored so long! Our government is based upon the principle that no man, or set of men, shall have exclusive privileges, and that taxation and representation are co-ordinate. But here is a body, self-existent, and perpetuating itself, not at all dependent upon the people, who are allowed to tax us just as much as they please, without our consent, and without any responsibility whatever! And this is not all: after leading a life of ignorance and fraud, they become high sheriffs, to exercise the highest functions of the executive government. But they will not even do that which the law requires them to do, but most grossly and corruptly *sell the office to the highest bidder!* We calmly put it to every man of self-respect—every lover of order—every respecter of morals, if this infamous excrescence on our republican constitution should not be speedily removed as a "nuisance," utterly incompatible with our safety and happiness? Oh! but then, perhaps if a convention was called, the 31,000 slaveholders might be deprived of their exclusive privileges also! So the 600,000 must put up with all these existing and increasing abuses, for we learn that the office of clerk is also begun to be bought and sold! But what else are we to look for but gross fraud, corruption, and crime, where slavery exists, and where the most "respectable men" avow force as the supreme law of the land?

Surely those who sow the wind, shall reap the whirlwind!

MURDER.

We learn that the citizens of Georgetown, Scott County, Kentucky, rather encouraged the murder of the poor Irishman, who beat C. in a drunken frolic! Come, Mr. C. and E., can't you make out a case of "incendiarism" against this humble practitioner of the shelalah? These Georgetown fellows were the most rampant agents in the affair of the 18th! Of course they will acquit the murderer: the poor devil who was shot down in cold blood was a "nuisance!" What right had he to keep a doggery in that refined city; and beat respectable men who happened to get drunk in his house as a compliment? Won't Messrs. F. and others call upon the other Irish in the burgh, and order them in a friendly manner to be off? Has not Mr. R. S., got well enough, after his hard ride on the 18th, to call upon his fellow slave-traders in Fayette to gallop around the country to muster the faithful? Surely one good turn deserves another! No doubt Messrs. Hunt, Dudley, and Waters, would consent to act as a committee, for party considerations ought not to be allowed to interfere in so grave a matter; and when the Irish are to be mobbed and murdered, it ought certainly to be done "*in a dignified manner!*"

My name is not Bently!

Many of the Kentucky editors undertake to invite strangers to come and see slavery, and then they will not think so hardly of it! A Louisville paper asks Horace Greeley to come and see, promising him "that he shall not be mobbed, tarred-and-feathered, roasted, nor eaten alive by the slaveholders." The impudence of the slaveocrats reminds us of a certain man named Bently. He was a most confirmed drunkard, but would never drink with a friend, or in public, and always bitterly denied, when caught a little too steep, ever having tasted liquor. One day some bad witnesses, as Horace would no doubt be, concealed themselves in his room, and when the liquor was running down his throat, seized him with his arm crooked and his mouth open, and holding him fast, asked him, with an air of triumph; "Ah, Bently, have we caught you at last—you never drink, ha?" Now one would suppose that Bently would have acknowledged the corn. Not he! with the most grave and impassable face, he calmly, and in a "dignified manner," said, "Gentlemen, my name is not Bently!"

The Mason Meeting.

The slaveholders seem to be very anxious to make themselves out afraid of their slaves! Is it not enough to be despicable, without courting contempt and aspiring to be ridiculous?

Penitentiary and Slave Labor.

We give to-day in our columns, from the Vicksburgh Sentinel, an article over the signature "True Democratic Mechanic," and also from the Washington Union, a resolution of the New York democracy.

The Vicksburgh mechanic can very well see how *penitentiary labor*, when a man works for mere food and shelter, and coarse clothing, comes into powerful competition with his *free labor*. Slave labor is but another word expressing the identical thing. Now the New York boys suppose, that making the penitentiary labor *free* would injure them; the Mississippi boy imagines just the contrary! He supposes very rightly, that a man at liberty to do as he pleases would hardly put up with the wages of the convict and the slave! Can it be possible that the democrats of New York are sappy enough to think, that Mason and Dixon's line protects them from the hard competition of slave labor? or do they in good faith believe, that the free negro would work for less wages than the slave, and thus produce a cheaper article to come in competition with, and undersell the products of the white free laborer of the North? They must either be knaves or fools!

There is but one class of men in the North, who are apparently interested in slavery—the manufacturers. Because slaves and slave-owners are consumers of their goods, and not competitors. But in reality, this monopoly is no equivalent for the increased capacity of purchase, which would ensue if the South were free. In the long run, Nature's laws, justice, and enlightened political economy, are the same. The more production in the world the better, provided just and enlightened laws make a fair distribution of wealth.

LEXINGTON, TUESDAY, DECEMBER 9.

AN APPEAL TO ALL THE FOLLOWERS OF CHRIST IN THE AMERICAN UNION.

To all the adherents of the Christian religion, Catholic and Protestant, in the American Union, the writer of this article would respectfully represent, that he is but a single individual of humble pretensions struggling with honest zeal for the liberties of his country and the common rights of all mankind. He sets up no claims to piety or purity of life; but whilst he is himself subject to all the infirmities of our common nature, he believes in an omnipotent and benevolent God over-ruling the universe by fixed and eternal laws. He believes that man's greatest happiness consists in a wise understanding and a strict observance of all the laws of his being, moral, mental, and physical; which are best set forth in the Christian code of ethics. He believes that the Christian religion is the truest basis of justice, mercy, truth, and happiness, known among men. As a politician especially, does he regard Christian morality as the basis of national and constitutional *liberty*. He believes, that liberty of conscience was the antecedent of civil liberty, and that to Christianity did our fathers owe the emigration from the Old World, and our national independence in the New. He believes that there is now a crisis in the affairs of our nation, which calls for the united efforts of all good men to save us from dishonor and ruin.

Slavery is our great national sin, and must be destroyed, or we are lost. From a small cloud, not larger than a man's hand, it has overspread the whole heavens. Three millions of our fellow men, all children of the same Father, are held in absolute servitude, and the most unqualified despotism. By a strange oversight, or self-avenging criminality of our fathers, an anti-republican, unequal, sham representation has given the slaveocracy a concentrated power which subjects the additional fifteen million of whites of this nation to the caprice and rule of some *three hundred and fifty thousand slaveholders*. They monopolize the principal offices of honor and profit, control our foreign relations, and internal policy of economical progress They have forced us into unjust wars—national bad faith—and large and unnecessary expenditures of money. They have violated, time after time, the national and state Constitutions. They have trampled under foot all of the cardinal principles of our inherited liberty—freedom of the press—liberty of speech—trial by jury—the habeas corpus, and that clause of the constitution which gives to the citizens of the several states the rights and privileges of citizens of each state. They have murdered our citizens—imprisoned our seamen—and denied us all redress in the courts of national judicature, by forcibly and illegally expelling our ambassadors—thus failing in the comity, observed sacred by all nations, civilized, and savage, till now! All this have we borne, in magnanimous forbearance, or tame subserviency; till remonstrance is regarded as criminal; and it has become the common law of the land, in all the states, to murder in cold blood, and in a calm and "dignified manner," any American freeman, who has the spirit to exercise the constitutional, and natural, and inalienable rights of free thought and manly utterance!

Now, in the name of that religion which teaches us to love our neighbor as ourself—to do unto others as we would have others should do unto us—to break every yoke, and let the oppressed go free—we pray every follower of Christ to bear testimony against this crime against man and God: which fills our souls with cruelty and crime—stains our hands with blood—and overthrows every principle of national and constitutional liberty, for which the good and great souled patriots of all ages laid down their lives, and for which our fathers suffered, bled, and died.

We pray you to set your faces against all those professed followers of Christ, who betray him in the house of his friends, and make God out the founder of an institution which causes the most refined, enlightened, and "respectable men" in the state of Kentucky, where slavery exists in its most modified and lenient supremacy, to raise the black and bloody flag of "death to liberty of speech and the press!"

We pray you in the name of liberty—our country—our common humanity—and the God of all, who is no respecter of persons—to come to our help!

We know that in 1776 the prayers of the Church, went up from the closet, the altar, and from the field of battle to the Great Arbiter of the destinies of war; we believe that a time of equal danger and awful responsibility is at hand; and we now ask that the prayers of the universal Church be uttered in the cause of liberty once more.

And as we believe that it is not only our duty to pray but to act, we respectfully submit for your serious consideration, the following suggestions:

I. That all ministers of religion, all over the Union, either in their sermons or in their prayers, once on every Sabbath solemnly warn their hearers against the *special sin of slavery*.

II. That in all religious journals, a column be devoted to slavery—its economical statistics—and to moral remonstrance.

III. That in all addresses of religious bodies, oral or written, when moral conduct is touched upon, that a solemn and special denunciation of slavery be made.

IV. In the exercise of the elective franchise, that each christian will honestly endeavor so to use that great and responsible privilege as, by all honorable, just, and *constitutional* means, to destroy slavery in this nation.

We suggest, with great diffidence, for the consideration of Christians, *a board of home missions*, founded as follows: A common treasury, sustained by all sects of Christians, to be located in the city of New York. From this shall be sustained, at fair wages, as many missionaries, in the slave states, as the funds of the society, or the interest thereof when vested in stocks, will sustain. 1. Let an equal number of each sect represented be elected. 2. Let the ministers living in slave states be preferred, if they can be procured. 3. Let them be instructed never to speak of slavery in the presence of blacks or slaves. 4. Let them for the present be confined to the states of Maryland, Virginia, and Kentucky. Let them be instructed to preach in the counties where there are the fewest slaves. 5. Let them be men of ability, and, though not fanatical, self-sacrificing, and well versed in the political and economical bearings of slavery, as well as in its moral influences, so that they may be able to show the non-slaveholder how slavery impoverishes his family; excludes them from schools, churches, the honors of the state, and the general advantages of civilization.

We believe that a scheme of this kind would do infinite good. There could be no pretext for violence on the part of slaveholders, because the blacks would never hear. It would arouse a generous shame in the bosoms of our own clergy, and force many to make sacrifices in the cause of religion and liberty.

Now, once more, in great yearning of spirit for the liberty of our country, the happiness of mankind, and the glory of God, we pray you to question each one his own conscience. Never let it be said that our country called on us for help, in great woe, and none heeded her voice!

We ask all the friends of Constitutional liberty, and pure Christianity, to give the above an insertion in their religious and political journals—a request never before made by us.

TOLERATION.

The Catholic Advocate, of Louisville, gives his Protestant brethren, of the True Catholic, some hard hits. Let each sect stand by its own name and doctrines, and let others alone. There is work enough to be done against the common enemy, without fighting each other. We despise persecution for opinion's sake, birth's sake, or nation's sake, or any other sake. Let virtue only be honored! Native American, where are you?

LEXINGTON, TUESDAY, DECEMBER 16.

HOGS GOING FROM TENNESSEE TO CINCINNATI.

Several editors who violently oppose emancipation and free labor, wonder at the fact of a drove of fat hogs passing through Frankfort, to Cincinnati, Ohio, from Tennessee. Now, these hogs, after passing some hundreds of miles, at a great expense, to Cincinnati, are slain, packed, and sent right along side the place whence they started, on to the great marts of commerce! So, cotton is carried from New Orleans to Lowell, made into coarse negro shirting, and sent back to whence it started! Can there be a stronger proof of the advantages of free over slave labor than this? In Louisville you pay about ten cents a head for killing hogs; in Cincinnati, the killer pays, on the contrary, the seller ten cents a head for the privilege of killing. Why the difference? In Cincinnati the hair is made into mattrasses, the bristles into brushes, the blood into some chemical preparations, the hoofs into glue, the fat into lard and oil. In Louisville "Canaan" can't or won't do all these things; hence hogs come from Tennessee, pass Louisville, and go on to Cincinnati! And is a man to be mobbed and murdered for seeing these things, and crying out against them?

Hogs have almost ceased going over the mountains; we foresaw this when we opposed the railroad. They are too poor to buy.

The time is not far distant when hemp will cease to be manufactured in the interior of Kentucky, and, perhaps, even in the state! Alas, our poor, slave ridden state!

INGRATITUDE.—THE ASS'S KICK

One of the greatest trials to which we have ever been subjected, in a somewhat eventful life, is the ingratitude of men whom we have, in what they may call our better days, befriended. We are not the man to reproach any one with favors conferred; such a thing is repugnant to every generous mind. Yet, when ridicule is attempted, and insult added to injury, forbearance ceases to be a virtue, by giving impunity to crime. We care not for the relentless and uncalled for war, which the editor of the American Democrat has waged, with a bitter vindictiveness for which we know no cause, upon us ever since we were overpowered by a heartless mob; but when he resorts to misrepresentation to show his subserviency to the stronger party, he merits contempt and indignation. If we had gained but one subscriber since our misfortune, a generous mind would have forborne the taunt; if we had gained more, as is the truth, an honest man would have spurned the calumny. When Mr. E. Bryant was turned out of office by Mr. Tyler, homeless, friendless, and poor, our bowels of compassion were moved, and we contributed about seventy dollars out of our pocket to his penny sheet, the "Whig Rally," a page of which we never read, to keep his body and soul together! Now, when he sees us robbed of thousands of dollars by a band of mobites; slandered and persecuted on all sides, without crime—struggling almost single-handed against the most powerful and relentless despotism that the world has seen—he comes forward with a mean insinuation, the cowardly shadow of a lie, and gives us the ass's kick!

FREEDOM AND INSANITY.

We believe that we have before somewhere noticed the argument attempted to be drawn from the sixth census in favor of slavery, because it was there proven, from figures, that there were more insane, blind, and deaf blacks among the free, than among the same number of slaves. Mr. E. Jarvis, of Dorchester, Massachusetts, in a pamphlet now before us, extracted from the "American Journal of the Medical Sciences," printed at Philadelphia, 1844, proves conclusively, by a direct reference to many towns in the several states North, that the census is grossly incorrect. Every grade of error prevails; sometimes *seven times* as many insane blacks are reported, as actually existed—all told—sane and insane. He concludes, however, with every man acquainted with the incapability of the negro's constitution to stand cold, that a comparison of the northern free blacks in a cold climate with slaves in a hot climate, where nature has evidently designed them to live, would prove nothing, even if the facts were as stated by the census, which they are not!

Mr. Jarvis then takes up the southern free and slave blacks, upon the data that all the slave blacks are supported at private expense, and that the free fall into the public charge, and forms the following table :

State or Territory.	Slaves.	Insane at private charge.	One in	Free colored population.	Insane at public charge.	One in
Dist. Columbia,	4,694	4	1173	8,361	3	2787
Florida, . .	25,717	12	2146	817	0	
Arkansas, . .	19,935	13	1533	465	8	58
Missouri, . .	58,240	50	1164	1,574	18	87
Kentucky, . .	182,258	132	1380	7,317	48	152
Tennessee, .	183.059	124	1476	5,524	28	198
Mississippi,	195,211	66	2957	1,366	16	85
Louisiana, . .	168,452	38	7657	25,502	7	3643
Alabama, . .	253,532	100	2532	203,9	25	81
Georgia, . .	280,944	108	2601	2,753	26	105
South Carolina,	327,038	121	2702	8,276	16	517
North Carolina,	295,817	192	1280	22,732	29	7839
Virginia, . .	448,987	327	1372	49,842	54	923
Maryland, . .	89,495	99	904	62,020	42	1576
Delaware, . .	2,605	21	134	16,919	7	2417
Slave States, .	2,485.984	1407	1766	215,507	327	659

From this table it appears that in all the slave states there is one slave in every 1766 insane, and one free black in every 659 insane. Now there is no force nor data of just comparison in any of these tables. All the free blacks are not supported at public charge. In Kentucky, and we presume in all the slave states, the masters liberating, are bound to maintain the freed man : so that he comes not to the public charge. And then, again, the *old* and *useless* are generally set free ; and an inaccurate census would prove nothing in comparing the worn-out and the miserable, struggling with a new life and poverty in old age, without vigor or self-reliance, with young classes of slaves. So if you go to the North, still a difficulty exists ; many of the free there have been slaves, and are unfitted by *slavery*, not by *nature*, for freedom ! Again, who can say whether the sufferings of the body may not be intolerable, whilst the mind is comparatively at ease,—or the mind wrecked with suffering, whilst the body is at ease ?—and which of the two is the greater woe ? and which first produces madness ? And should it turn out that despotism favors mental sanity; and liberty, insanity ; what then ? Shall we confine it to the blacks, or shall a Nicholas take the reins of national control ? Many of the most eminent British statesmen went mad. Intelligent foreigners, travelling among us, note that the faces of our people express disquietude,—that whilst we possess more physical comforts than the old monarchies, we seem to be far less mentally happy. It is natural that where fortune and all offices of honor and profit are open to the lowest individual, that there should be great energy of character, restlessness, and posting in the race ; it seems to be a reproach to a man to be behind in a race in a Republic, whilst the monarchist consoles himself that he *could win if he was allowed !* The Yankee studies or labors for long hours ; the German or Frenchman sings or smokes, or fiddles, when the time of recreation comes. What then, shall republicanism be given up ? By no means. The same reasons would impel us back once more to the savage state. We should think that republics were more subject to insanity : despotisms more liable to idiocy. The one loses mind at intervals, through over-wrought action of the brain : the other falls into stupidity, through inaction and original want of brain !

But it is time every where to cease talking about the blacks. The great question is now, whether African slavery shall be destroyed, or American liberty be lost !

Janus-Face.

If "constitutional legal liberty" be a gem of such estimable
price, where were those dainty spoken men when it was trampled
into the mire on the 18th of August, 1845 ? Because we would
not betray the liberty of the press and quietly submit to the
slave despotism, which we well knew slumbered with its Cerberian heads and Cyclopean strength in every valley, and on every
hill-top south of Mason and Dixon's line, the Whig was ready
to denounce us as being of that egotistical class of conceited
madcaps, who press into the first ranks of every cause, and injure it by their rashness ! How dare he now to come forward
and find every thing lovely and glorious in Hampden's laying
down his life for "constitutional liberty?" Is not this rank
incendiarism ? Will not the slaveholders of Virginia taste of
his blood ?

LEXINGTON, TUESDAY, DECEMBER 23.

The Louisville Institute.

Since our last notice of this extraordinary gathering of the
knights of the scalpel and balances, fifty names have been added
to the list of students. It now stands at 350, whilst Transylvania numbers about 150. For our part, we think the lives
and safety of our people in imminent danger ! Would it not
be well to appoint a committee of our most "respectable citizens," to proceed forthwith to Louisville, and abate the "nuisance ?"

The Response.

Well, the response to our appeal, which has come from conventions and meetings has filled a side of our journal for two
months ! In the whole north not one meeting has stood by the
Robbers ; and but *one* so-called Whig press in all the free states

—the *New York Courier and Enquirer*—has justified the rebels! Out of all Kentucky, one hundred counties, but four or five have sustained the mob by *doubtful* majorities, *leaving about ninety-five against them!* Not one meeting in the slave states, leaving out Kentucky, has stood by the assassins; whilst all the manly portion of the press, whig and democratic, have denounced them—in Baltimore, in St. Louis, in Louisville, and other places! If the Courier and Enquirer and the Philadelphia dinner committee prefer to honor those, who stood a thousand against one sick man—contending for *their* liberty as well as his own—we shall not on that account, or for any man's sneers or blame, be jostled from the firm stand where honor and conscience place us! Against them, too, as against the rebels of the 18th, we are ready to appeal to "Kentucky and to the world," and with unbroken faith, to abide the verdict!

RELIGION AND POLITICS.—THE W. UNION.

Religion and politics, from time immemorial, and, in all nations, till the United States sprung into an independent existence, have been intimately united. The Jewish government was a theocracy. In the most celebrated nations religion and temporal affairs were intimately united, and the most eminent statesmen aspired to sacerdotal honors, as the first among men. The Pope is a temporal prince, as well as a teacher of divinity. The English church acknowledges the king or queen as its temporal and spiritual head; and the high dignitaries of the church compose, in part, the House of Lords, one of the co-equal branches of legislation, and the highest court of judicature. The same thing prevails among savage and civilized nations; and, during the last war, no prophet exercised as much power as the illustrious Tecumseh. The prominent nations of antiquity invoked the gods in great emergencies of civil administration, and solemnly implored their protection in peace and in war. The rape of Helen was deemed impious, and the cause of the destruction of Troy, which fell, all powerful as it was, under the wide-spread and indignant enthusiasm of confederated Greece. The very last great struggle for national regeneration among men, the French revolution, was caused by the decay of religious feeling; and it owes its bloody and unsatisfactory result to impiety, and a defiance of the living God.

It is too true that ambitious men, insinuating themselves into sacred places, have often polluted them with blood and crime; but it would be extreme hardihood to attribute to religion those relentless persecutions and selfish cruelties, which, it seems plain, would have been far more rampant if unrestrained by her divine institutions.

The persecutions which our fathers received in the old world from the English and Scottish churches, made us jealous of priestly rule. We declared in our Constitution, that there should never be any *"religious test;"* and that "Congress shall make no law respecting an establishment of religion, or prohibiting the free exercise thereof." The same provisions were followed up in most of the state constitutions; in Kentucky, and other states, clergymen are excluded from legislative power.

Now part of this is right, and part, in our judgment, utterly wrong. As, on the one hand, we readily agree that a man's faith should not be the ground of giving him privileges not allowed to one of another faith; so a man's faith should not disqualify him for office, or take from him privileges which other men of a different faith enjoy. And whilst we cheerfully agree, that "no religious test" should prevail, and "no law respecting an establishment of religion, or prohibiting the free exercise thereof" be made, we deny the justice, or policy, of excluding clergymen from office.

The equilibrium of the different sects is our security against religious supremacy and intolerance; and as it protects us out of doors, so would it protect us in legislative halls. It is admitted, on all hands, that never before, in the history of nations, has any government become so suddenly corrupt as ours. We know that the first minds of the Union attribute this lamentable state of affairs to slavery. Well, that may be true; but if common opinion, and the constitutional disqualification, had not driven our intelligent and large-souled divines from legislative halls, who does not believe that the warning voice of religion, and mercy, and far-sighted self-interest might have checked, if not destroyed, this national and deadly crime?

But a new era is dawning upon us. Standing, as we do, upon the very eve of national dissolution, and a total overthrow of republican liberty, the veil, which knavish or short-sighted men would throw around the religious sentiment of our people, and the national conscience is to be rent asunder for ever! It will no longer answer the purpose of our God-defying rulers to attempt to smother every movement of virtuous sensibility, and manly truth, by crying out "*fanaticism!*" The lovers of mankind begin to give way to the undying virtues of the human soul, and to cry out, "What shall we do to be saved?" For they feel—they know—that great and imminent danger is at hand! The counter cry is also heard from the cravens of power, who have too long trampled upon all things, human and divine, "What have we to do with thee, Jesus, thou son of God, most high? We beseech thee, torment us not!"

A Mistake.

A paragraph is going the rounds of the papers to the effect "that the slaveholders having driven us and our press out of the state, are making it a precedent to do the same with other presses." It is true they have stolen our press—and there are men enough in *Lexington* to *put* us out! but here we are, and there are not men enough in *Kentucky* to "*drive*" us out of the state!!

The Lowell Offering, for November, 1845.

Is before us. We do not propose to speak of the literary merits of this little monthly; it has been lauded by better judges than we profess to be, and we will only say that we deem it superior to many other periodicals of much higher pretensions.

We were never more convinced of the "progressive" movement of modern times, than when looking in person on those lovely females of Lowell, and other portions of the North.

We conceive that the factory system in the United States has proved:

That labor and refinement are not incompatible.

That labor is forwarded by intelligence and virtue.

That physical beauty is forwarded by moderate toil.

That the mind may be instructed, the morals cultivated, and the physical development be, fully attained, during a course of self-sustaining labor.

That the interests of capital and labor are inseparable, and not necessarily antagonistic.

That association in large numbers does not necessarily demoralize. On the contrary: That association aids economical accumulation, and improves the mind, and manners, and person, under Christian guidance.

That cities are not necessarily abodes of vice.

That inequality of fortune, and idleness, and wealth, on one hand, and pinching poverty on the other, are the greatest causes of crime and wretchedness.

If these statements be true, as we feel confident the factory towns and associations prove, what are Christians and patriotic statesmen to do? We answer: remove all oppression from labor: legislate for its elevation and success: without touching upon the rights of capital. Give fair play to isolated labor.

Thus will the rich be made secure, and the poor placed above want: and man's greatest happiness be achieved!

We would say something about the beauty of factory girls, who are given to free and wholesome exercise—for we profess to be a critical judge of these things—but we should be voted a "mad incendiary," and so we keep dark!

———

VIEWS OF AMERICAN CONSTITUTIONAL LAW IN ITS BEARING UPON AMERICAN SLAVERY, BY WM. GOODELL ; UTICA, N. Y., 1845.

This work, like Mr. Spooner's and Jay's, is able and instructive. But it is of no use to argue after that manner. The disease is of the *heart, and not of the head!* We tell you, that the American people know well enough that the bloody stain is upon them! but they love its taint! If we can't arouse the conscience, and ennoble the heart, our labor is lost. Heaven inspire our souls, and may the voices of the mighty dead and living, thunder in our ears, till our hearts shall be moved to be just and fear not!

LEXINGTON, WEDNESDAY, DEC. 31.

"Look at Her, and see where She·stands!"

Massachusetts is full of great men. She has great scholars, great merchants, great mechanics, great divines, and above all, a great laboring class. Her intelligence, her philanthropy, her religion, her virtue, her wealth, and above all, her love of liberty, place her prominently before the eyes of men. Standing as she did, at the head of the revolutionary movement, she has pursued unfalteringly the impulses of her own glorious, self-creating destiny. She declared all men equally entitled to life, liberty, and the pursuit of happiness, and she has lived up to her declaration, and proved the high aspirations of the soul, true, by untold blessings, which cluster around the altar of her faith. We are free to confess, that when we went up to Massachusetts, and saw her "as she stood," with her people, her wealth, her improvements, her arts, her soul-stirring monuments of gallant achievement, the heavy and painful aspiration weighed upon our spirits, "O, that our native state was like this!"

We have just finished reading in the Free State Rally, the speech of Stephen C. Phillips, delivered in Boston, on the 18th day of Nov., 1845, on the annexation of Texas. We do not know when we were so moved by any speech! How shall we speak of this man? True, generous, lofty, intelligent, great-souled, are tame words in connexion with him! He knows the crisis is at hand. He knows what Massachusetts is. He knows what Massachusetts has done. He is her son. He loves the glory of his native land. The map of the United States is before him—stretching from the frozen to the torrid zone, from sea to sea, from the rising to the going down of the sun! embracing all climates and soils. Here lie the widest plains, the longest and highest ranges of mountains, the largest and most far-reaching rivers, the sublimest scenery! Inland seas, great sea coast, Harper's ferry, the mammoth cave, the Falls of Niagara, the great prairies of the west, in giant nature appealing eternally to the depths of the human mind, seem to make us the nation of God on earth !

Century after century had come and gone, nations had been born and had died, governments formed and perished, philosophers, and statesmen, and scholars, had reasoned, and studied, and concentrated the wisdom of ages, and the experience of untold years, and the art of printing had fixed them and spread them among the masses of men, and the Christian code had taught them the individual worth of man, equally entitled to the goods of earth, and the divine favor and glorious immortality. But old worn out forms—the cast off crysalis of regenerated man obstructed the new expansion of his higher nature, and he found not in Europe, nor Asia, nor the isles of the sea, nor Africa, a home.

Then for the first time, and in the nick of the necessity, this new world was opened up to the view, and this glorious theatre spread out to liberty and virtue!

He came through much suffering and wo, for it must needs be through fire that the soul is purified, that man might remember the God of his being forever, and that not by blind chance do the good things of earth abound. Yet more, we did not walk into an uninterrupted paradise, lest we might forget the hand of oppression ; it was once more stretched out over us, till our fathers called again upon the God of all to witness the justice of their cause, and having sealed their faith with their blood, they left us FREE ! Mr. Philips sees this. He knows that justice is the only basis of lasting security—that liberty dies, when justice is lost. He feels the golden rule, do unto others as you would they should do unto you. He knows that his security consists in making others secure : and that when his neighbor falls under oppression or despotism, he must fall next ! He feels that when *constitutional* liberty is gone, *liberty* is gone ! That the arbitrary will of numbers is the most damnable of all despotisms ! He knows that the resolution of the last congress, annexing Texas, a foreign slave nation to us, was not only a criminal attack on the rights of man, but in the teeth of the American Constitution, which makes the senate, the representative of the states, the only power capable of acquiring or losing territory, through treaties with foreign nations.

He is wise enough to know that a sufferance of a *single* despotic wrong, is the loss of *all rights !* He looks to Massachusetts where she stood, and then again where she will stand, when a great unconstitutional slave despotism spreads in lengthening pall of crime and wo over a once free continent, and liberty be known no more! When Massachusetts shall be dwarfed to a point, and Faneuil Hall be filled with slaves, and the eyes of bondmen look up upon Bunker Hill, and base bodies sink down into voiceless wo! Is that man eloquent? Yes; there were no remnant of the God-like spirit in piteous nature, if he were not. He proudly raises his eyes to "Webster and Adams," and damns the traitor who would basely stoop from the field of freedom's battle, and cries "all is not lost!" Go then, thou old and scarred veteran, once more to the field of thy soul's love—the war for the right—and let thy death eclipse the glory of thy life! Webster! Now if indeed thou art *the man* of the age and of the world, we tell you, the world and the age, and all coming ages, call for such a man! Defender of the Constitution! speak now if thou art the Olympian, in the divine power of truth, liberty, and law. Let thy voice, in thunder tones, shake the continent from its sleep of half a century, and make the old Bastile of slavery crumble to its very foundations! Look back to the dungeon—the scaffold—the battle-field:—the spirits of the great dead walk unavenged among us! Hear! "Don't give up the ship!" "Live or die, I am for the Declaration!" "Give me liberty, or give me death!" "In the name of the living God, I come!" Millions of eyes from the unmeasured abyss of the dread future, are turned to Massachusetts— to her God-like sons—well then let them "*look at her and see where she stands !*"

PROF. THOMAS D. MITCHELL.

The lecture of this gentleman, published by the medical class of Transylvania is before us. The lecture is as good as might be expected upon so common-place a theme—"the reciprocal obligations of professors and pupils." We have heard Professor M. on other occasions, and deem him an able lecturer. We regret to see his allusion to the Louisville Institute: we know how hard it is to bear reproach and detraction, (if such have been used,) yet commend what we do not always practice, magnanimous forbearance. Prof. M. states the number of students at from 150 to 200; this is enough in all conscience! This number added to the 350 at Louisville, would make 550 students of medicine now at *public* schools in our State! We intend no reproach upon the profession when we say, they had better be running the plough, throwing the shuttle, or pushing the plane. We are selfish enough, however, to wish our schools prosperity. Of all producers of wealth, education is the cause of the greatest nett accumulation. A few talented men, without any raw material but brains, and a few books, may bring millions to a city; to say nothing of health, cultivation, and renown: and we say this, feeling that the medical school was the cause in part of the overthrow of our press.

The people of the South may be proud and tyrannical, if you please, but not utterly *contemptible ;* they will not honor a man for mean subserviency, even to slavery! The Lexington school we hope will flourish; but the mob of the 18th has fixed a stain upon this city which all time cannot eradicate! She may not feel it just now ; bnt it will rise up in the minds of the young and true-hearted, that here was plotted the foulest deed that the American sun has yet looked upon !

> " There's blood upon that dinted sword,
> A stain its steel can never lose! "

LEXINGTON, FEBRUARY 4, 1848.

Fourier Association—the Harbinger.

We give place below to some strictures upon us, because of our article in the 18th No. upon Fourierism. We number among our warmest personal and political friends, some men and women holding the doctrine of "Association." The Harbinger has condescended to notice our efforts in the cause of liberty, and to award us a position far above our merits (although we feel that we deserve somewhat the sympathies of all true men); we shall therefore take censure with the same spirit that we do praise, being neither elated by one, nor depressed by the other.

We are not learned in metaphysical disputation; and have no taste or time for the trial, and no ambition to triumph in speculative philanthropy. Seeing great and pressing evils lying across our path in life, we cannot from our organization go round them, and we would not if we could. We shall deem ourselves happy, when our lamp is extinguished, if it shall be said of us, there was one who dared to do *right*, at whatever cost of personal and spiritual care. We think we have fully proved to the world, or that very small portion of it to whom we are known, that we shall not sacrifice an honest and manly expression of our sentiments to *friend* or *foe*. It is far easier in life to cater to the crimes and *delusions* of men, than to incur their censures, by a faithful setting forth of the right and the true, as we see it. We do not profess to be *wise* but *honest*. If any other man, or set of men, shall be gifted with a broader insight into the nature of things, than we,—much more if by self-sacrifice they shall lead the way to *truth and happiness*, which are the temple of the living God—none shall exceed us in profound admiration and reverence.

We aspire not to the "profundity" of "philosophy," and have no reverence for the "ridiculous." If we are not "clear-sighted" and "qualified," we submit that "philanthropy" should forbear the *reproach*. As to matters of "faith" we are used to hold it "unphilosophical" to *condemn* for any *faith*. We were foolish enough to believe that men were *responsible* for *not* acting up to the faith or the conscience that is in them. If faith be a crime, then is many an honest man damned! Can the word "*infamous*" apply to *faith* in any case whatever? For our part we are prepared to condemn neither Malthus nor Fourier.

The truth is, we did not approach the subject of association with "levity." We gave our candid opinion of it with freedom, because of our sympathy for *general humanity* without the bounds of "Kentucky." It is the sick who need a physician; if the wound is not to be probed, it is not necessary to call him. If association be founded upon the nature of man, our mistake or shallow ideas, will not retard its success, for we did not profess to "*understand*" it. If it be *not* founded on the nature of man, it were better that all should receive a timely warning, that they were entering on an unknown sea, full of whirlpools and breakers! If we had treated the subject with a "sneer," we should have found it easier, and have been sufficiently *common place!* We did not *utter* it, because we did *not feel* it. On the contrary, wherever we see an honest spirit striving for the removal of those thousand ills, which press upon humanity, he has our respect and sympathy. True philanthropy may cause the cold-hearted to mock, but is never *ridiculous.* The World's convention! What is there in it to cause "levity?" The Harbinger cannot vindicate it from cachinnation! Association is different; it attempts to *do:* it is not mere *words!* Heaven forbid that we should throw cold water upon any attempt to raise fallen man! We say again, they may succeed; we hope they may; but yet we want faith. Brothers, be prepared on all hands; let the good that ye do be your reward; for hope unattained is an ashen apple to hungry lips!

Let us see. The associationists claim "social equality." Now, if sociability is founded upon the same principle as "friendship, which acknowledges equality wherever it meets with sympathies"—and it can be founded upon no other—and there is an admitted difference in "tastes," and consequently in *sympathies,* how "in the name of all the gods at once" is "social equality" possible? "Equality of conditions," we both agree, is impossible! "Equality of rights," is attainable; for that we contend. The socialists overlook this *possible,* for the equality of sociality, which is *impossible!* The meaning of the Declaration of Independence is *true.* The word "*equal*" was not the word which ought to have been used, because in one sense it is not true, and gives room for cavil. It is not possible, perhaps, to find a single word to fill its place. The idea contended for is, that all men are, or ought to be, allowed the free and untrammeled use of spirit and body, so far as is compatible with the law of nature and of God. In other words, no man, or set of men, ought to put a disqualification on another, which God has not put upon him. That law which makes me a lord of England, is unequal, because whatever merit B has, who was born at the same time, he cannot be a lord! That law which gives me the property of my father and thus gives me an advantage over B who is poor, makes our conditions *unequal* in fact. Yet it may still be just, and in accordance with the Declaration of 1776; because there is nothing in the laws why B might not have been equally wealthy. B's father

was a spendthrift, and mine economical! Does nature object
to such a law? Never! We oppose slavery, not because it
obstructs us in the race of life; for it does not, seeing we had
the vantage ground by birth; but because it is at war with
nature and the laws of nature's God. We leave it to unpreju-
diced minds to say, who stands upon the true ground of reform,
we, or the associationists? Our "Familism," by the laws of
our state, if not *Catholic*, was so favored that we had "a higher
place than our neighbors;" but we scorned to use factitious
advantages : we preferred to come down into the broad republican arena which Deity spreads out to the sons of men, and
contend for honor, prosperity, and happiness. The arrow, if it
were poisoned, which we trust it was not, falls harmless at our
feet! Our readers will see, that we embraced in our word "refinement," not mere conventionalisms, but, in addition, natural
organic sensibility, so that the criticism of our reviewer does not
reach us.

We say "the cook and washer-woman are," in one sense,
"menials," but that *no* "stigma" rests upon them, rightly. One
of the great evils of slavery is, that it *heightens* the base prejudices, which exist in even free states, making all those employments dishonorable, by association of ideas, in which slaves are
employed. For our own part, we admit the "social equality"
of washer-women and cooks, when they are of similar tastes
and accomplishments with ourself : although the difference of
employments would require some sacrifice of convenience in
enjoying their company. The consequences would be, that
unless there was a purer and nobler spirit, or a more lovely personage, in the working woman, we should assort with the lassies
nearest at hand. The worst deception in the world, is that
wherewith we deceive ourselves. We are not creatures of pure
reason or pure justice; we are governed much by the imagination. If it sometimes underrates one class, it also overrates
another class. Many a man marries "the ideal" and goes out
at the elbows, and with an empty bread-basket because of the
"Divinity" of his wife. Whilst many another man marries
"the cook or the washer-woman" and grows fat, seeing that he
knows who is the father of the "little blessing" that squalls in
the cradle!

With regard to the ultimate perfection of mankind and entire
happiness we are skeptics! Deity has laid down certain laws,

which makes our happiness but an *approximation* to bliss.
The Christian religion teaches the same doctrine. Faith will
not cure us of evil. The violation of natural laws brings woe,
whether our intentions be, metaphysically speaking, good or
bad! We must be not only conscientious, but *wise*. We regard virtue as another term for knowledge and conformity to
the law of nature. The epitaph by Burns, sums up our faith
in this respect: if we insert *virtuous* for "honest," which is
limited in its meaning:

> "Here lies a (virtuous) man, * * *
> If there's another world, he lives in bliss,
> If there is none, he made the best of this."

Of course we put virtue here in its largest sense, including
an expansive conformity to all the laws of our moral, intellectual and physical existence. Nations will rise and fall, be
happy, or miserable, in as far as they are wise and virtuous.
We have no guaranty that the printing press will necessarily
preserve and increase knowledge and virtue. This nation now
is preaching democracy and liberty, and complacently extending
one of the most damning despotisms the world has seen! We
cannot escape the awful retribution of this monstrous violation
of all the laws of God and nature. It does not need a resolution or special judgment of God to effect this: our hand is
thrust into the fire, and surely it will be utterly destroyed unless
we speedily withdraw it! Heaven help us, if a sin-hating God
shall bare his red right arm.

LEXINGTON, WEDNESDAY, FEB. 11.

Elijah Hart.

Our correspondent talks plainly. We like that. There
is some hope for a man, however wrong, if he be frank and
honest.

We have never, however, advocated the abolition of the death
penalty, although some writers in the True American look that
way. It is not plain that the abolition of the death penalty

would increase crime, but we are not prepared now to make new issues.

We *are* the advocates of universal suffrage.

We are in favor of the abolition of slavery because it is the mother of "ignorance and corruption," first, to all the blacks, and next, of necessity, to most of the whites. The common school system has not succeeded in a single slave state; and never will succeed in one of them. It is the interest of slaveholders to keep non-slaveholders ignorant, else slavery would be overthrown in a day. Abolish slavery, and you abolish the "school of revenge and bloodshed."

We are more opposed to "amalgamation" than Mr. Hart; and because we are opposed to amalgamation we oppose slavery; for while that exists, it goes on infinitely faster than in a state of freedom! The danger is not in setting men free, but in holding them in slavery. Let any man look around him; how few crimes are committed by free blacks, in comparison with the slaves! In the West Indies there were from six to eight blacks to one white; here it is the reverse. Yet in the Islands, although the masters bitterly opposed emancipation, and the blacks regarded the boon of liberty as coming solely from the central government, yet not *a single emeute* or outbreak has ever taken place!

Then let us hear no more of this silly cry of the danger of freedom. Love begets love, and justice begets justice. Will any man deny the proposition in terms? Then why beat the bush for a raw head and bloody bones to frighten women and children? All that is wanting to make Kentucky free is the WILL. If justice be of God, its fruits must be peace, happiness, and eternal prosperity.

LEXINGTON, WEDNESDAY, JAN. 21.

CROW-FOOT SKETCHES.

Chestnut street, Philadelphia, is the sheep walk of the hautton, for man is gregarious, and so is a sheep; man has wool on his head, so has a sheep; a sheep has a leader, and the rest follow; man has a leader, and all the rest follow; a sheep has horns—enough said!

When we were a school boy we used to put a drop of ink on a sheet of white paper, and then fold it down and press it; the line of flection passing through the drop, strange and fantastic figures were the result. These we used to call crow-foot sketches.

There are crow foot sketches in Chestnut; things human and inhuman; such things as are described in the books; and such things as are not described at all.

We say nothing now of the men; when they are once done for, there is no cure. Lord Chesterfield hoped that regard for the opposite sex might effect something, and put his son under the tutelage of "fine women;" but it would not do. Man must be original and self-relying or nothing. Not so the women; they look to us for their every help, and improve by precept.

But, for the sights in Chestnut street: And first, we saw women, thick and thin, fat and lean, high and low, angular, rectangular, and triangular. We saw a nose with a face to it, and a face without a nose; a neck without a head on it, then a head without a neck—a lard keg and the human face divine in awful and mysterious junction—as some ass said of Ole Bull and his fiddle, "it was hard to say where the fiddle ceased and the man began"—so of the keg and the face! We saw old "gals," from one to three in a squad, lean, dry, and sallow, a drop of rain missing once the head, would never touch in its descent. Their eyes wore a fixed and lack-lustre cast; and if by some chance they fell upon that "other part of mankind which is not a woman," they spoke in unmistakable language, "Sir, you will be d——d for this." Some had thin and wind blown hair, wiry, like a cataract of cork screws—some plaited, some crisped; and then there was a lassie with yellow mane, which showered its voluminous folds in all directions, like the fiery beams of the autumn sun. Some were *fat*—not plump; yes, by Jove, *fat*—a fat woman has no soul; immortality is swallowed up of mortality; we tell you they will go to sleep, and a shower bath can't wake them! We saw three women in a row; they were of the same size, had the same step, all loaded with cotton bales; and they beckoned to the east, and then to the west. Did you ever see three cradlers abreast in a wheat field? They are all *au-fait* at the stroke; like soldiers, they keep time, and respond to the flam of the drum sticks! We saw dresses of all sorts and colors, one, two, and three stories high; one of mud, one of brick, and one of stone. Out upon such horrid architecture! If a woman is a ball, or a triangle, or a square, or any other geometrical figure, the more clothes she puts on, the more breaks in the outline, the more colors, the better; for if she be a monster in form, a clothes horse is the lovelier sight. But if she be a woman, of divine image, simplicity—simplicity—simplicity is all.

We saw some skins like old leather; some chalky, and some laid down in brick-dust; and indigo about the eyes. Take care there! "Wolf in the camp!" We leaned our arm against the column at Jones', and for an hour let our eyes fall with the freedom of a stranger, upon this stream of caricatures, till we felt like swearing by the mammoth cave, the wild crab-apple orchard, the racoon dog, the best rifle, the snapping turtle, and the half horse and half alligator, and the small touch of an earthquake, that there was not a pretty woman out of old Kaintuck, when we were of a sudden smoothed down like a frill under a hot iron! We saw her coming at last; she was half an inch above medium size, and would weigh more than she seemed—which a practised eye gathers from the momentum, as truly as from the scales—the movement cannot be imitated. There was the whole outline of the woman, with no breaks in the dress, neither in the edge nor color. The bonnet was of dark crimson velvet, with a red, graceful feather hugging it around unostentatiously; a dress of a warm color, and elastic texture, closing at the round wrists with clasps, swelling with the shoulders, gently shrinking with the waist, widening once more, and then with the undulations of the walk closing in sympathetically with the loveliest feet and ankles, in saucy boots of the same hue of the dress—a scarf thrown over the shoulders, so as to form a pretext for bringing the well chiselled hands to a clasp at the zone. It may be that a band of polished gold or brilliants shone through the intervals of the wrist bands; and the all-pervading colored gloves, we know, concealed the offerings of the happy lover. There were features, not classic, but passionate, and full of poetry and soul; the large and expressive mouth; eyes large, wide apart, and wide awake, under seemingly sleepy lids; rich auburn hair, so judiciously braided as to fill out to perfection of outline, a most beautiful head. She seemed to walk, all intent on her own sweet thoughts, as if conscious of the inexhaustible treasures of her own being. With one glance she knocked the crow foot sketches into a cocked hat, and "Mrs. Peck's husband" was a dead man!

LEXINGTON, WEDNESDAY, FEB. 18.

W. Z. T. AND THE CHRISTIAN INTELLIGENCER.

There is no true-hearted man in our state, who is not proud in his secret thoughts, that there is one Kentuckian who stands up under all difficulties, and truly and boldly defends the liberty of the press and eternal justice.

The time has not yet come when Evan Stevenson is to receive his full reward. But come it must as sure as any thing noble yet remains in the hearts of men, or Deity watches over the things of His own creation.

Mr. T. speaks in seeming coolness, and we will show him that we can do so too.

Mr. T. says he has been for some years past in "favor of gradual emancipation." Has he *begun* his system of gradualism? When will he begin? Has he liberated his own slaves? Has he freed any portion of them? Has he fixed a time when all or any portion of them are to be free? If not, then we confess that we are a more ultra-abolitionist than he. Has he urged emancipation upon the state at large? Has he proposed his plan of gradualism? When does he advise its commencement? Is he prepared to vote out his views? If not, he is far less "*rash*" than we: he has a prudence that would make Falstaff himself shed tears of admiration!

Mr. T. says our abolitionism comes from the love of "*black* men," his abolitionism from the love of the "*white* man." Where does Mr. T. get this information of our views, since he admits he does not read our paper?

We are not a professed Christian as Mr. T. is: we do not read our Bible so much: perhaps Christ did die for "white men" only, not for the love of the blacks. The Mogul, the Malay, the Indian, perhaps they are not all children of the same Father—the God of all. That may be a good reason for his loving only white men. But we protest against his giving our *motives* as they do *not* exist. We go for the abolition of slavery, not because the slave is *black* or *white*—not because we love the black man best, for we do not love him as well, we confess we are full of prejudice,—but because *it is just*—because it is honest—and because honesty is the best policy. If this is ultra, truth is ultra, and we are ultra.

Mr. T. thinks that sentiments similar to his were fast gaining preponderance in the state till our "ultraisms" caused a retrograde movement in public sentiment. Now, if this be true, we ought to be a great favorite with the perpetualists: we deserve a statue.

If Mr. T. will read the history of British emancipation, he will find that the same song was sung in England: and Wilberforce and Clarkson were ever reproached with causing "a retrograde movement." Yet emancipation came at last in spite of the efforts of the abolitionists to the contrary. So here in Kentucky, emancipation will come at last in spite of our ultraisms, and Mr. T.'s *gradualisms!*

Public sentiment is "morbid," says Mr. T.; it is diseased. Well, then, it needs a physician: a diseased mind needs truth to cure it: for truth is the mind's only medicine. Now we call upon Mr. T. in the kindest spirit, to show wherein our doctrines want truth; and if he does, we pledge ourselves to come over to it. Will he do as much?

We have "fretted off the bridle and thrown it away." We go free from the errors of habit—of education—of dogmatism: we seek after the right only, and having found it, we speak out, like a free-born man what we think as we see it. We are of Jefferson's opinion, that "error may be safely tolerated, if reason is left free to combat it." If we have gone into any excesses, we should be glad to have Mr. T. to point them out, and we promise reform. Yes, we are "rash and reckless" of the denunciations of the worshippers of error and crime. We return blow for blow: we send back bitter words against calumny; but under the holy influences of right and kindness, we are as tame as the shorn lamb. So that brother T. may *come it over us with as much effect* as he did over brother Evans—and no more.

The Rochester American,

Severely criticises our reply to the Albany invitation. As to all the bad taste of the thing, we plead guilty. When we sit as a stern critic upon our own composition, we are often ready to go as far as the farthest in denunciation of our style. It is very easy, at any rate, for a man with his feet upon the fender, or on somebody's writing table, to talk very philosophically about the proper means of overthrowing a despotism which the men of '76, great as they were, *dared not attack!*

No one despises *mere words* more than we do; but unhappily we have *nothing else to use.* The Rochester paper will hardly advise us to take up a meat axe and cut away at the American people—will it? Well, if we have nothing but words, it seems to us right, that we should array them into all sorts of single and double files, platoons, and hollow squares, making as "big a show" as the nature of the case will allow! What says the American?

Our *modesty* would not originally have allowed us to mention ourselves in the day-time with Washington; but since the American ventures the comparison, let him remember, that Washington lived only to put himself at the head of forces already arrayed—to fall in with a public sentiment already made. The sword was the thing he was called to use, not *words!* Now as to dying, we are as fond of life as any man; we know how to enjoy it; and as long as we can avoid the grim monster, without incurring greater evils, we shall not be slow to give him the slip! But yet, with the American's permission, we think that we shall not be driven from our defence of the right to use *words, great, huge swelling words,* if it please us, to avoid even the risk of a physical stoppage of the pipe of enunciation.

So much for matters of taste!

As to the denial of our proposition, that "if they are not freemen, who tamely submit to the loss of one right, then are the American people slaves," we stand prepared to defend it by all sorts of speech; the premise, the copula, and the conclusion; by all sorts of rhetoric, logic, and syllogisms. Nay, if the American prefer it, we will use something more than words: we will maintain it with fists, the shelalah, the small sword, the single stick, the big sword, and double sticks, the guard and the prenez garde ; and if its editor will only come on to Kentucky, on that subject, he shall have a "free fight!"

The patriots of '76 did not deem the tax on tea a great sum to pay, to be sure ; but then the *right* to tax them by parliament, without their being represented, necessarily involved the right to "tax them in all cases whatever." If they had tamely submitted to the loss of this right, would they not have been slaves? Wilkes and the British people deemed it their right to discuss publicly, in word and in print, the measures and men of government : and in this contest, sustained themselves against the combined power of kings, lords, and commons. Well, had he and the British people tamely submitted to the loss of this one right, would they not have been slaves?

The despotism of Charles, perhaps, did not touch Sidney, and Hampden, and Russell, *personally ;* but when they saw a great constitutional and legal principle, day after day violated, they deemed that he who tamely submitted to the loss of one great right—for the king even was bound by the constitution—*was not a freeman !* If the British nation had not aroused itself and vindicated the right, would they not have been slaves?

It seems to us, that the "American" confounds *private forbearance* with *public servility.* If a man steals our purse, we may tamely submit to it, and yet be free. Why? Because we may at any time vindicate our right, or guard against its loss. But if a people allow a despot to lay unjust tribute upon them, they are slaves, because they both lose the *will* and the *power* of self-vindication ! The American people see the slaveholders violate the Constitution, openly and palpably : they allow them to introduce a slave state into the Union : they not only show the spirit of slaves, base submission to a monstrous and radical wrong—but they place themselves in a position less capable of resisting than ever ! Wherein then are they different from the meanest African? You may say that there is a latent power which they *can* exercise some of these times—so may say the slave—yet nevertheless they are slaves. The constitution of Kentucky gives us the right "freely to write or speak on all subjects whatever," being responsible, of course, for its abuse, to the laws, and a jury of our peers. But of this right we are forcibly stript by the slaveholders : and are we not then a slave? They have taken our property with impunity, and we have no redress : are we not a slave? We hold our life at their good will and pleasure, without fear of law and retribution on them for taking it away : are we not then a slave? And if we cry out then not exactly to suit the nervous sensibility of the Rochester American—it censures ! It does not see the good taste of making such a hellabaloo !

The signers of the Declaration of Independence had the *bad taste* to pledge "*their lives.*" Two of the most eloquent speakers of the age had the *bad taste* to say—one : "survive or perish—live or die ;" the other—"give me liberty or give me death." The American's memory is as blunt as its logic ! Of course all these men were cowards !

It would no doubt be more agreeable to the quiet sensibilities of Messrs. Webb, Mann, and ourself, to look a Frenchman and an Englishman in the face, and lay it on some poor foxy-headed African, as being the *slave.* Yet the truth shall be told, wince who may. However much we may cloak ourselves in the huge phrase of dignified manhood, WE ARE THE SLAVES ! and more shame to us, WE WERE ONCE FREE !

The Anti-Slavery Reporter,

Thinks our remarks in New York, concerning the Liberty party, *ungenerous.* We do not denounce the motives of the Liberty party, on the contrary, we commend them. We do not say of them that no enlightened and consistent abolitionist can approve *their* plan, as the Reporter says of *ours.* We *think* we are right ; it speaks as if it *knew* it was right ; who is most *generous ?*

There are many reasons why black suffrage should be advocated in New York, yet refused here. The blacks in New York are free, in Kentucky they are slaves. The blacks in New York are generally educated; in Kentucky they are not. The blacks in New York are few; in Kentucky many. Besides, we may all admit that the cat ought to be belled : but who is able to bell her ? Perhaps the Reporter can pull out Leviathan with a hook ? We cannot ! We shall try to maintain our independence and impartiality ; we shall be forced into controversy with no party, unless they trample upon the great principles of constitutional liberty and justice. We have defended the Liberty party, when it was worth our head to dare it : we shall not now be turned aside by unkind words, from honoring those who have borne much calumny for conscience's sake. We spoke of the Liberty party, because of their greater number, and consequent importance, not as being less patriotic than the Garrisonians. But enough of this, whilst the *foe* is in the field.

The Baltimore Saturday Visitor, and the Liberty of the Press.

The battle rages apace : and again and again, Americans, you hear and must as surely decide, "under which King Bezonian, speak or die "—liberty or slavery? Those who have read Mr. Snodgrass's journal, will bear unqualified testimony to its dove-like spirit and patient Christian tone, yet this does not avail, and Lynx-eyed despotism has found out that he is in *earnest*, and means to *act*, and he too is marked for ruin.

Mark the fiend-like language of Clagett's resolution, "*best to convict him*." Here the legislature sits as judge and jury, and the liberty of a citizen is proposed to be taken away without a hearing ! And this is a free land, is it? This is the mob spirit of Kentucky—the spirit of lynch-law—the spirit of slavery. How long, sons of '76—children of Washington and Lafayette —shall we crouch under the despotism of three hundred and fifty thousand slaveholders ?

> Come, ye craven millions, why sit ye in stolid,
> Gaze till "they have bouud us hand and foot? "
> "Men at sometimes are masters of their fates,
> The fault, dear Brutus, is not in our stars
> But in ourselves, that we are underlings.
> Brutus and Cæsar: What should be in that Cæsar,
> Why should that name be sounded more than yours?
> Write them together, yours is as fair a name ;
> Sound them, it doth become the mouth as well;
> Weigh them, it is as heavy ; conjure them,
> Brutus will start a spirit soon as Cæsar.

> Now, in the name of all the Gods, at once,
> Upon what meat doth this our Cæsar feed,
> That he is grown so great? Age thou art shamed,
> Rome thou hast lost the breed of noble bloods!"
>   "I cannot tell what you and other men
> Think of this life; but for my single self
> I had as lief not be, as to be
> In awe of such a thing as myself,
>   I was born as free as Cæsar."

Such is the language of a British subject. We call ourselves freemen—we value our own constitution—we enact our own laws—yet a few men, elevated from the common mass only by trampling under foot all the principles which republics hold as sacred, come upon us at their own good will and pleasure, and rob us of our property—imprison our persons, and destroy our lives! Will not some Cromwell—some Cæsar—some Nicholas, come and purge us of this living lie—this foul hypocrisy—this base pollution of all that is glorious and manly?

> * * * * * "Knew I an hundred men
> Despairing, but not palsied by despair,
> This arm should shake the kingdoms of the world."

Is this the language of a British subject? And do we sit here with eighteen millions of men, tamely bowing our heads to the tender mercies of relentless tyrants, and yet dare look *men* in the face and call ourselves *free*?

> "Awake, (not Greece, she is awake!)
>   Awake my spirit, think through whom
> Thy life-blood tracks its parent lake,
>   And then strike home."

Is this the language of a British subject? Americans from what blood do you track your parent lake? Go destroy the memorials of the gallant dead, which shame us in our apostacy, and make us more miserable by contrast, in this well of our infamy!

> "Not thirty tyrants now enforce the chain,
> But every carle can lord it o'er thy land;
> Nor rise thy sons, but idly rail in vain,
> Trembling beneath the scourge of Turkish band,
> From birth to death enslaved; in *word*, in *deed* unmanned."

LEXINGTON, WEDNESDAY, FEB. 25.

Who is Guilty?

The people will remember that there are several correspondents for this paper, one of whom has thought proper to denounce slave traders with great bitterness. For our part, we entirely dissent from this ; we cannot see for our life, how they are more guilty than those who, by their *vote*, and the *musket,* and the *pulpit*, make it *legal !* Is the principal worse in the eye of reason, or the common law, than the aider and abettor ? Not at all. So we see no impropriety in catching slaves with dogs, if it be just to catch them at all ! We hate *cant* and *hypocrisy !* We love plain, outspoken villany more : it is safer and less subversive of the idea that man is born of God, and not inevitably destined for the devil !

Abbott Lawrence's Letters to Wm. C. Rives.

We have read these two letters with great care. The reputation of Mr. Lawrence as a clear-headed business man, entitles his opinions to at least a candid consideration, whilst his courtesy and liberality as a gentleman, demand of us terms of delicate respect. It is not the province of this journal to discuss topics of mere economical interests, upon which the two great parties of this nation are divided ; we therefore avoid an analysis of Mr. Lawrence's theory of a tariff and "reciprocity treaties." Suffice it to say, that we do not dissent from him in a single position taken. We are honestly of opinion that a tariff of discriminating duties, for the purpose of sustaining and *creating* home manufactures, is equally beneficial to capital and to *labor*, which is the main point ; well paid labor being the first element of national and individual progress. By creating *new* places for work, you do not diminish the *old;* and it seems to us that a man who places two manufactories where only one existed before, is equally entitled to the honor of benefactor of the race, as "he who causes two blades of grass to grow where there was but one before."

It is plain, as Mr. L. says, that Great Britain does all her free trade in her literature, not in her halls of legislation. Far less can it be said of other nations, that they are for free trade; for they seem rather to be verging towards a more restrictive system. But even were it otherwise, we deny that it is our policy to go for free trade. We take the broad ground, that if every nation in the world were to abolish tariffs, we should hold on. We say that all commerce consisting in exchanges between nations, of other than exotic things, is a loss to one or both. Any marine, other than a productive one, by fisheries, &c., is a dead loss to mankind, to the whole amount of all the ships and outfits, the food and clothing of the men, and the labor. The more of man's wants that can be supplied in his own home, and nation, the better for him and the better for mankind.

Let us descend from theory to practice. New England has a poor soil; but she has *learning*, skill, and water power. It is her interest, then, to make every thing she wants within her own borders, according to the general theory. Poor as her soil is, it is her interest to till it to the best advantage, rather than let it lie waste, relying for exchange of cloths for Western provisions. But her population rises to the point of subsistence, where her soil ceases to afford food for her people; what then? They must emigrate, starve, or manufacture, and by an exchange of those manufactured articles, get food. Here our theory is fully sustained. Kentucky sends her beef and pork there, and gets manufactured goods in exchange. New England does well; she *pursues* general principles and gets rich. But how is it with Kentucky? She, by violating general principles, is kept, with all her advantages of soil, comparatively poor; because she bears the expense of all the *exchange*. Our hats, &c., cost us *more* than the farmers of New England, and our beef sells for less. A hat in Boston costs the farmer four or five dollars; us six or ten. The Boston and New York farmers get five or six cents for their pound of beef; that pays for the hats. The Kentuckian gets but three cents for his pound of beef, at New York or Boston, where we now drive, it costing him three cents carriage! These are *facts!* Now, by a division of labor, in consequence of home manufactures, on as good a farm, with the same labor, the Massachusetts man enjoys twice the amount of the physical wants as the Kentuckian; for every want supplied is a positive pleasure.

Mr. L. tells us to educate our children and put wheels on our water courses, and then we will fare as well as Massachusetts. True; but not the whole truth. We would fare better, just as much better as our land is richer than the land of Massachusetts. But why did not Abbott Lawrence tell us that slaves were not, and could not become equal to Massachusetts freemen? and of course, education never would become general, and wheels never be put upon our water courses? Mr. Lawrence does not fear competition in manufactures from us. Of course not; for he knows just as well as we do, that slaves would not manufacture if they could; and could not if they would!

No; Mr. Lawrence knows, and W. C. Rives knows, and we know, that any slave state is just now by slavery what he predicts America would be by the loss of the tariff! We are *provincial;* an agricultural people, without division of labor, and without capital, and must ever remain so through all time, while slavery lasts. And we now, before all America—since Mr. Lawrence has presumed to instruct the South—put the question to him, and demand of him as a gentleman and an honest man, if our position is not true? and, if it is, that he say—yes!

Mr. Lawrence may not be of that number, but we know that many Northern capitalists are, who think that slavery is a benefit to them, though a curse to us!

We attempted briefly in our New York speech to meet that opinion. We say, in all confidence, that the ground then taken by us is true and incontrovertible. What is the continent, with all its soil and minerals, without labor? What sort of customers are the Indians to New York and Boston? Slavery is wearing out the soil of the South; "her millions are inert, tame Indians!" Give us free labor and that we will manufacture much more than now, is true; but still we will be, in the main, an *agricultural* people, because we have the soil and the climate. We will have, by the energy and intelligence of free labor, quadruple what we have now, to exchange for northern manufactures.

The products of labor are in a *geometrical,* not a *simple* ratio to its increased energy, for, after the body is clothed and fed, all the rest is clear gain. Thus, A and B make five hats a day, or two bushels of wheat—enough to clothe and feed them in the rudest style—they have nothing to exchange for luxuries. C and D make ten hats, or four bushels of wheat per day; they have as much to expend in luxuries as A and B had to expend in necessaries; but E and F, by skill and education, and superior energy and mechanism applied to arts and manufactures, make fifteen hats, or six bushels of wheat a day. Now, C and D do not enjoy simply double of A and B; by laying up their surplus they may grow a million times more wealthy, instead of just *twice* as wealthy, although making but just twice as much per day! E and F, by making a third more than C and D, are not just in that proportion better citizens, in an economical point of view, than C and D, for they are consuming no more than C and D, whilst they are making a third more! Practically they would be as far ahead, in the long run, of C and D, as C and D were of A and B! We repeat then, that the accumulations of wealth are not in a simple, but in a geometrical ratio to the talent and energy of the laborer; and this difference is greater than any man can imagine or calculate. Its results, however, break upon us with astounding reality when we see Massachusetts, a mere speck on the map of the Union, making in 1845 ninety millions of dollars worth of manufactures, whilst the whole cotton crop amounted to several millions less.

Massachusetts has seven hundred miles of railroad, more, by some hundreds, than all the railroads south of Mason and Dixon's line!

But we have said enough. We regretted to see Mr. Lawrence yielding to the Texas usurpation with a facility unworthy the noble name he bears. He may be a shrewd merchant and manufacturer, and see "new markets" opened up in Texas for New England enterprise. But justice and lasting prosperity go in the long run together; reason proves it—history proves it, the Bible proves it—the undying promptings of the immortal soul prove it. We tell Mr. Lawrence, in all humility and reciprocal kindness, that he is receiving from the South the shirt of Nessus; such prosperity is the fruit of crime, and madness, pain, and despair follow in its train! When he sees Mr. Rives, let him whisper into his ear one word—worth a thousand of his letters, *able* as they are—"*Make Virginia free!*"

CROW-FOOT SKETCHES.

Philadelphia is complained of as being too rectangular; and no doubt, so far as mere beauty is concerned, the objection is good. It is rarely that cities like St. Petersburgh are created; they may be rather said to grow, controled on all sides by obstructions without, and certain conflicting laws within. It is of no use to talk then of parallel right-lined streets; the thing is donè; but by all that is sacred in the sublime and beautiful, why are immense blocks of buildings put up as much alike as two peas, or right and left eyes? Is there no individuality in the Quaker city? Does everybody copy the Smith—the wealthy, or the Brown—the traveller abroad? Is there no genius, no personality in these people? Is there no variety in stone, in brick, in paint, in outline? If not for the sake of violating all nature's laws, what is it for? If for nothing else than to save time, that a man might know his own, would not some slight mark be advisable? Mr. Brown turns the knob and walks right into Mrs. Smith's, and before she can say, " who's that?" has his arms around her : " Oh dear!" cries Mrs. Smith, with a voice liked crushed sand, or squeaking hinges. " I beg ten thousand pardons," cries Mr. Brown, disentranced by these unusual notes —"thought it was Mrs. Brown—wrong door I see." We once heard of a case of a man's walking up three pair of stairs, shutting the door, and attempting to push his head into a night cap already filled with a most lovely face and dewy lips—of course he had mistaken the house !

Philadelphia has many small parks which atone somewhat for this tameness of structure. The old United States Bank and the Mint are her principal public structures; they are of a classic model, but not very imposing. The Girard College is in the suburbs, I presume, the most beautiful specimen of art in America. It is of the Grecian order after the manner of the Parthenon. It is of hewn granite, with a colonnade of Corinthian columns all round, eleven on each side, and six on each of the gables.

The building is nearly complete, with marble floors, arched ceilings, winding arched stairs of stone, and covered with granite tiles. Thus making the building entirely of stone, and of course fire proof. The building will be entered at the gables over flights of steps, passing into a vestibule or court lighted from the roof; with winding stairs leading to the several stories; you can enter any of the twelve principal rooms, without passing through one to the other. The building is heated with air flues from a single stove in the basement; seems gloomy within; of course from its model better suited to inspire awe and a sense of mystery and sublimity, than well arranged with light and air, for school rooms. The whole, however, viewed from without, is the most lovely and perfect building we ever saw, the eye seems never satisfied with gazing, and its beautiful harmony of proportion wins upon the spirit the more it is studied. Certainly we know but one edifice which surpasses it in exquisite grace and symmetry of outline, and that is the work of which Burns speaks, as nature's "first," and made by no "prentice hand"— and about her there are some curves which the volutes of the Corinthian capitals do not begin to rival, from which Burke drew his idea of "the line of Beauty."

The main edifice is flanked on both sides by two regular buildings of granite plain parallelograms intended for dormitories, all fire proof. The whole are to be surrounded by highly ornamented landscape gardens.

Since New York has made her Croton water works, Philadelphia says little of Fairmont: and Basil Hall might travel the country in some complacency of spirit, without having his self-love injured by "Pray, Mr. Hall, have you seen the water works?"

Fairmont is a beautiful place, and worth a visit yet.

The Mint is remarkable for the simplicity, and finish, and perfection of its engine and machinery: and its collection of ancient and modern coins is truly interesting.

Peale's Museum in this city is a good one, now removed to the old Masonic Hall, on Chestnut street, and deserves to be sustained for its own merits, as well as on account of its gentlemanly and spirited proprietor.

It is well known that the Academy of Fine Arts in Philadelphia was lately burnt, and most of its marbles entirely destroyed. I remember to have visited it in 1840, and I felt on revisiting it like returning to the tomb of some lost friend, finding it in ruins, and covered with grass and coarse weeds, and its inscriptions gone !

It was the best collection in America. But as the women have taken it in hand, we trust it will soon surpass its original excellence; for although there are many statues lost for ever, there is genius enough now in existence to equal them. I reverence the olden time only for its excellence, not for its age.

There is still a beautiful marble copy of the original Venus di Medicis; and as this celebrated statue has won the unmixed admiration of ages, I studied it somewhat with a view to see if possible what there was in it peculiar.

There is no question but that the Caucasian, or Pelasgian, race of men is the first in mental and physical development. The climate of Greece was favorable to luxurious and graceful development: the people were not over-worked, and yet exercised sufficiently for health and free and equal distribution of muscle. The public amusements, and the universal habits of the Grecian people, and above all their natural and free clothing, the loose zone and sandal, instead of the corset and spring-soled pinching shoe—all favored physical beauty.

The Greek artist had the advantage, from the habits of the people, of studying the best models of the best race : and the consequences are " the Venus."

The head of this statue, like that of all the statues of the ancients where mere beauty, or the sensual is impersonated, is rather small and oval ; the forehead is shaped in harmony with the chin to produce the full effects of an oval face: the intellectual development of the head is sacrificed to the beautiful and sensual, in contradistinction to the beautiful in sentiment and intellect. In male figures, the opposite course is pursued ; and in the Minerva the same masculine style of head is kept up.

The reader must not suppose me a phrenologist; I think nothing yet has been produced to entitle phrenology to the title of *science*. I believe the brain acts as a whole ; still certain forms of head to a practised eye indicate intellectual and moral differences, with a force amounting, in nine cases out of ten, to a conviction in the mind of the beholder; though those convictions may not always be truths. I do not contend that an intellectual head and face are necessarily wanting in beauty— such beauty as creates love. A merely beautiful woman, with no great intellect, generally knows her true strength, and no divided thoughts interrupt the sensation produced on our sex. A woman of beauty, and intellect, and sentiment, may divert us a long time without inflaming us ; a nice sense of propriety or pride may induce her to spare us ; but when she does choose to play the lover, and is fairly taken herself, she has far more power than your *mere* beauty. So that in looking on the Venus, I venture to say that the head and face do not equal our *living* ideal of the beautiful; yet in statuary where *quiescent* matter is without the play of feature, which reveals the soul, it is perhaps the true in loveliness. The remainder of this statue is faultless in our eyes. The roundness of the shoulders is not to us a defect : it is graceful, and indicates *physical vigor.* I have seen statues which were more impressive at first glance, more rich in animal fulness and budding vitality, yet the modest swell and tapering limbs here more interest the mind, and take at last a stronger hold upon the soul.

The statue, all know, is nude, and *entirely* made after the manner of the ancients ; the head is turned aside, as if startled by an intruder; and both hands are instinctively brought to shield, where " concealing is most revealing ;" and the person slightly shrinking, gives that show of modesty which above all things so moves our sex.

On the whole, the artist must have been a man of eminent genius of course ; and that he studied long and well, and availed himself of all nature's secret stores, is proven by the test of time and the verdict of mankind.

It would be well if some of our modern women could occasionally see this statue to find where a woman's waist ought to be ; and learn that a wasp, though the very acme of contrasts, is not the most beautiful thing in nature, by a *bustle full.*

There were many paintings, etc., in the Rotunda, the part left unburnt, worthy of notice, had we time and space. The colossal group in the centre of the room seemed to have much merit ; and one of the female figures, on the right hand, prostrate on the ground with the face hid on her arm, seemed full of grace and of unequalled attitude.

Peale's Gallery, on Chestnut street, has nothing that struck me as worthy of special remark, unless it be the horse and rider attacked by an anaconda.

I saw nothing in the city that more interested me than the

manufactories. I was particularly pleased with Lovering & Co.'s sugar refinery, and Coffin & Co.'s soap and candle factory.

The sugar refinery is a fine comment upon the system of slave labor. The sugar is carried to Philadelphia and refined, and then returned once more to New Orleans for sale and home and foreign consumption. The reason! Slaves are not taught chemistry nor mechanics, and *can't* do the work: the whites, if learned enough, *won't.*

Philadelphia is said to be the first manufacturing city in the Union; and in spite of her inland position is steadily and securely advancing in wealth and population. Her charitable institutions are highly creditable to her. Her alms house, penitentiary, lunatic asylum, etc., are worthy of the age, and deserve farther notice.

LEXINGTON, WEDNESDAY, MARCH 4.

SABBATH CONVENTION.

This convention met in Frankfort, Kentucky, on February 10th, 1846, composed of two hundred and three delegates, including ministers, laymen, and moralists. Governor Owsley was chosen President, and Col. Wm. Rodes, William Richardson, Rev. Jacob Creath, David Thornton, and Major Samuel McCown, were made Vice Presidents; and Rev. Thomas S. Malcolm, and Hon. Benj. Monroe, Secretaries. It was composed of Christians and others, without reference to sect or party. Spirited resolutions were passed, and an impressive address sent out to the people of Kentucky.

This convention meets the cordial approbation of every good and reflecting mind. Its influence will be felt in causing the Sabbath to be observed. The necessity of resting one day in seven—in pausing in the mad vortex of business and pleasure, and reflecting upon man's *duties* to man and to God—in elevating the affections and the aspirations of the heart, and purifying the soul, has not only been commanded in the Bible, but has met the individual approbation of the wise in all ages. We are opposed to *formal* religion, or formal morality ; yet we gladly wish every aid to fix our thoughts and assist reflection. We believe the better part of our nature, under fair play, will ever triumph ; and our aspirations for the glory and happiness of *all men* are incessant.

The Sedition Law.

It will be seen from the act of the Kentucky legislature, in to-day's paper, that the sedition law has dwindled down into a very harmless affair. After the infamous and cowardly mob of the 18th, and the re-appearance of the True American, the poor mobbites, who have become the laughing stock of the very boys in the streets, some of them having been even hung in effigy, seeing that they had taken off inert types in the absence of the legal owner, appropriating them to their own use, whilst the living editor was walking about among them—consoled themselves by nodding their heads and saying, "never mind, we'll have him in the penitentiary yet." Sure enough, when the legislature met, a bill was brought in, utterly destroying the liberty of the press, and making the circulation of the Bible, and the Declaration of Independence, by being " *calculated* to excite slaves to insubordination !"—PENAL !

The Tobacco Interest in the State were the foremost in this matter, with some honorable exceptions. But failing to play the tyrant over their own citizens by disregarding every principle of reason, justice, the common law, the constitution, and common sense, in their usual spirit of kicking the breeches of Northern men, they extended their laws over the *Free States.* Of course when it came to the lower house this Quixotic law was cut up—" gutted," as some of the members vaunted. The nation will no doubt be surprised to find the more numerous body of the Legislature, composed mostly of young men, sitting as censors, and correcting the follies of grave senators ! But they must remember, that the Senate is of the old dynasty, and knows not of the young Giant Liberty, which is arousing itself among the *people* of the present generation. We had the pleasure of looking in upon the House, and hearing many members priding themselves that the monster " was gutted—made its dying effort—never to rally again." And so we venture to say it will be for ever. In the meantime, we ask *the five hundred thousand white non-slaveholders to make those tools of slave-holders, who were willing to sell our liberties for gold, meet the doom of traitors! and whenever they present themselves at the polls for office, let us see if we can't find some other men than they, to represent* FREEMEN. For we now, since the Kentucky legislature has refused to stand by the usurpation of the 18th of August, giving an earnest that the laws will be *vindicated*, are proud to say, that *Kentucky is yet free*, to us the *whites*, at least. God speed the time when not a *slave* of any color shall desecrate her lovely soil and glorious name!

The liberty of the press was most ably sustained by the mountains where few slaves exist. We are glad of this, for it proves that the *true issue* begins to be understood, and that we, the *non-slaveholders* of this State, are destined to overthrow slavery. *We have the power;* when we understand each other, *will we use it.* The legislature having very justly passed full laws to punish all the abuses of the press and *the exciting slaves to insurrection,* we suppose we shall have no more Lynchers using the plea of *necessity* for their *cowardly plots of assassination*!

CORRECTION—T. F. MARSHALL.

A report has been going the rounds of the papers to the effect, that we had shot Mr. Marshall in a duel. Our friends are aware, whilst we are ever ready to defend our legal and natural rights, by all the power that God has given us, that we have abandoned that *bloody child* of *barbarism* and *Slavery, the duel.* We trust that we are as magnanimous over a fallen foe, as we are ready to resist a powerful one: and Mr. Marshall's misfortunes have stripped us of what resentment we felt that we had a right to indulge towards him, for his unrelenting persecution of us in our hour of prostration and weakness.

And were it otherwise, feeling ourselves deeply wronged, we had but to sit still as we were compelled to, and see those awful and startling denunciations of Scripture, "Vengeance is mine and I will repay," and such like phrases, *literally fulfilled!*

Not one year has passed since the mob of the 18th, and yet

we have lived to see some of its most prominent advocates drinking the bitter cup which they would have thrust upon us. Some have been publicly disgraced'; some have suffered the loss of friends and family ; some have been reduced to poverty ; some have gone to that bourne whence no traveller returns ; and some are now walking about among men, in the full tide of reason and strength, with the horrid image of inevitable death before their eyes, with haggard countenances, showing their consciences are bloody with the crime of proposed murder !— living over the four days and more, which they inflicted on a supposed dying man ! However much we attempt to dispel *the idea of a Special Providence, when men see these things,* reflection will seize on the mind—remorse upon the soul. And we venture to say, that not one of all those triumphant thousands, who, in August perpetrated the foulest crime known among men, will pass away, without bitterly regretting that day ; for, as we foretold, it shall " BE ACCURSED." And when any of those evils arise, to which all men are liable in the course of nature, *they shall then remember, and we shall be avenged !*

LEXINGTON, WEDNESDAY, MARCH 11.

EXTRAORDINARY EXCITEMENT IN HARRODSBURG, AND IN THE COUNTY OF MERCER, KENTUCKY.—THE SLAVEOCRACY CHECKMATED—A "NUISANCE" ABATED !*

" We stop the press" to give our readers an account of a tremendous excitement among the people of Harrodsburg and Mercer county, Kentucky.

For some time past, J. A. G., Esq., a wealthy slaveholder, living three miles from the town of Harrodsburg, had evinced a most *aristocratical* anti-equality, anti-republican bearing. There were unmistakeable signs, for several months past, of deep indignation among the people, till at length an *overt act* on Mr. G.'s part precipitated matters; as it was plain that Mr. G. was a madman and fanatic, stirring up one class against

---

* The style of the Kentucky Press after the 18th of August.

another to the danger of all social harmony and the lives of the citizens of Mercer.

On the night of ——— Mr. G.'s daughter, a very accomplished and fashionable woman, was married to Mr. ———, and the wedding was celebrated at the father's house, in the presence of a very *select* company. It was soon ascertained that the students of Bacon College,* and divers other *people* of Mercer were utterly slighted by Mr. G., and that the chance of getting any part of the wedding cake was hopeless. Some of the most "*respectable*" of the people forthwith got in private caucus, without "distinction of party," to see what was best to be done to allay the public excitement ; or since it was evident that the excitement was hourly increasing, and it was feared that some lawless violence might ensue, it was thought that "a more *general meeting of the people* was advisable." In pursuance of this determination on the part of the secret committee, all of whom were *personal enemies* of Mr. G., yet, still moved by the most generous and patriotic motives, a large and "highly respectable" meeting was assembled at ———.

The great White Owl was called to the chair, and Black Hawk appointed secretary. On motion of the Hon. John Barleycorn, it was unanimously

"I. *Resolved*, That J. A. G., Esq., in giving a supper to a *select* company, to the exclusion of the *people*, exciting a deep and dangerous jealousy between the good citizens of Mercer, and thus endangering the lives of the men, women, and children, was "*a madman and a fanatic.*

"II. *Resolved*, That said supper be immediately 'abated as a nuisance,' 'peaceably if we can, forcibly if we must.'

"III. *Resolved*, That this meeting be a committee forthwith to execute said resolutions."

These resolusions, after a long, and calm, and patriotic report from the Hon. John Barleycorn, were unanimously adopted, amidst most deafening applause. The meeting, having first disguised themselves with masks, and being provided with all sorts of musical and unmusical instruments, among which were horns and pans, and horse rattles, and divers unknown har-

* The President Shannon not long since delivered an address upon the "Philosophy of Slavery!" An address now, upon the child of that address, *mobs*, should follow!

monics, proceeded from the town of Harrodsburg, in double file, to the number of about two hundred, three miles into the country, to the splendid mansion of Mr. G.

The most profound silence and the utmost good order prevailed, until they had surrounded the house. It was now thought just and equitable to give Mr. G. some opportunity of voluntarily abating the nuisance, by a removal of the supper, whereupon the most unutterable discord of unearthly sounds, rent the dull ear of night, that ever broke upon the startled nerves of beatic wassailers! The dance was stopped; and the glad notes of youth, mirth, and love, froze into inarticulate whispers; the bridegroom stood as a pillar of salt: and the lovely bride seemed a statue—Niobe in tears! The indignant pater familiæ rushed to the door, gun in hand, and threatened them with instant vengeance, unless they immediately retired! The people, nowise daunted, drily remarked, that they had brought along some of those sorts of things themselves, and that Mr. G., himself a Kentuckian, should know Kentuckians better; and neither he, nor ten thousand such, should drive them from their purpose. That their bread-baskets were empty, and it was for him to say, whether they should be filled with bread or balls—but be filled they must! And if blood was shed, it should be upon his, G.'s head, who had provoked the assault by first arming his house. It was plain that his purposes were infamous, else he would not have armed himself! and they concluded by appealing to Kentucky and to the world.

Mr. G., seeing the contest hopeless, as it was now impossible to send out for neighboring slaveholders and fellow aristocrats, sullenly retired into the parlor to explain his ill-success, when another fiendish clash of hellish harmonies silenced all once more!

Mrs. G., with a woman's tact, hastily sent them a waiter of bread, bacon, and whisky; they threw the waiter, and meats, and bottles, indignantly away! This action on the part of Mrs. G., was "very imprudent," and tended "to increase the excitement against her husband, already very great." The great White Owl mysteriously "shook his head," and was heard to utter words full of ominous deprecations, "most unhappy, unfortunate man!" After these words were heard, it was manifestly all over with poor G.! Forming themselves into their original order, they proceeded, in double file, into the house, and into the supper room.

The procession was headed by two tall, gaunt fellows, in women's clothes, with caps, and most *capacious pockets*. Without ceremony the stack cakes were thrust into these; then followed pyramids of candies, wreaths of flowers, lemon puddings, Charlottes à la Russe, and the untold paraphernalia of a wedding supper. The great pockets, still greedy as the grave, like Milton's hell, stood, within the lowest deep, a lower deep, still opening to devour! The table being stripped of its wines and eatables—utterly gutted, to a cricket's supper—the procession, in the most " *calm and dignified manner*," * retired.

As an impartial conductor of the press, we congratulate the country, North and South, upon the peaceable abatement of this insufferable nuisance. No doubt some of the ultra and fanatical slaveholders of the South, will attempt to characterize this movement on the part of the *people*, as a mob, and it is very probable that some of the pro-slavery fanatics in Kentucky will echo these insolent misrepresentations. But every impartial man will see that Mr. G. had become intolerable; and such conduct Mr. Walsh has thought to be "necessarily exceptive" in states where men are born free and equal! " *There was not the least outbreak, nor the least violence used, but only so much force used as was necessary to abate the nuisance, and no more!*" And, as a friend of Mr. G.'s, we tell him, that he ought to congratulate himself that his life was spared! For a just public will see that Mr. G. was doing wrong, and was plainly an incendiary; else why did he keep that gun, and other dangerous weapons, to kill his fellow citizens with? The brave men who thus risked their lives in the defence of their most sacred rights will receive their just reward in the grateful appreciation of posterity!

Cavillers will no doubt ask, why did not the people resort to the *laws*, instead of taking the remedy into their own hands? But the truth is, there was no law to meet the case. The con-

---

* It may be contended here by some, that these pockets were intended as a burlesque upon "bustles," and an insult to the ladies; not so—not so. But then, on the other hand, what right had the women at G.'s to pile the agony so high? We triumphantly ask the question of all impartial men!

stitution guarantied to Mr. G. the right, we admit, to eat the proceeds of his own labor, and to invite whom he pleased to partake; and it is true, that a man's house, by the common law, is his castle, and the occasion of a wedding party most sacred. Yet it does not follow, therefore, that Mr. G. has a right in the exercise of this privilege to array one class against another, and bring republican equality—another constitutional right—into disrepute, and thus endanger the whole community. And it is clearly better that Mr. G. and his whole family, men, women, and children, should have been murdered outright, than that the peace and happiness of the whole people should have been disturbed by his "mad and incendiary" supper! It may be true, that no such thing could have taken place in England or France—or in many other countries, savage, or civilized; but then we must remember, that they are filled with tyrants and slavery; and we are *all* free; and *equality* and *justice* are the very basis of our government!

We know that our press has been threatened with violence, because we did not think proper to denounce Mr. G. in his day of popularity and power. But this cry arises from political and *party* enmity, because we have ever been the devoted friend of liberty and the whig party!

Mr. G. is a *whig*, yet we have ever been ready to offer him up as a sacrifice to *principle;* and although his services to the party in times past have been equal to his ability, yet we did not scruple on that account to hand him over to the tender mercies of the democratic party, so soon as he became a traitor to liberty and the *people.*

We conclude by congratulating the people upon the "orderly and dignified manner" in which this whole matter has been conducted; and we assure them that we shall continue, without fear or reward, to maintain one *independent* press in our noble state, and ever dauntlessly contend for the *Constitution* and the *laws*."

N. B. Since writing the above, some evil-minded persons, no doubt with a view of discrediting the glorious affair of yesterday, tripped up an old cake-woman's heels, overturned her basket, and in the confusion. gathered up her cakes, and made off with them! Whereupon the people again met, and the same officers of the meeting presiding. it was unanimously

Resolved: I. " That the carrying off of the cakes by a set of low and vulgar raggamuffin slaveholders had nothing to do with the gentlemanly and orderly meeting of the people, who robbed the supper-table the night before.

"II. Resolved, That we organize ourselves into an armed police, to prevent any further violence in the tripping up of old women's heels, and the low-minded stealing of cakes!

"III. Resolved, That these resolutions be published in the True American."

The meeting then adjourned; the canaille were then taken up, and heavily fined; and when this sheet went to press, the utmost quiet and good order prevailed. Yet, to prevent the recurrence of the unhappy scenes, would it not be well for the next Legislature to make *wedding suppers* FELONIOUS?

SLAVEHOLDING INSOLENCE.

We all remember the assertion of R. W., a few years ago, published in pamphlet form, that, free white laboring men were "*white negroes!*" and we have lately heard our class—the non-slaveholders—termed, in derision, "*tame Indians!*" Is not this insolence insufferable? How much longer will slaveholders add insult to their other crimes against us?

They first monopolize all the land; refusing to sell, or rent an acre to the poor, at any price; they prevent us from becoming mechanics and manufacturers, by driving out all our consumers and filling their places with slaves; they take our school fund, for which our fathers fought and freely bled; and when they have by the ruinous competition of unpaid wages, and compulsory labor, reduced us to poverty and ignorance, they add insult to injury by calling us "white negroes" and "tame Indians!"

They fill all the offices of honor and profit with slaveholders, and have a portion of the judicial power, *self-elective;* and when we venture to set up a press—a constitutional right—to complain of all this rank tyranny, they come upon us and mob us, "in a calm and dignified manner!" These aristocrats try, and acquit themselves; why? because they are slaveholders; and the judges and jury are also slaveholders. But when a

few of the common people assemble together, and by the same
appeal to original rights endeavor to get rid of what they deem
an equal nuisance to a free press, commit a less criminal act,
these same slaveholders are up in arms, come upon them, and
fine them to the extent of the law. Is not such conduct out-
rageous tyranny? Let each free born white Kentuckian remember these things, and tell them to his neighbors, and to his
children. Let the seeds of a virtuous indignation sprout into
mature growth, and in due time meet this insufferable despotism at the *ballot-box.* Let us stand upon the constitution
and the laws, if our rights are further trenched upon; teach
these contemning tyrants that *our* hearts are as brave as *theirs,*
our privileges as dear, *our* homes as loved, *our* hearths as sacred, and that come what may, *slavery shall die,* and **Ken-**
tuckians shall be free!

Crow-Foot Sketches.

I profess to be rather an amateur than a connoisseur in the
fine arts: still I have a mode of judging for myself: at all events
I know what pleases me, and why it pleases me. I hold that
art can never surpass nature. I may stand alone in this theory,
but still there I stand. It is true, I believe, that many times art
may surpass ordinary nature; but somewhere in her great and
varied storehouse, there is the type of excellence. In my last,
in giving my views about the Venus di Medicis, I followed out
the theory of attaining the truly beautiful. We are too often
led astray by authority: some flippant critic makes a remark;
some fashionable men or women take it up; and some eau de
Cologne poet perpetuates it! Thus we hear of a woman's
mouth like a *Cherry!* The artist takes it up; and in a great
many portraits which I have seen, in public places and private
houses, this absurd idea has been carried out literally, and we
find the divine features of woman marred by "a little mouth
like a ring." Now any man of sense and taste is utterly horri-
fied at this. The truth is, a large mouth is truly beautiful.
The expression of the face depends upon the mouth—the play
of the infinite muscles of the lips as moved by various passions.
I had rather observe a woman's mouth to see if she loved me,

than even the eye : the one can be held *steadily*, the other cannot, when they are moved. If this be true, as every *observer* will attest, what shall we say of " a cherry mouth ? " Oh ! oh !

I was induced to make these remarks in consequence of seeing Anelli's Dream. If *nature be the true standard* of excellence, it must be subjected to severe criticism.

The artist has attempted an ambitious painting, " The End of the World," on colossal canvas. Now I contend that a painting cannot be natural and allegorical at once. He represents the world, or a part of it, on fire, and the people flying in great crowds—to the churches? no ! but to an *allegory*—a woman dressed in white robes—" representing the church ! " Does not every one *feel* the absurdity of this? I could give what I deem many other grave faults, but my limits forbid. Many of the figures are very well drawn ; others are not : some admirably outstanding by the right use of light and shade ; others are chalky. It is on the whole, an interesting painting, and being the *"End of the World"* will do for the *prudish* of course to look at ! Although there are some figures that would put the Venus to the blush ! Just as many modest women will not go to the theatre, who do not scruple to see the circus horses ! or live Indians ! or rather their tails of horse hair or peacock feathers !

But enough of pictures. The Blockley Alms House stands beyond the Schuylkill on high and pleasant ground in sight of Philadelphia. It is an immense quadrangular building, three stories high, inclosing an interior space of several acres. It is owned by the county of Philadelphia, and appropriated exclusively to the paupers of that county. The institution is managed by a steward, accountant, agent, etc., including a resident physician. They manufacture, and cultivate a farm.

The officers are very polite, and Dr. P., the resident physician, showed me through the whole building. Everything appeared clean and comfortable, beyond my expectations. The food is good and abundant. The great mass eat in common ; and the cooking, tabling, etc., was done on the most wholesale and economical plan. The inmates were divided out into different groups for sitting and sleeping. I saw some real " old soldiers " who, chewing tobacco, smoking around the stove, telling tales, or reading to each other, seemed to take life fairly enough ! A department is devoted to the insane. The arrangements here were limited; too many together, and not sufficiently assorted according to their different diseases. The physician spoke of a contemplated enlargement of this department. When asked if the malformation of the heads, many of which were remarkable, were confirmatory of the theory of phrenology? he answered, *No!* And thus confirmed my theory of craniology, or the general necessary quantity of brain, *acting as a whole.*

It was painful to see the sick females in the hospital—the awful sequences of crime and destitution. The most aggravated diseases seized upon some: and I was told that the great majority of "women about town" died young, or fell at last into the poor house, either insane, or horribly diseased!

Seven apartments were filled with young women and young infants; and it would have done an old bachelor good to have seen twenty or thirty cradles all going at once; while anti-Malthusians might learn a solemn lesson; for here were sometimes twins in the cradle, and not a penny in the pocket! The children were, some of them at least, bright-eyed and beautiful; and might well have stood as arguments to Richard the Third's theory!

The sight of the orphan children, from four to nine years old, was truly touching in every respect. One little girl was in tears, because her former nurse had left her; and she had not yet learned in the bitter school of adversity that for her friendship was forbidden. Ah! who can fathom the bitterness of that poor child's heart? Her *governess* was to her, home, sister, brother, mother, and playmate, and *she* was taken away!

I know not how it is with others, but no sermon ever reaches me as the simple sight of orphans. If we are angry, our wrath is subdued: if we are sorrowful, it is purified: if we are proud, we are humbled: if hard-hearted and selfish, we are melted down. Well may it be said that charity covers a multitude of sins: well may we claim future reward for relieving the sorrowful hearts of "these little ones." I have seen women in all phases and in all places; but never seemed they to us so divine, as when engaged in this special charity of "visiting the orphan." The commonest features are lighted up with a benign and holy radiance, till they pass from homely to comely, and from comely to divine!

LEXINGTON, WEDNESDAY, MARCH 25.

JOHN H. PLEASANTS, THE MARTYR.

When we received the news of Mr. Pleasant's murder, we felt instinctively that he had died like his illustrious namesake, because of his denunciation of slavery. Being without an exchange from Virginia, we waited with deep anxiety to hear the *real* cause of that tragical affair. For we knew too well the jesuitical Machiavelism of the South to expect truth through the regular channel of the press! We have gone through the same sort of usage ourselves, and, therefore, can speak knowingly.

We give in another column our authority for what we say; and do not doubt it was worse than it is represented. Will not some friend send us the Richmond Enquirer, that we may see how a brave and sensitive soul has been forced to die? How is the state of the case? Mr. Pleasants is admitted on all hands, to have been a man, noble, brave, and chivalric. In the day of his power, his opponents were silent as the grave, or dealt in far off side blow calumny. But Mr. P. sees slavery eating up his once proud native state, in whose fair character and enduring prosperity, the honor of his *name*, and the hope of his children, are identified, and he dares like a man, and true patriot to speak out against the mountain curse and giant lie! Forthwith old feuds are renewed; cowardly blood hounds rage afresh; bitter, vindictive, calumnious words pierce his fiery spirit to the quick; no friend now comes up to his vindication; sullen silence and distrust, or secret connivance, seize upon the mass of his quondam partizans. We would that he had had the unbending spirit to have hurled back taunt for taunt, and, reposing on the consciousness of the great and indestructible right, had stood up only in his own defence! But he did not; in a moment of despair and wounded pride, he hurries *unequally armed* to the *unequal combat—and Virginia's hope is gone!*

Does the public know that an "artillery sword" is as formidable as a bowie knife; and that a sword cane is the meanest of all weapons? But enough. Slavery demanded the sacrifice!

and sooner or later they would have had it! Therefore it is vain now to ask why this thing was not stopped? Or at all events, why less deadly weapons were not insisted upon? Slavery! *Slavery!*

Reader, have you read the funeral obsequies of this noble man? Could you contain yourself? Did you hear his address to his old and honored mother? Did you feel in your inmost soul his words to his orphan son? Then can you form some conception of the costly sacrifices which the South demands to be given up to her *only God!*

ALIEN AND SEDITION LAW AGAIN.

Horace Greely's reporters have been expelled from the gallery of the house of representatives! What right had Greely to expose the drunkenness, vulgarity, and stolidity of the slaveocracy, and its Northern bootlicks? Is this not a free country? Is it not the land of the rights of man? Is not this the home of the oppressed? A plague on all tyrants! Have we not a right to enslave whom we please?

PRAYER AND SLAVERY.

There are many men professing the Christian religion, who also profess to believe slavery a divine institution! Now we have lived thus long, and never yet have heard a prayer offered up to God in its behalf! *If it is of God, Christians pray for it!* Try it; it will strengthen your faith, and purify your soul.

O, thou omnipotent and benevolent God, who hast made all men of one flesh, thou father of all nations, we do most devoutly beseech thee to defend and strengthen thy institution, American slavery! Do thou, O Lord, tighten the chains of our black brethren, and cause slavery to increase and multiply throughout the world! And whereas many nations of the earth have loved their neighbors as themselves, and have done unto others as they would that others should do unto them, and have broken every bond, and have let the oppressed go free, do thou, O God, turn their hearts from their evil ways, and let them seize once more upon the weak and defenceless, and subject them to eternal servitude !

And O God! although thou hast commanded us not to muzzle even the poor ox that treadeth out the corn, yet let them labor unceasingly without reward, and let their own husbands, and wives, and children, be sold into distant lands without crime, that thy name may be glorified, and that unbelievers may be confounded, and forced to confess that indeed thou art a God of justice and mercy! Stop, stop, O God, the escape from the prison house, by which thousands of these "*accursed*" men flee into foreign countries, where nothing but tyranny reigns ; and compel them to enjoy the unequalled blessings of our own *free* land !

Whereas our rulers in the Alabama legislature have emancipated a black man, because of some eminent public service, thus bringing thy holy name into shame, do thou, O God, change their hearts, melt them into mercy, and into obedience to thy will, and cause them speedily to restore the chain to that unfortunate soul ! And O God, thou searcher of all hearts, since many of thine own professed followers—when they come to lie down on the bed of death, and enter upon that bourne whence no traveller returns, where every one shall be called to account for the deeds done in the body, whether they be good or whether they be evil—emancipate their fellow men, failing in faith, and given over to hardness of heart, and blindness of perception of the truth, do thou, O God, be merciful to them, and the poor recipients of their deceitful philanthropy, *and let the chain enter in the flesh, and the iron into the soul for ever !*

SISMONDI'S ITALIAN REPUBLICS.

This able work should be read by every lover of liberty. Sismondi and Guizot both argue that slavery was the cause of the overthrow of the Roman republic. The captives taken in foreign wars were reduced to slavery, farm was added to farm, and villa to villa, till the whole of Italy was populated by imperious, indolent masters on one hand, and abject servile cultivators of the soil on the other. The mechanic arts decayed; the yeomanry and middle class—the curia became almost extinct. Labor everywhere became dishonorable.

Hence, when in the time of the emperors, it became necessary to fill up the legions, foreign troops were taken into pay. And at last, when the Barbarians made an irruption into Italy, there was no seeming resistance. Province after province fell before the invaders; town after town was sacked and pillaged, till the central city, the "mistress of the world" was herself enslaved! Tiberius Gracchus foresaw this event. He first admitted the freedmen into the class of voters; and still seeing that class decay, by the spread of slaves and the extinction of the middle class (the same process which is now going on in all the slave states), he proposed the Agrarian law as a desperate remedy to save the republic from certan ruin; "For is it not better," said he, "to have a freeman on your soil instead of a slave, who will be a soldier in time of danger, than to hold large tracts of land for the benefit of the first invader?" But the slave-owners rose upon him, and in the most "dignified and calm manner," murdered him! And the consequence was as Gracchus had foretold.

Invasion came; the slaves welcomed any change, and the masters were neither capable of making, nor did they make any resistance. Their palaces were plundered, and they and their children in turn reduced to slavery. Thus did nature purge herself of the slough of her violated laws; and such is our fate, unless we return to justice and eternal truth! For nearly ten centuries after Julius Cæsar, the Roman empire suffered the purgatory of her crimes! At last, when anarchy became utterly intolerable, justice began to be done. The necessity of self-protection caused men to *free their slaves*, and make soldiers of them. They collected in walled towns, and the arts began to rise once more, till a common interest enabled the small republics to resist the ravages of foreign and domestic robbers. Thus slavery destroyed Italy, and *liberty and justice restored it!*

Americans, look back through all history and read your destiny! "Why will ye die?"

JUSTICE.

We give our readers in another column an act of the last Kentucky Legislature, entitled, "An act to amend the penal laws." Justice is usually regarded as the highest attribute of God, without which we cannot imagine his existence. The Heathen of old regarded justice as the highest attribute of man. Aristides won the proudest title of all the ancients, for he was called *the just*. The Heathen also represented justice as the chief virtue of legislators and judges. The celebrated court of Areopagus, which was *legislative* and judicial, sat in the night, that it might have no respect to persons. And the image of justice was represented as *blind*, weighing evidence, without respect to time, place, or the circumstances of the accused. The Scriptures bitterly denounce the unjust judge; and all men have united in severe condemnation of partial judges. Why? Because occupying posts of honor and responsibility, their injustice is more terrible, because wide-spread and remediless! Legislators occupy the same place as judges, and are amenable to the same moral standard as the judiciary.

We then ask our legislators if the law above cited is *just*? Every one will at once answer, *no!* How then can they hope to escape from the violated laws of conscience and the indignation of men? A man who receives an indirect pecuniary reward for selling justice, is equally criminal with the one who receives a bribe direct for a perverted judgment, or betrays his country for gold, or takes pay for imbruing his hands in the blood of innocent men. The legislature was, no doubt, induced to pass this law in order *to secure their tenure of slaves*. But it cannot be rightly pleaded, that one injustice is necessary to maintain another. On the contrary, this eternal violation of all the laws of justice, and conscience, for the maintenance of slavery, should open the eyes of the most blind, to the iniquity of a system, which tramples under foot the best feelings of the heart, the firmest conclusions of reason, and builds its Juggernaut upon the crushed instincts and holiest aspirations of the human soul. It was a noble saying of an old Roman statesman, that such an act was seemingly "*expedient*, but *not right*." What did he tacitly acknowledge? *That right was in the long run expedient.*

We hear continual cries among slaveholders, that freed blacks are incapable of taking care of themselves. As honest men, then, *they* are bound to open up to them every road to improvement, which does not trench upon the rights of others. But say some, it is *wrong* to make or deal in spirituous liquors. Well, then, the whites should be subject to the *same* penalties. If laws are made for the protection of the weak—what a perversion of all things, Human and Divine, to punish the weak, merely because we have the power instead of protecting them against power? The greatest injustice in this act, however, is in its *penalties* which may deprive a man of his liberty for giving a brother man a glass of " *Hard Cider !*" Does slavery require such propping up as this? And are there Divines who yet contend that it is of God?

The clause selling emigrants—black citizens of the sister States—into slavery, for exercising a clear constitutional right, is not only infamous, but being as it is clearly contrary to that clause of the U. S. Constitution which says, " the citizens of each State shall be entitled to all privileges and immunities of citizens in the several States," we hope will never be attempted to be executed.

We know some contend that blacks, or free negroes, are not " *citizens,*" within the meaning of the constitution. But will any man point out any absurdity for which slaveholders will not contend? Have they not gravely contended that slavery is of God? Have they not contended that Africans were not men —and that, too, with the best blood of the South flowing in their veins? Who shall be surprised, then, that they contend that blacks are not, and *cannot be* " *citizens.*" But test their argument. Suppose Jews become odious in Kentucky, and a law is passed denying Jews citizenship, and subjecting them to slavery if found in our State ; would not the constitution of the Union step in to save a New York Jew from a Kentucky dungeon, or life long slavery? Suppose the same of a Dutchman, or an Irishman, or a Yankee, or a Catholic, or a Protestant, who happened to become odious in a particular State ; would not the National constitution fly to the rescue? Yes, so long as the humblest citizen of the humblest State in the Union, shall be compelled to fight the battles of Kentucky, so long should the national government protect him in his rights, natural and civil. And when this Union shall fail in this first purpose of its creation, by playing the slave of Tyrants, we say let it perish! In some of the States of this Union, blacks are as much "citizens" as any member of the legislature is a citizen of Kentucky. And Massachusetts would have just as much right under the constitution, and natural law, and more too, to imprison Messrs. Hardin and Dixon, or sell them for life, for *being slaveholders*, as Kentucky has to do the same thing to men guilty of being "*free and black.*"

As a friend of our fellow men, even of slaveholders, we would rather that these things should not be! But as an advocate of universal liberty, we are not disturbed, because these repeated acts of outrage, and God-defying injustice, may be necessary to arouse the Christian world to the damning sin of slavery; to teach the great mass of Americans, that there is not, and cannot be any compromise between liberty and slavery; and, that if *they* themselves would continue *free, slavery must die!*

CROW-FOOT SKETCHES.

" Think'st because thou art virtuous,
There shall be no more cakes and ale?
Yes, by St. Anne, and ginger shall be hot
In the mouth too!"

The Wistar parties in the Quaker City, were originally intended, we are told, to bring a few friends together, successively at each others houses, at stated periods, to enjoy society, rather than the luxuries of the table; but, alas! for the "uneradicable taint of sin," they have degenerated into regular set suppers and honest eating. How could it be otherwise when women are excluded? Without women there is no poetry, no imagination, no soul; conversation slackens into monosyllables; and oysters and grapes are sweeter than the tones of things with beards on! In vain may distinguished strangers be sought out to give these banqueting soirées piquancy; women are not there, and the light is out! Yet Philadelphia aspires to literary reputation. though I deem her, in this respect, behind both New York and Boston. I know not upon what the men most vaunt themselves; but the women claim to be lovelier and more tasteful in their dress, equipage, houses, and so on, than those in the great Gotham. But I found the Gothamites rather snubbing the Philadelphians as *provincial.* Certainly there is a staid and formal subservience to rule in Philadelphia, far less captivating than the bold, dashing originality and variety of the New Yorkers. I shall not now speak of those agreeable and long to be remembered acquaintances, who honored me with their hospitality and consideration. Invited by a friend to look in upon a private Polka party at the Assembly Rooms, I readily consented. The building is large, and handsomely fitted up with a great profusion of mirrors, which of all other furniture produces the most brilliant effect. Most exquisite music was streaming from the band, and many sets, after the manner of quadrilles, were luxuriating in this most sensual of dances. Being a man of no great modesty, and not at all afraid to look a woman in the face, I advanced half way up the room, that I might take an ocular survey of all the inmates. I must be frank enough to admit that in dress the women were up to my fullest expectation. Most of them had the good sense to study general effect, and dress of course without any regard to fashion; each one consulting her own form and complexion. In the ornaments of the hair this was very remarkably the case. The hair was generally braided, and so arranged as to give tone to the head. I have occasionally seen hair that might be let down into curls with good effect. When a woman is rather full in person, quiet in manners, and has a *very luxuriant* head of hair, she may venture upon this hazardous experiment. But if a woman be frisky, lean, and thinly covered with Esau's wear, she must spare me! The polka is a compound of the waltz, and free and general attitudinizing. The head, the arms, the feet, and bustle, are in most animated commotion, and there is a mingling of hands, waists, curls, and whiskers, that curdles the blood of the most veteran surgeon. Most exquisite, delicious entanglement, who would hesitate to put the Gordian knot to the sword? A very graceful *pretty* woman may dance the polka; a very ugly one ought not; a very modest one will not! But I am a backwoodsman; and in the South an oriental idea of woman's exclusiveness too much prevails. When the woman I love dances the polka with some "goatee" satyr, we should like first to serve an apprenticeship to Captain Brighthorn's stoicism!

Brighthorn was an Indian Platonist; he took his guest to a running stream and thrust his walking cane into the crystal tide : "See there," said he. "Well," said the white man. He then withdrew his cane : "What do you see now?" said the stoic. The white buried the jealousies of civilization in his assumed determination : he looked into the water, and into the face of the "Platonist," and said no more. I say no more !

The Jew's ball was at the Musical Fund Hall. It was composed of that peculiar people, with a large infusion of invited guests. The women were more "assorted" from fashionable to respectable. They were generally good-looking—few impressive. The Jews have generally black eyes. I like a dark grey, a chestnut, or any transparent color, better. In a truly fine eye,.there is great expansion of the iris, which by exposing more of the pupil, gives to passion its manifestation, and a deepening of color and variation of hue, as the soul is more touched. The polka, the waltz, and quadrilles were here danced. Amid music, and bright eyes, and sweet voices, I was well nigh giving up my first impressions of Philadelphia, and I forgot for a while the fresh fawn-like fairies of my forest home.

That night my pillow was as hard as a chestnut log, and my bed, some how or other, brought to my mind an old fellow called in olden times, Procrustes ! I was as uneasy as a horse in running water; my eyes closed in vain against intrusive images, and sleep checked not the tide of thought.

I wandered alone in a spacious room, gorgeously and luxuriously fitted up—but,

> "I felt like one who treads alone
> Some banquet hall deserted,
> Whose lights are fled, whose garland's dead,
> And all but he departed."

I strode the room in sullen silence, interrupted by long, deep, and heart-breaking sighs. From out of the floor—by that facility which dreams allow, there rose a most beautiful woman, clothed in pure white; the face seemed like one whom I had passionately loved in early life; yet I knew her not; her eyes were filled with sympathizing tears, and a most sad and melancholy expression clouded her otherwise most angelic features. "Oh, restless, unhappy man, what would you have?" Timidly raising my eyes to hers, by association perhaps, I ventured to reply, "*Beauty*." Immediately she sank into the floor; a bright light filled the whole room; and the most exquisitely beautiful women that eye hath seen, or heart conceived, sprang as lilies from the field, or tulips from the loam, on an April day. Their eyes were upon me with a deep, liquid, unmistakable beam of love. I clasped one, and then another, in eager, burning embrace. But, alas! when touched, their features grew coarse and disgusting, and the mellow, hesitating tones of love croaked unwelcome discord! My soul filled with sad satiety. They were gone!

Once more came up that sweet melancholy face: "What now? not yet happy—what will you have?" *Pleasure;* I answered, in a fretful tone—and she was gone. The walls were gone; and I stood on a hill of gently graceful acclivity, and a magnificent city sprang up to my astonished vision; and golden cupolas, and jewelled spires, and flashing minarets, rose on all sides to the deep blue Heavens. I was in an elegant coach, and fiery blooded steeds bore me, with eagle speed along a forest arched road of unresisting smoothness, to the suburbs. It seemed full blossomed June; and a grassy lawn of velvet touch spread before me, till it was lost in the obstruction of nature's myriad trees and flowers. The sun's rays evaporated the vegetable juices, and gave the atmosphere that wiry spider web motion which tokens full spring, and invites to coolness of shade and luxurious repose. Pavilions were spread at pleasant intervals, with music, dancing, and all the varieties of delicate food. All things were full of joy and life; but the butterfly was absorbed in its own delicious tonguing of flowers; bird answered to bird; and lovely couples of men and women seemed gazing in each other's faces, in rapturous confidence; and from all animated nature there came no glance of recognition—no note of sympathy to me! Deep melancholy seized upon my inmost soul; and I was in the dusky hall once more!

Again my melancholy guardian looked upon me and once more questioned me. I answered through clenched teeth— *Glory.* Immediately there stood before me a most majestic woman. She wore a simple riband bound around her temples. Taking hold of it—as a conjurer draws tow from his mouth converting it into brilliant silk—she tore the ornament from her temples: and with most sweet sounds, wreaths of gems, flowers, and coronets of most inconceivable lustre, fell around me thick as leaves in wintry weather. On some were written in electric brightness "Thou wer't not born to die"—"The saviour of his country"—"Immortality."

Then came a deep and far-off shout, as if the great deep was broken up : and myriad voices greeted me : and mid martial music and banners flying, they bound the wreaths upon my brow! And men and women gazed upon me with a fixed and distant and respectful gaze. But my heart was frozen beneath the sunny current of general admiration! In untold isolation and bitterness of soul I sought once more the deserted hall! And again arose the accustomed face. "What now, impious man? thou hast had pleasure, and beauty, and glory, and still dost thou provoke the gods with thy insatiable desires?" The tone was not at all in accordance with the divine and pure loveliness of her seraphic face. Tears now in turn streamed from my eyes ; my heart seemed to have melted with an indefinable aspiration—tell me, I pray, who thou art—and grant me yet one more request—*thy pure love!* With most ineffable archness of manner she brushed back the profuse curls, which masked her face, and laying her hand upon my shoulder, she breathed deliciously, "I am M——y, your wife! you runaway rascal!"

I bit about four square inches of cloth and feathers out of Jones' pillow!

LEXINGTON, WEDNESDAY, APRIL 1.

DEBATE ON SLAVERY, CINCINNATI, 1845, UPON THE QUESTION : IS SLAVEHOLDING IN ITSELF SINFUL, AND THE RELATION BETWEEN MASTER AND SLAVE A SINFUL RELATION? AFFIRMATIVE, REV. J. BLANCHARD, PASTOR OF THE SIXTH PRESBYTERIAN CHURCH, CINCINNATI. NEGATIVE, N. L. RICE, D. D., PASTOR OF THE CENTRAL PRESBYTERIAN CHURCH, CINCINNATI.

This is an octavo volume of four hundred and eighty pages. We read at the time of the debate a current report of it. We are glad the debate has taken place. We rejoice at its publication and its large sale. We give a heading of the work, that every Kentuckian and every American may know where to get it. We fear nothing from the discussion of slavery : we hope all things from its thorough investigation. We know Mr. Blanchard, and we know Mr. Rice. Mr. Rice was our school-mate, rather older than ourself. We remember him as a quiet silent bright black-eyed boy, who was evidently a *thinker*. We are tenacious of our school-boy attachments; we were, there-fore, pained at the position which he has thought proper to assume with regard to the great question of the rights of man. For upon this question we know neither father nor mother. nor sister nor brother, but deserting all, we cling to the higher, holier vindication of the universal brotherhood of men, without which those endearing names are swept away by every breeze of popular caprice. Mr. Blanchard is barely known to us; yet the cause 'is a species of freemasonry, that assures us of a noble nature, and a firm basis of confidence and friendship. We will not say, therefore, that we are an impartial critic. We are not. A tory of the Revolution was hardly a just historian of the whigs of that day ; far less was the whig an impartial judge of the motives and merits of the tory. We speak, therefore, of Mr. Rice with the barrier of eternal principles separating us. He advocates the cause of despotism and irresponsible power; we of liberty and self-government. If Mr. Rice proves his case, an African is not the only sufferer; we and our children are also to reap the bitter fruits of the horrible truth. If Mr. Rice maintains his position, the American Revolution was a crime and a failure ; the blood that stains the hands of our fathers, and every life lost in that contest, is a murder upon their souls ! The assumption of the British government to tax us in all cases whatever, according to Mr. Rice, was not itself sinful and oppressive, because the relation between the oppressor and the oppressed was not necessarily sinful, but might have existed in a harmless state ! They taxed us only for our own good, of which they were to be the *sole judges*. If Mr. Rice is right, the theory that government is instituted by the authority of the governed is wrong. If Mr. Rice is true, the dogma that all men are entitled by nature to life, liberty, and happiness is false. If Mr. Rice is correct, the idea that society is formed for the better security of natural rights is miserably false ! But we cannot pursue this subject : every one feels and knows that he cannot overturn these self-evident truths. It therefore only remains for us to follow Mr. Rice tediously through his whole volume, and to expose his shallow sophistry—his absurdities—his false assumptions—his perverted facts! We are vain enough to believe that in our Philadelphia lecture, we have in a short, and incontrovertable argument, maintained successfully, that "slaveholding is in itself sinful."

We shall now follow Mr. Rice and attempt to prove that its concomitants—its sequences, are such as we had a right to suppose would flow from a fountain of unmixed tyranny. We venture not to follow in Mr. Blanchard's tracks. He has, in a giant stride, passed over the whole ground. We need not say that he has not left Mr. Rice burying ground! The sophist and dialectician, and special pleader, has been met by his equal in all these, and a *man* in *soul*, and an *orator* in *speech*. Living in a slave state, we shall attempt to reveal some things which were hidden from Mr. B.'s eye, whilst doffing the *gown*, we can strike where *clerical brotherhood* forbade. In following Mr. Rice, we will attempt no system of generalization, but meet his arguments and assertions as they come, the important and the trivial. This method, so opposite to our taste, and destructive of our time, we pursue, because many minds, which it is important for us to reach, are rarely touched by a more logical method.

We commence with Mr. Rice's first speech, and shall take one each week, till we pass through the whole book.

We war not upon the christian religion, but upon its abusers, not upon its supporters, but upon its traitors! The church has a right to ask of a man of the world, a respectful and unwavering vindication of the christian religion; the statesman, and the man of the world, have a right to demand of the church, that it be pure, and betray not the rights of man, and thereby the cause of God!

Mr. B. having led off: Mr. R. begins by alluding to the correspondence; it did not originate with him; he had no desire "to engage in a public discussion of the claims of abolitionism." True Mr. R. knew it a hard case; he felt, no doubt, that he was selling his birth-right for a mess of pottage, for a little brief notoriety, he was sowing a harvest of coming infamy through all time! For is not the advocate of slavery the enemy of the human race? and will they not heap up unmeasured curses upon the man who shall attempt to mar the image of God, and reduce them to the level of the beasts of the field, who, when the belly is full and the body warm, lie down in sleep—aspire not—and hope not for elevation, now, or hereafter?

He here begins to play the sophist, the dialectician, the logist. For remember, reader, the question is not " the claims of abolitionism." If abolitionism be shown wrong, Mr. R.'s proposition is not advanced one step, for it may be proved damnable, and slavery still be not of God! So, when you press a slaveholder, and are about to corner him, and impale him as well nigh infamous, he escapes by flying the track, for immediately he discovers that the English are no better than they ought to be! The mines of Cornwall are disemboweled, the ranker atmosphere of Leeds is vented upon you! It is true *we* are murderers, but *they* are parricides! If *true*, is the murder atoned? Is it any the less a murder, because a more gross outrage has been committed elsewhere? The devils in hell, Milton tells us, love company!

We pardon the frailty of poor human nature. But the argument, the fact stands untouched, eternally unshaken!

Mr. R. admits that something is to be hoped from *moral* discussion. " We thank thee, Jew!" The slaveholders hate this more than all other arguments. The shrewd Macchiavelian will tell you, touch the *economical question* if you want to effect anything, but you injure the cause by making a moral question of it! The highway robber will listen very coldly to "the calm, dispassionate" attempt to convince him, that his *gain* in the long run would be, to deliver up! But denounce him, and above all show him the halter, and he will begin to squirm! We think with Mr. R. the halter is the better argument!

Mr. R. complains, that Mr. B. won't talk " abstractions;" he gives some of the realities of slavery! Mr. R., no doubt, is against slavery in the "*abstract!*" Very good! only talk, Mr. B., about a thing *that never existed and cannot exist*, and we, who have the stain upon our garments, will be very much obliged to you! Do, now, Mr. B., come to the "*definition*," I hate those gory locks! Mr. R. feels that he has to encounter prejudice! Indeed! the human soul revolts at tyranny, neither does it love its advocate: even a *stranger* will not soften down into pleasant smiles!

How will you work it now, my worthy and acute sophist, to

get on the blind side of your audience? By all means, raise your crest; get the jockey word; claim that the advocate of slavery is the friend of liberty; and that the advocate of liberty is the friend of slavery! To be sure this would be presuming a great deal upon the gullibility of your audience; but then man loves to be humbugged! We thank God that there are few men living who venture to be the pure, unmixed friends of slavery; and that they yet have respect enough for virtue to assume her livery! While there is life there is hope!

The question is not whether it is right to force a free man, charged with no crime, into slavery!" Indeed! say you so? then all slavery *not of crime* falls to the ground! Come home then, Mr. Rice, according to this admission, there is not a rightful slave in Kentucky, come home and help us to purge her of this usurpation! We refer our readers to our Philadelphia lecture for further elucidation of this point. For the title being bad, all its *modes* of *transfer* are bad. The civil and common law says: " Non alienum, plus ipse habet." Mr. R. deems that he is not about to justify those who, at a future day, may enslave our children;" yet he is justifying a similar thing—present slavery, being *future* to the first usurpers, though *present* to us! Is not this contemptible?

To reduce a man to slavery, he admits, " is a crime of the first magnitude." " It would be very wicked in me, whether by force or fraud, to reduce a rich man to poverty, but how far I am bound to enrich a man, reduced to poverty by others, is a very different question." This is a specimen of Mr. Rice's mode of argument. This is one of his sophistries. These are the things which we intend to use up!

Mr. Rice is not bound to raise a man reduced to poverty, by the fraud or force of another—unless he has some, or all of the goods taken away from the poor victim of fraud or force! In that case, as the reverend gentleman seems to be very obtuse in discerning the right, we venture, unasked, to tell him what he ought to do—*give up the stolen and robbed plunder!* If men see great principles of morals at once, as he contends, we are uncharitable enough to believe that he sees this thing as we do!

Again, if a rich man is reduced to poverty by fraud or force, and Mr. R. has none of the tainted goods—there is another duty imposed upon him—*to use all the power God has given him, to cause the robber to restore !*

As he is dull, we put it thus : if Mr. Rice has a slave reduced to slavery by fraud or force, for anything else than debt and crime, restore him to his liberty ! If Kentuckians hold slaves on any other terms—vote to restore them to their liberty ! If we have all been equally guilty of the robbery—let us all share the loss—and " let justice be done, though the heavens fall."

We put it to all impartial men, if Mr. Rice's sophism is not exploded ?

Mr. R. says : " The question is not, whether the laws by which slavery is regulated are just or not ? For by that rule the *conjugal* and *parental relations* are in themselves sinful !" Let's strip him. again ! Now we both agree that man is by *nature, free ;* that being nature, then is not sinful. Again : marriage is by nature, we both agree, a right relation *independent of law,* and of course not *sinful.* Now the law takes hold of the free man, and makes him a slave—which Mr. Rice admits " to be a crime of the first magnitude." Where then is the crime ? In the law, of course ! repeal the law and the crime ceases—the injury ceases ! Now, once more the parental relation and the marriage relation, was a good and pure one : but the Roman law comes in, says Mr. R., and gives the father power of life over his child, and the husband power to degrade and tyrannize over the wife. Indeed ! what is the remedy? Repeal the laws giving the improper power, and its conjugal relation, and the parental relation is not objectionable ! But now mark the culminating point of the sophistry ! Therefore, marriage, parental guardianship, and slavery, are not in themselves sinful ! It should have been stated thus : Therefore the marriage, and the parental relation, and LIBERTY, are not in themselves sinful ! For just so far as the law touched liberty at all, as well as the marriage relation, it contaminated it. It laid its foul hand upon the freeman, and degraded him into a slave. It laid its foul hand upon the husband, and changed his love into brutality. It laid its foul hand upon the parent, and he forgot the *father by becoming a master.* We say then, with Mr. Blanchard, the laws are the basis, the bone and sinew, the flesh and blood, of slavery ; dissolve them, and slavery falls --*natural right* is untrammeled—and the thing " in itself is not sinful," *because it is no more.*

We should deem ourselves unhappy in being a slave, but most of all would the bitter iron enter into our soul, to find ourself thrust through to the vitals with such shallow sophistry as this!

Mr. Rice presses Mr. B. upon the subject of the marriage relation, and gets an advantage of him. He loves to run into collateral discussion, he is acute, but never profound; never expansive. No man denies that the marriage relation is a natural relation; its validity in the eyes of God and nature, consists in its purity and undying devotion, not, in its publicity. Its publicity and form of ceremonial, are subjects of human legislation, to ascertain the duties and legal responsibilities of the parties, and to prevent so far as we can by law and public opinion, the facilities and consequent temptations to concubinage. To say that marriage may be abused, is not, logically speaking, true at all. Like truth, or charity, or wisdom, it is eternal. Pure love, chaste fidelity, may be departed from; those professing marriage may turn traitors to it; they may reap the bitter fruits of their crime; the laws may fail to enforce the demands of the natural contract; but still the original type of a possible state of existence remains pure and unsullied, *not in itself sinful*. Not so of slavery. You may be forced by law to, or in your *natural despotism* of superior force, you may clothe and feed me, and be kind in all other respects, and teach me to read, and learn me to be religious, and allow me a full equivalent for my work. Yet, if I am a slave, if I may not indulge my own idea of life, liberty, and the pursuit of happiness, then I am deeply injured, and, according to Mr. Rice's admission, I am suffering the greatest of criminal inflictions!

Mr. R. goes on to say, that as the laws of slavery have been variant in different countries, and in the same country at different times—the relation between master and the slave remaining the same—the laws may be unjust, and the relation may not be in itself sinful! Now if this is not arrant nonsense, then we are, indeed, "a madman and a fanatic!" Now a master being one existence, and the slave another, and *both being men* —what does the word master or slave mean, except *relation?* The relation not being *natural*, but legal, is of course determined by law, and *nothing else.* Let us apply a few grains of common sense!

The master in Russia may make the serf, sow, cut wood, or spin

—yet he may not sell him from the soil ; the master in Kentucky may do all that the Russian may do ; and yet sell the slaves from off the soil, and separate families. Is there any sensible man who fails to see a *degree of crime* here greater than in Russia ? And if he does, in what does it consist ? Why of course in the *legal relation*. You may enact law after law, controlling the absolute control of one man over another, till the veriest slave insensibly rises to the rank of a freeman—and as the last feather breaks the camel's back, so the last removal restores him to his legs ! How then can "the laws be unjust, and the relation may not be in itself sinful ?"

Again : "A master, a father, or a husband, may be cruel, but is the master obliged to treat his slave cruelly ?"

We answer yes ! He cannot cease to be cruel except by ceasing to be a *master !* He "must not of necessity starve or abuse them !" But then by holding them absolutely to his will, he increases the chances of abuse, and his own imprudence whatever may be the slave's prudence, is the *slave's starvation !* Besides, as law makers, we are liable for all the abuses of slavery. If I vote for a law that Mr. Rice should violate with impunity the most chaste woman in Kentucky, I should hardly shield myself from the condemnation of mankind, because Mr. Rice, obeying a higher moral law, thought fit not to indulge in crime ! For our part we have never indulged in denouncing slave traders, as Mr. R. seems disposed to make them the scape-goats of slavery, because we see no difference in the eye of reason between the slave trader and the man who stands by with his vote and his musket to allow the trader to do it with safety ! On the contrary, the man who holds the resisting victim is worse than the ravisher ! Because he aids and abets the damnable deed without temptation. Mr. R. is less guilty only because he *does reap* advantage from the slave trade ! Why hypocritically denounce the slave trade yet refuse to pass laws for its abolition ? The cloak is too transparent to dupe the blind !

He could find many instances of abuse of the marriage and parental relation. A man murdered his wife and three children in Cincinnati ! Well, what is the remedy ? *Punishment !*

Is the slave trade punished ? No ! Again, if slavery did not exist could the slave trade be carried on ? If marriage did not exist, nevertheless, would not the murder of women increase instead of abate!?   Are we never to have done with this shallow sophistry? Is it at all wonderful that Mr. B. *wept*, in the great indignation which springs up in every pure and unsullied soul at this *repeated desecration* of the marriage and filial relation!

Mr. R. says "the slave trader is looked upon by decent men in the slaveholding states with disgust." He will allow us to say that decent men in slaveholding States are sadly in the *minority*, or else his statement is false! There have been two well known slave traders elected to the legislature from Fayette county, within the last few years; and this is a common thing; there are several in the legislature now! We are prepared to *give names* if called upon!

Mr. R. imputes the increase of the slave trade to abolitionists, "they rivet the chains and aggravate every evil attending his condition!" "And upon those who provoke men rests in no small degree the responsibility of increasing the sufferings of the slaves." *We deny the facts, and we deny the conclusion!* Mr. Rice distinctly states in several places that the condition of the slave is improving. We say so too; but we say that this improvement is owing to the discussion of abolitionists! For Mr. Rice will hardly be able to convince men that the slaveholders are such monsters as to be insensible to shame and general indignation! It is true, as Mr. B. says, that amidst all the amelioration of the institutions of mankind, American slavery is now as it was in Rome, still crime, and unimproved, because it is crime; and in crime the only reformation is total abandonment of the criminal action. The spirit of the slave laws is the same—the spirit of the master is the same--the condition of the slave is only a little better now, by compulsion, by the outward pressure of abolitionists, and the inward pressure of danger. The spirit of slaveholders is indeed provoked and Mr. R. very well explains what they would do, if they were secure of the power, and could shun the indignation of men. The discussion is not criminal. A robber takes my purse, and lets my person pass—the hue and cry is raised—and for fear I may testify against him—he murders me! Who is responsible for the murder? The robber? or the indignant executors of law and justice? Is it better to let robbery go unpunished?—or is it better to denounce it and bring the murderer to justice, at the expense of a few innocent victims of his fear or revenge?

Clearly stop his robbery at all hazards! "Partial evil is universal good," says Pope. But here not even partial evil arises; for Mr. Rice himself admits that the treatment of slaves has improved lately since the origin of abolitionism. Whilst we believe that, as God lives or is just, slavery will fall under the searching discussion which is spreading everywhere throughout the world!

Again Mr. R. says, "The question before us is not whether it is right to treat slaves as mere *chattels personal*?" Yes that is the question! Mr. B. has shown that such is the decision of the American courts. How does he get over the *fact*, reader? He says a man ought to be excluded from the Church, who would treat a horse cruelly. "Yet it is not a sin to own a horse!" Let us see: a dog buries a bone; it is not a sin to rob a dog of his bone! Therefore it is not a sin to rob a *man* of his property. A squirrel lays up hickory nuts; it is not a sin to rob a squirrel of his nuts. Ergo, it is not a sin to rob a man of his earnings! Now in order to make the case parallel it must be shown that the man is no more than a horse, a dog, or a squirrel! that he has no memory—no sense of injury—no aspiration, but to fill the belly and keep warm. Does Mr. R. contend that a man is no better than a beast? Will our readers pardon us for thus trespassing upon their time and sense?

"The question is not whether a great amount of sin is in fact committed in connexion with slaveholding."

Do you think he does not come back to the *parental* and *conjugal* relations again? The wickedness done in the last, when overt, is *punished*. The wickedness done in slavery, is legalized and goes *unpunished* by *law*, in *this world!* One may starve, rape, and murder one's slave and go unwhipt of justice. If we are caught starving, by the *whites*, we may get the full *equivalent* in *money*, if any one thinks proper to sue us, and sell the slave of another. If one rapes, it is nobody's business. If we murder, we have but to exclude *white* testimony. We said years ago that we *knew* of five murders of slaves, and not a single punishment. If ever a master was hung for murdering a slave in any portion of the world for the last six thousand years, we never heard of it. "But the sin is not in the relation!!!"

"Nor is the question before us whether slavery is an evil? *It is an evil*." "I thank thee, Jew, for teaching me that word."

Now if slavery is an evil, here is an end of the matter. Is not sophism dead, and absurdity buried? Not at all! May not a thing be *evil* in itself, (for mark the word *"slavery"* is the *"evil"* —not the relation—not the abuse, not the laws of its existence *"slavery is an evil"*)—and yet not be *sinful* in itself? Now if slavery be the cause of evil, it is an *agent*, and is *sinful*. But if slavery be the *effect*, which is an evil, the *master* is sinful. And as slavery is not of itself an entity, an existence, independent of man, but is a modification or sequence of his acts, it is a voluntary evil on the master's part; and if it is a *voluntary evil*, whether moral or physical, it is *sinful!* And from this conclusion when Mr. Rice once admits slavery to be an *evil*, he cannot escape; *we have him on the hip!* If I break my arm by accident, it is evil, but no *sin;* but if I voluntarily break my arm it is a sin and an evil. The will to do, whether it be to cause evil to the body or to the soul, is *sin.* And as slavery cannot be conceived as existing without the will "slavery is the being unconditionally subject to the will of another," and slavery is an evil—then slavery is a voluntary evil, and Mr. Rice stands pinioned by his own showing.

Mr. R. having admitted slavery to be an evil, feels of course bound to do something, but is "not willing to upturn the foundation of society in order to overturn it." Indeed! In what country has it been found necessary to upturn the foundation of society to overthrow slavery? All the ancient Republics *perished* because of *slavery!* The Italian Republics never began to spring up from anarchy, and robbery, and desolation, till slavery perished. England abolished slavery; and yet she stands. France and other nations; and yet they stand. St. Domingo would not overthrow it, and she fell! Thirteen of these states overturned it and yet they stand. All America but Brazil and the American Union have overturned it, yet they stand! Is there an instance in history where the overthrow of slavery overthrew the nation? No, not one! What are you afraid of, Mr. Rice? Afraid of the counsel of the wise? They warn you to act. Afraid of History? She proclaims in trumpet tones—act! Afraid of virtue? She beseeches you, by all her inviting loveliness—to act! Afraid of justice? She demands it—act! Afraid of God? He commands you, as you have a soul to be saved—act!

But "he will not do evil that good may come!" No! **But**

he does evil that *evil* may come!—evil—the one and undying evil! Nothing but evil! No, Mr. Rice, don't do evil, but have faith in the human soul, in justice, in mercy, in man, in God: do right though the heavens fall!

" The question does not relate to the duty or policy of Kentucky, or any other state, concerning slavery." " The duty of the state is one thing: the duty of individuals quite another." We deny the proposition utterly: the dáty of individuals and of the state are "one and inseparable, now and for ever." We call for proof!

Lastly. "We are not to discuss the merits of any *system of slavery*, Roman, Spanish, English, or American." Let Mr. R. congratulate himself! Neither does he understand what is meant by a *system* of slavery! We will do for him what he cannot do for himself: we will attempt to tell him what a system of slavery is. If I come upon Mr. R. in a free country, or state of nature, and by my own power reduce him to slavery contrary to law, or natural right, that is simply slavery. But if the government take it up, and stand by me with the law and the musket, and enable me and others to enslave him and others, with impunity—that is a *system of slavery*. The first seems to be bad enough—the second is as bad as anything can be! No doubt Mr. Rice hates to look it in the face!

Mr. Rice then comes to the question as stated in the caption. And here for the present we leave him.

LEXINGTON, WEDNESDAY, APRIL 8.

The True American.

When we first proposed publishing this journal, we had promised coadjutors, and an *engaged editor*, as our prospectus set forth. The reasons which caused these men to desert us, if satisfactory to themselves, are so to us! Duties and responsibilities have thus, however, been imposed upon us, which in the beginning we did not anticipate; and the conducting of a newspaper is neither suited to our early habits, our tastes, nor our necessities. We do not, however, underrate the post of editor of an enlightened and virtue-teaching journal. If to do good is honorable, then few positions can be more respectable than this. But still the daily and crude spreading of one's thoughts before men, prevents that concentrated utterance, which only can place the author among those, who are to live in the far future. If fame were our sole goddess, we should raise some other banner; but there is a higher heaven even than that where glory enthrones herself. To *Truth immortal* have we sworn undying allegiance. Wherever she leads, we follow.

The True American is devoted to the highest interests of Kentucky; but not confined to state action only. In the national government is a higher ground, which must determine our ultimate destiny. The title of our paper, then, is designed to embody the spirit of the whole movement. The cause of liberty is expansive—*American :* and the American, to fulfil his high destiny among men, must be *True.*

The extraordinary success of this paper, proves that not in vain is the appeal to the nobler passions of the human heart, the higher aspirations of the soul. The response has come back in encouraging tones, from our own "dark and bloody ground"—from the states of the free, and from the far-off lands of century-seated tyranny. Thanks, fellow-men, that you have stood by us and the cause!

We have made suitable arrangements to make this one of the best journals in the Union. We to-day improve its typographical features; and we trust, hereafter, its spirit will be consonant with its incarnation.

Since our reduction of the price to non-slaveholders, small farmers, and mechanics in slave states, our circulation has rapidly increased, at *home* as well as abroad. We begin to prove to conceited and vindictive detractors from our political sagacity, that in our appeal to those who are to gain by freedom, the *white laborers* of America, as well as the black, we are not a "*madman,*" if "a fanatic."

The New Hampshire victory marks the beginning of progress! and the Texas usurpation shall be death to slavery, instead of its triumph!

In the wrongs which we have borne at the hands of the slave power, you have our hostages, that we shall be true to the cause of human freedom. Time will prove, if we are not equal to the occasion, that at least we were not over sensitive in calling for our country's reformation, nor blind to the coming revolution; which must be safe and glorious for our country and mankind, because based upon truth and justice, and nature's law.

Crow-Foot Sketches.

New York, including Brooklyn and the suburbs, contains about four hundred and fifty thousand people. She has the first harbor in America; and being the entrepot of the western continent, she must grow with the widening prosperity and development of our extraordinary people. The time is not distant when she will be, what London now is, the commercial emporium of the world. The United States is already the second commercial power on earth; and if the Union lasts, she will soon reign the unrivalled mistress of commerce; and become the first nation on the globe, in power, numbers, and civilization. New York city will be to America, what America is to other nations; and if she shall not be, as the Parisians now claim, the "brain," she will be the heart of mankind. Already she gives earnest of coming glory. It is the only city in the Union which excites in one an idea of the sublime, arising from immensity and mystery. A forest of ships surrounds her as a wall, and all tongues of the earth are heard in mingled murmurs within her massive masses of palaces and hovels.

Broadway is a magnificent street, and worthy of the magniloquent commendations of the children of Gotham.

The Battery, the Bowling Green, the Park, the breadth of the way, the churches, the walks, the founts of water, the old and dusky, the splendidly new buildings, of every hue and form, make Broadway a most picturesque and agreeable place.

Her floods of moving men and women of all climes and hues, and fashions of habiliment, faces, fortunes, and hopes, increase the interest. Everything is colossal: her palaces, her prisons, her water-works, her omnibuses, her masses of people—all indicate a giant city.

The works of man are greatly prominent here: man himself is lost in his aggregate manifestation. All the inhabitants of many a self-elated village might repose within the walls of the

Astor House; and governors, members of Congress, bishops, generals, great scholars, sprigs of European nobility, and Messrs. Smith and Brown, sit down to the same table, in unnoted individuality; and the head waiter is as much observed as the "observed of all observers!" Few men or women create a sensation in New York. We have even seen Mr. Webster sit down to table, and not a fork or knife was seen to rest from its labors.

When I was in New York, a college boy, I felt all the solitude of our forest wild, and longed for the woods, and the far-reaching prairie, that I might feel my individuality once more. I now welcomed her solitudes of men, that I might be alone to my own thoughts and acts, shielded from the annoying inquisitiveness of the "great unwashed."

When one looks upon the mass of human beings here congregated, his first suggestion is, how do all these live? And this question is not answered till the immense holds of her forest shipping are seen to disgorge the products and manufactures of a great portion of the globe.

New York turns her eyes towards the East, and regards all America as *provincial*. Except when some exciting topic is up at Washington, the eyes of all the Union are upon her. Her journals begin to give tone to the politics of the country—her fashions are those of the republic—her moneyed and commercial powers are spread throughout the land. She begins to be *felt;* and the time is not far distant, when she will be, in America, what Paris is in Europe. But enough of her totality.

The houses in New York are more magnificent than those in the Quaker city. The dwellings more palace-like, of more variety of form, and of better material: red sand stone, and granite, being more largely used than red brick. The equipages are more stylish, and the dresses and furniture more costly, if not more tasteful. The best specimens of statues, and paintings, which I saw, were in private houses, and the Academy of Design had only casts of plaster, with no marbles.

The taste for statues seems to be on the increase in New York, as well as elsewhere in America; and her great wealth allows her to gratify her taste. At P.'s and Gen. T.'s I saw some beautiful specimens of the divine art. Mr. and Mrs. Kean, late Miss Ellen Tree, were playing at the Park Theatre to crowded and fashionable houses. The women were dressed as for balls, and "loomed up" in great profusion of silks and diamonds. Their eyes fell upon one with electric sympathy, with souls warmed by the Mesmeric influence, of full and rounded persons, rose-stained arms, and peach-blossom'd cheeks! Heaven forgive them for my sin of thought! The music of the orchestra was very fine, and the scenic representations unequalled, it is said, in our land.

Mrs. Kean, whom we saw also in Ion, now playing the Queen in Richard the Third, met very well our idea of a finished actress. Her person and features, at first common and uninteresting, reflect the beauties of a cultivated mind, and an impassioned soul, and become at length quite interesting. Mr. Kean's impersonation of a hunch-backed Richard, is admirable. He looks, and conceives, and acts the King well, in all his dark sinuosities in *council,* and bold courage in action, but injures the effect by his r-r-rolling enunciation! I never could conceive how a really sensible man could fall into this cold shower-bath of all real passion. How would a man be received by the woman of his love, if he was to pour out his soul in this wise? " t-r-uest, dea-r-est love of my l-i-f-e!" Pshaw!

Declaim as we may against the theatre, it cannot be denied that it is a most captivating amusement. The glorious, the intellectual, the ideal, the *sensual,* are combined in such delicious perfection and heightened power, that we fear poor humanity cannot resist the temptation to seek them out here! But still my frank judgment demands of me to say, that I cannot look upon the drama, in theatrical impersonation, as any thing else than the most seductive enemy of womanly purity, and heroic manly virtue!

LEXINGTON, WEDNESDAY, APRIL 15.

RICE AND BLANCHARD'S DEBATE ON SLAVERY.

(Continued Review.)

Nature purges herself of her violated laws, and the time has come for the stern application of the means. Slavery demands not a *prosecutor* but an *executioner*. If the injuries we have received at its hands fit us for the task, we are content to yield to the demands of fate. If we shall be found an uncompromising enemy of slavery; if our faculties, whatever they are, are sharpened to the searching out of its dark hiding places, to the sparing of neither church nor state, nor hoary custom—nor of the sophistry, cant, or hypocrisy which labors to shield it—let slaveholders thank themselves for maturing us in the school of their own wiles, for the determination which leads us on in this eternal war!

Against Mr. Rice we have not the least ill feeling. To be sure, we are roused at *wrong;* but then again, we know that his own conscience sits as a stern vindicator of Heaven's right, and his punishment is inevitable. If at times, then, we use words of indignation, it is in view of the injustice of the whole system of American slavery, which looms up in all its horrors, and makes us strike unconsciously through him at the world's enemy.

Mr. Rice we regard as a third or fourth rate man in general debate; as a moralist, far inferior to Fuller, and infinitely behind Wayland. When we laboriously pursue him, then, through this large volume, it is because he sums up the vulgar, current vindications of slavery; and we find it convenient to answer them here.

Mr. Rice is not a bad man. No doubt he prefers doing good to sustaining evil. He is a preacher of the doctrines of Jesus Christ. But he is not of the temperament of Paul; and has not the spirit of a martyr. It would rejoice his inmost soul, unquestionably, to see slavery fall. He feels it to be an "evil, a sin, an incubus," upon the spirit of his church, and the diffusion and practice of religious truth; but, to attack it, would send him, as he thinks, like "a squirrel with the wind in his tail, over the Ohio!" Yet the great world *is* attacking slavery. If it be proved damnable, the church South stands in the same category. What, therefore, is to be done? They must defend themselves, lest a white cravat become disreputable, and the boys in the streets hoot at a black gown! This is Mr. Rice's position; it is the position of a great number of southern Christians. We pity them from our soul! They stand the unwilling watch-dogs over a doomed flock! We would, but cannot spare them. The same impulse which makes us pity

them, demands of us the sacrifice. Nature, and nature's God
call for redress. The cry of millions rings unceasingly in our
ears, and the hand of destiny is upon us! We speak not in
the impulse of a wild patriotism; we, and those who act with
us, are not special, but general, yet the no less inevitable agents
of Providence. The time in the history of the world for the
overthrow of slavery is come; and no power on earth or in
Heaven can stay it; for God, in the very necessity of his Being,
has willed it!

Mr. Rice, having, by nine stated propositions, narrowed the
discussion, giving them up as lost to him, and incapable of defence, proceeds to state what is the question. "It is stated by
the Rev. Thomas E. Thomas, a prominent abolitionist, in the
following language: 'That question now in process of investigation among American churches, is this, and no other: Are
professed Christians in our respective connexions, who hold
their fellow-men as slaves, thereby guilty of a sin, which demands the cognizance of the church; and after due admoni-
tion, the application of discipline?' In order to get at slaveholding, he must have a *definition*. Well, what is it? He
gives Paley: Slavery is 'an obligation on the part of the slave
to labor for the master without consent or contract.'" Now,
Mr. R. is logician enough to know that this definition is a *petitio principii*, a begging of the question. Mr. Blanchard very
truly objects to it, as a definition, because it is too general, including persons who are not slaves. For instance, children
under majority, are precisely included. The definition is false
in all the respects of a definition. It includes persons not
slaves; it creates conditions not essential to slavery; and is
untrue in its *main* assumption. The condition, an "obligation," as Paley observes, arises from crime, captivity, and death;
but slavery exists in America when it is not pretended that
crime, captivity, or debt exists.

This definition makes an essential condition, which is false.
The main assumption, that slavery is an "obligation," is false,
by the final clause, "without consent or contract." Now, in all
cases of forfeiture of liberty by debt and crime, *there is consent.*
And therefore, the definition clashes in itself; and is false in the
main part. Captivity is not a ground of slavery, *as all now admit*, and therefore has nothing to do with it. We are not first-
rate at definitions, but we can beat Paley: thus, "Slavery is

the WANT of *obligation* on the part of the slave, forced to labor
for the master without consent or contract!" We throw out
this as our definition of slavery. Mr. Rice is welcome to its
conclusions.

Yet this is not a perfect definition of slavery; for, notwithstanding Mr. Rice's question, "is any thing included in slaveholding except the claim of one man to the services of another?"
a woman is frequently held in slavery only to answer the criminal lusts of the master!

We attempt, therefore, an improvement upon our definition:
"Slavery is the want of obligation on the part of the slave, to
be subject, yet, by force, or law, or both, made subject, to the
will of the master, without consent or contract." Mr. Rice
may take our definition, or give us a better. *His* definition is
"*rich*." "By slaveholding, then, I understand, the claim of the
master to the services of the slave, with the corresponding obligation on the part of the master, to treat the slave kindly, and to
provide him with abundant food and raiment during life, and
with religious instruction!" *Page* 33. Do we place Mr. Rice
too low, when we call him a third or fourth rate mind? Let us
paraphrase his definition; we can make it more true without
departing from its form, thus: "By slave-holding, then, I understand, the claim of the master to the chastity of the slave,
with *corresponding obligation* on the part of the master, to
treat the slave kindly, and to provide her with abundant food,
and raiment during life, and with religious instruction!" We
then ask, in his own language, "Are there any circumstances
which can justify such a claim? or is the claim in itself sinful,
and the relation founded on it a sinful relation?" Yet this is
the real relation of every slave woman in America, and not a
law in a single state interposes the least restraint! And in
Kentucky Mr. Rice and myself are bound to stand by with the
musket, and perfect the wishes of the ravisher! For, if the
slave resist, the master may murder her; if she call upon her
husband, or sister, or brother, or mother, or son, to help, the
master may call upon us to come to the rescue! And, because
we cry out against this damnable complexity of crime, in tones
not altogether measured and musical to the ear of the criminal,
we are "rash and imprudent," and Mr. Rice is not very sure,
indeed he rather thinks, we deserve to be murdered!

Mr. Rice then says: "Let it be distinctly understood, that if slave-holding is in itself sinful, it is sinful under all circumstances, and must be immediately abandoned, without regard to circumstances." In our review, in a previous number of this paper, we proved slavery sinful by Mr. R.'s own admission. He is therefore. by his own showing, bound to immediate emancipation! He shall not escape condemnation. Now we do not assent to the rule, that a thing is right or wrong, independent of circumstances. On the contrary, *circumstances* and *motives* influence, more or less, all human acts, and determine, to a great extent, their guilt, or goodness. For instance: some whites travelling in Africa; one of the servants took an African's wood by force. The injured man rallied his party, and was coming down to kill the whole company. When the whites saw the Africans coming, they flogged the servant *most unmercifully*, which at length appeased the enemy. Now, the taking a few chunks of wood from a log, at other times and places, would have hardly attracted notice; yet, here it was just to punish him severely; nothing less would have saved life!

Now we will not say, that there is no *circumstance* which would justify a man in holding a slave. But we know what we say, when we declare, that we never have known a case in Kentucky, where Mr. Rice can legitimately act, where every moment of slaveholding was not sinful!

We say, that there *is not the least danger in immediate emancipation in Kentucky*. Reasoning *a priori*, will a man murder you *because* you are his friend? because you are just? because you do a godlike action? because you are merciful? No! Has history proved it dangerous to emancipate? On the contrary, emancipation has always, without a single exception, been *safe*. How dare Mr. Rice to assume any such false sequence, as that emancipation was dangerous? How does he avoid the conclusion in reality? Not because it is *unsafe*, but because it would run counter to his prejudices; "those states are bound to liberate all their slaves, and grant them the right to vote, and to fill any office within the gift of the people." Well, does he deny the *right* of the last proposition? Not at all! He reproaches Mr. Blanchard very justly for not carrying it out in Ohio. So that it is plain that Mr. Rice does not search for truth, but caters to the base prejudices of his audience for temporary victory!

Now, whether the African should be allowed to vote or not,

is not at all material to the question, "Whether slavery is in itself sinful?" And if they were to remain among us till doomsday, without the power of voting or filling office, we maintain that slavery is equally sinful. What sort of religion or morality is that, which says to a man, because you will not be entirely virtuous, therefore it is no use to leave off murder or robbery; because you lie, you may steal! because you keep a mistress, you may therefore murder your wife, or sell your country for gold? Does not every man see the absurdity of such arguments? In Massachusetts and New York, and some other states, Africans vote; yet New York and Massachusetts dare look decent men in the face, and call upon the name of the living God!

Color may be a very good reason for a negro pew in the church of Christ, for no doubt there will be a negro pew also in heaven! But when Mr. Rice comes into the arena of world-wide morality, he must lay aside his bigotry! Boyer and family were entertained by the royal family of France, upon terms of social equality; and Alexander Dumas, a half-blood, is one of the most sought after aristocrats in Paris; whilst even in New Orleans, a very reputable man is said to have committed perjury in order to indulge in the delicacies of legal amalgamation! So that Mr. Rice must take care else he will have the chivalry on his back—something harder to put up with than a black coat! Why then do we not advocate immediate emancipation? We do. We practise our own teaching. And having given our advice and example, we say to weak human nature, if you won't do *all* the right, let us as a state, agree to a scheme, which will finally effect the whole right. We prefer a half loaf to no bread. We prefer freedom in thirty years, to slavery for ever! If the blacks are unfit for freedom now, the sooner we cease to *cause* their unfitness, the sooner it will cease! The sooner they are free, the sooner they will be enlightened; the sooner they are enlightened, the sooner will they be capable of self-government.

We are free to confess that slavery cannot be abolished without some temporary ills, some self-sacrifice, some penal consequences. To maintain the contrary, would be to maintain that it was no violation of nature's laws, which have ever a penalty. The taking medicine is an evil, but it saves from death! If there were no violation of moral or physical laws, there were no pain, no disease, and consequently no need of a remedy! Slavery is a deadly disease: it must be cured, or the patient dies! There is no other alternative. We are now suffering its way-side calamities—all bad enough—but its catastrophe is as certain as it is insufferable and disastrous.

Mr. Rice opposes abolitionism, " not because it tends to abolish slavery, but because it tends to perpetuate slavery, and to aggravate its evils." Mr. Rice, this is love's labor lost! The slaveholders will not thank you for your pains! And he is confirmed in his belief by men in the free states. Yes, many men in the free states are slave-traders, cotton planters, and sleeping partners of slave plantations and slaves! Many are indirectly interested in slavery. Many are inately base; and some few are blinded by the calumnies of slaveholders and their parasites! If the Union shall be dissolved, it will not come of abolitionism, but of slavery. The crime is of slavery, and slavery will reap its bitter fruits.

In reply to the argument, that slavery mars the marriage tie, and makes children illegitimate, Mr. Rice denies, on the ground that marriage exists of God, and not of man. True, marriage is literally of the soul, and not of the municipal law. But. when slavery usurps a higher power than that of the Bible, and separates by its will whom God has joined together, does it not stand responsible for the real outrage to the person and the spirit of the slave by taking the wife from the nuptial bed, and forcing her to the master's bed of lust? And for the guilt of soul, when the separated couples are thus tempted by the strong impulses of nature, to form new alliances, whilst the old parties are yet alive? Mr. Rice may say that Christians need not do all the law allows them to do. True, but then they are responsible by their voice and their practice, for all the crimes which are perpetrated by the facilities and *infirmities* of " *this relation.*"

Slave children are neither legitimate nor illegitimate : because the law does not take cognizance of the relation of marriage in blacks at all. But so far as marriage is a protection to children, by defining their rights, it is all lost to slave children. Neither the father nor the mother has the care of the child, even when known to be their joint issue. And whilst the parents may be Christians, the master may be an infidel ; and whilst the parents may inculcate chastity the master may play the jesuitical seducer, or the unrestrained violator of female purity ! So that Mr. Rice must give up Christian morality or yield up slavery: for they are as far apart as virtue and vice ! As to the names of slaves, it is a small matter. True, masters are not in the habit of naming them just as *they* please ; where there are causes for a different course—then the course is different ! For instance, if a mother wishes to name a child after a friend or a relation, and calls him Joe, Joe will be the name, unless there is another Joe on the same place, black or white ; then the child must be called something else. If the name is too *long* for speedy calling, it is knocked down to something *short*. This is tyranny in small things. Slavery is nothing else.

Mr. R. then assumes the *offensive*. "My first argument is founded upon the admitted fact, that the great principles of morality are written upon the human heart, and when presented do commend themselves to the understandings and the consciences of all men, unless we except the most degraded." "But the doctrine that slaveholding is in itself sinful, has not thus commended itself to the great mass, even of the wise and good. Therefore it is not true." We thank thee ! Yes, the great principles of morality do commend themselves to the consciences and convictions of men ; and we assert boldly, that slavery *does so present itself as sinful*. At the time of the revolution, when our own difficulties taught us, in sincerity, to examine our hearts, the conviction was unanimous, that *all men* are created free and equal, and that man cannot hold property in man. We heard then nothing of the contemptible plea that slavery is not "*in itself sinful*." It was only when we grew strong in physical force, and abandoned, and "most degraded," that we began to preach this heresy of conscience. Yes, slaveholding does present itself to our conscience as the greatest of crimes. For whilst we have violated, and continue to violate, many of the great precepts of christianity and conscience, we felt that slaveholding was too bare-faced, and impudently criminal, for a reasonable share of self-respect ; and therefore we abandoned it ! Yes, we know some of the *secrets* of the prison-house, and we say, in all candor, that we never, till within a few years, heard of a man who believed, or pretended to believe, that slavery was right. We would to-morrow submit the question to the men of the 18th, who were murderers in heart, and believe that not five men of all those thousands who were " so degraded," would conscientiously deny that slavery is wrong—sinfully wrong.

So that Mr. Rice is caught in his own trap! We know not what the Jews did; whom the God of the universe has accepted. and whom he has rejected, no man knows, or can know. But if a slaveholder can enter the kingdom of heaven, let the vilest sinner take courage: for there is no deed so damnable but that its penalties may be shirked! We speak of wilful *perpetualist* slaveholders! For we are willing to admit that there are many good men who are slaveholders. For who is without sin? There is every grade of christianity, from the most benevolent master, denying himself the powers of the law, to him who goes the full length of its dark chain!

Mr. R.'s second ground is: "There never was and never can be, a man, or class of men, heretical on one fundamental point of faith, morals, and yet sound on all the other doctrines of the Bible, and on all other important principles of morality." But slaveholders are sound on all other parts of morality; and of consequence slaveholding cannot be a sin. That is the sum of the argument.

Now, this is almost too deep in theology for us of the world. Yet we venture to deny the predicate and the conclusion. Catholics hold that Protestants are vitally wrong on many leading or "fundamental points of faith and morals." Yet there are as many good Christians and virtuous Catholics, as Protestants. And vice versâ. We are astonished that Mr. Rice should have ventured upon so broad an assertion, knowing the great number of religious sects, from the Trinitarians to the Unitarians; many, in all of which sects, we trust, he is willing to admit, are good and moral men.

But if we *mend* Mr. Rice's proposition, by excluding *faith*, and putting simply great or fundamental points of *morals;* still it is by no means a logical argument. Because it assumes that slaveholding Christians are as good men in other respects as non-slaveholding Christians, *which is denied.* But yet, if we allow his assumption, still is the argument inconclusive; because slavery is so mixed up with law and government, and the old Jewish customs, that the clearest minds, though they feel something is wrong—something " *evil* "—are not capable of saying where it is, or what it is. And in illustration of this fact, we might produce many whole nations by law violating cardinal principles of morality. Even Mr. Rice is so absurd as to assert, that the moral obligations of the state are different from those of the individuals of it !

The dogged pertinacity with which Mr. Rice repeats these propositions, throughout his subsequent speeches, is truly astonishing, and proves that he is either a very dull man, or presumes much upon the gross stupidity of his audience.

Since Mr. Rice is so reliant upon natural instincts and consciousness, for the discernment of great principles of morals, we presume that he would have some faith in the instinctive perceptions of slaves to find out who were their true friends. If so, we venture to say of the three millions of American slaves, if all had heard this debate, not *one* would have concluded that Mr. Rice was their friend at all—far less, a better friend than Mr. Blanchard. And if he is indeed a better friend of the slave than abolitionists, then may the Africans cry out with undying energy, " Save us—save us, from our friends ! " As to runaway slaves never hearing the Gospel in Canada, if Mr. Rice rightly reads it, we venture that not a single African will ever grieve himself to death, if he never hears the gospel, in the tide of times !

Having gone through his first speech, we shall reserve for another paper the continuation of this review.

LEXINGTON, WEDNESDAY, APRIL 22.

SLAVEHOLDING MADNESS AND FANATICISM.

We call the attention of our readers to Mr. S. M.'s letter. It proves to what excess the human mind may reach in a bad cause !

This man is surprised to see us " fighting against God " in attempting emancipation ! Does not he know that thirteen states of this Union are free of slaves ? Have they fought successfully against God ? The majority of civilized nations have abolished slavery. Have they fought successfully against God ?

M. contends, that God cursed the sons of Canaan, and put a black mark upon them, that the world should know that whomsoever the Lord curses, he will curse! What arrant nonsense is this? Have not a majority of the slaves in the world been white? Where, then, is the mark of the curse? Are there not many colors—every shade, from white to black, and are not all, yes, every one, enslaved? How then can we know the accursed? The exhortation to servants, or slaves, to be obedient to their masters, is similar to the injunction to " be subject to the powers that be." Will any sane man, therefore, submit to all iniquities and oppressions of government, under this command? Was our revolution criminal? The *spirit* of the rule only must be kept in view. Well, if God wills slavery, according to M., till he thinks proper to change it, who can say but that he is now commencing the great work? Let M. take care lest he resist the will of God at *his own* hazard!

Such doctrines as are held in this letter, and taught by learned divines, make God out the most merciless of tyrants, and fill our madhouses with miserable lunatics!

RICHMOND, KY., APRIL 2d, 1846.

MR. C. M. CLAY—SIR:

You surprise me to see you fighting against God; or do you expect to bless those whom God curses; or do you intend to alter or abolish the decrees of God at your will? When the old servant of God cursed his son Canaan, and told him that a servant of servants he should be to his brethren, are you so presumptuous as not to be willing for the Lord's will to be done on earth as it is in heaven? Why, sir, he has put a black mark upon them, that all the world should know, that whomsoever the Lord blesses he will bless, and whomsoever the Lord curses he will curse. And it is clear and plain that the Lord sanctions slavery, for when he came upon the earth and found them slaves, he never forbade it, but told the servants to be subject to their masters in all things. Now, sir, it appears clear and plain that God intends them to be slaves, until he changes or alters his decrees. Let any man deny it, if he pleases; it will be at his own hazard.

S. M.

RICE AND BLANCHARD'S DEBATE ON SLAVERY.

CONTINUED REVIEW.

In following Mr. Rice, we shall frequently use Mr. Blanchard's arguments as well as our own. We do not flatter ourself that we can improve upon his refutation, but we may vary the mode, and thus reach various minds.

Mr. Rice attempts to avoid the conclusions of abolitionism by putting the extreme case, that the slave has a right to regain his liberty by flight or force. Now we never shrink from conclusions which follow upon justice and right. We say the slave has the same revolutionary ultimatum that all other men have —the same that our fathers of 1776 had. But we know it would not be expedient for the American slave to resort to the ultima ratio Regum. He would be over-matched; and the consequences would be disastrous to white and black. As a member of a slave state, bound up in its welfare, and identified in interest with the whites, we should not hesitate to resist a slave insurrection. Though we are free to confess, that were we a member of a free state, with our family and relatives and friends, and clear of the United States Constitution, we should not feel ourselves bound to fight the battles of the *oppressor*. This argument of Mr. R.'s illustrates the fable of the ox, the farmer, and the lawyer. When Mr. Rice's ancestors were gored in the cause of liberty and self-government, we heard nothing of this shuddering at the horrid crime of self-vindication! This is not a pleasant subject to us. It is one which we have ever avoided, but since Mr. R. has voluntarily put it in print, we have answered it fully, as we do not intend to slur any of his arguments, least of all those which we deem most powerful!

Mr. R. denies that the Bible authorizes physical resistance to tyranny; we think differently, and there's an end of it. There is not, and never has been, a nation on earth that does not act upon the principle of self-defence. And if any tyranny under heaven warrants resistance, the American slave system is the thing! If Mr. Rice is right, then were Washington, and Madison, and Adams, and Franklin, and Jefferson, and their compeers, murderers, and, by his construction of Christianity, the present recipients of eternal damnation; for they died covered with blood, and with consciences glorying in their perpetrations. We do not agree with Mr. B. that the duty of abolitionists ceases before the black is entitled to political equality. On the contrary, we must either yield up the republican theory, that a majority, under constitutional restrictions, must rule, or we must recognise the only other alternative, that the bayonet is the only proper source of power. Now, since Mr. Rice denies the latter as Christian, will he be so kind in his great wisdom as to give us a substitute for the first? For, however much he may use the Greek and Hebrew, to gull his followers, the world will hardly be held in check by cant, prestiges, and syllogisms. As to this question about naturalization, it may be summed up in a few words. Every man, as soon as he becomes a bonâ fide inhabitant of a country for life, should have a right to assist in the government of the country. Aliens and denizens, not being compelled to fight or pay taxes, should not be allowed to vote. This may seem radical ground; but it is right and, therefore, safe. It is only hoary error and usurpation, in church or state, which fear first principles, and their stern application.

We content ourselves with stating these collateral questions in a concise manner, as a book would not be too much for their full discussion.

Mr. R. squirms whenever slavery practically is held up to view. He cries incessantly for abstraction; when he can't get that, he goes back to his favorite marriage and parental relation! Why this nonsense? It is just as good a plea to cry out against God for giving us existence because we may be murdered! Existence, marriage, and children, are good things, but not free from the abuses of bad men. Slavery is not good even when free from *abuse*. Yes, in its most simple form, "slavery in itself," to us, is the sum of all evils, for you may take away marriage, and parents, and even existence, but leave us, while life does last, our *liberty!*

But give Mr. R. the full benefit of his Hindoo marriage, and we would say, sooner than the widow should be put to death on the decease of her husband, let marriage perish from the face of the earth! So of slavery, sooner than have it, with its ever attendant abuses, let it perish! How, then, has his shallow sophistry advanced him?

Nothing is more true than that a man may swallow a camel and strain at a gnat. Mr. R. admits that "speculating" in human beings is damnable. Let us see. A comes upon me and robs me of my liberty; B comes and buys me, and sells me to C for a profit; which man injures me most? Answer conscience, answer reason, answer slave! Of course A is the greater enemy. If A takes all my goods by robbery, and B speculate upon them, which is the most criminal? Of course, A; because it becomes a matter of utter indifference to me whether A, B, or C, have them, so they pass beyond my control. But a man's liberty is worth more than property; *a fortiori* then, much more is the slave trader more virtuous than the slaveholder. Nay, if a slave trader, denouncing slavery as a crime, and refusing to own slaves, was to confine his trade at *home*, and to *whole* families, selling from a bad master to a good one, we should place him infinitely above Mr. R., the slaveholder and defender of slavery! But Mr. R. admits slave trading to be "in itself sinful," *ergo*, slaveholding. or "slavery, is in itself sinful." q. e. d.

The time is at hand when the white cravat and the black gown, and the slave coffle, shall be classed together in the detestation of mankind, unless the Bible defenders of slavery be stripped of the sheep's clothing, that men may discriminate and see who it is that dare desecrate the temples of the living God, and turn its heavenly fold into a charnel house of blood, despair, and death.

Mr. R. here admits that slavery is daily becoming more tolerable in all the South. Indeed! The chain is not tightened then, as he alleged in his first speech, by discussion and denunciation! The Bible, he tells us, has done the work! It has, in spite of its recreant guardians, stood a living fire, wasting away the bulwarks of time-honored oppression! Give us the Bible; and Heaven speed the day when its traitor priests shall be sent scudding across Mason and Dixon's line, "like squirrels with the wind in their tails!" It is bad enough to flee from duty, but doubly infamous to make our cowardice the bulwark of oppression and wo!

Mr. Rice, in connexion with Mr. B.'s remark that *partus sequitur ventrem*, and that slavery places human beings among the *cattle*, admits, that if *this* is true, slavery is detestable! Now, if Mr. Rice can cite a single state in the Union where a slave is better protected by law than "*cattle*," we yield the whole ground! He cannot. Shall the world hear it? The

virtue of the brute creation is better protected than that of the
human race! No, Mr. Rice, the slave is. not placed " among
cattle," but *below them;* whilst as a being of consciousness and
immortal nature, his condition is as far below the beast of the
field, under a bad though *law-abiding* master, as the earth is
below the heavens! If to place a slave *among* brutes is detestable, to place him *below* the brutes, is, *a fortiori* (Mr. R. loves
a syllogism!) more detestable. If one is sinful, the other is altogether sinful. Q. E. D. And over this damnable system, if we
do not roar as any sucking dove, Mr. R. does not see but that it
would be very right to *murder us!* And yet he preaches *non-
resistance!* Out upon such Janus-faced morality!

" The Christians of the South are waking up to a sense of
their obligation to have the gospel of Christ proclaimed to the
slave as well as to the master." Alas, alas! so much the worse
for them; better never hear of God than to know him as an
unrelenting and eternal tyrant. Far better

> " A 'friendless slave, a child without a sire,
> Whose mortal life and momentary fire
> Lights to the grave his chance-created form,
> As ocean's wrecks illuminate the storm!' "

Give us back our ignorance, our sufferings, our crimes, but
for heaven's sake, destroy not all hopes of a God of justice, and
mercy, and rest, beyond the grave!

Mr. Rice sips comfort from the saying of a reverend Monsieur
Griffin, who did " not see that the efforts in favor of immediate
emancipation have effected any thing but rivet the chains of the
poor slave!" Now, if slavery be *right,* the tighter the chain is
riveted the better; God forbid that the wrong should break
loose. And if slavery be of God, why " poor slave?" It is
plain that the reverend Monsieur Griffin was rather a transpa-
rently weak brother, and short of sight. If the blind lead the
blind, they will surely fall into the ditch together.

We are glad to get safely past Mr. R.'s complaints of want of
something tangible in Mr. B. to his *third* proposition. There
are revivals of religion in slaveholding churches, and slaveholders are accepted of God, but God accepts not sinners, therefore,
slaveholders are not sinners! There is a form of logic called
petitio principii, a begging of the question; but this syllogism
is most too strong, even for logic! The boys have a better

nomenclature; they would call it "coming the giraffe!" The swell mob would illustrate it by putting thumb on nose and twirling somewhat significantly the four digits. The Rounders would denounce it as a "fiery facias;" and some very grave and respectable magistrates, whom we know, would content themselves after this sort, "non compos mentis!" We have done.

Brother, a parting word. You are in a bad cause. Be warned:

> "Ah, Tam! ah Tam! thou'll get thy fairin,
> In hell they'll roast thee like a herrin!"

CROW-FOOT SKETCHES.—NEW YORK.

What is music? No one can tell us. I have heard eloquence, and read the first poems of human genius; I have gazed for long hours upon all lovely nature, and the divine creations of art, yet nothing so moves me as music. Though I cannot describe it, I can feel it. Shakspeare has it, "If music be the food of love play on." No one doubts that the features of the one we love, grow yet more lovely under its influence. The ancients, who illustrated all the phases of human passion and action by fable, had it that the wild beasts were tamed under the subduing strains of the harp of Orpheus. So in war, we hear of the stirring drum and thrilling fife. How is this? Whence all these conflicting influences? Would it be a definition of music to say, the inarticulate voice of the passions? It is certain that it is like the natural cries of pleasure or wo. It quickens every passion of the human soul. Certainly much of its power arises from exciting the principle of association. When the Swiss hear the *Ranz des Vaches*, their native mountains are spread out before them in vivid, seeming reality, and tears of fond remembrance suffuse their eyes. All the passionate love of glory, and turbid ambition is quickened to madness in the Frenchman when he hears the Marseillaise. Even the rude Yankee Doodle fires the patriotic ardor and military pride of brother Jonathan. There is an air which invariably brings to my mind the battles of the Duke of Marlborough; whilst another pictures to me a sylvan rill, boyish years, and a blue-eyed girl of twelve summers. Of the ambitious, who has not listened to strains of satanic energy, of despair, or elated hope of undying fame ? Melancholy! bitter are thy tones, when the wintry wind hurries in heart-chilling blasts through the shattered lattice of what was once home, when they of other years are gone ! Oh love, and crime, and poverty, and misery, and death, who has heard, unshaken, your many-tongued utterances ? The many-voiced wind, the creaking forest trees, the gurgling brook, the rushing ocean, the roaring cannon, the crashing thunder, the cricket's chirp, the liquid notes of sylvan birds, the voice of woman's love—if these speak a language, what is it ? Now, it seems to me, that instrumental combined music must have something like this for a base, or foundation point. If so, there is much playing after the manner of what is called *execution*, which is a waste of so much wind and cat-gut. " Cruning to a body's self," as Burns has it, is better than this. Is there not some affectation in all this ecstacy about " forty cats a fighting ?" Or is music like cooking, which can be so scrambled up with condiments, that one may unknowingly eat his grandmother's leg ? It is of no use however to ask these questions, for the grand altos and furiosos will write me down " semplice ; " and every head-nudger cry out, ass !

However I may miss the mark in talking about music, I know something about " the voice that made those sounds more sweet "—woman. I cannot, therefore, agree with the apostate Jew, and northern renegade, southern boot lick, and servant-maid poetaster, Park Benjamin, that there is no beauty in New York. It is true that there is not that fairy-like, shadowy beauty which we find in the South, which, as frail wild flowers, almost buds, blows, and perishes in a day. But you find in New York fine, vigorous, elastic, rounded persons ; intellectual, variant, piquant faces ; and a great many of them women that seem fit for other things than to look upon. So Gotham may say with any city in America " stand out my shin."

I cannot say always with Wirt, "Objects loom large at a distance ; " or, in more poetical language, with Campbell,

> " 'Tis distance lends enchantment to the view,
> And robes the mountain in its azure hue,"

for, at a social party at L.'s I met many literary persons whom I had long known through their writings, and whom I had afar off, long time imaged to my mind's eye ; yet I found them all I could have wished. Among them were Miss S., Mrs. K., Miss F., Miss L., Mrs. S. S., Mrs. O., etc. And then there were of the sterner sex, H., P., H., the artist, etc.

I envy the East her ocean, her oysters, and her literary women. There is talent in the West of the highest order, but our people are too happy to write. When our cities become crowded with an energetic, pleasure-loving, ambitious, property proud population, then there will arise a class of writers far superior even, we believe, to any the world has yet heard. There is a magnificent substratum of mind in the West yet to be built upon, as expansive as our boundless and ever various and gigantic nature. We are already on the horizon, and "Westward the star of empire wends its way."

LEXINGTON, WEDNESDAY, APRIL 29.

Speech of Henry Wilson of Mass.

Since noticing some extracts of this speech, the whole of it, and the preamble and resolutions have come to hand. The resolutions of Mr. Culver, of New-York, concerning the overthrow of slavery in the District of Columbia, and this move in the Massachusetts Legislature, in addition to many other evidences too numerous to mention, prove what we have for years foreseen and most ardently hoped for, that the great Whig party, as in 1776, will soon rally on the great principle of *resistance to tyranny and the rights of man.* If not in 1848, in 1852, parties will be fairly made up upon this sole issue. The result we venture to predict. The majority of the present Whig party, a large minority of the Democrats, and no inconsiderable number of the Liberty party and Garrisonian abolitionists, will ultimately unite on some man and *elect him.* Slavery will be abolished in the District. The effort to introduce Cuba, or California, or Mexico, as slave states, will prove abortive. They may come in, but *they will have to come in free.* The coastwise slave trade will be abolished. The supreme court will be filled, as vacancies occur, with true free-born men, rightly interpreting the Constitution in its true spirit of liberty. The South will bluster, but *not dare to sever the Union.* All the grain-growing states will enter on schemes of gradual or immediate emancipation. The internal slave-trade will be abolished; the Constitution changed, taking away slave representation. The clause requiring the return of fugitive slaves will be repealed. Slavery will retire into the cotton and sugar region and there die. The republic will be redeemed, and " universal liberty" be spread over this north continent.

If this does not happen, then will the slave power increase; Cuba, Mexico and California come in as slave states. The South will rule with an iron hand, joined with the commercial and manufacturing interests of the North : the great mass of Americans, north and south, will be reduced to real slavery. The South will become more and more worn-out, more corrupt, and seek more and more the expansion of the government patronage, and offices of profit, for her broken-down aristocracy.

Foreign invasion, insurrection, and anarchy, will come upon us singly, or in mass, and despotism will swallow up *this long-lived lie !*

Well then, we say with Mr. Wilson, let the Whigs raise their colors, " constitutional resistance to the slave power, and the utter overthrow of slavery." Yes, it is our " inevitable destiny ;" let it come : the sooner the better ! The party has no chance for but four southern states; in trying to gain them, which hereafter will be very doubtful, it will lose New-York and Pennsylvania, and thus lose the battle ! We say the Whig party will never rise except upon the battle cry of " *constitutional liberty;*" if it seeks any other it deserves defeat, just as certainly as it will meet it ! Up, then, and to the battle-field ! " On, Stanley—on!"

LEXINGTON, WEDNESDAY, MAY 13.

The Massachusetts Resolution.

Since our last the Senate has rejected the resolution of Mr. Wilson by a small majority. This conduct on their part does not alter our opinion of Massachusetts: we believe her *people* are right, and not yet degenerate sons of glorious sires.

Does the Senate, in its affected regard for Southern rights, forget, that in refusing us their countenance, they are assisting in oppressing nearly eight millions of men? Are all their sympathies with the slaveholder? Are they so in love with tyranny, as not to see our wounds and hear our cries? Or is there something worse behind the scene? Is the great popular party of this union to be told outright, that the *tariff* and *cotton*-spinning are to be purchased by the sacrifice of the *liberties* of the country?

Let these men beware, lest they push our endurance to the quick! We have heretofore held to the "conservative" course through all its trials; there are thousands like us, who have done so through hope of a returning sense of justice and mercy in the capitalists of this country. But if the *capital* of the North has taken its ground of *a firm alliance with the slave despotism of the South,* we say, with language laden with the groans and sufferings of millions—*beware!*

This material temple of a nation's embodiment, we aspire to see eminently decked out in all the tasteful and luxurious adornment of which the genius of man is capable; but if all this is to be done only by the crushed affections, the stifled aspirations, the beggared bodies, and the brutified souls of the laboring millions, we say—no!—*never!*

ROBERT WALSH.

This European correspondent of the National Intelligencer, in the case of the Polish Revolution, speaks out the instincts of his servile spirit! It makes one's blood curdle to listen to his cold, snake-like fawning upon aristocracy and despotism—giving the lie to all the generous sympathies and noble humanities which should characterize a countryman of Washington. Yet, on the whole, we are glad of this, if our once free people may be aware at last of all the dark and destroying influences which are secretly entangling them!

Rice and Blanchard's Debate on Slavery.

Heathenism was far preferable to slaveholding Christianity. The gods of old were never contemptible, and heroic virtues were the fruit of their worship. But the sneaking, snivelling meanness of slaveholding Christians brings the right into contempt, and makes virtue ridiculous. To avoid the odious imputation of alliance with such time-servers, men seek crime and open wickedness, in order to preserve some self-respect, and attain to something of respectability. We see a reward of fifty dollars offered for the best tract upon *dancing ;* whilst the omniferous curse of *slavery* slumbers with the consecrated shrines of hoary impunity! Will not infidelity and bloody and foul vice sweep with untold horrors our devoted land? The salt has lost its savor ; the great and glorious flag of Christianity is struck down : and men wander in the dark, and horror and despair begin to fill the world!

In treating with ridicule Mr. Rice's third argument, we took not the easiest, though the most deserved, method of refutation.

Slaveholders are accepted of God ; but God receives not sinners ; therefore slaveholders are not sinners, and, of course, slavery, in itself, not sinful. We said Mr. R. here assumes the whole ground in controversy, and upon this assumption builds up a sort of syllogism to blind the weak-minded.

Who dare say that this or that man is accepted of God? Who dare venture to assert that God accepts not sinners? This is not the doctrine of the Bible. No man knows the Father save the Son ; and no man doeth good, no, not one ; this we understand to be the teaching of the Christian religion.

So far from this being true, we are told of many of the choice followers of God in olden times, perpetrating crimes which would disgrace a modern bandit! Yet they were better than other nations ; we are worse!

But the Christian is a newer and a better code of morals than the Jewish dispensation ; and it knows not slavery, nor its advocates. By the fruit shall the tree be known. If so, what are the fruits of slavery? Every crime known among men follows

swiftly at its heels.   And the church has become literally a den
of thieves, money changers, and robbers !   We speak not in
terms of vindictive denunciation, but use simply terms which
are necessary to the conveying of the sense.   Usury, contrary
to law and gospel, has become a highly reputable calling among
Southern churchmen ; shaving notes, and brokerage, and " salt-
ing," are right holy things !   A mercenary spirit pervades the
church.   They flatter their pride, by great temples built with
hands, and filled with *negro pews !*   And the voice is no longer
of one crying in the wilderness, clothed in sack-cloth and
ashes, but the cry is of *gold*, and where it cries loudest, there is
" *the call !* "   Robbing, stealing, or counterfeiting a half dollar,
will send a poor devil to the penitentiary, but the taking all the
half dollars that a man may earn in a life time—the seizing on
the man himself, controlling his will, his action, his morals, his
mind, his soul, for the basest and most mercenary purposes—
this is a godly and Christian thing, a sweet morsel in the fastidious jaws of the church !

We say, then, that slaveholders are not accepted of God, unless he loves sinners par excellence !   Yet we do not say, that
slaveholders are all damned for ever, any more than all murderers and parricides are all sent to Hell !   Nay, so far from being
thus uncharitable, we are willing to admit that even a Bible
defender of slavery, by repentance, and the great goodness of
God, may be saved—the hardest case of all !

We despise your slaveholding religion !   Here, on the Sabbath preceding the mob of the 18th of August, when murder
was avowedly contemplated from seven churches, which continually annoy us with their everlasting bell-ringing, went up
the ordinary cant to a sin-hating God, and not one, so far as
we are informed, ventured to warn the people to keep their
hands clear of the blood of an innocent man !   Words are impotent to characterize such Judas Iscariotism !   If we were a murderer, a robber, a ravisher, a house burner, a seller of our country
for gold, a parricide, a robber of the grave, a desecrator of the
temples of God, they would have flocked around us, as buzzards
over a dead ass !   But as we stood for the rights of man, the
liberties of our country, and the *purity* of Christianity, they
were silent ; as dumb dogs they opened not their Mouths ; or,
like some of old, cried out bitterly, we know not the man ; cru-
cify him for he blasphemes !   And are these men the only con-

servators of liberty and religion among men ; the brothers of martyrs ; the sons of the self-sacrificing and crucified Christ !

We alter the syllogism thus : These Southern slaveholding churches are sinners. God accepts not sinners, therefore slaveholding is not of God, and slaveholding is in itself sinful !

We come now to Mr. R.'s fourth argument—the *golden rule*. " Therefore, all things whatsoever ye would that men should do to you, do ye even so to them." Matt. vii. 12.

Now, this rule, it seems to me, is the very gist of Christianity. If the Jewish system was ferocious and tyrannical, here was the new and better system of love and justice. If the Jewish system *modified* the system of slavery, and made it far better than that of the surrounding nations, here was a code of morals utterly abolishing it. Does Mr. Rice yield to the rule—does he give way to the dictates of conscience—will he allow the justice, " consistent with paramount duties," of enslaving himself or his children ? Oh no, not he ! But he slopes out of the difficulty thus : A slave *has* a hard master ; he begs you to buy him ; you are not able without some pecuniary sacrifice ; yet, to prevent him from being torn from those he loves, you buy him, and take his services as an equivalent ; have you sinned by thus slaveholding ? By no means.

This is the argument. Mr. R. has taken the most favorable case possible in the nature of things. We are glad of it ; for if we can overturn him here again, we have him on the hip, and slavery itself *is* sinful.

Now, in a government of laws of Mr. R.'s own enacting, before he can claim the virtue of the good act above cited, he must prove that he has done what he could as a citizen by his vote and by solemn protest against slavery to overturn it. But the Christian slaveholders have not done this ; therefore their peace-offering is tainted with crime, and not acceptable to God. God cannot be cheated with half-way repentance, or partial reform : the evil thing must be put away utterly.

But even if he shall have voted against it, and shall have on all suitable occasions, lifted up his voice against it, and shall have been actuated by the best motives in purchasing the slave, still he is doing a *criminal act*, because he has become a *participant in crime*. His example, and his sanction, outweigh the *special* good. If the act of freeing a man from bondage was praiseworthy, it is vitiated by the price. The Holy Ghost

cannot be bought with money. So the great claims of humanity forbid a reward for doing justice or mercy. We fall into a
stream, and we promise Mr. Rice if he will save us at the risk
of his life, we will give him our whole estate : he saves us, and
and we comply, and we and our family are reduced to beggary.
Does not every one see that Mr. Rice has done a great injustice,
although we might continue grateful for life saved ? God im-
planted in him a principle which required of him to save us if
consistent with is "paramount duties." The preservation of his
own life, his services for the support of his own family, &c., were
to be duly considered, and if they would not allow him to venture for us, well. But if he did venture, and saved us, all nature
cries aloud against any remuneration, other than what we might
voluntarily bestow.

Again : We are about to be murdered and robbed on the
highway : Mr. Rice, being stronger than the robber, repels him
at our instance, and simply robs us, sparing our life ; we are
grateful, but still he is a robber ! So, if being a slave to a hard
master, he buys us at our solicitation, and continues the slavery,
he is still in *degree* only less guilty than the first master. For
slavery being a *malum in se*, to which, in the nature of things,
the will of the slave cannot be gained, all *participation* in it is
sinful. Then slaveholding is, in the most favorable circumstances, sinful,—" in itself," therefore " sinful."

Abolitionists feeling the truth that all slaveholding was sinful, and knowing the criminality of example and sanction have
refused to pay the master for the slave : because it would seem
to recognise his *right* to enslave. They are wrong here, because
if we ransom our friend from the Algerines, we, by paying the
cost, manifest the injury done to him in his personal liberty
We are not a participant in his enslavement. But if we hold him
in slavery ourself, we become, under whatever pretext, *participes criminis :* and therefore guilty. We lay down the broad
rule, then, that the eternal laws of our nature impose positive
duties upon us, which, consistent with the paramount regard to
self, friends, and country, we are bound to render to the meanest of men : and *to demand or receive an equivalent in money
or service, is criminal in the eyes of nature and of God.*

We illustrate our proposition once more, by the common plea
for exorbitant usury, that " the man needed it, else he would
not have agreed to pay the per cent."

Now, if A be in a strait, we are bound to aid him " consistently with our paramount duties ;" but if under the pretence of
aiding, we avail ourself of his necessities to impoverish him,
we are damnably criminal, however much we may cloak ourself in the assertion that we acted by his persuasion. All men
instinctively feel this, without being able to give the reason.
For no man is grateful to the *usurer*, and *rightly !* So when
you come to sift the secret thoughts of the slave, no matter
under what circumstances enslaved and transferred, there will
be something still galling in the yoke, which dries up the well
of gratitude.

We confess this proposition has cost us hours of long and
labored thought ; but we trust we have sifted out its sophistry
and exposed its falsehood. If so, we have taken the ground
from under the slaveholding church and left them naked and
defenceless to the indignation of men !

With regard to all instances where the laws throw obstacles
in the way of emancipation, some of which Mr. Rice has enumerated with some show of force, it aids nothing in proving
slaveholding not in itself sinful ; for if it turn out that the master acts from *compulsion*, then he is not a free agent, and of
course not responsible. But wherever a man can emancipate,
he is bound to do so even at great self-sacrifice. We utterly
dissent from the idea that any man was bound to go from the
free states to New-Orleans to inherit slaves there. He should
have done as Palfrey, of Boston, have gone and brought them
into freedom in other states ; or, if his circumstances would not
have allowed it, then he should have borne solemn testimony
in the face of the world against slavery, and have washed his
hands of the crime! *For a special and limited charity is*
forbidden at the expense of the violation of the great and uni-
versal laws of right ! And the man in this and all similar
cases, violates the spirit and letter of the golden rule, which
requires us to abstain from all participation in tyranny and
crime ! Heaven help us to its speedy appreciation and rigid
practice : then shall the right triumph, and slavery die !

LEXINGTON, WEDNESDAY, MAY 20.

RICE AND BLANCHARD'S DEBATE ON SLAVERY.

CONTINUED REVIEW.

This is the Sabbath day. All visible nature smiles harmoniously with the sublime quietude which God infuses into the souls of his true worshippers. His material representative, the life sustaining sun, glows warm in the heavens, and, by sea and shore, each mute and living thing responds to the jubilation of universal nature. Not on such a day as this, has ever "fool said in his heart, there is no God!" The heavens and the earth do not more fully declare his glorious Being, than the willing instincts of the grateful soul proclaim him a God of *life, liberty*, and *love!* Oh my soul! how shall they, who this day assuming to be his priests on earth, are busily engaged in reversing these divine characteristics, answer at the final account? Christianity, that broke down form, and ceremony, and *caste*, majestically simple and sublime emanation from the Father of *all* men living, and having its being in universal love, how this day are bloody hands laid upon thy pure robes! how are thy sacred temples desecrated!

The religion—that was designed to progress and expand itself with the progress of nature and man's civilization, that once poured, as a great river, its pure waters of life-giving energy, or like some great oak, spread out its fruit and shade for the protection and sustainment of man—has gone back into the ragged and cast-off vestments of past ages! stagnates in fetid pools, where are generated deadly miasmas and slimy monsters; or, like parasitic moss, has seized on existing establishments to cover up abuses, or suck the life-sap from every glorious manifestation of moral principle! Oh Christianity, the religion of the soul, of nature, and of God, who shall deliver thee from this death? Not in temples made with hands do we this day worship; eternal and unchangeable are the manifestations of God's goodness; the heavens and the earth are spread out before us; our spirit, ever thirsting for communion with the Infinite, here drinks unmeasured fulness! From the everlasting depths of the universe comes a voice,—*goodness* is the only worship of God! To be good is to be great—to fill the aspirations of earthly fame; they who seal up a fountain of tears, shall there be embalmed for ever: but they who cause to run this blood of the soul, shall be wasted with it, and be no more! To be *good*, is to be immortal; in the world of spirits, it is the food of the soul; the bread that multiplies by being broken; an emanation of the Deity, it must return to its fountain once more, and be eternal, for it is God!

If all this be not the creation of a heat-oppressed brain, then is slavery not of God, but diametrical to his every nature, and "in itself sinful!" Mr. Rice, in his fifth speech, after complaining of Mr. Blanchard's portraying the *sequences*, but what he calls the *abuses* of slavery, asks, "Is every master a heinous and scandalous sinner, however kindly he may treat his slaves, and however conscientiously he may afford them religious instruction?" We answer, no: not a *heinous* sinner, but still a *sinner!* He may be a very good man, worldly speaking —a good father, a good citizen, an honest man, a pleasant companion, a faithful husband, industrious, truthful, economical, intelligent—but not *pious;* not pleasing to God, because there is one thing lacking—he is still a *master!* He has *usurped powers;* he has another man's labor; he muzzles the ox that treads out the grain; he takes away the germ of manhood; he denies the equality of men, and the brotherhood of God's children; he brutifies man's nature; he puts him below the beasts! he mars the human will, subverts the principle of free agency, and destroys in consequence, the moral government of God. Yes, he is a *sinner!*

No doubt, the old friend of Gov. Cole thought he was doing God's service towards his slaves—"treating them kindly, and giving them religious instruction." But, when stript of his deceptions, when, like the rich man in the scriptures, who asked, Lord, what else am I to do? there was a *lust of gain* lying at the bottom of the whole thing! The young man was *silent*—so was the old Christian; he saw, for the first time, that it was selfishness—a lust of money or dominion—that influenced him, and the requirement of all to be given up was "a hard saying!"

"Is a man to be condemned as a sinner, simply because he is a slaveholder?" Yes! Mr. Rice. There is no help for it. God has decreed it! Nature swears it! Man's every instinct and immortal aspiration, echoes the damning yes ! The church, if she would, cannot shirk the test. She must either exclude slaveholding Christians, or fall ! The morality of the people is ahead of the church. The Christian religion will not fall: no, never! But it will put on some other outward dress. It will have *new* teachers. There is a new era in the development of man's moral nature, of science, of politics, of civilization. The old creeds, forms, and abuses of the church, will become the cast-off shells of the new born chrysalis of expanded progression. As sure as God, the church South, so far as it is wedded to *slavery*, must fall ! If it does not voluntarily change its position, so much the worse for us: so much the worse for liberty: so much the worse for morals : so much the worse for the souls of men. Through more suffering, and tears, and blood, and crime, and woe, we shall pass, as by fire, into the new era. But heaven nor hell can stay our onward march !

" Must every man holding this relation, forthwith dissolve it, without regard to circumstances ?" Yes, that is it. As to revolutionizing society, that is all stuff, a worn-out lie ! It answered its day ; it was *in use* some years ago, but British, and other national emancipation, have buried it so deep in the things that were, that Mr. Rice, and the whole church South, cannot resurrect it. It is worn thread-bare : it will no longer clothe a *savage*, far less a *Christian* ! There are more men in France given to adultery and fornication, than there are men in the South given to slaveholding. proportionate to number. What is to become of this illicit connexion ; what of these victims of sin ? Would Mr. Rice advise their " *turning loose ?*" Many of them are helpless women, without " capacity to take care of themselves," would he revolutionize society ? Would he preach immediate reform ? Yes, as a man and a Christian, yes ! Those who are unable, by long departure from the right, to take care of themselves, should be taken care of by their destroyers. So of the slaves, " poor things ;" cannot help reach them, as well in a state of freedom, as in a state of slavery ? Then, why not act now, to-day ? We honestly believe, that if every slave under the whole heavens, were liberated this hour, that it would be infinitely better for master· and slave, and all mankind. Yet, because of man's selfishness, and unbelief, and unyielding habits, if we cannot bring an immediate, we will take gradual emancipation, so that at last the right be done !

Mr. Rice asks if we would insist on the doctrine that all men

are born free and equal; would we have every young woman
in England claim to be in all respects equal to Victoria? Yes!
Men are not equal, and cannot be equal, in personal and moral
and intellectual development. God has made them unequal in
this respect; and this inequality seems necessary in the pyra-
midical structure of creation—God being the head. But the
Declaration of Independence asserts a truth—a *practical* truth
—the *political* equality of men.

Our fathers of '76, met to talk and act about *government*,
and their language was directed to that end. They denied
that George had more *natural* right to govern than Jefferson.
Does Mr. R. deny this? He dare not! So far as Queen Victoria,
is Queen of England by the *consent* of a majority of her subjects,
she is the Queen by their *will*, not by *nature*. Nay, if a nation
choose, for supposed or real expediency, to say that a certain
family shall supply a ruler by birth, for a succession of ages,
it does not contradict the doctrine of natural political right and
equality; because the right of each one being king or queen, is
waived by *consent*. But if George or Victoria claims this place
upon any other ground than the will and consent of their people, then is their sovereignty null and void, and ought to fall.
So if it turn out that slavery exists by the *consent* of the enslaved, which in the nature of things is *impossible*, then is
slavery right, and natural equality not violated! But if slavery
be claimed on any other ground, such as the *divine right* of
masters or kings, then is it an usurpation, in violation of natural
political equality, and ought to perish.

"Every king or emperor of Europe that exercises *arbitrary*
power" is, of course, a "sinner." If his subjects *assent* to his
exercise of power, it is not *arbitrary*. If the subjects do not
assent, but are subjected to arbitrary power by force, latent or
overt, then is every king and emperor, so governing, an *usurper
tyrant, criminal,* and "*sinner.*" Wherever we find a monarch
governing in the affections and by the consent of his subjects, we
find a good man: wherever we find a master doing the same
thing in regard to slavery, slavery ceases, and the man is no
longer *master,* nor *sinner!* No *arbitrary* monarch, however
good he may be, can be worthy of the admiration of men! He
not only *unmans* his people, but by withholding a *constitutional*
government, he deprives them of their *natural right,* which all
his failure to abuse power, or all his positive beneficence cannot

counterbalance. But, above all, he subjects them to the chances and, by the nature of things, to the *certainty* of tyranny in his *successors.* If he resigns his power and leaves no successors, then he tacitly yields up his assumed sovereignty to its legitimate owners—the *people.* It is unworthy of Mr. Rice, or any other man, in this age of intelligence and advanced understanding of human rights, affecting to teach others, to be groping about in the dark himself. The man who undertakes, in this republic, to discuss questions of such magnitude, should blush to be continually stranded in the shallow waters of hoary error and stupidity.

"How far may circumstances and the good of society justify restricting the privileges or liberties of men ?"

We are silly enough to suppose this problem solved by every philosophical mind and passing scholar for the last half century at least. Force, or its representative, law, in *religion,* and in *government,* should go just so far as to prevent one individual from trampling upon the rights of another, and no farther. A man yields up to society only so much of his liberty as is necessary to protect the remainder. A government which leaves us not as much protection against the trespass of another as we had in a state of anarchy- or nature, is an usurpation, and ought to perish. *Slavery is that government !*

The false positions of abolitionism have no doubt done harm, but the discussion of slavery has done infinite good. True abolitionism is good ; impracticable discussion and action better than none, for they elicit the true and the practicable. Tyranny always grows more violent when attacked ; but when the friends of freedom are once aroused, it shall surely fall. If the trumpet is never sounded, the forces cannot move to battle ; and if the battle is not fought, victory is not won. The bitterness with which slaveholders denounce abolitionists, shows that their arrows have reached the vitals ; weapons which only penetrate the armor never cause the wearer to cry out. So far as the abolitionists have assaulted slavery in an unconstitutional way, by "stealing slaves," resistance to the laws, and assaults upon the Christian religion, they have done harm, but still less harm than good ; for any thing is better than lethargy. But they who have at great personal sacrifice earnestly cried out against our national crime, shall be ranked with the benefactors of mankind. Neither do we find fault with the *manner*, so that the truth be made sure; for Christ, the mildest and most patient being the world ever saw, dealt at times in the most scathing denunciation that ever startled the ears of men! If the cry of fire be not rung into the ears of the listless slumberer, he will be burnt in his bed!

If we knew any language more terrific than we have ever used towards slavery, we would hail it as heaven's help!

> " Could I embody and embosom now
> That which is most within me—could I wreak
> My thoughts upon expression, and thus throw
> Soul, heart, mind, passions, feelings, strong or weak.
> All that I would have sought, and all I seek,
> Bear, know, feel, and yet breathe—into one word,
> And that one word were Lightning, I would speak ;
> But as it is, I live and die unheard,
> With a most voiceless thought, sheathing it as a sword."

With regard to the numerous instances of special cruelty which Mr. Rice undertakes to refute, it is all love's labor lost: the main stem of slavery is the sum of all evil—we need waste no words upon its branches and leaves.

Mr. Rice asks, " Am I here to defend any *system* of slavery ? " No! by no means ! Mr. Rice is not yet so abandoned : he has not the brass of the Carolina school! That would be too bad, even for Mr. Rice! He is here to apologize for the false position of his church, and to whitewash slaveholding Christians ! You can't do it, Mr. Rice. The sooner you retreat, the better. The sooner the church retreats the better.

" I believe that the state of Kentucky would do wisely to get rid of it. I do desire that it should everywhere come to an end." Then out spoke the heart of the *man*, when was lost the armor of the *churchman!* What! if it be not in itself sinful ? If it be of God, why should it come to an end? No, Mr. Rice, we hold you to your premise, if it be of God, if it is sanctioned by the Christian code, if this cant about " the curse of Canaan " be not " madness and fanaticism," we hold you to your creed. We forbid you to wish its overthrow ! We demand of you to utter daily your prayers to the God of all nations, that the prison-house be strengthened, and the chains more heavily forged ! seeing that the " Peculiar Institution " is set on by a great army of spirited and determined men—swearing by the heavens, and the earth, and the soul of man, that it shall die ! They who are not for us are against us, say the friends of liberty; so say also the foes of human rights. God is on one side or the other, he cannot be neutral in such a contest; wide as heaven is from hell is the space which divides liberty from despotism. "You cannot serve God and mammon!" You must pray for the breaking of every bond, and that the oppressed go free: or else, that despotism set in terrors upon the hearts of men, the iron enter into the flesh, and despair and death into the immortal soul!

LEXINGTON, WEDNESDAY, MAY 27.

The United States an Elective Monarchy.

The experiment of self-government and republicanism in the United States has failed! We know what we say. Every essential guaranty of liberty has long since fallen, and now not even a *show* of regard for constitutional government is left us.

Trial by jury has been and is now denied in more than half of the states! The right of *habeas corpus* has been and is now denied in more than half of the states! The liberty of speech and of the press has been and is now denied in more than half of the states! The clause of the Constitution, which says, "No person shall be deprived of life, liberty, or property, without due process of law," has been and is now violated in a majority of the states, in the District of Columbia, and in the Territories.

That clause of the Constitution which says, "This Constitution, and the laws of the United States which shall be made in pursuance thereof, shall be the supreme law of the land, anything in the Constitution or laws of any state notwithstanding," has been and is now habitually violated North and South.

That clause in the Constitution which says, "The citizens of each state shall be entitled to all the privileges and immunities of citizens in the several states," has been and is now set at defiance.

That clause which says, "A person charged in any state with treason, felony, or other crime, who shall flee from justice, and be found in another state, on demand of the executive authority of the state from which he fled, shall be delivered up, to be removed to the state having jurisdiction of the crime," has been and is now habitually violated.

That clause of the Constitution which says, "The judicial power shall extend to all cases in law and equity—between citizens of different states," has been and is now habitually violated.

That clause of the Constitution which prescribes the mode of electing the President, has been and is now habitually violated.

That clause of the Constitution which says, "No state shall emit bills of credit," has been and is now habitually violated.

That clause of the Constitution which says, "Representatives shall be apportioned among the several states, according to their respective numbers," has been, in the case of Texas, flagrantly violated.

That clause of the Constitution which says, "No person shall be a Senator, who shall not have been *nine years* a citizen of the United States," has been, in the case of Texas, flagrantly violated.

That clause of the Constitution which says, the President "Shall have power, by and with the consent and advice of the Senate, to make treaties, provided two-thirds of the Senators present concur," was, in the case of Texas annexation, flagrantly violated.

That clause of the Constitution which separates the executive and legislative powers of the government, and gives to Congress only the power "to declare war," in the case of the march into the Mexican border, and making military posts in the bounds, and on the undisputed soil of a nation, at peace with us by solemn treaties of friendship and amity, is grossly violated. And when we remember that all this despotism is imposed upon us to sustain African "slavery, the lowest, the most unmitigated, the basest, the world has seen!" we are ready almost to declare ourselves in all respects absolved from any allegiance to the American Union.

In the name of the Constitution which has been overthrown; in the name of liberty which has been destroyed; in the name of the rights of man which have been trampled in the dust, we solemnly protest against the usurpations of the present administration. We only fail to use physical resistance because we are overpowered; yet, with the unconquerable spirit of our sires of '76, we call upon our fellow-citizens of America, to resort to the ballot-box, if possible, to restore the broken Constitution; and if we shall hopelessly fail, then let all lovers of liberty, and self-government, concentrate in some portion of the continent, and form a government for themselves.

The usurpation of Texas, it seems, was not enough for the insatiable appetite of slavery. *James K. Polk*, without any authority from this people, but in derogation of the sovereignty of the same, contrary to the solemn treaties of peace constitutionally made with our sister republic, Mexico—contrary to the laws of nature, of nations, and of God—has marched a hostile army into the Mexican territory beyond the Nueces, which is the farthest possible boundary of Texas, to Matamoras on the Rio Grande, driving women and children before him, for the sole purpose of enlarging the slave-market, and strengthening the despotism of the South.

Americans, sons of Washington, of Adams, of Franklin, of Jefferson, have we come to this? Shall we prove ourselves willing traitors to the liberties of men? Shall we shed our blood in such a damnable cause? No! let us rise in the once mighty strength of our illustrious sires, the unconquerable power of a just and free people, and say to these infamous tyrants, withdraw your army from another's soil, restore the bleeding Constitution of our unhappy country, and let slavery, the cause of all our woes, cease on the whole continent.

WAR MEETING.

On Saturday, the 16th of May, after notice previously given, the people of Lexington and Fayette county, met at the court house to take into consideration the affairs of the republic, (military despotism!) The house and galleries were full, but there was very little appearance of any other feeling but curiosity to learn and see.

General L. C. entered with hat in hand, and after a few faint calls, ascended the Tribune. He seemed to be evidently pressing himself up to the sticking point, against the true feelings of human nature, for the General, though a slaveholder, and Texas land speculator, is nevertheless a good fellow. He commenced by saying, that it was anticipated that officers of the meeting would have been selected, yet it was not important, and as it was expected that he would say something, he would proceed at once. The map of Texas was hung upon the wall, all that part of Mexico between the Nueces and the Rio Grande, called Texas, was put in *blue!* He asked for a rattan, and pushed without further preface in *medias res.* There, gentlemen, is a map of Texas, once the republic of the Lone Star, but now one of the states of this Union, and however much we once differed about it, *all* now must agree to stand for its brotherhood. [The General was for Clay and the Presidency, but that failing was for the *land.*]

The boundary of Texas begins here at the Sabine, and runs thence north and west, with the United States boundary line to the Rocky mountains, in latitude about 42°, four degrees further north than Lexington. From the mouth of the Sabine it runs along the Gulf of Mexico to the mouth of the Rio Grande, or Bravo, and with the Bravo, to its source in the Rocky Mountains, and its intersection with the United States line! (This boundary takes in a large portion, besides Texas, of the Mexican provinces of Cohahuila, Tamaulipas, and Santa Fe, upon which never was set the foot of a Texan, except as a prisoner! But the General loves land!)

General Taylor is a Kentuckian, and a good soldier, but he is evidently in a false position, perhaps ordered there by the Executive. Here is Matamoras, some twenty or thirty miles from the mouth of the Rio Grande, on the west bank of the river, in a sort of horse-shoe bend, on the east bank, is Gen. Taylor's army, some 2,200 strong, and well fortified, with his guns bearing upon the opposite city, and the guns of the city bearing upon his camp.

Here, about twenty or thirty miles on the Gulf, is Point Isabel, with the stores and ammunition, wagons, &c., approachable by sea, and by two routes by land from Corpus Christi. This is the place where Taylor ought to be. Because it forms the heel of a fan, with the fingers resting upon divers points upon the Mexican border, liable to attack in divers places, and thereby causing them to scatter their force along the whole river. He wished not to be critical. [The General wants, it is said, the command of the Kentucky forces! But so far as we can learn, there is a general disposition to confer the command upon us. First, because we are supposed to be, not an abler, but an *older* soldier, for the General, claims being a widower, to be but " but a boy!" and next, because the community would thus be rid of a man who is thought to be a thorn in the king's side ! If we make up our mind to fight in this cause at all, we think we shall outrank the General, we having commanded *uni-*

form, and the General having only commanded *corn-stalk* militia !)

But General Taylor, in leaving his post at Isabel, rendered himself liable to be cut off from provisions and recruits. For should the Mexicans intercept him in the rear, by taking Isabel, and thus preventing sea passage, and by stationing a detachment above Isabel, on the road to Corpus Christi, cut him off from land passage, his case is almost hopeless. For, although he and his officers are gallant and well disciplined, his men are mostly foreigners, too lazy to work on railroads, peckrock, or drive carts, and willing to enlist in order to get bread; although they were to wash their own clothes, and cook their own victuals, he much feared they would not be able to cut their way through the enemy, or advance upon Matamoras. For, although this white race, with blue, black, and *red*, and all sorts of eyes, were destined, as he believed, by God, to over-run and own the world, yet the Spaniards were not such mean soldiers at last; for *they believed* they were fighting for their religion, their altars, as well as their hearths! [Indeed! a strange belief, to be sure, General.] And in such a cause it was hard to whip any men. [Yes, truly.]

So, when the company was sent out to see if the troops had crossed the river, as it was reported, Capt. Thornton, no doubt acting upon this idea, contrary to the orders of Taylor and the advice of his guide, pushed into the enemy's whole army, intending, no doubt, to destroy the army at a blow, and make himself President. Of course he was knocked into a cocked hat in less than no time. He and his sixty men were killed and taken prisoners. To take Mexico we need 20,000 men as an advance guard, followed up with lengthening columns of fives and ten thousands in the rear. The General still, however, hoped for the best. Rapid reinforcements had been sent on from New Orleans, Mobile, and no doubt Texas and Mississippi. But the truth was, with a large and excited population of a *peculiar kind* at home, it was *not safe* to draw many men from the *South!* So that Kentucky and Tennessee ought to turn out! *as it was perfectly safe to spare any number of men from those warlike states.* He was himself willing to bear a hand if called on, and he supposed an indication of that kind on the part of Kentucky, at present, was enough.

We have given a very meagre sketch of the General's speech; we shall be pleased to report him from his own notes.

During the speech the United States flag was introduced with its stars and "*stripes*." It produced very little sensation, because every man present felt that the *cause* was bad, and the colors of the *free* desecrated!

Judge J. E. D. then, after some hesitatiion, moved that *Squire* Hickman take the chair, and Maj. C. C. R. be secretary, which was assented to. The *mobite* having taken the chair, Judge D. proceeded to make a few remarks previous to offering a resolution. He said he differed in some respects from the gallant General. He could not believe that Taylor was whipt, or Point Isabel taken. That the wagoners, and carpenters, and artillerists at Isabel would whip any amount of Mexicans. He then went on to review the Texan war, and to show the inferiority of the Mexican troops. He was willing to lay a wager that they were now whipt, and that Taylor had advanced over the river upon Matamoras. The object of the Judge seemed to be to arouse the flagging courage of the audience, which the General had caused to ebb considerably. The resolution was then read, in substance as follows:

Resolved, That we have heard with concern of the critical situation of the army of occupation, and of the call made upon the southern states for reinforcements; Kentucky claims also a share in the labor and the peril of arms, and holds herself ready to march at a moment's warning.

Resolved, That a copy of these resolutions be sent to the President of the United States, and that they be inserted in the city papers.

Mr. G. offered a preamble stating the wrongs received by the United States from Mexico, and justifying our *defence!* An universal murmur of dissent ran through the audience, and Mr. G. withdrew them without putting them to the vote! We were glad of this, for it saved us from inflicting a speech upon unwilling ears, and showed that our people, if *robbers*, were not willing to add hypocrisy and falsehood to bloody and merciless crime!

The resolutions were then voted, and the meeting, after Hail Columbia and *Yankee Doodle* were played, adjourned with a most dove-like quietness.

The heroes of the 18th were remarkably scarce. The venerable President was the only one we recognized!

What business had General Combs to give the lie to those redoubtable champions of their country's liberties, by saying that Kentucky would be *"perfectly safe"* with a large portion of her soldiers withdrawn! Now, the patriots of the 18th think just the contrary. They seem to think that it would be very dangerous for them to go to war leaving us in the rear! Well has some one pithily said, "a lie cannot live!"

Now, we wish to be distinctly understood. We say we have not the least shadow of title to the land west of the Nueces. The reason why General Taylor has pushed himself into this straight is, that he might, by threatening Matamoras, blockading the Rio Grande, and *occupying* the Mexican soil, *force* them to yield their just rights! We solemnly protest against the damning usurpation of James K. Polk in *making* war without the consent of Congress, passed in the most formal and solemn manner. At the same time, when we are actually at war, we are ready to defend our poor soldiers who have been forced by *death* from desertion into this unwilling danger!

If called upon by Governor Owsley to take our old command, or any other post, we are willing to do so; whilst we demand of Congress, as a citizen of a republic, where the highest and the lowest are equally entitled to be heard, to cause the President to withdraw his forces from the soil of a friendly sister republic, and punish him for his assumption of kingly power, in putting to death, without trial, American citizens, and making war without constitutional right!

RICE AND BLANCHARD'S DEBATE ON SLAVERY.

CONTINUED REVIEW.

There is in this debate good hearty quarreling, and brotherly insinuation of the lie direct, that shocks *our* sensibilities. "Brother" Rice, for the first time in his numerous debates, gets angry!

Mr. Rice contends that the slave is as well protected from cruelty in Kentucky as the child of the parent. We must attribute ignorance to Mr. Rice, to save him from the imputation

of falsehood.   When we come across such stuff as this, we lose
all patience.   Some few years ago Robert Wickliffe introduced
and carried through the legislature a law authorizing a slave to
be sold when cruelly treated.   But as every human cruelty,
specifically named, can be inflicted on the slave according to
law, there remains nothing else coming under the denomination
of " cruelty ;" unless it be to reduce the " poor slave" to a state
of freedom !   If a slave may be whipped to death, shot for insubordination, kept in utter ignorance, have his food and medicine prescribed, be raped with impunity, worked without wages,
and damned with all sorts of opprobrious epithets from infancy
to old age, is it not worse than nonsense to talk about any
other cruelty ?   Can any of this happen to the child, without
some redress ?   Why then will Mr. R. stultify himself ?

This is as barefaced a fiction, as the solemn vote of the 18th,
that we were an *insurrectionist ;* which not a single man present believed to be true !   The world has always underrated the
deep and unfathomable Machiavellism of slavery.   What was
the cause of our overthrow on the 18th ?   We had largely estimated the hellish baseness of slaveholders, but we *had infinitely
underrated it !*

He reiterates his *second argument.*   As we flatter ourselves
that we have effectually used that up, we pass on.

Mr. Rice again presses the right of blacks to vote.   We give
him rope in his eulogy upon the Declaration of Independence.
It is plainly *felo de se !*   If he is in earnest, he admits his own
crime ; if in irony, he wants the outspoken boldness of the
Carolina school to make his treason respectable !

It is true that in Kentucky there is no law to prevent slaves
from reading.   But slavery has a law of its own—Lynch law !
When Lewis Marshall, the father of T. F. Marshall, attempted
to teach a black school, John U. Waring and others, took a
rope and showed him a limb !   Yes, they played the game of
the 18th of August upon him !   These facts were related to me
by Waring himself, in the presence of D. McPayne.   Perhaps
Thomas' hereditary instincts led him to be on good terms with
Judge Lynch !   Again, when some members of the city council
of Lexington voted to allow a *free black* school even, they
were placarded in the streets by this same Judge Lynch !   So
far from letting slaves read, they won't allow free blacks to have
schools to read ; so far from letting free blacks read, they won't

let free *whites* read! Witness the stealing of the common
school fund, and the overthrow of the True American on the
18th!

Mr. Rice again pleads the *law* as a justification of Christians
in what he is forced to admit is criminal! In a country where
every voter is responsible for the laws, and those laws are found
to be criminal and infamous, cannot Mr. Rice see that he must
first prove that he has voted against the laws, and used all the
means consistent with his "paramount duties" for its repeal,
before he stands acquitted? Mr. Rice, by attempting to sanctify and whitewash slavery, and by denouncing the friends of
abolition, takes upon himself the damning guilt of the whole
system. We say of this action as we said of Junkins', we had
rather fill any other place, in the category of crime, than his.

The reverend gentleman takes up again the thread of his
third speech, and wishes to know what a Christian is to do,
where the laws will not allow emancipation. We will tell him.
Change the law. Do all you can, consistent with "paramount
duties," to change it. Tell the slave you have no right to his
services, farther than to pay the taxes, and provide for his support in old age. Pay him wages. Tell him how he can get
free if he wants to, by flying into the land of *English tyranny!*
Has your Christian slaveholder done this? No! Then he is
deceiving himself, or imposing upon the world.

Ex-Governor Cole told us that, after he had freed his slaves,
by taking them from Virginia to Illinois, in returning to Virginia, he stopped at the house of an old Presbyterian acquaintance, one of Mr. Rice's Christian slaveholders. The old
gentleman immediately began to protest that his slaves were a
tax upon him—he wished they were all free—he would set
them free at once, but, poor things, they could not take care of
themselves—if any one would take care of them, he would
liberate them that moment.

Mr. Cole listened very patiently till he was through with all
this usual *cant*, and then replied: "My Dear Sir, you deceive
yourself; you are not in earnest." "I call God to witness that
I am in earnest," said the Presbyterian. "Well, then," said the
Governor, "I pledge myself to take them, and take care of
them, and plant them with my freedmen in Illinois." "Up to
this time," said the ex-Governor, "my old friend had been in-

sisting upon my staying with him; my horse was at the stile; but after this he never said another word. I mounted my horse and as far as I could see him, he was gazing on the ground just as I left him." The old man had all along deceived himself! The human heart is desperately wicked—who can know it?

Mr. Rice then comes to his fifth argument against the doctrine of abolition: Because the doctrine of abolition leads men to pursue a different course from that of the apostles of Christ. Christ and the apostles went among the heathen, and denounced their superstition; whilst the abolitionists stay at a distance and remonstrate against it! Now this is too silly to come from even Mr. Rice.

If the cases are similar, it proves only that they lack the courage and self-sacrifice of Christ and Paul. So the Southern church are more cowardly even than abolitionists (for some of them have fallen martyrs to their opinions), but is the Christian religion therefore *false*, because its priests are *traitors?* But we utterly deny that it is the *duty* of abolitionists to come into the slave states. They have no more right to come here, and declaim against slavery, than we have to go to Russia and denounce despotism of the same sort there. The laws of comity, and of nations, and good sense, forbid this. The nation is also a slaveholder too, and Northern men ought to cease to hold slaves unconstitutionally in the District of Columbia before they can spare their missionaries here, even if it was proper. So far as slavery affects the nation, any citizen of the republic ought, at any place, to raise his voice against it; but so far as slavery is a municipal institution, confined to the states, there none but citizens have any right to cause popular agitation. The right, however, of free speech and thought at *home*, on any subject, and about any government, is one of the inalienable rights of man, and Mr. Rice is very silly in denouncing it.

Mr. Rice, in his zeal to taunt his *brother* of Ohio, forgets the pitiable dilemma in which he places himself. For, if it be right for abolitionists to come here and cry out against slavery, then all the uproarious objections made against it are criminal! If it be not safe, as he intimates, to do so, then are the slave states proved to be lawless murderers, violating the American Constitution, and the laws of God and nature! The truth is, Mr.

Rice, in his accusation against abolitionists, of a want of apostolic courage, seals his own condemnation; for he confesses, that if he were to preach, as he taunts them for not doing, that he and the other priests would be sent across the Ohio, "like squirrels with the wind in their tails!"

But Mr. Rice will soon be put to shame, unless we are very much mistaken, for we believe that the time is at hand, when the true followers of Christ will stand like Paul upon Mars Hill, and cry out with omnipotent power against this worse than Pagan crime! So that if we have not now shown his argument false, it will then prove itself so; for if a want of courage and home contact with slavery proves abolitionism spurious, when the bull is taken by the horns, it will then be proven the real thing! So the days of his fifth proposition, to say the least, are *numbered*. Nay, if we might be allowed to state our own case, is his fifth argument not already dead? For we declare as Paul: Ye men of Kentucky, we "perceive that in all things ye are too superstitious; for as I passed by and beheld your devotions, I found an altar with this inscription, *To the unknown God!*" For there is but one true and only God, the Father of all men—a God of justice, and no respecter of persons—a God hating oppression, and not at all tolerant of sin! Whereas the God whom ye worship, is a God of injustice and oppression, having respect to the color of the skin, and dooming a whole people to eternal slavery!

END OF TRUE AMERICAN.

ESSAYS, SPEECHES, &c.

BY C. M. CLAY.

SKETCH OF A SPEECH

Delivered on the 20th day of May, 1846, before 5,000 Kentuckians, in the City of Lexington.

Gen. Leslie Combs, having made a few remarks, concluded by saying, any person who chooses to address the people, or whom the people choose to hear, can now speak.

After a long and unanimous call, Mr. C. arose and said:

Men of Fayette. It is well-known to at least a portion of you, that no man has more steadily and unsparingly denounced this war than I. Both by speech and the pen, have I warned my countrymen of the calamity which is now upon us. At the White Sulphur Springs, I told you that in taking Texas, we took her war; and this position is now sustained by a leading Texan Senator, Gen. S. Houston, if the stern catastrophe left any longer room for speculation.

Up to the time that this war was legalized by congressional assumption, it continued to meet my uncompromising opposition.

But now, stern necessity leaves me no alternative ; *my country* calls for help, and, " right or wrong," I rally to her standard. Whatever difference of opinion may have honestly or dishonestly existed between us in matters of civil administration, is lost in the great first law of nations, as well as of individuals, and the instincts of self-preservation lead me to make common cause in the defence of our common country.

He shall be deemed the true friend of his country, who not only consistently warns her against evil, but rescues her from the danger of her errors or her crimes. And, as at no time have I sought individual popularity at the expense of the common good, so now I shall not claim exemption from common danger and equal sacrifice, upon the plea that others, and not I, are responsible for this thing.

It is the true glory of a free people, that we are not called upon to *execute* the mandate of an inexorable superior. It is our part to advise, as well as to act; and whilst I volunteer to risk my life in the battle field, I claim the right of a parting word in council.

It is now out of place to review the Texan controversy. Whether Texas was rightly admitted into this Union or not remains to other times and other places than now and here, for determination.

Thus much, however, I do say, that I am constrained to regard the river Nueces as the western boundary of Texas. We ask óf you that, whilst we fly to the rescue of our gallant army, that you place us on the safe ground of justice.

I go not as the enemy of the Catholic religion, nor the invader of a sister republic, in a war of aggression and rapine.

I ask that we conquer an honorable and speedy peace; and that our unhappy enemy shall not be forced to dishonorable terms.

I believe that an overpowering force, thrown at once into the Mexican dominions, will in the long run save treasure and blood.

I do not believe the war can last long, without bringing the allied nations of Christendom against us; and whatever success we may have had at other times, it is not now that we can hope to stand against the world in arms.

It was a good and wise custom among the Athenians, that he who advised the republic, should prove the fidelity of his counsel by personal execution. So now I fall into the ranks, as a private, with my blanket and canteen, giving practical illustration of that equality of privilege among men which I have ever advocated. If from the Executive, or the people, I shall receive promotion, I shall unaffectedly be gratified, for I regard the confidence and approbation of my countrymen as only less than the consciousness of having, partially at least, at all times discharged my duty to myself, to my family, to my country, and to God.

LETTER.

(From the New-York Tribune.)

CAMARGO, Mexico, December 10th, 1848.

P. C., MY DEAR SIR : Your letter, addressing some inqui-
ries to me, has just come to hand ; and I shall answer you in
the same frank and friendly manner in which they are put.

After some years of high-pressure life, I was glad once more
to get to myself and the woods ; and, whether ruminating by
day and night upon the wide-spread prairies of Texas, or pursuing the buffalo upon the Brazos and Colorado, or lassoing
the wild horse of the Nueces, à la Camanche, upon the "disputed" desert, I cared little for the newspapers, the vindication
of friends, or the denunciations of enemies. Coming to Camargo, I see steamboats, and hear bells ; and newspapers force
upon me the thought of politics once more.

Since I left home I have written no letters touching my views
upon political subjects ; and no one has had authority to speak
for me. If I live to return I shall, in due time, take care to
write and speak so as not to be misunderstood.

In the mean time, however, I have no secrets ; and I say in
answer to your first inquiry, "My opinions of the institution
of Slavery are unchanged." Whether I shall continue "to edit
the paper" or not, is problematical. It was never my original
design to do so. I think I can be more efficient in "exerting"
my "influence as heretofore for the establishment of freedom"
in other ways.

I have suffered enough to look charitably upon the "hasty
rebuke of the bigoted and contracted." I am willing to trust
to time and the unbiassed opinions of men for my final vindication.

In going into this war, I have not been impelled, as some of
my apologists would have it, by Constitutional ardor, or Southern education. Neither have I been lured by the vulgar ambi-

tion of military glory. I would far rather have been ADAMS at the vindication of the Right of Petition, than WELLINGTON at the battle of Waterloo.

I wished to *prove* to the *people* of the South that I warred not upon *them*, but upon *Slavery*—that a man might hate slavery and denounce tyrants without being the *enemy of his country*.

Besides, the instincts of self-preservation, or rather of national preservation, as well as history, teach me that a Constitutional declaration of war must be sustained by *all parties*. My action, therefore, is a corollary from the admission of the republican theory that a *legal majority must rule*. Have my denouncers found a *better* theory ?

I trust that, after a while, I shall convince those who have no interest in doing me injustice that I am not a "fanatic," for I have at all times stood by the broad landmarks which the laws of nations and custom and an enlightened morality have fixed as sacred from innovation ; nor an "egotist seeking temporary notoriety," for I have labored in obscure places, and been silent under reproach and calumny. Far less am I "a traitor to my country," for I have been ready to lay down my life at home and abroad, ever standing in her defence.

I thank you and those most sincerely who have not ceased to have "implicit faith in the purity of my motives." I am proud in the reflection, that if fate denies me the good fortune "to return and aid" in the emancipation of our loved country and the vindication of the universal liberties of men, the loftiest virtue known to the heroes of antiquity, "Mori pro patria," was imputed to me as my only crime.

When I *spoke* against the Mexican war I said that I would *fight* it. I am here to redeem my pledge. I saw in anticipation the noble dead whom *all* now mourn. The million taxes coming will arouse those who were insensible to national dishonor and personal woe. The people already begin to ask, what is all this for? I venture to say that the millions upon whom the burden of this war rests, will not love *slavery* the more that *it* has caused it. It lives only by the will of the *people :* then speed the day when from the St. John's to the Rio Grande, from the Atlantic to the Pacific, the sublime enunciation shall be made, America is FREE !

This, my undying aspiration, may be delusive. It may be

that our fathers were "impracticable enthusiasts"—that there is no hope of the amelioration of human society—that virtue and justice may not be possible foundations of human happiness and national prosperity—that America is not destined to mark a new era in the history of mankind;—still we may cherish those sublime principles which have in days gone by and will ever in the course of time act as sheet anchors of safety, upon which cavillers themselves rest, when the storm of passion, crime, and woe rages apace.

SURRENDER OF ENCARNACION.

LETTER FROM CASSIUS M. CLAY.

CITY OF MEXICO, July 15, 1847.

TO THE EDITORS OF THE PICAYUNE:

I have till now refrained from making anything public touching our capture. The probability that it might become the subject of legal investigation seemed to me to be a sufficient reason, among others, for silence.

But since the *merits* of our surrender have become the topic of discussion, any farther deference to personal delicacy becomes criminal injustice to those who have a right to claim of me, their immediate commander, whatever protection my humble ability can afford them. I therefore merge the imputation of egotism and self-elation in the higher necessity of discharging a duty to the living who do not, and the dead, who cannot speak for themselves.

If the failure of our superior officers to exchange us, after three successful battles, and the capture of many prisoners of war, is necessary to the public service, requiring the soldier never to surrender, but in all cases to lay down his life, without regard to the inequality of numbers or the resulting good of the sacrifice, then, without a murmur, I submit to the sentence. But if this policy becomes not general, and is not deemed usual and necessary in war, then, on the part of myself and my brave companions in arms, some of whom have gone from the loathsome prisons of Mexico, where praise nor blame can never reach them, I protest against it as a condemnation without a trial, and a penalty without a crime.

You term the surrender at Encarnacion an "honorable capitulation." It is so. The mass of mankind judge of things by their *apparent* success or failure. With them victory is glory, and defeat disgrace. But with enlightened minds it is better to *deserve* success than to win it. Yet paradoxical as it may seem, I say that the expedition to Encarnacion not only deserved, but achieved success.

Lieut. Colonel Field, Surgeon Roberts, and Major Gaines will remember, that on the night preceding the adventure, it was urged that the reconnoitring party should consist of a large body, with artillery sufficient to hold the enemy in check till the arrival of reinforcements, or strong enough to retreat with its face to the foe. Or else it should be a small body, whose loss would not be materially felt by the army—a part of whom we might calculate from the superior speed of the horses and better address of the men, would return with the tidings of the enemy's position and force. The last alternative we were compelled to adopt, and the result was as foretold. We found the enemy, and *sent back word of his approach.* Whether this reasoning be in accordance with military science or not, and how far the success of the glorious battle of Buena Vista was owing to this timely warning, I leave abler strategists than I to determine.

But why anticipate capture? The country through which we had to pass was a grass covered plain, shut out by mountains, where there was no growth of wood to conceal us. We were compelled to go to fixed and well known places for water, surrounded by rancheros, who were ever ready and not slow in giving timely notice of our approach. The night before reaching Encarnacion, we had resolved, according to the Spartan maxim, continually to change our camp to avoid surprise, and to move, if necessary, twice a night, to prevent the peasantry's knowing our whereabouts.

That we camped two nights successively in Encarnacion, the cause in part of our capture, was rather the result of fortune than design on our part; for we had on the 22d advanced ten miles in the direction of Salido, intending to attack two hundred men whom we learned were stationed there; but night, storm, and darkness coming on, we were compelled, having no guide, to return, against the protest of some and our previous rules of action, to Encarnacion. The idea of putting out picket guards in a plain of twenty miles diameter, intersected by roads in all directions, is absurd. And had a picket guard given an alarm in the night the result would have been the same, for we would not have left our castle till morning, till we saw the enemy, and knew their force.

Seventy-one men and officers, all told, held General Miñon and three thousand regular and veteran troops, as numbered by himself, at bay, from dawn till noon of the 23d day of January. Without half as many rounds of shot as there were opposing foes, without water, without provisions, one hundred and ten miles from camp, without the remotest *probability* of reinforcement, we unanimously determined to *exact* "the most honorable terms of capitulation known to nations," or sell our lives like men who held the faith that honor is the only necessity.

Holding a Mexican chief of equal rank with our commandant as a hostage, Major Gaines and General Minon concluded the following terms of capitulation :

First. The most honorable treatment as prisoners of war known to nations.

Second. Private property to be strictly respected.

Third. Our Mexican guide to receive a fair trial in the civil courts.

When we remember that Taylor fought at Buena Vista, at a liberal computation *one* to *four*, and had his hands full, and that we stood less than *one* to *forty-two* of the enemy, under their most gallant chief, I hazard the assertion that in the history of the Mexican war there will have been no exhibition of nobler gallantry than was displayed at the capitulation of Encarnacion.

Accept assurances of my lasting gratitude, that you have, with Mrs. Hemans, in the "Captive Knight," entered into a prisoner's griefs, and magnanimously vindicated our claims upon our country's justice ; for all that is generally deemed remunerative in war falls to the lot of others, but

> "The worm, the canker, and the grief,
> Are ours alone."

Ever your ob't servant,

C. M. CLAY.

LETTER.

The Editors of the Christian Reflector :

Gentlemen,—In your paper of January 6th instant, which you have forwarded me, you have commented freely upon my volunteering in the Mexican war. The spirit of your remarks, though mixed with censure, commands my respect. Denunciation from other quarters has also reached me, which I regard with philosophic indifference. Neither flattery nor denunciation, at home or abroad, shall move me from the advocacy of such principles as I choose to advocate, nor the use of such *means* as I choose to use, for their ultimate success. I am a private man —a candidate for no office : I ask no man for his vote, or his purse. In the discharge of my duty as a citizen of a republic, I have attempted to be intelligent ; I certainly have *labored.* I have spent my money and my time, foregone tolerable chances of elevation to office, suffered somewhat in feeling, in name, and in person, in vindicating principles—surely, I ought to be *honest.* If any man knows of any proofs of integrity and sincerity which I have not yet given, and will write them down, I will attempt them : I am not too old yet to learn, nor too conceited to be advised. In attempting to overthrow slavery, I expected to meet the ill-will and violence of those who were gainers by slavery. But to find those who profess to be anti-slavery men, and who are certainly interested in the establishment of liberty in America, watching my every word and act, with uncompromising hatred and denunciation, astounds me. No doubt some who hate the *South,* who have calculated the cost of the Union, and desire its dissolution, are disappointed in not finding me prepared to forget, that the slaves, the masters, and the non-slaveholders of the South, by such an event, would be involved perhaps in one common ruin. I come not to destroy, but to save. If liberty and this Union cannot co-exist, then I confess I am in despair. If with all our *natural,* social, and political advantages, some of which can never be renewed in all coming time, we cannot carry out the principles of 1776, then I confess I have no hope of their ultimate triumph.

What is the basis of Republicanism? That the majority, in constitutional form, rule. That the end of government is to secure the rights of all, minorities as well as majorities. But suppose the imperfections of humanity cause government to fall short of the protection of all the citizens, what are you to do? Give it all up in despair and return to anarchy or despotism? Surely not. What then? Simply if we cannot do as we the minority please, let the majority do as they please. Have you, gentlemen, found a better rule of action than this? Have you knowingly and in good faith entered into the partnership of the American government? You have agreed to play; you have put up the stakes; you have lost. What say you? will you pay up? A grumbles, and swears, and pays up: B pays up with a gentlemanly grace. Which is the honest man, A, or B? You and I and the American people have formed this governmental partnership; we have agreed to play; we have put up the stakes; we have knowingly said, whatever the legal majorities enact, that we will abide by. Congress says there shall be war with Mexico: we have said we are opposed to war with Mexico: we have done our duty: we have played the game; and have lost. Shall we pay? I say, yes: you say, no. "Logic" brings us just to this point: shall we do what we agreed to do? You say no: I say yes. There is an end of it. You must either go with the government, or *dissolve* the government. For my part, great evils as were the Texas iniquity and the Mexican war, they were yet more sufferable than *revolution*. There is no middle ground. If you refuse to pay when you lose, there is an end of all playing. If you refuse to carry out the enactments of the government, then there is an end of all government. Well, the regular army ought to fight: not you—a volunteer. Why the regular? Because he is paid for it? Shall a man be excused for the violation of a principle because he is *paid*? If I committed a crime in joining the army, then did every soldier who believed the war unjust commit the same crime. If I committed a crime in going to the war, then did every man in America denying the justice of the war, who paid taxes, or gave aid and comfort to the army, commit the same crime.

If there was a man opposing the justice of the war, who did

not use all the energies and means, which, after providing for himself and his, he owes to universal man, in aid of the Mexicans, and against the American army, that man committed the same crime. I go boldly a step further ; every man, believing the war unjust, unless a non-resistant, who did not take up arms against the Americans, and who was not ready to peril his life in the Mexican cause, committed the same crime. Let impartial reason, then, determine who has been the victim of "logic," you, or I. Once more. The jury is the legal creature of government: the prisoner has undergone a fair trial : he is condemned to death. You think the man innocent: or you are opposed to capital punishment : will you hang him ? If you think with me, you will : if not, you will go guilty away, and let me do it. You are a coward in such case. I say, either *hang* him, or *help* him.

Once more. Congress lays a tariff upon foreign sugar: it robs you to sustain slave-labor. Will you pay ? You have never thought of doing otherwise. Then you have committed the same crime for which I am denounced. Will I pay it ? Yes. Because it is the *law*. But, say you, I pay it, because I cannot help it. Indeed ! There was in Boston once a set of men, who, when an unjust tax was laid upon them, said, we will die, but pay no tax. Which were the nobler, you or your ancestors ? " Logic " places you in the dilemma of denouncing your ancestors : or by admitting that the cases are dissimilar, you lose your argument.

In a republic, it is the duty of every one to advocate what he deems right : but when the public will has been declared in legal form, though it be opposed to his, we ought in good faith to carry it out, dissolve the government—or leave the country. It does not follow that you, or thousands of others, ought to have gone to the war. You and they may have been more useful in other vocations. But you, and every other man in this republic who votes or partakes of its protection, should have aided and abetted me and the army who did war, until the proper authorities should have concluded a peace, or the public legal will have changed. It suited my temperament to play the soldier : yours to be tax-payer. I trust we have both discharged our whole duty. In going to the war, then, it was possible to have been consistently an anti-slavery man. My *motives*, then, and not the *act*, must determine my *consistency*. Now long before the declaration of war, I avowed in public speeches in the North, that I would go to it. Why was I not then denounced? The earnestness that I displayed in this cause gave me the reputation of being a fanatic. The untold woes which have come upon us by the annexation of Texas, were long since seen by me. I would that I had possessed eloquence equal to the infinite issue—that our nation had been spared her great crime—that the Constitution of my country were yet unbroken—that our public faith were yet inviolate—that these millions of treasure had been spent in the liberation of the children of our own soil— that the blood of the great dead had not been shed in vain—that the tears of widows and orphans had not moistened so many hearths, now desolate for ever!

Believing with Channing, that the triumphs of war are third rate in the scale of human greatness, and that even then to be glorious, they must be just, it seems hardly possible that I should have been seduced from the path of duty by the "mad spirit of war." If I was ambitious, there was some peculiarity in my taste: they who reaped the laurels of the war, sought other places than the *ranks*, in which to win fame. With so many inducements to ignoble ease—with the often avowed sentiment that the mere desire for military glory was a vulgar ambition, it seems hardly possible that I was "intoxicated with the mad spirit of war." I said to the people of Fayette, I go to this war with my political opinions unchanged. I wrote to the Tribune, from Camargo, "my opinions are unchanged." Once more on my native soil, after long suffering in a cause, which I did all possible in the nature of things to avoid, I say to the same people, my opinions are unchanged. Is it, then, so hard a thing to believe in the honesty of a man with all these proofs of integrity graven on the annals of the country? Are men engaged in a common cause to be thus trammeled by narrow views of means? So long as one is believed to be honest, and right in the main, is he to be forced to look through the brazen spectacles of every madman who has set up his bedroom Utopia? Have I one set of opinions for the North, and another for the South? If I love the South, and because I love her would make her free, am I not allowed to convince her that it is slavery which I hate, not her *people*? Must I stand by the inalienable duties which birthplace imposes upon the true of all lands—to struggle for a higher destiny—or must I flee from the hard and unwilling task, and become in other countries a pensioner upon the blood-bought liberties of nobler men? Have I omnipotence to speak vitality into a dying community? or must I intelligently use the *means* of influencing their wills, that they may be convinced and be saved?

I have done. There is a class of men in the North whose good opinion I am unwilling to lose, who cannot just now appreciate my position. These, this letter, and my future conduct, will, I trust, make my friends. There is another class who have no intention now, or hereafter, to do me justice. Our aims are not, and never can be the same. For them I have no reproaches. Bitter words are to be used only by those who have nothing to extenuate in the difficult drama of life. I am not of them: I have never assumed to be *infallible*. As a man, I have never attempted more than a balance sheet in morals. But as a politician, in degenerate times, I have borne an *unsullied banner:* my highest ambition, my holiest hope is, that it may at last be triumphant—that as it is now, so may it be eternally the same.

C. M. CLAY.

Lexington, 1847.

(From the Louisville Examiner.)

C. M. CLAY.

The friends of freedom will be glad to hear again from one of its truest champions. Unchanged in mind and purpose, he is fired by as holy a zeal for the good cause as man ever felt.

His reception in Kentucky has been of the warmest character. At Lexington, it *was* a grand fete. All parties and all classes joined to meet and greet Cassius M. Clay. The truth is, the people love and respect the man.

Nor let any one suppose that this results from his *military* services! He had no opportunity to win warrior fame. It was the spirit of generosity and self-sacrifice—the remembrance of his fight in a holier battle than war ever witnessed—which bade the people hail his return home with so wide and earnest an enthusiasm.

And it is a good omen—this honorable acknowledgment of past injustice, and shaking of hands over past divisions. It shows that the hour *is* when men may consider the right, and struggle honestly for it. Let us welcome this change as the dawn of a better day, and labor together to hasten its full and more glorious opening.

———

(For the Examiner.)

To the Subscribers of the True American.

Compatriots:—The True American has ceased to exist; but it was not in vain that it was established by me, and so liberally sustained by you.

The true friends of the South were not behind their brothers of the free states in feeling the evils of slavery. Not content with infecting the pulpit, the legislative hall, and the social circle, it breathed upon the liberty of the press, and despairing silence sat upon millions. Here and there, at long intervals, some one more daring than the rest gave utterance to the holiest instincts of nature, and spoke out against the giant curse. It was but a momentary ripple on a vast sea, whose waters again subsided into more than original stagnation.

In all the South there was not a single press where the right could be vindicated, or calm reasoning allowed. In the year 1845 I ventured single-handed into this fearful contest. Holding in mind the examples of those who in all ages had vindicated the liberties of men, I had counted the cost, and was prepared for the catastrophe.

The American people know the result. The God of battles has stood by the right. The *liberty* of the press is, for the first time since 1776, established in the South. Not only in my own state, but in the national capital and divers other places, "men may freely speak and write upon any subject whatever," being responsible only to the *laws*.

The "Examiner" has succeeded the "True American." My detention in a Mexican prison delayed my return longer than was anticipated ; the editor of the " Examiner " has forestalled my wishes, and is now fulfilling all my obligations to my subscribers by substituting his paper for mine. Those who have seen both papers will not regret the change. I ask for him the continuation of that generous support in that cause which was in me shown dear to so many noble Americans. The first scene in the drama is accomplished ; brighter hopes dawn upon Kentucky and the American republic. The extraordinary events at home and abroad for the last few years have aroused the consciences and startled the minds of millions. Go read Guizot's History of Civilization, and take courage. Faith in the progress of mankind is no longer the dream of "*fanatics.*"

The spirit of large and liberal inquiry and consequent amelioration is moving all nations. The land of '76 cannot long follow in the unwilling wake of transatlantic despotism in se curing the *liberties of men*. A great destiny awaits us. America will yet be FREE !

CASSIUS M. CLAY.

Lexington, Ky., Dec. 18*th*, 1847.

SPEECH OF COL. W. H. CAPERTON,

AT RICHMOND, KY.

FEBRUARY 7th, 1848.

CAPTAIN CLAY:

As the organ of your old neighbors and friends of your
native county, I congratulate you on your return to your home
and to your family. This very large assembly has come out to
extend to you a hearty welcome. These, your friends, never
doubted your patriotism, or the purity of the motives which influenced you to volunteer your services to fight the battles of
your country. From the moment you set out for Mexico, they
took the deepest interest in your welfare, and kept a constant
eye on your movements. They heard with deep regret of your
captivity. They felt for you the greatest sympathy. Long
before you were released from your galling captivity, they heard
through your brother captives of your noble and generous conduct towards your soldiers. They have informed us, that at
the most critical period of your captivity, a bloody order was
given by the commander of the Mexican forces, to put to immediate death those under your command, and that you, with a
magnanimity and self-devotion never surpassed, presented yourself a victim to appease this cruel thirst for blood, and exclaimed,
"Don't kill the men, they are innocent, I only am responsible."
And they heard, too, sir, that with remarkable promptness and
presence of mind, you ordered your men to prostrate themselves
upon the ground, and that this order having been promptly
obeyed, enabled you to intercede with the Mexican commander
so as to save your own life and that of your soldiers. This
conduct of yours, this self-devotion, challenges our highest admiration, and has electrified every patriotic bosom in the whole
country. This single act, as great as it was, does not stand
alone, as we are informed by your fellow-prisoners. They inform us, that you shared your purse with them ; then sold your

mule, and your horse, and divided the proceeds to the last cent ; and then, sir, that you shared your clothes with your soldiers.

Although in thus placing yourself between the Mexican lance and your soldiers, and by these disinterested acts of kindness and benevolence to your men, you may not have gained laurels as bright and dazzling as those won on the field of battle in storming a battery, or leading out a sortie, yet, sir, they will live longer and fresher in the memory of your countrymen, than any fame acquired in the heat and excitement of battle.

Whilst undergoing your loathsome imprisonment, your countrymen were gaining brilliant and unparalleled victories over your captors. To be deprived of sharing in these stirring events, was, we are sure, chafing to your proud spirit. None of these great victories, however, restored you to your liberty—this you negotiated yourself, stipulating with the enemy, if the terms you made were not confirmed by the commander of the American forces, that you would voluntarily return a prisoner to the enemy's camp. They were confirmed, and you are again restored to your family and your friends.

From our long and intimate acquaintance, it is a source of high gratification to me, that I am the organ of my fellow-citizens in extending to you this welcome. In conclusion, sir, I again, in behalf of these, your friends, congratulate you on your return to your home, your family, and your native county. Old Madison is proud of you as one of her sons, and you are doubly welcome among us.

C. M. CLAY'S REPLY.

Col. Caperton, Ladies, and Fellow Citiizens :

I am not insensible to appreciation from any portion of my countrymen, but to be thus remembered and thus welcomed here in the home of my nativity and youth, and early manhood, touches me deeply and gratefully. But doubly grateful, sir, are these kind words coming from one whom I have so long intimately cherished as a sincere and abiding friend. If I have been ambitious of gaining your confidence and esteem, my countrymen, my hopes and aspirations are accomplished. Be-

tween *us*, there is no place for form and ceremony ; I am proud
of the heartfelt expressions of sympathy and congratulation of
you who have known me longest and best ; I am amply rewarded for all the hardships and dangers of the past.

Some of you know that no man in America more opposed
the Mexican war than I. But when it was *legitimated* by
the *constitutional will of the people*—when my country called
for help—as a common soldier, I entered the ranks. Unmerited
praise is to me the severest censure ; I will not deny, therefore,
that whilst I was prepared with my blanket, and tin cup, and
knapsack, I expected a higher position. I thought that I had
personal claims upon the Governor of Kentucky, for a field
appointment : whilst my ability to fill such a place was, I flat-
tered myself, in no quarter denied. In the discharge of my *duty*,
in peace or war, I trust that I look not to personal suffering ;
with some mortification of spirit, but with unshaken purpose, I
took post in the ranks. Lieutenant J. S. Jackson, then
captain of the "Old Infantry," with a magnanimity of soul
rarely equalled in all time, resigned his place, and took the
ranks : and I was unanimously elected captain. Such self-
sacrifice of one gallant spirit, was more gratifying to my ambition than if I had worn the proudest badges of honor that governor or president can bestow upon those who worship not at
the shrine of *truth*, but of *power*. That enmity which saw
me cut off from all hopes of elevation to civil offices, which had
destroyed my property, calumniated my reputation, and subjected my person and life to legalized outlawry, was still insatiate, and with fiendish rancour pursued me still. They
attempted to dissolve my company, trusting once more to reduce
me to the ranks, where they hoped that the hardships of the
camp and climate, would accomplish what violence had failed
to effect, and that death would free them from one whose vindication of justice and humanity had made "a thorn in the
king's side." A thing before unheard of, civil opinions were attempted to disqualify me for military promotion. Handbills denouncing me, after the stereotyped manner, were freely circulated at home, and sent to the Heads of Departments at Washington, to the President, and to the officers of the invading army
in Mexico.

Thanks to the great-souled army of America, such contemptible malice was duly estimated. Before I arrived at San Anto-

nio de Bejar, Gen. Wool had determined to detach me from the Kentucky regiment, then lying at Lavaca, and destined to Gen. Taylor's column, where it was supposed the fighting was all over, after the battle of Monterey, and take my company with him to Chihuahua. Nothing but the sickness of my men at Lavaca prevented this design. The attempt to prejudice me at home, by asserting that I had gone to San Antonio, under pretence of a buffalo hunt, to intrigue with Gen. Wool, was one more link only in the system of calumny, which will pursue me through life, or so long as I vindicate the *true interests* of Kentucky. When I left the regiment at Crockett, their point of destination was San Antonio! So a lie cannot always live! At Camargo General Patterson once more offered, voluntarily to take my company with him to Tampico, which I declined. By my request, that true-souled old soldier, General Taylor, ordered me up to the head of the column at Saltillo, when I was put on severe duty at an advanced post, to watch the approach of the enemy, by Gen. Butler. Thus every general, under whose command I came, showed a magnanimous disposition to allow me, with my very insignificant command, every possible chance of distinction. But fortune was against me. To relieve the army from the dangers and unpleasant anticipations of surprise, for it was reported continually that Santa Anna was advancing in force, the gallant Jno P. Gaines volunteered to find the enemy at all hazards, if he was on the road from San Luis Potosi to Saltillo. He did me the honor once more to take me as his commanding captain. The event of the surrender of Encarnacion is to you well-known. The grounds of defence, upon which that act rests, will be found in my letter to the New Orleans Picayune. That seventy-one men and officers should hold three thousand regular Mexican cavalry at bay from light till noon, and finally make terms of the most honorable treatment, presents a spectacle of the moral sublime, unsurpassed by the heroism of the bloodiest battles. In sending back Captain Henry, through eighty armed lancers, one hundred and fifty miles from camp, with three thousand enemies in the rear, was displayed a rare feat of individual daring, and the object of our mission accomplished. Your allusion to my action on that occasion, and the testimony of my fellow-prisoners generally, as well as the previous comments of some others. induce me here to relate the exact particulars of that adventure. The soldiers, with Captain Danley, and the subordinate officers, were on foot, marching by two's. Major Gaines, and Borland, Captain Henry, and myself, were on horseback at the head of the column. The Mexican lancers mounted, were in open files on both sides of the soldiers, with a van and rear guard. Captain H., having been taken prisoner at Mier, and having escaped from the castle of Perote, and being recognised by the Mexicans, feared that he would be put to death, as the expedition to Mier was disavowed by Texas. Major Gaines thought there was no danger of his life, but permitted Henry to change horses with him, as the two Majors only had been allowed to retain their American horses. Henry also asked my advice : I agreed with him that his life was in imminent peril —told him I should be glad for our friends to know of the advance of the army—but declined urging him one way or the other in an affair of so much danger. Henry agreed, at length, to run. I told Capt. H. to speak low, as the Mexican lieutenant, I was convinced, understood English, although he denied all knowledge of the language. This the lientenant overheard, and reported it to Col. Sambranino, the commanding officer of the guard. He immediately ordered Messrs. Gaines and Borland, under a strong guard, ahead, uncovered his pistols, and commanded the guard to open the ranks, so as to be out of arm's reach of our men. Seeing their preparations, we supposed the time had come for Capt. H.'s death, and he, riding down the ranks, under pretence of arranging the men by twos, according to order, gave spurs to his horse, and escaped. The Colonel supposed that we were plotting to rise upon the guard, and Henry's running, confirmed him in the opinion. He ordered the lancers to charge : which they promptly obeyed—having retired before far enough to allow some momentum in the advance. I was alone, and about twenty yards ahead, I rode back and ordered the men to lie down, which they promptly did—told the Colonel they were innocent—that I only was responsible. He then told three lancers to lance me ! One at each side and one in the rear, he with his pistol at my breast, and the lieutenant with his sabre also drawn, placed me in no very agreeable attitude. Seeing that the soldiers were safe, as they began to tie them, I assure you that I was not slow in talking in my own defence— I avowed that I knew of H.'s design to escape—that I had not advised him one way or the other—that he had a right to act independently, and, by the laws of war, I could not be responsible for another's act—that there was no intention to rise upon● the guard—that to kill me would be murder—that I was of noble family at home—and that my death would be amply avenged by my countrymen. Believing, no doubt, from my manner, that I told the *truth*, they spared my life. They tied me for a few moments—then released me, when the Colonel embraced me, and asked my pardon for the indignity. They released the officers who were on foot, and also tied that night, but kept the soldiers tied for two days longer. That the lives of my command were saved by my presence of mind, and frank confession, I honestly believe. I admit, to use the language of my friend, Col. C——s, that if " I was not scared, I stood in great bodily apprehension." But, to be serious, whatever fears of death I might have had, I am proud to say, never outweighed my sense of *truth* and *justice*. Whatever, then, my enemies shall deduct from my courage, they must place to the credit of my superior moral powers, and become, unconsciously, my loftiest eulogists. Our long and painful march to San Luis Potosi, and thence to Mexico, our imprisonment, and final release, are well-known. It is but just to the Mexicans to say, that in allowing our soldiers eighteen cents a day, they gave them the same that they give their own soldiers, who do not require half as much food as our own men, whilst our being strangers prevented us from buying as much food, with the same money. The hardships of the route through the desert, were shared by their own soldiers. In a word, there were many instances of Spanish generosity during our captivity, and our hardships were not unreasonable, when we remember that their own men were *starving*, in the defence of their homes and their religion.

That Santa Anna was sincerely courteous and full of fair promises, as he was going on " to drive Taylor over the Sabine," seems natural : that he should have broken all his engagements with us afterwards, can only be accounted for upon the supposition that he wished to hold us as hostages for his safety, in case he fell into our hands. The Governor of Mexico, at Toluca, is entitled to our lasting gratitude for sending us to Scott on parole, the man who could thus trust others, is himself, of necessity of a great and noble soul.

In giving public expressions of thanks to Gen. Worth, for his solicitude in our behalf, we did not intend to reflect upon other officers, some of whom did display the same remembrance of us. So far as I was concerned I did not blame Gen. Scott for any dereliction of duty. It was not to be supposed that the General-in-chief had much time to think of the release of a few hundred men. His failure to mention Santa Anna's breach of the ninth article, however, was to us a sore mortification. Although his efforts for our liberation were such as, perhaps, are usual in such cases, it seemed to us, who were continually threatened with assassination, that we were *neglected :* and it was some consolation to our pride to know that to ourselves only we owed our own liberation at last.

I have thus 'ventured here among you, my neighbors and friends, to indulge in these personal adventures ; because, while on the one hand I am unwilling to receive credit for more than I deserve, on the other I have done too little in the military way to submit to unjust detraction. And justice to my noble companions in arms leads me freely to declare, that they who died in the swamps and deserts of Texas, in the loathsome prisons of Mexico, and in the discharge of the every-day duties of the camp, deserve the same hold on the memory and gratitude of their countrymen, as they who nobly laid down their lives on the field of battle.

It is no doubt expected of me to give some ideas of Mexico, and the present war. Mexico extends from about latitude 16° north to 42°, from the Gulf of Mexico to the Pacific; and was in extent, before the loss of Texas, about as large as the United States. It embraces all the climates of all the world : and rises in temperature from the tropical plains of Vera Cruz and Acapulco to the regions of perpetual snow. The Rocky mountains, which separate us from Oregon, extend through all Mexico : and her whole surface is composed of table lands and mountains, which rise in steps from the gulf, and the Rio Grande, to the highest level ; and then descend in regular gradation once more to the Pacific. She has no navigable streams, and the mountains and arid plains compose, I should imagine, nine-tenths of the whole territory. It is now three hundred years since the Spanish conquest, and her population has long since reached that barrier where nature imposes eternal obstacles to further progress—where the whole products of the earth are economically consumed by the people. No doubt better modes of agriculture would increase her population, but at present, to use the language of Malthus, she has reached the *point of subsistence.* It is true, that the remote provinces of California and New Mexico, and those bordering upon the Rio Grande, and subject to Indian invasion, contain some uncultivated lands; but the proposition, as above stated, applies to the mass of Mexico. For, in the greater portion of the whole republic, women and children may be seen picking up grains of corn in the highways; and the rinds of fruit thrown in the streets are immediately seized and consumed. So soon as you cross the Rio Grande you feel yourself in a foreign land. Mexico has no forests. It is true, that along the streams and on the mountain tops there are trees; but you are struck with this great characteristic, that the land is bald of trees. The numerous varieties of the cactus of all sizes, intermixed with palmetto, stunted or long grass, covers the whole land. You are among a people of a novel color and a strange language. The very birds, and beasts, and dogs, seem different. The partridge, the lark, the blackbird, differ in size and plumage, and sing differently from ours. The buildings are of Moorish and Spanish build. The goats and the sheep feed together. The bricks are of clay and straw, sun-dried. The women go with earthern vessels to the well, just as Rachael was seen of old in the time of the Patriarchs of Judea. The roofs of the houses are flat and places of recreation: and the people wear sandals as in the East, in olden time. Wheat, Indian corn, and herds of cattle, sheep, and goats, and the banana, and red pepper, and garlic, and onions, are the principal sources of subsistence. The products of the mines are the principal articles of foreign exchange, added to woods, besides tallow and cochineal.

The extreme dryness of Mexico makes irrigation necessary in most of the country; and the scarcity of water, and the habits of the people, collect the inhabitants into cities or villages. The land itself is owned by a few large proprietors; not the least of whom are the priests. The great mass of the people are serfs, with but few more rights than American slaves. It is true, that the children of serfs are not of necessity also serfs, but debt brings slavery, and the wages allowed by law almost always perpetuate it. *Here, then, is the secret of the success of our arms.* I conversed freely with the tenantry and soldiers in all Mexico, and where they are not filled with religious enthusiasm against us, they say they care not who rule them, American, or Mexican masters. If all the Mexican soldiers were freeholders and freemen, not one of all the American army could escape from her borders. The soldiers are caught up in the haciendas and the streets of towns, by force confined in some prison, or monastery, there drilled, clothed, armed, and then sent on to the regular army. Such men avow their resolution to desert, or run, on the first occasion. Of near a thousand soldiers, sent from Toluca to the aid of Santa Anna at Mexico, not one hundred stood the battle.

The whole people do not exceed eight millions, of these about two millions are white and mixed blood, the remainder are native Indians. I never, in all Mexico, with the exception of foreigners in the capital, saw a single white man at work. Wherever there is slavery, there is labor dishonorable; it is more creditable to rob than to work! Yet Mexico surpasses the slave states of America in manufactures! As Rome was overrun by the Barbarians, so is Mexico now by the Americans; the slaves will not fight—the masters are too few to defend the country. Bigotry of religion has abased the mind—the corruptions of the church have destroyed the morals of the people—the oppressions of the masters have exhausted the lands. Mexico is decreasing in population and resources. Since her independence, her revenues are falling off—her villages are decaying—her public works falling to ruin. She has lived by the sword—she must perish by the sword. *The time for her to die has come!* Yet, like South Carolina, she talks large. She whipped Spain—Spain whipped France—France the world—and of consequence, Mexico is the mistress of the world! Yet, fifty thousand Americans conquer eight millions of souls! The clergy plunder the people—the army now begin to plunder the clergy—whilst independent robbers begin to plunder the government, the clergy, and the people. Such is the fearful retribution of nature's violated laws. Seeing Texas, that it was a lovely land, we coveted our neighbor's goods—seeing the weakness of Mexico. we took it by force. Though a whig, I do not stand here as a partizan. I shall speak with the freedom of history. I have no sympathy with this late outcry against President Polk, as bringing on this war. I shall do the President the justice to say, that in all Mexico I never heard the first man allege the march of Taylor to the Rio Grande, as the cause of offence, or of the war. I am not going to debate the worn out topic of the annexation of Texas—the melancholy and disgraceful causes that led to the consummation of the iniquity. All America knew that foreign territory could not be acquired, except by TREATY—and a TREATY could only be made by the SENATE and PRESIDENT. But slavery demanded a sacrifice of the Constitution : it was made then, it always has been, and always will be made, so long as the slave power rules this nation. In taking Texas, you took the WAR. So said the Mexican Minister, so said Houston, President of Texas, so said conventions of several sovereign states, so said common sense. That actual hostilities might have been avoided by the President, confining the army to the left bank of the Nueces, or to Corpus Christi even, I have not the least doubt. But the good-natured President, no doubt, thought a little more robbery was all right. Texas claimed to the Rio Grande. I'll take the Rio Grande, and then, being in possession, will hold it with a peace. What was the claim of Texas to the once province of Mexico ? Conquest, and no other. How far did she conquer ? To the Nueces, and no further. Her expedition to Santa Fe and Mier, both signally failed. San Patricio is on the east bank of the Nueces. I have been there myself—there is not a single house or improvement on its west side ! I say, when our army marched into the Mexican territory, and planted her batteries, bearing upon the Plaza of Matamoras, amidst the people fleeing from their cotton and sugar fields, that the President of the United States made actual war upon Mexico. Every man in America knows this to be true. Will a lie live for ever ? The President, no doubt, usurped power belonging only to Congress, but Congress had just usurped power belonging to the Senate—the Constitution had been overthrown. The nation is corrupt—to talk of impeachment is worse than nonsense. Let the guiltless throw the first stone ! The National Intelligencer has found out that Mr. Polk is a despot, and our government a despotism ! Indeed ! When the liberty of the press was attempted to be overthrown in Kentucky, he closed his columns to my defence, but he allowed a Paris correspondent to apologize for the act, by quoting the despotisms of Europe ! And now he begins to find out that there is danger of despotism in these States ! Sagacious editor ! Far-seeing patriot ! Ten thousand men have been slain—one hundred millions of money have been spent

—a standing army of one hundred thousand men is asked for—the purse and person of the reviewer are in danger! What shall be done? Why—send for Mr. Walsh! These things are common in Europe!

But we are at war, how shall we get out of it? Do you want more land? The appetite of the great slave champion himself is glutted at last? Mr. Thompson says that slavery cannot extend into Mexico. Why? They have there reached that delightful condition, upon which Southern patriots love to dwell. *Free labor* is at the *starving point.* Slave labor won't pay—it cannot therefore exist. Mexico can't help us—she may cherish some recollections of by whom it was, that she was robbed of a province as large as France. Therefore Mr. Calhoun begins to perceive danger to our republican institutions!

Texas cannot claim beyond the Nueces. If more is acquired, it is by my blood and treasure, by your blood and treasure —it is ours—not one foot belongs to Texas. It is *free* territory —*free* under the Constitution of the United States. It needs no Wilmot proviso. Will the North be for ever thus gulled. Is she knave, or fool?

Total annexation! We want to extend free institutions over poor Mexico, we want to give the gospel to the miserable heathen! Is the spirit of hypocritical and fiendish propagandism never to die? You have lost ten thousand men and one hundred millions of money, and have possession of some four or five of the most insignificant of the twenty-four Mexican states! Will you work the sum? Have you counted the cost of this so great philanthropy? Can you levy the expenses of the war from the duties at the seaports, when commerce has ceased? Will the mines be worked when plunder stands with greedy hands to seize the accumulations of labor? Will you forage on the enemy? Will one man sow, when another reaps? Let me tell you, all hopes of drawing revenue from Mexico are delusive. Levy contribution, forage, distress the enemy, compel a peace! A neighbor of mine learned that sheep would kill briars. After a time, I said "Neighbor, how went the experiment? did you kill the briars?" "Oh yes," said he, "*but they killed the sheep too!*" If eight millions of people could be united to us on equal terms, enjoying security of property, freedom of the press and of religion, it might well compensate for the blood which has been spilt, the desolation of farms and villages, the pangs and tears of widows and orphans, the myriad calamities which the war here and in Mexico brings in its train. But will it be done? The past gives no assurances of such things. The South has shown no such greatness of soul; she has not done for the children of her own soil what she proposes to aliens of other lands. The North has given us no such evidence of independence of spirit. She has, on all occasions when a deed of oppression was to be done, been ready to calculate how many coppers it would bring into her coffers. Give her the price of blood, and she is always contemptibly tame.

A line of defence seems full of similar objections to a war "in the vitals" of the country. It would take nearly the same number of troops; deprive us of the little help we may now receive from levies upon the enemy, whilst it would allow concentration of their forces and attack upon us in detail. A total withdrawal of the army east of the Nueces river seems to be puerile and absurd. If Mr. Clay had taken the ground of his Lexington speech before the last presidential election, we might have been saved from this war. But it comes too late. The moral power of the nation is weaker now than it was then. The lives of our people have been sacrificed, our treasure has been expended. I agree that in an unjust war, we cannot claim indemnity for our own expenditures. But then Mexico owes us from three to five millions of money, on the old score. She has accumulated upon us robbery and insult; and now, when we have the power to right ourselves, and all the evils of war are accomplished, we must grow suddenly "*magnanimous!*"

I shall not speak of the beauties of California, of the ports of San Diego and San Francisco; nor of the south pass over the Rocky Mountains, which leads through present Mexican territory; nor of the mines of New Mexico, nor of the navigation of the Rio Grande, as inducements to shed blood and do injustice. But blood having already been shed, and injustice already done, I would claim my rights. I contend that the line proposed by the President of the United States, running with the Rio Grande from its mouth to latitude 32° north, and thence due west to the Pacific, is not too much indemnity for what Mexico owes. I would for this pay her not one cent. If you want to pay her, pay her for Texas. But these provinces have never been a source of power to her, and never will be. She has not extended to them the protection of the federal government; they are subject to Indian attack and pillage; they have few people, and would never throw a disturbing force into our councils.

What claim does Mexico set up to them? Has she any other than conquest? Has she allowed any Indian of the country to retain a fee simple in the soil of their ancestors? Why, then, show "*magnanimity*" to those who have never shown it to others? I have not now, and never have had much respect for any other claim than that of *labor* upon the soil. Mexico can not cultivate this country; we can, and will; if not now, here-after—as certainly as fate. Will we ever have a better title than now? Will we ever be in a better condition to assert our will than now? Then why not say, as Mr. Poinsett advises, to Mexico: "You owe us so much money; you refuse to pay us; we will take to this line; attack us at your peril!"

The present standing army is sufficient for the purpose. Dis-miss your volunteers, and take secure "interior posts of de-fence" and offence. Proceed as you do against the Indians. Go not to the line, but in *striking distance*. Mexico can never march large armies to the border. She has neither commissary nor quartermaster departments; her soldiers are paid, and each man finds his own shelter and food by daily purchase or rob-bery. They cannot make long marches in large masses; they would not if they could. Such is the course of policy recom-mended by those who know them best. Such would I recom-mend. The Nueces is the western boundary of Texas; let the balance be formed into new states—into *free* states. Texas never conquered a foot of land beyond the Nueces except Cor-pus Christi. The remainder belongs to the provinces of Ta-maulipas, Coahuila, Chihuahua, and New Mexico. She has no more right to that than she has to the Federal district of the United States, or of the Mexican republic. Slavery ought not longer to be fed at the expense of the honor, the liberties, and the blood of this republic. "The area of freedom" is to be ex-tended indeed. Cant must at last have an end. The free mil-lions of this continent will not be the hacks of slavery for ever. The hand of destiny is upon us; Mexico is not ours as yet. The time will however come when our republic will spread over the whole continent. The Texan precedent of Congres-sional annexation, will, to the slave states prove a two edged sword. Every national crime, like individual sin, must meet its penalty, and slavery will find at last its grave in the land of its promised security !

The majority of this people made this war legitimate ; a majority are now, it is said, against it. By what theory of republicanism is the President allowed to carry it on ? Shall we never cease to believe, that the world was made for Cæsar ? Shall we for ever ask what will the President do ? For my part I see too much subservience to men in all parties. I will allow no man to dictate to me what I am to think or what I am to do. I regard the ground of Mr. Clay as too narrow for a great party to stand upon. Let no man assume the prerogatives of Congress. Let the circumstances of the war determine its mode of termination. If I will not allow Mr. Clay to give me my political opinions, far less will I submit to the dictation of an irresponsible clique to whip me into the support of *men*. When I go into the Presidential canvass I want to *win*. I don't want a man tied hand and foot and shorn of his strength, for my champion. Give me an honest man, a sensible man, who will let me think for myself, and carry out my mature judgment, as it is indicated by a Congress fresh from the people—if such an one can be found—he is my man for president. Old party hacks, who have life estates in *particular men*—political parasites, who live upon the vitality of others, may denounce *independent* men as *knaves* and *fools*, but in my opinion they will at last go to bed supperless. I rejoice to think it so. That all party feeling or party organization will be broken down in the next canvass, I do not expect or believe, but that new elements of vitality and patriotism will be infused into the general government I heartily hope. What if those who sought political capital by the war, should be overthrown at last by *one whom the war has made !* Surely there is retribution even in this world !

I have thus, fellow-citizens, glanced at some of the stirring topics of the times. I have spoken boldly and honestly. In this day's manifestation of approbation of my conduct you impose upon me new obligations to stand by the right in times to come. The time is at hand when, whatever of patriotism and manliness of thought there is in your state will be severely tested. I trust I will ever be found trying to do my whole duty.

I thank you, ladies, Colonel Caperton, and fellow-citizens, once more, and bid you adieu.

MEXICO.

Address before the Mercantile Library Association of Baltimore, March 6, 1848.

LADIES AND GENTLEMEN OF THE SOCIETY, AND FELLOW-CITIZENS:

MEXICO is the second power of the North American continent. It is washed by the Gulf of Mexico on the east, and by the Pacific ocean on the west: and extends from the republic of Guatemala, in about latitude 16°, to the United States, in latitude 42° north. It is subdivided into twenty-four states and provinces, including the federal district: and, since the disruption of Texas, contains about one and a half millions of square miles. The great Rocky mountains run from north to south through all Mexico—spread out into several parallel or slightly divergent chains, which widen into table-lands six or eight thousand feet above the level of the sea, or with serrated and impassable heights border level plains, which descend by steps to both seas. Not only its great extent, but its altitude under the same parallel of latitude, gives Mexico all the climates of the world. From the low lands of Vera Cruz, and Acapulco, of suffocating heat and tropical vegetation, you pass to Mexico, and Toluca, through every grade of temperature, till you are stopped on the heights of Orizaba, Popocatapetl, and Toluca, more than seventeen thousand feet above the level of the sea— regions of eternal snow and sterility. The fruits, and melons, and vegetables of all climes, are found here. The great articles of subsistence are wheat, Indian corn, the potato, the banana, pepper, onions, and garlic; and barley, used exclusively for horses. Humboldt has estimated the banana to yield more food to the acre than the potato, the most fruitful of European crops. This, however, as a food, exclusive of more costly products, is not to be envied by any people; For Mr. Malthus has demonstrated the evil of any people living upon the lowest in price in the scale of foods. For when the lowest fails there is no possible substitute : the poor not being able to go back and purchase wheat, or dear food, in a famine. Whereas, those who live habitually upon flesh, or wheat flour, or Indian corn, can substitute oats, barley, and potatoes for a time, for their ordinary provisions during a scarcity of these last. The famine of Ireland was foretold by this great man : for the potato crop failing, no cheaper substitute was possible : and the consequence in the long run will be death, till there are only enough to live upon the old kinds of produce. The maguey, or American aloe, is the source of the principal Mexican drink. This plant grows in the driest places, and amidst the most abrupt steeps and rocky wastes. When it is ready to flower, not at the age of a century, as is generally supposed in this country, but somewhere from seven to fifteen years of its growth, the flower bud is scooped out into a kind of bowl, into which the sap, which was about to push up the immense flower stem of thirty or forty feet, now daily flows to the immense total quantity of from twenty to fifty gallons. The plant thus exhausted dies. This juice is taken up by a gourd siphon of the length and thickness of a man's arm (suction being applied through a small hole by the human mouth), emptied into hog-skin sacks, and then taken to the cities, and put into wooden or earthen vessels. After the vinous fermentation takes place, it is fit for use ; being in color and taste something between still beer and crab cider ; and certainly a very wholesome and agreeable beverage in warm climates. This liquor composes the staple of all " coffee houses ;" is called pulque ; and the vending-shops are called pulquerias. Here, as in most countries, is done the loafing, quarreling, and killing. The signs which indicate these earthly hells are, however, more honest than those of our country. I have seen over the doors signs with mad buffalo bulls, rattlesnakes, and wild Camanche Indians, with knives dripping with the blood of their victims : certainly very fit emblems of the destroyer within !

Mexico produces for home consumption, in addition to the articles I have already named, sugar, cotton, tobacco, and wine, and brandy, and muschal. She exports, principally, the precious metals, cochineal—which feeds upon the cactus—beautiful woods, hides, tallow, vanilla, indigo, jalap, and pimento. Fine wine is made at Parras, in Coahuila, near Saltillo, and in other portions of the country ; but I believe none is exported.

The mines of Mexico have fallen off in their proceeds since the revolution. During the civil wars much machinery was destroyed, and the lower mines filled with water; and much capital withdrawn from these investments by the expulsion of the Spaniards. The system of mining is also defective. When a mine has ceased to be worked for a few months, any informant may apply to the board of mines and have it condemned to his own use. Of course, such insecurity of property discourages heavy investments. Owing to all these causes the product of the mines has fallen from more than twenty millions yearly to an average of less than twelve millions, since Mexican independence. There is no reason to believe, however, that Mexico is exhausted in this respect. Under a stable government, no doubt she is capable of producing as much as ever; for her treasures are untold, and undiscovered; and her whole surface indicates metallic formations. Mining countries are, however, always poor. Nature never aggregates all her wealth. Franklin's system of mining was, no doubt, the best—never to go more than ten or twelve inches below the surface of the soil. Agriculture is the greatest source of national wealth.

After all, Mexico is rather picturesque and lovely, than possessed of great elements of wealth and civilization. When we add up her mountains, her volcanic rocks, her arid plains, and the pestilential marshes of Vera Cruz and the western coast, I venture to say that nine-tenths of her whole surface is unproductive of human food. It is true, there are some extraordinary and very fertile spots, where there is water; but they are thinly scattered over vast space, and are small in extent. She has no navigable rivers, inland seas, and bays—those arteries of civilization. It is true the Rio Grande, on the east, and the Colorado of the west, are capable of being navigated with steamboats; but they are very inferior channels of commerce. Vera Cruz is the best harbor in the direction of Europe; and even here none but vessels lying under the lee of the castle, are safe in a severe gale. I believe the first class of vessels cannot enter the harbor at all. The harbors of Acapulco and San Diego, and San Francisco, of the west, are splendid places of anchorage; but they are far removed from the present sites of production. Even her grateful climate is a barrier to progress. For altitude, whilst it refreshes, enervates; the light pressure of the atmosphere relaxes the muscles and unfits men for active and laborious exertion. *Repose* broods over all nature; the trees struggle through centuries to their dwarfed maturity. The Indian shrinks from the vertical sun into his mud hut, or the plantain shade; the wealthy Mexican retires into thick walls to his daily siesta; the beasts of the field even, seem to dread locomotion. With drooping ears and sullen mien, the ass and the mule wend on with drowsy pace—seem like fixed points on some far ascent—or raise columns of sublimated sand, immoveable on the distant horizon. The gurgling brooks are here silent in their parched channels; and the very birds—nature's glad choristers of other lands—are mute in the drooping shrubs. As mind and matter are mysteriously united, and their cognate laws little known, so is there a large and unexplained field of unknown truths, upon which man, and climate, and soil, rest. Whether man be descended from a single stock, or many embryos, in far-distant lands, it matters not. For untold ages the whites of the temperate climes have poured themselves, by war and peaceful immigration, into the hot wastes of southern Asia and the rich plains of India. Again and again have Africa, and the isles of the sea, of similar structure and temperature, been inundated from southern Europe and Asia Minor; yet how few of the Caucasian race now people those vast regions! So it has been, and so will it be in all coming time.

Around inland seas and rivers, those channels of rapid transmission of physical and mental wealth, has civilization ever loved to hover. If the Mexican aborigines had had these also, in addition to their pleasant climate and facile production, they would no doubt long since have rivaled China, if not Asia Minor, and Southern Europe. But without these, they had gone far ahead of all other American nations. At the time of the Spanish conquest, in 1519–'20, the Aztecs lived in cities, and cultivated the soil. The ruins of cities, pyramids, idols, and antiquarian relics, described by Stephens, Humboldt, and others, show advanced architecture, and progress beyond the savage life of hunters, and the wanderings of shepherds. Montezuma was not a chief, ruling by the willing love and admiration of his people, but by the sword. He was a great king. He had learned the too often attendant evil of civilization, oppression, the subjugation of the minds and bodies of others to individual wants. That a superior race, however, once possessed Mexico,

I have no idea: far less, the least proof. Semi-barbarous nations, have frequently excelled in particular arts. All Europe cannot rival the shawls of Cashmere : and France, and England, and the United States, have in vain attempted the Rebosa of Mexico. Yet the Rebosa is of Indian manufacture. The ruins of ancient works in Mexico, then show nothing which the Aztecs may not have done ; whilst the "Sun Dial," and "Stone of Sacrifice," yet seen in the city of Montezuma, show art in the use of the chisel, unsurpassed by any shown by Stephens, or others. That Mexico has continued to progress since the conquest, is equally certain, as that civilization has advanced in the whole world from time immemorial, as it will do in the main in all coming time. They who then used bows and arrows, now use fire-arms. They who were wrapped in skins, and ornamented with dyed feathers and shells, now are clothed in woolens, cottons, and silks, and adorned with gold, silver, and precious stones. Mud and cane wrought hovels are substituted by palaces of marble and stone. Rude hieroglyphics yield to letters and words, those ready exponents of thought and things. Laws, feebly executed, and not very distinctly or wisely conceived, 'tis true, but on the whole salutary in protecting life, property, and character, bear rule, instead of the mad will of a pampered despot. The bloodless idolatries of the Catholic religion, bad as they are, are yet surely something better than the nightmare terrors of heathen idols, and the bloody offerings to insatiate gods of stone. Mexico then may be ranked among the civilized nations. A very silly fellow can see that Mexico is not equal, in development, to the United States. A good man will not readily denounce a whole people ; whilst the wise and philosophical will look to the point whence a people started, and be cautious of placing down dogmatical barriers to future progress.

The Mexican people number about eight millions of souls: five and a half of these are pure Indians, and from two to three millions whites, Africans, and mixed bloods. The Africans are very few in number, and are rarely seen, except in the lowlands of the coast. No doubt I shall startle many Americans when I say that Mexico nearly equals the slave states of this Union, in civilization. I know what I say. First in the mechanic arts, take all that Mexico makes in her borders, and all that the South makes in her borders, and Mexico is superior. She equals us in the making of hats and boots, and surpasses us far in the making of shoes: all the shoes of the women are made at home. She excels the South in saddlery —in the making of cotton, woolen and silk goods—in manufactures of steel and iron, of gold and silver, and jewelry. In architecture, she is ahead of the South. The city of Mexico, in beauty, extent, sewers, water works, public walks, durability, and taste, is ahead of any city in the South. The hacienda of the Mexican, is more magnificent than the homestead in Virginia, or the plantation house in Louisiana. The tenantry, and serfs, are better sheltered than the slaves of the South.

In agriculture, the South has better tools; but they are of "Yankee" make. But in ponds, in stone fencing, hedging, and ditching, in putting in wheat, and gathering it into stacks and barns, I have never in America seen anything to equal Mexico. In physical well-being, then, Mexico has more advanced than the South. In civil liberty, how do they stand? Mexico has no jury, I grant you, but then she boasts not the honored Judge Lynch of the South! Mexico has more robberies of property : the South more destruction of human life. There are more men killed in the South by the duel and the street rencontre, than there are by robbery and murder in Mexico. Mexico allows not the duel, nor divorce—those ever attendants of barbarism. The South is horribly permissive of both. I have not the least patience with those who compare the serfdom of Mexico with the slavery of the South. I shall not attempt to vindicate the oppressions of Mexico. The apology for crime, that it is shared by others, is the poor vindication of thieves ; and the miserable consolation of damned spirits! Whatever force there is in the feeble artillery of bitter words, I would for ever thunder into the unwilling ears of tyranny and crime, in whatever land they may be found, or under whatever Protean names they may attempt to hide themselves. Let us see then. In Mexico, if you take and use my labor, the accumulations of the expended "sweat of my face"—my *property*, you are bound to pay me, in default of other *property*, your *labor*. Is there, then, any hardship in this? No. I say, in whatever land this law does not prevail, there justice does not prevail. Here is foreknowledge and consent on the part of the serf, to pay labor for property already used that rightly belonged to another. In Mexico, then,

debt and slavery are one.   In a lecture which I had the honor
to deliver a few years ago, in the city of Philadelphia, I think I
incontestibly showed that this was the only legitimate base of
slavery possible in the nature of things.   In America, I believe
that it is not pretended that the slave *"owes"* the master anything.   Even the ingenuity of Messrs. McDuffie and Hammond
have not yet so made it appear : though I confess, from the past,
there seems to be imminent probability that they will after a
while cause logic so to bear them out.   The children of the
serf are free.   The children of the slave are slaves.   The serf
of Mexico may work out his freedom : all the mines of Mexico
are not legally equal to the liberation of a single American
slave.   In America, slaves are almost regarded, in every sense,
as chattels ; the beasts of the field are as well protected by law
as the slaves of this nation.   I say, then, what I have before at
other times and places uttered to unwilling ears, *American
slavery is the most despotic of known governments, the most
uncompromising of world-wide oppression.*   Mexico, then, in
the security of her person and property, is as civilized as the
South.   If it be possible to draw a distinction between political
and civil rights, the South might at first blush to arrogate supremacy over Mexico : if so, it takes the ever-watchful death-
struggle of ten millions of northern freemen to effect even that.
For long years the right of petition, one *mode* of the liberty of
speech and of the press, without which all government is impossible, was lost in the Union itself.   When Santa Anna made
a forced contribution in Mexico, to sustain his newly-raised
troops, he turned all the editors but the government organ out
of doors, and closed their presses.

To question the tyranny of Don Antonio Lopez de Santa
Anna, was regarded by him as a *"nuisance."*   But still the
presses of the states continued to denounce him.   In my state
and in yours, my noble audience, the liberty of the press is
inviolate.   But how many, alas! of the fifteen southern states
can say the same ?   The military dictator of Mexico sends
Almonte and Arista to prison : South Carolina and Louisiana
with far less show of justice, banish the envoys of Massachusetts for ever from their borders.   Whilst "citizens" of so called
free and independent states, contrary to the laws of nature, the
rights of nations, and the express declaration of the Constitution of the United States, lie imprisoned without crime, in the
dungeons of the South.

Mexico, I imagine, prints as many books as the South. There are as many Mexicans of the present generation learning to read and write as there are Whites and Blacks in the slave states, according to population. It is true, I have no statistics to prove so grave an assertion : but the Mexicans live in cities and villages, and of late years, schools are everywhere established. In both nations there is much ignorance. In Mexico there is a determination on all hands to spread learning among the people. In the slave states, on the contrary, there is a predominant party, the slaveholders, who have determined systematically to oppose the education of the people. I foretold years ago the loss of the school fund in Kentucky. That state which nature has overflowed with every natural source of wealth and civilization, has not a single cent set aside for the education of her people !

I say, then, the cry of our people, who are vociferous for the conquest of Mexico, under pretence of extending the "area of freedom," comes in most questionable shape. I recommend such to one Robert Burns, who thus aspired :

> " Oh wad some power the giftie gie us,
> To see oursels as ithers see us ;"

or to that higher source of moral precept :

> " Thou hypocrite: first cast out the beam out of thine own eye : and then shalt thou see clearly to cast out the mote out of the eye of thy brother."

Mexico has struggled on through many obstacles to her present state. Spain brought not liberty, but a change of masters. The chiefs of hostile tribes were put to death. Their idols were broken ; and their cities and dwellings razed to the ground. It was the policy of the Spaniards to destroy all mementos of her religion, government, and past history. The Indians were forced into villages for police purposes, and to use their unpaid labor. The whole land was divided among the conquerors. Communications with foreigners were entirely cut off ; education discouraged. Every thing that Spain could make, or raise on the soil was forbidden in Mexico, to foster the monopoly of the mother country. The very vines and olive trees were plucked up under this grinding system of exclusion. Hand in hand with political oppression, went religious intolerance and fraud. Not only was freedom of conscience disallowed, but the reading of the Bible even forbidden. The mind was first made weak and pliant by vain and silly ceremonies, and then the persons of the many made subservient to the wants and appetites of the governing few. Spain built churches and public roads, and waterworks and bridges—a huge body of nationality—but infused into it no soul. No. Without liberty there is no progress. For three centuries Mexico lay prostrate under the leaden hand of despotism. The arm of the Father of nations is not shortened. Nature for ever purges herself of her violated laws.

About 1810 the spirit of the people had outgrown the feeble grasp of the tyrant. After many hard-fought battles, in 1820, independence was established. In 1824, after the usurpation, and speedy overthrow of the emperor Iturbide, a constitutional government was formed: modeled after our federal system. That men, unaccustomed to self-government, should at once secure liberty, was not to be expected. In 1836 Santa Anna, after many revolutions, established Centralism; and in 1838 proclaimed the basis of Tucubaya, which, under the forms of law, clothed him with unlimited power. "But freedom's battle, once begun," is ever onward. Like Iturbide, he was readily overthrown; and after many defeats, Mexico still struggles on to ultimate liberty. Whether she shall fall into the American Union, or maintain her separate nationality, Mexico has sworn eternal enmity to tyrants. That a few of the priests, and some remnants of the old Spanish families, desire a monarchy, is true, but they are a most insignificant part of the nation. The most of the intelligence and patriotism of Mexico belongs to the democratic party, who war against centralism and solitary rule: who are, in other words, for a constitutional republic. They are alike the foes of despotism, in church and state. The army composed of broken down politicians, bankrupts in fortune, and successful robbers, a few gallant men, of course, excepted, are for any man who will plunder priest or layman for their benefit. Among these stands Santa Anna, "proudly pre-eminent." The most skilful of rogues—the most successful of robbers—the falsest of villains—yet, in talents, far ahead of his nation—he has been the pride, the curse, and the final ruin of his country. Overthrown by Paredes—an exile during the battles of Palo Alto and Resaca—a solitary and miserable fugitive from the vengeance of his countrymen—his statues overthrown—his leg lately buried with the honors of war, amid the tears and admiration of a whole people, now exhumed, and cast, with insult and execration, into the streets, to be devoured by the dogs and vultures—in Catholic countries, the most impious desecration of the dead—he returns alone once more, and places himself in the presidential chair, and at the head of the patriot army of Mexico. In opposition to the democratic party, then in the ascendant in most of the states—in spite of the priests, whom he had plundered, and canaille, whom he had abused and insulted—in a few months he raises sixty thousand troops, and fights the three great battles of Buena Vista, Cerro Gordo, and Mexico. After the battle of Cerro Gordo, the last hope of successful resistance to the American invader seemed lost in the bosoms of the most hopeful patriots. A thousand armed men could have captured the capital of the republic. The city authorities having, no doubt, the fate of Vera Cruz within memory, sent word to Santa Anna not to enter the walls of Mexico. He treated their command with supreme contempt. A daily pronunciamento, and revolution, was expected in the city: in which, it was supposed, Congress, then in session, would take a prominent part. Yet, with about three thousand men, ragged, hungry, and spirit broken, and a few pieces of artillery, he marched into a city of three hundred thousand souls.

Affecting to resign his command, the conspirators were lulled to inactivity, when, in a few days, by the congress of the nation, he was clothed with *absolute power*—excepting only the authority to make peace with the Northern invaders. In a few months more he is at the head of an army of thirty thousand troops—levies forced contributions upon the city, and pays his contractors, and his followers. The hatred of the Americans was only a little less than the enmity to this incarnation of centralism and tyranny. The states lent him feeble aid: his camp was full of traitors: the battle came on: the day went against him. He plundered the treasury—opened the prisons to the sacking of the capital—fled in the night—and once more from the wilds of Puebla, addressed, through the press which he had before silenced, in patriotic and hopeful strains, his oft deluded countrymen. He resigns his presidency and leadership in the army, affects humility and self-sacrifice—but in a few weeks more I left him behind me in Mexico, marching with a few needy followers against Anaya, and Peña y Peña, legal and adopted successors, to re-establish himself in the dictatorial power! Such is Santa Anna. It is not wonderful, then, that he should have been an insuperable obstacle to the liberties of Mexico.

In 1824, in her Constitution, Mexico inserted a clause of prospective emancipation. In 1829 liberty was proclaimed by President Bocanegra throughout the republic. In 1830, and in 1836, these noble laws were attempted to be fully enforced. Then, and not till then, to our shame be it spoken, began the war with our race. Mexico complains that we set upon her in her *minority*, and that we have not shown the magnanimity of *equal battle*. Her resistance to us is called foolishness, and her patriotism is, to us, Spanish obstinacy. A people who again and again risked all that was sacred for great principles and the integrity of their empire, however feeble in execution, is to the foolish only, an object of contempt. With an empty treasury, with a desolated country, with her villages destroyed, her cities in ruins, her capital threatened by the invader, with a hundred thousand troops—thinned with ball, disease, and famine—at last killed and dispersed, she declares once more against a humiliating and dishonorable peace. New Mexico, said she, has ever shown herself loyal to the Mexican nation; often neglected, and never fully defended by the central power, she had yet shown herself ready to make any sacrifice in the defence of the common liberties; sooner than yield up their countrymen—who sought perpetual alliance with the Mexican people, to the invader—they would all be involved in one common ruin. I quote from memory, but such is the spirit of this ever-glorious response of the Mexican nation to Mr. Trist's proposed treaty of peace. A nation capable of such magnanimity of soul can never be permanently enslaved.

I have thus attempted an outline of the progress of Mexico in physical, social, and political development—all which may be summed up in the one word, civilization. I shall now take a pictorial view of some things difficult to group; and though unimportant in themselves, yet, perhaps not uninteresting to a portion of my audience.

So soon as you approach the Rio Grande you feel that you are in a strange land. The live oaks, the cotton woods, and long moss, which border the streams of Texas, decline into that peculiar and not very easily described mixture of stunted thorns, shrubs, and various cacti, which constitute the Mexican chaporal. The buffaloes, the wild horses and cattle, the antelopes and deer, which enliven the wild wastes of the Nueces and Rio Grande, disappear. You are once more in the haunts of men—the confines of civilization. But it is a civilization of a new type. You see people of a copper color, and an unknown language. The mass of the men and women are bare-legged, and wear sandals. The men are clad in white trowsers; sometimes open at the sides, or closed with showy buttons, bound round the waist with a red or blue sash, or scarf; in their shirt sleeves of white cotton, or robed in a serape, or a tight fitting roundabout of white. They wear broad brimmed hats, with conical crowns, and hat-bands of wrought silver wire, or fur of animals. The women are seen in many-colored petticoats, of white, blue, red, and yellow, with similar scarfs round the waist; white chemise; bare arms and bust, with the rebosa covering the head, shoulders, bosom, and flowing gracefully to the ground. The hair of the men is cut short; but that of the women is divided into two plaits, ornamented with red ribband, and falling full length down the neck and back. The Mexicans are less in stature than we; have small feet, and hands, round limbs, and are graceful in movements of person, and courteous in manners. The natives of wealth, as well as the Spaniards, are cosmopolitan in their dress, except that no class wears bonnets. The Mexican women of Spanish ancestry are generally brunettes, with black hair and bright, black eyes; but some of them are the fairest blondes, with blue eyes and auburn hair. Some of the native Indians of the highlands, as in the mountains of Toluca, are nearly white, of a warm, red complexion, like the people near Lima, in South America; these are also beautiful in feature, and have none of the characteristic features of the Indian races. Chocolate, with cold bread, or toast, is the universal breakfast of Mexico; then comes dinner, of meats, vegetables, and fruits; then chocolate once more at night, before going to bed. Some add a more substantial breakfast, but rarely ever supper. From twelve, to four or five in the afternoon, the better classes are never seen. Then every one that can raise a coach goes to the public drive, called the Pasao. There they occasionally draw up in a circle, around some jets-d'eau, or statues of stone, salute each other by a gentle wave of the fingers of the hand, pass a few common place compliments, and drive off again, till dusk hurries them into the city. The men, on horseback, or in carriages, go through the same routine of salutation and recreation. When the shades of evening begin to lengthen, in all the principal cities of Mexico, may be seen in the balconies, leaning on the ballusters, thousands of as lovely women as the world can boast, with long flowing hair, bare arms, and irresistible eyes. The humbler classes go on foot to the Alamedas, or public walks. These are everywhere seen in Mexican cities; full of trees and flowers, and stone seats, and gravel walks, statues, and jets-d'eau of cool waters. In such places is most of the courting done; and I am told that many a match has been made, and agreed upon, and even consummated by the church ceremony, before the parties have ever exchanged a word. But these I imagine are extreme cases. Still, dinner and evening parties, and free conversation between young people, are almost unknown in Mexico. At the theatres, and in their carriages, or on feast days—at times in the balconies, are women seen in full dress, when all the mines of Mexico are worn. Bull and cock fights, monte banks, theatres, and religious processions, are the public and principal amusements of Mexico. The Catholic religion, like the Heathenism of Greece and Rome, seems every where to foster rather a refined sensualism than the pleasures of the intellect and the family affections—which are the true conservators of morals. Passing into the country you are met at every turn by caravans of mules, bearing on their large and gay pack-saddles of colored cloth, merchandise, the products of the mines, and the fruits of the soil. The Mexicans might justly be characterized as the nation of mule-drivers. Like the Arabs, they lead an adventurous and romantic life. They eat and sleep generally in the open air, turn out their mules to graze, and by the light of wood fires play monte, or the Mexican guitar. They go with arms; for which they have frequent use in the long and dangerous defiles of unpeopled mountains, or the dark and tangled thickets, where robbers find easy ambuscade for attack, and concealment from the arm of the law. The villages are built mostly of sun-dried bricks, composed of clay and straw. They have wooden carts and wagons on the farms; and wooden ploughs are seen every where, drawn by oxen in the fields. The goats and sheep feed together in the same flock, and the watch-fires of the shepherds are seen nightly in the mountains.

The roofs of the houses are flat, and of oriental or Moorish models. The palmetto, the orange, the citron, and the banana, remind you of Eastern climes—the land of the Arabian Nights, whilst the women are seen in long lines along the running streams washing their garments, or bearing great earthern cans to the walls for water; just as Rachel was seen by Jacob of old, in Judea. There are no chimneys in Mexican houses; and from the thickness of the walls they are sufficiently warm in winter, and cool in summer. The coal used for cooking is brought on the backs of mules or asses from the mountains. Go into the houses of the poor, and you find them sitting on skins of animals dressed with the hair all retained. Meat is served up in small earthern platters, with a great profusion of red pepper; a separate dish is given each guest. The hand is knife and fork; and the tortilla, bread and spoon. This is homely fare; but when the appetite is good, and the hostess a beautiful woman, it is by no means unpleasant. A few pictures of saints, crosses, and beads, occasional bedsteads with serape bed coverlids, and an earthern water vessel for water, and another for pulque, are the usual furniture. The kitchen has nothing peculiar but the metate. This is a square stone of a few feet, with another stone three sided like a prism, and of the size of an ordinary bread-roller: between these stones the Indian corn, first softened in boiling water, is rubbed into a malleable paste; this is patted between the hands into the size of buckwheat cakes, and then cooked half done on a baking plane of earthenware or iron. This bread is the far-famed tortilla; the food of the great mass of the Mexican people: the making of these is the chief employment of a woman's every-day life. The most remarkable feature of Mexican scenery is the want of trees. Except along the mountain tops and running streams there are no trees in Mexico. Over the wide waste of mountain and plain are interminably spread the cactus, the palmetto, the aloe, tall and stinted grass, and rocky surfaces. The birds are different in size and plumage from ours. The quail is crested like the peacock. The blackbird is larger, and the lark less, and both have a different note from ours. The raven is the same, but far more gentle. The vulture, and the Mexican eagle differ from ours; and are everywhere seen; even in cities, on the tops of houses and churches. I saw no crows in Mexico. In the low lands of Acapulco and Vera Cruz, the parrot and paroquets keep up an eternal clatter. On the Rio Grande, the blackbird pours forth a continual strain of not unpleasant music. Several species of nightingales are seen and heard in all parts of Mexico. In the interior of Mexico, however, as I have before remarked, there sits eternal silence and repose upon all nature. The melancholy notes of a small ring-dove but add to the feeling of desolation. After a few days' travel from Camargo, you see the mountains of Monterey: some of them are ever in sight. After being six months on the plains of Arkansas and Texas, I shall never forget my sensations upon first seeing the blue tops of these bold, serrated, and lofty piles. The vast height of the mountains of Mexico produces a continual optical illusion: they always seem nearer than they are. Thus you travel for days, it seems, under the shadow of some lofty peak, that interminably recedes as you approach. Mirage, that interesting novelty of great sandy plains, is common in Mexico. No country in the world is more picturesque than Mexico. You wind along rocky beds of mountain streams, steep defiles, and deep-washed barancas, till, suddenly turning some corner of a mountain, the most lovely valley of cultivated fields, lakes, streams, herds, villas, and minaretted cities, breaks at full view upon the captivated eye. The largest wheat and corn fields in the world, I imagine, are here. The mountain streams are dammed up with huge masonry; and, during the dry season, poured out to irrigate the soil. Two or more crops in one year, are common all over Mexico. The fields are fenced with stone, or with ditches and embankments, covered with cactus, or the aloe, or thorn. In these walls of stone are numerous grey squirrels. The flowers and ornamental shrubs of Mexico, are justly celebrated for their variety, beauty, and delicate texture. In the quadrangular colonnades of wealthy Mexican houses, these flowers for ever bloom in vases of Tuscan mould and beauty. Even the Indian in the market place is sheltered from the sun's rays, by a parasol made of the flower of the maguey and wreaths of rustic flowers. Upon these the humming-bird, of great variety of species, and beautiful plumage, feed. Except on the mountain heights, no dews fall. The twilights are lovely, and the nights brilliant; you may read a newspaper by the light of the moon; and sleep with impunity in the open air. Nowhere else have I seen so many stars in the heavens, and the planets so moonlike.

Many of the customs of Spain followed her people into the new world. The serenade is not uncommon. Of course I have been to fandangos. The earth is cleared off smoothly in a circular form, as large as a city ball room : in the centre is placed a vessel of oil, with a large wick, which with the moon gives sufficient light. Wooden seats are placed around the circle. All the lassies of the villa, with their near relatives, are gathered together. Introductions are not used : but if the lady refuses to dance, no insult is meant or received; there must be some safe-guard against uninteresting ugliness, or impertinence. Waltzes, fandangos, country dances, and a dance resembling a quadrille, with a waltz, are all to be seen; of these, the waltz is the favorite.

> " Those waltz now, who never waltzed before ;
> And those who always waltzed, now waltz the more."

Everybody, old and young, falls into the magic circle—and late does revelry " vex the dull ear of night." If your lady has deigned to dance with you, you are expected to treat her to refreshments of coffee, chocolate, nuts, and fruits, which are always vended at hand. Of the Mexican women, of all others, full of simplicity, confidence, and warmth of soul, it may be said :

> " If they love—they love : you may depend on it ;
> But if they don't—they don't ; and there's an end on it."

After all that has been said of the Mexicans, I believe there are no women less mercenary in their loves. But when love is gone, all is gone; they know no law but that of the affections. They remain long neglected, with the most philosophical, or rather the most unphilosophical devotion to their lords. On the battle-field, even, they are shot down attending to the wounded and the dying. And on the march they follow the impressed soldier for hundreds of miles, suffering all sorts of fatigue, exposure, and privation. When we were prisoners, women followed on foot eight hundred miles, keeping up with the cavalry, suffering for food and water, and deeming it all a pleasant duty, in devotion to their lovers and husbands. Surely, of all worlds, these are the angels. The kindness of the Mexican women to distressed foreigners, so much talked of, is, I imagine, the result of the sympathy of the sexes, and is not confined to any nation. Foreigners are always favorites with women; and not long since some very poor specimens of the genus homo, in the persons of Mexican prisoners of war, were great lions, in the eyes of southern women of America. The love of novelty, however, is not confined to either sex, but is a trait of our common nature.

The farm-houses of the poor are called ranchos, or ranches; and the abodes of the wealthy, haciendas. Mexico is owned by a few large landed proprietors; of whom the priests are not the least portion. Whole square leagues, and entire villages are owned by a single proprietor. Every hacienda has its church and its priest, who is chain-forger for the whole village. If a young couple are to be married, he must have, at all events, a certain sum of money; no matter how far out of the means of the parties; the hacienda man advances the amount, and the young lovers are serfs for life. Is a mother, or sister, or lover dead? before the burial, the same tragedy is again enacted by these Cerberian watch-dogs of power in all lands. These serfs, and oppressed tenantry, form the great mass of the Mexican nation. From these are taken the soldiers for the army, and the police—for their police officers are soldiers.

Voluntary enlistments are exceedingly few. The recruiting officer takes not, as with us, the banner and music to lure the soldier to slavery: but the musket and lance are ready substitutes. They are forced from family and home into large monasteries, quartres, and prisons; where they are drilled, clothed, armed, and then sent on to the regular army. The sergeants are all armed with long "hickories," to punish the careless and the unruly. Here, then, is the secret of the success of American arms. *The defenders of Mexico are slaves.* I conversed freely with the soldiers and the peasantry, from the Rio Grande to Toluca, and they everywhere avowed their determination, not to fight for the rights which they never shared: and declared, that they would desert whenever they had an opportunity. What was it to them whether their masters were Americans, or Mexicans? Of about one thousand men sent from Toluca to Mexico, to Santa Anna's assistance, not one hundred stood the battle. This is the reason why Rome fell an easy conquest to her barbarian invaders. The slaves of her great villas would not defend her; the masters were too few— they could not. Had the cultivators of Italian soil been free- men, Cæsar would never have crossed the Rubicon; nor the barbarians the Alps or the Danube. Rome might have yet been the mistress of cities, and the Romans the conquerors of the world. If Mexico had been just, she would not now have been at the feet of the Americans. Were her eight millions of people freemen and landholders, scarcely one of all our army would escape to tell the tale of our defeat. The church has degraded the minds of the people, and plundered their persons. The army begins to plunder the church : and independent rob- bers to make war on people, church, and government, whilst the Americans are plundering all. They who sow the wind, shall reap the whirlwind! They who live by the sword, shall perish by the sword! I shall not here make speculations upon the future destiny of Mexico, in the spirit of a partizan politi- cian. But these speculations are subjects for the philosopher as well as the statesman. No doubt the climate and soil of Mexico compel her to a higher civilization. The mountains, by some unanalyzed law of nature, do not breed slaves for ever. If Mexico maintains her nationality now, she will hereafter not be so easy a prey to American rapacity. Bitter experience will bring her wisdom; and adversity will teach her to be *just*. There is a party in Mexico for freedom of the press, and reli- gious toleration. With these come power which the bayonet cannot give, nor take away. Her people live in villages and cities, eminently well situated for general education. We will teach them a more liberal system of finance and civil adminis- tration. There are some noble spirits in Mexico, who conceive her true destiny : let them struggle on as they have begun. Freedom of internal commerce, equal taxation, trial by jury, general education, freedom of the press, and of religion, are all that are wanting to make Mexico great. These are much— very much, I know ; but I trust they are not unattainable even by Mexico. At all events, the time for the absorption of Mexico by the American Union has not yet come. Slavery will find no ally in Mexico. The shrewd defenders of the "peculiar insti- tution" see this. The North is yet in her nonage : she has not yet begun to feel her power. Besides, she is contemptibly time-serving: adversity will cure her of that at last. When we become *free indeed*, then will our example be more powerful than our arms. Mexico will then become a willing bride, and the Union be consummated. Canada, and Russia in America, will precede, or follow. Thus will civilization, which the wisest and coldest philosophers and statesmen have determined to have been progressing from the remotest time, move steadily on. May our loved and favored land lead on ever, as of yore, the vanguard of the only truly glorious army, who shall at last establish "the liberties of men" on earth!

ADDRESS

At the Musical Fund Hall, Philadelphia, January 14, 1846, before the Board of Home Missions of the M. E. Church and the People; for the benefit of the Poor.

Labor, the basis of the rights of property, cannot be the subject of property.

REVEREND SIRS, LADIES, AND GENTLEMEN OF PHILADELPHIA.

The motives which have impelled me to appear before you, are these: In the first place, I am not insensible to the claims of humanity, and I am happy in being able to alleviate in some measure, the physical sufferings of the unfortunate poor. I would also bear testimony, by my acceptance of this invitation, to the gratitude which I owe in common with the American people, to the Methodist Episcopal Church, for the advance which it has made and is making in vindicating religious and political liberty. But above all, am I here to proclaim, before an audience little used to such subjects, the eternal rights of man, and the justice and necessity of universal liberty.

I am no "fanatic." I war not upon society, upon government, upon the churches, upon the family relations, upon the rights of property, upon the liberty of conscience, or the freedom of speech. I am, on the contrary, the friend of all these; and because I am so, I would place them on the ever-enduring basis of nature's laws.

In the effort to vindicate the proposition that "labor, the basis of the rights of property, cannot be the subject of property," I shall resort to no new methods of reason or of authority; but planting myself upon History, the Bible, the laws of Nations, the dicta of learned men, and right, reason, and conscience, I shall stand, or fall.

That labor is a natural law, has never been questioned. Assuming the broad ground, that man's highest happiness consists in a wise understanding of, and a strict conformity to nature's laws, labor cannot be a *curse*. On the contrary, necessary as it is to our very existence, to mental, moral, and physical development, I am constrained to regard it as eminently honorable and an absolute blessing. And with great deference, I undertake to state it as the Bible doctrine. The Mosaic history is eminently figurative, elliptical, and general. From the necessity of the case, its right meaning must be drawn from liberal interpretation, assisted by reason and a large understanding of Nature. The first chapter of Genesis is a general account of the creation. The second gives the reason of man's creation ; verse fifth ;—"And there was not a man to *till the ground.*" And again, verse fifteenth :—" And the Lord took the man and put him into the garden of Eden, to *dress it and to keep it.*" Now here was a law of Nature, or of man's being, imposed upon him *before* there was any alleged transgression on his part. It is sufficient for us to note this fact : whether Deity made man the highest link of animated nature, to adorn and beautify physical nature for his own gratification, or for man's gratification, pursuing what seems to be a general design, that the greatest possible number of animal existences should fill the earth, is not important to the main issue. It is true, that in the third chapter and seventeenth verse, we have, "Cursed is the ground for thy sake, in sorrow shalt thou eat of it, all the days of thy life," and verse eighteenth, "Thorns and thistles shall it bring forth to thee, and thou shalt eat of the herb of the field ;" and nineteenth, "In the sweat of thy face shalt thou eat bread, till thou return to the ground, for out of it wast thou taken, for dust thou art, and unto dust shalt thou return." But then another law had come into play. Man had sought knowledge, and knew good and evil ; his wants had increased ; and of course his labors must be commensurate with his new necessities. In the first existence, nudity was not objectionable ; but as his knowledge increased and consequent refinement, "they sewed fig-leaves together and made themselves aprons ; and still advancing, they "made coats of skins and clothed them."

I say then, that labor was thus far only a curse, that it became with man's greater knowledge, and consequent wants, a more urgent necessity, which could not be resisted with impunity. So that at last it falls in with the first stated general proposition, that as one of nature's laws, it contributes to man's highest happiness, and is a benevolent and sacred attribute of his being.

But whether labor be a blessing or a curse, we assert that it is the basis of property, *personal* and *real*.

That labor is the source of the right to personal property, has been admitted by all writers on property, without a dissenting voice. The wild fruits which a man gathers, the fish which he catches, the game which he kills, the skins with which he clothes himself, the bows and arrows which he fashions from the woods, are all allowed rightfully to belong to him, who upon them expended his labor—" the sweat of his face."

Such is reason and conscience, and such the law of the whole world. That labor is the basis of right to real estate—to land, is not so universally admitted, and demands a more thorough demonstration and proof.

The common right of all mankind to the land, is based upon reason, natural law, and the Divine grant. The first chapter of Genesis, twenty-eighth verse, says, " Replenish the earth, and *subdue it*." It is not disputed, then, that there was a common right of man to the use of the earth : the difficulty is to find authority for a *separate use* or *property* in land.

Upon this subject there have been four leading theories :

1. Tacit consent.
2. The leave of God.
3. The law of the land.
4. Labor.

The first, " Tacit consent," is false in fact, and in principle. Land was appropriated by men and nations, without the consent of others. Nor could *assent be presumed*, because there was no notice given, nor did any portion of mankind *know* what the other was doing.

The second, " Leave of God," or as others have it, " The necessity of the case," is too indefinite, if true ; and cannot be a standard of action. Besides the rule destroys itself. For if I claim land upon the ground of necessity, or the leave of God, the first comer might justly put in the same plea, and so subdivide it indefinitely ; and each claiming *necessity* with no other arbiter, force would determine the last square foot necessary to sustain life.

It seems to me more true, as well as more philosophical, to say that inasmuch as land could not be productive or useful without *division* or *property* in it, that *necessity*, or *the leave* or *will of God* is the reason for *separate use;* not the right which determines the particular owner.

The third theory, " The law of the land," as Paley contends, is false. For whether law be " a rule of action prescribed by a superior to an inferior," or whether it be, as we regard it in Republics, " the constitutional will of the people," it may still be *wrong ;* and frequently *is* wrong; and that which is wrong cannot constitute the basis of *right*—of *rights of property,* or of any other rights. Paley felt the absurdity of the rule, and very justly remarks, " The principles we have laid down upon this subject, apparently tend to a conclusion of which a bad use is apt to be made."

He then illustrates his meaning by the limitation and minority laws, and asserts that a man ought to pay an honest debt, *in spite of those laws,* which were intended to protect him *against* frauds, not *in* frauds; and concludes, " that so long, therefore, as we keep within the design and intention of a law, that law will justify us as well in *foro conscientiæ,* as in *foro humano,* whatever be the equity or expediency of the law itself."

I pronounce such a standard of human action false and infamous! It is enough to say that no man on earth ever did conscientiously act upon such a rule of conduct. On the contrary, courts of *equity* exist in all civilized nations, expressly, by a wise appeal to reason and conscience, to relieve men from the injustice and wrong of " the law of the land." I prefer the language of Dymond, " The proposition, therefore, as a general rule, is sound. *He possesses a right to property to whom the law of the land assigns it.* This, however, is only a general rule." And he goes on to say, that the evils which result from the laws of property must be remedied by "*virtue* in individuals." I would say, then, that the law of the land is good in "*foro humano,*" but not good in "*foro conscientiæ,*" as a rule of action I deem it generally good. A citizen should be very cautious how he undertakes to set up conscience and reason against the law of the land ; yet when the law of the land runs counter to conscience and reason, he should not violate the law, but seek its change after the manner which the organic law of his nation prescribes. There are a few extreme cases in which the law may be justly violated ; the violators preferring its penalties, to the inflictions of an injured conscience ; and in every such case the transgressor should weigh well *whether it is bet-*

ter *that anarchy should prevail, by the overthrow of all govern-*
ment, or the assertion and vindication of his principle remain
in abeyance ? For that seems to be the ultimate test of the propriety of resistance in any case to " the law of the land."

It seems to me, then, that Paley has utterly failed to sustain
his position; for it depends upon the assumption, that the law
is ever right, which is proven false, by the fact that the law of
the land changes ; maintaining at different times under similar
circumstances, opposite principles. But right is ever unchang-
ably the same.

Then is there a higher standard of action ; reason, the law
of nature, and the will of God, which must sustain us in the
"*forum of conscience.*"

The fourth theory, "Labor," Mr. Locke's ground we deem
true. As it is admitted on all hands that there is a necessity
for division of land among nations and individuals, it seems
that labor is the true basis of ownership. And as the wild ap-
ples, wild animals, and forest wood became the subject of individual property, and the common right which all mankind had
in them thereby extinguished, so the land when occupied and
improved by the sinews of a man, and watered with " the sweat
of his face," became his.

The usages of nations have been in the main, in accordance
with this theory.

1. Conquest. Bad.

2. Grant of the Pope. " Ac de apostolica potestatis pleni-
tudo." Bad.

3. Discovery. A certain outlay of labor. Good.

4. Exploration. For the same reason. Better.

5. Beneficial possession. Best.

6. Purchase, gift, inheritance, will—all good, *being mere*
modes ; where the original title was good.

This tabular view shows the usages of nations. The two
first grounds of property in land being false in fact. have been
rejected by modern civilization. The rest being in accordance
with our rule, are retained by the common consent of mankind.

I cannot refrain from alluding just here to our right to Oregon. It is ours by the absorption of the Spanish and French
priority of *discovery*—ours by the *exploration* of Gray, Lewis,
and Clark—ours by the *beneficial occupancy* of Astor, and the
legitimate expansion of our border people—ours by the will of

God, the laws of nature, and our own good swords, if the worst comes to the worst! At the same time, having acknowledged a joint right of occupancy on the part of Great Britain by treaty, we owe her something for her improvements—her partial expenditure of labor. As a Christian nation we would stand condemned before God and man, if we refused now to treat, or submit to *arbitration*.

Not only the practice of nations, but learned authorities of all times sustain me in my position. The Bible: Jacob claimed a right to a well because his father (Isaac), had dug it; and this claim was deemed good by the Philistines. *Blackstone:* "Bodily labor bestowed upon any subject, which before lay in common to all men, is universally allowed to give the fairest and most reasonable title to our exclusive property therein." *Vattel* says the cultivation of the earth, "Is an obligation imposed by nature on mankind." "The earth belongs to all men in general." That nations not cultivating the earth, ancient Germans, and modern Tartars, would be justly limited to soil sufficient for *cultivation*, in spite of the ordinary law of nations, *possession*. That Peru and Mexico being tilled, were robbed by the Spaniards! but the American savages, not working the ground, were rightly ousted. J. B. Say, takes it for granted that labor is a good title to land.

If then by reason, by the law of nations, the practice of States, and by all learned authority, labor is the basis of property—if my lot is mine because of the exertions of my sinews —"the sweat of my face"—*my labor, a fortiori*, by the strongest proof known in logic, the clearest demonstrations known to intellect, you cannot without injustice take my person—my sinews—my labor.

Labor, then, and its proceeds, are his, whose hands perform it. It is the most sacred of all property and cannot be alienated by slaves or individuals, by any other rules than those which govern the alienation of other kinds of property. Slavery then cannot exist except for crime, or by the voluntary consent of the enslaved.

The following are the grounds of slavery at any time urged by mankind.

1. Conquest.
2. Difference of religion.
3. The right of the parent to sell his child.

4. Inferiority of the different species of the genus homo.

5. Inheritance, gift, will, purchase, *Secondary Bases.*

6. Debt.

7. Crime.

8. Voluntary consent.

The first five bases of slavery, in this tabular view are *false*, being in opposition to our former demonstration ; the last three bases are good for the opposite reason.

1. Conquest, for long ages, was the prolific source of slavery. It proceeded upon the principle, that "*might gives right ;*" it admitted no other standard of action among men, no other God in the world but *force.* The advocates of slavery, by making conquest, or subjecting captives to servitude, attempted to defend the practice on the ground of philanthropy, that it was more lenient than putting to death ; and it was *necessary* to enslave them in order to *save* life. Montesquieu, with a most summary and sarcastic ramark, topples over the whole structure : "It is proven *unnecessary*, because in fact *they were not killed.*"

It is enough to say of this ground of slavery that it has long since ceased, by the law of nations ; captives being exchanged in war, or liberated when peace ensues.

2. Difference of religion, though practised among the Jews and other ancient nations, and assumed in modern times as a reason of enslavement by the Pope of Rome, and even by Louis XIV., of France, is so manifestly unjust and absurd, that now none are so poor as to do it reverence ! The Catholic Church has abandoned the pretension ; and no monarch or goverament in the world, savage or civilized, would•ever think of urging such a plea for the enslavement of their fellow-men.

3. The right of the father to sell his child, prevailed longer and more universally than either of the other customs ; and exists in practice, to some extent, at the present time. Its fal-lacy is not so apparent, because the true and false are mingled, and their separation is a task of some skill and difficulty. The right of the parent to the use of the labor of the child for cer-tain periods, termed minority, differing among different nations, is not disputed. And the question may be asked, if I have the right to the labor of my child for twenty-one years, why not for life? And if *I* have the right, why not the privilege of selling it to *another ?* The difficulty of this whole matter vanishes, by reference to the rule first laid down by me. *Labor is the basis*

of property. During the infancy and childhood of the off-spring, the parent by the laws of nature and civil society, is required to expend his labor for the benefit of the child; and so the child, as soon as able, is by the same laws bound to return an equal amount of labor. And upon this basis the parent has a right to the labor of the child for a limited term of years, and during that time may use, hire, or sell the child justly. But as in no case, an expenditure in infancy, can equal life-long slavery; the sale for life is unjust and void. Men have acted upon this rule in the apprentice system; and service up to twenty-one years of the age of the apprentice, is generally deemed an equivalent for a common education, a good trade, and sustenance and clothing during the helplessness of infancy.

It is enough to say of this basis of slavery, then, that it is unjust; and has in practice been abandoned in all civilized nations.

4. The inferiority of the different species of man, whether real or assumed, has been made the ground of enslavement.

Were I here merely to defend a theory, I might very ably maintain the proposition that there is no difference in the races of men, that they are of equal capacity of elevation and civilization, all children of the same father, *Adam.* But if I know myself, I seek earnestly after the truth, and wherever she leads me I follow.

I am a friend of the Bible, an adherent of the Christian philosophy. If they are based upon the eternal laws of nature, man cannot overthrow them, for they are Divine. For God is true and consistent; he cannot put one doctrine in a book, and another in nature. And as books are mediate and nature immediate, one comes to me through the translation of languages and the agency of men; the other one the same through all eternity, "without variableness or shadow of change," is the truly Divine, and the test of conscience, and human belief, and action. If astronomy, and geology, and physiology, sustain the Bible, it will stand; if not, *not.*

So far, then, astronomy and geology have been said by the most learned to sustain the Mosaic history, though at first seemingly variant; whether Mahomet has gone to the mountain, or the mountain to Mahomet, they are together, and strengthened in the union.

I say, then, that from all the lights which are before me, there are distinct species of the genus homo. I believe the Caucasian, the Mogul, the Malay, the Indian, and Negro races are different species of the Genus Man, just as the terrier, the spaniel, the grey-hound, the pointer, are different species of the same canine genus.

I am farther of the opinion that the Caucasian, or white, is the superior race; of a larger and better formed brain; of more beautiful form, and more exquisite structure. Modern discoveries prove that the builders of the Pyramids, and Egyptian founders of science and letters, were *Whites*. And this long disputed problem being settled, History now unites in making the Caucasian race, the first in civilization through all past time.

As I said in the beginning of this lecture, the Mosaic history is highly figurative, and *general*.

In the begining God created the type of mankind, Adam, who represented his capabilities for good and evil, and his general destiny. But we are also bound to believe that distinct pairs were created by general or special Providence in different portions of the earth, suitable to its climate and physical differences.

Such is a summary of my opinions upon the *difference* of races. As to the *inferiority* of races, I am also of the opinion that the Caucasian is the first; whilst we know that myriad causes may depress one species, and elevate another, *till they meet upon a common level.*

Whilst I grant, then, that "The inferiority of races" exists, I utterly deny, that it is a good basis of enslavement. We are all still *men*—children of the same Father—the God of all—subject to good and evil on earth, and the same destiny in a future life. If I can, on this plea, enslave the African, I can, upon the same ground, enslave the Mogul, the Malay, the Indian. Yes, if it be a sound basis of action, that because a man is inferior to another, he may be enslaved by another, then there is but one law on earth, and that is *power*. The very object of all government is to protect the weak, the "*inferior ;*" reason, the Divine law, and the undying instincts of the human soul; all cry out against the infamy and crime of trampling upon the weak, the helpless, and the poor. Montesquieu, in speaking of prejudice and contempt, and "inferiority of races, as a reason of enslavement of our fellow-men," breaks out into the most exquisite, and scathing irony : "It is hardly to be supposed that God, who is a wise being, should place a soul, especially a good soul, in such a black, ugly body." "It is impossible to suppose that these creatures are men, because, allowing them to be men, a suspicion would follow, that we ourselves are not Christians !"

So the old Spaniards, when they had oppressed for centuries the Spaniards of the New World, denying them education, and legislation, and destroying their every means of economical progress, even pulling up their olive trees, that Spain might have a monopoly—in the Spanish Cortes, in the face of the world, had the frontless impudence and God-defying falsity, to say that the American Spaniards *were not men !* And so say Hammond and McDuffie, and that school, after similar oppressions of the American Blacks! But natural causes are operating, which, when reason, humanity, and religion fail, will yet *purge us of this lie !*

Conquest, difference of religion, the right of the father to sell the child, and the inferiority of different species of the genus homo, are proven false grounds of slavery.

5. The secondary basis : inheritance, gift, will, and purchase, being merely *modes* of transfer of a thing, cannot be good. For where there is no right, it cannot be transferred ; in other words, the title conveyed is just as good as it was before conveyance, and no more so.* And a title being bad all its modes of perpetuation are bad. For example : I might show in fact that M. Van Buren willed, gave, and sold, and that my father had a claim which I inherited, to Daniel Webster, and James K. Polk, and John C. Calhoun, and Henry Clay ; and it might be proven that I had paid ten thousand dollars to Mr. Van Buren for these men ; and yet I could not hold them as slaves, because neither my father, whose heir I was, nor Mr. Van Buren, whose assignee I was, had any title; and of course none could accrue to me.

All these grounds, then, upon which slavery is attempted to be held, crumble into dust before the force of reason and justice.

6. Debt is good. Because I having used the property, the labor of another, and failing to pay the equivalent, it is just that my labor should be taken as the only remaining means of

---

* The doctrine of the Civil Code, or Roman Law, as well as of the Common Law, is " Nemo plus juris in alium transferre potest quam ipse habet."

remuneration. But even this basis of slavery, such is the love of liberty among men, is now almost universally done away with among men.

7. Crime, is a true basis of slavery. By the social compact a man may forfeit his life, by crime; and as the greater includes the less, he may of course forfeit his *labor*. The government may use it in a penitentiary, or elsewhere, or sell the criminal to an individual.

8. Voluntary consent is no doubt a basis of slavery. For, as a man may give away his property, so he may give away his labor, and become a slave. But as he may resume his liberty whenever it suits him, this state of being can hardly be ranked under the head of slavery. For the obligation to serve ceases with the will. Nor can it be urged that a man *sold himself*, for, a sale to be valid, must be fair; the seller must be shown to have received an equivalent; but, as a slave cannot hold property, he cannot of course have received the price of his liberty, and the *contract is void*. Neither can it be urged that some immaterial equivalent may have been given and received. For we cannot imagine such a case. "What is a man profited if he shall gain the whole world, and lose his own soul?"

The ancients did, indeed, allow of this kind of voluntary enslavement, yet such a slave was held in utter infamy, because they contended, that in selling himself, he endangered the liberties of others. They felt the evil, but gave a wrong reason; its utter injustice and violation of natural law, and good reason, were the cause of its *hardship*, and made it, in truth, *void*.

Having gone through all the grounds of slavery, and shown their utter falsity—for it is not contended by any one that slavery in the United States exists for crime, for debt, or by voluntary consent of the enslaved—the whole fabric by which three millions of men are held in absolute servitude in these States, crumbles into dust!

Nor do I stand sustained by reason and nature only, but I am fortified in my impregnable fortress by the greatest names and the most illustrious enunciations of men.

All authors unite in the declaration, that government was formed for the better preservation of natural rights. And we declared as a nation, that the only authority arose, not from the

Divine right of kings, or priests, or hoary usage, but from "*the consent of the governed.*" We cannot, therefore, claim to govern men for *their own good*, but only *by their voluntary consent*. Far less can we, under the pretence of protecting a man, or any set of men in their natural rights, *utterly destroy them*.

What, then, are man's natural rights? What the illustrious enunciations of God and man?

Paley: "Natural rights are a man's right to his life, limbs, and liberty."

Blackstone: "For the principal aim of society is to protect individuals in the enjoyment of those absolute rights which were invested in them by the immortal laws of nature."

Thomas Paine: "Man has no property in man; neither has a generation any property in the generation which are to follow." Roger Sherman, and James Madison, and others, used the same language, "I deny that man can have property in man."

Dymond: "It were humiliating to set about the *proof*, that the slave system is incompatible with Christianity." "Christianity condemns the system; and no further inquiry about rectitude remains."

The French Convention, 1789: I. "Men are born and always continue free and equal in respect to their rights. Civil distinctions, therefore, can only be founded on public utility."

II. "The end of all political associations is the preservation of the natural rights of man; and these rights are liberty, property, security, and resistance of oppression."

III. "Political liberty consists in the power of doing whatever does not injure another."

But above these and all, is the Declaration of 1776: "All men are created equal—are endowed with certain inalienable rights; among these are life, liberty, and the pursuit of happiness."

And still higher, is the New Testament: "*Love thy neighbor as thyself!*"

I have taken slavery in its simplest form—*the taking of another's labor*. I say nothing of its sequences—crime, poverty, woe, and death! I have shown it opposed to the most illustrious enunciations, human and Divine—in violation of the common law—the laws of nations and of reason—subversive of all our ideas of right—and repugnant to the conscience, and every aspiration of the immortal soul. Before God and man, I denounce " *slavery as being in itself sinful.*" Yes, " Slavery ; I denounce you wherever thou art," whether in church or state, upheld by *false* religion, or *unjust* law—LET IT DIE !

LINES TO C. M. C.

BY MRS. E. J. EAMES.

I.

BRAVE heart, and truly noble! that didst single
  From all Earth's lofty aims the loftiest one,
Pursuing it by means which might not mingle
  With views less generous:—nobly hast thou done!
And dared and striven—through every obstacle:—
And steadfastly resisting, through each ill,
  The Wrong and False. Sure, thou hast read and pondered
With highest wisdom on those words divine—
  " Love one another ;"—therefore ne'er hath wandered
The star that led thy spirit to the shrine
  Of holiest Truth! Still may the Angels have
Their charge o'er thee. Still (with the hope sublime
  To serve thy race) mayest thou all danger brave
And win thy way, now, and through future time!

II.

  For Truth—Truth pure and indestructible—
Is the strong ark wherein thy safety lies:—
Even 'mid the slanders of fierce enemies
  Shalt thou be armed with hero-courage still
T' oppose the Wrong—and pray God speed the Right
Now steadily upon the wondrous light
  Of Freedom, in the Future, fix thy glance—
Then, animated by the grandest dream—
  The noblest earthly hope—still to advance
(With fearless will) the Cause that must redeem
  The promise written on the Nation's scroll—
  The pledge that in the Country of the Free
Men shall have Equal Rights! Courage, O ardent soul!
Press onward—onward still! and thou shalt reach the goal!